PAGE
24

ON THE ROAD

YOUR COMPLETE DESTINATION GUIDE
In-depth reviews, detailed listings
and insider tips

Georgia
p26

Azerbaijan
p198

Armenia
p121

Nagorno-
Karabakh
p269

Azerbaijan
p198

D0030986

Directory A–Z 294
Transport 300
Health 308
Language 310
Index 320
Map Legend 327

Health

THIS EDITION WRITTEN AND RESEARCHED BY

John Noble
Michael Kohn, Danielle Systermans

welcome to Georgia, Armenia & Azerbaijan

A Feast for the Eyes

Few travellers are prepared for this region's beauty. The Great Caucasus strides from the Black Sea to the Caspian in a sequence of dramatic icy peaks, green river valleys and quaint, remote villages. Further south the Lesser Caucasus and the Armenian Plateau are geographically complex areas of rugged mountains, lush valleys, rocky gorges and arid semideserts. Beautiful architecture is often perched in the most picturesque locations throughout.

Hosts Supreme

This region, smaller than the UK, takes in three distinct countries (two Christian, one Islamic); three breakaway territories;

at least 16 local languages; and a melange of Russian, Persian, Turkish and other influences. But common to them all are deep-rooted traditions of hospitality. Travellers are warmly received everywhere, and the enjoyment of tasty, fresh local food and wine with your local hosts is something you won't quickly forget.

The Great Outdoors

In the Great Caucasus, Georgia's Svaneti, Kazbegi and Tusheti regions and Azerbaijan's Quba hinterland are strung with spectacular walking and riding routes, good for day trips and (in Georgia) village-to-village treks. There's excellent walking in Caucasus foothill areas and the Lesser

With breathtaking natural beauty, wonderfully hospitable people, quaintly charming architecture and cosmopolitan capitals, the three small South Caucasus nations are just waiting to be explored.

(left) Tsminda Sameba Church (p88), Kazbegi, Georgia
(below) Azeri babushka dolls

Caucasus in Armenia and southern Georgia. Thousands of pilgrims ascend Azerbaijan's 'holy mountain', Babadağ, every year, while around 5000 mountaineers reach the top of Kazbek, one of Georgia's handful of over-5000m peaks. You can set your adrenalin pumping by rafting on several of Georgia's rivers, paragliding in its skies, or delving underground in Armenia's many caves.

Food for the Mind

Forts, monasteries, mosques, churches and excavations pepper the region; history buffs will love disentangling their Bagratids from their Bolsheviks. The cities boast well-presented museums and classy concerts, dance and theatre; smaller regional museums show local culture and notables.

Cultural Crossroads

South Caucasus travel weaves you between cosmopolitan, modernising capitals and slow-paced countryside where most families live off their land. Social attitudes remain traditional, with family networks supreme and most women marrying early. This is a cultural crossroads where Europe meets Asia and tomorrow mingles with yesterday, where tourism infrastructure is improving but travel still presents a few challenges. It is perfect for those who like to explore beyond the beaten path and enjoy a warm local welcome at the end of a day's journey.

❭Georgia, Armenia & Azerbaijan

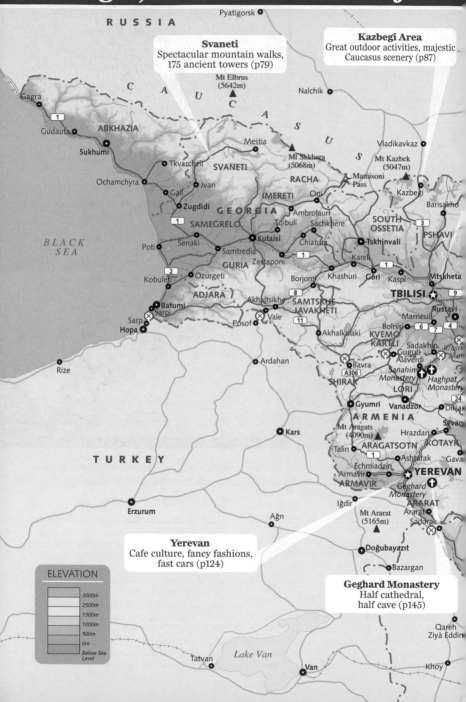

Svaneti
Spectacular mountain walks,
175 ancient towers (p79)

Kazbegi Area
Great outdoor activities, majestic
Caucasus scenery (p87)

RUSSIA

Pyatigorsk

Nalchik

C A U C A S U S

Mt Elbrus
(5642m)

Vladikavkaz

Gagra

Gudauta

ABKHAZIA

Sukhumi

Mestia

SVANETI

Mt Shkhara
(5068m)

RACHA

Mt Kazbek
(5047m)

Mamisoni
Pass

Kazbegi

Barisakho

Tkvarcheli

Ochamchyra

Jvari

Galı

Oni

IMERETI

SOUTH
OSSETIA

PSHAVI

Zugdidi

GEORGIA

Ambrolauri

Tqibuli

Sachkhere

SAMEGRELO

Chiatura

Tskhinvali

BLACK
SEA

Poti

Senaki

Samtredia

Kutaisi

Karel

Mtskheta

Zestaponi

GURIA

Khashuri

Gori

Kaspi

Borjomi

Ozurgeti

Kobuleti

ADJARA

Akhaltsikhe

SAMTSKHE-
JAVAKHETI

TBILISI

Marneuli

Rustavi

Batumi

Sarpi

Vale

Bolnisi

KVEMO
KARTLI

Sarp

Hopa

Posof

Akhalkalaki

Sadakhlo

Krasn
Mos

Rize

Ardahan

Bavra

Guguti

Alaverdi

A306

SHIRAK

Sanahin
Monastery

Haghpat
Monastery

LORI

Gyumri

Vanadzor

Dilijan

Kars

Mt Aragats
(4090m)

ARMENIA

Sevan

Hrazdan

KOTAYK

Talin

ARAGATSOTN

Gavar

TURKEY

Echmiadzin

Ashtarak

Armavir

YEREVAN

Erzurum

ARMAVIR

Geghard
Monastery

ARARAT

Ağrı

Iğdir

Mt Ararat
(5165m)

Ararat

Sadarak

Doğubayazıt

Yerevan
Cafe culture, fancy fashions,
fast cars (p124)

Bazargan

Geghard Monastery
Half cathedral,
half cave (p145)

ELEVATION

3000m
2500m
1500m
1000m
500m
0m
Below Sea
Level

Tatvan

Lake Van

Van

Khoy

Qareh
Ziyâ Eddin

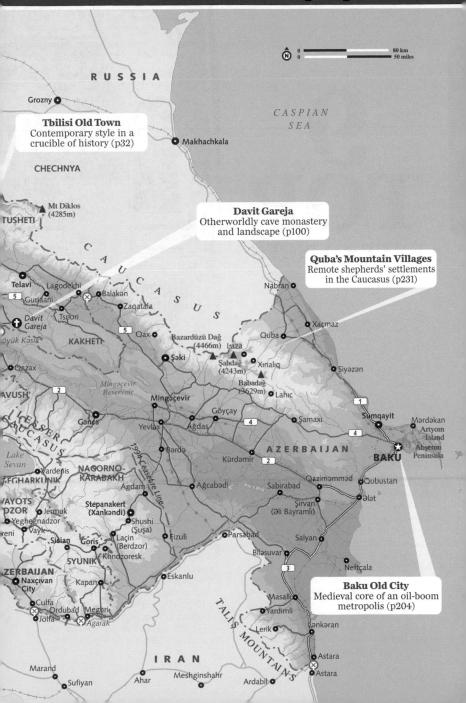

Tbilisi Old Town
Contemporary style in a crucible of history (p32)

Davit Gareja
Otherworldly cave monastery and landscape (p100)

Quba's Mountain Villages
Remote shepherds' settlements in the Caucasus (p231)

Baku Old City
Medieval core of an oil-boom metropolis (p204)

0   80 km
0   50 miles

RUSSIA

Grozny

CASPIAN SEA

Makhachkala

CHECHNYA

Mt Diklos
(4285m)

TUSHETI

C A U C A S U S

Telavi   Lagodekhi
Gurjaani   Balakən
Zaqatala
Davit   Tsnori
Gareja   Qax
Büyük Kəsik   KAKHETI

Bazardüzü Dağ
(4466m)   Laza
Şəki   Xınalıq
Şahdağ
(4243m)
Babadağ
(3629m)   Lahıc

Nabran

Quba   Xaçmaz

Siyəzən

Mingəçevir
Reservoir
Mingəçevir

Qazax

LESSER

CAUCASUS

Gəncə   Yevlax   Ağdaş
Göyçay

Şamaxı

Sumqayıt

Mərdəkan
Artyom
Island
Abşeron
Peninsula

BAKU

Lake
Sevan   Vardenis

NAGORNO-
KARABAKH

Bərdə

Kürdəmir

AZERBAIJAN

TEGHARKUNIK

Agdam
Stepanakert
(Xankəndi)

Ağcabədi

Qazımməmməd   Qobustan

Sabirabad
Şirvan
(Əli Bayramlı)   Ələt

VAYOTS
DZOR   Jermuk
Yeghegnadzor
Vayk

Shushi
(Şuşa)
Laçın
(Berdzor)

Fizuli   Parsabad

Salyan

Sisian   Goris
Khndzoresk

SYUNIK

Eskanlu

Biləsuvar

Neftçala

ZERBAIJAN
Naxçıvan
City   Kapan

Masallı
Yardımlı

Culfa   Ordubad   Meghri
Jolfa   Agarak

TALIS

Lerik   Lənkəran

MOUNTAINS

IRAN

Astara
Astara

Marand

Sufiyan   Ahar   Meshginshahr   Ardabil

9 TOP
EXPERIENCES

Tbilisi Old Town

1 Nowhere better blends the romance of Georgia's past with its striving for a new future than Tbilisi's Old Town (p32). Winding lanes lined by rakishly leaning houses lead past tranquil old stone churches to shady squares and glimpses of the ultracontemporary Peace Bridge spanning the Mtkvari River. Casual cafes and bohemian bars rub shoulders with trendy lounge-clubs, folksy carpet shops, new travellers' hostels and small, quirky hotels. The aeons-old silhouette of Nariqala Fortress supervises everything, while Georgia's 21st-century Presidential Palace, with its egg-shaped glass dome, looks on from over the river.

Svaneti

2 The mysterious mountain valleys of Svaneti (p79) sit high in the Caucasus, surrounded by spectacular snowy peaks, alpine meadows and thick forests – a paradise for walkers in summer. Long isolated and insulated from the outside world, Svaneti has its own language and a strongly traditional culture, symbolised by the 175 *koshkebi* (ancient stone defensive towers) that stand picturesquely in its villages, and the 1000-year-old frescoes in its churches. Accessible only by a long road trip until recently, Svaneti also has daily small-plane flights from Tbilisi.

Geghard Monastery

3 Half cathedral, half cave, Geghard (p145) is a spooky, dimly lit sanctuary, where voices bounce off walls, sunbeams shoot through the narrow windows and droplets of water ooze through the walls. Ancient *khatch-kars* (carved stone crosses) surrounding the church, and crosses carved into the 800-year-old walls, are testament to centuries of pious visitors. Walking through the church you half expect to find Indiana Jones busting the stone floor open to reveal lost treasures.

Kazbegi Area

4 Just a couple of hours' drive from Tbilisi, the small town of Kazbegi (p84) is the hub of one of the region's most spectacular, yet easily accessed, high-mountain zones. The sight of Tsminda Sameba Church silhouetted on its hilltop against the massive snow-covered cone of Mt Kazbek is Georgia's most iconic image. Numerous walking, horse and mountain-bike routes lead along steep-sided valleys and up to glaciers, waterfalls, mountain passes and isolated villages – just ideal for getting a taste of the high Caucasus.

Yerevan Street Life

5 Street life in Yerevan (p139) is slow-paced, often involving long hours spent lingering over coffee or beer in the city's numerous outdoor cafes. The cafe scene gets going in late afternoon and builds to a crescendo by evening, ending some time before dawn. The cafe crowds mass around Opera Sq, the Ring Park or Republic Sq, occasionally passing by Northern Ave to preen and parade their latest fashions.

Quba's Mountain Villages

6 Behind the peaceable country town of Quba (p231), woodland glades and sheep-nibbled hillsides lead up into the foothills of the Great Caucasus. Here, separated by dramatic canyons and wild river valleys, lie a scattering of remote shepherd villages, some speaking their own unique languages. Best known of these is Xınalıq, where stacked, grey-stone houses constitute what, by some definitions, is 'Europe's highest village'. Even more remote are timeless gems such as Qriz and Buduq while, slightly further afield, Laza has one of the most spectacular backdrops of any Caucasian mountain settlement.

Baku Old City

7 Huddled behind a battlement-topped arc of city wall, Baku's Unesco-listed core (p204) is a world away from the traffic and bustle of the surrounding oil-boom city. The winding alleys follow a crooked medieval logic, while the stone buildings run the gamut of eras, from the ancient Maiden's Tower to brand-new, pseudo-classical townhouses via a selection of 19th-century homes and austere mini-mosques. Added to the mix are several caravanserais, a 15th-century palace complex and a whole range of carpet shops all gently spiced with cafes and little hotels.

Davit Gareja

8 With a spectacular setting in remote, arid lands near Georgia's border with Azerbaijan, these much revered cave monasteries (p100) were carved out of the hillsides long, long ago. They became a cradle of medieval monastic culture and fresco painting. Saints' tombs, vivid 1000-year-old murals, an otherworldly landscape and the very idea that people voluntarily chose – and still choose – to live in desert caves, all combine to make visiting Davit Gareja (an easy day trip from Tbilisi, Telavi or Sighnaghi) a startling experience today.

Armenian Monasteries

9 Armenia's rich collection of ancient churches and monasteries is a world treasure that has developed over thousands of years of architectural tinkering. The general layout and design are almost universal and you'll soon become accustomed to seeing the ubiquitous conical roof, resembling Mt Ararat. Closer inspection reveals that each monastery has its own unique character and design variation. Location also differentiates Armenia's monasteries, ranging from Tatev's mountaintop perch (pictured left; p184) to Nora-vank's desert canyon (p174) and the iconic Khor Virap (p151) with the backdrop of Mt Ararat.

need to know

Time

» GMT + 4 hours

» Daylight saving period (Armenia and Azerbaijan only): GMT + 5 hours, last Sunday in March to last Sunday in October.

Money

» ATMs and money-changing offices widely available. Credit cards accepted at some hotels, restaurants and shops, mainly in the capitals.

When to Go

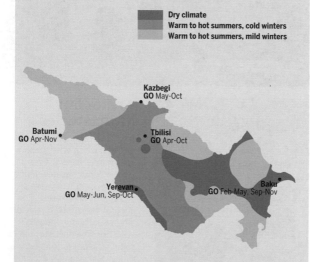

Dry climate
Warm to hot summers, cold winters
Warm to hot summers, mild winters

Kazbegi
GO May-Oct

Batumi
GO Apr-Nov

Tbilisi
GO Apr-Oct

Yerevan
GO May-Jun, Sep-Oct

Baku
GO Feb-May, Sep-Nov

Your Daily Budget

Budget less than
US$40

» Hostels, homestays, budget guesthouses and B&Bs average around US$15 per person

» Save on meals by staying in accommodation where you can cook

Midrange
US$100

» Doubles average around US$75 in comfortable hotels, US$50 (including two meals) in good guesthouses

» You can afford at least one good restaurant meal daily, and some guides and long-distance taxis

Top End more than
US$200

» Doubles in luxury hotels start around US$150

» Eat wherever you like, take taxis everywhere

High Season
(Jul–Aug)

» Locals' holiday time; tourist accommodation is crowded

» Visit mountain areas now; the only assured snow-free months for hiking in the high Caucasus

» Capitals and other lowlands unpleasantly hot and humid

Shoulder Seasons (May–Jun & Sep–Oct)

» The most pleasant temperatures in the lowlands

» Upland areas can be cool; some walking trails only open June to September

» May is the rainiest month

Low Season
(Nov–Apr)

» Winter sports Jan–Mar; most mountain-village lodgings close

» Inland often below freezing Dec–Feb

» Tbilisi: wet and slushy; Yerevan: icy; Baku: cold and windy

» Wintry weather often lasts into April

Toilets

» Public toilets are rare. Larger bus stations usually have them, often with squat toilets.

Water

» Tap water is generally safe to drink in Georgia and Azerbaijan's mountain areas, but not in Armenia, Baku or lowland Azerbaijan. Bottled water is widely available.

Mobile Phones

» If your phone is unlocked for international use, local SIM cards, available in each country, are the cheapest way to go.

Driving

» Drive on the right; steering wheel is on the left side of car. Allow time to adapt to local driving styles. Roads are steadily improving.

Websites

» **Georgia** (www.georgia.travel) Official tourism site.

» **Armenia Information** (www.armenia info.am) Tourist info.

» **MCTAR** (www.azerbaijan.tourism.az) Azerbaijan's tourism site.

» **Lonely Planet** (lonelyplanet.com) Destination info, Thorn Tree forum and more.

» **Caucasian Knot** (www.eng.kavkaz-uzel.ru) News.

» **Eurasianet** (www.eurasianet.org) Features.

» **IWPR** (http://iwpr.net/programme/caucasus) Caucasus bridge-building.

Don't Leave Home Without...

» Torch
» Universal sink plug
» Sturdy shoes
» Rainproof jacket
» Sunglasses and hat
» Long skirt and long-sleeved tops for women
» Good-quality spare batteries
» Towel
» Comprehensive insurance
» Two debit/credit cards, preferably one MasterCard, one Visa

Important Numbers

Country code Armenia	⌕374
Country code Azerbaijan	⌕994
Country code Georgia	⌕995
Emergency	⌕103 (Georgia ⌕113)
International access code	⌕00

Arriving in the Region

» **Tbilisi International Airport** (p53) Buses run to the city centre 7am to 10pm. Taxis (20 minutes) cost US$15 to US$18.

» **Zvartnots Airport, Yerevan** (p144) Minibuses run to Zoravar Andranik metro station. Taxis to the city centre (20 minutes) cost US$16 booked inside the airport, but as little as US$6 outside.

» **Heydar Əliyev Airport, Baku** (p223) Buses run to the city centre (one hour) 6.30am to 7.30pm. Taxis cost around US$30.

Getting Around

Marshrutky (minibuses) and buses provide the main transport within the region. These are inexpensive, reasonably quick (*marshrutky* more so than buses), and fairly frequent along the more major routes.

Trains provide less frequent, slower service on some routes (Georgia has the most extensive network). They are generally more comfortable and a bit cheaper than *marshrutky*. Overnight trains are a convenient option between Tbilisi and Yerevan, Baku, Batumi or Zugdidi, and between Baku and Lənkoran, Gəncə or Şəki.

Long-distance taxis can be surprisingly inexpensive, especially if shared. A taxi from Tbilisi to Yerevan, for example, normally costs US$100 to US$125.

Intraregional flights connect Tbilisi with Yerevan and Baku, and (in summer) Batumi with Baku. There are a few domestic flights in Georgia and Azerbaijan.

There is no direct transport between Armenia and Azerbaijan.

if you like...

Walking & Horse Riding

The Great Caucasus has many wonderful routes along its valleys and over its passes. Many routes are suitable for horses as well as walkers, with riding or pack horses quite widely available.

Svaneti Many varied trails in this spectacular region of green valleys, snowy peaks and picturesque villages (p79)

Kazbegi Area A quick climb to Tsminda Sameba Church or longer hikes to Gergeti Glacier, along the lovely Sno and Truso valleys, or over passes to remote Khevsur villages (p87)

Quba hinterland Homestay treks link some of Azerbaijan's loveliest mountain villages (p231)

Tusheti Beautiful mountain area with fine village-to-village walking and the region's best longer trek, five days to, or from, Khevsureti (p90)

Tatev Valley and hill walks amid gorgeous southern Armenian scenery (p184)

Borjomi-Kharagauli National Park Well-marked trails of up to three days across forested hills and alpine meadows (p104)

Mt Babadağ Join pilgrims trekking up Azerbaijan's 'holy mountain' (p235)

Architecture

If old stone buildings and carving shiver your spine, you're in the right place. The medieval architecture of Georgia and Armenia, in particular, is outstanding.

Vardzia An entire medieval town carved into a cliff face (p107)

Geghard Monastery Chapels and churches hewn from the rock, and stunning *khatchkars* (p145)

Mtskheta The mother of early Georgian churches and grand Svetitskhoveli Cathedral (p54)

Debed Canyon The beautiful medieval monasteries of Sanahin and Haghpat (p168)

Baku Old City A mysterious tower, 15th-century palace and medieval minarets, within photogenic crenellated walls (p204)

Tatev Great fortified monastery on a fairy-tale natural rock fortress (p184)

Shatili Unique agglomeration of defensive towers forming a single fortresslike whole (p89)

Gandzasar Monastery Excellent Armenian architecture with rich friezes and magnificent detail (p276)

Şəki Caravanserais, mosques and an extraordinarily decorated khan's place, inside sturdy fortress walls (p238)

Urban Vibes

The three large, contemporary-cum-old-fashioned capitals are keys to their countries, quite distinct from each other and the rural expanses beyond.

Tbilisi The most charming and intimate of the three, with an extensive old town, and surprisingly villagelike neighbourhoods strung along the Mtkvari valley. Aeons of history, a smattering of standout new architecture, and plenty of slick, bohemian or in-between restaurants and bars (p30)

Yerevan A mainly 19th- and 20th-century city, with broad avenues and squares, Yerevan has heaps of museums, monuments, theatres and clubs. Citizens like to don high fashion, speed along the boulevards and idle hours away at pavement cafes (p124)

Baku The biggest and fastest changing of the three, Caspian-side Baku contrasts a fascinating old town with grand century-old mansions and dazzling 21st-century glass towers. It has top-notch restaurants and appealing cafes but its suave lounge bars cater more to nouveaux riches than bohemian travellers (p231)

» Traditional Armenian food (p192)

Eating

Each country has its own spicy, herby cuisine but common to all is the freshness: most ingredients come straight from the garden or market. Georgian food is especially tasty with its imaginative use of walnuts, garlic and melted mountain cheeses.

Georgian homestays & guesthouses In Georgia many of your best meals will be in locals' homes, where they'll be prepared with special care because you are a guest (p115)

Barbecued meats All three countries relish skewer-barbecued meats. Called *khoravats* in Armenia (p192), *shashlyk* in Azerbaijan (p263) and *mtsvadi* in Georgia (p114), they're available almost everywhere and always make a satisfying meal served with a selection of salads and fresh-baked breads

Dolma Another classic regional dish, comprising vine-leaf parcels or various vegetables, stuffed with rice, minced meat and herbs. Especially popular in Azerbaijan (p263) and Armenia (p192), which both think they invented it

Khachapuri Georgia's everfilling, ever-calorific, ever-tasty cheese pies (p45)

Remarkable Landscapes

With low population density, small-scale agriculture and only scattered industry, the human impact on the landscape is relatively low-key. Indeed, it often enhances the spectacle of snow-capped mountains, green valleys, rocky canyons and arid semi-deserts.

Great Caucasus From Abkhazia in the west to Xınalıq in the east, the southern flank of Europe's highest mountain range is a magnificent sequence of high peaks, green valleys and remote villages

Lesser Caucasus The Lesser Caucasus encompasses beautiful diversity, from the forests and alpine meadows of Borjomi-Kharagauli National Park (p104) to the dry mountains and lovely valleys around Jermuk (p178) and Yeghegnadzor (p174), and the deep gorges and wild peaks of Kelbajar (p276)

Mud & fire The geology that gives Azerbaijan its petrochemicals also produces such weird phenomena as a spontaneously burning hillside (Yanar Dağ, p226), water that 'catches fire' (near Astara, p254), and the mud volcanoes near Qobustan (p227)

Wine, Cognac & Other Drinks

Georgians have been making wine for 7000 years and it plays a central, unforgettable role in their culture. Armenia's *konyak* (brandy) was famously favoured by Winston Churchill. Azerbaijan's national drink is tea. There's vodka and beer everywhere.

Kakheti Georgia's prime winegrowing region, with lots of wineries to visit (p99) and even sleep at – imbibe steadily all day long, if you like

Yerevan Brandy Company Armenian brandy is a world-beater and the makers of the premier brand, Ararat, offer fun tours with generous tastings (p128)

Supra Any Georgian *supra* (feast) involves numerous toasts, usually directed by a *tamada* (toastmaster) – a quintessential experience (p115)

Azerbaijan teahouses Teahouses are central to Azerbaijani culture: the traditional *çayxana* is essentially a male-only institution, but a new breed of upmarket *çay evi* is modernising the concept, at least for the wealthy

month by month

Top Events

1 Tbilisoba, October

2 Kakheti Grape Harvest, October

3 Art-Gene Festival, July

4 High Fest, October

5 Gabala International Music Festival, August

January

The coldest month. Expect snow and below-freezing temperatures over much of the region. Winter sports get going. Georgians and Armenians celebrate Christmas, with the devout going on fasts of varying rigour for days or weeks beforehand.

New Year

Cities are prettily decorated, with fireworks launching the year. Georgians may gather for post-midnight feasts. In Armenia children receive gifts from Dzmer Papik (Santa Claus/Grandpa Winter) on New Year's Eve; families and friends visit and exchange gifts over several days until Christmas (6 January).

Armenian Christmas (Surb Tsnund)

Hymns and psalms ring out from churches, where part of the ritual is the blessing of water to mark Epiphany (Jesus' baptism), with which Christmas is combined. Families gather for Christmas Eve dinners, where the traditional main dish is fish and rice (6 January).

Georgian Christmas (Shoba)

On 7 January. Flag-carrying, carol-singing crowds make Alilo (Alleluia) walks through the streets, with children wearing white robes. For some, the festive season continues to 14 January, 'Old New Year', the year's start on the Julian Calendar used by the Georgian Orthodox Church.

Martyrs' Day

20 January. A national day of mourning in Azerbaijan, commemorating the 1990 massacre of Baku civilians by Soviet troops. Bakuvians head up to the Şahidlər Xiyabani memorial in a major commemoration.

February

It is still very cold but the winter sports season is in full swing; this is usually the optimal month for skiing at Georgia's and Armenia's ski stations.

Skiing

The season runs from about late December to the end of March at the Georgian resorts of Gudauri (p84), Bakuriani (p105) and Mestia (p80), and Armenia's Jermuk (p178) and Tsaghkadzor (p156), but February generally has the best snow conditions.

Surp Sargis Don

The Day of St Sargis, a handsome warrior saint, is popular among unmarried Armenians: tradition tells that the person who gives them water in their dreams this night will be their spouse. It falls nine weeks before Easter (between 18 January and 23 February).

Trndez

This Armenian religious festival of the Purification falls on 14 February. Bonfires are lit and people leap over them for protection from the evil eye, illness and poisons. Trndez also signals the approach of spring.

March

It's starting to get a little less cold, but don't expect anything above 10°C except perhaps on the coasts.

★ Women's Day

On 8 March. Celebrated throughout the region with flowers and presents given to female colleagues and friends, and lots of flower stalls on the streets. It's a public holiday in Georgia and Armenia.

★ Noruz Bayramı

Azerbaijan's biggest celebration, a week either side of the spring equinox (night of 20 to 21 March), marks the Persian solar New Year and the coming of spring. Traditions include preparing special rice dishes and cleansing the spirit by jumping over bonfires on the Tuesday night before the equinox.

April

Temperatures may climb to 20°C in lowland areas. Spring rains and melting snows bring bigger, faster rivers and the start of the main white-water rafting season in Georgia (until July).

◉ Armenian Easter (Zatik)

Happens on the same variable date as Roman Catholic and Protestant Easter (see p296). On Palm Sunday (Tsaghkazard), a week earlier, trees are brought into churches and hung with fruit. Easter tables in homes are laid with red-painted eggs on beds of lentil shoots grown during the Lenten fast.

◉ Georgian Easter (Aghdgoma)

The Eastern Orthodox Easter can happen up to five weeks after the Western

one (see p296). Churches hold special services on Passion Thursday (with Last Supper ceremonies) and Good Friday, notably at Svetitskhoveli Cathedral, Mtskheta (p54).

◉ Genocide Memorial Day

On 24 April, thousands of Armenians make a procession to Yerevan's genocide memorial, Tsitsernakaberd (p133). The date is the anniversary of the arrest of Armenian leaders in Istanbul in 1915, generally considered to mark the start of the genocide.

May

Spring rains continue but lowland temperatures become pleasant and the countryside blooms with flowers. Walking trails in mountain areas start to open up. Generally an enjoyable time to visit the region.

★ Victory Day

The anniversary of the Nazi surrender to the USSR on 9 May 1945 is still commemorated throughout the region. It's particularly interesting in Nagorno-Karabakh (p269), where 9 May is also the anniversary of the Armenian capture of Shushi in 1992, a turning-point in the Karabakh War.

June

One of the best months. Temperatures get up to 30°C in most areas; spring rains have eased off. Walking season in the mountains gets into its stride, although some

high passes are only accessible in July and August.

🏃 Abano Pass Opens

The only road into the beautiful Georgian mountain region of Tusheti (p90), via the nerve-jangling 2900m Abano Pass, normally opens from June to October. Dates depend on the weather, of course.

July

It can get too hot (above 35°C) in the capitals and lowlands, but this is a great time to head to the mountains or the seaside.

☆ Golden Apricot International Film Festival

Yerevan hosts the region's biggest international film fest (www.gaiff.am), under the theme Crossroads of Cultures and Civilisations, over a week in early or mid-July. Launched in 2004, by 2011 it was showing over 170 feature and documentary films from dozens of countries.

☆ Art-Gene Festival

This very popular folk festival (www.artgeni.ge; p41) tours Georgia and culminates with several days of music, cooking, arts and crafts in Tbilisi.

☆ Black Sea Jazz Festival

International jazz artists gather in Georgia's main coastal resort, Batumi, for a week of rhythm, improvisation and fun in late July (www.batumijazz.ge).

Kvirikoba

Georgian countryside festivals usually combine Christian devotion with merrymaking and pagan roots, and Kvirikoba at Kala village on 28 July, one of Svaneti's biggest gatherings, is no exception. Liturgy, blessings, bell-ringing, animal sacrifice and a boulder-tossing contest are followed by feasting and song.

Ramazan

During the Islamic month of Ramazan (Ramadan; see p296 for dates), many Muslims refrain from eating, drinking and smoking during daylight. The fast is not strictly observed throughout Azerbaijan, but many people fast for at least part of Ramazan. Ramazan Bayram, the day after Ramazan, sees widespread feasting.

Vardavar (Transfiguration)

The big summer holiday in Armenia, 14 weeks after Easter. In a throwback to the legendary love-spreading technique of pre-Christian goddess Astgik, kids and teenagers throw water on everyone, and no-one takes offence (much). It's hilarious but not a day for nonstay-fast colours.

August

The weather is the same as July's and this is the big local holiday month, with people flocking to coasts, lakes and mountains. Accommodation in these areas, and transport to them, are at their busiest.

Batumi Season

Georgia's attractive main coastal resort (p72) fills up with holidaymakers from Georgia, Armenia and beyond in July and, especially, August. Much of Tbilisi's nightlife migrates here for the season, adding to the party atmosphere.

Gabala International Music Festival

This top-class international smorgasbord of mainly classical music (www.gabala internationalmusicfestival .com) rings out at Qəbələ (p236) in Azerbaijan between late July and mid-August.

Tushetoba

A part-traditional, part-touristic, Georgian mountain festival at Omalo, Tusheti (p90), on the first Saturday in August (sometimes the last Saturday in July). It features folk music and dancing, traditional sports like horse racing and archery, and the chance to shear your own sheep.

Astvatsatsin

This Armenian festival devoted to the Virgin Mary is celebrated on the Sunday nearest to 15 August. It marks the beginning of the harvest season, with priests blessing grapes in churches.

Mariamoba (Assumption)

One of the biggest holidays in Georgia, especially eastern Georgia, celebrating the Assumption of the Virgin Mary into heaven (28 August). People attend church services and light candles, then gather for family picnics. Sheep may be slaughtered at churches, and then eaten in the gatherings.

September

Temperatures subside a little from their August heights, making for excellent weather. The main local holiday season is over. This is the last full month of the walking season in many mountain areas.

Alaverdoba

The September religious-cum-social festivities of Alaverdoba at Alaverdi Cathedral (p95) in Kakheti last three weeks, climaxing on 14 September, with people coming from remote mountain areas to celebrate.

October

Autumn is here, with temperatures ranging between 10°C and 20°C in most areas. This is the season of harvest festivals and still a nice time to be here.

Kakheti Grape Harvest

The picking and pressing of grapes in Georgia's main wine-producing region, Kakheti (p92), lasts from about 20 September to 20 October. Feasts, musical events and other celebrations go hand-in-hand with the harvest, and it's easy for visitors to join in both the harvest and the partying.

High Fest

The region's top international theatre festival (www.highfest.am) brings a broad range of dramatic companies from around 30 countries to Yerevan, during the first 10 days of October.

Armenian Harvest Festivals

Almost every village and small town in Armenia holds a harvest festival. You'll see singing, dancing and plenty of fresh fruits and vegetables, and the preparation of traditional dishes. In the wine-growing village of Areni (Vayots Dzor) the festivities focus on wine.

Svetitskhovloba (Mtskhetoba)

The Day of Svetitskhoveli Cathedral (p54), 14 October, sees the town of Mtskheta and its people returning to the middle ages with medieval dress, decorations and re-enactments. The Catholicos-Patriarch of the Georgian Church prays for the 12 Orthodox Apostles to give their protection to Georgia.

Gurban Bayramı

The Muslim Festival of Sacrifice (for dates, see p296) commemorates Abraham's test of faith when God ordered him to sacrifice his son Isaac. Azerbaijanis visit family and friends, and the head of the household traditionally slaughters a sheep, which forms the basis of a grand feast.

Baku Jazz Festival

Dates may vary (the second half of October in recent years) and may not be announced till close to the event, but this festival (http://bjf.az) draws some top-notch artists. Participants in recent years have included Al Di Meola, Herbie Hancock and Aziza Mustafadeh.

Tbilisoba

Tbilisi's biggest festivity (http://tbilisoba.ge), with the whole city coming out to party for a week in late October. Food, wine, music (including a jazz festival), dance, exhibitions, martial arts displays and more (p41).

November

Winter is closing in. The days are shortening and the weather is pretty much like March.

Aşura

This solemn Shiite holy day (see p296 for dates) commemorates Imam Hussein's martyrdom in AD 680. Azerbaijani religious authorities suggest that the pious give blood rather than indulging in Iranian-style self-flagellating processions, which are only likely in Muslim hot spots like Nardaran (p226).

Giorgoba (St George's Day)

Georgia celebrates two days of its patron saint, St George, 6 May and 23 November. Both see people attending church and family feasts; 23 November is the more widely celebrated, particularly in eastern Georgia. The president pardons some lucky convicts and concerts are held in Tbilisi.

December

Winter is well and truly here. Temperatures are down around zero in most places.

Tbilisi International Film Festival

Showcases recent movies, mainly Georgian, regional and European, over a week in the last quarter of the year. Dates vary, but in recent years it has been during the first week of December. See www.tbilisifilm festival.ge.

itineraries

Whether you have six days or 60, these itineraries provide a starting point for the trip of a lifetime. Want more inspiration? Head online to lonelyplanet. com/thorntree to chat with other travellers.

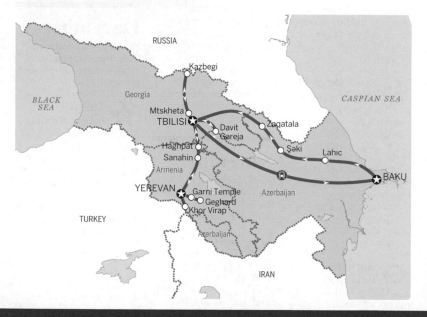

Two Weeks
A Taste of Everything

> You can get a taste of all three countries in two weeks, but do organise your Azerbaijan visa in advance. Starting in Yerevan and finishing in Baku, or vice versa, if you can arrange it, will save backtracking. Otherwise, three days in and around the Georgian capital **Tbilisi**, the region's most attractive city, is the obvious starter. Take day trips to **Davit Gareja** cave monastery and/or the old Georgian capital **Mtskheta**. Next head up to **Kazbegi** for two or three days in the spectacular Great Caucasus. Return to Tbilisi and head off to **Baku** by road or the night train, explore the bustling Azerbaijani capital for a day or two, and return to Tbilisi by the 'country route' through quaint **Lahıc** and lovely **Şəki** and **Zaqatala**. Now head south into Armenia, visiting the World Heritage monasteries of **Haghpat** and **Sanahin** en route to the capital **Yerevan**. In three days here you can venture out to **Garni Temple** and **Geghard** and **Khor Virap** monasteries as well as enjoy the city's cafes, shops and museums.

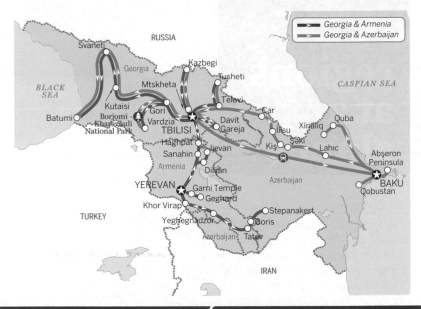

Three to Four Weeks
Georgia & Azerbaijan

Begin with three days in attractive **Tbilisi**, taking a day trip to **Davit Gareja** or **Mtskheta**. Head up to **Kazbegi** for a couple of days in the wonderful Caucasus, then take the overnight Tbilisi–**Baku** train. Spend two or three days soaking up the buzz of Azerbaijan's capital, with side trips to the **Abşeron Peninsula** and/or the petroglyphs and mud volcanoes of **Qobustan**. Head up to the carpetmaking town of **Quba** and to mountain villages beyond such as **Xınalıq** for Azerbaijan's best hiking. Return to Baku and head northwest to quaint **Lahıc**, another base for good walks. Continue to lovely **Şəki** and, if time's on your side, linger at Caucasus foothill villages such as **Kiş**, **İlisu** or **Car**. Re-enter Georgia at Lagodekhi and spend two or three days tasting the wines and sights of Kakheti from **Telavi**. After another night or two in Tbilisi, travel west to the spectacular valleys, villages and mountains of **Svaneti**, visiting **Gori** and **Kutaisi** on the way or way back.

If time allows, detour to spectacular, remote **Tusheti** (from Kakheti), or **Borjomi-Kharagauli National Park** and **Vardzia** in southwest Georgia, or the fun Black Sea resort of **Batumi**.

Three to Four Weeks
Georgia & Armenia

For a three-week itinerary, start easy with three days in attractive **Tbilisi**, taking a day trip to **Davit Gareja** or **Mtskheta**. Head up to **Kazbegi** for a couple of days for a taste of the wonderful Caucasus, then return to Tbilisi and south into Armenia. Check out **Haghpat** and **Sanahin** monasteries in the Debed Canyon, then enjoy **Yerevan's** food, cafes, museums and shops for about three days, with outings to **Garni Temple** and **Geghard** and **Khor Virap** monasteries. Explore southern Armenia for about four days, focusing on the **Yeghegnadzor** area (monasteries, lovely walks and wineries), slow-paced **Goris** and spectacular **Tatev**. Return to Yerevan and Tbilisi and head out to the stunningly beautiful Caucasus enclave of **Svaneti**, visiting **Gori** and **Kutaisi** on the way or way back. Spend your last couple of days enjoying the wines and sights of Kakheti from **Telavi**.

With an extra week, take your pick of side trips to **Stepanakert** in Nagorno-Karabakh (from Goris); northeast Armenia's intriguing **Dilijan** and **Ijevan** areas; **Borjomi-Kharagauli National Park** and **Vardzia** cave city in southwest Georgia; the enjoyable Black Sea resort of **Batumi**; or spectacular, remote **Tusheti** (from Kakheti).

regions at a glance

Wherever you go in the South Caucasus, two of your strongest impressions will be the epic mountain scenery and wonderfully hospitable people. The spectacular Great Caucasus makes for wonderful hiking in Georgia and Azerbaijan. Armenia and Nagorno-Karabakh are a crinkled jigsaw of mountains, valleys, plateaus and gorges, with good day walks.

Fans of ancient churches, monasteries, carvings and frescoes will adore Georgia, Armenia and Nagorno-Karabakh; Muslim Azerbaijan has its own sprinkling of palaces, mosques, forts and caravanserais.

Georgia is the most visited country, with good tourism infrastructure. Travel is easy enough in Armenia, though fellow travellers are few. Azerbaijan is the least touristed, and rewards travellers who like a challenge. Nagorno-Karabakh remains an adventure, though infrastructure is improving rapidly.

Georgia

Scenery ✓✓✓
Hospitality ✓✓✓
Outdoor Activities ✓✓✓

Scenery
The Great Caucasus takes the breath away with its snowy peaks, green valleys and quaint stone villages. The lowlands are strewn with vineyards, rivers, forests and rocky canyons. And the Georgian habit of building churches and castles on picturesque perches only enhances nature.

Hospitality
Georgians believe guests are gifts, so providing hospitality is both customary and a pleasure. You'll be delighted everywhere by the warmth of your welcome, at its best when you share locals' food and their beloved wine.

Outdoor Activities
Hiking, horse riding or climbing in the Great Caucasus is truly spectacular. There is also excellent walking in areas like Borjomi-Kharagauli National Park, Samegrelo and Vardzia. Rafting and paragliding out of Tbilisi are growing in popularity. Winter brings good skiing and ski-touring.

p26

Armenia

Sacred Sites ✓✓✓
Hiking ✓✓
Food ✓✓✓

Azerbaijan

Scenery ✓✓
Earth & Fire ✓✓
Architecture ✓✓

Nagorno-Karabakh

Historic Sites ✓✓
Monasteries ✓✓
Museums ✓✓

Sacred Sites

More than 1700 years of Christian heritage has left Armenia with a rich collection of ancient churches and monasteries, many still active places of worship. Follow Armenians to the most sacred place in the country, holy Echmiadzin near Yerevan.

Hiking

Armenia offers plenty of scope for light hiking and backpacking trips. There are good walks around Dilijan, Ijevan and Tatev, and a more strenuous hike to the top of Mt Aragats.

Food

Some of your best memories of Armenia will be at the dinner table as Armenian cuisine offers a marvellous array of grilled meats, fresh vegetables and sweet, fruit vodkas. Yerevan has the best selection of restaurants, but for an authentic experience try dinner at a family-run homestay.

p121

Scenery

With dizzy Caucasian peaks, bald sheep-mown highlands, Caspian beaches, bucolic woodland meadows and craggy desert badlands, Azerbaijan packs in an astonishing variety of landscapes into a remarkably small space.

Earth & Fire

If you're looking for offbeat curiosities, seek out Azerbaijan's gurgling mud volcanoes or investigate the unusual selection of fire phenomena including 'inflammable' rivers, burning hillsides and a classic fire temple that seems designed for a movie set.

Architecture

Baku's rash of dazzling 21st-century constructions contrast boldly with the city's stately century-old 'oil-boom' mansions, some grand Stalinist constructions and a Unesco-protected medieval Old City still enclosed within crenellated stone walls.

p198

Historic Sites

Step back in time at Shushi, one of the most historic towns in the Caucasus, with fortifications and houses that date back to the mid-18th century. Much older is Tigranakert, an ancient city founded by Tigran the Great.

Monasteries

Monasteries such as Gandzasar and Dadivank are fine examples of the centuries-old Armenian architectural craft. Amaras Monastery, founded by St Gregory the Illuminator in the early 4th century, is more modest in size but one of the world's oldest Christian sites.

Museums

There's a surprising number of excellent museums in Karabakh, including history museums in Shushi, Tigranakert and Stepanakert. Visit the Museum of Fallen Soldiers in Stepanakert for a touching exhibit on the still-recent Karabakh War.

p269

Look out for these icons:

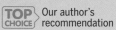 Our author's recommendation

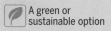 A green or sustainable option

 No payment required

GEORGIA 26
TBILISI 30
AROUND TBILISI 54
Mtskheta 54
Gori 57
Around Gori 59
WESTERN GEORGIA 60
Kutaisi 60
Around Kutaisi 63
Poti 65
Kolkheti National Park 66
Zugdidi 66
ABKHAZIA 68
Sukhumi 69
Northwest of Sukhumi 71
ADJARA 72
Batumi 72
Around Batumi 78
GREAT CAUCASUS 79
Svaneti 79
Georgian Military
Highway 84
Khevsureti 89
Tusheti 90
KAKHETI 92
Telavi 92
Around Telavi 95
Sighnaghi 97
Around Sighnaghi 100
Davit Gareja 100
Lagodekhi
Protected Areas 101
SAMTSKHE-JAVAKHETI .. 101
Borjomi 102

Borjomi-Kharagauli
National Park 104
Bakuriani 105
Akhaltsikhe 106
Vardzia 107
Sapara Monastery 108
UNDERSTAND GEORGIA .. 108
Georgia Today 108
History 109
Arts 112
Food & Drink 114
SURVIVAL GUIDE 115
Directory A–Z 115

ARMENIA 121
YEREVAN 124
AROUND YEREVAN 145
Garni Temple 145
Geghard Monastery 145
Zvartnots Cathedral 147
Echmiadzin 148
Sardarapat 149
Ashtarak 149
Byurakan & Around 150
Mt Aragats 151
Khor Virap Monastery 151
NORTHERN ARMENIA 152
Lake Sevan 152
Sevan 153
Around Lake Sevan 155
Tsaghkadzor 156
Dilijan 157
Haghartsin 159
Goshavank 160
Ijevan 160

See the Index for a full list of destinations covered in this book.

On the Road

Yenokavan & Around 162
Vanadzor 163
Stepanavan & Around 165
Debed Canyon 167
Gyumri 169
Marmashen 173
Harichavank 173
SOUTHERN ARMENIA 173
Areni 173
Noravank 174
Yeghegnadzor & Around . . 174
Yeghegis & Around 177
Vayk & Around 177
Jermuk 178
Sisian 179
Around Sisian 180
Goris 180
Around Goris 183
Tatev 184
Kapan 185
Meghri 186
UNDERSTAND ARMENIA . . 187
Armenia Today 187
History 188
Arts 190
Food & Drink 192
SURVIVAL GUIDE 193
Directory A–Z 193

AZERBAIJAN 198
BAKU (BAKI) 202
AROUND BAKU 224
Abşeron Peninsula 224
Baku to Qobustan 227

Şirvan National Park 228
NORTHERN AZERBAIJAN . . 228
Baku to Quba 228
Quba 230
Around Quba 231
NORTHWESTERN
AZERBAIJAN 233
Baku to İsmayıllı 233
İsmayıllı 233
Around İsmayıllı 234
Qəbələ 236
Oğuz 237
Şəki 238
Around Şəki 244
Qax 244
Around Qax 244
Zaqatala 245
Around Zaqatala 247
Balakən 247
CENTRAL AZERBAIJAN . . . 248
Gəncə 248
Around Gəncə 250
SOUTHERN AZERBAIJAN . . 250
Masallı & Around 250
Lənkəran 251
Lerik & Around 253
Astara 254
NAXÇIVAN 254
Naxçivan City 255
Naxçivan City to
Ordubad 258
Naxçivan City to Turkey . . . 259
UNDERSTAND
AZERBAIJAN 260
Azerbaijan Today 260

History 260
Arts 262
Food & Drink 263
SURVIVAL GUIDE 264
Directory A–Z 264

**NAGORNO-
KARABAKH 269**
Stepanakert 270
Shushi 273
Southern Karabakh 275
Northeast Karabakh 275
Northwest Karabakh 276
Kelbajar 276
UNDERSTAND
NAGORNO-KARABAKH . . . 277
History 277
Nagorno-Karabakh Today . . 277
SURVIVAL GUIDE 278
Directory A–Z 278

Georgia

Includes »

Tbilisi...................................30
Mtskheta 54
Gori 57
Kutaisi...........................60
Zugdidi..........................66
Abkhazia.......................68
Sukhumi.........................69
Batumi 72
Svaneti..........................79
Kazbegi..........................84
Shatili.............................89
Tusheti 90
Kakheti...........................92
Davit Gareja 100
Borjomi 102
Borjomi-Kharagauli NP 104
Vardzia..........................107

Best Places to Stay

» Dzveli Batumi (p73)

» Boombully Rooms & Hostel (p42)

» Skadaveli Guesthouse (p42)

» Nikolaishvili Winery (p99)

Best Places to Eat

» Pur-Pur (p44)

» Puris Sakhli (p45)

» Temraz Nijaradz (p83)

Why Go?

From its sublimely perched old churches and watchtowers dotting fantastic mountain scenery to its green valleys spread with vineyards, Georgia (Saqartvelo, საქართველო) is one of the most beautiful countries on earth and a marvellous canvas for walkers, horse riders, skiers, rafters and paragliders. Equally special are its proud, high-spirited, cultured people: Georgia claims to be the birthplace of wine, and this is a place where guests are considered blessings and hospitality is the very stuff of life.

A deeply complicated history has given Georgia a wonderful heritage of architecture and art, from cave cities to the inimitable canvases of Pirosmani. Tbilisi, the capital, is still redolent of an age-old Eurasian crossroads. But this is also a country striving for a place in the 21st-century Western world, with eye-catching new buildings, a minimal crime rate and a heap of new facilities for the tourists who are a big part of its future.

When to Go

The ideal seasons are from mid-May to early July and from early September to mid-October, when it's generally warm and sunny. Most of July and August can be uncomfortably humid, and lowland temperatures can reach 40°C. However, this is an excellent time to be in the mountains, and it's the peak season on the Black Sea.

Early autumn brings the festive wine harvest in Kakheti, from about 20 September to 20 October. The eastern half of Georgia often suffers below-freezing temperatures between December and February.

Connections

Tbilisi has direct flights to/from numerous European cities, several in the Middle East and Kazakhstan, and even Ürümqi in China. Batumi has direct flights to/from Istanbul, Tel Aviv, Moscow and several Ukrainian cities. Both Tbilisi and Batumi have Baku flights, and Tbilisi has flights to/from Yerevan.

The busy Sarpi border crossing to/from Turkey is used by buses between Tbilisi and Istanbul as well as shorter-distance services. Some Georgia–Turkey transport also crosses the Vale–Posof border near Akhaltsikhe.

Marshrutky (public minivans), taxis and a train connect Tbilisi with Yerevan via the Sadakhlo border. There is also *marshrutka* service between Akhaltsikhe, Gyumri and Yerevan via the Zhdanovi–Bavra border.

An overnight train runs between Tbilisi and Baku, as do buses and *marshrutky* via the Tsiteli Khidi (Krasny Most, Red Bridge) border. The more attractive route to/from Azerbaijan, via Lagodekhi, Balakən and Zaqatala, is a matter of several *marshrutky* or taxi hops.

ITINERARIES

Three Days

Focus on Tbilisi, the fascinating capital, with an outing to Mtskheta and a day trip to the spectacular Davit Gareja cave monastery.

One Week

Starting with Tbilisi, you have time to visit the mountains and another region too. Opt for two or three nights in either Kazbegi or Svaneti (to fit Svaneti into this schedule you'll have to fly at least one-way). Have a couple of nights in the eastern wine-growing region of Kakheti (including a visit to Davit Gareja), or head to the cave city Vardzia via Borjomi and maybe have a day walking in Borjomi-Kharagauli National Park.

Two Weeks

You can fit in all the destinations of the one-week itinerary, plus Gori, Kutaisi and the Black Sea resort of Batumi.

Visas

Many nationalities need no visa for stays up to 360 days. Those who do need visas can obtain them on arrival at Tbilisi airport or road entry points into Georgia (50 GEL for 90-day single-entry visas), or beforehand from Georgian embassies or consulates. Visas on arrival are not available for those coming by train or sea. See p119 for further details.

RESOURCES

Georgia
(www.georgia.travel)

Agency of Protected Areas
(www.apa.gov.ge)

National Agency for Cultural Heritage Preservation
(www.heritagesites.ge)

Georgia & South Caucasus
(georgien.blogspot.com)

Civil.ge (www.civil.ge)

Fast Facts

» **Country code** ☏995
» **Population** 4.47 million
» **Currency** Lari (GEL)
» **Language** Georgian
» **Emergency** ☏113

Exchange Rates

Australia	A$1	1.77 GEL
Canada	C$1	1.69 GEL
Euro zone	€1	2.36 GEL
Japan	¥100	2.16 GEL
NZ	NZ$1	1.41 GEL
UK	UK£1	2.70 GEL
USA	US$1	1.66 GEL

Set Your Budget

» **Budget accommodation** 25 GEL per person
» **Two-course meal** 12 GEL
» **Museum** 3 GEL
» **Beer** 1.50 GEL per bottle
» **100km marshrutka ride** 10 GEL

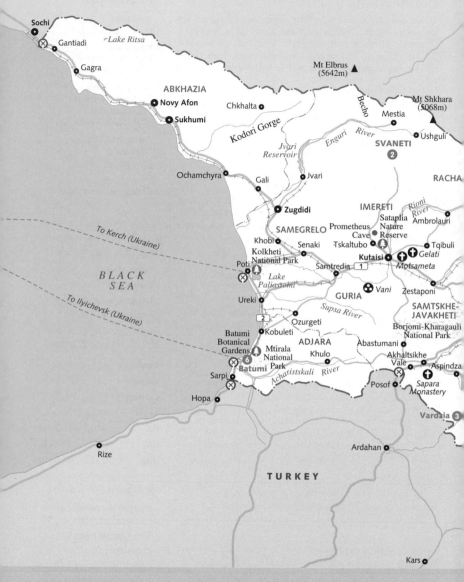

Georgia Highlights

1 Enjoy the Old Town, Mtkvari River, fine restaurants and fun bars of **Tbilisi** (p30), the most charming Caucasian capital

2 Discover unique Svan culture, ancient defensive towers and wonderful walking amid Georgia's finest alpine scenery in **Svaneti** (p79)

3 Explore **Vardzia** (p107), an entire medieval city carved out of a cliff face

4 Catch the breath-taking sight of Tsminda Sameba Church silhouetted against legendary Mt Kazbek while hiking around **Kazbegi** (p84)

RUSSIA

Nalchik

Grozny

Nazran

Vladikavkaz

Mamisoni
Pass

Mt Kazbek
(5047m)

Larsi

Shatili

Kazbegi ④

Mt Diklos
(4285m)

Roki
Tunnel

Jvari Pass

KHEVSURETI

TUSHETI ⑦

Oni

KHEVI

Barisakho

Dartlo

Shenaqo

Liakhvi

Gudauri

Omalo

Sachkhere

Didi

SOUTH
OSSETIA

Georgian
Military
Highway

PSHAVI

Chiatura

Kvirila

Likhi Range

Tskhinvali

Pasanauri

Alaverdi
Cathedral

Gremi

Nekresi
Monastery

Khashuri

Kareli

Uplistsikhe

Ananuri

Akhmeta

Lagodekhi
Protected Areas

Gori

Mtkvari
River

Ikalto

Telavi

Tsinandali

Lagodekhi

Borjomi

Ateni
Sioni

Mtskheta

Akhali Shuamta &
Dzveli Shuamta

Bakuriani

TBILISI ①
Tbilisi Airport

Sagarejo

Gurjaani

Balakən

Tsalka

Rustavi

Sighnaghi

Tsnori

Bodbe Convent

Bolnisi

Gardabani

Davit
Gareja ⑤

Mirzaani

Lake
Paravani

KVEMO
KARTLI

Marneuli

Böyük Kəsik

Dedoplistskaro

Akhalkalaki

Guguti

Sadakhlo

Tsiteli Khidi
(Krasny Most)

KAKHETI ⑧

Ninotsminda

Bagratashen

Bavra

(Border
closed)

AZERBAIJAN

(Border
closed)

Gyumri

Vanadzor

ARMENIA

Gəncə

⑤ Visit the ancient, highly
revered cave monastery of
Davit Gareja (p100) in its
unique setting

⑥ Soak up the party
atmosphere in **Batumi** (p72),
Georgia's lovable Black Sea
'summer capital', against a
backdrop of mist-wrapped
green hills

⑦ Hike the spectacular,
remote, pristine region of high-
mountain **Tusheti** (p90)

⑧ Spend your days sipping
the **wines of Kakheti** (p99) in
the home of Georgian wine

TBILISI

📋 32 / POP 1.1 MILLION

With a quarter of Georgia's population, Tbilisi (თბილისი) is the place where Georgians gravitate for action and excitement. The city brims with history and has a dramatic setting on hillsides either side of the swift Mtkvari River. Its Old Town, at the narrowest part of the valley, is still redolent of an ancient Eurasian crossroads, with winding lanes, old balconied houses, leafy squares, handsome churches and countless busy bars and cafes, all overlooked by the 17-centuries-old Nariqala Fortress.

Tbilisi is also a modern city trying to move forward in the 21st century after the strife and stagnation of the late 20th. Its streets are crowded with pedestrians, construction debris and hurtling or crawling traffic. Flagship building projects, from a new cathedral and presidential palace to revamped parks and museums, coexist with crowded old markets, confusing bus stations and shabby Soviet apartment blocks.

Tbilisi is still the beating heart of the South Caucasus and should not be missed by any visitor.

Tbilisi

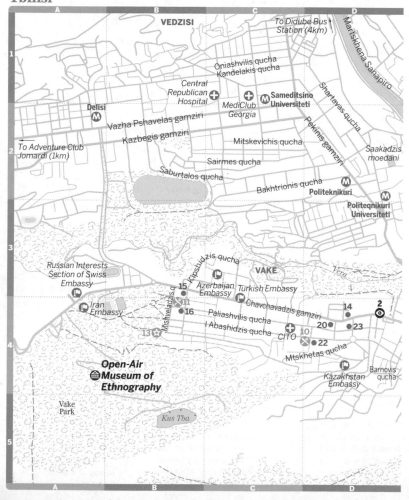

History

Evidence of settlement in the area stretches back to the 4th century BC, but Georgians like the legend that King Vakhtang Gorgasali of Kartli founded Tbilisi in the 5th century. The story runs that when the king was hunting, a wounded deer fell into a hot sulphur spring and was miraculously healed. In fact Gorgasali won the town back from the Persians, and moved his capital here from Mtskheta in the late 5th century. But there's no doubt that it was Tbilisi's magnificent hot springs that gave the city its name (the Georgian *tbili* means warm).

In 645 Arabs captured Tbilisi and kept it as an emirate for four centuries, but in 1122 King David the Builder (Davit Aghmashenebeli) took the city and made it capital of a united Georgia, building a palace near the Metekhi Church. David invited Armenian artisans and traders to settle in the city, and Armenians remained highly influential here until the 20th century. Under David and his great-granddaughter Queen Tamar, Georgia enjoyed its medieval golden age and Tbilisi developed into a multiethnic city of 80,000 people, known for its production of weapons, jewellery, leather and silk clothing. The golden age was ended with a vengeance by

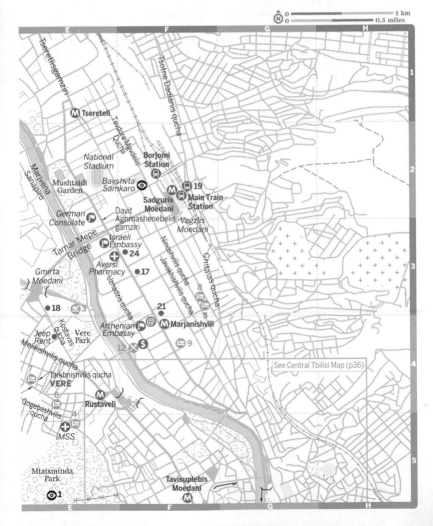

the Mongols in 1235, followed in turn by the Black Death, then conqueror Timur (Tamerlane), who destroyed the city in 1386, and the Persians, who captured it in the 1540s.

Tbilisi recovered somewhat under the Persians during the 17th and 18th centuries, and in 1762 it became capital of an independent eastern Georgia under King Erekle II. Erekle's protector Russia, however, withdrew its troops to fight the Turks, allowing Agha Mohamed Khan to inflict Persia's most devastating assault in 1795. His army killed tens of thousands and burnt Tbilisi to the ground; few buildings today predate 1795 in any substantial form. Russia annexed Georgia in 1800 and recreated Tbilisi in the imperial mould, laying out wide streets and squares. By 1899, Tbilisi had 172,000 people, one-third of them Armenian and a quarter each Georgian and Russian.

The Soviet era saw huge growth and relative prosperity: the city's population passed one million in the 1970s as Georgians flooded in from the countryside. Tbilisi became a centre of opposition to the late Soviet regime, culminating in 19 deaths when troops dispersed hunger strikers at the Parliament building on 9 April 1989. Parliament declared Georgian independence two years later. Rebellion against President Zviad Gamsakhurdia erupted in fierce fighting on Tbilisi's streets in December 1991, destroying several central landmark buildings.

The 1990s were dark years in Tbilisi – literally, with frequent power cuts blacking out the city – as living standards sank and corruption and crime became rife. In the Rose Revolution of 2003, protesting crowds filled central Tbilisi and finally poured into parliament to drive out President Eduard Shevardnadze. Since then, crime has almost disappeared and Tbilisi has enjoyed a flood of investment and refurbishment, although prosperity is still barely trickling down to the less advantaged sectors of the population.

◉ Sights

The Old Town, where Tbilisi began, is the most fascinating area for exploring. There's also plenty to see in the 19th-century city focused on Rustavelis gamziri and in the Avlabari area on the left bank of the Mtkvari. Most churches are open daylight hours every day.

OLD TOWN ჯაღა

Tbilisi grew up below the walls of the Nariqala Fortress, which stands on the Sololaki ridge above the west side of the Mtkvari. The twisting alleys of the Old Town (Qala) are still full of hidden courtyards and carved

Tbilisi

◎ **Top Sights**
   Open-Air Museum of
   Ethnography A4

◉ **Sights**
  1 Ferris Wheel E5
  2 Tbilisi State University D4

✪ **Activities, Courses & Tours**
  3 Laguna Vere Pool E3

🛏 **Sleeping**
  4 Betsy's Hotel E5
  5 Dodo's Dormitory F3
  6 Hotel British House E4
  7 Hotel Vere Inn E4
  8 Irine Japaridze's Boarding House F3
  9 Sky Hostel F4

✕ **Eating**
  10 Cafe Tartine D4
  11 Il Garage B4

  12 Shemoikhede Genatsvale F4

✪ **Entertainment**
  13 33a B4
  Georgia National Music Center .... (see 17)

ℹ **Information**
  14 Levon Travel D4
  15 X-Tour B3

ℹ **Transport**
  16 Air Baltic B4
  17 Airzena Georgian Airways F3
  18 Arkia E3
  19 Avtosadguri Dedaqalaqi F2
  20 AZAL (Azerbaijan Airlines) D4
  21 Belavia F3
     BMI .... (see 23)
  22 Czech Airlines D4
  23 Lufthansa D4
  24 Turkish Airlines F3

wooden balconies leaning at rakish angles. Though almost no buildings here survived the Persian sacking of 1795, many date from soon after that and still have the Eurasian character of earlier times.

Kote Abkhazi   STREET
(Map p36) The main thoroughfare of the Old Town, winding down from Tavisuplebis moedani and strung with assorted shops and eateries, is Kote Abkhazi, formerly Leselidze. Towards the bottom of the street stands the large, disused Armenian **Norasheni Church**, dating from 1793, with the smaller **Jvaris Mama Church** next door on a site where a church has stood since the 5th century. The current Jvaris Mama dates from the 16th century and its interior is almost completely covered in recently restored frescoes in striking reds, golds and blues: the atmosphere is exquisitely pious and calm. A little further down Kote Abkhazi is Tbilisi's main **synagogue**, a welcoming place built in 1904.

Shavteli, Erekle II & Sioni   AREA
(Map p36) This string of narrow, traffic-free streets paralleling the river was the heaving commercial hub of the Old Town in medieval times. At the north end of Shavteli you'll find the quirkiest building in Tbilisi, the rakishly leaning **Clock Tower**. Like something out of a fairy tale, it faithfully evokes the spirit of the celebrated Tbilisi Marionette Theatre beside it.

Just south stands the lovely little **Anchiskhati Basilica**, Tbilisi's oldest surviving church, built by King Gorgasali's son Dachi in the 6th century. The name comes from the icon of Anchi Cathedral in Klarjeti (now in Turkey), brought here in the 17th century and now in Tbilisi's Fine Arts Museum. The church is a three-nave basilica that has been restored several times: the brick pillars and upper walls date from the 17th century. Further down Shavteli is a peaceful little park, **Erekle II moedani**, facing the walled **residence of the Catholicos-Patriarch** (head of the Georgian church).

The street Erekle II gives access to the **Peace Bridge** (Mshvidobis Khidi), an elegant glass-and-steel footbridge over the Mtkvari, designed by Italian Michele De Lu-cchi and opened in 2010 – now unfortunately nicknamed the Always Bridge, for its undeniable resemblance to a giant sanitary towel. Erekle II continues past cafes and galleries into Sioni, where the **Sioni Cathedral** was originally built in the 6th and 7th centuries. It has been destroyed and rebuilt many times and what you see today is mainly 13th century, though the southern chapel was built and the cupola restored in 1657. A bronze grille to the left of the icon screen displays a replica of the sacred cross of St Nino which, according to legend, is made from vine branches bound with the saint's own hair. The real thing is apparently kept safe inside.

The **Tbilisi History Museum** (Sioni 8), housed in an old caravanserai, will be worth a visit when it eventually opens after refurbishment. Just past here Sharden and Bambis rigi, two parallel streets lined with fashionable cafes and bars, branch off Sioni and emerge on the busy intersection known as Meidan.

Meidan & Around   AREA
(Map p36) Meidan is now a rather bland, traffic-infested junction beside the Metekhi Bridge but was once the setting of Tbilisi's bustling bazaar. Just above it is the large **Armenian Cathedral of St George** (Samghebro), founded in 1251 (although the current structure is mainly 18th century). Its surprisingly small, smoke-blackened interior has a few interesting frescoes. King Erekle II's famed Armenian court poet Sayat Nova was killed here during the Persian invasion of 1795 and his tomb is just outside the main door.

Samghebro leads south to Tbilisi's celebrated sulphur baths, the **Abanotubani**. Alexandre Dumas and Pushkin both bathed here, the latter describing it as the best bath he'd ever had. Most of the bathhouses are subterranean, with beehive domes rising at ground level. Many date back to the 17th century. Outwardly the most impressive, the aboveground **Orbeliani Baths** (Abano; ☉8am-10pm), has a Central Asian feel to its blue-tile façade. See p41 for information on using the baths.

A short distance uphill behind the baths is the red-brick **mosque** (Botanikuri), the only mosque in Tbilisi that survived Lavrenty Beria's purges of the 1930s. It was built in 1895 and, unusually, Shia and Sunni Muslims pray together here. The interior is prettily frescoed and visitors are welcome to enter (after removing shoes). At the top of this street are Tbilisi's **Botanical Gardens** (Botanikuri; admission 1 GEL; ☉9am-8pm). It's easy to wander for an enjoyable hour or two in these extensive, waterfall-dotted gardens,

GEORGIAN STREET NAMES

The spelling of Georgian street names varies slightly, depending on whether words such as *qucha* (street), *gamziri* (avenue) or *moedani* (square) are present. In Georgian, Sioni Street is Sionis qucha. To simplify matters, we use noninflected names in addresses – for example Sioni rather than Sionis qucha – unless there is more than one street with the same name (for example Chavchavadzis qucha and Chavchavadzis gamziri).

which were opened in 1845 in former royal gardens.

NARIQALA FORTRESS & AROUND

FREE **Nariqala Fortress** FORTRESS
(Map p36; Orpiri; ⊙9am-9pm) Dominating the Old Town skyline, Nariqala dates right back to the 4th century, when it was a Persian citadel. The most direct way up to it is by the street beside the Armenian Cathedral of St George. The tower foundations and most of the present walls were built in the 8th century by the Arab emirs, whose palace was inside the fortress. Subsequently Georgians, Turks and Persians captured and patched up Nariqala, but in 1827 a huge explosion of Russian munitions stored here ruined not only the fortress but also the **Church of St Nicholas** inside it. The church was rebuilt in the 1990s with the help of funding from a police chief. There are superb views over Tbilisi from the top of the fortress.

Kartlis Deda MONUMENT
(Mother Georgia; Map p36) From outside the fortress entrance, you can follow a path west to the statue of Mother Georgia. As attractive as a 20m aluminium woman can be, this symbol of Tbilisi holds a sword in one hand and a cup of wine in the other – a classic metaphor for the Georgian character, warmly welcoming guests and passionately fighting off enemies. A few muggings were reported up here a few years ago, so it's probably wise to stay alert – but your main challenge is likely to be steering clear of canoodling couples hoping for a bit of privacy. Past Mother Georgia are the ruins of the **Shahtakhti (Shah's Throne) fortress**, which housed an Arab observatory.

AVLABARI

Avlabari is the dramatically located slice of Tbilisi above the cliffs on the left (east) bank of the Mtkvari, across the **Metekhi Bridge** from the Old Town. At least twice foreign invaders (the roaming Central Asian conqueror Jalaledin in 1226, and the Persians in 1522) used the bridge for forcible conversion of Georgians to Islam (those who resisted were tossed into the river).

Metekhi Church CHURCH
(Map p36; Metekhis aghmarti) The Metekhi Church, and the 1960s equestrian **statue of King Vakhtang Gorgasali** beside it, occupy the strategic rocky outcrop above the Metekhi Bridge. This is where Vakhtang Gorgasali built his palace and the site's original church, when he made Tbilisi his capital in the 5th century. King David the Builder had a palace and church here too – they were destroyed during the Mongol invasion in 1235. The existing church was built by King Demetre Tavdadebuli (the Self-Sacrificing) between 1278 and 1289, and has been reconstructed many times since. It is thought to be a deliberate copy of King David's 12th-century church. The tomb of the Christian martyr St Shushanik – tortured by her husband in 544 for refusing to convert to Zoroastrianism – is to the left of the icon screen.

Rike Park PARK
(Map p36) This attractive flowery expanse north of the Metekhi Bridge lights up with an entertaining fountains, music and laser show every evening from about 8pm to 11pm. The Peace Bridge connects the park to the west bank of the Mtkvari.

Tsminda Sameba Cathedral CATHEDRAL
(Holy Trinity Cathedral; Map p36; Samreklo) The biggest symbol of Georgia's post-Soviet religious revival rises high on Elia Hill above Avlabari. Tsminda Sameba, an unmissable landmark by night and day, was consecrated in 2004 after a decade of building. A massive expression of traditional Georgian architectural forms in concrete, brick, granite and marble, it rises 84m to the top of the gold-covered cross above its central dome.

The cathedral is five aisles wide but its emphasis is on verticality, with a result like one single, many-bulwarked tower. The huge dome creates a larger, much brighter central space than you'll find in most Georgian churches. A big new illuminated manuscript of the New Testament, on calf-leather parchment in a jewel-studded, gilded-silver cover, stands in a glass case to the right of the icon screen. There's a whole large second church beneath the main one, down 81 steps from the west end. Designed by Archil Mindiashvili, the building was paid for mostly by anonymous donations. Some controversy surrounded its construction on the site of an old Armenian cemetery.

Presidential Palace PALACE
(Map p36; Tsutsqiridze) Not far below the cathedral, Georgia's new presidential palace (not open to visitors) is an equally unmissable landmark, with its ultraclassical portico surmounted by a large, egg-shaped, glass dome – another creation of Michele De Lucchi.

RUSTAVELI

Tbilisi's main artery, **Rustavelis gamziri**, is named after the national bard, Shota Rustaveli, and runs 1.5km north from Tavisuplebis moedani to Rustavelis moedani. Laid out by the Russians in the 19th century, it's strung with elegant and important buildings. It's also a fast traffic route, dangerous to cross except by four pedestrian underpasses. **Tavisuplebis moedani** (Liberty Sq; Map p36), with the old city hall on its south side, was Lenin Sq in Soviet times. Georgia's last Lenin statue, toppled in 1990, stood where the golden St George now spears his dragon.

TOP CHOICE **Museum of Georgia** MUSEUM
(Map p36; www.museum.ge; Rustaveli 3; admission 5 GEL; ⊙11am-5.30pm Tue-Sun) The impressive national museum reopened in 2011 after a five-year refurbishment. A major highlight is the Archaeological Treasury, displaying a wealth of pre-Christian gold, silver and precious-stone work from burials between the 3rd millennium BC and the 4th century AD. Most stunning are the fabulously worked gold adornments from Colchis (western Georgia) from the 8th to 3rd centuries BC. The rest of the museum has a huge collection of historical and ethnographic material, including a hall on the Soviet occupation and another full of the historic photos of Dmitry Yermakov which document Georgia and the South Caucasus a century ago.

TOP CHOICE **National Gallery** GALLERY
(Map p36; Rustaveli 11; admission 5 GEL; ⊙11am-5.30pm Tue-Sun) Brand new in 2011, the National Gallery is entered from the park beside the Kashveti Church and is well worth an hour of your time. For most visitors the highlight is the hall full of wonderful canvases by Georgia's best known painter Pirosmani (Niko Pirosmanashvili, 1862–1918), ranging from his celebrated animal and feast scenes to lesser-known portraits and rural-life canvases. There's also a good selection of work by other top 20th-century Georgian artists such as Lado Gudiashvili, Elene Akhvlediani and David Kakabadze.

Fine Arts Museum MUSEUM
(Map p36; ☑2999909; Gudiashvili 1; admission 3 GEL, guide per group 10 GEL; ⊙11am-4pm Tue-Sun) Just off Tavisuplebis moedani, this is a comprehensive if underwhelmingly presented storehouse of Georgian art and artisanry from several centuries BC up to the 20th century. The major highlight is the Treasury section, only enterable with a guide (you can reserve an English-speaking guide in advance to avoid waiting at busy times). This contains a great wealth of icons, crosses and jewellery in precious metals and stones from all over Georgia and old Georgian churches and monasteries on what is now Turkish territory. Many of Georgia's most sacred and revered objects are here. Don't miss the beautiful little pectoral cross of Queen Tamar, set with four emeralds, five rubies and six pearls – the only known personal relic of the great 12th-century monarch. Another interesting section covers 19th-century Persian and Azerbaijani art and crafts. The building was once a seminary: Stalin studied for the priesthood here from 1894 to 1898 until expelled for revolutionary activities.

Parliament Building HISTORIC BUILDING
(Map p36; Rustaveli 8) The high-arched Parliament building has seen momentous events, including the deaths of 19 Georgian hunger strikers on 9 April 1989; Georgia's independence declaration on 9 April 1991; and the Rose Revolution on 22 November 2003. It was constructed between 1938 and 1953 for Georgia's Soviet government, became the seat of Georgia's Parliament after independence, and has been the venue of many antigovernment protests ever since late Soviet times. With the moving of Parliament to Kutaisi, planned for 2012, the building will take on a new role (undecided at the time of writing). A small monument in front of it, and paving stones and glass panels set at irregular angles, commemorate the dead of 1989.

Central Tbilisi

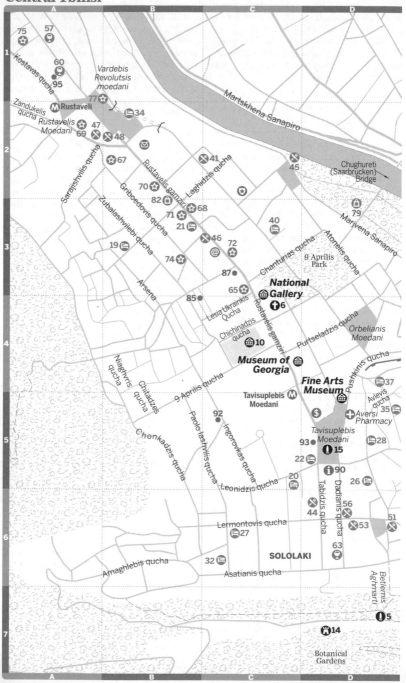

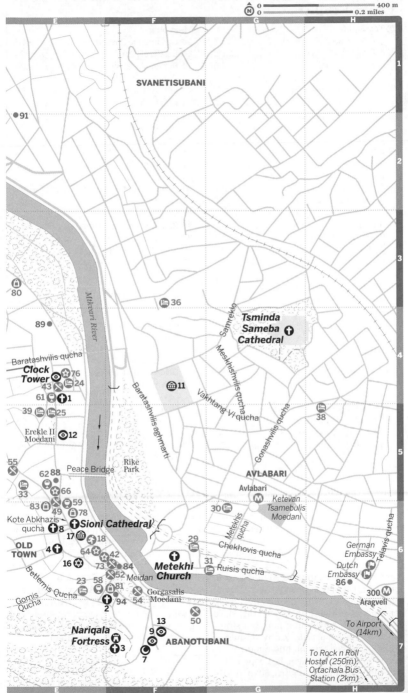

0 400 m
0 0.2 miles

SVANETISUBANI

●91

80

89●

Baratashvilis qucha
*Clock
Tower* ◉ 76
43 ✕ 24
61 ♛ ⓪1
39 🖻 25

Erekle II ◉12
Moedani

55
✕
33 🖻
62 88
66 ★
83 🔒 59
49 ✕ 78
Kote Abkhazis
qucha ⓪8 ♔*Sioni Cathedral*

OLD
TOWN 4⓪
16 ⚽
64 ★ 42
23 58 73 🕍 84
Bettlemis Qucha 52 *Meidan*
Gomis 81
Qucha 94 54
2

Nariqala 🏰
Fortress 3

13
9 ◉
7

ABANOTUBANI

🖻36

Tsminda
Sameba
Cathedral 🕀

🏛11

Samrekho

Meskhishvilis qucha

Vakhtang VI qucha

Gonashvilis qucha

🖻
38

Rike
Park

Peace Bridge

AVLABARI

Avlabari
Ⓜ Ketevan
Tsamebulis
30🖻 Moedani

Metekhis qucha

29
🖻
31 Chekhovis qucha
🖻 Ruisis qucha

Metekhi
Church 🕀

Gorgasalis
Moedani

✕
50

German
Embassy
Dutch
Embassy 🖻
86●

elavis qucha

300 Ⓜ
Aragveli

To Airport
(14km)

To Rock n Roll
Hostel (250m);
Ortachala Bus
Station (2km)

Mtkvari River

Baratashvilis aghmarti

Central Tbilisi

◎ **Top Sights**

Clock Tower	E4
Fine Arts Museum	D5
Metekhi Church	F6
Museum of Georgia	C4
Nariqala Fortress	F7
National Gallery	C3
Sioni Cathedral	E6
Tsminda Sameba Cathedral	G4

◎ **Sights**

1	Anchiskhati Basilica	E4
2	Armenian Cathedral of St George	F7
3	Church of St Nicholas	F7
4	Jvaris Mama Church	E6
5	Kartlis Deda	D7
6	Kashveti Church	C4
7	Mosque	F7
8	Norasheni Church	E6
9	Orbeliani Baths	F7
10	Parliament Building	C4
11	Presidential Palace	F4
12	Residence of the Catholicos-Patriarch	E5
13	Royal Bath	F7
14	Shahtakhti Fortress	D7
15	St George & Dragon Monument	D5
16	Synagogue	E6
17	Tbilisi History Museum	E6

✈ **Activities, Courses & Tours**

	Courtyard by Marriott	(see 22)
	Radisson Blu Iveria Hotel	(see 34)
18	Vanilla Sky	E6

🛏 **Sleeping**

19	Beaumonde Guest House	B3
20	Big Star Hostel	C5
21	Boombully Rooms & Hostel	B3
22	Courtyard by Marriott	D5
23	Friends Hostel	E6
24	Hotel Ambasadori	E4
25	Hotel Charm	E5
26	Hotel City	D5
27	Hotel David	C6
28	Hotel Dzveli Ubani	D5
29	Hotel Kopala	F6
30	Hotel Lile	G6
31	Hotel Old Metekhi	G6
32	Nest Hostel	C6
33	Old Town Hostel	E5
34	Radisson Blu Iveria Hotel	B2
35	Skadaveli Guesthouse	D5
36	Soul House Hostel	F3
37	Star Hostel	D4
38	Tbilisi Hostel	H5
39	Villa Mtiebi	E5
40	Why Not? Tbilisi Legend Hostel	C3

🍴 **Eating**

41	Baan Thai Cuisine	C2
42	Brasserie L'Express	F6
43	Café Gabriadze	E4
	Caliban's Coffeehouse	(see 82)
44	Downtown	D6
	Dzveli Metekhi	(see 31)
45	Dzveli Sakhli	C2
46	Entrée	C3
	Hotel Kopala	(see 29)
47	Khinkal Centre	A2
48	Khinklis Sakhli	B2

Kashveti Church CHURCH

(Map p36) Almost opposite the Parliament building, the Kashveti Church stands on a spot where it is said pagan rituals used to take place. The first church here is supposed to have been built in the 6th century by Davit Gareja, one of the ascetic 'Syrian fathers' who returned from the Middle East to spread Christianity in Georgia. According to legend, a nun accused him of impregnating her. He replied that if this were true, she'd give birth to a baby, and if not, to a stone, which duly happened. Kashveti means 'Stone Birth'. The existing 1910 building, designed by Leopold Bielfeld, is a copy of the 11th-century Samtavisi Church, 60km northwest of Tbilisi.

MT MTATSMINDA

Mtatsminda is the hill topped by the 210m-high TV mast looming over central Tbilisi from the west. **Mtatsminda Park** (Map p30; www.park.ge; ◷noon-9pm) spreads over more than 1 sq km at the top of the hill, with plenty of funfair attractions. To use the attractions you must buy a card (1 GEL) at the entrance and put credit on it. The best views are from the huge **Ferris wheel** (per person 5.50 GEL), as trees obscure the panoramas elsewhere. Buses 90 and 124 go up to the park from Leonidze off Tavisuplebis moedani.

VAKE ვაკე

Considered Tbilisi's most prestigious neighbourhood, Vake is an amalgam of apartment

49 Luca Polare E5
50 Puris Sakhli F7
51 Pur-Pur..D6
52 Qalaquri Samikitno.................................F6
53 Racha...D6
54 Restorani Alani...F6
55 Shemoikhede Genatsvale.....................E5
56 Teremok...D6

🍸 **Drinking**
57 Art Café A1
58 Bude Bar...E6
59 Café Kala E6
60 Dublin A1
61 Hangar Bar...E4
62 Moulin Electrique....................................E5
    Oxygen Bar..(see 34)
    Pur-Pur ....(see 51)
63 Salve...D6

🎭 **Entertainment**
64 Bamba Station...E6
65 GURU Club C3
66 Missoni E5
67 New Cafe Gallery B2
68 Paliashvili Opera & Ballet
    Theatre...B3
69 Pantomime Theatre A2
70 Restaurant Chakrulo..............................B2
71 Rock Club B3
72 Rustaveli Theatre C3
73 Safe...E6
74 State Conservatoire B3
75 Success...A1
76 Tbilisi Marionette Theatre E4
77 Vernisage A1

🛍 **Shopping**
78 Caucasian Carpets.................................E6
79 Dry Bridge Market...................................D3
    Gallery ....(see 82)
80 Geoland..E3
81 Meidan 91...F6
82 Prospero's Books.....................................B3
83 Vinotheca...E6

ℹ **Information**
    Beeline ....(see 87)
    Canadian Consulate.....................(see 82)
84 Caucasus Travel.......................................F6
85 Explore Georgia..B4
86 Fedex..H6
87 Geocell...C3
88 GeorgiCa Travel.......................................E5
    Magti ....(see 46)
89 Ministry of Culture &
    Monument Protection.........................E4
    Post Office ....(see 87)
90 Tourism Information Centre D5
91 Wild Georgia E2

ℹ **Transport**
92 Aerosvit...C5
93 Avis..D5
    Hertz...(see 84)
    Pegasus Airlines..........................(see 22)
    S7 Airlines.......................................(see 26)
    SCAT..(see 92)
94 Sixt F6
95 Ukraine International Airlines A1
    Vanilla Sky ....(see 18)

blocks, houses, restaurants, cafes, shops, parks and busy traffic. You can get to Vake's main avenue, Chavchavadzis gamziri, by bus 61 from Tavisuplebis moedani and north on Rustaveli, or bus 59 north on Davit Aghmashenebeli on the east side of the Mtkvari.

Tbilisi State University UNIVERSITY
(Map p30) The elegant, neoclassical main building of Tbilisi State University, Georgia's biggest educational institution, stands near the start of Chavchavadzis gamziri. It was built in 1906 as a school for the nobility.

Open-Air Museum of Ethnography MUSEUM
(Map p30; Kus Tba 1; admission 1.50 GEL, tour per group 10 GEL; ⏰10.30am-6pm Jun-Sep, to 5pm Oct-May) About 3km uphill from attractive Vake

Park is the Open-Air Museum of Ethnography. This collection of nearly 70 traditional, mostly wooden houses from around Georgia is spread over a wooded hillside with good views, and makes for an enjoyable visit. The most interesting exhibits are in the lower section (near the entrance), where the buildings are kitted out with fine traditional furnishings, rugs and utensils. Tours are available in English, French and German. You can walk up to the museum from Vake Park, which is about 2km past the university, or take bus 61 to the petrol station 200m past the large Iranian embassy, then walk or take a taxi 2km up the road between the concrete pillars opposite.

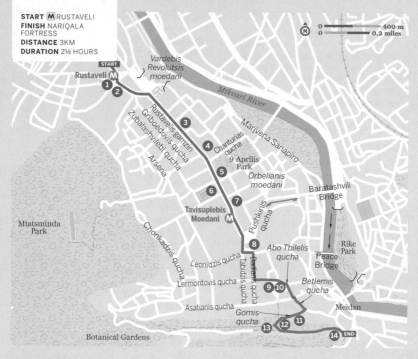

Walking Tour
Tbilisi New & Old

❯ This walk takes you along Tbilisi's main
avenue and into the twisting lanes of the
Old Town, then up to Nariqala Fortress with
its great panoramas.

Start at the **1** **monument to Shota
Rustaveli** outside Rustaveli metro station.
Pass the Stalinist **2** **Academy of Sciences**
at Rustaveli 52, with an informal souvenir
market outside, then walk along Rustaveli to
imbibe the busy atmosphere of Tbilisi's main
artery. The street is strung with handsome
and important buildings such as the Moorish-
style **3** **Opera House**, built in 1896; the
baroque-cum-rococo **4** **Rustaveli Theatre**
(1901); the **5** **Kashveti Church**, the
6 **Parliament building** and the **7** **Museum of Georgia**.

Rustaveli ends at wide **8** **Tavisuplebis
moedani** with its landmark St George and
Dragon monument.

Head up Dadiani and go left at the first
crossroads. This brings you to the charming,
leafy square **9** **Gudiashvilis baghi** where, if

it's past noon, you can stop for refreshments
at the appropriately charming **10** **Pur-Pur**.

Continue down Abo Tbileli, across Ieru-
salimi and up Betlemi. Turn right after Hotel
ZP and right again along Gomi.

In 100m you'll see the partly reconstructed
5th-to-7th-century **11** **Ateshgah Fire Temple** up on your left, a brick cube that is a very
rare example of a Zoroastrian temple in Georgia. A further 100m brings you to the 18th-
century **12** **Betlemi Church**, with beautiful
bright frescoes.

Behind the church, a metal staircase and
winding footpath lead up the hillside to the
13 **Kartlis Deda** (Mother Georgia) monument. A few muggings were reported up here
a few years ago, so it's sensible to stay alert.

From Mother Georgia it's 500m east along
a road and footpath round the side of the hill
to **14** **Nariqala Fortress**.

🏃 Activities

Adventure Club

Jomardi
RAFTING, EQUIPMENT RENTAL

(off Map p30; ☑2319101, 599141160; www.adventure.ge; Vazha Pshavela 93, Saburtalo; Ⓜ Vazha-Pshavela) Georgia's many rivers can provide exciting rides for rafters of all levels. Jomardi is the longest-established and most reputed operator, with English-speaking guides available. A half-day trip to the Mtiuletis Aragvi or Pshavis Aragvi north of Tbilisi, suitable for any level, costs 35 GEL per person, plus 10 GEL to 20 GEL for transport (depending on group size). The season runs from late April to October (best until July). Trips go most often at weekends. Jomardi can also provide challenges for experienced rafters on the Mtkvari River near Borjomi and Vardzia (April and May), and the Rioni River in western Georgia (June to November).

Jomardi also rents sleeping bags (per day 5 GEL), sleeping mats (3 GEL), three-person tents (10 GEL), mountain bikes (30 GEL), skiing gear (skis, boots and poles 22 GEL) and mountaineering equipment.

Abanotubani
BATHHOUSES

Any time of year is good for a traditional bath and massage experience at Tbilisi's famed sulphur baths. The **Orbeliani Baths** (Map p36; Abano; per hr communal pools 3 GEL, private cabins 20-50 GEL; ⊙8am-10pm) have inexpensive male or female communal pools; an invigorating massage is 10/15 GEL in public/private areas. The **Royal Bath** (Map p36; Grishashvili 1; private rooms 50-100 GEL; ⊙8am-11pm) has fancier private rooms only.

Extreme Team
BUNGEE JUMPING

(☑599622676, 592511001; geobungee@gmail.com) This group of experienced alpinists provides jumps for 50 GEL from noon every Sunday at Maglivi Bridge between Vake and Saburtalo. Search 'bungee jumping Tbilisi' on Facebook.

Irakli Kapanadze
PARAGLIDING

(☑599690769, 595424298; i_kapanadze@yahoo.com) Irakli is a highly experienced paraglider who takes inexperienced flyers on tandem flights in the Tbilisi Sea and Rustavi areas close to Tbilisi, from March to October, for 50 GEL (minimum two take-off attempts), or from Gudauri ski resort in winter for 100 GEL, transport included. He can also provide logistical support for groups of experienced pilots who want to fly in other areas including Gudauri (best August to mid-October) and Svaneti (best August and September). Paragliders should check www.xcaucasus.org. Irakli is also a top mountain and ski-touring guide.

Vanilla Sky
SCENIC FLIGHTS, BALLOONING

(Map p36; ☑2428428; www.vanillasky.ge; Bambis rigi 7; ⊙10am-6pm Mon-Fri, plus 11am-4pm Sat May-Oct) Offers sightseeing (and charter) flights in three-passenger Cessnas for €200 per hour from Natakhtari airfield, about 25km north of Tbilisi. A 12-passenger AN-2 biplane is €800 per hour. It also does hot-air balloon flights for up to three passengers for €425 per hour.

Swimming

In the heat of the Tbilisi summer, a cooling splash can be just the thing. **Laguna Vere Pool** (Map p30; Kostava 34; admission 10 GEL; ⊙8am-1pm & 2-9pm) is a mite antiquated but has a clean 50m by 25m open-air pool. First-time visitors must pay 5 GEL extra for a cursory medical inspection, available 8am to 3pm only.

Nonguests can use the super sky-level pool, sauna, solarium and gym at the **Radisson Blu Iveria Hotel** (Map p36; Vardebis Revolutsis moedani 1) for 90.60 GEL per day; the pool at the **Courtyard by Marriott** (Map p36; Tavisuplebis moedani 4) is 40 GEL.

✨ Festivals & Events

Art-Gene Festival
MUSIC, FOOD

(www.artgeni.ge) This hugely popular Georgian folk festival tours the country and culminates with several days of music (including trademark ethno-jam sessions), cooking, arts and crafts at Tbilisi's Open-Air Ethnographic Museum in July.

Tbilisoba
WINE, ARTS

(tbilisoba.ge) Tbilisi comes out to party for this festival of new wine and the city's founding, lasting a week in late October. There are *mtsvadi* (meat kebabs) and wine stalls everywhere, feasting rafts on the river, dance and martial arts in the streets, cheese and fruit festivals, concerts and more.

Tbilisi International Film Festival
FILM

(www.tbilisifilmfestival.ge) Showcases recent Georgian and international movies, in the last quarter of the year (dates vary).

🛏 Sleeping

There is a good range of places to stay in and around the areas of most interest to visitors, the Old Town and Rustavelis gamziri. These include a glut of backpacker hostels, of which those listed here are only a selection. Nearly all hostels offer good-value accommodation, with sturdy bunks in small or medium-size dorms, the odd private room, and shared kitchens, bathrooms and common areas. Hostel staff are usually young and welcoming, and many will go that extra mile to help you enjoy your time here to the full. Hostels, homestays and guesthouses in the following listings do not serve breakfast, unless stated otherwise.

Most midrange and top-end establishments accept credit cards. Although some places quote prices in euros or US dollars, you will normally be charged in lari, at current exchange rates.

OLD TOWN

TOP **Skadaveli**
CHOICE **Guesthouse** GUESTHOUSE **$$**
(Map p36; ☏595417333; www.ska.ge; Vertskhli 27; s/d/tr €20/30/30; ☸❄🖥) This Old Town hideaway has just four exceptionally attractive, good-value rooms with tasteful, contemporary furnishings and very comfy beds – plus a lovely wood-columned verandah for sitting out, and a good guest kitchen. All in amazing contrast to the dilapidated exterior of this 1860s building.

Hotel Ambasadori HOTEL **$$$**
(Map p36; ☏2920403; www.ambasadori.ge; Shavteli 13; r incl breakfast from US$209; ❄@🖥🏊) An elegant hotel in a great location overlooking the Mtkvari, the Ambasadori has a more personal atmosphere than the top-end chain hotels. In attractive fin-de-siècle style, it features well-equipped rooms with very comfortable beds, plus a rooftop pool overlooking the Anchiskhati Basilica. Service is polished, and the photos of old Tbilisi add character.

Hotel Charm BOUTIQUE HOTEL **$$**
(Map p36; ☏2986348; www.hotelcharm.ge; Chakhrukhadze 11; r incl breakfast US$40-80; ❄🖥) Atmospheric Charm is a converted family home in the Old Town, with parquet floors everywhere and a fine collection of art and antiques. There's a range of comfortable rooms at different prices. Top of the range includes a white Steinway.

Old Town Hostel HOSTEL **$**
(Map p36; ☏2986188, 571004002; tbilisioldtown hostel@gmail.com; Khodasheni 7; incl breakfast dm 25-30 GEL, d 70-100 GEL; ☸❄@🖥) A well-equipped hostel spread over two floors in a quiet lane, with a nice yard for sitting out. It has two private rooms and four dorms (one for women only) with good solid bunks and bright green bedding. Airport transfers and car trips to other Georgian destinations available.

Hotel City HOTEL **$$**
(Map p36; ☏2923871; www.hotelcity.ge; Abesadze 7; incl breakfast s/d US$100/120, superior US$120/140; ☸❄🖥) A pleasant small hotel offering good-sized, tasteful rooms on a quiet street. There's a good roof terrace.

Hotel Dzveli Ubani HOTEL **$$**
(Map p36; ☏2922404; www.dzveliubani.com.ge; Diumas 5; s/d incl breakfast US$50/60; ❄🖥) This small hotel has modest but cosy and well-equipped rooms. The top-floor mansard rooms are the most appealing.

Villa Mtiebi BOUTIQUE HOTEL **$$**
(Map p36; ☏2920340; www.hotelmtiebi.ge; Chakhrukhadze 10; s/d incl breakfast €65/75; ☸❄🖥) A small hotel that maintains its building's original art-nouveau elegance. Rooms are soundproofed and service is personal and attentive.

Star Hostel HOSTEL **$**
(Map p36; ☏2995099, 599971825; tbilisistarhos tel@gmail.com; Vertskhli 45; dm 25 GEL; ☸❄@🖥) Welcoming, 10-place hostel in an interesting Old Town house.

Friends Hostel HOSTEL **$**
(Map p36; ☏577652118; www.friendshostel.ge; Betlemi 28-30; dm €9.50-10.50, d €27.60; @🖥) In one of the quaintest parts of Old Tbilisi; includes a women's dorm and a bar.

RUSTAVELI & AROUND

TOP **Boombully Rooms**
CHOICE **& Hostel** HOSTEL **$**
(Map p36; ☏551100172, 595715745; boombully. com; Rustaveli 24; dm €14-16, d €33; ☸❄🖥) Boombully has a great location and welcoming young staff who often like to do things with their guests; eg cook or go out. There are comfy bunks in three different-sized dorms, and a good pine-panelled kitchen, all centred on a spacious, comfy sitting area. The atmosphere is friendly and relaxed, and it's one of Tbilisi's most popular hostels.

Why Not? Tbilisi Legend Hostel
HOSTEL $

(Map p36; ☑599007030; www.whynothostels.
com; Tabukashvili 15/4; incl breakfast dm €10-
12, d €30; ☺@☎) This fun, sociable hostel occupies a funky, spacious, two-level
house a block from Rustaveli. Run by a
friendly Polish and American team who
know Georgia well and are full of ideas for
things to do, it has nice big common areas
and the five dorms include one for women
only. Tea, coffee and washing machine are
included.

Betsy's Hotel
HOTEL $$

(Map p30; ☑2931404; www.betsyshotel.com;
Makashvili 32-34; s/d incl breakfast US$145/165;
☺✳@☎☒) An oasis of American-run effi-
ciency, Betsy's is a favourite with Georgia's
numerous international-agency workers.
The rooms are bright and very comfortable,
and some boast great views over the city.
The cocktail bar and restaurant (for guests
only) are both highly recommended, and
there's a small outdoor pool.

Hotel British House
BOUTIQUE HOTEL $$

(Map p30; ☑2988783; www.british-house.ge; Be-
linski 32; s/d incl breakfast US$90/105; ☺✳☎)
British-owned but Georgian-run, this elegant little hotel in a quiet, leafy part of Vere
has an exceptionally welcoming, homelike
atmosphere. The attractive, well-equipped
rooms have carpets and quality furnishings
including king-size beds, and antiques and
original art abound.

Radisson Blu Iveria Hotel
LUXURY HOTEL $$$

(Map p36; ☑2402200; radissonblu.com/hotel
-tbilisi; Vardebis Revolutsis moedani 1; r from
US$330; ☺✳@☎☒) The Radisson is a
Soviet-era tower on Rose Revolution Sq,
revamped as Tbilisi's most spectacular
hotel after years housing refugees from
Abkhazia. The excellent spa, pool, fitness
centre and bar on the 18th and 19th floors
are a highlight, with fabulous panoramas.
Rooms are supercomfortable and bright.
Has the good Italian **Filini Restaurant**
(mains 22-46 GEL) too.

Beaumonde Guest House
HOTEL $$

(Map p36; ☑2986003; www.beaumondehotel.com;
A Chavchavadzis qucha 11; s/d incl breakfast & dinner US$80/100; ✳@☎) This large, rambling,
family-run house has a welcoming atmosphere, the meals are good and the 19 rooms
(many with balconies) are comfortable and
big – some very big.

Courtyard by Marriott
LUXURY HOTEL $$$

(Map p36; ☑2779100; marriott.com/tbscy; Tavisu-
plebis moedani 4; r from US$242; ☺✳@☎☒)
The less expensive and less formal of Tbi-
lisi's two Marriotts, the Courtyard offers
typical international business-class rooms,
brightened by colourful art and 59 channels
of TV. A good indoor pool and fitness club
are included in rates.

Hotel David
HOTEL $$

(Map p36; ☑2935006; www.davidhotel.ge; Paolo
Iashvili 16A; s/d incl breakfast US$70/80; ✳☎) A
comfortable small hotel not far from Tavisuplebis moedani. Rooms have attractive
wooden furniture.

Nest Hostel
HOSTEL $

(Map p36; ☑598161771; www.nesthostel.ge; Paolo
Iashvili 23; dm/s/d 25/45/70 GEL; ☺@☎) A rambling, spacious, friendly place on a shady
street just beyond the main touristic bustle.
Has one women-only dorm.

Big Star Hostel
HOSTEL $

(Map p36; ☑2931511, 599971825; bigstarhostel@
gmail.com; Machabeli 2; dm 20 GEL, dm incl breakfast 25 GEL, d incl breakfast 56-72 GEL; ☺@☎)
Just off Tavisuplebis moedani; same owners
as Star Hostel.

EAST OF THE RIVER

Soul House Hostel
HOSTEL $

(Map p36; ☑598277898; www.facebook.com/soul
househosteltbilisi; Akhvlediani khevi 13; dm 25 GEL,
d 60-65 GEL; ✳@☎) A lovely, spacious house
in a quiet lane, Soul House will appeal to
travellers who like a bit of style. It has an
excellent, spacious, spotless kitchen, a
front-yard cafe and a piano in the comfy sitting area. The mother-and-daughter team
who run it are clued into all that's going
on around Tbilisi and have an interesting
events board to give you ideas.

Hotel Kopala
HOTEL $$

(Map p36; ☑2775520; www.kopala.ge; Chek-
hov 8/10; r incl breakfast €65-170; ☺✳@☎)
Classy Kopala's main Building A has one
of the loveliest positions in the city, above
the Metekhi Church. Some rooms here
(from €100) have balconies or vistas over
the Old Town. Other rooms (many are in
two further buildings on the same street)
don't enjoy the same vistas, but all are well
equipped and comfortable. Staff are ami-
able and efficient, and the restaurant is
excellent.

Dodo's Dormitory GUESTHOUSE $
(Map p30; ☑2954213, 579111221; www.dodosguest
house.com; Marjanishvili 38; per person 25-30 GEL;
☎) Dodo's is a good pick for budget travellers
who like a more spacious, less hectic atmosphere. The single-storey house has several
large dormitories with mostly single beds,
plus two kitchens and a shady courtyard for
sitting out. Members of the extremely helpful family speak excellent English, German
and Italian, and the leafy street is full of local life and food shops.

Irine Japaridze's Boarding House HOSTEL $
(Map p30; ☑2954716, 599111669; www.iverieli.nar
od.ru; irina5062@gmail.com; 3rd fl, Ninoshvili 19B;
dm/d 20/50 GEL; ☻✳☎) Artist Irine's two-
storey apartment is a colourful, well-run
place with a sociable atmosphere, always
busy with international backpackers. It has
10 dorms and rooms, four bathrooms, two
kitchens, and free tea and coffee. It's just off
Marjanishvili: go in the entrance with two
headless stone lions and up to the top of the
stairs.

Hotel Old Metekhi HOTEL $$
(Map p36; ☑2747431; www.oldmetekhi.ge; Metekhi
3; r incl breakfast US$60-100; ✳@☎) Perched
on a rocky cliff above the Mtkvari, this is
a traditional establishment favouring indi-
vidual attention over visitor numbers. The
14 rooms are comfortable and mostly good-
sized, but only a few enjoy river views.

Tbilisi Hostel HOSTEL $
(Map p30; ☑2747668, 598506969; www.tbilisihos
tel.com; Makhatis shesakhvevi 22; dm/d incl wine
25/60 GEL; @☎) A very sociable 'party hostel'
run by amiable young guys. The wine and
chacha (powerful grappalike liquor) flow,
and guests and hosts often prepare meals
together. In an untouristy neighbourhood
near Avlabari metro.

Hotel Lile HOTEL $$
(Map p36; ☑2773856; www.lilehotel.ge; Ghvinis
aghmarti 19; r 70-120 GEL; ✳) Friendly little Lile
is a short walk from the Old Town, close to
Avlabari metro. Rooms are modern, good
value and comfortable. No breakfast though.

Sky Hostel HOSTEL $
(Map p30; ☑577716575; www.skyhostel.ge; Davit
Aghmashenebeli 77; dm/s/d €10/22/30; ☎) A
welcoming place offering free airport pick-
ups. Go in the south end of Aghmashenebeli
77 to the pink building at the end of the
courtyard.

OTHER AREAS

Rock n Roll Hostel HOSTEL $
(off Map p36; ☑2457702, 574600066; www.face
book.com/hostelrocknroll; Qumsiashvili 1; dm/d
25/65 GEL; ☎) Rock n Roll is a 10-minute
walk southeast of the Old Town. The facilities are fairly standard but what's special is
the group of adventurous young guys who
run it, who are hooked into everything
that moves in 'extreme' sports (rafting, skiing, bungee jumping, mountain biking and
more) and music. Offers free airport pick-
ups too.

Hotel Vere Inn BOUTIQUE HOTEL $$
(Map p30; ☑2291252; www.tourvereinn.com; Barnov
53; r US$40-80; ✳☎) This pleasant hideaway
in Vere has just five imaginatively decorated
rooms. The friendly English-speaking owners
are full of useful information.

✗ Eating

Tbilisi eateries span a broad range from
traditional Georgian fare and atmosphere
to cool, European-style joints. There's also a
good cafe culture, and plenty of food shops
for self-caterers.

OLD TOWN

TOP CHOICE **Pur-Pur** INTERNATIONAL $$$
(Map p36; Abo Tbileli 1; mains 18-28 GEL; ⊗lunch
& dinner; ☎▯) With uniquely quaint design
that cleverly evokes the elegant charm of
19th-century Tbilisi, Pur-Pur is a cool and
classy haunt for culturally inclined Georgians, expats and visitors. The menu ranges
from pork in beer-and-mustard sauce to
baked apple with nuts and cream; the meat
assortment is an excellent starter.

TOP CHOICE **Shemoikhede
Genatsvale** GEORGIAN $$
(Map p36; www.gmcgroup.ge, in Georgian; Kote Ab-
khazi 25; mains 7-21 GEL; ⊗lunch & dinner; ☻▯)
The name means 'Drop in, Love' and this
restaurant makes good on that invitation
with terrific Georgian food in a fun but not
overwhelming tavern ambience. It's easiest
spotted by the Pirosmani painting of three
men and a dog displayed outside. *Khinkali*
(spicy dumplings; available here with potato
or mushroom stuffings as well as meat) are
one speciality but there are plenty of other
very good cold and hot Georgian dishes in-
cluding *mtsvadi* and *shkmeruli* (sizzling
chicken in garlic sauce). Wash it all down
with draft beer or good house wine.

KNOW YOUR KHACHAPURI

An excess of these is not the thing for slimmers, but Georgia's ubiquitous cheese pies are the perfect keep-me-going small meal, as well as playing a part in many a feast. Different regions have their own varieties, but you'll find many of them all around the country:

Khachapuri Acharuli The Adjaran variety is a large, boat-shaped calorie injection, overflowing with melted cheese and topped with butter and a runny egg.

Khachapuri Imeruli Relatively sedate, these round, flat pies from Imereti have melted cheese inside only.

Khachapuri Megruli Round pies from Samegrelo, with cheese in the middle and more cheese melted on top.

Khachapuri penovani Square and neatly folded into four quarters, with the cheese inside the lightish crust – particularly tasty!

Khachapuri achma Another large Adjaran concoction, with the dough and cheese in layers, lasagne-style.

Puris Sakhli GEORGIAN $$
(Map p36; www.mgroup.ge; Gorgasali 7; mains 6-20 GEL; ⊙lunch & dinner; 🅙) A short walk from the sulphur baths, brick-walled Puris Sakhli (Bread House – it has a bakery just inside the door) is one of Tbilisi's most popular and lively spots for a meal. The well-prepared dishes run the gamut of Georgian cuisine. There's live Georgian music in the back room nightly except Monday.

Restorani Alani OSSETIAN, GEORGIAN $
(Map p36; Gorgasali 1; mains 5-12 GEL; ⊙lunch & dinner; 🅙) This subterranean eating den (the sign is in Georgian, with red lettering) serves Ossetian food, which is pretty similar to Georgian, and it's some of the best and best-value restaurant fare you'll find in Georgia. Try the very tasty *chakapuli* (lamb with tarragon and plums) or *shkmeruli* and, if you have room, wind up with a *khabidzgina,* a filling Ossetian *khachapuri* (cheese pie). The house beer, Alani, slips down very nicely. Decor is of the heavy woodcarving and iron-lampshade genre, and the thankfully intermittent live music is straight out of a Soviet hotel restaurant.

Café Gabriadze CREATIVE GEORGIAN $$
(Map p36; Shavteli 13; mains 11-19 GEL; ⊙lunch & dinner; 🅙) Quirkily attractive little Café Gabriadze, under the same management as the neighbouring Tbilisi Marionette Theatre, makes a great place for lunch or dinner. It offers friendly service and Georgian food with original twists. Decor is on theatrical themes, full of intriguing details.

Qalaquri Samikitno GEORGIAN $
(Map p36; www.samikitno.ge; Meidan; mains 6-10 GEL; ⊙24hr; 🅢🅙) With large windows overlooking Meidan and the Metekhi Church, this cheerful, informal place serves up decent Georgian standards from *khachapuri* and *khinkali* to *mtsvadi* and *chakapuli.* And it never closes.

Brasserie L'Express INTERNATIONAL $$$
(Map p36; www.mgroup.ge; Sharden 14; mains 16-30 GEL; ⊙lunch & dinner; 🅙) Pedestrianised Sharden and parallel Bambis rigi are lined with fashionable cafes, bars and restaurants. L'Express is the best all-round bet for food, with well-prepared international dishes for light or heartier appetites. The steak wrap is pretty good.

Teremok RUSSIAN $
(Map p36; Dadiani 18; mains 2-15 GEL; ⊙lunch & dinner; 🅙🅙) This cosy little restaurant in Russian-cottage style specialises in tasty *bliny* (pancakes), which you can enjoy with mushrooms, meat, cream, jam, cheese, fruit or many other options. Plenty of other Russian and Ukrainian dishes are served too.

Racha GEORGIAN $
(Map p36; cnr Lermontov & Dadiani; mains 4-5 GEL; ⊙lunch & dinner) One of Tbilisi's last *duqani* (literally 'shop' but also meaning a cheap, traditional, basement eatery), Racha serves up tasty home-style Georgian staples such as *khinkali, mtsvadi, khachapuri* and *badrijani nigvzit* (aubergine slices with walnut-and-garlic paste) at great prices. Perhaps not a place for beginners: the menu is a board

written in Georgian and no one speaks any English.

Luca Polare
ICE CREAM $

(Map p36; Kote Abkhazi 34; per scoop 2.10 GEL; ▥) The creamy Italian-style ice cream at this little parlour makes the perfect cooler during your Old Town ramblings. Good coffee too.

RUSTAVELI & AROUND

Downtown
INTERNATIONAL $$

(Map p36; www.down-town.ge; G Tabidze 7; mains 13-24 GEL; ⊙breakfast, lunch & dinner Mon-Fri, lunch & dinner Sat & Sun; ☏▥) A spacious cafe-restaurant off Tavisuplebis moedani serving well-prepared dishes from pumpkin cream soup or chicken quesadillas to pancakes and pasta, for a more Georgian than international clientele. You can't beat it for a breakfast of bacon-and-cheese omelette or sunny-side-up eggs.

Dzveli Sakhli
GEORGIAN $$

(Map p36; ☏2365365; www.gmcgroup.ge, in Georgian; Marjvena Sanapiro 3; mains 10-25 GEL; ⊙lunch & dinner; ▥) The rambling 'Old House' serves authentic dishes from all over Georgia. There's Georgian music and dancing at 8pm nightly in the main dining hall, which has long banquet tables, ideal for small groups (best to reserve for these). For a quieter meal, choose the partly open-air riverside hall. Service can be slow but the food is worth a wait. You can order wine by the jug.

Khinklis Sakhli
SAKHINKLE $

(Map p36; Rustaveli 37; khinkali 0.40-0.80 GEL, mains 4.50-10 GEL; ⊙24hr) With its fish tanks, green carpets and red upholstered booths, the 'Khinkali House' is a Tbilisi institution where anyone and everyone goes by day or night for a fill of *khinkali* and draft beer (1.70 GEL). It's right beside the eastern end of a dank, gloomy pedestrian underpass beneath Vardebis Revolutsis moedani.

Khinkal Centre
SAKHINKLE $

(Map p36; Rustaveli 37; khinkali 0.30-0.60 GEL; ⊙lunch & dinner; ▥) This upstart *khinkali* rival, entered from the yard beside Khinklis Sakhli, has arguably tastier *khinkali* and more tasteful decor, but it's only open half as long.

Baan Thai Cuisine
THAI $$

(Map p36; Tabukashvili 35; mains 11-29 GEL; ⊙lunch & dinner; ⊖▰▥) Serves a full range of extremely good Thai dishes, all prepared with minimal oil and salt and no MSG, in unassuming surroundings.

Entrée
CAFE $

(Map p36; Rustaveli 20; baked goods 2-6 GEL; ⊖☏▰▥) Bright, French-run cafe with delicious baked goods and good, if expensive, coffee.

Caliban's Coffeehouse
CAFE $

(Map p36; Rustaveli 34; baguettes, cakes & coffees 3-7 GEL; ⊖☏▥) Caliban's is the cafe at Prospero's Books, with a leafy courtyard and a comfy indoor area ideal for sitting with a laptop and a pot of coffee.

EAST OF THE RIVER

Hotel Kopala
GEORGIAN $$$

(Map p36; ☏2775520; www.kopala.ge; Chekhov 8/10; mains 10-29 GEL; ⊙lunch & dinner; ▥) Hotel Kopala's restaurant has one of the best views in the city and serves some of the best Georgian food and wines with a fairly tranquil, polished ambience. It's very popular so it's worth reserving for dinner: if the weather's good, choose the fabulous open-air terrace.

Dzveli Metekhi
GEORGIAN, INTERNATIONAL $$

(Map p36; ☏2747404; www.oldmetekhi.ge; Metekhi 3; mains 8-25 GEL; ⊙lunch & dinner; ▥) This restaurant attached to the Hotel Old Metekhi has sought-after balcony tables with superb views over the Old Town (you need to reserve these in advance). The food is excellent Georgian and international fare (try the chicken in blueberry sauce), and there's a good wine list. Stick to the balcony area as the live music in the rear section can be painful.

Shemoikhede Genatsvale
GEORGIAN $$

(Map p30; www.gmcgroup.ge, in Georgian; Marjanishvili 5; mains 7-21 GEL; ⊙lunch & dinner; ⊖▥) Another branch of the excellent restaurant.

VAKE

Il Garage
ITALIAN $$

(Map p30; ☏577780090; Mosashvili 26; mains 12-20 GEL; ⊙lunch & dinner, closed Sun & Aug; ☏▰▥) Sardinian chefs whip up yummy concoctions of fresh pasta at this colourful haunt with half a dozen tables – it's worth reserving one of them.

Cafe Tartine
FRENCH $$

(Map p30; Abashidze 22; mains 10-18 GEL; ☏) A casual French bistro where expats and Georgians enjoy everything from breakfast to cocktails and quiches to snails.

Drinking

You are never far from places to go for a drink in Tbilisi. Most visitors will want to head to the pedestrianised Old Town streets Erekle II, Sharden and Bambis rigi, where al fresco cafes and bars offer great opportunities for people-watching. A more raucous evening can be had in the bars around Akhvlediani (formerly Perovskaya). Meanwhile, Tbilisi's clutch of hip, semi-underground venues such as Salve and Bude Bar are a must for those who want to sample a new generation of Georgian hospitality, usually till way past bedtime.

OLD TOWN

Salve
BAR

(Map p36; Dadiani 15; ⊙5pm-3am) This basement bar doesn't have a sign outside, and that's just how the patrons like it. Run by the ever-hospitable Gio and his family, Salve is a Tbilisi institution, popular with Georgian student types and younger expats. It's crowded most nights, and the eclectic music and mixed crowd make it the best place in town to meet people.

Moulin Electrique
BAR

(Map p36; Kote Abkhazi 28) This funky, relaxed little nook attracts a crowd of locals and travellers. The bar is comprised of stacks of old filing boxes, and bundles of old clothes form seats. There are tasty eats too.

Bude Bar
BAR

(Map p36; Gorgasali shesakhvevi 5; ⊙6pm-2am) Tucked into a lovely courtyard opposite the Armenian Cathedral of St George, this studenty bar is run by the young group of friends who own Nest Hostel. Small, and often eye-wateringly smoky, this place still has enough atmosphere to carry it off. Friday and Saturday nights see big crowds dancing to shuffled iPods until the small hours.

Café Kala
CAFE

(Map p36; Erekle II 8/10; ☎) Consistently one of the most popular bars, with a comfortable, arty atmosphere and live jazz from 9pm nightly. The food is pretty average.

Hangar Bar
PUB

(Map p36; www.thehangar.biz; Shavteli 20) An expat-favourite Irish-American pub that shows lots of TV sport and serves damn good burgers. It's always bustling and the welcoming staff speak perfect English. Often has a live band from 9pm in the second half of the week.

Pur-Pur
BAR

(Map p36; Abo Tbileli 1; ☎) The downstairs bar here has a younger crowd than the elegant restaurant, and interesting music nights at weekends.

PEROVSKAYA & AROUND

Although the street running north from Vardebis Revolutsis moedani has been called Akhvlediani for almost 20 years, everyone still calls it Perovskaya. With a few exceptions, the bars here and on neighbouring Qiacheli and Vashlovani are cheaper and seedier than in the Old Town, offering a near-identical mix of wooden interiors, cheap food and rock-cover bands.

Art Café
CAFE-BAR

(Map p36; Akhvlediani 15; ☎) Run by local artist Sandro Antadze, this relaxed cafe-bar is popular, unsurprisingly, with Tbilisi's arty crowd. There are regular exhibitions and tango classes, and most weekends see parties of some kind.

Dublin
BAR

(Map p36; Akhvlediani 8) A heady mix of live cover bands, young Georgians and raucous expats, the Dublin has been keeping its neighbours awake since 1990, and is crowded till late most evenings.

Success
GAY-FRIENDLY

(Map p36; Vashlovani 3; ⊙2pm-6am) Often described as Tbilisi's only gay bar, Success is really more of a place where it's OK to be out; public displays of affection are only ever seen at one of its extremely rare gay nights. It gets a good crowd dancing to house and disco on the weekends. Don't be alarmed by the massive pictures of Hollywood celebrities everywhere.

Oxygen Bar
BAR

(Map p36; radissonblu.com/hotel-tbilisi; Radisson Blu Iveria Hotel, Vardebis Revolutsis moedani 1; ☎) With imported beer selling for 11 GEL and bar food at more than 30 GEL, the sumptuous Oxygen Bar on the Radisson's 18th floor certainly isn't cheap, but the stunning views of the city, countryside and Caucasus might well seem worth it.

☆ Entertainment

You'll find listings and announcements online at www.facebook.com/tbilisi.whatson and www.info-tbilisi.com, and in the weekly English-language paper *Georgia Today* and the magazine *Tbilisi Out*.

Theatre

Rustaveli Theatre
DRAMA

(Map p36; ☑2726868; www.rustavelitheatre.ge; Rustaveli 17; ⊗closed Aug) Georgia has a long and illustrious theatrical tradition; the Rustaveli is internationally famed for the Shakespeare productions of Robert Sturua, its artistic director until 2011. Check for shows with simultaneous English translation.

Tbilisi Marionette Theatre
PUPPET THEATRE

(Map p36; ☑2986593; Shavteli 13; ⊗box office 11am-7pm) If you think puppets aren't your thing, think again. The shows at this little theatre, directed by Rezo Gabriadze, are awe-inspiringly original and moving. English subtitles appear on a screen. Book ahead.

Pantomime Theatre
DANCE

(Map p36; ☑2996314; Rustaveli 37) Panto here is nothing like the 'he's behind you' comedy familiar in the West. In fact, this theatre stages some of the most technically accomplished and beautiful interpretative dance shows found anywhere, dramatically reworking some of Georgia's most beloved poems and even the life of St George.

Live Music

Tbilisi has a thriving independent music scene, with everything from Britpop-revival to electro to Georgian folk fusion. But gigs often happen at short notice and may only be publicised through Facebook. Check out the **Rock Club** (Map p36; Rustaveli 28) for rock gigs, or **33a** (Map p30; Vake Park), an old open-air cinema that hosts a wide variety of live acts in the summer.

Tbilisi is a great place to enjoy classical music for next to nothing. Virtuoso performances are held almost nightly at the **State Conservatoire** (Map p36; Griboedov 8). World-class opera and ballet are staged at the **Georgia National Music Center** (Map p30; www.facebook.com/georgian.national.music.center; Davit Aghmashenebeli 127) while the **Paliashvili Opera & Ballet Theatre** (Map p36; Rustaveli 25) is being renovated.

Restaurant Chakrulo
TRADITIONAL MUSIC, DANCE

(Map p36; Rustaveli 38) This nicely presented cellar restaurant has live Georgian folk music, not overwhelmingly loud, nightly from 7pm, and dance performances at 10pm – Georgian dance Monday to Wednesday, and 'Arabic', featuring a candelabra-balancing belly dancer, Thursday to Saturday. The food (mains 7 GEL to 17 GEL) is Georgian or pizza.

Nightclubs

Tbilisi has an increasing number of places to spend a night on the tiles, though many are expensive, only open at weekends (typically 11pm to 6am Thursday to Saturday nights), and play only minimal techno and house.

At trendy Old Town lounge-clubs such as **Safe** (Map p36; Rkinis rigi 11), **Bamba Station** (Map p36; Bambis rigi 12) and **Missoni** (Map p36; Erekle II 11), you will have to dance around the tables and be prepared to wait for your drinks. **GURU Club** (Map p36; Rustaveli 12; ⊗closed Thu) regularly attracts well-known DJs from Europe.

New Cafe Gallery
CLUB

(Map p36; Rustaveli 48) A trendy, studenty crowd can be found at this venue run by a local artist. Cheaper and less pretentious than many Tbilisi clubs, it has regular weekend events including DJs and Latin parties, and features a nice terrace and interesting contemporary art.

Vernisage
CLUB

(Map p36; Vardebis Revolutsis moedani; admission 10 GEL) Not for the faint-hearted, Vernisage is in the warren of sub-basements below Rose Revolution Sq. Here, prostitutes and Turkish truck drivers compete for space on the *Saturday Night Fever* dance floor, and drinks are cheap. Go with a mixed group.

🛍 Shopping

Interesting shops purveying distinctive mementos, from drinking vessels to decorative swords, carpets to wine, are dotted along Rustaveli and around the Old Town.

TOP CHOICE Dry Bridge

Market
ARTS & CRAFTS, ANTIQUES

(Map p36; 9 Martis Park; ⊗11am-5pm Mon-Fri, 9am-6pm Sat & Sun) You'll find all kinds of knick-knacks and charming miscellanea at this open-air market – original art, decorative drinking horns and daggers, shaggy hats, accordions, as well as china, glass and silver being sold off by impoverished old folk.

Geoland
MAPS

(Map p36; www.geoland.ge; Telegrapis chikhi 3; ⊗10am-2pm & 3-7pm Mon-Fri) Georgia's best mapmaker, Geoland sells its own excellent 1:500,000 country map, four Travel maps showing regions at larger scale (1:250,000), a Tbilisi city map, and 1:50,000 hiking maps of the Borjomi, Kazbegi and Tusheti areas, for 8 GEL to 9.50 GEL each. It can also print you 1:50,000 sheets of other areas for about 22 GEL each.

Vinotheca   WINE
(Map p36; Kote Abkhazi 33; ☺10am-2am) A very accommodating wine shop with lots of wines to taste. Bottles start around 8 GEL, though staff have a talent for persuading you to spend more than you planned. They'll pack bottles for carrying home.

Gallery   ARTS & CRAFTS
(Map p36; Rustaveli 34) In the courtyard next to Prospero's Books, this gallery offers a range of funky items, from bronze sculptures and enamelled jewellery to hand-dyed silk scarves. All created by Tbilisi designers.

Prospero's Books   BOOKS
(Map p36; www.prosperosbookshop.com; Rustaveli 34; ☺10am-9pm) This English-language bookshop has a good selection of titles relating to Georgia and the South Caucasus.

Caucasian Carpets   CARPETS
(Map p36; Erekle II 8/10) Has the best selection of any Old Town carpet shop, with colourful rugs from Georgia, Azerbaijan, Iran and Central Asia, starting around US$250.

Meidan 91   ARTS & CRAFTS
(Map p36; Meidan) Touted as the oldest carpet shop in the South Caucasus, Meidan 91 is an Aladdin's cave of old and new carpets, samovars and fantastic old shepherds' wool coats.

ℹ Information

Dangers & Annoyances

Tbilisi, like Georgia as a whole, feels very safe. Just exercise normal vigilance as you would in any new foreign city. Take a taxi if you're uneasy about walking or taking public transport.

Internet Access

Internet cafe (Map p30; Davit Aghmashenebeli 108; per hr 1.20 GEL; ☺9am-10pm)

Internet cafe (Map p36; Rustaveli 18; per hr 2 GEL; ☺10am-11pm Mon-Fri, 11am-11pm Sat & Sun; ☻) Clean, English-speaking facility; does photocopies too.

Medical Services

The following private Western-standard medical facilities have 24-hour emergency service and English-speaking doctors.

CITO (Map p30; ☑2290671; www.cito.com; Paliashvili 40, Vake; ☺9am-6pm Mon-Fri, to 3pm Sat) Has a GP and specialists, dental service and a good laboratory; expect to pay 30 GEL to 90 GEL for initial consultations.

IMSS (Map p30; ☑2920928; www.imss.ge; Makashvili 31; ☺24hr) Consultations (US$49, follow-up US$30) and 24-hour inpatient care available with EU- or US-trained doctors.

MediClub Georgia (Map p30; ☑2251991, emergency 599581991; www.mediclubgeorgia. ge; Tashkent 22A, Saburtalo; ☺9am-6pm Mon-Fri, 9.30am-1.30pm Sat) The place of choice for serious issues.

Standards at the **Central Republican Hospital** (Map p30; ☑2390237; Vazha-Pshavela 29, Saburtalo) have improved considerably and it's cheaper than the private facilities.

Medicines are widely available at pharmacies (*aptiaqi* in Georgian, but often signed 'Apotheka'), including Aversi, open 24 hours.

Aversi (Davit Aghmashenebeli 146)

Aversi (Pushkin 11)

Money

Tbilisi is full of ATMs issuing lari on MasterCard, Visa, Cirrus and Maestro cards. There are also plenty of exchange offices (including at every metro station and the main bus stations) where you can buy lari for cash euros, US dollars and often roubles, sterling, Armenian drams or Azerbaijani manat. The airport has several ATMs and two 24-hour bank branches offering currency exchange. The main train station has an ATM on level 1, and there are several exchange offices, typically open 9am to 9pm, across the street outside.

Some ATMs, including those of **TBC Bank** (Marjanishvili Map p30; Marjanishvili 7; Rustaveli Map p36; Rustaveli 1; Airport Tbilisi airport), dispense US dollars as well as lari.

Post

Fedex (Map p36; www.fedex.com; Ketevan Tsamebulis gamziri 39)

Post office (Map p36; Rustaveli 14; ☺9am-1pm & 2-6pm Mon-Fri, 9.30am-1pm & 2-5pm Sat) You can send mail from here while the main post office (Map p36; Rustaveli 31) is closed for refurbishment.

Telephone

These are the downtown offices of the three mobile networks:

Beeline (Bilaini; Map p36; www.beeline.ge; Rustaveli 14; ☺10am-5pm)

Geocell (Map p36; www.geocell.ge; Rustaveli 14; ☺9am-9pm)

Magti (Map p36; www.magticom.ge; Rustaveli 22; ☺9am-7pm Mon-Sat, to 6pm Sun)

Tourist Information

Tourism Information Centre (Map p36; ☑2436969; Tavisuplebis moedani; ☺10am-6pm) Has printed material on all parts of

Georgia (if in stock) and staff who may or may not give helpful, accurate answers to questions. Also two touch-screen internet-connected computers (free). The branch at the airport is open 24 hours.

Travel Agencies

Good local agents can take the organisational hassle out of anything from a city tour to a hiking expedition, and good guides can open your eyes to things you'd otherwise never know. A typical day trip with the top agencies from Tbilisi for four people costs 300 GEL to 400 GEL. Typical office hours are 10am to 6pm Monday to Friday, and 10am to 2pm Saturday.

Caucasus Travel (Map p36; www.caucasus travel.com; Kote Abkhazi 44) Long-established, very professional Caucasus Travel can set up just about any group or individual trip, from self-drive jeep tours to climbing awesome Ushba.

Explore Georgia (Map p36; www.exploregeor gia.com; Shevchenko 5/41) An experienced specialist in activity-based travel, including climbing, hiking, horse riding, bird-watching and archaeological tours.

GeorgiCa Travel (Map p36; www.georgica travel.ge; Erekle II 5) Professional GeorgiCa offers a full range of cultural and adventure trips, and will happily construct tailor-made itineraries, combining Georgia with Armenia and/or Azerbaijan if you like.

Levon Travel (Map p30; www.levontravel.ge; Chavchavadzis gamziri 20) A US-based outfit, Levon runs tours in Georgia and offers good deals on air tickets, especially to and from North America.

Wild Georgia (Map p36; www.wildgeorgia.ge; Tsinamdzghvrishvili 17) Enthusiastic, experienced, high-end boutique agency specialising in hiking and horse riding in Tusheti.

❶ Getting There & Away

Air

Tbilisi International Airport (☑2433141; www. tbilisiairport.com), 15km east of the centre, has plenty of international flights (see p301 for more information). Domestic flights head to Batumi and Mestia, and in summer sometimes to Tusheti.

Airline offices in Tbilisi:

Aerosvit (Map p36; www.aerosvit.com; Contact Travel Agency, Ingorokva 12)
Air Astana (www.airastana.com; Airport)
Air Baltic (Map p30; ☑2152997; www.airbal tic.com; Paliashvili 72, Vake)
Airzena Georgian Airways (Map p30; ☑2485560; www.georgian-airways.com; Davit Aghmashenebeli 127)

Arkia (Map p30; www.arkia.com; Fresh Travel, Kostava 63)
Armavia (www.u8.am; Airport)
AZAL (Azerbaijan Airlines; Map p30; www.azal. az; Chavchavadzis gamziri 28)
Belavia (Map p30; http://belavia.by; Intex, Davit Aghmashenebeli 95A)
BMI (Map p30; www.flybmi.com; Paliashvili 15, Vake)
Czech Airlines (Map p30; www.csa.cz; Berika International, Mtskheta 2, Vake)
Lufthansa (Map p30; www.lufthansa.com; Paliashvili 15, Vake)
Pegasus Airlines (Map p36; ☑2400400; www. flypgs.com; Courtyard by Marriott, Tavisuplebis moedani 4)
S7 Airlines (Map p36; www.s7.ru; Abesadze 5)
SCAT (Map p36; www.scat.kz, in Russian; Contact Travel Agency, Ingorokva 12)
Turkish Airlines (Map p30; www.turkishair lines.com; Davit Aghmashenebeli 147)
Ukraine International Airlines (Map p30; www.flyuia.com; Ekaladze 3)
Vanilla Sky (Map p36; www.vanillasky.ge; ☑2428428; Bambis rigi 7)

Bus & Marshrutka

Tbilisi has two main long-distance bus and marshrutka stations. Sprawling **Didube** (off Map p30; Tsereteli; Ⓜ Didube), outside Didube metro station, is the main hub for national services. The first yard outside the metro exit tunnel has marshrutka to Akhaltsikhe, Bakuriani, Batumi, Borjomi, Kutaisi and Vardzia. A second yard, across a small road and behind a line of buildings, has marshrutky to Mtskheta and Kazbegi, and the bus to Barisakho. For further services, walk 300m along the above-mentioned small road. Here you'll find the Okriba bus station on your left, with Batumi, Kutaisi and Zugdidi marshrutky; and a yard on the right with Gori marshrutky.

Ortachala (off Map p36; Gulia 1), about 2.5km southeast of the Old Town, has services for Kakheti, Armenia, Azerbaijan, Turkey and Greece. Marshrutky to Telavi, Yerevan and Zaqatala leave from out the front; other services go from inside. You can reach Ortachala on bus 55 from Baratashvili, near Tavisuplebis moedani in central Tbilisi. Heading to Baratashvili from Ortachala, catch bus 55 going to the left on the street outside. Marshrutka 150 runs between Ortachala and Didube, passing Marjanishvili (with its budget accommodation) en route.

Further useful marshrutky leave from in front of the main train station; from **Avtosadguri Dedaqalaqi** (Map p30; Tsotne Dadiani) outside the train station's level 3; and from the street

DOMESTIC MARSHRUTKY & BUSES FROM TBILISI

DESTINATION	DEPARTURE POINT	FARE (GEL)	DURATION (HR)	DEPARTURES
Akhaltsikhe	Didube	12	4	M hourly 8am-7pm
Bakuriani	Didube	11	4	M 9am & 11am
Barisakho	Didube	5	3½	B 3pm Thu-Tue
Batumi	Didube	20	6	M half-hourly 8am-8.30pm
Borjomi	Didube	8	3	M hourly 8am-7pm
Gori	Didube	4	1¼	M every 30min 8am-7.30pm
Kazbegi	Didube	10	3	M hourly 9am-5pm
Kutaisi	Didube	10	4	M at least hourly 8am-7pm
Lagodekhi	Isani	7	2½	M about hourly 7.40am-6.40pm
Mestia	Train station (Tevdore Mgvdeli near Bavshvta Samkaro store)	30	11-12	M 6am*
Mtskheta	Didube	1	30min	M every 15min 7.30am-8.30pm
Poti	Dedaqalaqi	15	5½	M 9am, 11am, 2pm, 5pm & 7pm
Sighnaghi	Isani	6	2	M about every 2hr 10am-6pm
Telavi	Ortachala	7	1¾	M hourly 7am-6pm
Tsiteli Khidi (Krasny Most, Red Bridge; Azerbaijan border)	Train station (front)	4	1	M about hourly 5-8am, fewer till 5pm
Vardzia	Didube	16	6	M 10am
Zugdidi	Dedaqalaqi	15	6	M every 80min 8.20am-9.40pm; B 10am, noon, 2pm & 11pm

M *Marshrutka*

B Bus

* Be there by 5am, or ask someone to call **Gia Japaridze** (☎599606332, 595923870) to reserve seats.

behind the Chamber of Control of Georgia building behind Isani metro station.

For Baku, the few through services from Tbilisi can suffer delays at the border; it's often quicker to take a *marshrutka* to the border at Tsiteli Khidi and pick up onward transport on the other side. Start early in the day.

Remember: *marshrutky* may leave after or before scheduled times, depending on how quickly they fill up, and all schedules are subject to change!

An option for those wanting to see the sights of northern Armenia en route to Yerevan is the weekly one-way tour (100 GEL, 11 hours) organised by Yerevan's **Envoy Hostel** (www.envoyhostel.com), leaving Tbilisi (Tavisuplebis moedani) at 9am Saturday: reservations are essential.

INTERNATIONAL MARSHRUTKY & BUSES FROM TBILISI

DESTINATION	DEPARTURE POINT	FARE	DURATION (HR)	DEPARTURES
Ankara	Ortachala	US$40	20	B about 4 daily**
Ardahan	Ortachala	US$35	7	B 8am***
Athens	Ortachala	US$100-110	42	B about 5 a week**
Baku (via Tsiteli Khidi & Gəncə)	Ortachala	30 GEL	10	M 11am; B 4.30pm
Istanbul	Ortachala	US$35-45	26	B about 6 daily**
Trabzon	Ortachala	US$25-30	10	B same as for Istanbul
Yerevan****	Ortachala	30 GEL	6	M hourly 8am-noon
	Train station (front)	30 GEL	6	M 10am, 11am, 1pm, 3pm & 5pm
Zaqatala (Azerbaijan; via Lagodekhi)	Ortachala	10 GEL	3-4	M 8.30am

M *Marshrutka*

B Bus

** Via Sarpi border point. From mid-September to mid-June departures to Turkey and Greece are much reduced – usually a couple daily to Istanbul, one to Ankara, and one or two weekly for Athens.

*** Via Vale–Posof border crossing; company Özlem Ardahan; service may drop to one weekly from mid-September to mid-June (you can still reach Ardahan from Akhaltsikhe).

**** Via Sadakhlo border point, Vanadzor, Sevan; if you get off before Yerevan, you still pay the full 30 GEL fare.

Car

The only sizeable independent local rental company, **Jeep Rent** (Map p30; www.jeeprent.ge; Office 25, Kostava 44), gets good reports from customers. It rents economy (up to €40 per day) and medium-size (up to €60) Toyotas and Hondas, and Nissan 4WDs (up to €75), with unlimited kilometres, insurance and a repair and replacement service. Pick-ups and drop-offs at Batumi, Poti and Georgia's road borders, and rentals into Armenia or Turkey, are available at extra cost. Minimum driver age is 23 and you'll normally have to leave a warranty deposit of US$200 in cash or by Visa or MasterCard.

Avis (Map p36; www.avis.com; Tavisuplebis moedani 4) Also at the airport.

Hertz (Map p36; www.hertz.com; Caucasus Travel, Kote Abkhazi 44)

Sixt (Map p36; www.sixt.com; Samghebro 5) Also at the airport.

Taxi

Typical one-way long-distance fares are 100 GEL to 120 GEL to Kazbegi, and 200 GEL to 250 GEL to Yerevan. A return trip to Davit Gareja should be 120 GEL. Your accommodation can often find drivers. You can also find drivers at the main bus and train stations, although they can be tough bargainers.

For some destinations you can get a place in a shared taxi, with four passengers splitting the fare. Shared taxis to Yerevan from Ortachala bus station should cost 40 GEL to 50 GEL per person, or to Lagodekhi from the street beside Isani metro 8 GEL to 10 GEL. Go early to maximise chances of finding one.

Train

Tbilisi's recently rebuilt **main train station** (Map p30; Sadguris moedani) is the railway hub of Georgia. The ticket counters are on level 3 (the top floor); platforms are on level 2. You can buy tickets here for any train trip in Georgia. You must show your passport when buying tickets.

Schedules change fairly often: some information is given in English on the **Georgian Railway** (www.railway.ge) website – click 'Online Tickets': the main Tbilisi station is listed here as Tbilisi-pass. For busy trains such as those to Baku, Yerevan, Batumi and Zugdidi, it's advisable to book tickets a day or two ahead – and as far ahead as possible for July and August. It is possible to buy tickets online at www.railway.ge, and from yellow NOVA machines in metro stations and some supermarkets: instructions are available in English but procedures are quite complicated and it's best to have help from a local.

The only international trains are the sleepers to Baku and Yerevan (tickets at window 14). Both are convenient ways of getting to their destinations. The Baku train (2nd/1st class 57/112 GEL, 14 to 18 hours) leaves at 4pm or 5pm daily: the carriages have air-con though this may be switched off for long periods. The train to Yerevan (4th/3rd/2nd/1st class 23/31/49/70 GEL, 13 hours), via Vanadzor and Gyumri, normally departs at 6pm every two days – on odd dates from Tbilisi to Yerevan and on even dates from Yerevan to Tbilisi. However, from mid-June to mid-September the normal train is usually replaced by a quicker daily service: in 2011 this left Tbilisi at 8.35pm (3rd/2nd/1st class 23/38/80 GEL, 10 hours).

Within Georgia, useful trains include overnight services to Zugdidi (seat/2nd/1st class 6/11/15 GEL, eight hours, 10.30pm) and Batumi (4th/3rd/2nd/1st class 14/15/23/40 GEL, eight hours, 11.50pm). This Batumi train has air-conditioned 1st- and 2nd-class compartments. Batumi usually appears as Makhinjauri in timetables.

Day trains, with seats only, include the 8.50am to Batumi (20 GEL, eight hours), the 2pm to Poti (10 GEL, 5½ hours), and the 9.05am to Kutaisi (5 GEL, 5¾ hours) and Zugdidi (6 GEL, 8¼ hours). Extra trains to Batumi run during the summer holiday season.

Elektrichky (slow electric trains with seating only) run to Borjomi (2 GEL, 4½ hours) at 7am and 4.35pm, and to Kutaisi (3.50 GEL, 5½ hours) at 4pm. For these you pay on the train.

See p306 for general information on train travel.

ⓘ Getting Around

To/From the Airport

Bus 37 (0.50 GEL, half-hourly, about 7am to 10pm) runs between the airport and the train station via Ketevan Tsamebulis moedani on the east side of the Mtkvari, and Baratashvili, Tavisuplebis m;odani and Rustaveli in the city centre; the same in reverse going out to the airport.

Trains to Tbilisi's main train station (0.50 GEL, 30 minutes) leave the shiny new station outside the airport terminal at 6.10am, 8.30am, 1.50pm

and 6.05pm. Further services may be introduced. Trains depart the main station for the airport at 5.30am, 7.50am, 1.10pm and 5.25pm.

The official taxi fare from the airport to the city centre or vice versa is 25 GEL (30 GEL at night), but going out to the airport, a taxi hailed on the street may only charge 20 GEL.

Public Transport

BUS & MARSHRUTKA

City buses (yellow; per ride 0.50 GEL) and *marshrutky* (0.80 GEL) provide an above-ground complement to the metro. Their route boards are in Georgian only, but route information at some bus stops is given in English as well as Georgian. Metromoney cards, for riding the Tbilisi metro, can be used on the yellow buses too.

Buses only stop at predetermined stops, but you can get on and off *marshrutky* anywhere along their route. Pay when you get off. To get the driver to stop, yell out '*Gaacheret!*' ('Stop!').

METRO

The efficient Tbilisi metro operates from 6am to midnight, and the two lines reach most important parts of the city, meeting at Sadguris Moedani station. To use the metro, buy a Metromoney card (2 GEL), and charge it up with credit for rides, at any metro station ticket office. You touch the card on a reader when you enter the metro. Your first ride of the day costs 0.50 GEL, your second 0.30 GEL, and any further rides the same day 0.20 GEL. You can sell your card back

Tbilisi Metro

ST NINO & THE CONVERSION OF GEORGIA

While some of the legends that have grown up around St Nino are ridiculously far-fetched, there is no doubt that Nino is the historical figure to whom the 4th-century Christian conversion of Iveria (eastern Georgia) can be attributed. Nino is believed to have hailed from Cappadocia in Turkey and a widespread version has it that she was the daughter of a Roman general, Zabulon, was brought up in Jerusalem under the eye of an uncle who was Patriarch of Jerusalem, and at the age of 14 experienced a vision of the Virgin telling her that her destiny was to convert the Iverians to Christianity.

Coming to Iveria in the 320s, Nino won respect from local people by her good deeds and miracles. At Mtskheta she won a royal convert when her prayers saved Queen Nana of Iveria from serious illness. Then King Mirian was struck blind while hunting, only for his sight to be miraculously restored after he prayed to the Christian God – leading to mass baptism in the Aragvi River for the folk of Mtskheta. Mirian made Christianity Iveria's official religion in about 327. The vine-leaf cross that the Virgin allegedly gave Nino (and which Nino later bound with her own hair) is kept at Sioni Cathedral in Tbilisi. She remains Georgia's most venerated saint, and is buried at Bodbe Convent in Kakheti.

within a month if you show the original purchase receipt.

English signage and announcements are being phased in alongside Georgian. Station names are announced at each stop, and just before the doors shut the next station is announced.

Taxi

Taxis are plentiful and almost always unmetered. Agree on the fare before getting in. The standard cost for a shortish ride (up to about 3km) is 3 GEL. Longer rides cost up to 7 GEL (10 GEL at night).

AROUND TBILISI

A cradle of Georgian culture, the region west and south of the capital is known as Kartli, after the mythical father of the Georgian people, Kartlos, whose progeny made their home at Mtskheta. Nobody can understand Georgian spirituality without visiting Mtskheta, where St Nino converted the Iverian kingdom to Christianity in the 4th century. By contrast Gori is best known as the town where Joseph Stalin was born in 1879.

Mtskheta მცხეთა

♪32 / POP 7700

Mtskheta has been Georgia's spiritual heart since Christianity was established here in about 327, and holds a near-mystical significance in Georgian culture. It was capital of most of eastern Georgia from about the 3rd century BC to the 5th century AD, when King Vakhtang Gorgasali switched his base to Tbilisi. It remained a spiritual capital,

however, and Mtskheta's Svetitskhoveli Cathedral is still the setting for important ceremonies of the Georgian Orthodox Church. Containing some of the oldest and most important churches in the country, and with an alluring setting where the Mtkvari and Aragvi Rivers meet, Mtskheta makes an easy and enjoyable day trip from Tbilisi. Unesco placed Mtskheta's historic churches on its World Heritage in Danger list in 2009, citing deterioration of stonework and frescoes and loss of authenticity due to work on the buildings.

⊙ Sights

Svetitskhoveli Cathedral CATHEDRAL
(Arsukidze; ⊙8am-8pm) This grand (and for its time, enormous) building dates from the 11th century, early in the golden age of Georgian church architecture. It has an elongated cross plan and is adorned with beautiful stone carving outside and in.

According to tradition, Christ's robe lies buried beneath the cathedral. Apparently a Mtskheta Jew, Elioz, was in Jerusalem at the time of the Crucifixion and returned with the robe to Mtskheta. His sister Sidonia took it from him and immediately died in a passion of faith. The robe was buried with her and as years passed, people forgot the exact site. When King Mirian decided to build the first church at Mtskheta in the 4th century, the wooden column designed to stand in its centre could not be raised from the ground. But after an all-night prayer vigil by St Nino, the column miraculously moved of its own accord to the burial site of Sidonia and the robe. The column subsequently worked many miracles and Svetitskhoveli means 'Life-Giving Column'.

In the 5th century Vakhtang Gorgasali replaced Mirian's original church with a stone one, whose modest remains are visible to the left of the cathedral today. The present building was constructed between 1010 and 1029 under Patriarch Melqisedek, and is still one of the most beautiful churches in the country. The defensive wall around it was built in 1787.

Christ's robe is believed to lie in the nave beneath a square, towerlike pillar that is decorated with colourful if faded frescoes of the conversion of Kartli. The tomb of Erekle II, king of Kartli and Kakheti from 1762 to 1798, lies before the icon screen (marked with his birth and death dates, 1720 and 1798). Vakhtang Gorgasali's tomb is behind this, with a raised flagstone and carved stone sword.

Jvari Church   CHURCH

(Holy Cross; ⊘9am-7pm) Visible for miles around on its hilltop overlooking Mtskheta from the east, the Jvari Church is, to many Georgians, the holiest of holies. Jvari stands where King Mirian erected a sacred wooden cross soon after his conversion by St Nino in the 4th century. Between 585 and 604 Stepanoz I, the *eristavi* (duke) of Kartli, constructed the church over the cross.

Jvari is a beautifully symmetrical little building and a classic of early Georgian tetraconch design. It has a cross-shaped plan with four equal arms, the angles between them being filled in with corner rooms, and the low dome sits on a squat, octagonal drum. The interior is rather bare, but the site provides spectacular views over Mtskheta and the convergence of the Aragvi and Mtkvari Rivers. The road up to the church from Mtskheta takes a highly circuitous route; a taxi costs 20 GEL to 25 GEL return trip, including waiting time. If you're feeling

Around Tbilisi

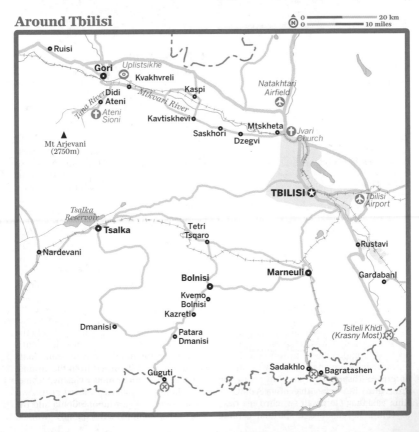

Mtskheta

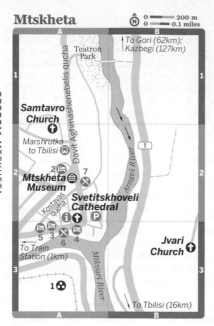

Teatron Park

To Gori (62km); Kazbegi (127km)

Samtavro Church

Marshrutka to Tbilisi

Mtskheta Museum

Svetitskhoveli Cathedral

Jvari Church

To Train Station (1km)

To Tbilisi (16km)

Mtskheta

◉ Top Sights

Jvari Church B3
Mtskheta Museum A2
Samtavro Church A2
Svetitskhoveli Cathedral.....................A2

◉ Sights

1 Armaztsikhe-Bagineti A3

🛏 Sleeping

2 Eto Manjavidze A2
3 Gulo Merebashvili...............................A3
4 Hotel Tamarindi...................................A3
5 Nana Machitadze.................................A3

✕ Eating

6 Old Taverna...A3
7 Opizani..A2

energetic, you can walk from Mtskheta in about one hour by crossing the footbridge from Teatron Park, walking about 1km down the busy highway, then heading up the hillside to the church.

Samtavro Church   CHURCH
(Davit Aghmashenebelis qucha; ⊙8am-8pm) This large church, now part of a nunnery, was built in the 1130s and was once the palace church of the lords of Mtskheta. King Mirian and Queen Nana are buried in its southwest corner, under a stone canopy. The little church in the grounds, Tsminda Nino, dates from the 4th century and stands on a spot where St Nino is said to have prayed.

Mtskheta Museum   MUSEUM
(Davit Aghmashenebelis qucha 54; admission 3 GEL; ⊙10am-5pm Tue-Sat) The museum has an interesting collection of archaeological finds, labelled in English and Georgian, from the Mtskheta area, which has been inhabited for several millennia. Highlights include an elaborately worked Bronze Age ritual belt, and a miniature mother-of-pearl Iranian sun temple from the 3rd or 4th century AD, found in the Samtavro cemetery.

Pre-Christian sites   ARCHAEOLOGICAL SITES
Several pre-Christian sites have been excavated in the area. Most interesting is the excavated residence of early Iverian kings at **Armaztsikhe-Bagineti** on the south side of the Mtkvari, which includes remains of baths, a temple and a wine cellar.

🛏 Sleeping

Mtskheta is an easy day trip from Tbilisi, but if you fancy getting away from the city it has a small central hotel and some good, welcoming, very clean homestays (with shared bathrooms).

Eto Manjavidze   HOMESTAY $
(☑2512463, 595909396; Karibche 6; per person 20-30 GEL; 🛜) Very friendly household with the upper floor given over to guests – three double rooms and spacious sitting areas.

Hotel Tamarindi   HOTEL $
(☑2512764, 579037772; www.tamarindi.ucoz.com; Arsukidze 23; per person incl breakfast 25-30 GEL; ❄@🛜) This small hotel has comfy rooms and a kitchen and washing machine for guests. Host Jemal speaks a little English and offers day trips.

Gulo Merebashvili   HOMESTAY $
(☑2322636; Arsukidze 15; per person 20-25 GEL) Gulo speaks no English but is a great communicator and has a small guest kitchen.

Nana Machitadze   HOMESTAY $
(☑2512413, 599353104; Gamsakhurdia 14; per person 20-25 GEL; 🛜) Good, spacious accommodation with a kitchen, sitting room and washing machine for guests. Cable internet available for laptops; German spoken.

✗ Eating

Mtskheta is famous for its *lobio* (beans with herbs and spices), which can be found in any local restaurant, served in a traditional clay pot.

Old Taverna GEORGIAN $$
(Arsukidze; mains 5-10 GEL) This friendly little place serves good Georgian dishes such as *ostri* (spicy meat in a tomato-based sauce), *mtsvadi, khachapuri* and mushroom dishes. In good weather it's lovely to sit outside facing Svetitskhoveli.

Opizani GEORGIAN $$
(Mamulashvili; mains 8-15 GEL; ☺lunch & dinner) A larger, fancier, new place in an attractive stone, tile and wood building, with a wide range of Georgian dishes and wines.

❶ Information

Tourism Information Centre (☑2322128; mtskhetatic@yahoo.com; Arsukidze 3; ☺10am-6pm; ☎) Has helpful English-speaking staff, full information on the area, and free internet-connected computers and wi-fi.

❶ Getting There & Away

Marshrutky to Tbilisi leave about every 15 minutes from 7.30am to 8pm from the bus stop on Davit Aghmashenebeli. No *marshrutky* go from Mtskheta town to Gori or beyond, but you may be able to flag one down on Hwy 1. A few trains a day stop at Mtskheta station (on the south side of the Mtkvari, about a 15-minute walk from the centre) including *elektrichky* to Gori (1 GEL, one hour) and Borjomi (2 GEL, four hours) at 7.21am and 4.57pm.

Gori გორი

☑370 / POP 45,000

Gori, 80km west of Tbilisi, has long been synonymous with just one man: this is the town where Stalin was born and went to school. The large museum devoted to Stalin, opened in Soviet times, is still Gori's best known attraction, but there are also several intriguing older historical attractions close by.

In the 2008 war over South Ossetia (whose border is 30km north of Gori), Gori was bombed by Russia, with at least 20 civilians killed, and most of the population fled before the town fell under Russian control for 10 days. Rows of single-storey refugee houses visible from the Tbilisi–Gori highway, and from the road into Gori from the highway, are reminders of that war.

The centre of town is the wide Stalinis moedani (Stalin Sq). The main street, Stalinis gamziri (Stalin Ave), runs 600m north from here to the large Stalin Museum, and 700m south to a bridge over the Mtkvari River.

◉ Sights

TOP CHOICE ›**Stalin Museum** MUSEUM
(www.stalinmuseum.ge; Stalinis gamziri 32; admission incl photo permission & guide in English, German or French 10 GEL, incl train carriage 15 GEL; ☺10am-6pm) One of Georgia's most interesting museums, this impressive 1957 building exudes a faintly religious air. The visit includes the tiny wood-and-mudbrick house where Stalin's parents rented the single room where they lived for the first four years of his life. This stands in front of the main museum building, under its own templelike superstructure. The rest of the poor neighbourhood in which it stood was demolished in the 1930s as Gori was redesigned to glorify its famous son.

The museum charts Stalin's journey from the Gori church school to leadership of the USSR, the Yalta Conference at the end of WWII and his death in 1953. It now gives a slightly less starry-eyed account of his career than it used to, with guides referring to the purges, the Gulag and his 1939 pact with Hitler. A small two-room section beside the foot of the main stairs is devoted to political repression under Stalin.

Upstairs, the first hall details Stalin's childhood and adolescence, including his rather cringeworthy pastoral poetry, and then his early revolutionary activities in Georgia, organising unions and setting up illegal printing presses. Stalin's involvement with Lenin is detailed, taking us through Stalin's seven jail terms under the tsarist authorities (six of them in Siberia), the revolution of 1917, the Civil War and Lenin's death in 1924. This hall displays the text of Lenin's 1922 political testament that described Stalin as too coarse and power-hungry, advising Communist Party members to remove Stalin from the post of General Secretary.

One room is devoted to a bronze copy of Stalin's eerie death mask, lying in state. The next one has a reconstruction of his first office in the Kremlin, as People's Commissar for Nationalities in 1918, plus personal memorabilia such as his pipes and glasses, and a large collection of tributes and gifts from world leaders and other Bolsheviks.

To one side of the museum is **Stalin's train carriage**, in which he travelled to the Yalta Conference in 1945 (he didn't like flying). Apparently bulletproof, its elegant interior includes a bathtub and a primitive air-conditioning system.

FREE Gori Fortress FORTRESS
(⊘24hr) This oval citadel stands atop the hill at the heart of Gori, a short walk through the streets west from Stalinis gamziri. A fortification existed here in ancient times but most of the present building dates from the Middle Ages, with 17th-century additions. There are fine views from the fortress and it's a good place to be around sunset. At the northeast foot of the fortress, a circle of mutilated metal warriors forms an eerie memorial to those lost in the 2008 war.

War Museum MUSEUM
(admission 3 GEL; Stalinis gamziri 19; ⊘10am-5pm Mon-Sat) This museum, 400m south of the Stalin Museum, is mostly devoted to Gori people's involvement in WWII, but also contains a small display on the 2008 war. A makeover is in the offing, presumably to downplay the Soviet side of things and up-play the Georgian. Outside is a memorial with a long list of local people who died in the fighting over Abkhazia and South Ossetia in the 1990s.

🛏 Sleeping

Gori has a smattering of hotels, and several guesthouses with shared bathrooms.

Hotel Victoria HOTEL $$
(☏275586; victoria_gori@mail.com; Tamar Mepi 76; r 80-140 GEL; ❈🗺) Only a few years old, the Victoria is already due for renovation, though it still offers large, clean, comfy and bright rooms. It's 200m east off southern Stalinis gamziri. Breakfast is 10 GEL.

Hotel Georgia HOTEL $$
(☏275756; www.hotelgeorgia.blogspot.com; Stalinis gamziri 28; r 70-90 GEL; ❈🗺) A stone's throw from the Stalin Museum, Gori's newest hotel has plain but quite comfy rooms. Only the *luks* (deluxe) pair have air-con. Breakfast is 5 GEL.

Guesthouse Luka GUESTHOUSE $
(☏278758, 598552053; Aghmashenebeli 19; per person incl light breakfast 20 GEL; @🗺) Plain but clean, neat rooms in a small street north of the bus station and market. There is a small pool.

Guesthouse Ketino GUESTHOUSE $$
(☏276806; Tbilisis chikhi 1; per person incl light breakfast 30 GEL; @) This three-room guesthouse is in a lane off Tbilisi (the continuation of Stalinis gamziri), 700m north of the Stalin Museum.

Hotel Intourist HOTEL $
(☏272676; Stalinis gamziri 26; r 30 GEL) Modernised rooms for 80 GEL to 120 GEL may eventually open; meantime, only very shabby rooms without hot water are available. Next to Hotel Georgia.

🍴 Eating

Hunter GEORGIAN $$
(Stalinis gamziri 6; mains 5-14 GEL; ⊘lunch & dinner; 🍴) With a window display of stuffed animals and a log-cabin-style interior with antlers and furs, Hunter serves up excellent dishes from straightforward *mtsvadi* and *khinkali* to specialities such as duck in *tqemali* (plum sauce). It has a picture menu and friendly staff who speak some English. It's 300m south of Stalinis moedani.

Kafe Sport GEORGIAN $$
(Stalinis gamziri 11; mains 4-15 GEL; 🛜🍴) A large, bright place just south of Stalinis moedani. It does good Georgian fare including *ojakhuri* (a meat-and-potatoes dish), trout and *shkmeruli*, and is popular with locals for evening drinks.

Cake House CAFE $
(Stalinis gamziri 22; khachapuri or pizza 4-5 GEL; 🍴) A pine-panelled cafe between the Stalin Museum and Stalinis moedani, serving sickly cakes as well as *khachapuri* and reasonable pizza.

ℹ Information

Tourism Information Centre (☏270776; ticgori@gmail.com; Kutaisi 23A; ⊘10am-7pm) Behind the Stalin Museum; has masses of info on the area.

ℹ Getting There & Away

Gori's bus station is 500m west of Stalinis moedani, along Chavchavadze. *Marshrutky* (4 GEL, 1¼ hours) and buses (3.50 GEL, 1½ to two hours) to Tbilisi leave about every half-hour from 7am to 1pm and then a few more times until 6pm. There are three or four daily *marshrutky* to Borjomi (5 GEL, 1¾ hours), and one in the morning (it can be as early as 7am) to Kutaisi (8 GEL, 2½ hours) and Batumi (15 GEL, five hours).

About 10 daily trains head east to Tbilisi (4 GEL to 32 GEL, one to 1¼ hours) from **Gori station**

(Gorijvari), across the Mtkvari from the south end of Stalinis gamziri. Westbound, they head to Borjomi (1 GEL, three hours) or other towns in western Georgia.

Around Gori

UPLISTSIKHE უფლისციხე

This fascinating and once enormous **cave city** (admission 3 GEL, guide in English 15 GEL; ☺10am-6pm) affords expansive views along the Mtkvari valley from its site on the river's north bank, 10km east of Gori. Between the 6th century BC and 1st century AD, Uplistsikhe developed into one of the chief political and religious centres of pre-Christian Kartli, with temples dedicated principally to the sun goddess. After the Arabs occupied Tbilisi in AD 645, Uplistsikhe became the residence of the Christian kings of Kartli and an important trade centre, with a main caravan road from Asia to Europe running through it. At its peak Uplistskhe housed 20,000 people. Its importance declined after King David the Builder retook Tbilisi in 1122 and it was irrevocably destroyed by the Mongols in 1240. What you visit today is the 40,000-sq-metre Shida Qalaqi, or Inner City, less than half of the original whole. Almost everything here has been uncovered by archaeologists since 1957, when only the tops of a few caves were visible. The many round pits dug in Uplistsikhe's rock are thought to have been used for corn storage or for sacrificial purposes; tadpole-shaped pits may have been ovens.

To enter by the old main track into Uplistiskhe, go about 5m up the rocks opposite the toilets and cafe at the entrance, and follow the rock-cut path to the left. Metal-railed steps lead up through what was the **main gate**, with the excavated **main tower** of the Shida Qalaqi's defensive walls sitting under a corrugated roof to the right. Ahead you'll find a cave overlooking the river, with a pointed arch carved in the rock above it, and a ceiling carved with octagonal Roman-style designs. Known as the **Theatre**, this is probably a temple from the 1st or 2nd century AD, where religious mystery plays may have been performed.

Returning towards the main gate, turn left to wind your way up the main street. Down to the right is the large pre-Christian **Temple of Makvliani**, with an inner recess behind an arched portico. The open hall in front has stone seats for priests.

A little further up on the left is the big hall known as **Tamaris Darbazi** (Hall of Queen Tamar). Here, behind two columns cut from the rock, is a stone seat dating from antiquity. The stone ceiling is cut to look like wooden beams, and there is a hole to let smoke out and light in. This was almost certainly a pagan temple, though Georgia's great Christian Queen Tamar may have used it later. To its left is an open area with stone niches along one side, thought to have once been a pharmacy or dovecote. A large cave building to the right of Tamaris Darbazi was probably a **sun temple** used for animal sacrifices, and later converted into a Christian basilica.

The church near the top of the hill is the 10th-century **Uplistsulis Eklesia** (Prince's Church). This triple-church basilica was built over what was probably Upliistsikhe's most important pagan temple.

On your way back down, don't miss the long **tunnel** running down to the Mtkvari, an emergency escape route that could also have been used for carrying water up to the city. Its entrance is behind a reconstructed wall beside the old main gate.

ⓘ Getting There & Away

A return taxi from Gori, including waiting time, normally costs 30 GEL. *Marshrutky* leave Gori bus station a few times a day for Kvakhvreli (1 GEL, 20 minutes), the village across the Mtkvari River from Uplistsikhe – a 2km walk from the site.

ATENI SIONI ატენის სიონი

This impressively ancient **church** (⊙9am-6pm) has a beautiful setting above a bend of the pretty, grapevine-strewn Tana valley, surrounded by high hills and cliffs, 12km south of Gori.

Ateni Sioni was built in the 7th century and modelled on Mtskheta's Jvari Church. Beautiful reliefs of stags, a hunting scene and a knight were carved into the exterior walls later. Inside, the 11th-century frescoes, depicting biblical scenes and Georgian rulers, are among the finest medieval art in the country. They have been painstakingly preserved to prevent further fading, although there are no plans to restore them to their full glory, as it is precisely their ancient nature that makes them interesting.

A return taxi from Gori to the church should cost about 30 GEL, or 40 GEL if combined with Uplistsikhe. Alternatively, buses run from Gori bus station to Ateni Sioni (0.80 GEL, 30 minutes) hourly from 7am to 6pm.

WESTERN GEORGIA

Famous as the destination of Jason and the Argonauts in their search for the Golden Fleece, western Georgia is home to Georgia's second-largest city, Kutaisi, and is full of historical, architectural and natural riches. It's also an area where the government is investing a lot in the future: Kutaisi is scheduled to become the seat of Georgia's parliament in 2012, a new coastal resort is under construction at Anaklia (just south of the Abkhazian border) and a brand-new city of 500,000 people, Lazica, is planned nearby.

The region has always acted as a conduit for influences from the west, from the Ancient Greeks to St Nino to the Ottoman Turks. It was for long periods ruled separately from eastern Georgia, but was also where the great united Georgian kingdom of the 11th and 12th centuries made its start.

Kutaisi ქუთაისი

✓431 / POP 199,000

Capital at various times of several historical kingdoms within Georgia, Kutaisi has a rich and fascinating history, much of which is apparent to visitors. The transfer of Georgia's parliament from Tbilisi to brand-new quarters in Kutaisi, scheduled for 2012, should help revitalise the city after years of post-Soviet industrial malaise.

Kutaisi is built around the Rioni River, with the city centre, first developed in the 17th century, on its left bank. To its north, the right bank rises up to an older area where the landmark Bagrati Cathedral overlooks the city.

History

Kutaisi was one of the main cities of the ancient kingdom of Colchis, and a settlement has existed here for nearly 4000 years. At the end of the 8th century AD, Leon II, king of Abkhazia, transferred his capital from Anakopia to Kutaisi. In 1001 Abkhazia's Bagrat III inherited the eastern Georgian kingdom of Kartli, uniting western and eastern Georgia for the first time in many centuries. It was in Kutaisi that Bagrat's descendant David the Builder was crowned Georgian king in 1089. Kutaisi remained the political and cultural centre of Georgia until 1122, when David liberated Tbilisi from Arab rule.

Kutaisi resumed as capital of the western region when Georgia was divided in the 15th century after the Mongol and Timurid invasions. It was occupied by the Ottomans in 1669, then captured by Georgian and Russian forces in 1770. Under the Soviet regime Kutaisi became Georgia's second most important industrial centre.

◎ Sights

Everyone will want to see Bagrati Cathedral, while those with more time will also enjoy the Historical Museum, the busy **market** between Paliashvili and Lermontov, and the attractive, recently spruced-up area around **Kutaisis bulvari** park, with its opera house, theatre, art museum and more.

FREE **Bagrati Cathedral**   CATHEDRAL
(Bagrati; ⊙9am-8pm) From the Jachvis Khidi (Chain Bridge), you can walk up cobbled

Western Georgia

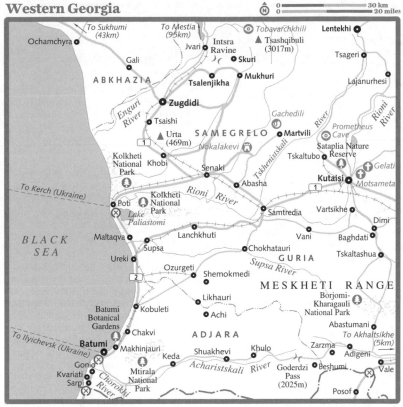

streets lined with attractive houses and gardens to the stately ruins of the Bagrati Cathedral on Ukimerioni Hill.

Bagrati was built in 1003 by Bagrat III. A great dome rose over the centre of the cathedral, but in 1692 a Turkish explosion brought down both dome and ceiling to leave the cathedral in a ruined state. The cathedral is now being completely restored, with the aim of returning it to its original form. Unfortunately, this contributed to Unesco placing Bagrati Cathedral on its World Heritage in Danger list in 2010, due to threats to the 'integrity and authenticity of the site'.

The ruined **palace-citadel** immediately east of the cathedral dates back to the 6th century. It was ruined in 1769 by bombardment from the forces of Solomon I of Imereti and the Russian General Todtleben as they fought to take Kutaisi from the Turks. But you can see wine cellars at the west end

of the palace, a church in the middle, and parts of the medieval walls.

Kutaisi Historical Museum MUSEUM
(Tbilisi 1; admission 3 GEL, tour in English, French or German 15 GEL; ☺10am-6pm) The history museum has superb collections from all around western Georgia and is well worth your time, but a guided tour is a good idea as labelling is poor. The highlight is the Treasury section, with a marvellous exhibition of icons and crosses in precious metals and jewels, including a large, reputedly miracle-working icon from the Bagrati Cathedral. The rest of the collection ranges from a famous 7th-century BC androgynous fertility god figurine to medieval weaponry, historical art, manuscripts going back to the 10th century and even the first telephone used in Kutaisi.

Kutaisi

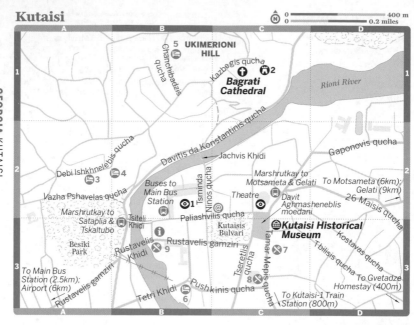

🛏 Sleeping

The selection of hotels is rapidly improving, and a slew of homestays and guesthouses provides budget accommodation.

Hotel Old Town   HOTEL $$
(☏251451, 593408445; dzvelikalaki@gmail.com; Grishashvili 3/4; incl breakfast s 90-110 GEL, d 120-145 GEL, ste 160-175 GEL; ❄🛜) This well-run, centrally located little hotel provides comfortable, carpeted, modern rooms in a variety of tasteful styles. Some have balconies or hydromassage showers, and there's a neat little cafe-bar too.

Hotel Rcheuli Palace   HISTORIC HOTEL $$
(☏252710; www.rcheuli.ge; Grigol Khandzteli 21B; s/d incl breakfast from 90/110 GEL; ❄🛜) Though a little out of the centre (west of the river, about 1km south of the Rustaveli Bridge), the Rcheuli Palace will surely be Kutaisi's most stylish lodging once fully completed (probably by 2012). With massively thick walls and brick arches everywhere, it's set in a former military barracks dating from 1860. Opened in 2010 with 15 spacious, carpeted rooms in contemporary style, it's expanding to 36, with a bar, swimming pool, tennis court and public restaurant.

Giorgi's Homestay   HOMESTAY $
(☏243720, 595591511; giorgihomestay14@yahoo.com; Chanchibadze 14; per person with/without breakfast 30/20 GEL; @) Hospitable, English-speaking Giorgi Giorgadze and his family provide clean, sizeable rooms in their ample house on Ukimerioni Hill. Giorgi offers plenty of travel and sightseeing tips and help, and the breakfasts are substantial. Guests can use a kitchen, and the shared bathrooms are sparkling clean.

Gvetadze Homestay   HOMESTAY $
(☏243007; Tbilisi 3rd Lane No 6; per person 15 GEL) Suliko and Mediko Gvetadze provide a friendly welcome at their house, 800m east of Davit Aghmasheneblis moedani, in the side street opposite Tbilisi 100. Meals are available at a modest extra charge, and the wine flows freely! It can squeeze in about 10 people when busy. The shared bathroom has been modernised.

Argo Palace   HOTEL $$
(☏248395, 599376525; Debi Ishkhnelebi 16; per person incl 0/1/2 meals 30/35/50 GEL) This new place on Ukimerioni Hill offers 16 clean, pleasant, en suite rooms in pastel shades, and a terrace with views over the river and city centre. There's a good, bright dining room and Ana, the teenage granddaughter

Kutaisi

◎ **Top Sights**
- Bagrati Cathedral C1
- Kutaisi Historical Museum................ C3

◎ **Sights**
- 1 Market B2
- 2 Palace-citadel C1

🛌 **Sleeping**
- 3 Argo Palace A2
- 4 Beka Hotel... B2
- 5 Giorgi's Homestay B1
- 6 Hotel Old Town B3

✕ **Eating**
- 7 Baraka C3
- 8 Flamingo C3
- 9 Mirzaani Brewery............................... B3

🛈 **Transport**
- Buses to Kutaisi-1 Train Station . (see 9)

of the family, speaks English. There is also a slightly cheaper guesthouse, with shared bathrooms, next door at No 16.

Beka Hotel   HOTEL **$$**
(✆246923; Debi Ishkhnelebi 26; per person incl 0/1/2 meals 35/40/50 GEL) An impressive white mansion run by a friendly Russian- and Georgian-speaking family, the Beka has 16 good, spick-and-span rooms, eight of them with balconies overlooking the river and city centre. Meals are good, too.

✕ Eating

Kutaisi's mostly uninspiring selection of eateries will certainly improve when Parliament hits town.

Mirzaani Brewery   GEORGIAN **$$**
(www.mirzaani.ge; Rustaveli 9; mains 5-13 GEL; ☺lunch & dinner; 🗐) With three floors of well-spaced tables, two of them with ample terraces, this is the choice spot to eat. There's a wide selection of mainly Georgian dishes from cold starters such as *basturma* (air-dried cured beef) or cauliflower in walnut sauce, to hot mains such as barbecued veal or roasted mushrooms with potatoes – plus mugs of Mirzaani's house beer and a long wine list.

Baraka   GEORGIAN **$**
(Tamar Mepe 3; mains 5-8 GEL; ☺lunch & dinner) This pleasant, brick-arched place does good *khachapuri* and other dishes including

trout and *kubdari* (a *khachapuri*-like pie with minced-meat filling). Popular for ice cream, too. Look for its red-neon name sign.

Flamingo   GEORGIAN **$**
(cnr Tamar Mepe & Pushkin; mains 2-6 GEL; ☺lunch & dinner) Economical self-service place; one of several cheap eateries around this street junction.

🛈 Information

Internet cafe (Detsky Mir, Paliashvili; per hr 1.20 GEL; ☺9am-9pm)
Tourism Information Centre (✆241103; tickutaisi@gmail.com; cnr Rustaveli & Paliashvili; ☺10am-7pm) Very helpful office in colourful, purpose-built premises in the heart of town.

🛈 Getting There & Around

Marshrutky from Kutaisi's **main bus station** (Chavchavadzis gamziri 67), 3km southwest of the centre behind a McDonald's, go to Tbilisi (10 GEL, four hours, 12 daily), Gori (8 GEL, 2½ hours, noon), Zugdidi (7 GEL, two hours, 12 daily), Batumi (10 GEL, 2½ hours, nine daily), Poti (7 GEL, 2½ hours, 12 daily) and Borjomi (8 GEL, three hours, 8.20am, 8.50am and 1.30pm). You can find long-distance taxis here.

Kutaisi-1 train station (Tamar Mepe), less than 1km south of the centre, has trains to Tbilisi at 12.57pm (3rd clas; 5 GEL, 5½ hours) and 12.30am (2nd class; 10 GEL, six hours), two daily to Batumi (Makhinjauri; 2 GEL to 4 GEL, three to four hours) and one at 12.20pm to Zugdidi (2 GEL, 3½ hours).

In 2011 **Ural Airlines** (www.uralairlines.ru) and **S7 Airlines** (www.s7.ru) began flights from Moscow to Kutaisi airport, 6km west of the centre along the Samtredia road. Flights from other cities may start. The Irish carrier Ryanair has been among airlines linked with Kutaisi in media reports.

Bus 1 (0.30 GEL) runs from the bus station to the city centre (Mirzaani Brewery restaurant). Catch it across the road (Chavchavadze) from the bus station, going to the left. From the centre to the bus station, catch bus 1 at the west end of Paliashvili. From Kutaisi-1 to the centre, take bus 1 or 22 north on Tamar Mepe; from the centre to Kutaisi-1 catch them outside Mirzaani Brewery.

City taxis with numbers on top and on the door have meters and charge 0.60 GEL per kilometre.

Around Kutaisi

MOTSAMETA მოწამეთა
Little Motsameta **monastery** sits on a spectacular clifftop promontory above a bend of the Tskhaltsitela River, 6km from Kutaisi,

1.8km off the Gelati road. The river's name, 'Red Water', derives from an 8th-century Arab massacre. Among the victims were the brothers Davit and Konstantin Mkheidze, dukes of Argveti. Their bodies were thrown in the river, but the story goes that lions brought them up to the church where their bones were subsequently kept. If you crawl three times under the side altar where the bones are kept, your wish will supposedly be granted (this didn't work for your correspondent).

See the following Gelati section for transport information.

GELATI გელათი

Georgians have always had a talent for choosing beautiful locations for their churches and this monastery complex, on a wooded hillside 9km northeast of Kutaisi, is no exception.

Gelati was founded by King David the Builder in 1106 as a centre for Christian culture and Neoplatonist learning; its academy became, according to medieval chroniclers, 'a second Jerusalem'. Many Georgian rulers were buried here, including David himself and (according to her chronicler) Queen Tamar. In 1510 the Ottoman Turks set fire to the complex, but Bagrat III of Imereti subsequently restored it, and it became the residence of the West Georgian patriarch. The monks were cast out by the Communists in 1922, but the churches were reconsecrated in 1988 and President Saakashvili chose Gelati for his inauguration in 2004.

The interior of the main **Cathedral of the Virgin** is among the brightest and most colourful in Georgia. Among the frescoes, painted between the 12th and 18th centuries, note especially the line of seven noble figures on the north wall of the north transept: these include David the Builder (holding the church) and Bagrat III (with a cross over his left shoulder). Across the corner to the right of David are the Byzantine emperor Constantine and his wife, Helena. The apse holds a famous 1130s mosaic of the Virgin and Child, with Archangels Michael and Gabriel to the left and right respectively. If you visit during the Sunday-morning service from around 10am you'll be treated to beautiful Georgian chants.

Outside the cathedral's west door is the smaller **Church of St Nicholas**, built on an unusual arcaded base, and beyond that, the **Academy**, where philosophy, theology, sciences and painting were studied and important chronicles and translations written.

The Academy has recently been completely rebuilt after years as a roofless shell. To the left of the Academy, inside the **South Gate**, lies David the Builder's grave. David wanted to be buried here so that all who entered the monastery would step on his huge 3m tomb, a notably humble gesture for such a powerful man. Ironically, reverent visitors nowadays take great care *not* to step on the tomb.

ℹ Getting There & Away

Marshrutky to Gelati (1 GEL, 30 minutes) leave from Brose behind the big theatre in central Kutaisi at 8.30am, 11am, 2pm, 4pm and 6pm, passing the Motsameta turn-off en route. If you're visiting both places, it's mostly downhill walk of about one hour from Gelati to Motsameta, should the return *marshrutka* schedules not suit. On Saturday and Sunday there are direct *marshrutky* to Motsameta from Brose at 9am, 12.30pm and 3pm.

A taxi from Kutaisi to Gelati and back should cost about 20 GEL, or 25 GEL with Motsameta too.

SATAPLIA NATURE RESERVE

სათაფლიას სახელმწიფო ნაკრძალი

This 3.5-sq-km **reserve** (admission 6 GEL; ☺10am-6pm Wed-Mon), 9km northwest of Kutaisi, has recently been developed for visitors and is a big hit with Georgian tourists. Its star features are a couple of dozen 120-million-year-old, fossilised **dinosaur footprints** (well displayed in a protective building), and an attractively lit 300m-long **cave** with a small underground river and plenty of stalactites and stalagmites. The reserve is covered in thick, subtropical Colchic forest and has a couple of panoramic lookout points. *Marshrutka* 45 (1 GEL, 30 minutes) goes hourly to Sataplia from the west side of the Tsiteli Khidi (Red Bridge) in Kutaisi.

PROMETHEUS CAVE პრომეთეუს მღვიმე

At Kumistavi, 20km northwest of Kutaisi, this 1.2km-long **cave** (☺11am-4pm Tue-Sun) is more beautiful and impressive than the Sataplia cave. It was opened for tourist visits in 2011, initially free though a charge will probably be introduced. It's planned to make boat trips available on the lake inside the cave. *Marshrutky* 30, from near Kutaisi's Red Bridge, and 45 from Kutaisi's main bus station (both 1 GEL, 30 minutes) run to the spa town of Tskaltubo, where you can get a *marshrutka* 8km onward to Kumistavi (1 GEL, 20 minutes) from the central bazaar.

VANI ვანი

The site of this ancient city is 40km southwest of Kutaisi. The modern **museum** (admission 1.50 GEL, tour in Russian 10 GEL; ☺10am-4pm) here, labelled in English as well as Georgian, has spectacular exhibits.

Vani was one of the main centres of ancient Colchis, flourishing from the 8th to 1st centuries BC. Some speculate that it could have been the city of King Aeëtes, where Jason came in search of the Golden Fleece. Archaeologists have found remains of monumental architecture and opulent burials. Strong brick and mud walls with towers were built towards the end of Vani's life, when archaeologists think it may have become a kind of temple-city, dedicated principally to the goddess Levcoteia. The museum's most remarkable treasures are on its upper floor, where you can see fine bronze casts including a statue of a youth, and a mix of originals and copies of fabulous gold adornments with incredibly fine animal designs. The first excavations at Vani took place in the 1890s, after locals reported gold ornaments being washed down the hill after heavy rains.

The site itself is not developed for visitors but you can make out some temple areas, defensive walls and a deep ritual well, as well as a small city gate and a section of paved street.

Marshrutky to Vani (3 GEL, 1½ hours) leave Kutaisi's main bus station hourly from 7am to 1pm (except 10am). From Vani's bus station, it's about a 15-minute walk to the museum. A taxi from Kutaisi is about 50 GEL return.

Poti ფოთი

📱493 / POP 48,000

Poti, Georgia's main port, is visited by travellers for two main reasons: the Ukraine ferry and the nearby Kolkheti National Park.

Once a centre of the Ottoman slave trade, Poti developed after coming under Russian control in 1828. In 2008 Russian forces controlled Poti for a month and sank several Georgian naval vessels in the port.

The centre of the city is marked by Poti's cathedral, which is modelled on Istanbul's Hagia Sofia and was completed in 1907. Ten streets radiate from Rustavelis rkali (Rustaveli Circle), the very large roundabout surrounding the cathedral. Davit Aghmashenebeli, the main street, runs northwest from here across a branch of the Rioni River to reach a junction after 1.5km. Here Gegidze heads to the right (east), while the port is 400m to the west. Parnavazi runs 600m eastward from Rustavelis rkali, through the market area, to a square with another bridge leading to the train station on Reqvava.

🛏 Sleeping & Eating

Mosquitoes can be a nuisance here.

Porto Hotel HOTEL $$
(📱577161016; Akaki; r 90-140 GEL; ❄🖭) This recently opened pale-blue hotel 600m south of Rustavelis rkali has just six very pleasant, thickly carpeted, well-equipped rooms with carved wooden furniture. Meals are available.

JASON & THE GOLDEN FLEECE

In the Ancient Greek myth of the Golden Fleece, Jason, a prince of Thessaly, responds to his uncle Pelias' challenge to go to the land of Colchis, on the eastern shores of the Black Sea, to find the Golden Fleece. (Colchis was a historical kingdom occupying most of western Georgia in antiquity.) Jason had a special ship, the *Argo,* built to carry him and 49 other adventurous young Greek rowers, thenceforth known as the Argonauts. After various tribulations, they reached the kingdom of Colchis and sailed up the Phasis River (the present-day Rioni), where they were received by King Aeëtes in his capital (possibly Vani or Kutaisi). Aeëtes agreed to give up the fleece if Jason could yoke two fire-breathing bulls to a plough, and then sow the teeth of a dragon from which a crop of armed men would spring. Jason secretly promised marriage to Aeëtes' daughter Medea, who had conceived a violent passion for him, in return for help from her skills in magic. Medea gave Jason a charm which enabled him to survive Aeëtes' tests and to take the fleece from the dragon that guarded it.

The Golden Fleece itself is related to real mountain traditions: in Svaneti and Racha, people sifted for gold in mountain rivers by placing a sheepskin, in which tiny nuggets of gold would collect, across the rocks. This technique still exists today in the Caucasus.

Tim Severin's *The Jason Voyage* (1986) tells the story of a modern-day row from Greece to Georgia in a smaller replica of the *Argo.*

Hotel Anchor   HOTEL $$
(☎226000; tamrikosaba@mail.ru; Gegidze 90; incl breakfast s 90-100 GEL, d 100-120 GEL; ❀❂) Modern hotel near the port, with good, clean, sizeable rooms and a reasonable restaurant. Some desk staff speak a little English.

Apartment   APARTMENT $$
(☎599777692; Room 12, Gegidze 20; s/d/tr US$30/50/50) Russian-speaking Nona Topuria rents out this adequate one-bedroom apartment, with shower, next to the Malibu bar. If your Russian is non-existent, call her and say, 'Nona, hotel?'

Aragvi   GEORGIAN $$
(Gegidze 18; mains 5-10 GEL; ☺lunch & dinner) About 100m past Hotel Anchor, Aragvi serves up decent Georgian dishes amid decor of antlers and swords.

❶ Getting There & Around

Poti's main *marshrutka* terminal, about 300m west from the train station along Reqvava, has departures to Zugdidi (6 GEL, 1½ hours, 11 daily), Kutaisi (7 GEL, two hours, 17 daily), Tbilisi (15 GEL, 5½ hours, five daily) and Batumi (6 GEL, 1½ hours, 11 daily).

UkrFerry (www.ukrferry.com) operates approximately weekly ferries between Poti and Kerch, Ukraine (US$140 to US$320, 20 hours). UkrFerry's agent in Poti is **Instra** (☎221060; Gegidze 20).

Marshrutka 25 (0.50 GEL) runs from the market on Parnavazi to Gegidze.

Kolkheti National Park
კოლხეთის ეროვნული პარკი

This 285-sq-km **national park** (www.apa.gov.ge) encompasses three separate areas of coastline and wetlands north and southeast of Poti. The southeastern area, focused on Lake Paliastomi, is of most interest to visitors, thanks to its large bird population. The most interesting months to visit are January to May, when swans, geese, ducks, and rare pelicans, storks and booted eagles winter here. From May to September, one-hour dolphin-spotting trips on the Black Sea (up to six people 195 GEL) are offered by the **visitors centre** (☎577101896; Guria 222; ☺10am-7pm Mon-Fri, by arrangement Sat & Sun), 4km south of the centre of Poti on the Batumi road. The visitors centre sells an English-language field guide to the park's birds and organises trips on Lake Paliastomi

by pontoon boat (up to six people 100 GEL per hour) or catamaran (up to six people 145 GEL per hour). It also rents kayaks (15 GEL for three hours).

Hotel Paliastomi (☎555159775; r 20-120 GEL; ❀), near the main access point to Lake Paliastomi, 1.5km south of the visitors centre, has nice pine-panelled or blue-painted aircon rooms in its main building, and older but adequate rooms in brick-and-wood cottages. Meals are available at the hotel and in Restaurant Iasoni, under the same management, 100m away on the main road. *Marshrutky* 16 and 20 from Poti (0.50 GEL) will stop at the visitors centre or the turning to the hotel and lake. Catch them on Parnavazi in the market area, or on Akaki heading south off Rustavelis rkali.

Zugdidi ზუგდიდი
☎415 / POP 69,000

The main city of Samegrelo (Mingrelia), Zugdidi is 108km northwest of Kutaisi. The nearest Georgian city to Abkhazia, it has absorbed a high number of refugees since the 1990s. Today it's a bustling town that serves as a stepping stone for getting to Svaneti or Abkhazia, and a base for exploring the less known attractions of Samegrelo.

The central boulevard, running southwest to northeast, is Zviad Gamsakhurdias gamziri, named after Mingrelian Zviad Gamsakhurdia, post-Soviet Georgia's ultra-nationalist first president.

◉ Sights

Dadiani Museum   MUSEUM
(admission 2 GEL; ☺10am-5.30pm Tue-Sun) The palace of the Dadiani family (old lords of Samegrelo), a castlelike building in a park 500m beyond the north end of Zviad Gamsakhurdia, is now a museum. As well as interesting 19th-century paintings of the Caucasus region and plenty of fine furniture and crockery, it contains one of Napoleon Bonaparte's three bronze death masks, acquired via a marriage between a Dadiani and a descendant of Napoleon's sister. The wooded botanical gardens beside the park are worth a stroll.

▣ Sleeping

Zugdidi Hostel   HOSTEL $
(☎579792002, 591654036; www.zugdidihostel.com; Griboedov 1; dm 20 GEL; ❂) Guests are treated more like friends than customers at

this very hospitable hostel, and the young owners are keen to show you the best of Samegrelo. The house, with a garden, beds (not bunks), kitchen and good shared bathrooms, is in a quiet street 1km from the southern end of Zviad Gamsakhurdia. They can meet you on arrival in Zugdidi, and can get *marshrutky* to Mestia to pick you up at the hostel.

Hotel Zugdidi　　　　　　　HOTEL **$$**
(☏254242; Kostava 5A; r 50-70 GEL; ✳️🛜) One block along Rustaveli from Zviad Gamsakhurdia then a few steps south on Kostava, this hotel occupies the top two floors of a four-storey building. The 12 rooms are clean, parquet-floored and quite presentable. There's a cafe-bar with all meals available.

Eating

Host　　　　　　　　GEORGIAN **$$$**
(Kostava 34; mains 5-20 GEL; 🛜🛵) This popular, three-floor, brick-walled establishment stands just off the fountain circle at the south end of Zviad Gamsakhurdia. Service is friendly and the range of good Georgian dishes includes interesting Mingrelian specialities such as *elarji* (cornmeal porridge with melted cheese) and *gebjalia* (boiled *sulguni* cheese with yoghurt and mint).

Taverna Pirate　　　　　　GEORGIAN **$**
(Rustaveli 85; mains 4-10 GEL; 🛵) A cheaper but still pleasant restaurant with a maritime theme and Mingrelian as well as other Georgian dishes. The *lobiani* (a *khachapuri*-like pie with a bean filling) is good. It's 1.5 blocks east off northern Zviad Gamsakhurdia.

ℹ️ Information
Internet Cafe 33 (Zviad Gamsakhurdia 28; per hr 1 GEL; ⊘24hr)

ℹ️ Getting There & Away
The main *marshrutka* terminal is outside the train station, which is 1km west along Rustaveli from Zviad Gamsakhurdia. *Marshrutky* and some buses leave for Kutaisi (7 GEL, two hours, 12

WORTH A TRIP

SECRETS OF SAMEGRELO

The Samegrelo countryside, with the Caucasus foothills rising above 3000m in the north, is full of beautiful spots little known to outsiders. The best way to get out to them is on a trip with the enthusiasts from **Zugdidi Hostel** (☏579792002, 591654036; www.zugdidihostel.com). They charge 100 GEL to 250 GEL for day trips for two or three people.

South from Zugdidi, the main highway towards Senaki passes **Tsaishi**, with hot springs where you can swim, and the 469m hill **Urta** with caves, waterfalls and great views to the main Caucasus range. Beyond Senaki, 60km from Zugdidi, is picturesque **Nokalakevi** (admission 3 GEL, English-speaking guide 15 GEL; ⊘10am-2pm & 3.30-5pm Tue-Sun), an ancient Colchian royal town and fortress. A tunnel leads down to the Tekhura River from the grassy grounds and admission includes an interesting archaeological museum. Excavations are ongoing (see www.nokalakevi.org).

Martvili Monastery, 20km beyond Nokalakevi, was a centre of medieval Georgian culture, and its cathedral, with many interesting murals, dates from the 7th century. Near Martvili are the **Gachedili waterfalls**, a good picnic spot with recently discovered dinosaur footprints nearby.

The area around the villages of **Skuri** and **Mukhuri**, about 30km northeast of Zugdidi, is dotted with caves, rivers, wild woodlands, mineral springs and swimming spots, and makes another great day out. There's a good 14km valley and forest hike in the **Intsra ravine** and near the head of the river you'll find Kuakantsalia, a large boulder that figures in a local David-and-Goliath-type legend and will rock at the push of a finger but won't topple even with the heave of a shoulder.

The beautiful, remote mountain lakes of **Tobavarchkhili**, at an altitude of 2650m, are best visited on a camping trip, as they're reached by a 30km jeep drive north from Mukhuri, followed by a 10km walk to the lakes. Legend has it that if you jump into one of the lakes, or shout near it, it will start to rain. A natural staircase climbs to the top of **Mt Tsashqibuli** (3017m), 4km southeast of the first lake. It's possible to walk on from Tobavarchkhili over to Khaishi in Svaneti.

THE ABKHAZIA CONFLICT

The Abkhaz are linguistically distinct from the Georgians, their language being one of the northwestern Caucasus family (although Russian is now the most common language in Abkhazia). During the Middle Ages, Abkhazia was an important kingdom of Christian Georgia. It came under Ottoman rule in the 15th century, then Russian rule in the 19th century. After Soviet power arrived in 1921, Abkhazia signed a treaty of union with Georgia, but in 1931 it was downgraded to an autonomous region within Georgia. From the late 1930s to early 1950s, Stalin's Georgian henchman Lavrenty Beria oversaw the migration of many Georgians into Abkhazia. From the late 1970s the Abkhaz began to agitate for more rights. In the 1980s and early 1990s the rise of anti-Soviet nationalism in Georgia fuelled tensions. By 1989 only 18% of Abkhazia's population was Abkhaz; 46% was Georgian.

The first violent clashes between Abkhaz and Georgians left 16 dead in Sukhumi in 1989. In 1990 Abkhazia's Abkhaz-dominated Supreme Soviet unilaterally declared Abkhazia a separate Soviet republic, independent of Georgia. Real conflict broke out in August 1992 when the Georgian National Guard entered southern Abkhazia and then moved on to occupy Sukhumi. Abkhazia was plunged into a year of fighting, in which about 8000 people died, with the civilian population suffering terribly. The Abkhaz were aided by fighters from the Russian Caucasus, principally Chechens, and by Russian weaponry, obtained officially or unofficially, and on some occasions by Russian armed forces. Both sides terrorised civilians and committed appalling atrocities. The Georgians drove most Abkhaz out of Sukhumi when they occupied the city. In September 1993 the Abkhaz attacked Sukhumi in violation of a truce and drove the Georgian forces and almost all of Abkhazia's Georgian population (about 230,000 people) out of Abkhazia. Many refugees died while crossing the mountains to Svaneti and Samegrelo.

Only in Abkhazia's southern Gali district have significant numbers (around 40,000) since returned. The rest have had to try to make new lives elsewhere in Georgia.

After the 1992–93 war, Russia imposed trade sanctions on Abkhazia, but Vladimir Putin changed Russia's stance when he entered the Kremlin in 2000, seeking to use Abkhazia for leverage over Georgia. Abkhazians were offered Russian passports from 2001. In 2008 Russia removed trade sanctions. Any hopes of Abkhaz–Georgian reconciliation almost disappeared with the 2008 South Ossetia War, during which Russian forces came from Abkhazia to attack Georgian military installations in western Georgia. Soon after the war, Russia recognised the independence which Abkhazia had formally declared in 1999. (Only Venezuela, Nicaragua and Nauru have since followed Russia's lead.) Russia has stepped up aid, investment and its military presence in the territory, stationing anti-aircraft missiles and a few thousand troops in Abkhazia.

Ethnic Abkhaz still constitute less than half of Abkhazia's much reduced population but they dominate the government. They do not appear to want annexation by Russia.

daily), Poti (6 GEL, 1½ hours, 14 daily), Batumi (12 GEL, three hours, 14 daily), Tbilisi (15 GEL, 5½ hours, 14 daily) and Mestia (15 GEL to 20 GEL, about six hours, from 6am). *Marshrutky* to Mestia leave when full, which can happen as early as 6.30am when the night train from Tbilisi arrives. You should certainly be there by 8am, though you may still have to wait a few hours before you get moving. They usually charge foreigners 20 GEL and Georgians 15 GEL.

A night train to Tbilisi (seat/2nd/1st class 6/11/15 GEL, 8½ hours) departs Zugdidi at 10.30pm. There's also a day train to Tbilisi (seat 6 GEL, eight hours) at 10.25am, and an *elektrichka* to Kutaisi (2 GEL, 3½ hours, 7.15am).

ABKHAZIA

The greatest tragedy to befall Georgia since its independence is the secession of Abkhazia (Apsny or Apswa in Abkhazian, Apkhazeti in Georgian), and the bloodshed and misery this has brought about.

Once the jewel of the 'Soviet Riviera' along the Black Sea coast, today this de facto independent republic is still getting over the devastation of the 1992–93 war, with less than half its prewar population of 535,000. Russian tourism, investment and aid have boomed since the 2008 South Ossetia War. By 2011 Abkhazia was internally much more stable, with few reports of gangsterism or violent incidents. It had also become relatively easy for foreign travellers to visit, although the British **Foreign Office** (www.fco.gov.uk) and US **State Department** (travel.state.gov) still advised against it.

Abkhazia's towns still have a strangely underpopulated feel, but the coast and countryside are beautiful, and just being inside this curious territory with a throwback Soviet atmosphere is an intriguing experience.

Check recent news and travellers' reports, such as on the Thorn Tree forum on lonely planet.com. It is always possible that tensions or violence may flare up again in the southern Gali region or elsewhere in Abkhazia. Abkhazia's official tourism site, http://abkhazia.travel, is worth a look but is not always up to date.

❶ Information

MONEY

Abkhazia's currency is the Russian rouble (US$1 is worth around R30 at 2012 rates). You can change cash US dollars, and often euros, at banks and money changers, but Abkhazia's few ATMs do not accept foreign cards. Bring some roubles (obtainable at many moneychangers in Georgia) to keep you going on arrival.

TELEPHONE

Abkhazia uses the Russian country code, ☎7. At research time it was not possible to call from Georgia to Abkhazia except for the southern Gali district, which was within reach of Georgian mobile networks.

VISAS

The first step to visiting Abkhazia is to obtain a visa. The easiest method is through one of Abkhazia's representatives abroad, listed on the website of the **Abkhazia Foreign Ministry** (☎840-2263948, 2265792, 2267069, 2262426; www.mfaabkhazia.net; ulitsa Lakoba 21, Sukhumi; ⊙9.30am-6pm Mon-Fri). At research time the representatives in the UK, Germany, Turkey, Greece and Russia were able to issue visas. The UK representative was accepting email applications comprising a form found on www.mfaabkhazia.net and a scan of your passport's personal details page, with a fee of £15 (for a 30-day single-entry visa) plus postage to send you the visa. Abkhazia visas are single pieces of paper, not stuck into your passport.

Alternatively, you can apply by email to the Foreign Ministry itself, using the same form from its website. Within five working days you should receive by email a permit enabling you to cross the border into Abkhazia. This is not your actual visa: once inside Abkhazia, you must go to the Foreign Ministry in Sukhumi to obtain a form for the nearby **Sberbank** (ploshchad Konstitutsii 1, Sukhumi; ⊙9.30am-2pm & 3-4.30pm Mon-Fri), where you pay in roubles for the visa (a 30-day single-entry visa costs the equivalent of US$20). Then return to the ministry with the bank receipt to obtain the visa itself. You'll need the visa when you leave Abkhazia, and you should obtain it as soon as possible, as accommodation places may ask to see it.

It's best to apply in advance to allow for possible delays, follow-up phone calls or repeat applications. The Foreign Ministry often doesn't answer the phone: just keep trying.

Georgia permits foreigners to enter Abkhazia by the Enguri Bridge border point near Zugdidi, but treats entry to Abkhazia by the Psou River border with Russia as illegal entry into Georgia, which carries a maximum penalty of five years' imprisonment. If you enter Abkhazia from Russia, don't try to continue across Abkhazia's southern border into undisputed Georgia. You will need at least a double-entry Russian visa in advance, so that you can return to Russia.

Sukhumi

☎840 / POP 40,000 (ESTIMATED)

Abkhazia's capital (Sukhumi or Sukhum in Russian, Sokhumi in Georgian, Akwa in Abkhaz) has a gorgeous setting on a bay backed by hills thick with luxuriant semitropical vegetation. Reconstruction is finally picking up pace, but many buildings still stand empty or ruined, including landmarks such as the Government House on ploshchad Svobody (gutted when the Abkhaz took the city in September 1993).

Ruins of the Greek trading port Dioskuria lie beneath Sukhumi Bay. After periods of Roman, Byzantine, Arab, Abkhazian and Turkish domination, Sukhumi was taken by the Russians in 1810. By 1989 it had a multiethnic population of 120,000, but it was badly damaged during the fighting between 1989 and 1993, when its large Georgian population was driven out.

The main streets are ulitsa Lakoba, one to two blocks inland from the seafront boulevard (naberezhnaya Makhadzhirov), and prospekt Leona which runs down across Lakoba to Makhadzhirov.

◉ Sights

The well-kept **Botanical Gardens** (cnr prospekt Leona & ulitsa Gulia; admission R120, English-language tour R800; ⊙10am-6pm) are well worth a stroll. **Alleya Slavy** (Glory Alley), a park on

SUKHUMI'S SPACE MONKEYS

Sukhumi's Monkey Colony, officially the Abkhazia Academy of Sciences Research Institute of Experimental Pathology & Therapy, was renowned in Soviet times for training monkey astronauts (eight from here made space flights in the 1980s) and as a centre for medical research using monkeys. At its peak 5000 monkeys were kept here. The institute is widely believed to have been the home of a freakish Stalin-era experiment in inseminating female monkeys with human sperm, with the aim of creating a strong-bodied, weak-brained subcaste to help build the glorious Soviet future.

The institute has fallen on hard times but hopes for a revival based on participation in Russia's Mars-500 project, which is preparing for possible future Mars expeditions. Today the colony has around 300 African and Asian monkeys in sad, smelly cages, and a three-room museum with displays and documents on monkeys and its own history.

the north side of ulitsa Lakoba, is the burial site of many Abkhaz who died in the 1992–93 fighting. **Sukhumi Fort**, on the seafront west of ulitsa Sakharova, is a Russian rebuilding of a Turkish fort built on the site of a Roman one. The remains are meagre. The collections of the **Abkhazian State Museum** (prospekt Leona 22) will be worth perusing when it eventually reopens after refurbishment.

🛏 Sleeping & Eating

Numerous families rent rooms to tourists, including several on ulitsa Akirtaa in the eastern Turbaza district. Look for signs in Russian saying *sdayutsya komnaty* (or minor variations thereon).

Coming from Gali, you can get off your *marshrutka* under the railway bridge just after the road bends away from the coast. Walk east along Akirtaa, to the left of a dilapidated block of flats.

Hotel Ritsa   HOTEL $$
(☎2233242; www.hotel-ritsa.ru; prospekt Leona 2; incl breakfast s R1750-3000, d R2500-3900; ✳) Originally opened in 1913, the elegant white Ritsa stands on the corner of the seaside boulevard and is the top hotel in town. The more-expensive rooms have sea-view balconies. It also houses European and Abkhazian restaurants and a cafe.

Hotel Sukhum   BOUTIQUE HOTEL $$
(☎9409274182; www.otel-sukhum.ru, in Russian; ulitsa Naberezhnaya 9; incl breakfast d R2900-3500, q R2900-4900; ✳✳📶) Excellent small, modern hotel beside the Basla River at the east end of central Sukhum.

Hotel Inter-Sukhum   HOTEL $$
(☎2260062; intersukhum.su, in Russian; ulitsa Lakoba 109; s/d incl breakfast R1300/1700; ✳📶) The rooms at this larger, newish hotel are

terminally bland, but they're clean and secure with small balconies and comfy beds, and the seafront is 100m away.

Homestay   HOMESTAY $
(ulitsa Akirtaa 55; per person R400-500) The Kvitsinia family has a variety of decent, clean rooms, with shared bathrooms and a small guest kitchen. The twin teenage daughters speak good English.

Nartaa   CAFE $
(naberezhnaya Makhadzhirov btwn ulitsa Aidgylara & ulitsa Konfederatov; mains R75-190) There are plenty of cafes, bars and restaurants on naberezhnaya Makhadzhirov and lower prospekt Leona. Most close about 9pm. Wood-built Nartaa, with tables on various verandahs and small pavilions, does excellent food at small prices, including *shashlyk* (shish kebab), salads and a good *kartofel* (potato) side dish.

ℹ Information

Prospekt Mira, one block inland from ulitsa Lakoba, has a handful of internet places and bookshops (where you might find a city map) on the quiet couple of blocks west of Leona.

ℹ Getting There & Away

The 20-minute taxi ride from Zugdidi to Abkhazia's southern border at the Enguri Bridge (Enguris Khidi) costs 10 GEL. There are also *marshrutky* (1 GEL, every two hours 7am to 3pm) from a small street off the south side of Rustaveli in Zugdidi, just west of the river. At the border you show your documents at a Georgian police post, then walk across the 1km bridge and show them again at the Abkhazian border post, which is run by the Russian FSB (State Security Service). They may call the Foreign Ministry in Sukhumi before letting you proceed. Most people crossing here are Mingrelian Georgians travelling to or from their properties in the Gali area, home to most of Abkhazia's remaining Georgian population.

From the border you can take a *marshrutka* (R50, 30 minutes), shared taxi (around R75) or taxi (around R300) to the sadly dilapidated town of Gali (Gal in Abkhazian), 15km northwest. Buses to Sukhumi (R105, two to 2½ hours) leave Gali's bus station about hourly from 11am to 5pm. You may also find buses or *marshrutky* leaving from the post office or from the Chernomorsky Bank. A taxi from Gali to Sukhumi costs anywhere between R1000 and R2000, and about half that to Ochamchyra (R500 to R1000), from where *marshrutky* or buses head to Sukhumi (R54, one hour) about hourly until about 6pm.

The last *marshrutky* from Gali to the border, and from the border to Zugdidi, can leave any time from about 4pm. Taxis are always available for both legs.

From Sukhumi's **bus & train station** (ulitsa Dzidzaria), in the northwest of town, buses and *marshrutky* run northwest to Novy Afon (R50, 30 minutes), Gagra (R100, 1½ to two hours), and the Psou border (R130, 2½ hours), about every half-hour, 6.30am to 3.30pm. There are also a few services to Sochi (R220, about 3½ hours) in Russia. Services south to Gali (R105, two to 2½ hours) leave about hourly from 6am to 5pm.

Train service to Adler in Russia (just across the Psou border; R200), via Novy Afon and Gagra, resumed in 2011. There is also a Sukhumi–Moscow service. The nearest passenger airport is at Adler.

🅘 Getting Around

Trolleybuses 1, 3 and 4 (R3) run from the station to ulitsa Lakoba in the centre, and 3 continues east to ulitsa Akirtaa, as do 'Turbaza' *marshrutky* (R10). A taxi between the station and centre costs R80 to R100.

Northwest of Sukhumi

The coast northwest of Sukhumi is beautiful, with the thickly forested slopes of the Caucasus reaching right down to the shore in places.

NOVY AFON

This village 25km from Sukhumi makes a great day out. The multi-gold-domed **Novy Afon Monastery**, founded by Russian monks in the 19th century, stands out on the hillside, about a 15-minute walk up from the main road. Its cathedral has wonderfully colourful murals. From here it's a five-minute walk down to the 10th-century stone

Church of Simon the Zealot (Khram Simona Kananita), on the spot where this apostle was reputedly killed by Roman soldiers, and the **Museum of the Abkhazian Kingdom** (Muzey Abkhazskogo Tsarstva), with plenty of food, drink and souvenir stands in front. A path leads up beside the waterfall here to Psyrtskha train station, from which you can walk 20 minutes up a pretty river valley to **Simon the Zealot's Cave** (Grot Simona Kananita), where the saint reputedly lived.

In another direction from the museum and church, it's 500m to the impressive **Novy Afon Caves** (Novoafonskaya peshchera; admission R300; ⊘11am-4pm, closed Mon, Tue, Thu & Fri approx mid-Sep–mid-Jun), where a mini train carries visitors on a 1.4km underground journey. From here it's a 2.5km uphill walk to **Anakopia** (admission R100; ⊘10am-6pm), capital of Abkhazia in the 8th century AD. Inside the hilltop citadel are the ruins of an 8th-century cathedral and a recently rebuilt 11th-century watchtower with awesome views.

Several houses in Novy Afon rent rooms, typically for R300 per person. There are a couple of small hotels too.

LAKE RITSA

At Bzyb (or Bzypta), 70km from Sukhumi, a road heads off north to Lake Ritsa, amid beautiful Caucasus mountain scenery at an elevation of 950m. Stalin had a *dacha* (country cottage) on the far shore, which is visitable by boat. The 41km drive up to the lake, via gorges, waterfalls and the smaller Goluboe Ozero (Blue Lake), is spectacular. Day-trip coach tours designed for Russian tourists head to Ritsa from Sukhumi and the main resorts (R600 to R700).

GAGRA

✎840 / POP 8000

Abkhazia's main resort stretches about 8km along a stony beach below thickly forested mountains, about 85km from Sukhumi. The main **marshrutka stand** (ulitsa Demerdzhipa 30) is towards the south end of town, next to Kontinent supermarket; plenty of *marshrutky* run the length of town. In summer a daily **catamaran service** (www.katamaran.g-sochi.ru; ⊘May-Oct) between Gagra and Sochi (R500, 1½ hours) provides an alternative to the Psou road border, where peak-period queues can be hours long.

🛏 Sleeping & Eating

Hotel rates plummet outside the July-to-September high season.

There are dozens of homestays, most charging R300 per person, in houses along the main road and in side streets sch as ulitsa Sayat-Nova, 400m south of the *marshrutka* stand, and ulitsa Shapshugskaya, 800m north of the *marshrutka* stand.

Starye Gagry
HOTEL **$$**

(☏2340212; www.stgagra.ru, in Russian; r incl 2 meals R2860; ◷closed Nov-Apr; ▣) The Staraya Gagra (Old Gagra) district at the north end of town has a kind of dilapidated charm. This hotel is right by the sea, with 14 smallish but presentable sea-facing rooms in a log building. It also has a very pleasant half-open-air **restaurant** (mains R110-330) with dishes from trout to *shashlyk* to pizza.

Alex Beach Hotel
HOTEL **$$**

(☏2340686; www.hotelalex.ru, in Russian; ulitsa Zvanba 1; s/d incl 2 meals R3300/4400; ▣❋▣) A sparkling new hotel right by the beach, 2km north of the *marshrutka* stand. Some staff speak English.

ADJARA

The idiosyncratic southwestern corner of Georgia, Adjara (აჭარა; also spelt Achara, Ajara or Ajaria) has taken on the mantle of Georgia's holiday coast since the loss of Abkhazia. Batumi, Adjara's rapidly developing capital, is the destination of choice for most Georgians – and many Armenians and others from further afield – in search of summer fun, with a real party atmosphere in August.

Though Adjara's beaches are mostly stony, the semitropical climate is beautiful and the scenery gorgeous, with lush hills rising behind the coast, and peaks topping 3000m in the Lesser Caucasus inland.

Many travellers enter Georgia at the busy Sarpi border post with Turkey, just south of Batumi.

Under Ottoman control from the 16th century to 1878, most of Adjara's inhabitants were converted to Islam, but today Muslims comprise only about 30% of the population. Adjara has retained its Soviet-era status as an autonomous republic within Georgia: until 2004 its pro-Russian president, Aslan Abashidze, ran an authoritarian, corrupt regime backed by his own militia. A standoff between Abashidze and President Saakashvili raised fears of another Georgian civil war. However, Abashidze lost his crucial support from Russia and days later left for ignominious exile in Moscow, to the delight of Adjarans.

Batumi ბათუმი

☏422 / POP 121.000

With a backdrop of mist-wrapped hills, Georgia's summer holiday capital has sprouted new hotels and attractions like mushrooms in recent years, but it still owes much of its charm to the fin-de-siècle elegance of its original boom time a century ago.

For travellers arriving from Turkey, Batumi makes a great introduction to Georgia, with its relaxed atmosphere, plentiful accommodation, good restaurants and nightlife.

Batumi developed in the late 19th century as the western terminus of a railway from Baku that then carried one-fifth of the world's oil production. A pipeline and refinery built by Ludwig Nobel, brother of Swedish dynamite inventor Alfred, soon followed. Batumi gained free-port status and developed into a fashionable resort at the southern tip of the Russian empire. In Soviet times the nearby border with Turkey was closed, making Batumi a bit of a backwater, but it has since bounced back as a hub of commerce as well as tourism.

One of the first decisions of the post-Abashidze administration in 2004 was to make Batumi an attractive place to visit, something in which it has happily succeeded. Old buildings have been renovated and floodlit, bold and attractive new structures have joined them, and strolling around the leafy parks and low-rise central streets is a real pleasure.

◉ Sights & Activities

Batumis Bulvari
PARK, BEACH

(www.boulevard.ge) Everyone soon finds themselves strolling along Batumis bulvari, the park strip fronting the main beach, originally laid out in 1884 and now stretching 6km along the coast. With its trees, paths, fountains, cafes, beach bars and some quirky attractions, this is the life and soul of Batumi. You can rent **bicycles** (price negotiable) at a couple of spots. The **beach** itself is fine though stony – extremely busy in July and August, but kept clean. Near the northeast tip of the Bulvari you'll find a large **Ferris wheel** (per person 2 GEL); the 145m-high **Alphabet Tower**, a monument to Georgian script and culture with an observation deck and revolving restaurant; and a 7m-high ethereally moving metal sculpture of a man and woman by Tamar Kvesitadze, universally known as **Ali & Nino** after the protagonists of Kurban Said's marvellous novel of that name (see it after dark). Southward, on what's known as the New Boulevard, an ornamental lake hosts the **Dancing Fountains** (⊘9pm-midnight Jun-Oct), an entertaining laser, music and water show.

Evropas moedani   SQUARE
Broad, attractive Europe Sq sports musical fountains which are a magnet for kids on hot summer evenings. Towering over the square is the striking **Medea monument** to 'the person who brought Georgia closer to Europe', according to Batumi's mayor when it was unveiled in 2007. Sculpted by Davit Khmaladze, it controversially cost the Georgian government over 1 million GEL.

Nobel Technological Museum   MUSEUM
(Leselidze 3, Tamari district; admission 2 GEL; ⊘10am-6pm Tue-Sun) Batumi's newest and most interesting museum takes you back a century to when the city was in the vanguard of the international oil business, with investment from the Nobels and Rothschilds spawning technological innovations here. It also looks at the tea industry that grew up at the same time. It's 3km from the centre, just off the road to Makhinjauri train station (turn opposite Hotel Sanapiro).

6 Maisi Park   PARK
(Rustaveli) Sixth of May Park contains a lake, a modern **dolphinarium** (45min show adult/child 12 GEL/free; ⊘noon, 3pm & 6pm Tue-Sun) and a small **zoo** (adult/child 2 GEL/free; ⊘11am-8pm) of Georgian and international wildlife. At the dolphinarium you can also **swim with dolphins** (per 15min adult/12-18yr/under 12yr 150/100/60 GEL). Dolphinarium hours outside the summer season are variable.

Adjara Arts Museum   MUSEUM
(Gorgiladze 8; admission 2 GEL; ⊘11am-6pm Tue-Sun) Well displayed and lit, the collection covers Georgian art including works by Pirosmani and Akhvlediani, as well as 19th- and 20th-century European and Russian painting.

Mosque   MOSQUE
(Chkalov 6) Batumi's only surviving mosque, built in the 1860s, is finely painted in pinks, greens and blues, with Koranic calligraphy

on the walls. Friendly men often gather to socialise outside.

Sheraton Batumi Hotel   SWIMMING, SPA
(Rustaveli 28; nonguests pool incl 3-course lunch 50 GEL, spa 50 GEL) The Sheraton has a lovely large open-air pool in a garden setting in the Bulvari park, and an excellent spa.

Batumi Tennis Club   TENNIS
(Batumis bulvari; per hr for 2 incl racquets & balls 20 GEL; ⊘8am-9pm) Eight good hard courts.

Ice Rink   SKATING
(Baku; per hr incl skates 5 GEL; ⊘10am-6pm) You can ice skate all year round at this modern installation.

✦ Festivals & Events

Black Sea Jazz Festival   JAZZ
(www.batumijazz.ge) A week in late July.

Batumi International Art House Film Festival   FILM
(www.biaff.org) A week in late September.

🛏 Sleeping

Batumi has a large and ever-growing range of accommodation. Prices in many midrange and top-end hotels drop by around one-third outside the July–August peak season.

Budget-category places generally have shared bathrooms and don't serve meals but have guest kitchens.

TOP CHOICE **Dzveli Batumi**   GUESTHOUSE **$$**
(☑277157; www.welcome.ge/dzvelibatumi; Kostava 24; incl breakfast s €25-30, d/ste €40/100; ✳@🖥) Friendly and informative hosts Gocha and Irina offer half a dozen well-equipped, carpeted rooms in an old-town house, with assorted colour schemes and tasteful contemporary style. The breakfasts are excellent, they have a wine shop across the street, and more rooms are being added. A guesthouse with flair.

Hotel Rcheuli Villa   BOUTIQUE HOTEL **$$**
(☑270707; www.rcheuli.ge; Jordania 31; r/ste incl breakfast 150/240 GEL; ✳@🖥) A lovely pink-painted mansion, recently built but in old Batumi style, houses fine rooms with marble floors and elegant Italian-made, classical-style furnishings. Professional but friendly service helps make this one of the best bets in Batumi.

Batumi

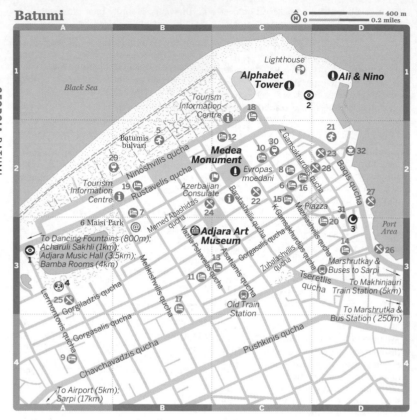

N 0   400 m
0   0.2 miles

Black Sea

Lighthouse

Alphabet Tower

Ali & Nino

Tourism Information Centre

Batumis bulvari

Medea Monument

Z Gamsakhurdias qucha

Ninoshvilis qucha

Evropas moedani

Tourism Information Centre

Rustavelis qucha

Azerbaijan Consulate

Baratashvilis qucha

K Gamsakhurdias qucha

Mazniashvilis qucha

Piazza

Baqis qucha

Port Area

6 Maisi Park

Memed Abashidzis qucha

Vazha Pshavelas qucha

Adjara Art Museum

To Dancing Fountains (800m);
Acharuli Sakhli (1km);
Adjara Music Hall (3.5km);
Bamba Rooms (4km)

Asatiani qucha

Gorgasalis qucha

Zubalashvilis qucha

Melnikshvilis qucha

Tseretlis qucha

Marshutkay & Buses to Sarpi

To Makhinjauri Train Station (5km)

Old Train Station

To Marshrutka & Bus Station (250m)

Lermontovis qucha

Gorgiladzis qucha

Gorgasalis qucha

Chavchavadzis qucha

Pushkinis qucha

To Airport (5km);
Sarpi (17km)

Boombully Beach Hostel
HOSTEL **$$**

(☑595715745; boombullybeach.com; Kldiashvili 32; dm €10.50-11, d €28.60; ✴☎) This 'party hostel' is brought to you by the people from the popular Boombully in Tbilisi. It has two bars, an open terrace, mixed and women's dorms, bikes for hire and plenty of ideas for enjoying Batumi by day and night.

Hotel Elegant
BOUTIQUE HOTEL **$$**

(☑274841; www.welcome.ge/elegant; Gorgasali 68; r incl breakfast 120-170 GEL; ✴☎) Opened in 2009, this appealing little hotel has just six rooms, allowing for an attentive touch from the friendly management. The comfortable rooms are in a variety of tasteful styles, and the original stained glass everywhere is an attractive feature.

Hotel Intourist Palace
LUXURY HOTEL **$$$**

(☑275525; www.intouristpalace.com; Ninoshvili 11; incl breakfast s US$177-248, d US$201-248, ste from US$354; ✴@☎☀) Palace is no exaggeration for this luxurious large hotel, from its gleaming marble lobby to the spacious, thickly carpeted rooms, some with balconies. The position facing the Bulvari park is superb, and facilities include a good spa and open-air pool (free for guests), two restaurants, a nightclub and a casino.

Gulnasi's Guesthouse
GUESTHOUSE **$**

(☑557965859; homestay@mail.ru; Lermontov 24A; per person 20 GEL; ✴☎) Gulnasi Miqeladze and her welcoming family run what's really a good-value budget hotel. The 18 rooms, on four floors, are bare but spotless and good-sized. There's free tea, coffee and wine tasting, and the family is full of helpful travel information. They also offer free pick-ups anywhere in Batumi on arrival, and great-value day trips (80 GEL for up to four passengers, including picnic) into lovely rural Adjara.

Batumi

◉ Top Sights
Adjara Art Museum B3
Ali & Nino... D1
Alphabet Tower C1
Medea Monument C2

◉ Sights
1 Dolphinarium A3
2 Ferris Wheel C1
3 Mosque... D3
4 Zoo.. A3

◔ Activities, Courses & Tours
5 Batumi Tennis Club................................ B2
Sheraton Batumi Hotel .... (see 19)

◔ Sleeping
6 Batumi Hostel C2
7 Boombully Beach Hostel B2
8 Dzveli Batumi.. C2
9 Gulnasi's Guesthouse A4
10 Hotel Alik C2
11 Hotel Elegant... B3
12 Hotel Intourist Palace........................... C2
13 Hotel Irise C3
14 Hotel Mercury D3

15 Hotel Rcheuli Villa C2
16 Hotel Ritsa C2
17 Light House Hotel................................... B3
18 Radisson Blu Hotel................................. C1
19 Sheraton Batumi Hotel.......................... B2
20 Siesta Hostel D3

◉ Eating
Bakuriani Winter Garden Café ..... (see 12)
21 Ice Rink.. D2
22 Kafe Literaturuli C2
23 Press Cafe.. D2
24 Privet iz Batuma..................................... B2
25 Retro A3
Ristorante Venezia.......................... (see 12)
26 Samikitno... D3
27 Sanapiro/Beregi D2
28 Shemoikhede Genatsvale...................... D2

◉ Drinking
29 Art Bulvari.. B2
30 Salve... C2

◉ Transport
31 Instra.. D2
32 Passenger Ferry Terminal..................... D2

Sheraton Batumi Hotel　　LUXURY HOTEL $$$
(☑229000; sheraton.com/batumi; Rustaveli 29; Aug s/d incl breakfast from US$295/330; ☀✵@ ☎✆) The faintly Chinese-looking Sheraton towers beside the Bulvari park and offers all the services and luxuries you'd expect. Rooms are stylish, spacious and well equipped, with supercomfortable beds. Many feature large ballerina photos in counterpoint to the large rock-star shots in the lobby. Facilities include outdoor and indoor pools (the latter in the spa), a nightclub and a 20th-floor restaurant with spectacular views. Big discounts are often available.

Radisson Blu Hotel　　LUXURY HOTEL $$$
(☑255555; www.radissonblu.com/hotel-batumi; Ninoshvili 1; s/d incl breakfast from US$265/285; ☀✵@☎✆) An eye-catching zigzag-shaped glass tower at the northeast end of the Bulvari, the Radisson was 2011's big addition to Batumi's skyline. Style is contemporary minimalist and rooms are large, all with floor-to-ceiling windows. The rooftop bar

is spectacular, and you can enjoy indoor or outdoor pools.

Hotel Alik　　HOTEL $$
(☑275802; www.hotelalik.gol.ge; Memed Abashidze 12; s/d incl breakfast from 150/160 GEL; ☀✵@ ☎✆) A bright, comfortable and quirkily designed central hotel where large faux-cactus lamps and gaudy bedspreads cohabit with Empire-style chairs. Services and facilities are good, including a bar, sauna and plunge pool.

Hotel Ritsa　　HOTEL $$
(☑273292; www.hotelritsa.com; Z Gamsakhurdia 16; r incl breakfast 110-150 GEL; ✵☎) This well-situated, 14-room hotel provides comfort and touches of belle époque style in a modern building, opened in 2006.

Hotel Irise　　HOTEL $$
(☑221301; www.irise.ge; Vazha Pshavela 39; r 80-120 GEL; ✵☎) Recently modernised Irise has 15 plain, well-kept rooms, mostly smallish and some with balconies.

Light House Hotel
HOTEL $$

(☑278218; www.lighthouse.ge; Kazbegi 4; r incl breakfast 80-180 GEL; ✳✿) This stylish hotel on a quiet street has just 10 rooms in a variety of eye-catching, modish styles and colours. A comfortable and friendly place to stay.

Hotel Mercury
HOTEL $$

(☑277501; www.hotelmercurybm.ge; Chavchavadze 10/12; r incl breakfast 50-70 GEL, ste 120 GEL; ✳@✿) The decent-sized and uncluttered rooms, some with balconies or large windows over the street, plus roof terrace, bar and sauna, make the 35-room Mercury reasonable value.

Batumi Hostel
HOSTEL $

(☑294286; www.facebook.com/batumihostel; Jordania 18; dm 20-25 GEL; ✿) Small place with friendly, helpful young owners.

Siesta Hostel
HOSTEL $

(☑277277; Zubalashvili 4A; dm €9.50-11; ✿) Can host 50 people.

🍴 Eating

Batumi is full of lively cafes and restaurants, most of them usually staying open till midnight or later. From July to September many more open up on the main beach, some making admirable efforts to create a tropical ambience.

Shemoikhede Genatsvale
GEORGIAN $$

(Jordania 8; www.gmcgroup.ge, in Georgian; mains 5-12 GEL; ⊘lunch & dinner; 🖱) This large, brick-walled eatery has a kind of tavern feel and a huge range of well-prepared Georgian dishes from *khinkali* or *badrijani nigvzit* to *mtsvadi,* trout or *chakapuli.*

Privet iz Batuma
CAFE $

(Memed Abashidze 39; mains 2-8 GEL; ⊘lunch & dinner; ✳🖱) A fashionable cafe with a pre-1917 theme and sailor-suited waiters, 'Hello from Batumi' is good for ice cream, cakes, salads, sandwiches, teas, coffees and alcoholic drinks. The interior is air-conditioned and there are outdoor tables too, but you may have to wait for seats on summer evenings.

Press Cafe
CAFE $

(Sabcho 2-1; www.facebook.com/pages/press-cafe; mains 2.50-7 GEL; ✿🖱) Apart from the best coffee in town, Press Cafe does good light eats from salads and sandwiches to pizza and pancakes. With chic red-and-black decor, it attracts some arty/scribey types and

also stages art exhibitions, movie nights and literary evenings.

Samikitno
GEORGIAN $$

(www.samikitno.ge; Baku; mains 7-12 GEL; ⊘24hr; 🖱) Conveniently sited where many *marshrutky* arrive from the east, and overlooking the harbour, Samikitno is a bright, cheerful place for Georgian meals and Georgian wine, with Georgian folk music and ballads in the evenings.

Acharuli Sakhli
GEORGIAN $$

(Sherif Khimshiashvili 10A; mains 6-12 GEL) A good spot for Georgian dishes including Adjaran specialities such as *iakhni* (a meat stew) and *sinori* (noodles baked in a butter, curd and garlic sauce). Some tables overlook the summer-evening Dancing Fountains show. A couple of musicians will play Adjaran music if paid. The pretty garden has an interesting exhibit of Adjaran architecture models.

Retro
SAKHACHAPURE $$

(Takaishvili 10; khachapuri Acharuli 5.45-12.45 GEL; 🖱) There's no better place than Batumi to decide whether you like *khachapuri Acharuli,* Adjara's large boat-shaped variety of Georgia's national fast food with a lightly fried egg on top. And there's no better place to try it than this neat place widely considered to make the best in town.

Kafe Literaturuli
CAFE $

(K Gamsakhurdia 18; cakes, pastries & hot drinks 2.50-6.50 GEL; ✿🖱) The Literary Cafe is a great stop for tea, coffee, white tablecloths and indulgent cakes and pastries, with a mildly artsy ambience.

Ristorante Venezia
ITALIAN $$$

(Hotel Intourist Palace, Ninoshvili 11; mains 10-30 GEL; ⊘lunch & dinner; 🖱) Classy service, excellent Italian food and a long wine list make this hotel restaurant overlooking the Bulvari park a fine dinner spot.

Bakuriani Winter Garden Café
CAFE $$

(Hotel Intourist Palace, Ninoshvili 11; cakes, sandwiches & salads 4-15 GEL; ✿🖱) A large conservatory style of cafe that's one of the most tranquil, comfortable (and expensive) in town. Open till 4am.

Sanapiro/Beregi
GEORGIAN $$

(☑31271; Baku 9; mains 7-12 GEL; 🖱) Right on the waterfront facing the harbour, this open-air pavilion has a fine location and respectable food (mainly Georgian standards).

Drinking & Entertainment

In summer Batumis bulvari is the nightlife capital of Georgia, with long lists of international DJs providing high-energy and chill-out beats, plus regular live performers. An annually changing assortment of fresh-air clubs and bars close to the beach has people partying till dawn every night. The clubs start to fill from 11pm, with admission normally 10 GEL to 15 GEL. Two of the biggest, most popular and most enduring spots are way down near the end of the New Boulevard – **Adjara Music Hall** (www.facebook.com/adjara musichall) and **Bamba Rooms**.

Art Bulvari   CAFE, MUSIC
(Batumis bulvari) A fun place for nocturnal drinks among the trees in the Bulvari park. There's live music and a small dance floor but you can also sit outside and enjoy the summer night. Plenty of food too.

Salve   BAR
(Memed Abashidze 10; mains 8-12 GEL; ⊘9am-last customer) This hip little bar, popular with travellers, has fin-de-siècle painted ceilings and three hand-carved bars. Often packed in the evening, it's a unique place where you can enjoy all manner of drinks or food, or sit with a coffee for an hour or two perusing books. Occasional art exhibits and live bands too.

ⓘ Information

You can change Turkish lira, euros and US dollars at offices around Tbilisis moedani, outside the bus station and elsewhere.

Adjara (www.tourismadjara.ge) Informative regional tourism website.

Internet cafe (Melikishvili 23; per hr 1.50 GEL; ⊘9am-midnight) An efficient spot equipped with scanners, photocopiers, Skype and more.

Tourism Information Centre (⊘9am-8pm mid-May–mid-Oct, 10am-6pm mid-Oct–mid-

May) Bulvari (✆577909091; Ninoshvili); Rustaveli (✆577909093; Rustaveli 30) These well-informed places provide good city maps and other material on Adjara in English.

ⓘ Getting There & Around

Air

Batumi International Airport (✆276649; www.batumiairport.com), 5km south of town, has a growing range of flights. Frequency increases in summer. **Airzena Georgian Airways** (www.georgian-airways.com) has at least four weekly flights to Tbilisi (one-way fares bought in advance start at 50 GEL), plus flights to Baku, Tel Aviv, Moscow and several Ukrainian cities. **Turkish Airlines** (www.turkishairlines.com) flies to Istanbul and **Aerosvit** (www.aerosvit.com) to Kiev.

Marshrutka 110 (0.40 GEL) runs to/from Tbilisis moedani via Chavchavadze; bus 10 (0.30 GEL) runs to/from Rustaveli.

Land

BUS, MARSHRUTKA & TAXI

Taxis to or from the Turkish border at Sarpi, 17km south, should cost 15 GEL. *Marshrutky* are 1 GEL; in Batumi they start from Tbilisis moedani. Bus 101 (0.80 GEL) runs from Sarpi to Makhinjauri train station via Chavchavadze, Tbilisis moedani and Baku (Baqis qucha) near the bus station, and vice versa. The border is open 24 hours daily and crossing it is normally straightforward, though there can be queues at weekends.

Many *marshrutky* arriving in Batumi from the east terminate on Baku just east of Chavchavadze. The main **marshrutka & bus station** (Maiakovski 1), 1km east of Tbilisis moedani, has departures to Tbilisi (20 GEL, six hours, hourly 7am to midnight), Kutaisi (10 GEL, 2½ hours, hourly 7am to 8pm), Khulo (5 GEL, two hours, every 40 minutes 8am to 6pm), Poti (6 GEL, 1½ hours, hourly 8am to 6pm), Zugdidi (12 GEL, three hours, four daily), and Akhaltsikhe (20 GEL, six hours, 8.30am and 10.30am) via Khashuri and Borjomi. Direct *marshrutky* to Akhaltsikhe by the scenic route through mountainous interior Adjara, via Khulo and the Goderdzi Pass, may start once a major

---

WORTH A TRIP

INLAND ADJARA

Mountainous inland Adjara is a different world from the coast. The heartland of Adjaran tradition, with graceful old stone bridges, wooden village houses clinging to steep slopes and beautifully carved 19th-century wooden mosques, it's home to the majority of Adjara's Muslims, principally in the Khulo district. The road through this area over to Akhaltsikhe in Samtskhe-Javakheti is being upgraded, and a small ski resort is being developed at the Goderdzi Pass. A good time to visit is for the **Shuamtoba festival** at Beshumi, a few kilometres south of the Goderdzi Pass, on the first weekend of August, featuring horse racing, folk music, craft exhibits, wrestling – and weddings!

upgrade of the very poor stretch between Khulo and Zarzma is completed (due by 2012). Meanwhile, from about May to September there's a *marshrutka* to Abastumani (18 GEL, six hours, 9am); if you get off at the Abastumani–Akhaltsikhe road, you should be able to pick up another *marshrutka* to Akhaltsikhe.

For Turkey a host of bus and *marshrutka* companies run from the bus station to Trabzon (20 GEL, about 3½ hours, at least hourly 8am to 1am). There are also six or more daily departures to Ankara (60 GEL, about 14 hours) and Istanbul (65 GEL to 70 GEL, about 20 hours). You will often save time without adding expense by taking bus 101 to the border, then a waiting Turkish minibus to Hopa, about 20km south, where there are frequent departures to many points around Turkey.

Further *marshrutky* to Tbilisi (hourly 7.30am to 11.30pm) and Trabzon (hourly 8am to 7pm) leave from the **old train station** (cnr Asatiani & Zubalashvili).

For city buses from the bus station it's best to walk out on to Baku, the main road 200m north. Here, bus 1 (0.30 GEL) heads to Rustaveli, and bus 101 and *marshrutky* 20 and 45 (0.40 GEL) run to Tbilisis moedani and on down Chavchavadze.

TRAIN

Batumi's Makhinjauri station is about 5km north of town. *Marshrutky* 20 and 150 (0.40 GEL) and bus 101 (0.30 GEL) run there from Tbilisis moedani. You can buy train tickets in town at the **post office** (Baratashvili 18; ⊙10am-5pm Mon-Sat). The comfortable sleeper train to Tbilisi (4th/3rd/2nd/1st class 14/15/23/40 GEL, 8½ hours) departs at 11.05pm; it's best to book ahead for this (and essential in summer). There's a 9am train to Tbilisi every two days most of the year, and up to four day trains every day in the summer holiday season. Two daily trains run to Kutaisi (2 GEL to 4 GEL, three to four hours). From about mid-June to mid-September there's a daily train all the way to Yerevan (3rd/2nd/1st class 45/70/161 GEL, 17 hours) via Tbilisi.

Sea

UkrFerry (www.ukrferry.com) operates one or two ferries a week from Batumi's sea port to Ilyichevsk, near Odessa, Ukraine, and back. One-way fares for the 50-hour sail are between US$140 and US$380, including three meals a day, depending on the ship and cabin. Most sailings also carry motorcycles (US$214) and cars (US$437). UkrFerry also has an approximately once-weekly service from Varna, Bulgaria, to Batumi (US$140 to US$320, 2½ days), but to get from Batumi to Varna you have to go via Ilyichevsk first. Schedules do change, however. UkrFerry tickets from Batumi are sold by **Instra** (☑274119; Kutaisi 34; ⊙10am-5pm), starting

two days before departure. At research time the ferries between Batumi's **passenger ferry terminal** (Baku 3) and Sochi in Russia were only open to CIS and Georgian citizens – check www.seaport-sochi.ru for information. See p303 for further details on sea services.

Around Batumi

SOUTH OF BATUMI

Gonio, 11km south of Batumi, and **Kvariati**, 4km beyond, on the road and *marshrutka* route to the Turkish border at Sarpi, have pebbly beaches with generally thinner crowds and cleaner water than Batumi. Tourism is developing, with some hotels and beach bars. Densely vegetated mountains slope right down to the coast at Kvariati. Beside the main road at Gonio, **Gonio-Apsarus Fortress** (admission 3 GEL; ⊙9am-6pm) is one of the finest surviving examples of Roman-Byzantine military architecture, covering 47,000 sq metres within an intact rectangle of high stone walls with 18 towers. Built by the Romans in the 1st century AD, it was occupied by the Byzantines in the 6th century and by the Ottomans in the 16th century. An interesting little museum sits in its midst, with a cross outside marking what's believed to be the grave of the Apostle Matthias.

Gonio and Kvariati have several hotels and plenty of rooms to let, many of them right on the beach. Next to Hotel Lazuri at Kvariati, **Merabi** (☑599954237; Kvariati 14; per person 15-30 GEL) has an assortment of decent, clean rooms with shared or private bathroom in two buildings near the beach and his house behind.

BATUMI BOTANICAL GARDENS

Nine kilometres north of town at Mtsvane Kontskhi, these **gardens** (admission 6 GEL; ⊙9am-8pm) are well worth a trip. With many semitropical and foreign species, the gardens cover a hillside rising straight out of the sea. It takes about 1½ hours to walk the main path at a leisurely pace. A decent, stony beach, much less busy than Batumi's, is down to the left of the entrance, and there's a handful of cafes and bars around there too.

Marshrutka 31 (0.60 GEL) runs there from Baku in Batumi, just east of Chavchavadze.

MTIRALA NATIONAL PARK

This 160-sq-km **national park** (☑577101844; www.mtiralapa.ge, www.apa.gov.ge)offers the chance to spend a day or two among unspoiled Adjaran hills and forests. The park has dense subtropical vegetation in its lower reaches and some beautiful rhododendron trees. The visitors centre (no English spoken at our last check) is about 25km northeast of Batumi. There are two main **walking routes** – an easy 2.5km (each way) trail to a 12m waterfall, and a harder 15km circular route, with 1150m of ascent, to a tourist shelter where you can sleep. The visitors centre has rooms with private bathroom (50 GEL), a guest kitchen and a camping area (free) with bathrooms. It also rents sleeping bags (per night 5 GEL) and tents (7 GEL). There are also a couple of guesthouses in nearby Chakvistavi village.

Marshrutka 122 (0.80 GEL) from Baku just east of Chavchavadze in Batumi goes to Chakvi, from where a taxi along the mostly unpaved road to the visitors centre is around 30 GEL.

GREAT CAUCASUS

A trip into the Great Caucasus along Georgia's northern border is a must for anyone who wants to experience the best of the country. Spectacular mountain scenery, wonderful walks and picturesque, traditional old villages with strange, tall defensive towers are all part of a trip to the Great Caucasus.

Georgia's very identity hinges on this mighty range that rises in Abkhazia, forms the border with Russia and runs the length of the country into Azerbaijan. The Caucasus includes the highest mountain in Europe, Mt Elbrus (5642m, on the Russian side of the border), and remains little touched by commercial development in a way the Alps can only dream about.

The most accessible destination is Kazbegi, reached by the dramatic Georgian Military Highway from Tbilisi, but other areas are more than worth the effort of getting there – including enigmatic Svaneti, a refuge for many things considered essentially Georgian, and beautiful, pristine Tusheti.

It's notably cooler in the mountain villages, which can be a blessed relief in August, and in the hills you should be equipped for bad weather any time. The best walking season is in most areas is from June to September. Some areas such as Khevsureti and Tusheti are only accessible for a few summer months.

Svaneti სვანეთი

Beautiful, wild and mysterious, Svaneti is an ancient land locked in the Caucasus, so remote that it was never tamed by any ruler, and even during the Soviet period it largely retained its traditional way of life. Uniquely picturesque villages and snow-covered peaks rising over 4000m above flower-strewn alpine meadows provide a superb backdrop to the many walking trails. Svaneti's emblem is the *koshki* (defensive stone tower), designed to house villagers at times of invasion and local strife (until recently Svaneti was renowned for its murderous blood-feuds). Around 175 *koshkebi*, most originally built between the 9th and 13th centuries, survive here today.

Svaneti's isolation meant that during the many invasions of Georgia over the centuries, icons and other religious artefacts were brought here for safekeeping, and many of them remain in private homes. Svaneti also has a rich church-art heritage of its own, and many tiny village churches boast frescoes 1000 years old. This mountain retreat is regarded by many as a bastion of Georgian traditions, such as can be witnessed at Svan festivals such as Kvirikoba (p17). Svans speak their own, unwritten, language, largely unintelligible to other Georgians. They live mainly from farming cattle and pigs, and, today, tourism.

Svaneti is divided into Upper (Zemo) and Lower (Kvemo) Svaneti. Upper Svaneti offers the best walking and climbing as well as the strongest traditions; it is very green, with subalpine forests of hornbeam, chestnut, spruce, pine and fir.

Svan food may be less elaborate than other varieties of Georgian cuisine, but is delicious when well done. Typical dishes include *kubdari* pies, *chvishdari* (cheese cooked inside maize bread) and *tashmujabi* (mashed potatoes with cheese).

MESTIA მესტია
☑ 410 / POP 2800

At an altitude of 1400m, Mestia is a conglomeration of at least 10 neighbourhoods, dotted with typical Svan towers which are picturesquely floodlit after dark. Government-sponsored tourism development has seen the area around the central square, Setis moedani, attractively spruced up, and an airport, ski station and hotels have all appeared in the last few years.

Svaneti

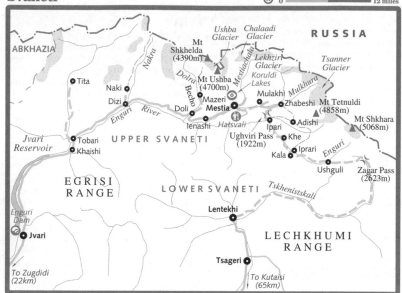

Sights & Activities

Museum of History & Ethnography MUSEUM
(Ioselani 7; admission incl guide, English- or Russian-speaking 3 GEL; ☺11am-6pm Tue-Sun) Mestia's excellent main museum is 600m south from Setis moedani, across two bridges. The Svans are reluctant to see their rich treasury of religious items moved from the villages, but the museum's collection is comprehensive, and labelled in English as well as Georgian. The exhibits include a historic collection of 1890s Svaneti photos by Italian Vittorio Sella, and a hall with reproductions of famed Svaneti church murals, but the highlight is the two-room treasury: here you can see a Persian silver jug given to Svaneti by Queen Tamar, a number of beautifully illuminated gospels, and golden altar crosses and chased-metal icons of amazingly high quality – all from the 9th to 14th centuries. One rare icon shows St George spearing the emperor Diocletian instead of his usual dragon.

Mikhail Khergiani Museum MUSEUM
(M Khergianis qucha; ☺11am-5pm Tue-Sun) Dedicated to a famous Svan mountaineer, this interesting little museum also exhibits woodcarving and other traditional Svaneti artefacts.

Hatsvali Ski Station SKIING
The ski station at Hatsvali, 8km south of Mestia up a good paved road, opened in 2010. The season runs from December or January to about early April. The station has a 300m beginners' slope, a 2565m blue run, a 1900m red run and a French-built chairlift. Taxis from town usually charge 80 GEL return. Equipment rental at the station costs 40 GEL per day for skis, boots and poles. Ski touring in Svaneti is possible towards the end of the season – contact **Svaneti Tourism Centre** (☎595358049; www.svanetitrek king.ge; Vittorio Sella 7) or **Irakli Kapanadze** (☎599690769, 595424298; i_kapanadze@yahoo. com) in Tbilisi; you need your own gear.

Sleeping & Eating

Mestia has dozens of guesthouses and homestays, most of them happy to provide as many or as few meals as you like, including picnic lunches. Most can arrange vehicles and/or guides for out-of-town trips and help with most things you might want to do. All those mentioned here have shared bathrooms with hot showers.

Roza Shukvani's Guesthouse GUESTHOUSE $
(☎599641455; www.roza-mestia.com; Vittorio Sella 17; per person 20 GEL; @) Terrific Svan meals (10 GEL) and a warm welcome from ever-helpful,

English-speaking Roza and her family make this one of Mestia's best places to stay. The spotless, spacious rooms are on the house's upper floor, which is dedicated to guests. Vittorio Sella runs up off the main street about 60m west of Setis moedani.

Nino Ratiani's Guesthouse GUESTHOUSE **$**
(☑599183555; www.svanetighouse.com; J Khaftani 1; per person incl breakfast 20-25 GEL, full board 35-40 GEL; @) Particularly good Svan food (including many vegetarian dishes), a hospitable welcome and six clean, cosy, smallish rooms make Nino's one of the best budget stays in town. Nino speaks some English and has mountain bikes to rent (25 GEL per day for guests, 35 GEL to 40 GEL for others). The house is 600m along the street towards Zugdidi from Setis moedani.

Guesthouse Seti GUESTHOUSE **$**
(☑599325219; setihouse@yahoo.com; Setis III chikhi 1; per person with 0/2/3 meals 25/40/50 GEL) This farmstead, just off the east side of Setis moedani, has its own Svan tower plus eight good guestrooms and three good bathrooms.

The friendly family serves plentiful, tasty food in a nice big dining room.

Villa Gabliani GUESTHOUSE **$**
(☑599569358; ciurigabliani1@rambler.ru; I Gabliani 20; per person with 0/2 meals 15/45 GEL; @) These teacher sisters speak good English and German, and their house has big, carpeted rooms, books on Svaneti in several languages, and a lovely verandah overlooking a garden of wild flowers and fruit trees, with the sound of a river below. It's 500m southwest of Setis moedani, near the hospital.

Iamze Japaridze HOMESTAY **$**
(☑790592040; apt 1, Kakhiani 49; per person with 0/2/3 meals 20/40/50 GEL) Big meals, clean, cosy rooms and delicious homemade cherry cognac are the successful recipe at Iamze's apartment, in the last building before the airport, 1.5km from the town centre. Iamze is usually home before 11am and after 6pm; at other times you'll find her in her shop beside the Tourism Information Centre on Setis moedani. Kitchen use available. Daughter-in-law **Irina** (☑598510402) speaks English.

GEORGIA SVANETI

WALKS AROUND MESTIA

Take local advice as you make your plans. Many routes are well signposted; others aren't. Your accommodation or the Tourism Information Centre will help you find a guide if you want one. The walking season lasts from about early June to mid-October, though some routes can be waterlogged early or late in that period. Check www.svanetitrekking.ge for route information and maps.

A moderately demanding half-day walk is up to the **cross** that's visible 900m above Mestia on the north side of the valley. The views get better as you go, and from the cross you can see the spectacular twin peaks of **Mt Ushba** (4700m), Georgia's toughest and most dangerous mountaineering challenge. From Setis moedani, walk 450m east along the main street then take the lane up to the left (Khergiani, becoming Lanchvali). Take the uphill option at all junctions, passing under an arch after about 350m. After 150m more the street becomes a footpath: follow this up and after 800m it bends to the right across the hillside, eventually meeting a jeep track. You can follow this, shortcutting some bends, all the way to the cross. The return trip from Mestia takes about five hours. With good weather and enough daylight and energy, you can continue to the **Koruldi Lakes**, a group of pristine small lakes about two hours beyond the cross and some 300m higher.

The walk to the **Chalaadi Glacier** is another good route, of about six hours return trip, taking you out past Mestia's airport and up the Mestiachala valley. Take your passport as Georgian border guards may want to check it. The last section is up through woods to the foot of the glacier. Watch out for rocks falling off the glacier in summer.

From about late July to late September you can spend a lovely two or three days walking to **Ushguli** if you start with a taxi as far as Ipari (Nakipari on some maps), about 20km southeast of Mestia. From Ipari the first stage takes you to **Adishi**, where there's good homestay accommodation with **Zhora Kaldani** (☑599187359; per person with 0/1/2 meals 20/30/40 GEL) or **Mukhran Avaliani** (☑599186793; per person with 0/1/2 meals 20/30/40 GEL). The second stage is from Adishi to **Iprari**, where **Ucha Margvelani** (☑599574783; per person with 0/1/2 meals 20/30/40 GEL) has a nice homestay. From Iprari it's three or four hours' walk to Ushguli.

Hotel Tetnuldi HOTEL $$
(☑790123344; www.tetnuldi.ge; Revez Margiani 9; incl breakfast s 120-130 GEL, d 150-170 GEL; ☻) The best of Mestia's hotels, opened in 2010, the Tetnuldi sits on a small hilltop, is built mainly in wood and has 34 good, bright rooms with balconies. Also here is the town's top **restaurant** (mains 5-10 GEL; ☐), serving Svan and Georgian food. You can rent mountain bikes for 5/40 GEL per hour/day.

Eka Chartolani's Guesthouse GUESTHOUSE $
(☑599726719; marfasvan@gmail.com; Vittorio Sella 8; per person with 0/2 meals 20/35 GEL) Hospitable, helpful, English-speaking Eka, who works in the Museum of History & Ethnography, has six rooms and makes delicious meals.

Manoni Ratiani HOMESTAY $
(☑599568417, 577568417; manonisvaneti@yahoo.com; Kakhiani 25; per person 20 GEL, half board 35-40 GEL, full board 45 GEL, camping per person 10 GEL; ☐) Has seven comfy, recently made-over rooms. Camping in the grassy garden includes hot shower and kitchen use. It's 1km east from Setis moedani, up a lane beside Kakhiani 31.

Nest Hostel HOSTEL $
(☑595414443; www.nesthostel.ge; Kakhiani 16; dm 25 GEL; ☐☎) Branch of Tbilisi's Nest Hostel, with a guest kitchen and a stock of books, a little over 1km from Setis moedani on the airport road.

Hotel Mestia HOTEL $$
(☑577721211; marika-japaridze@mail.ru; Setis moedani 27; s/d incl breakfast 80/100 GEL, full board 100/140 GEL) Has a prime position on the square. Rooms are plain and pine-furnished, with good firm beds. There's a restaurant, and a bar and duplex rooms are being added.

Cafe Ushba GEORGIAN $
(Tamar Mepe 7; mains 3-7 GEL) Good for a cheap meal, with a reasonable range of dishes from boiled potatoes and cheese to *chakapuli*. It's 200m east of Setis moedani.

Bazari MARKET $
(Tamar Mepe; ☺10am-9pm) Mestia's one-room food market, opposite Cafe Ushba, has a good selection of fresh veggies, fruit and cheese.

ℹ Information
Liberty Bank (Tamar Mepe 12) Has an ATM (not always working) and changes foreign currency; 150m east of Setis moedani.

Svaneti Tourism Centre (☑595358049; www.svanetitrekking.ge; Vittorio Sella 7) This NGO has helped to develop locally based tourism in Svaneti and has signposted many walking trails; it can provide guides, horses and vehicle transport within Svaneti. The office is open erratically and may only have Russian and Georgian speakers available, but you can make contact via the website, which is a great information source.

Tourism Information Centre (☑790357375; Setis moedani 2; ☺10am-7pm)

Training & Consultation Centre (Sgimieri; internet free; ☺noon-1pm)

ℹ Getting There & Around
Flights from Tbilisi to Mestia and back (75 GEL one-way) are operated daily except Tuesday and Thursday by a Canadian company, Kenn Borek Air, with a 15-seat plane. In Tbilisi tickets are sold by **Pegasus Airlines** (Map p36; ☑32-2400400; www.flypgs.com); in Mestia you can buy them at the airport, 2.5km east of the town centre. **Vanilla Sky** (Map p36; ☑32-2428428, www.vanillasky.ge) flies from Natakhtari airfield, about 25km north of Tbilisi, to Mestia and back with a 12-seat biplane on Friday and Sunday (100 GEL one-way including transfer to or from Tbilisi's Didube bus station). Schedules on both services may change and flights are sometimes cancelled because of weather conditions. A taxi from Mestia airport to the town centre should cost 10 GEL.

Getting to Mestia by road is part of the adventure of visiting Svaneti. The six-hour *marshrutka* trip from Zugdidi (see p67) traverses increasingly spectacular scenery heading up the Enguri and Mulkhura valleys. The road is normally kept open all year. There is also a daily *marshrutka* to Mestia from Tbilisi's train station, or you can take an overnight train to Zugdidi and then a *marshrutka* from there.

Returning, two *marshrutky* leave Setis moedani between 5am and 6am – one to Zugdidi (Georgian/foreigner 15/20 GEL, five hours), the other to Tbilisi (30 GEL, 11 to 12 hours). Further Zugdidi *marshrutky* may leave later if there are enough passengers. You can ask your accommodation to check times and reserve places.

Getting around Svaneti from Mestia, unless you're walking, usually means taxis. Your accommodation or the Tourism Information Centre can arrange drivers.

USHGULI უშგული
POP 290
Ushguli, a 47km drive southeast from Mestia, reaches up to 2100m above sea level and is claimed to be the highest permanently inhabited place in Europe. With more than 20 ancient Svan towers, it has been on the

Unesco World Heritage List since 1996. Set in the topmost reaches of the Enguri valley beneath the snow-covered massif of Mt Shkhara (5068m), Georgia's highest peak, it's a superbly picturesque and atmospheric spot – actually a conglomeration of four villages (from lowest to highest: Murqmeli, Chazhashi, Chvibiani and Zhibiani).

There's some wonderful walking around Ushguli: it takes about seven hours to walk 8km up the valley to the foot of the Shkhara glacier and back. One tower in Chazhashi houses Ushguli's main **Ethnographic Museum** (admission 3 GEL; ⊙10am-4pm Tue-Sun), with a superb collection of gold, silver and wooden icons and crosses dating back to the 12th century from Ushguli's seven churches. A second **ethnographic museum** (admission 3 GEL), in a *machubi* (traditional home shared between people and livestock) in Zhibiani, opens when you find someone with a key. At the top of Ushguli, beautifully situated on a hill looking up the valley to Mt Shkhara, is the 12th-century **Church of the Virgin Mary** (Lamaria), with a defensive tower next to it.

🛏 Sleeping & Eating

Ushguli has at least a dozen homestays and guesthouses, with shared bathrooms. Those listed here all have hot showers.

Temraz Nijaradze   HOMESTAY $
(☑790209719; Zhibiani; per person with 0/2/3 meals 20/40/50 GEL) Just below Lamaria church, Temraz' has four new rooms and awesomely delicious local food. The teenage kids speak a little English.

Tariel Nijaradze   HOMESTAY $
(☑599317086; Chvibiani; per person 20 GEL, meals each 10 GEL) Amiable Tariel's house, with plain, clean rooms, is the first on the right in Chvibiani. Tariel's son, sometimes present, speaks some English.

Dato Ratiani's Ushguli
Guesthouse Lileo   GUESTHOUSE $$
(☑599912256; lileo-ushguli.blogspot.com; Zhibiani; per person half/full board 50/60 GEL) One of the largest and most professional establishments, with 20 beds in smallish rooms, and excellent Svan cooking.

Kafe Koshki   GEORGIAN $
(Chvibiani; mains 3-7 GEL) This neat wooden cafe with jolly yellow sunshades serves good basic fare such as *kubdari, mtsvadi* and salads,

and has Natakhtari beer on tap. It closes about 8pm.

❶ Getting There & Away
A taxi or jeep day trip for up to four people from Mestia costs 150 GEL to 200 GEL; for one-way trips you shouldn't have to pay above 150 GEL. The drive along a mainly unpaved road takes about 2½ hours each way. The road is normally open all year except after heavy snows or landslides, but non-4WD vehicles can generally only manage it from about June to October (and they need high clearance). *Marshrutky* to Mestia (10 GEL) normally leave Ushguli about 9am Tuesday and Friday (days can vary with local demand), starting back from Mestia about 6pm. The rough track on from Ushguli to Lentekhi in Kvemo Svaneti (via the 2623m Zagar Pass) is normally only passable from about June to October.

BECHO ბეჩო
Becho, a community of several small villages strung up the Dolra valley west of Mestia, is a very beautiful and relatively little visited area with some wonderful walks. Bring your passport in case Georgian border guards want to see it. The valley is headed by the spectacular, twin-peaked **Ushba** (4700m). One lovely, well marked walk from **Mazeri** village leads up the Dolra River then up past waterfalls to the glacier on the west side of Ushba (about eight hours there and back). From about mid-June to mid-October you can walk from Mestia to Mazeri in about nine hours via the Guli Pass (the route diverges west from the Koruldi Lakes route at the Lamaaja ridge). A taxi day trip from Mestia to Mazeri costs 120 GEL to 150 GEL; a one-way trip should be a bit less.

🛏 Sleeping & Eating

Grand Hotel Ushba   LODGE $$
(☑790119192; www.grandhotelushba.com; incl breakfast s €44-64, d €54-74; ☺) A stylish, comfortable and hospitable mountain lodge in a gorgeous setting just outside Mazeri, with a restaurant serving good Svan food. It's a wonderful base for walking, skiing and a host of other trips and activities.

Giri Tserediani   HOMESTAY $
(☑790565820, 551161657; per person with 0/2/3 meals 35/40/50 GEL) This house in Nashtkoli, 2km south of Mazeri, has good, big, clean rooms. Giri and his son are both mountaineers and guides.

Georgian Military Highway საქართველოს სამხედრო გზა

This ancient passage across the Caucasus towards Vladikavkaz in Russia is a spectacular adventure. A track through the challenging mountain terrain was first properly engineered as a road in the 19th century with the Russian occupation of the Caucasus. The road clings to the side of the turquoise Zhinvali Reservoir and passes the sublime architecture of Ananuri and the ski resort of Gudauri before reaching its highest point, the Jvari (Cross) Pass. It then descends the Tergi valley to Kazbegi, a superb base for walking, climbing and bird-watching. The Russian border at Larsi, 15km beyond Kazbegi, was reopened to CIS and Georgian travellers in 2010 but remained closed to others.

ANANURI ანანური

This **fortress** with its churches, 66km north of Tbilisi, is a classic example of beautiful old Georgian architecture in a beautiful location, enhanced by the Zhinvali Reservoir that now spreads out below. The fortress belonged to the *eristavis* (dukes) of Aragvi, who ruled the land as far as the Tergi valley from the 13th to 18th centuries.

Within the fortress are two 17th-century churches, the larger of which, the **Assumption Church**, is covered with wonderful stone carving, including a large cross on every wall. Inside are vivid 17th- and 18th-century frescoes including a Last Judgement on the south wall. You can climb the tallest of the fortress towers, at the top end of the complex, for fine views: it was here that the last defenders were killed in 1739 when a rival *eristavi* set fire to Ananuri and murdered the Aragvi *eristavi's* family.

GUDAURI გუდაური

About 110km from Tbilisi, the Georgian Military Highway climbs 500m by a series of hairpins up to the ski resort of Gudauri, whose bare hillsides make for Georgia's best downhill ski runs. These total 16km of varied difficulty (blue, red and black), with good Doppelmayer chairlifts rising from 1990m to 3270m. Normally the ski season lasts from December to March or April, with the best snow in January and February. A one-day lift pass costs from 28 GEL to 33 GEL; ski- or snowboard-gear rental is 25 GEL to 50 GEL.

Gudauri also offers good freeriding, and heliskiing with the Georgian-French company **Heliksir** (www.heliksir.com; per half-day/day €450/600). Ski touring is best in March and usually possible into May: one of Georgia's top mountain guides, **Irakli Kapanadze** (☑599690769, 595424298; i_kapanadze@yahoo.com), organises trips for 100 GEL to 250 GEL per person per day, including transport from Tbilisi, guide(s) and accommodation.

🛏 Sleeping & Eating

Gudauri has about a dozen hotels. All the following can help with ski rental and instruction, and transfers from Tbilisi.

Hotel Gudauri Hut
HOTEL $$
(☑595939911; www.gudaurihut.com; d half board US$98) A friendly, medium-sized hotel a short distance up the road from the centre of the resort, Gudauri Hut offers pleasant, pine-furnished rooms with good views. It's run by Gia Apakidze, one of Georgia's top mountain guides, and his family. Gia also runs a free-ride school.

Hotel Shamo
HOTEL $$
(☑599500142; allgudauri.ge; s/d half board US$75/110; 😊🛜) Centrally located not far below the ski lifts, this is a less elaborate, more personal place with a sociable atmosphere. Owner Gela Burduli speaks good German and some English.

Hotel Truso
HOTEL $$
(☑599270051; www.hoteltruso.com; s/d 200/250 GEL) A quite stylish, more upmarket choice close to the resort centre. It has just 14 comfortable rooms and good service.

JVARI PASS ჯვრის უღელტეხილი

The Jvari (Cross) Pass starts about 4km after Gudauri; 2379m high, it takes its name from a cross placed here by King David the Builder. The present red stone cross, about 500m to the east above the road, was erected by General Yermolov in 1824. The pass stays open for all but a few days most years.

KAZBEGI (STEPANTSMINDA) ყაზბეგი (სტეფანწმინდა)
☑345 / POP 2700

This is most people's destination on the Georgian Military Highway: a valley town at about 1750m altitude, just 15km short of the Russian border, with the famous hilltop silhouette of Tsminda Sameba Church and the snowy peak of Mt Kazbek towering to the west. Now officially named Stepantsminda, but still commonly known as Kazbegi, it has

SOUTH OSSETIA

The breakaway region of South Ossetia, focus of the 2008 war between Georgia and Russia, stretches up to the main Caucasus ridge north of the Georgian town of Gori. At research time, South Ossetia was not letting any foreigners in from Georgia and this looked unlikely to change soon. It may be possible to enter South Ossetia from North Ossetia in Russia, although Georgia considers this illegal, and the British **Foreign Office** (www.fco.gov.uk) and US **State Department** (http://travel.state.gov) advise against all travel to both South Ossetia and North Ossetia for safety reasons.

South Ossetia's de facto authorities are reportedly keen to attract tourism. The first step towards visiting would be to contact the **South Ossetia Department of Tourism** (www.visitsouthossetia.com, http://minmol.org in Russian; ulitsa Osetinskaya 1, Tskhinvali). You would need a double- or multiple-entry Russian visa so that you can return to Russia. A daily bus service (R200, three hours) links Vladikavkaz in North Ossetia with the South Ossetian capital Tskhinvali, via the 4km Roki tunnel at the border. South Ossetia's currency is the Russian rouble. Central Tskhinvali has been extensively rebuilt since 2008 and the town has a couple of hotels: **Hotel Alan** (ulitsa Geroev 1; s/d with shared bathroom R400/800, r with private bathroom R1000-2000) and the cheaper **Hotel Ireston** (Teatralnaya ploshchad).

For travellers' experiences, search 'South Ossetia' on the Thorn Tree forum at lonely planet.com.

easy access from Tbilisi, plentiful inexpensive accommodation and great walking and mountain-biking in the area.

The highway brings you straight into the main square, Kazbegis moedani, with Hotel Stepantsminda on its west side. Be prepared for a bit of hustle from guesthouse owners and taxi drivers when you arrive. From the square Kazbegis qucha forks to the right, while the main road leads down over the Tergi River then continues north to the Russian border in the dramatic Dariali Gorge. Immediately after the Tergi bridge a side road turns up to Gergeti village on the west side of the valley, almost a suburb of Kazbegi.

◎ Sights

Stepantsminda History Museum MUSEUM
(Kazbegis qucha 2; admission 3 GEL; ◷10am-6pm) The museum is set in the childhood home of writer Alexander Kazbegi (1848–93), 300m north of Kazbegis moedani. Kazbegi made the unusual decision to become a shepherd after studying in Tbilisi, St Petersburg and Moscow. Later he worked as a journalist and wrote the novels and plays that made him famous. The museum's ground floor contains photos, paintings, traditional clothing and domestic artefacts documenting local life; the upstairs is devoted to the man. His grave lies under a large stone sculpture near the fence outside: he asked to be buried where he could see Mt Kazbek. To one side is a **church**, dated 1809–11, with a striking

relief of two lions above its door. To its east and west are the tombs of Alexander's father and mother.

🛏 Sleeping & Eating

Kazbegi is very well supplied with guesthouses and homestays, all providing meals. Those mentioned here are just a selection and (except where stated) have shared bathrooms with hot showers. Many are closed outside the main season (May to early November).

The eating-out choices boil down to a handful of cafes around Kazbegis moedani, serving staples such as *khachapuri, khinkali, mtsvadi* and salads.

Nazi Chkareuli GUESTHOUSE **$**
(Guesthouse Gergeti; ✆252480, 598382700; ssujashvili@yahoo.co.uk; Gergeti; per person 15 GEL, incl breakfast/2/3 meals 20/25/35 GEL; @) Nazi's house is a backpackers' favourite for its good prices, good meals and sociable atmosphere, with beds squeezed into every available room. Daughter **Shorena** (✆599265813), there in summer, speaks English. Walk up towards Gergeti and turn left along the second street.

Diana Pitskhelauri GUESTHOUSE **$**
(✆599570313, 598522525; Vazha Pshavela 64; per person half board 35 GEL; @) Terrific meals, a welcoming hostess and big, comfy, clean rooms in a new house make this one of the best picks even though no English is spoken. From Kazbegis moedani go up the street

opposite Hotel Stepantsminda, then 750m to the right. The house is on the left at the end of the street.

Nunu's Guesthouse GUESTHOUSE **$**
(☑558358535, 599570915; per person 20 GEL, half board 35 GEL; @) A good option just 50m up the street opposite Hotel Stepantsminda, with a friendly family and mountain views from the balcony. Daughter Gvantsa speaks English. They have their own jeep for outings.

Tamuna Sujashvili GUESTHOUSE **$$**
(☑252588, 599174613; Vazha Pshavela 40; per person half board 45 GEL; @) This two-storey house has five large, bright, very clean rooms, three showers and an upstairs balcony with mountain views. Go up the street opposite Hotel Stepantsminda, then 100m to the right.

Guest House Emma GUESTHOUSE **$**
(☑598236596; per person half board 25 GEL) Excellent food and a couple of large rooms. Turn right off Kazbegis qucha by Shop Tourist, go left at the top of the street and the house is the second on the right (through a gate).

Stefan Pitskhelauri
GUESTHOUSE $

(☎599183245; Stepantsmindis qucha; per person half board 40 GEL) A nice house built as tourist accommodation with great views and clean, bright rooms with private bathroom. From Kazbegis moedani go 350m back towards Tbilisi then nearly 1km uphill to the left. The house is just behind the Alpine Ecology Institute.

Meri & Gennady Chopiashvili
HOMESTAY $

(☎599415934, 593199200; per person half board 35 GEL; ❀) Friendly couple with three rooms (two with good views), and decent simple food. It's through a green gate, 60m up beside the Kazalikashvili museum on Vazha Pshavela.

Luiza's B&B Guesthouse
GUESTHOUSE $

(☎252353, 599928554; Vazha Pshavela 38; per person half board 35-45 GEL) Luiza speaks German and a little English, and two of her rooms have good new private bathrooms. Next to Tamuna Sujashvili's.

Rezo & Ramazi Gomiashvili
GUESTHOUSE $

(☎599153639; lia-kazbegi@mail.ru; per person 15 GEL, half board 30-35 GEL; ❀) Four rooms for up to four people each, and three bathrooms. Through the left-hand green gates, on the left 200m up the road towards Gergeti.

Guest House Ira & Dato
HOMESTAY $

(☎599584340; per person 15-20 GEL, half board 25-30 GEL; ❀) Simple place with decent food towards the northeast edge of town. Dato is an ambulance and taxi driver.

❶ Information
Liberty Bank (Kazbegis qucha 11) There was still no ATM in Kazbegi by 2011 but this bank exchanges euros and US dollars, and gives Visa and MasterCard cash advances.

Mountain Travel Agency (☎555649291; dkhetaguri@gmail.com; internet per 30min 2 GEL; ☉May-Nov) This agency, in a tiny office between Kazbegis moedani and the Tergi bridge, can provide most things you might need for trips out of Kazbegi, including mountain bikes (per hour/day 7/40 GEL), horses, hiking maps, hiking and climbing guides (around €400 per group for ascents of Mt Kazbek), and camping and climbing equipment. It plans to open a camping ground in Gergeti, with a cafe and on-site tents.

❶ Getting There & Away
Marshrutky to Tbilisi (10 GEL, three hours) are timetabled at 8am, 9am, 10am, 12.30pm, 3.30pm, 5pm and sometimes 6pm. A taxi to or from Tbilisi can cost anywhere between 80 GEL and 120 GEL.

AROUND KAZBEGI
There are many wonderful walks and some good mountain-bike and horse routes in the valleys and mountains around Kazbegi. Taxis to outlying destinations are available on Kazbegis moedani but you may get better prices through your accommodation. The walking and climbing season is from May or June to October or November, depending on the weather.

GERGETI GLACIER
If you're up for another 900m of ascent from Tsminda Sameba (p88), this quite strenuous walk rewards with spectacular views. The path heads straight up the ridge behind the church; an alternative route, more protected on windy days, runs up the left flank of the ridge. The two meet at a cairn at 2960m altitude, from where a path leads on up towards the left side of the Gergeti (Ortsveri) Glacier. Head up here for about one hour for views of the glacier, then return. Allow up to nine hours to get up there from Kazbegi and down again the same day.

If you have a day in hand and are experienced on ice or have a good guide, and preferably an ice axe and crampons, it's possible, with a further 600m of ascent, to cross the glacier and climb to the **Meteo Station** (Betlemi Hut; dm fl/bed 20/25 GEL; ☉May-Nov), a former weather station at 3652m where you can sleep. The station has around 50 beds and space for a total 200 people. Bring food, a warm sleeping bag and cooking gear. Camping is free but the wind can be fierce.

SNO VALLEY & ARKHOTI
The Sno valley runs southeast off the Georgian Military Highway 4km south of Kazbegi. The small village of **Juta** (2150m), inhabited by Khevsurs from over the mountains to the east, is about 15km along the unpaved valley road and a starting point for some great hikes. A taxi day trip from Kazbegi to Juta with a few hours' wait costs 60 GEL to 70 GEL; a one-way trip can cost anything from 35 GEL.

One beautiful short walk from Juta goes southeast up the Chaukhi valley to the foot of **Mt Chaukhi** (3842m), a multipinnacled peak popular with climbers, 1½ hours from Juta. With more time you can continue up the valley to the 3338m **Chaukhi Pass**, and in a long day you can get over the pass and down to Roshka in Khevsureti.

DON'T MISS

TSMINDA SAMEBA CHURCH

The 14th-century Holy Trinity Church above Kazbegi at 2200m has become almost a symbol of Georgia for its beauty, piety and the fierce determination involved in building it on such a lofty, isolated perch. In 1988 the Soviet authorities constructed a cable-car line to the church, with one station behind Kazbegi's History Museum and the other right next to Tsminda Sameba. The people of Kazbegi felt it defiled their sacred place and soon destroyed it.

Vakhushti Batonishvili wrote in the 18th century that in times of danger the treasures from Mtskheta, as well as St Nino's cross, were kept at Tsminda Sameba for safety. The beautifully weathered stone church and bell tower are decorated with intriguing carvings, one on the bell tower appearing to show two dinosaurs. The church interior is not particularly unusual, but certainly worth a look.

There are several ways of walking up to the church from Kazbegi. For the shortest and steepest, walk up through Gergeti village to a T-junction 1.25km from the highway (80m after signs indicating the car track to the right). Go 80m left from the T-junction, then 80m to the right and take a narrow path between metal posts. The path passes under a couple of wire fences and climbs steeply to join the car track after 350m. Follow the car track uphill to the fourth right-hand zigzag, where a path heads off up to the left: this reaches the church after a steep upward 700m – approximately one hour from Kazbegi.

For an alternative route avoiding the steepest parts and taking about half an hour longer, turn right at the previously mentioned T-junction in Gergeti, and go immediately up a narrow path to the left. Follow this up and out of the village to meet the vehicle track after 600m. Go left up the vehicle track and follow it up through the woods for approximately 2.5km until it emerges in a grassy clearing. About 150m along the clearing, a path starts up into the trees on the left. Take this and after five steep minutes you'll rejoin the vehicle track in grassy meadows with the church in view to the left – just 10 minutes' more walk.

A return-trip taxi to Tsminda Sameba from Kazbegi costs 40 GEL to 50 GEL.

A 10- to 12-hour walk eastward from Juta leads over the 3287m **Arkhotistavi Pass** to the intriguing **Arkhoti** area, with no roads and three Khevsur villages: Chimgha, Akhieli and Amgha. From Arkhoti you can cross the Blosghele Pass south to Roshka. The Chaukhi and Arkhotistavi passes are passable from about July to mid-October. Horse rental in Juta costs around 100 GEL to the Chaukhi Pass (one-way), 150 GEL to Roshka (one-way) and 200 GEL to Arkhoti and back.

Juta has several places to stay, most only open from July to September. Amiable **Soso Arabuli** (☑555690045, 577306574; per person half or full board 30 GEL) has a tin-roofed red house just above the river at the top end of the village, with a hot shower and indoor squat toilet; he's there all year. **Levan Arabuli** (☑555487468; per person with 0/2 meals 25/35 GEL) has a new, four-room, wooden cottage with hot shower by the bridge at the bottom of Juta. He and his friendly, well-travelled family speak Hebrew and Swedish. Beautifully located **Zeta**

Camp (☑577501057; www.zeta.ge; per person incl 3 meals 40 GEL), a 10-minute walk above the village, provides tents, meals and hot showers, but you need your own sleeping bag and mat. In Akhieli, **Mar Narozauli** (☑555496663; per person half board 30-35 GEL) has good accommodation with a hot shower, in a former UN building.

TRUSO VALLEY

This beautiful valley, source of the Tergi River, heads west off the Georgian Military Highway 17km south of Kazbegi. A good plan is to drive to Okrokana, 5km up the valley, then walk or ride to Abano village, 8km further. You'll pass mineral-water geysers, ancient towers and abandoned villages once inhabited by Ossetians. Truso is also noted for bird-watching. Georgian soldiers will probably prevent you from going much beyond Abano (the South Ossetia border is close). A return-trip taxi to Okrokano should be 70 GEL or 80 GEL including waiting time.

Khevsureti ხევსურეთი

Sparsely populated Khevsureti, bordering Chechnya (Russia), is home to some fantastic defensive architecture, a part-animist religion, and spectacular scenery of steep, forested valleys and blooming mountain pastures, as well as being credited with inventing *khinkali* dumplings.

Men in this remote area were still wearing chain mail well into the 20th century, but today Khevsureti's old culture is only clinging to life and very few villages have permanent inhabitants. Shepherds bring their flocks up from Kakheti from about June to September, when tourism also provides an income for a few families. Khevsureti makes a great trip but bring at least some food with you, and some warm clothes as it can get cold at night even in summer.

The road to Khevsureti turns northeast off the Georgian Military Highway shortly before the Zhinvali Reservoir and runs up the Pshavis Aragvi valley towards Khevsureti's largest village, **Barisakho** (population 200), about 100km from Tbilisi. At **Korsha**, 2km past Barisakho, there's a small but interesting **museum** (admission free) of Khevsur life, with armour, weapons, traditional clothing and photos; to visit, ask at curator Shota Arabuli's guesthouse, three doors away. There's no mobile-phone signal anywhere past Korsha. From Korsha it's about 8km up to **Roshka**, a small, muddy village off the main road, on walking routes towards the Chaukhi Pass and Arkhoti.

After Korsha the road becomes 4WD-only as it climbs to the 2676m **Datvisjvari Pass** (open about May to November) and then descends the Argun valley to **Shatili**, 150km from Tbilisi. Shatili's old town, built between the 7th and 13th centuries, is a unique agglomeration of tall *koshkebi* (towers) clinging together on a rocky outcrop to form a single fortresslike whole. It was abandoned between the 1960s and '80s, and the new village, of about 20 houses, is just around the hill. But several towers have been restored to accommodate tourists. In August or September (dates vary) you might run into the **Shatiloba festival**, with folk music and dance, horse races and Georgian wrestling.

From Shatili the road continues 3km northeast then veers south just before the Chechnya border. At the bend, the **Anatori Crypts**, medieval communal tombs with human bones still visible, sit on a promontory above the gorge: in times of plague, infected villagers would voluntarily enter these tombs and wait for death. The road

---

MT KAZBEK

This 5047m extinct volcano towering west of Kazbegi has much folk history. The Greek Prometheus was supposedly chained up here for stealing fire from the gods, as was the Georgian Amirani, for challenging God's omnipotence. Amirani's legendary abode was somewhere near the Betlemi (Bethlehem) cave, 4000m above sea level, where resided a hermit and many very sacred objects – Christ's manger, Abraham's tent and a dove-rocked golden cradle whose sight would blind a human being. There were taboos against hunting on the mountain and climbing it. Not surprisingly, the first to conquer Kazbek's peak were foreigners: Freshfield, Tucker and Moore of the London Alpine Club in 1868.

There is indeed a cave at 4000m, near the Meteo Station, which serves as the base for Kazbek ascents today. Somewhere around 5000 people a year climb to Kazbek's summit but it's not for everyone: this is a challenging mountaineering experience that requires fitness and acclimatisation to altitude. At the Meteo Station you may be able to join a group heading to the summit for 50 GEL to 100 GEL – but to ensure guide services you should organise them beforehand with agencies such as Tbilisi-based **Explore Georgia** (www.exploregeorgia.com) or **Mountain Travel Agency** (☑555649291; dkhe taguri@gmail.com) in Kazbegi.

The ascent is technically straightforward, though there is some danger in crevasses. It generally takes three or four days from Kazbegi, with nights spent at the Meteo Station. The second day is usually spent acclimatising with climbs to the Maili Plateau (4500m) or Ortsveri Peak (4365m). On day three you start for the summit from the Meteo Station in the early hours of the morning. The ascent takes around six hours, with the steep final 150m involving about three rope lengths of 35- to 40-degree ice. The descent to the Meteo Station for the third night takes up to another six hours.

Khevsureti & Tusheti

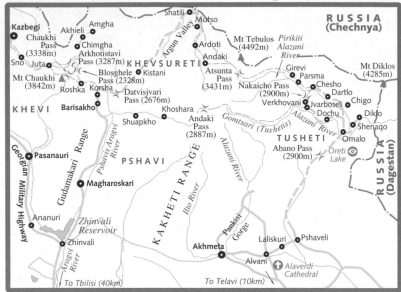

continues 9km up the Andaki valley to tiny **Mutso**, where the spectacular abandoned old village on a steep rock pinnacle contains several more bone-laden stone crypts. A foot trail continues up and over the very steep **Atsunta Pass** (3431m) into Tusheti.

🛏 Sleeping & Eating

In Korsha, Shota Arabuli, curator of the museum, has a good six-room **guesthouse** (☎790503134, 595503134; mamukaarabuli@yahoo. com; per person with 0/2/3 meals 15/30/40 GEL) with a hot shower, washing machine and plenty of Shota's own art.

In Roshka, photographer **Shota Tsik-lauri** (☎599399789; per person full board 40 GEL) has four guestrooms and good food in his comfy house at the top of the village. There's another guesthouse at Gudani, just off the main road about 7km past Korsha.

Shatili's *koshki*-guesthouses normally cost 25 GEL per person, or 30 GEL with a simple meal (when available) of something such as bread, cheese and *khachapuri* or *khinkali*. **Dato Jalabauri** (☎598127614; www.jalabauri. ge, in Georgian) has a particularly good one, a wonderfully atmospheric place to stay with 19 beds in several rooms, electricity and a good hot shower and seat toilet. Dato's own

house is the last on the left in the new part of Shatili, past the school.

ℹ Getting There & Away

A bus leaves Barisakho for Tbilisi's Didube bus station (5 GEL, 3½ hours) at about 8pm daily except Wednesday, heading back from Didube about 3pm. Zhinvali-based 4WD driver **Pridon Gogishvili** (☎599956562, 790956562), speaking Georgian and Russian, makes regular trips to Shatili: he charges 300 GEL for an overnight return trip from Tbilisi for up to three passengers (four at a squeeze), or 250 GEL one-way in either direction. The Tbilisi–Shatili drive takes six hours. In summer there is sometimes a weekly *marshrutka* between Didube and Shatili; otherwise, without a 4WD vehicle, beyond Barisakho it's a question of walking or trying to get a lift with one of the few passing vehicles (be prepared to camp).

Tusheti თუშეთი

Tucked into Georgia's far northeast corner, Tusheti has become a very popular summer hiking and horse-trekking area, but remains one of the country's most fascinating and pristine high-mountain regions. The single road to Tusheti, over the nerve-jangling 2900m Abano Pass from Kakheti, is 4WD-only and passable only from about early

June to early October. Evidence of Tusheti's old animist religion is plentiful in the form of stone shrines called *khatebi*, decked with the horns of sacrificed goats or sheep, which women are not permitted to approach. Defensive *koshkebi*, centuries old, still stand in many villages.

Today most Tusheti folk only go up to Tusheti in summer, to graze their sheep or cattle, attend festivals, cater for tourists and generally reconnect with their roots. Many have winter homes around Akhmeta and Alvani in Kakheti.

Tusheti has two main river valleys – the Pirikiti Alazani and the more southerly Gomtsari (Tushetis) Alazani – which meet below Omalo, the biggest village, then flow east into Dagestan (Russia). The scenery everywhere is a spectacular mix of snow-covered rocky peaks, deep gorges and steep, grassy hillsides where distant flocks of sheep appear as slowly shifting patterns of white specks.

◎ Sights & Activities

Most of the villages are around 2000m above sea level and sit above near-sheer hillsides or nestle down by one of the rivers. There's a particularly splendid group of old towers, known as Keseloebi, on the crag at **Zemo Omalo**, the upper part of Omalo. **Shenaqo**, a few kilometres east of Omalo, is one of the prettiest villages, with houses of stone, slate and rickety wooden balconies grouped below Tusheti's only functioning church. Just outside **Diklo**, 4km northeast of Shenaqo, is an old fortress perched on a spectacular rock promontory. **Dartlo**, 12km northwest of Omalo in the Pirikiti Alazani valley, has another spectacular tower grouping, overlooked by the single tall tower of **Kvavlo** 350m above.

Walking routes are innumerable though signage is erratic. Omalo to Shenaqo and Shenaqo to Diklo are two good short walks of a couple of hours each (one-way) on vehicle tracks. **Oreti Lake**, about five hours' walk south of Omalo, is a beautiful destination and the trail there is well marked; you can camp overnight if you like. A good longer route (about five days) starts in Omalo, runs up the Pirikiti Alazani valley to Dartlo and Chesho, then crosses the 2900m Nakaicho Pass over to Verkhovani and returns down the Gomtsari Alazani valley.

The track up the Pirikiti Alazani valley beyond Chesho, through Parsma and Girevi,

eventually leads to the 3431m Atsunta Pass, a very steep and demanding route over into Khevsureti. The Atsunta is normally open for walkers and pack horses from about early July to mid-September. It's a trek of about five days all the way from Omalo to Shatili in Khevsureti.

Horses are available in Omalo, Shenaqo and Chesho for between 35 GEL and 45 GEL per day.

Wild Georgia (www.wildgeorgia.ge), run by a Tusheti native, the fluent English-speaking Eka Chvritidze, is the main agency specialising in Tusheti tours and treks. Swiss company **Alpin Travel** (www.alpintravel.ch) organises one-week Tusheti heliskiing holidays in February and March for €4850, with accommodation and meals on the Chavchavadze estate at Tsinandali, Kakheti.

🛏 Sleeping & Eating

Tusheti has plenty of guesthouses and homestays, and a few modest 'hotels', all with shared bathrooms. They're open only when the road is open and some don't get going till July. All the following have hot showers (some wood-fired), and nearly all have seat toilets.

OMALO

Hotel Keselo   HOTEL $
(✆598941270, 577472111; arshaulidze@yahoo.com; Kvemo Omalo; per person 20 GEL) The yellow Keselo, at the top of Kvemo (Lower) Omalo, has comfy beds in half a dozen rooms, and reasonable food (meals 10 GEL).

Kamsuri   GUESTHOUSE $
(✆595544111; www.tusheti.ge; Kvemo Omalo; per person 20-25 GEL, with 2/3 meals 40/50 GEL) A recently built, three-storey white house with seven good rooms.

Hotel Tusheti   HOTEL $
(✆599231132; per person 20-30 GEL, half board 60-70 GEL) By the road about 1.5km before you reach Kvemo Omalo, this largeish wooden building has 10 rooms but maintains a homey atmosphere.

Shinay   GUESTHOUSE $$
(✆595262046; hotelshinay@gmail.com; Zemo Omalo; r full board 50 GEL, d/tr with bathroom incl breakfast 120/150 GEL, full board 140/170 GEL) The fanciest place in Tusheti, this stone-and-wood house includes three rooms with private bathrooms.

SHENAQO

Nino & Zauri Imedadze HOMESTAY $
(☑598313055; per person 20 GEL) Clean, basic rooms in a quaint, traditional wooden house, with an outdoor squat toilet. Serves delicious, large meals (10 GEL).

Old Tusheti HOMESTAY $
(☑558272006; per person half board 30 GEL) Host Eldar Buqvaidze cooks up good, plentiful meals and plays the balalaika.

DARTLO

Hotel Samtsikhe HOTEL $
(☑599118993; per person with 1/2/3 meals 35/50/65 GEL) Comprises six houses just above the ruined Russian church at the foot of the village, some with carved wooden balconies and pine-panelled rooms. Beds are comfy.

Hotel Dartlo HOTEL $
(☑598174966; www.dartlo.ge; per person incl 0/2/3 meals 20/40/45 GEL) At the top of the village, with fine views from its balcony. Offers jeep tours.

OTHER VILLAGES

In Chesho, **Qomito** (☑555570512, 591257402; per person 20-25 GEL, with 2/3 meals 40/50 GEL) is a substantial three-storey wooden house, just above a rushing stream. It has four guestrooms, a relaxed atmosphere and horses for rent.

One of the best places in the Gomtsari Alazani valley is **Sargiri** (☑555300221; per person incl 0/2/3 meals 20/40/50 GEL) in Alisgori, just outside Jvarboseli. There are also guesthouses or homestays at Verkhovani and Dochu.

A good stop before or after trips to Tusheti is **Darejan's Guesthouse** (☑599139494; per person full board 50 GEL; @) in Laliskuri, a few kilometres east of Alvani. The friendly English-speaking family here has six big, bright rooms and can pick you up from Alvani and organise Tusheti transport.

ⓘ Information

Tusheti Protected Areas Visitors Centre
(☑577101892; www.apa.gov.ge; ☺10am-6pm) This centre about 1km south of Omalo has plentiful displays, maps and material on Tusheti, and can provide walking route and accommodation information, and help arrange guides, horses (35 GEL to 45 GEL per day) and vehicle transport.

TushetiGuide (http://tushetiguide.org.ge, www.facebook.com/tusheti.guide) Useful pages of a Tusheti tourism NGO.

ⓘ Getting There & Away

When the Abano Pass is open, 4WDs run daily to Tusheti from the central crossroads in Alvani, 22km northwest of Telavi, charging 200 GEL for three or four passengers to Omalo. You can also organise one to bring you back. Try to be at Alvani by 9am; taxis to Alvani from Telavi are 15 GEL. *Marshrutky* from Telavi's old bus station to Alvani (1.30 GEL, 45 minutes) don't start till 8.45am. The spectacular drive to Tusheti takes about 4½ hours.

It's possible to find 4WDs for the same price from Telavi, but make sure your driver knows the road to Tusheti. It has many vertiginous preci-pices and steep hairpin bends – not recommended for any driver who doesn't know it well.

Vanilla Sky (☑32-2428428, www.vanillasky. ge) sometimes operates flights to Omalo in August from Natakhtari airfield near Tbilisi, for around 100 GEL one-way.

KAKHETI

The eastern region of Kakheti (კახეთი) is Georgia's premier wine-producing region. Almost everywhere you go here, you'll be invited to drink a glass of wine and it's easy to find yourself wandering around in a semipermanent mellow haze.

Kakheti is also rich in history and was an independent or semi-independent kingdom for long periods. Here you'll find the incredible monastery complex of Davit Gareja, the picturesque hilltop town of Sighnaghi, and many beautiful churches, castles and mansions around the main town, Telavi.

Telavi თელავი
☑350 / POP 21,000

The largest town in Kakheti, Telavi is set in the vineyard-strewn Alazani valley, between the Gombori Mountains and the Caucasus (visible to the northeast). It's the perfect base for exploring the historical, architectural and viticultural riches of Kakheti.

History

Telavi was one of Georgia's main medieval trade centres, but it was caught in the onslaught of the 13th-century Mongol invasion and then was twice devastated by Persia's Shah Abbas I in the early 17th century (Abbas killed around 60,000 Kakhetians and carted another 100,000 off to Persia). In 1744 Nader Shah of Persia installed the local prince Erekle II in Telavi as ruler of Kakheti. In 1762 Erekle united Kakheti with Kartli, to the west, as a more or less independent state, ruling with a progressive Westernising policy. Erekle still occupies an honoured place in Kakheti annals.

◉ Sights

Batonistsikhe Castle   CASTLE, PALACE
(admission 2 GEL, English- or German-speaking guide 15 GEL; ◷10am-6pm Tue-Sun) Batonistsikhe was the residence of the Kakhetian kings in the 17th and 18th centuries, built when King Archil II transferred his court back to Telavi from Gremi in 1672. Inside the castle yard is a Persian-style palace that was rebuilt by Erekle II, who was born and died here. Its central throne room holds many historical portraits including one of Erekle himself (above the throne).

The castle precinct contains the remains of the dilapidated Archil Church and a single-naved royal chapel, with holes for firearms in the walls, built by Erekle II in 1758. Included in the admission price are an art museum, with Georgian and western European paintings, and a history museum, in ugly modern buildings behind the palace.

🛌 Sleeping

Most places can organise taxi trips around the area's sights and/or wineries at reasonable prices.

TOP CHOICE **Tushishvili Guesthouse**   GUESTHOUSE $
(☎271909, 577756625; www.globalsalsa.com/telavi; Nadikvari 15; per person with/without breakfast 25/20 GEL; @🛜🏊) This welcoming house is an established travellers' favourite and justly so. Hostess Svetlana speaks some English and German, prepares fabulous dinners (with/without meat & wine 15/10 GEL), and is more than helpful in organising local taxi trips and getting transport information. There's even a small pool in the garden.

Guesthouse Nelly   GUESTHOUSE $
(☎272594, 599581820; Chonkadze 11; per person half board 35 GEL; @) The seven big, bright rooms here share three good bathrooms. Nelly cooks excellent Georgian meals with fresh, local ingredients, and the wine flows. Nelly and her husband speak a little English and German, and they have a jeep for tours.

Hotel Rcheuli Marani   HOTEL $$
(☎273030; www.rcheuli.ge; Chavchavadze 154; r incl breakfast 80-100 GEL; ❄@🛜) The best

Kakheti

N   0 _____ 20 km
    0 _____ 12 miles

Telavi

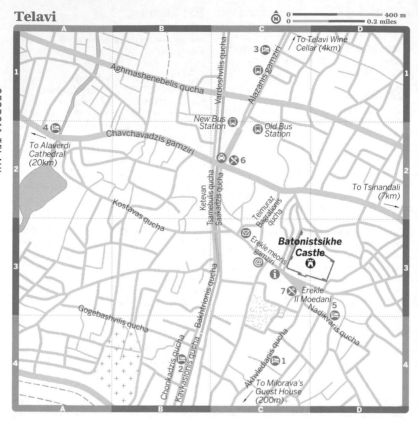

hotel in town is 800m west of the bus stations. Many of the pleasing, carpeted rooms are equipped with big balconies, and prints of paintings by top Georgian artists add a welcome arty touch. The hotel also has the best restaurant in town.

Eto's Guesthouse GUESTHOUSE **$**
(☑277070, 599782050; eto.neka@yahoo.com; Akhvlediani 27; per person 20 GEL; @) This friendly place has four bright, clean rooms sharing a good bathroom and a nice garden where you can sit out under a big apricot tree. Meals (breakfast 5 GEL, dinner 10 GEL) are made from fresh local produce; guests can use the kitchen if they wish.

Milorava's Guest House GUESTHOUSE **$**
(☑271257, 599170047; www.miloravagh.ge; Akhvlediani 67; per person 20 GEL, half board 40 GEL) Can accommodate six or seven people in comfy

beds in a cottage beside the garden. Good meals and an amiable, helpful host.

Hotel Alazani Valley HOTEL **$$**
(☑274144; www.elgitour.ge; Alazanis gamziri 75; incl breakfast r 50-80 GEL, ste 90-100 GEL; ✳@☎) This early-21st-century hotel has a spiffy lobby, comfy if uninspired rooms, friendly English-speaking staff, and a **restaurant** (mains 7-12 GEL) with a wide-ranging Georgian menu.

✗ Eating

Restaurant provision is thin, but if you're in a guesthouse you'll usually eat excellently.

Restaurant Old Marani GEORGIAN, RUSSIAN **$$$**
(Hotel Rcheuli Marani, Chavchavadze 154; mains 7-18 GEL; 🅙) Telavi's best eatery is this brick-cellar hotel restaurant incorporating an old wine cellar. A good range of Georgian and Russian dishes is on offer.

Telavi

◉ **Top Sights**

Batonistsikhe Castle D3

🛏 **Sleeping**

1 Eto's Guesthouse C4
2 Guesthouse Nelly B4
3 Hotel Alazani Valley............................C1
4 Hotel Rcheuli Marani.........................A2
5 Tushishvili Guesthouse.....................D3

🍴 **Eating**

6 Bazari...C2
7 Kafe..C3
Restaurant Old Marani.............. (see 4)

Kafe CAFE $

(Erekle II moedani; mains 4-7 GEL) This spot does good coffee and average *khachapuri,* pizza and *chakapuli.* It's nice to sit at its outside tables on a cool evening.

Bazari MARKET $

(cnr Chavchavadze & Alazanis gamziri; ⊙7am-6pm) Telavi's busy market bursts with fresh produce from the area's villages.

ℹ Information

Internet (Erekle meoris gamziri 3; internet per hr 1.20 GEL; ⊙10am-midnight)

Tourism Information Centre (☎275317; Erekle II moedani 9; ⊙10am-4pm Mon-Fri) Upstairs in a verandahed building on the main square.

ℹ Getting There & Away

Marshrutky to Tbilisi (7 GEL, 1¾ hours) go at least hourly from 6am to about 6pm from a yard below Alazanis gamziri 73. Shared taxis to Tbilisi (10 GEL) wait at the top of Alazanis gamziri.

The **new bus station** (Alazanis gamziri) has *marshrutky* to Lagodekhi (6 GEL, 1¾ hours, 7.30am, 8.30am, 8.40am and 1.30pm), Napareuli (2 GEL, 45 minutes, every one or 1½ hours 8am to 6pm) and Tsnori (4 GEL, 1¼ hours, 7.30am, 7.50am and 8.30am). The old bus station, on a lane opposite the new bus station, has *marshrutky* to Alaverdi Cathedral (1.30 GEL, every half-hour 8.45am to 5.15pm), Tsinandali (0.80 GEL, every half-hour 7.30am to 5pm), Kvareli (3 GEL, 1½ hours, every half-hour 9.30am to 5.30pm) and Sighnaghi (4.50 GEL, 1½ hours, 3pm), and further services to Tsnori (11am, 1.30pm) and Lagodekhi (3pm). For Sighnaghi you can also take a *marshrutka* to Tsnori, then a *marshrutka* or taxi 6km up the hill to Sighnaghi.

Around Telavi

The villages and lovely countryside around Telavi are full of fascinating places to visit. Public transport reaches many of them, but you can pack a lot more into your day by taking a taxi tour. Telavi drivers will take you to several of the following destinations in one trip, calling in at a couple of wineries too, for 60 to 70 GEL. Knowledgeable, English-speaking **David Luashvili** (☎593761216, 551300620; purgatorium@rambler.ru) is a recommended driver-guide.

IKALTO MONASTERY

იყალთოს მონასტერი

This monastery, beautifully situated in a cypress grove 8km northwest of Telavi, was one of two famous medieval Georgian academies, the other being Gelati. Shota Rustaveli, the national poet, is thought to have studied here. The monastery was founded in the 6th century by Zenon, one of the 13 Syrian fathers. Six hundred years later, King David the Builder invited the philosopher Arsen Ikaltoeli to establish an academy here, where the doctrines of Neoplatonism were expounded. In 1616 the complex was devastated by the Persians.

The main **Transfiguration Church** was built in the 8th and 9th centuries, over an earlier church where Zenon was buried. The brick cupola and whitewash were added in the 19th century. To the east, the small **Sameba (Trinity) Church** dates from the 6th century but has been extensively rebuilt over time. Check the interesting small relief of three saints at the top of its facade. The single-naved **Kvelatsminda** (St Mary's Church), to the south, dates from the 12th and 13th centuries. The roofless building behind this was the **Academy**.

Ikalto is 2km uphill from the 'Monastery Ikalto' sign on the Akhmeta road. Alaverdi-bound *marshrutky* will drop you at the turn-off.

ALAVERDI CATHEDRAL

ალავერდის საკათედრო ტაძარი

At the beginning of the 11th century, when Georgia was entering its cultural and political golden age, King Kvirike of Kakheti had a majestic cathedral built – at 50m high it remained the tallest church in Georgia for nearly a millennium. **Alaverdi Cathedral** (⊙8am-7pm), 20km northwest of Telavi, is Kakheti's main spiritual centre. The exterior is classically proportioned with majestic

HARVEST TIME

A very good time to visit Kakheti is during the *rtveli* (grape harvest) from about 20 September to 20 October, when grapes are picked and pressed, to the accompaniment of feasts, musical events and other celebrations. Many accommodation places can organise for you to join in the harvest and the partying.

rounded arches but minimal decoration, typical of Kakhetian churches. Inside, the structure has a beautiful spacious harmony, and light streams in from the 16-windowed cupola. The cathedral was damaged by several earthquakes and a severe 19th-century whitewashing. Some frescoes were uncovered from beneath the whitewash in 1966. Note the 16th-century St George and dragon over the west door. The Virgin and Child above the altar is from the 11th century.

Other buildings in the cathedral compound include the summer palace of Shah Abbas' governor (now restored as the bishop's residence), a bathhouse, a bell tower and the Alaverdi Marani winery (not generally open to visitors).

The September festivities of **Alaverdoba** last three weeks, with people coming from remote mountain areas to worship and celebrate.

GREMI გრემი

This picturesque brick **citadel** (admission to tower 3 GEL; ⊙9am-6pm) stands beside the Telavi–Kvareli road, 19km from Telavi. Kvareli-bound *marshrutky* from Telavi will stop here.

From 1466 to 1672 Gremi was the capital of Kakheti, but all that remains of its market, baths, caravanserai, palace and houses after its devastation by Shah Abbas in 1616 are some not-very-distinctive ruins. The citadel, however, still stands. By the road below it stands a large portrait of the Kakhetian Queen Ketevan, who was tortured to death by Abbas for refusing to renounce Christianity. Within the citadel, the **Church of the Archangels** was built in 1565 by King Levan (who is buried inside) and contains frescoes painted in 1577. You can climb up in the adjacent 15th-century **tower-palace**: a structure in one room was thought to be a bread

oven, but on examination turned out to be a tunnel. Although not yet fully excavated, it's thought to emerge in the yard outside – from where another tunnel leads down to the foot of the walls where in past centuries the Intsoba River flowed.

NEKRESI MONASTERY

ნეკრესის მონასტერი

Nekresi's early Georgian architecture and the views across the vineyard-dotted Alazani valley from its hillside-woodland site are marvellous. The monastery is 4km off the Kvareli road from a turning 10km past Gremi (Kvareli-bound *marshrutky* from Telavi will drop you at the turn-off). Vehicles must park 1.5km before the monastery, but from there *marshrutky* (1 GEL return) shuttle up and down the hill from about 8am to 5pm.

One of the very first Georgian churches was built at Nekresi in the 4th century. In the 6th century one of the 13 Syrian fathers, Abibos, who converted many of the highland Georgians, founded a monastery here. Considerable repair and reconstruction has been done in the last few years.

The first church you reach at the monastery is a three-church basilica from the 8th and 9th centuries, with a plan unique to early Georgian churches, the three naves being divided by solid walls into what are effectively three churches. Nekresi's tiny first church stands in the centre of the complex, immediately above the church shop. It's an extremely small basilica, many times reconstructed, with unusual open arches in the walls. Inside, steps lead down to a lower chapel or vault. Beside this church is a reconstructed 9th-century bishop's palace complete with a *marani* (wine cellar) and a 16th-century tower. Immediately east is the main **Church of the Assumption**, another triple-church basilica from the 6th to 7th centuries, with some 17th-century murals adorning its smoke-blackened interior.

TSINANDALI წინანდალი

This village, home of a famous white wine and site of the **Chavchavadze family estate** (www.tsinandali.com; gardens 2 GEL, museum incl guide in Georgian, English or Russian 5 GEL, incl tasting 1/several wines 7/20 GEL; ⊙10am-7pm), lies 7km southeast of Telavi. Prince Alexander Chavchavadze (1786–1846) was the son of Georgia's first ambassador to Russia and godson of Catherine the Great, and also a poet and antitsarist activist (for which he spent time in exile). His daughter Nino married the Russian poet and diplomat Alexander Griboedov in the family chapel here.

In 1854 Lezgin tribesmen from the Dagestan mountains ransacked the Chavchavadze house, kidnapping 23 women and children. Alexander's son David had to mortgage the house to raise the ransom. The hostages were returned, but David was unable to repay the loan and the house passed to Tsar Alexander III. The main room of the house is now a **museum**, with interesting paintings and photos of people and events associated with the house, including the Lezgin raid. It also stages some good art exhibitions. The tour includes the **Tsinandali Winery**, founded by Alexander's father in part of the 200,000-sq-metre park, which no longer makes wine but has a 16,500-bottle collection dating back to 1814.

The park is beautifully laid out in an English style, with venerable trees and exotic plants such as ginkgo, sequoia and yucca.

AKHALI SHUAMTA & DZVELI SHUAMTA
ახალი შუამთა და ძველი შუამთა

The churches of Akhali (New) Shuamta and Dzveli (Old) Shuamta are fine works of Georgian architecture among beautiful woodlands off the Gombori road west of Telavi.

The convent of **Akhali Shuamta** (⊙9am-7pm), 11km from Telavi, was founded in the 16th century by the Kakhetian Queen Tinatin and is now a convent again after serving as an orphanage in Soviet times. Wait at the inner gate for one of the nuns to greet you and show you the church (some of them speak English). The church has a cruciform design with a high cupola and large crosses inscribed on its extremities. The fine 16th-century frescoes portray Tinatin, her husband King Levan II and their son Alexander, as well as biblical scenes. Tinatin and the poet Alexander Chavchavadze are both buried here.

The three stone churches of **Dzveli Shuamta**, 1.8km up the road past Akhali Shuamta, formed part of a monastery founded way back in the 5th century. Nearest to the road is a three-naved 5th- to 6th-century basilica, in a style typical of the earliest period of Georgian Christianity. The next is a 7th-century tetraconch church with a plan derived from the Jvari Church near Mtskheta.

Third is another tetraconch church from the same period.

Marshrutky to Tetritsklebi leaving Telavi's new bus station at 8am and 2pm can drop you at the Shuamta turn-off, 500m from Akhali Shuamta. A return-trip taxi from Telavi is about 10 GEL.

Sighnaghi სიღნაღი

📞355 / POP 2000

Sighnaghi is the prettiest town in Kakheti, sitting on a hilltop 60km southeast of Telavi and full of 18th- and 19th-century architecture with a distinctly Italianate feel. A big tourism-oriented renovation program has seen a rash of new accommodation and eating options spring up, but the town's original style has been maintained, with handsome galleried houses around a series of appealing plazas.

Sighnaghi has wonderful views over surrounding hills, the Alazani valley and the Caucasus beyond. The town was originally developed in the 18th century by King Erekle II, in part as a refuge for the area's populace against Lezgin and Persian attacks. The name Sighnaghi comes from the Turkish *siğinak* (shelter).

⊙ Sights & Activities

Sighnaghi Museum   MUSEUM

(Rustavelis chikhi 8; admission 3 GEL; ⊙11am-5pm Tue-Sun) This excellent, well-displayed, modern museum has good exhibits on Kakheti archaeology and history, and a room of 16 paintings by the great Kakheti-born artist Pirosmani – the biggest collection of his work after the National Gallery in Tbilisi. Explanatory information is in English as well as Georgian.

Walls & Churches   ARCHITECTURE

Most of Erekle II's 4km-circumference **defensive wall** still stands, with 23 towers and each of its six gates named after a local village. Part of the wall runs along Chavchavadze on the hilltop on the northwest side of town, where you can enter the tiny **Stepan Tsminda Church** inside a tower. The 19th-century **Tsminda Giorgi Church** (Gorgasali) abuts another stretch of wall, lower down on the northeast side of town. A little further down you can climb up inside one **tower** and walk atop the walls down to the gate over the Tsnori road.

Pheasant's Tears   WINERY
(Baratashvili 18; www.pheasantstears.com; 5-wine tasting for groups per person 10 GEL; ⊙10am-7pm or later) This local Georgian-American-Swedish joint venture makes excellent organic wine by the traditional *qvevri* method, in which wine is fermented in clay pots buried underground, and offers tastings for groups at its attractive premises in town (which are also an art gallery and carpet shop). Independent travellers can often be catered for too. It also offers vineyard visits and wine tours.

🛌 Sleeping

Sighnaghi has a few good hotels, and plenty of guesthouses and homestays (with shared bathrooms), several of them on the north side of town on Tsminda Giorgi, which runs west just below the archway at the top of Gorgasali (the Tsnori road).

David Zandarashvili's   GUESTHOUSE $
(Hotel Family; ☑231029, 599750510; davidzandar ashvili@yahoo.com; Tsminda Giorgi 11; per person 20 GEL, incl breakfast & dinner 35 GEL; @🛜) This very hospitable and helpful family provides good rooms, great food and wine, and fine panoramas from the balcony, and is deservedly a travellers' favourite. They are adding rooms with private bathroom too.

Hostel Tura   HOSTEL $
(☑555616611, 568440633; www.facebook.com/hostel.tura, hosteltura.blogspot.com; Kedeli; per person 25 GEL; @🛜) A fun, friendly hostel at Kedeli, 3km south of Sighnagi off the Tbilisi road, Tura is run by young Americans who offer bike rentals (10 GEL per day), occasional cooking evenings and fascinating day trips (see Tura Tours, p100).

Hotel Old Sighnaghi   HOTEL $$
(☑598770101; www.transservice.ge; Dadiani 19; r incl breakfast 70-150 GEL; ⊖✳🛜) In a former carpet factory facing the central Bebris Park, this place has amiable management and attractive brick-walled, wood-beamed rooms with plenty of carpets on the walls. It has a basement restaurant, and a hand-knitted carpet workshop on-site.

Hotel Solomoni 1805   HOTEL $$
(☑231025; solomoni1805@gmail.com; Aghmash-enebelis moedani 1; r incl breakfast US$100; ⊖🛜) A good, modern, central, 13-room hotel, with comfy, thickly carpeted rooms in a classical style. Most have balconies and are well equipped with comforts such as dressing gowns and tea- and coffee-makers. There's also a good Georgian **restaurant** (mains 7-20 GEL; 🍴).

Hotel Maia   GUESTHOUSE $
(☑599554371; Tsminda Giorgi 7; per person 25 GEL, incl breakfast/half board 30/35 GEL) This modest-looking red-brick building has three cosy, good-sized rooms inside, sharing a good bathroom, and beautiful views from the balcony. Guests can use the large, clean kitchen if they wish, and/or learn Georgian cooking.

Hotel Pirosmani   HOTEL $$
(☑243030; www.rcheuli.ge; Aghmashenebelis mo-edani 6; r incl breakfast r 85-175 GEL; ✳) A comfortable central hotel with professional but friendly service; more-expensive rooms have appealing walnut furniture. Also has a good Georgian **restaurant** (mains 8-25 GEL; 🍴).

Nana's Guesthouse   GUESTHOUSE $
(☑599795093; kkshvl@yahoo.com; Sarajishvili 2; per person 20-25 GEL, s/d with private bathroom 30/60 GEL; @🛜) English-speaking Nana Ko-kiashvili has four nice big rooms and wide balconies in her fine old house overlooking the central Bebris Park, and provides good, home-cooked, local food (breakfast/dinner 10/15 GEL).

Bobo Guest House   GUESTHOUSE $
(☑551581950; Aghmashenebeli 20; per person incl breakfast 25 GEL) Just up the hill behind the tourist office, Bobo is a friendly spot with two nice big rooms upstairs in an attractive wooden house.

🍴 Eating & Drinking

Wine World   GEORGIAN $$
(Dadiani 9; mains 6-16 GEL; ⊙lunch & dinner; 🍴) Facing Bebris Park, Wine World has a contemporary setting of music videos and white-brick pillars in which to sample any of 125 wines (7 GEL to 60 GEL per bottle, 4 GEL to 5 GEL for a two-glass tasting), along with salads and trout, quail, pork, chicken or mushroom dishes.

Restaurant Natakhtari   GEORGIAN $$
(Kostava 1; mains 5-12 GEL; ⊙lunch & dinner) A clean, pleasant, brick-and-stone-walled spot serving typical Georgian dishes, starting with *khinkali* at 0.50 GEL each. Carafes of local wine are just 3 GEL.

ℹ Information

Discover Sighnaghi (☑599554371; discover signagi@yahoo.com; Erekle II moedani) Next

KAKHETI WINERIES

Visiting a few of Kakheti's wineries is a must while you're here. Evidence of winemaking in Kakheti goes back about 7000 years, and with 225 sq km of vineyards today, this is a region where wine plays a big part in daily life even by Georgian standards.

Georgian wine always used to taste sweet to Western palates, but Russia's ban on Georgian wine imports in 2006 spurred production of more refined wines using modern technologies, bottled for Western and Asian markets and typically selling at 10 GEL to 20 GEL in Georgian wine shops. Meanwhile, the age-old local method of fermenting wine in *qvevri* (large clay pots buried in the ground) continues unabated, producing quite drinkable, very inexpensive wine that's normally sold in plastic containers. In a *qvevri*, the crushed grapes are fermented for around six months before the juice is drawn off to make wine, and what's left is distilled into the potent, grappa-like *chacha*.

Around 500 of the world's 2000 grape varieties are Georgian, and 38 of them are used in commercial production today. The most widely used are the white Rkatsiteli and Mtsvane, and the red Saperavi. The fragrant white Kisi grape, grown only around three villages near Alvani, has a growing band of fans. Some European grapes are now grown too, so you may come across blends such as Saperavi-Merlot or Rkatsiteli-Chardonnay.

Kakheti's five main appellations of origin are Tsinandali, producing a dry white from Rkatsiteli grapes mixed with 15% to 20% Mtsvane; Mukuzani (quality dry Saperavi reds); Kindzmarauli (dry and semisweet Saperavi reds); Akhasheni (dry Saperavi reds); and Napareuli (whites and Saperavi reds).

Many Kakheti wineries welcome visitors for tours and tastings, and some even have hotels or guesthouses. It's generally best to call ahead, in the morning or the day before, to arrange tastings. Here are five recommended and varied wineries in the Telavi area:

Nikolaishvili Winery (Tsinandlis Edemi; ✆350-235200, 599260215; nik.nikolaishvili@gmail.com; Tsinandali; tasting 5 GEL; ☉daily) This small, family-run winery in Tsinandali village, 7km southeast of Telavi, makes Kakhetian wine in *qvevri* and 'European' wine in wooden casks. It has a pretty garden and several **rooms** (per person full board 70 GEL; ☎) with shared bathrooms, making an excellent, relaxed choice for those who want to stay and get a feel for Kakhetian wine traditions. Georgian cooking lessons available too.

Telavi Wine Cellar (Telavis Ghvinis Marani; ✆350-236111; www.tewincel.com; Kurgelauri; tour & tasting per person €11; ☉10am-4pm Mon-Fri) A relatively small-scale operation producing good wines under the Marani, Kondoli and Satrapezo labels by varied techniques: stainless-steel tanks, oak vats and *qvevri*. About 4km northeast of central Telavi on the Kvareli road.

Shumi (✆350-275333; factory@shumi.ge; Tsinandali; ☉10am-6pm Mon-Fri) A popular smallish winery with a good little wine museum.

Twins Old Cellar (✆350-270337, 599186414; www.cellar.ge; Napareuli; tour & tasting 10 GEL) A family-run operation making *qvevri* wine, a 23km drive north of Telavi. Call the winemaker, **Beqa** (✆595337688) beforehand. A hotel (rooms including breakfast 50 GEL to 100 GEL) has eight good, wood-beamed rooms overlooking vineyards.

Schuchmann (✆790557045; www.schuchmann-wines.com; Kisiskhevi; tour & tasting per person 35 GEL, incl lunch 60 GEL) A quality modern operation 5km southeast of central Telavi, founded by a German wine connoisseur and producing wine under the Schuchmann and Vinoterra labels. It has a nice hotel (rooms including breakfast 170GEL to 240 GEL, suites 330 GEL to 450 GEL).

You'll find plentiful information on Georgian wine at www.winetours.ge.

door to the Tourism Information Centre, this agency offers trips in the area including a three-winery outing with tasting of 10 wines for 120 GEL to 150 GEL, for up to four people.

Internet cafe (Dadiani 9; internet per hr 2 GEL; ⊙10.30am-11pm) Sharing a courtyard with Wine World, this spacious facility also stages art exhibitions.

Tourism Information Centre (☑232414, 535532414; Erekle II moedani; ⊙10am-7pm)

Tura Tours (☑555616611, 568440633; www. facebook.com/hostel.tura, hosteltura.blogspot. com) Based at Hostel Tura, these people make fascinating day trips to little-known destinations around eastern Kakheti, including isolated cave monasteries and the Vashlovani Protected Areas with their desertlike landscape, canyons and mud volcanoes. Prices from 25 GEL to 100 GEL per person, depending on trip and numbers.

❶ Getting There & Away

Marshrutky depart from the yard behind the police station on Erekle II moedani. Destinations include Tbilisi (6 GEL, 1¾ hours, six daily), Telavi (4.50 GEL, 1½ hours, 9.15am Monday to Saturday) and Tsnori (1 GEL, 30 minutes, every half-hour 9.45am to 5.45pm Monday to Friday). From Tsnori, *marshrutky* run to Telavi about six times daily, and to Lagodekhi about hourly, 9am to 8pm.

Around Sighnaghi

BODBE CONVENT ბოდბის მონასტერი
Bodbe Convent is 2km south of Sighnaghi, an enjoyable walk on country roads. Set among tall cypresses, the convent is dedicated to St Nino, who is buried here. The little church was originally built, over the saint's grave, by King Mirian in the 4th century. It has been rebuilt and renovated several times since. Nino's tomb, partly silver-covered, with a bejewelled turquoise cloisonné halo, is in a small chapel in its southeast corner. The murals were painted in 1823 by Bishop John Maqashvili. Through an opening in a wall just northeast of the church, and then down a steep path of 800m, you can reach a small chapel built over St Nino's Spring, which burst forth after she prayed on this spot. Pilgrims queue up to drink and splash themselves with the holy water.

MIRZAANI მირზაანი
Fans of the artist Pirosmani will enjoy a trip to his childhood home, now the **Niko Pirosmanashvili State Museum** (admission 3 GEL; ⊙10am-5pm Tue-Sun), in Mirzaani, 10km south of Sighnaghi. Paintings by Pirosmani and other Georgian artists, plus a collection of handmade carpets, are on view. Take a taxi.

Davit Gareja დავით გარეჯა

On the border with Azerbaijan, Davit (or David) Gareja (or Gareji) is one of the most remarkable of Georgia's historic sites, and makes a great day trip from Tbilisi, Sighnaghi or Telavi. Comprising about 15 old monasteries spread over a remote area, its uniqueness is heightened by a lunar, semidesert landscape that turns green and blooms with flowers in early summer. Two of the key monasteries, and the most visited, are Lavra (the only inhabited one today), and, on the hill above it, Udabno, which has beautiful frescoes.

Lavra, the first monastery here, was founded by Davit Gareja, one of the 13 ascetic Syrian fathers who returned from the Middle East to spread Christianity in Georgia in the 6th century. The religious complex grew until monasteries were spread over a wide area. Manuscripts were translated and copied, and a celebrated Georgian school of fresco painting flourished here. The monasteries were destroyed by the Mongols in 1265, revived in the early 14th century by Giorgi V the Brilliant, sacked by Timur, and then suffered their worst moment of all on Easter night 1615 when Shah Abbas' soldiers killed 6000 monks and destroyed many of their artistic treasures. The monasteries never regained their former importance, though they remained operational until the end of the 19th century. During the Soviet era the area was used for military exercises and the monasteries were neglected and vandalised. The Lavra monastery has since seen a good deal of restoration and is now again inhabited by monks.

It takes two to three hours to explore Lavra and Udabno at a leisurely pace. Entrance to both is free.

LAVRA
The Lavra monastery is on three levels, with buildings dating from many periods. The watchtower and outer walls are from the 18th century. You enter by a gateway decorated with reliefs illustrating stories of the monks' harmony with the natural world. Inside you descend to a courtyard with the caves of Davit and his Kakhetian disciple Lukiane along one side, and the 6th-century cave church **Peristsvaleba** (Transfiguration

Church) on the other side. Inside the Perists-valeba are the tombs of Davit (on the right), Lukiane and another Kakhetian companion, Dodo. Some of the caves in the rock above those of Davit and Lukiane are inhabited by monks, so you should avoid making too much noise.

UDABNO

To reach Udabno, take the uphill path beside the church shop outside Lavra. Watch out for poisonous vipers on this route, including in the caves and especially from April to June. When you come level with a watchtower overlooking Lavra, take the path straight up the hill. In about 10 minutes you reach a metal railing. Follow this to the top of the ridge, then along the far side of the ridge (where the railing deteriorates to a series of posts). The plains now spread below you are in Azerbaijan, and the caves above the path are the Udabno monastery. Some still contain 10th- to 13th-century frescoes, the most outstanding being about halfway along the hillside. Fifty metres past the cave numbered 50 in green paint, a side path heads up and back to cave No 36, the monastery's **refectory**, where the monks had to kneel to eat at low stone tables. It's decorated with beautiful light-toned frescoes, the principal one being an 11th-century Last Supper. Further up above here are the **Annunciation Church** (cave 42), with very striking frescoes in blacks, blues and yellows showing Christ and his disciples; and **St George's Church** (cave 41). Return down to the main path and continue 20m to the left to Udabno's **main church**. Paintings here show Davit Gareja and Lukiane surrounded by deer, depicting the story that deer gave them milk when they were wandering hungry in this remote wilderness. Below them are Kakhetian princes.

The path eventually climbs to a stone chapel on the hilltop, then heads down past a cave known as Davit's Tears (with a spring inside) and the top of Lavra monastery, to the watchtower you passed earlier. The monks' water-channel system enabled them to grow gardens and make wine.

❶ Getting There & Away

There's no public transport to the remote site, but a taxi day trip costs around 120 GEL from Tbilisi, or 100 GEL from Sighnaghi (about two hours' drive from either place). You can save a bit by taking a *marshrutka* to Sagarejo on the Tbilisi–Sighnaghi road, then a taxi from there to Davit Gareja (50 GEL to 60 GEL return trip).

Lagodekhi Protected Areas ლაგოდეხის დაცული ტერიტორიები

This remote, 244-sq-km **nature reserve** (www.apa.gov.ge) climbs to heights of over 3000m in the Caucasus, above the small town of Lagodekhi in Kakheti's far eastern corner. If you're heading this way to or from Azerbaijan, it's a worthwhile stop. The reserve features deep river valleys, alpine lakes and some of Georgia's best-preserved forests. There are good day hikes to waterfalls, and from July to September a 25km trail is open from Lagodekhi to Lake Khala-Khel on the Russian border (three days return trip, with an ascent of 2500m). Information is available at the helpful, English-speaking **visitors centre** (☏577101890; Vashlovani 197; ☺8am-10pm) at the park entrance, 2km up from the main road in Lagodekhi. It also rents tents (per day 10 GEL), sleeping bags (5 GEL) and horses (50 GEL).

Lagodekhi has several decent accommodation options. **Hotel Lagodekhi** (☏555380126; Iras Bakhtan; r incl breakfast 50 GEL) is on the central square; **Hotel Lile** (☏599580963; Aghmashenebeli 93; per person 25 GEL, half board 45 GEL) is 600m from the visitors centre (with shared bathrooms); and the **visitors centre** (r 50-70 GEL) itself has a guest kitchen.

Marshrutky leave Lagodekhi's bus station for Tbilisi (7 GEL, 2½ hours, 14 daily) and Telavi (6 GEL, 1¾ hours, five daily). For Sighnaghi take a taxi (25 GEL), or a Tbilisi-bound *marshrutka* to Tsnori (5 GEL, 30 minutes) then a *marshrutka* or taxi 6km up the hill to Sighnaghi.

A taxi to or from the Azerbaijan border at **Matsimi**, 4km southeast of Lagodekhi, costs 4 GEL. From the Azerbaijan side of the border you can take a taxi to Balakan (AZN4) or Zaqatala (around AZN10) – sharing is possible. You'll find moneychangers on the Georgian side of the border only. There's a **Liberty Bank ATM** (Qiziki 23) in Lagodekhi.

SAMTSKHE-JAVAKHETI

The tongue-twisting southern flank of Georgia is a highly scenic region whose biggest attractions are the spectacular cave city of Vardzia and beautiful Borjomi-Kharagauli

National Park, which offers some of the best hiking in Georgia. Landscapes are very varied, from the alpine forests and meadows around Borjomi and Bakuriani to the bare volcanic canyons of the Vardzia area.

Historically known as Meskheti, Samtskhe-Javakheti (სამცხე-ჯავახეთი) was part of Tao-Klarjeti, a cradle of medieval Georgian culture that extended well into what's now northeast Turkey. Tao-Klarjeti fell under Ottoman rule from the 1550s to the 1870s, was briefly part of independent Georgia after the Russian Revolution, and was then divided between Turkey and Bolshevik Georgia in 1921.

Javakheti is the more elevated southeastern half of Samtskhe-Javakheti. Bordering Armenia, it has a majority Armenian population, a struggling economy and rumblings of political discontent, with calls for more local autonomy.

Borjomi ბორჯომი

📋 367 / POP 14,000

Famous throughout the former Soviet Union for its salty-sour, love-it-or-hate-it fizzy mineral water, Borjomi is a likeable little resort town in the very green valley of the swift Mtkvari River, 850m above sea level. The town dates from 1829, when some soldiers discovered a health-giving mineral spring here. A Russian governor of the Caucasus, Count Vorontsov, developed Borjomi as a resort, one that became particularly fashionable after Duke Mikhail Romanov (brother of Tsar Alexander II) took a liking to it. In the 1890s Duke Mikhail built a summer residence, the Likani Palace, 2km west of Borjomi's centre. It's now a Georgian presidential residence.

After the USSR collapsed, Borjomi's flow of visitors slowed to a trickle, but things have looked up since the town's facilities were smartened up a few years ago. It's popular with Georgians coming to imbibe the waters and with people visiting the Borjomi-Kharagauli National Park, right on Borjomi's doorstep. Borjomi is also a good jumping-off point for Vardzia.

The main street, Rustaveli, runs along the northern bank of the Mtkvari. Just before you reach the heart of town (coming from the Tbilisi direction), a white suspension bridge crosses the river to the southern half of town, where Borjomi Park train station and the mineral water park are. Rustaveli becomes Meskheti 300m west of the bridge, continuing 300m more to the bus station and then a further 1km to the national park visitors centre.

⊙ Sights

Mineral Water Park PARK
(9 Aprili; admission Jun-Sep 0.50 GEL, Oct-May free; ⊙6am-midnight Jun-Sep, 9am-10pm Oct-May) Borjomi's mineral water park occupies a narrow, wooded valley and is a lovely place to walk. This was where the original mineral spring was discovered, and named Yekaterinsky Spring after the governor's daughter, who was cured here. The park itself dates from 1850. To reach it, cross the little Borjomula River just east of Borjomi Park station, turn right along 9 Aprili and go 600m. Warm mineral water flows from taps in a pavilion straight in front of the entrance (you can fill bottles with it). Most of the park's facilities – cafes, funfair attractions, a cinema and a cable car (1 GEL each way) which will carry you up to a hilltop Ferris wheel – only operate from about late June to early September. If you walk about 3km upstream through the park, you'll find a small, natural, spring-fed swimming pool with a constant temperature of about 27°C.

A second public **mineral-water spring** (this one cold) emerges inside a metal cage over the Borjomula River just outside the park: cross the footbridge opposite 9 Aprili 46, then go left for about 40m. The Borjomi bottling plants draw their water from other mineral springs – there are about 40 in the area.

Borjomi Museum of Local Lore MUSEUM
(Tsminda Nino 5; admission 3 GEL, tour in English or Hebrew 15 GEL; ⊙10am-7pm Jun-Sep, to 5pm Oct-May) Housed in the former Romanov offices, off the western end of Rustaveli, the diverse collection includes the first-ever bottle of Borjomi mineral water (1890) and other displays on the waters, plus china and glass from the Romanov palace, and sizeable exhibits of stuffed wildlife and historical paintings (mostly Soviet).

🛏 Sleeping

Borjomi has a handful of hotels, and more than 100 guesthouses and homestays (with shared bathrooms).

Hotel Borjomi HOTEL $$
(📋222212; Tsminda Nino 3; r 60-110 GEL, incl breakfast 70-120; ✲🖥) Next to the museum, this

Samtskhe-Javakheti

characterful and well-managed small hotel occupies an attractive tsarist-era mansion. The rooms are carpeted and spacious, and most have fans as well as air-con.

Hotel Victoria
GUESTHOUSE $

(📞222631, 593120283; Kostava 31; per person 20 GEL; @🛜) Has four excellent-value rooms with pine floors and walls on the top floor – three doubles and one for six. No food available, though. It's 200m up the hill from the south side of the suspension bridge.

Marina Zulmatashvili's Homestay
HOMESTAY $

(📞222323, 598184550; Shroma 2; per person with/without breakfast 25/20 GEL; ♨@🛜) One of the best homestays, in a welcoming, cosy house with three upstairs guestrooms. From the south side of the suspension bridge, follow Kostava until it bends left downhill. Here fork right along an unpaved street, turn right at the end, then take the first left. The

house is 60m along on the left. If full, they can find you rooms in other houses nearby.

Borjomis Kheoba
HOTEL $$

(📞223072; www.borjomiskheoba.com; Rustaveli 107A; s/d US$53/80, incl breakfast US$65/90, full board US$75/100; 🛜❄) Sharing its building with a medical centre and spa (run separately), this good modern hotel has an indoor pool and a gym (both open to hotel guests only), restaurant and bar. The comfy rooms boast top-end touches such as toiletries, hairdryers and heated towel rails.

Leo's Homestay
HOMESTAY $

(📞220018, 593981595; jango.geo@gmail.com; Pirosmani 18; per person with/without breakfast 25/20 GEL; 🛜) The English-speaking son of the family, Levan, loves hosting travellers and showing them lost fortresses and other little-known places around Borjomi. His mum serves up terrific breakfasts. Up to three rooms are available in their simple house (head up Tabidze beside the Aversi pharmacy on Rustaveli, and ask directions). Guests can also use the kitchen. Search 'Leo's Homestay' on Facebook.

Borjomi Hostel　　　　　　　　HOSTEL $
(☑222387, 558595580; Kostava 17; www.facebook. com/borjomihostel, www.borjomihostel.com; dm/d 20/60 GEL; @☎) A popular little hostel facing the Kostava Garden, a short walk south of the suspension bridge.

Saojakho Hotel　　　　　　　　HOTEL $$
(☑220780; Kostava 2; r 60 GEL) A small, family-run hotel between Borjomi Park station and the suspension bridge. Rooms are cosy and recently decorated, and some have balconies. No food, though.

✖ Eating

Taverna Nia　　　　　　　　GEORGIAN $$
(Robakidze 1A; mains 5-15 GEL; ☺lunch & dinner; 🗐) In a two-storey house with attractive wooden balconies, just west from the south end of the suspension bridge, Nia serves excellent Georgian cuisine, including meat and cheese from the owners' farm. It's popular with locals and can be packed on holidays.

Merabico's　　　　　　　　GEORGIAN $
(Kostavas Baghi; mains 5-7 GEL) This small eatery in the park opposite Borjomi Park station does presentable *mtsvadi*, trout, *khachapuri* and salads. It's nice to sit on its roof terrace with a draft beer (1.50 GEL). It closes about 9pm.

Inka Cafe　　　　　　　　CAFE $$
(9 Aprili 2; khachapuri or pizza 8-13 GEL; ☜) This smart, wood-panelled cafe, with sepia-tint photos of Tsarist-era Borjomi, does real coffee (4 GEL) and reasonable light meals and cakes.

Pesvebi　　　　　　　　GEORGIAN $
(Borjomi Park station; mains 4-10 GEL; 🗐) A largeish restaurant in the station building, serving good Georgian dishes in something of a party atmosphere in the evenings, when there's live music and dancing.

❶ Information

Internet cafe (Rustaveli 26; per hr 2 GEL; ☺10am-10pm) Next to the tourist office.

Tourist Information Centre (☑221397; Rustaveli; ☺10am-9pm Jun-Oct, to 6pm Nov-May) Helpful and informative, in a glass pavilion near the north side of the suspension bridge.

❶ Getting There & Away

From Borjomi's **bus station** (Meskheti 8) there are *marshrutky* to Tbilisi (8 GEL, three hours, 14 daily), Akhaltsikhe (4 GEL, one hour, about hourly), Bakuriani (3 GEL, one hour, eight daily), Gori (5 GEL, 1½ hours, 7.30am and 10.45am) and Batumi (17 GEL, five hours, 9am). Frequent *marshrutky* also run to Khashuri (2 GEL, 30 minutes, every 30 minutes 9.30am to 5.30pm), 32km northeast of Borjomi, where you can change for Tbilisi, Kutaisi, Zugdidi or Batumi.

From about June to September a *marshrutka* normally runs a day trip to Vardzia (30 GEL return), leaving Borjomi bus station at 8.45am and stopping at other sights such as Khertvisi Fortress en route. You can confirm schedules, and book seats, at the tourist office.

Slow *elektrichka* trains from Borjomi Park station, just east of the suspension bridge, leave for Tbilisi (2 GEL, 4¾ hours) at 7am and 4.40pm.

Borjomi-Kharagauli National Park ბორჯომ-ხარაგაულის ეროვნული პარკი

The ranges of the Lesser Caucasus in southern Georgia are less well known and less high than the Great Caucasus, but they still contain some very beautiful and wild country. Borjomi-Kharagauli National Park provides the perfect chance to get out into this landscape. The park spreads over more than 850 sq km of forested hills and alpine meadows up to 2642m high, north and west of Borjomi.

The park is crisscrossed by nine walking trails of various lengths, most of them well marked and some suitable for horses as well as hikers. Most trails are open from May to October or November. Overnight accommodation is available at five basic shelters, and camping is also possible. Park wildlife includes about 90 brown bears.

The **park office and visitors centre** (☑367-222117, 577101857; www.nationalpark.ge, www.ata.ge, greenborjomi@gmail.com; Meskheti 23, Borjomi; ☺10am-7pm Mon-Fri, to 4pm Sat & Sun, closed Sat & Sun Nov-Mar) is 1km west of central Borjomi (2 GEL by taxi). It provides a free trail map, issues the free permits you need for visiting the park, and can furnish all the information you need, including on horse rentals (50 GEL per day) and drinking water sources along the trails. You can pay here for any nights in the park, and rent tents (10 GEL per night) and sleeping bags

(5 GEL per night). Park permits are also available at Marelisi, just outside the park's northern boundary.

Trail 1 (Likani to Marelisi) is a 40km, three-day route crossing the park from south to north via Mt Lomis Mta (2187m). A taxi from Borjomi to its start (2km off the Borjomi–Akhaltsikhe road) should be 5 GEL. A popular day route of five or six hours, with an ascent of 800m, follows Trail 1 up to a clearing about 1760m high, then turns down Trail 6 to come out on the Akhaltsikhe road at Qvabiskhevi. Don't miss the turning (next to a large park map) where Trail 1 heads off left uphill from the vehicle track that you have followed for the walk's first 2.7km or so.

You can make Trails 1 and 6 into a two-day hike by continuing up Trail 1 to the Lomis Mta tourist shelter for the night. The longest and hardest route is Trail 2 (Atskuri to Marelisi), a north–south route of 50km taking three or four days.

🛌 Sleeping & Eating

Four basic wooden **tourist shelters** (per person 10 GEL) provide accommodation inside the park. They have spring water but you need to carry a sleeping bag, food and cooking gear. You can also sleep at the ranger shelter near the park's highest point, Mt Sametskhvareo, but there's no water there. **Camping** (per person 5 GEL) is allowed around the shelters, or at the park entrances at Qvabiskhevi, Atskuri and Marelisi.

The park has partner guesthouses in some villages around its periphery, providing convenient accommodation before or after park visits. They include **Marelisi Guesthouse** (✑599951421; per person full board 53 GEL) at Marelisi, recommended for its excellent food; **Nick & George Guesthouse** (✑599916237; maitsuradze@mail.ru; per person 30 GEL, meals each 10-20 GEL) at Atskuri, with horse rides; and two places at Likani, 2km west of the park office: **Hotel Mostioni** (Hotel Motion; ✑367-221999, 599170403; motionge@mail.ru; Meskheti 54, Likani; per person full board 60-70 GEL) and **Hotel Villa Likani** (✑367-223413; www.villalikani.com; Meskheti 56, Likani; per person full board 80 GEL; 🛜).

ℹ️ Getting There & Away

Marshrutky running between Borjomi and Akhaltsikhe will drop you off or pick you up at the turn-offs for the park's Likani, Qvabiskhevi or Atskuri entry points. The first two are about 2km off the Borjomi–Akhaltsikhe road, the third about 500m.

Marelisi village is 4km south of Marelisi station on the Tbilisi–Kutaisi railway (3½ hours from Tbilisi, with three trains daily in each direction).

Bakuriani ბაკურიანი
✑367 / POP 2700

Thirty kilometres up a winding road through pine-clad hills southeast of Borjomi, Bakuriani is the cheaper and more locally popular and family-oriented of Georgia's two main ski resorts. Bakuriani has a mountain-village atmosphere and the area is also good for mountain walks in summer.

Approaching the centre of town from Borjomi, you'll turn right (south) up the main street, Tavisupleba. After 500m Tamar Mepe turns right to the bus station, 120m away, and Tavisupleba continues as Aghmashenebeli. There's an informative **Tourism Information Centre** (✑240037; bakuriani.cenn.org; Aghmashenebeli 2; internet per hr 2 GEL; ☉10am-6pm Mon-Fri) at this corner, with internet available and a good map for sale showing day walks.

The ski season usually lasts from mid-December to late March. The main runs are **Didveli**, 1.8km long with a cable car (5 GEL), on the south side of town, and **Kokhta Gora** on the east side, 1.2km long with a chairlift, which was due to reopen for the 2012 season after modernisation. The **Otsdokhutmetriani** beginners' slopes, with toboggan as well as ski runs, are closer to the centre. Ski- or snowboard-gear rental costs 15 to 25 GEL per day at the lifts, but you can get older gear for around 8 GEL in town. Snowboards may be in short supply. Taxis to the lifts (8 GEL to Didveli) have ski racks. Instruction costs around 20 GEL per hour.

🛌 Sleeping & Eating

In the ski season almost every house in Bakuriani has rooms to let, for as little as 10 GEL per person. Many guesthouses and small and large hotels are scattered around the centre, up Aghmashenebeli, and along a ring road leading out to Kokhta Gora. Many close outside the ski season though plenty are open in July and August. The following are all smaller establishments with a friendly welcome.

Hotel New House   HOTEL **$$**
(✑599201720; www.bakuriani-newhouse.ge, in Georgian; newhousebakuriani@gmail.com; Tavisupleba 29;

d/with full board ski season US$50/100, summer 50/100 GEL; ☎) Just off the main street, New House has a log fire in the lobby-cum-lounge, pleasant, clean rooms with polished wood floors, and table tennis downstairs. It's open all year.

Hotel Apollon HOTEL **$$**
(☎599571108; www.apollon.ge; Aghmashenebeli 21; per person full board ski season US$45-65, other seasons US$35-40; ☎) Very comfy, pine-floored rooms with balconies and comfortable wooden beds, satisfying meals in a cosy dining room, and billiards and table tennis for your spare moments. It's 800m up the hill from the centre, and open all year.

Edelweiss Guest House GUESTHOUSE **$$**
(☎599506349; www.welcome.ge/edelweiss; Mta 19; r full board summer 50-60 GEL) Just 200m west (up the hill) from the bus station, this has good, spacious rooms. It sometimes closes in the shoulder seasons between summer and ski time.

Most visitors eat at their accommodation but there are several cafes and bars along Tavisupleba/Aghmashenebeli. A pleasant log-cabin-style spot, **Teremok** (Tavisupleba 19; mains 6-15 GEL; 📖) has a huge choice of Russian and Ukrainian food, from pancakes and *vareniki* (meat or cheese dumplings) to hearty meat dishes.

❶ Getting There & Away

Marshrutky run to Borjomi (3 GEL, one hour) at least four times daily (the last not before 5pm), and to Tbilisi (11 GEL, four hours) at least three times. In the ski season services are more frequent. A taxi to or from Borjomi costs 25 GEL.

Slow but scenic trains run to Bakuriani (2 GEL, 2½ hours) from Borjomi's Chyornaya Rechka station (2km east of Borjomi centre) at 7.15am and 11.15am, returning from Bakuriani at 10.10am and 2.10pm.

Akhaltsikhe ახალციხე

📞365 / POP 17,000

The capital and biggest town of Samtskhe-Javakheti, Akhaltsikhe means 'New Castle' in Georgian. In fact the castle that dominates the town dates from the 12th century. The local power here from the 13th to 17th centuries was the Jakeli family, but from 1688 to 1828 it was the centre of a *pashalik* (an Ottoman administrative area governed by a *pasha*). Today Akhaltsikhe has a sizeable

Armenian population. Little of its Soviet-era industry remains. For travellers, Akhaltsikhe is mainly a staging post towards the cave city at Vardzia.

The bus station is on a square on the north side of the Potskhovi River. Cross the bridge over the river and bear right at two forks and you'll be on the main street, Kostava.

◉ Sights

Rabati OLD TOWN
A wander around Akhaltsikhe's *rabati* (old town), with its multicultural architecture, is worthwhile. The district is on a hill on the north side of the Potskhovi, immediately northwest of the bridge. Rare examples of *darbazebi* (traditional Georgian houses) cluster around the castle, which houses, among other things, a mosque from 1752, the ruins of a *medrese* (Islamic school), and the **Ivane Javakhishvili Samtskhe-Javakheti History Museum** (admission 3 GEL, tour in English 10 GEL; Kharischirashvili 1; ⊙10am-5pm Tue-Sun). The museum spans the millennia with jewellery, pottery, manuscripts, coins, weaponry, clothing and a large collection of century-old carpets. The guided tour brings it more alive. The *rabati* also has a synagogue, an Armenian church and a Catholic church.

🛏 Sleeping

Hotel Prestizhi HOTEL **$$**
(☎593937125; prestige.hot@mail.ru; Rustaveli 76; r 40-60 GEL; @) About 1km east of the centre on the Vardzia road, the Prestizhi has good, big, comfy rooms with large paintings in reasonable taste. Rooms facing away from the street have balconies. Breakfast and dinner available.

Hotel Rio HOTEL **$$**
(☎593276169; www.riohotelakhaltsikhe.com; Akhalkalaki Hwy 1; r US$37-62; @🛜🏊) Near the river on the east side of town, the almost-new Rio offers spotless rooms and a decent restaurant. The lovely-looking indoor pool is however not always operational.

Hotel Meskheti HOTEL **$**
(☎220420; Kostava 10; r 30 GEL) This ancient ex-Intourist hotel is cheap, central and decent value. The rooms are moderately comfortable, with hot showers.

✖ Eating

Pizzeria S&L PIZZERIA **$$**
(Rustaveli 120; pizza 8-15 GEL; ⊙lunch & dinner) The pizzas at this barlike eatery, 400m east

of Hotel Prestizhi, are probably the best feeds you'll get in Akhaltsikhe. You might as well go for the pizza S&L (with everything). More-traditional Georgian fare is served downstairs.

Paemani CAFE $
(Kostava 41; mains 2-8 GEL) A bright spot for *khachapuri* and beer almost opposite Hotel Meskheti, with glass tables, shiny chrome chairs and restrained background music.

ⓘ Getting There & Away

The busy **bus station** (Tamarashvili) has *marshrutky* to Borjomi (4 GEL, one hour, 16 daily), Tbilisi (12 GEL, four hours, 14 daily), Batumi via Khashuri (20 GEL, six hours, 8.30am and 11.30am), Kutaisi (10 GEL, 3½ hours, four daily), Vardzia (4 GEL, 1½ hours, 10.30am, 12.20pm, 4pm and 5.30pm) and, in Armenia, Gyumri (18 GEL, four hours, 7am) and Yerevan (25 GEL, seven hours, 7.30am). For Turkey via the Vale–Posof border crossing, 20km southwest of Akhaltsikhe, Özlem Ardahan runs a daily bus (departing 2pm at research time) to Istanbul (US$50, 24 hours) via Ardahan (US$20, three hours), Erzurum and Ankara; Koch Ardahan has two further buses at variable times to Ardahan. *Marshrutky* run from Akhaltsikhe to Vale (1 GEL, 15 minutes, about hourly till 5pm), 7km before the border, but there's no public transport except taxis for the 20km between Vale and Posof (Turkey).

At research time there was no direct service west to Batumi by the scenic road through the Adjara mountains, but this may change when a major upgrade of the Goderdzi Pass section is completed (due by 2012). Meanwhile, from about May to September, if you can get to Adigeni, 28km west of Akhaltsikhe, by 9am, you should be able to pick up the daily Abastumani–Batumi *marshrutka* there (it leaves Abastumani at 8.30am).

Vardzia ვარძია

The 60km drive into the wilderness from Akhaltsikhe to the cave city of Vardzia is as dramatic as any in Georgia outside the Great Caucasus. The road follows the course of the upper Mtkvari, passing through narrow canyons and then veering south at Aspindza along a particularly beautiful valley cutting like a green ribbon between arid, rocky hillsides. There are several places of interest along the way: taxi drivers are often happy to stop at one or two of them for no extra charge. It's possible to see Vardzia in a day trip from Akhaltsikhe or Borjomi, but the

Vardzia area is a magical one, and an overnight (or longer) stay is well worthwhile.

Forty-five kilometres from Akhaltsikhe you reach the impressive 10th- to 14th-century **Khertvisi Fortress**, where the road to Akhalkalaki and Armenia diverges east from the Vardzia road. From the fortress's west end a steep tunnel (negotiable with care) leads down towards the Paravani River on its north side – probably once used both for water supplies and as an emergency escape route.

Two kilometres past Khertvisi, over above the west side of the Mtkvari, are the **Gelsunda Caves**, a medieval cave-dwelling complex with some unusual stone doors. Another 6km brings you to a stone enclosure beside the road, which is an old **slave market and caravanserai**. Almost opposite is the turning to the village of Nakalakevi, whose name means 'a city used to be here'. The city in question was **Tsunda**, capital of Javakheti until the 9th century, whose remains are actually just east of the north end of Tmogvi village, 1km further along the road. It's worth stopping to see Tsunda's beautifully ornamented 12th-century **Church of St John the Baptist**, with, curiously enough, a medieval stone lavatory next to it.

Two kilometres beyond Tmogvi village, atop a high rocky hill on the other side of the river (which flows far below in a gorge), is the near-impregnable **Tmogvi Castle**, which was already an important fortification by the 10th century. About 2km past this, up to the left of the road, is **Vanis Qvabebi** (Vani Caves), a cave monastery that predated Vardzia by four centuries, with a maze of tunnels inside the rock. Long abandoned, it's almost as intriguing as Vardzia itself and far less visited. If you want to get up to the little white domed church high up the cliff, ask for keys at the office at Vardzia. Tmogvi Castle and Vanis Qvabebi both make great half-day walks from Vardzia; from Tmogvi you can even continue north on marked trails as far as Gelsunda.

The cave city of **Vardzia** (admission 3 GEL, Georgian- or Russian-speaking guide 15 GEL; ☉9am-6pm), 2km past Vanis Qvabebi, is a cultural symbol with a special place in the hearts of Georgians. King Giorgi III built a fortification here in the 12th century, and his daughter, Queen Tamar, established a monastery that grew into a virtual holy city housing perhaps 2000 monks, renowned as a spiritual bastion of Georgia and of

Christendom's eastern frontier. The remarkable feature of Vardzia as it developed in Tamar's reign was that the inhabitants lived in dwellings carved from the rock and ranging over 13 floors. Altogether there are 119 cave groups, with 409 rooms, 13 churches and 25 wine cellars! Vardzia suffered a major earthquake in 1283, which shook away the outer walls of many caves. As Georgia suffered successive waves of invaders, the monastery itself declined. In 1551 the Georgians were defeated by the Persians in a battle in the caves themselves, and Vardzia was looted. Today Vardzia is again a working monastery, with some caves inhabited by monks.

Guides, available at the ticket office, don't speak English but they have keys to some passages and caves that you can't otherwise enter.

At the heart of the cave complex is the **Church of the Assumption**, with its two-arched portico. The facade of the church has gone, but the inside is beautiful. Frescoes painted between 1184 and 1186, the period of the church's construction, portray many New Testament scenes and, on the north wall, Giorgi III and Tamar before she married (shown by the fact that she is not wearing a wimple). The door to the left of the church door leads into a long tunnel (perhaps 150m) which climbs steps inside the rock and emerges well above the church.

Zemo (Upper) Vardzia, a 2km walk west from the Vardzia bridge, is a working nunnery with fruit orchards, a trout farm and an 11th-century church with some good carvings.

🛏 Sleeping & Eating

There are also a couple of guesthouses in Tmogvi.

Valodia's Cottage   GUESTHOUSE $
(☑599116207; per person 15 GEL) Up garden steps just above the east side of the bridge at Vardzia, this house has four clean, basic rooms with comfy beds, sharing bathrooms, and a downstairs **cafe** (mains 3-6 GEL) serving good trout, *khachapuri* and salads. No hot water when we stayed, though. Ask here or at the Koriskhevi guesthouse about possible bicycle rental and rafting on the Mtkvari.

Koriskhevi   GUESTHOUSE $
(☑599116207; per person 25-30 GEL) Run by the same family as Valodia's Cottage, Koriskhevi is 2.5km further up the Mtkvari valley, a nice new, single-storey, pine building in

riverside gardens. The 10 rooms have private hot-water bathrooms and there's a garden restaurant.

ℹ Getting There & Away

The first *marshrutka* leaving Akhaltsikhe, at 10.30am, reaches Vardzia around noon, giving you just enough time to see the cave city and catch the last *marshrutka* back at 3pm (earlier ones are at 8.30am, 9.30am and 1pm, and there's also one at 9.45am to Tbilisi). But a day trip is more comfortable and enjoyable by taxi, for 40 GEL to 50 GEL return trip from Akhaltsikhe. There's also a summer day trip *marshrutka* service from Borjomi.

Sapara Monastery
საფარის მონასტერი

Rivalling Vardzia as one of the most beautiful places in the region (and receiving just a fraction of its visitors), Sapara Monastery has a dramatic position clinging to the edge of a cliff about 12km southeast of Akhaltsikhe. It has existed from at least the 9th century, and has numbered many important Georgian church figures among its monks. At the end of the 13th century Sapara became a possession of the Jakeli family, whose leader, Sargis Jakeli, was adept at staying on good terms with the Mongols, which enabled Samtskhe to enjoy a peace unusual for the time. Sargis' son Beka built the largest of Sapara's 12 churches, **St Saba's Church**, which contains high-quality frescoes.

The first church on the left as you enter the complex is **St Stephen's**. To the south is the earliest surviving structure, the 10th-century **Dormition Church**. Three of the fine stone reliefs from this are now in the Fine Arts Museum in Tbilisi, and two are in the museum in Akhaltsikhe.

The drive is beautiful, and you'll have great views of the monastery 2km before you reach it. Taxis charge around 20 GEL return trip from Alkhaltsikhe (60 GEL or 70 GEL if combined with Vardzia).

UNDERSTAND GEORGIA

Georgia Today

Since Georgia lost the 'Five Day War' with Russia over the breakaway region of South Ossetia in August 2008, Russia has stationed missile systems and several thousand troops in both South Ossetia and the other break-away Georgian region, Abkhazia. Many Georgians are preoccupied that Russia may one day seek to take control of Georgia as Russia seeks to reassert its influence over the former USSR. Though Georgia and al-most all the rest of the world continue to consider South Ossetia and Abkhazia as parts of Georgia, both are in practice very much Russian satellites. Russia recognised both as independent states after the 2008 war and it now provides about half of Abk-hazia's budget and virtually all of South Os-setia's. In 2011 Russia's then Prime Minister Vladimir Putin openly aired the possibility of Russia annexing South Ossetia.

Within Georgia, the leadership of Mikheil Saakashvili since the Rose Revolution in 2003 divided opinion. Many welcomed his purges on corruption and crime, which have made Georgia one of the world's saf-est countries and turned the police into an organisation that can be trusted. Many like the freer and fairer elections, the boom in tourism (which employed 60,000 by 2011, according to the government) and the new prestige buildings brightening up cities such as Tbilisi, Batumi and Kutaisi.

For others, Saakashvili is an autocratic hothead who tossed away any chance of bringing South Ossetia and Abkhazia back into the Georgian fold, through an impetu-ous assault on South Ossetia that gave Rus-sia an excuse to invade Georgia in 2008. Critics say too much power and influence is wielded by a small circle of politicians and their allies. They point to the economic stagnation of Georgia's countryside, where small family-owned farms have replaced Soviet collective farms but suffer from lack of investment. They complain about the lack of opportunity and support for the under-educated and the over-40s.

Georgia rates high on international charts for ease of doing business, and its Gross Do-mestic Product nearly trebled from 2003 to 2010. But unemployment in 2010 was still 16%, and around 25% in the cities. Nearly half of all Georgians depend entirely on their own farms for subsistence. The basic old-age pension in 2011 was just 100 GEL (about US$60) a month.

Protesters with diverse grievances have frequently blocked Tbilisi's main avenue, Rustaveli, sometimes for days on end. Saa-kashvili often claimed the protests were fomented by Russia, and Georgia has more than once been criticised by bodies such as Human Rights Watch for using excessive force against political demonstrators.

Georgia's constitution barred Saakashvili from standing for a third presidential term in 2013. Many suspected that he might, ironically, take a leaf out of Putin's book and try to become prime minister – a post whose powers were greatly boosted by reforms in 2010. Possible contenders for the presidency in 2013 include Gigi Ugulava, mayor of Tbi-lisi since 2006, and Bidzina (Boris) Ivanish-vili, Georgia's richest man.

History

Georgians live and breathe their history as a vital key to their identities today.

Early Kingdoms

The Georgians know themselves as Kartve-lebi and their country as Saqartvelo (land of the Kartvelebi), tracing their origins to Noah's great-great-grandson Kartlos. In classical times the two principal kingdoms in the territory were Colchis in the west (site of Greek colonies), and Kartli (also known as Iveria or Iberia) in the east, south and some areas in modern Turkey and Armenia.

When King Mirian and Queen Nana of Kartli were converted to Christianity by St Nino in the early 4th century, Georgia became the second kingdom to adopt the Christian faith, a quarter-century after Ar-menia. In the 5th century, western Georgia became tied to the expanding Byzantine Em-pire, while Kartli fell under Persian control. King Vakhtang Gorgasali of Kartli (c 447–502) drove the Persians out and moved his capital from Mtskheta to Tbilisi. But the Per-sians soon returned, to be replaced in 654 by the Arabs, who set up an emirate at Tbilisi. Western Georgia managed to fight off the Arabs.

The Golden Age

Resistance to the Arabs was spearheaded by the Bagrationi dynasty of Tao-Klarjeti, a col-lection of principalities straddling what are now southwest Georgia and northeast Tur-key. They later added Kartli to their posses-sions, and when in 1001 these were inherited by King Bagrat III of Abkhazia (northwest Georgia), most of Georgia became united under one rule. The Seljuk Turk invasion set things back, but the Seljuks were gradually

GEORGIA & ST GEORGE

St George is Georgia's patron saint (as well as England's, Portugal's, Beirut's, Bulgaria's, Catalonia's and Malta's), but the legendary dragon-slayer was probably not responsible for the country-name Georgia. Georgians themselves call their country Saqartvelo. The English word 'Georgia', along with the French Georgie, German Georgien and similar names in other tongues, probably stems instead from the Persian name for Georgians, *gurj*, which was picked up by medieval crusaders.

According to widely accepted accounts, St George was a senior officer in the army of the Roman emperor Diocletian. He was executed in 303 in Nicomedia (modern Izmit, Turkey) after suffering terrible tortures, for standing up against Diocletian's persecution of Christians. He soon became venerated as a Christian martyr and it was St Nino, the bringer of Christianity to Georgia in the 320s, who first popularised St George among Georgians. Today Georgia celebrates two St George's Days each year – 6 May, the anniversary of his execution, and 23 November, commemorating his torture on a wheel of swords.

As for the dragon, the legend (first known in a 10th-century Georgian text) tells that the beast was hanging out beside the water source of the city of Silene, requiring the offering of a sheep or child to distract it whenever the townspeople needed water. The day came when the princess of Silene drew the short straw, but luckily St George came riding by, crossed himself, lanced the dragon, saved the princess and converted Silene to Christianity.

driven out by the young king Davit Aghmashenebeli (David the Builder; 1089–1125), who defeated them at Didgori in 1122, recaptured nearby Tbilisi and made it his capital.

Davit made Georgia the major Caucasian power and a centre of Christian culture. Georgia reached its zenith under his great-granddaughter Queen Tamar (1184–1213), whose writ extended over much of present-day Azerbaijan and Armenia, plus parts of Turkey and southern Russia. Tamar is still so revered that Georgians today call her, without irony, King Tamar!

Death, Destruction & Division

The golden age ended violently with the arrival of the Mongols in the 1220s. King Giorgi the Brilliant (1314–46) shook off the Mongol yoke, but then came the Black Death, followed by the Central Asian destroyer Timur (Tamerlane), who attacked eight times between 1386 and 1403.

Devastated Georgia split into four main kingdoms: Kartli and Kakheti in the east, Imereti in the northwest and Samtskhe in the southwest. From the 16th to 18th centuries western Georgian statelets generally fell under Ottoman Turkish dominion, and eastern ones were subject to the Persian Safavids. In 1744 a new Persian conqueror, Nader Shah, installed local Bagratid princes as kings of Kartli and Kakheti. One of these,

Erekle II, ruled both kingdoms as a semi-independent state from 1762.

Russian Rule

Russian troops crossed the Caucasus for the first time in 1770 to get involved in Imereti's liberation from the Turks. At the Treaty of Georgievsk in 1783, Erekle II accepted Russian suzerainty over eastern Georgia in return for protection against his Muslim enemies. Russia went on to annex all the Georgian kingdoms and princedoms during the 19th century, replacing the local or Turkish rulers with its own military governors.

In the wake of the Russian Revolution, Georgia was briefly independent under a Menshevik government from 1918 to 1921, but was invaded by the Red Army and incorporated into the new USSR in 1922. During the 1930s, like everywhere else in the USSR, Georgia suffered from the Great Terror unleashed by Joseph Stalin, a cobbler's son from the Georgian town of Gori who had managed to take control of the largest country on earth.

Stalin died in 1953, and the 1960s and '70s are looked back on with nostalgia by older Georgians as a time of public order, peace and high living standards. Yet by the mid-1980s Mikhail Gorbachev began his policies of reform and the USSR disintegrated in just seven years.

Independence: From Dream to Nightmare

Georgia's bubbling independence movement became an unstoppable force after the deaths of 19 hunger strikers when Soviet troops broke up a protest in Tbilisi on 9 April 1989. Georgia's now anti-Communist government, led by the nationalist Zviad Gamsakhurdia, declared independence on 9 April 1991. Almost immediately Georgia descended into chaos. Street fighting overtook central Tbilisi in December 1991 as rebels battled to overthrow Gamsakhurdia. He fled to Chechnya and was replaced by a military council, which gained an international respectability when Eduard Shevardnadze, a Georgian who had been Gorbachev's foreign minister, agreed to lead it.

Shevardnadze was elected head of state in October 1992 and his presence did wonders for Georgia's reputation abroad. But internal conflicts got worse. A truce in June 1992 halted a separatist conflict in the region of South Ossetia, which had an ethnic Ossetian majority and a Georgian minority. But in August 1992 an even more serious conflict erupted in Abkhazia. For more details about this bitter ethnic war, see p68.

In September 1993 Georgia suffered a comprehensive defeat in Abkhazia, leaving Abkhazia as well as South Ossetia de facto independent. Virtually all Abkhazia's ethnic Georgian population, about 230,000 people, was driven out of the territory – a desperate humanitarian and economic burden for Georgia, whose economy was already on the brink of collapse. Gamsakhurdia meanwhile tried to unseat Shevardnadze: a short civil war in western Georgia was only ended by Shevardnadze's quick negotiation of support from Russian troops already in the country. Gamsakhurdia died on 31 December 1993, possibly by his own hand.

The Rose Revolution

For a decade after the Abkhazia disaster, Georgia oscillated between periods of relative peace and security and terrible crime waves, gang warfare, kidnappings, infrastructure collapse and rampant corruption. Shevardnadze staved off a total collapse into anarchy, but by the early 21st century Georgians had lost all faith in him.

Badly flawed parliamentary elections in November 2003 were the focus for a mass protest movement that turned into a bloodless coup, named the Rose Revolution after the flowers carried by the demonstrators. Protestors outside parliament in Tbilisi vowed to stay there until Shevardnadze resigned. Led by Mikheil Saakashvili, a US-educated lawyer who now headed the opposition National Movement, the unarmed throng finally invaded parliament on 22 November. Shevardnadze announced his resignation the next morning.

The 36-year-old Saakashvili won presidential elections in January 2004 by a landslide, appointed a team of young, energetic, outward-looking ministers, set about liberalising the economy, and announced campaigns against the plague of corruption. Within a short time almost the entire notoriously corrupt police force was sacked and replaced with much better paid, better trained officers. (By 2011 Georgia had risen from 133rd to 64th in Transparency International's corruption rankings.) Foreign aid and investment in telecoms, electricity, transport and construction helped the economy, and roads were improved and electricity shortages ended, but levels of poverty and unemployment stayed high.

Saakashvili quickly faced down the semi-separatist strongman of Georgia's southwestern region of Adjara, Aslan Abashidze. Just when it seemed Georgia might be plunged into another civil war, Abashidze backed down and left for exile in Russia. Other opposition to Saakashvili coalesced around issues of poverty and government authoritarianism. Protests in Tbilisi in 2007 were dispersed by riot police. Saakashvili then called a snap presidential election for January 2008, and won it with 53% of the vote.

GEORGIA HISTORY

HAVE YOUR SAY

Found a fantastic restaurant that you're longing to share with the world? Disagree with our recommendations? Or just want to talk about your most recent trip?

Whatever your reason, head to lonelyplanet.com, where you can post a review, ask or answer a question on the Thorntree forum, comment on a blog, or share your photos and tips on Groups. Or you can simply spend time chatting with like-minded travellers. So go on, have your say.

War with Russia

The Saakashvili government had a strong pro-Western, especially pro-US, foreign policy, with ambitions to join NATO and the EU. This spooked a Russia led by ex-KGB officer Vladimir Putin. Saakashvili also began manoeuvring to bring the Russian-backed breakaway regions of Abkhazia and South Ossetia back under Tbilisi's control. Mounting tensions saw sporadic violence in South Ossetia, a Russian ban on imports of Georgian wine and mineral water, the closure of the Russia–Georgia border and, in July 2008, large-scale military exercises by both Georgia (near Tbilisi) and Russia (near its border with South Ossetia). Putin developed a deep personal dislike of Saakashvili: he was famously quoted as saying he would 'hang Saakashvili by the balls'.

On 7 August 2008 Georgia launched a massive shelling of the South Ossetian capital, Tskhinvali. Georgian troops entered Tskhinvali next day, but by 10 August they were driven out of South Ossetia by a rapidly arriving Russian army and aerial bombardment. Russian planes, and land forces moving through South Ossetia and Abkhazia, went on to bomb or occupy Georgian military airfields and bases as well as the towns of Gori, Zugdidi, Poti and Senaki. From Gori the Russians moved towards Tbilisi, but halted 45km from the Georgian capital. On 12 August French President Nicolas Sarkozy negotiated a ceasefire, but the ethnic cleansing of most of South Ossetia's 20,000-strong ethnic-Georgian population by South Ossetian forces (often with Russian connivance) continued into November. Refugees from South Ossetia swelled the number of refugees within Georgia to some 250,000. In 2011 more than 100,000 of these were still living in temporary accommodation, where many of them had been since they were driven from Abkhazia in 1993.

The August war claimed about 850 lives (half of them civilians), slightly fewer than the 1991–92 South Ossetian conflict. South Ossetia's population has recently been estimated at about 30,000, down from 70,000 in 2008 and 98,000 in 1990.

Georgia left the Russia-dominated Commonwealth of Independent States (comprising all 15 former Soviet republics except Estonia, Latvia and Lithuania) in 2009.

Arts

Georgians are an incredibly expressive people. Music, dance, song and poetry all play big parts in their lives.

Music & Dance

Live music is always close at hand in Georgia. *Supras* (feasts) may often be extended by polyphonic (multivoiced) singing round the table. Mentioned by Xenophon as long ago as 400 BC, Georgian polyphonic singing used to accompany every aspect of daily life, and the songs survive in various genres: *supruli* (songs for the table, the most famous being *Mravalzhamier,* 'Many Years'), *mushuri* (working songs), *satrpialo* (love songs) and *sagmiro* (epic songs). Folk festivals, such as Tbilisi's Art-Gene Festival, are great opportunities to hear the best folk singers and musicians, as is the October grape harvest season in Kakheti. For a good introduction to Georgian polyphonic singing, check out the two one-hour programs in BBC Radio 3's 'World Routes' series, available at www.bbc.co.uk.

Sagalobeli (ethereally beautiful church chants) have been part of Georgian life for at least 1500 years. Excellent choirs accompany services in the country's most important churches: the best time to catch them is Sunday morning between about 9am and noon.

Georgia's exciting traditions of folk dance range from lyrical love stories to dramatic, leaping demonstrations of male agility, usually with beautiful costumes and an accompaniment of string and wind instruments and drums. Top professional groups such as Erisioni and the Sukhishvili Georgian National Ballet often tour overseas, but don't miss them if they happen to be performing back home.

Jazz is also popular (Tbilisi and Batumi host annual festivals), while minimal techno is the optimal beat for many Tbilisi and Batumi clubbers. The most beloved rock artist is still Irakli Charkviani, even though he died in 2006.

Classical composer Zakaria Paliashvili is famous for his operas *Abesalom and Eteri* (1919) and *Daisi* (1923). Leading contemporary composer Gia Kancheli, born in 1935, has been described as 'turning the sounds of silence into music'.

Visual Arts

Many Georgian churches are adorned with wonderful old frescoes. The golden age of religious art in Georgia was the 11th to 13th centuries, when Georgian painters employed the Byzantine iconographic system and also portrayed local subjects such as Georgian monarchs and saints. There were two main fresco schools: one at Davit Gareja cave monastery and the other at the monasteries of Tao-Klarjeti (southwest Georgia and northeast Turkey). During the same period artists and metalsmiths were creating beautiful icons from jewels and precious metals that remain among Georgia's greatest treasures today.

Perhaps the last major artist in the fresco-painting tradition was one who painted scenes of everyday life in restaurants and bars in Tbilisi. The self-taught Niko Pirosmani (1862–1918) expressed the essential spirit of Georgian life in a direct and enchanting way. After his death in poverty and obscurity, his work was acclaimed by the leading Georgian modernists Davit Kakabadze, Lado Gudiashvili and Shalva Kikodze, all of whom were influenced by the artistic innovation they encountered in early-20th-century Paris. Their associate Elene Akhvlediani painted colourful scenes of old Tbilisi and Georgian historic sites that still have a lot of appeal. All these artists are well represented in Tbilisi's excellent National Gallery, opened in 2011. The Sighnaghi Museum has another good Pirosmani collection.

Literature

For a language with only a few million speakers, Georgian has an amazingly rich literature. In the 12th century Shota Rustaveli, a member of Queen Tamar's court, wrote *The Knight* (or *Man*) *in the Tiger's* (or *Panther's*) *Skin,* an epic of chivalry that every Georgian can quote from. This classic was first translated into English in 1912 by Marjory Wardrop, who learned Georgian by comparing a Georgian bible to an English one.

Nikoloz Baratashvili (1817–45) personified the romanticism that entered Georgian literature in the early 19th century. Headed by Ilia Chavchavadze and Akaki Tsereteli, the Tergdaleulebi movement promoted educational and political reform in Georgia after imbibing liberal ideas in Russia. Some later 19th-century writers turned to the mountains for inspiration – notably Alexander Kazbegi, novelist and dramatist, and Vazha Pshavela, whom many consider the greatest Georgian poet after Rustaveli.

The symbolist Blue Horn group was the principal poetic movement of the early 20th century. One leading member, Titsian Tabidze, was arrested and shot in the purges of 1937. Another, Paolo Iashvili, killed himself at a Writers' Union meeting when he heard of Tabidze's death. Galaktion Tabidze (1892–1959), a superbly lyrical writer who also committed suicide, was probably Georgia's best-loved poet of the 20th century.

Mikheil Javakhishvili (1880–1937) took the Georgian novel to new levels with vivid, ironic tales of city and country, peasant and aristocrat in tsarist and Soviet times, including *Arsena Marabdeli,* based on a real-life Georgian Robin Hood figure. Javakhishvili was executed by the Soviet regime. Konstantin Gamsakhurdia (1893–1975) brought new subtlety of phrasing to Georgian prose with his historical novels, among them *Davit Aghmashenebeli,* and somehow managed to survive Stalin. Nodar Dumbadze (1928–84) portrayed post-WW II life with humour and melancholy, and is one of the most popular Georgian novelists: *The Law of Eternity* and *Granny, Iliko, Ilarion and I* are among his novels available in English.

Leading post-Soviet writers include novelist, playwright and travel writer Davit Turashvili, and novelist Aka Morchiladze, whose *Santa Esperanza* (2004) is not exactly a book but actually a traveller's bag containing 36 booklets and maps about an imaginary island in the Black Sea, readable in any order.

Cinema

Georgian cinema enjoyed a golden age from the late 1960s to the 1980s, when Georgian directors working in Moscow or Tbilisi created dozens of films distinct from the general socialist-realist run of Soviet movies. They won international awards with brilliant visual imagery, lively characters, original cinematic languages and much use of allegory, fable and dreams to provide a platform for people's real concerns while trying not to fall foul of the Soviet authorities. Italian director Federico Fellini was a noted fan, praising Georgian cinema's ability to combine philosophy with childlike innocence.

Perhaps the greatest maestro was the Tbilisi-born Armenian Sergei Paradjanov (p190). Tengiz Abuladze's *Repentance* (1984) was ground-breaking in opening up the Soviet past – it's a black portrait of a dictatorial politician clearly based on Stalin's Georgian henchman Lavrenty Beria. Other leading directors included Otar Iosseliani (*There Lived a Songthrush,* 1970), Eldar Shengelaia (*The Blue Mountains,* 1983) and Giorgi Shengelaia (*Pirosmani,* 1969).

Soviet artistic repression and then Georgia's impoverished, anarchic condition in the 1990s saw many leading lights of Georgian cinema move to Western Europe. Iosseliani has made many feature films in France, including the internationally successful *Favourites of the Moon* (1984), and *Chantrapas* (2010), which is about a young director who leaves Soviet Georgia to live in France… Gela Babluani's *The Legacy* (2006), another French production, is a blackly humorous tale of three French travellers caught up in a murderous Svaneti blood feud.

Home-grown Georgian cinema has begun a comeback. It gets a reasonable amount of screen time among the Hollywood stuff at Georgia's few cinemas. Levan Zaqareishvili's successful *Tbilisi-Tbilisi* (2005) is a gritty portrait of urban life centred on a penniless film-maker. The conflicts of the 1990s and their fallout are treated in films such as Giorgi Ovashvili's *The Other Bank* (2008), about family divisions caused by the Abkhazia conflict, and Levan Tutberidze's *A Trip to Karabakh* (2005).

Theatre

Tbilisi boasts an amazingly lively theatrical scene for a city of its size. Four directors dominate the story of Georgian theatre: Kote Marjanishvili and Sandro Akhmeteli in the 1920s and '30s, and Misha Tumanishvili and Robert Sturua since the 1970s, all of whom contributed to Georgia's love affair with Shakespeare. Sturua's *Richard III* (1980) and *The Caucasian Chalk Circle* (1975) daringly burlesqued dictatorial regimes and won worldwide acclaim, as did his 1986 *Hamlet* in London, starring Alan Rickman. Sturua was director of Tbilisi's Rustaveli National Theatre from 1980 until 2011.

Food & Drink

Georgian food is a unique expression of the land and its people – diverse, fresh, imaginative, filling, often spicy – and with the hospitality and drinks that often go hand-in-hand,

eating is a central component of Georgian culture.

Georgians eat and drink at all times of the day, and most restaurants keep suitably long hours, typically 9am or 10am to 11pm without any break.

Tbilisi has the best selection and variety of restaurants, but eateries around the country have improved a lot. Outside Tbilisi, restaurants are almost universally cheap – a full slap-up feast will rarely be more than 20 GEL per person.

The best Georgian food you eat, however, will often be in homestays and guesthouses, where you can enjoy home-cooked fare with that genuine touch of Georgian hospitality.

At the bottom of the Georgian restaurant chain are the *sakhachapure* and the *sakhinkle,* cheap eateries where *khachapuri* or *khinkali* are, respectively, the staple dishes.

Staples & Specialities

The great staple for everybody, travellers and locals, is the *khachapuri,* essentially a cheese pie (see p45).

The second most common dish is *khinkali* (spicy dumplings, usually with a minced-meat filling, although potato and/ or mushroom fillings are quite widely available). These are usually served without any accompaniment, but are surprisingly tasty with a dose of pepper. You're not supposed to eat the doughy nexus at the top of the dumpling, though this being Georgia, a few people do. It's virtually impossible to order fewer than five *khinkali* at a time, even though they are quite substantial.

A great snack-on-the-go is *churchkhela,* a string of walnuts coated in a sort of pinkish caramel made from grape juice. Nicknamed Georgian Snickers, you'll often see it hanging, sausagelike, at roadside stalls or markets.

Starters to a larger meal may include the delectable *badrijani nigvzit* – (aubergine slices with walnut-and-garlic paste), *lobio* (bean paste or stew with herbs and spices) and *mkhali/pkhali,* which are pastes combining vegetables such as aubergine, spinach or beetroot with walnuts, garlic and herbs. The finest fresh bread to accompany a Georgian meal is *chotis* (or *tonis*) *puri* – long white loaves baked from wheat flour, water and salt (no fat or oil) in a dedicated oven called a *tone.* *Chotis puri* is welcomed by Jewish travellers because it is kosher.

More substantial Georgian dishes include the *mtsvadi* (shish kebab) and a variety of

EATING PRICE RANGES

In this chapter the following price indicators are used in Eating sections to indicate the price of a single main dish:

PRICE RANGE	TBILISI	ELSEWHERE
budget ($)	<9 GEL	<7.50 GEL
midrange ($$)	9 GEL-19 GEL	7.50 GEL-12 GEL
top end ($$$)	>19 GEL	>12 GEL

lamb, chicken, beef or turkey dishes in spicy, herby sauces or stews – see our Menu Decoder (p117) for descriptions of the most popular dishes.

Religious-minded Georgians may abstain from meat, eggs and dairy products on Wednesdays, Fridays and during certain periods such as those leading up to Christmas and Easter. The Fasting Menus available in many restaurants are designed for them but they make life easier for year-round vegetarians too.

The Supra & Toasts

While strictly speaking the word *supra* (feast, literally 'tablecloth') applies to any meeting where food and drink are consumed, the full works means staggering amounts to eat and drink. A selection of cold dishes will be followed by two or three hot courses as well as some kind of dessert. Make sure you try everything, as much to temper the onslaught of concomitant alcohol as to keep your hosts happy.

Bear in mind that Georgians toast only their enemies with beer. Wine or spirits are the only drinks to toast your friends with. However, you should only drink them when someone proposes a toast. This can be a surprisingly serious, lengthy and poetic matter, even at small gatherings of three or four friends. Larger gatherings will have a designated *tamada* (toastmaster), and some complex *supras* will involve an *alaverdi,* a second man whose role it is to elaborate on the toast, while a *merikipe* is there to pour the wine. If you are toasted, do not reply immediately but wait for others to add their wishes before simply thanking them – you should wait a while and then ask the *tamada* if you can make a toast in reply.

Drinks

Georgia claims to be the birthplace of wine (*ghvino* in Georgian), which is a national

passion, especially in Kakheti, the principal growing region (see Kakheti Wineries, p99). A popular spin-off of winemaking is the grappalike firewater, *chacha,* running at 45% to 55% alcohol content. Vodka is also common throughout the country.

Beer is a popular thirst-quencher: the two commonest Georgian beers are Kazbegi and the slightly smoother, creamier Natakhtari.

Georgia's favourite nonalcoholic drink is Borjomi, a salty mineral water which was the beverage of choice for every Soviet leader from Lenin on. It polarises opinion, and is certainly an acquired taste. Nabeghlavi is a less salty alternative. Georgians often state that tap water is safe to drink throughout the country, a claim that is hard to verify though we have never heard of anyone getting sick from drinking tap water. Various uncarbonated bottled waters are also available.

SURVIVAL GUIDE

Directory A–Z

Accommodation

Peak season in most of the country is July and August, when it's often worth calling ahead to secure a room in any particular place. Seasonal variations in room rates are uncommon, though it's sometimes possible to secure a discount at quiet times.

Camping There are very few organised camping grounds but equally few restrictions on wild camping. Be sensible about where you camp – in the mountains, dogs or even bears or wolves might be a threat. If in doubt ask locals.

Guesthouses Rooms in someone's house, usually with the owners living on the premises. Guesthouses are often enjoyable places to stay, not least for the contact you'll have with local people and the chance to eat home-cooked food. Bathrooms are usually shared; kitchens may be available for guests' use. Typical price: 20 GEL to 25 GEL per person; meals 5 GEL to 10 GEL each.

Homestays Very similar to guesthouses except that they're often slightly cheaper and you are more likely to share space with family members (in guesthouses, family and guest areas tend to be distinct).

Hostels The first travellers' hostel in Georgia opened in 2010. By the end of 2011 there were about 30 in the country (the majority in Tbilisi), with more sure to open. Hostels provide dormitory beds or bunks, sometimes a couple of private double rooms, and shared bathrooms and kitchens. They're economical and good places to meet other travellers, and most of them are run by young Georgians who like hosting and helping international guests. Typical price: 20 GEL to 25 GEL per person.

Hotels There are now many good, small or medium-sized midrange hotels with character in cities and towns around the country, and a handful of superluxury top-end places in Tbilisi and Batumi. Hotels nearly always have private bathrooms and usually on-site restaurants. Double-room prices start at around 60 GEL and are rarely above 200 GEL except in top-end places.

Activities

» Peter Nasmyth's *Walking in the Caucasus: Georgia* is an excellent guide to over 40 day walks all around the country.
» The **Agency of Protected Areas website** (www.apa.gov.ge) has useful maps and field guides.
» Good resources for bird-watchers include *Bird-watching Guide to Georgia, Raptors & Owls of Georgia* and *Vultures of Georgia,* all by Lexo Gavashelishvili and others.

» Walkers should give dogs a wide berth everywhere: Georgian mountain dogs are bred for fending off wolves.

Business Hours

Reviews in this chapter only list opening hours where they differ significantly from the following typical hours:

Airline offices 10am to 6pm Monday to Friday, 10.30am to 5pm Saturday

Banks 9.30am to 5.30pm Monday to Friday

Bars noon to 2am

Cafes 10am to 10pm

Shops Food 9am to 9pm, other 10am to 7pm Monday to Saturday

Restaurants Breakfast 9am to 11am, lunch/dinner 11am to 11pm

Customs Regulations

Valuable works of art or antiques require a licence from the **Ministry of Culture & Monument Protection** (Map p36; www.mcs. gov.ge; Sanapiro 4, Tbilisi) if you want to take them out of Georgia. Some galleries and shops will provide this, but private vendors are unlikely to. You may have to pay a heavy export duty.

Embassies & Consulates

Foreign representation in Georgia includes the following (all are embassies and in Tbilisi, unless stated):

Armenia (Map p30; ☑32-2950977; www.arme nianembassy.ge; Tetelashvili 4, Marjanishvili area; ⊙consular section 10am-1pm Mon-Fri)

Azerbaijan Embassy (Map p30; ☑32-2253526; www.azembassy.ge; Bldg 1, Block II, Kipshidze, Vake; ⊙visa applications 10am-noon Mon, Wed & Fri); Consulate (☑422-276700; Dumbadze 14, Batumi)

ACCOMMODATION PRICE RANGES

In this chapter the following price indicators are used in Sleeping sections to indicate the cost of a room for two people, including taxes but without meals:

PRICE RANGE	TBILISI	ELSEWHERE
budget ($)	<70 GEL	<50 GEL
midrange ($$)	70 GEL-300 GEL	50 GEL-300 GEL
top end ($$$)	>300 GEL	>300 GEL

MENU DECODER

Georgian menus often look daunting, even if there's an English translation available, but this list explains a large proportion of most menus.

ajika	chilli-and-herb paste
apkhazura	spicy meatballs/sausage
badrijani (nigvzit)	aubergine (in slices with walnut-and-garlic paste)
bazhe	walnut sauce
chakapuli	lamb with tarragon and plums
chakhokhbili	chicken or turkey in tomato sauce
chakhrakuli	lamb ribs stewed with tomato, herbs and spices
chanakhi	lamb with potatoes, aubergine and tomatoes
chashashuli	meat or mushrooms, with veggies in a spicy sauce
chebureki	triangular pies stuffed with minced meat
chikhirtma	chicken broth
churchkhela	string of walnuts coated in a sort of caramel made from grape juice
ghani	maize porridge
kababi	doner kebabs
khachapuri	cheese pie
kharcho	soup with rice, beef and spices
khinkali	spicy dumplings with a meat, potato or mushroom filling
kupati	sausage
lobio	bean paste or stew with herbs and spices
lomi	millet or maize porridge
matsoni	sour yoghurt drink usually consumed at breakfast
mchadi	maize bread
mkhali/pkhali	beetroot, spinach or aubergine paste with crushed walnuts, garlic and herbs
mtsvadi (ghoris/khbos)	shish kebab, shashlyk (from pork/beef)
ojakhuri	meat goulash
ostri	spiced meat in a tomato-based sauce
plovi	rice with meat, mushrooms or fruit
satsivi	cold turkey or chicken in a spicy walnut sauce, traditionally a New Year dish
shkmeruli	chicken in garlic sauce
soko	mushrooms
sulguni	smoked cheese
suneli	a spicy paste
tqemali	plum sauce

Canada (Map p36; ☎32-2982072; ccogeorgia@gmail.com; 3rd fl, Rustaveli 34)

France (☎32-2721490; www.ambafrance-ge.org; Krtsanisi 49; ☺9am-1pm & 2-6pm Mon-Thu, to 4.30pm Fri)

Germany (www.tiflis.diplo.de); Embassy (Map p36; ☎32-2447300; Sheraton Metechi Palace Hotel, Telavi 20; ☺8.30am-5.30pm Mon-Thu, to 2.30pm Fri); Consulate (Map p30; ☎32-2435399; Davit Aghmashenebeli 166; ☺2-3pm Tue & Thu)

Iran (Map p30; ☑32-2913656; iranemb@geo. net.ge; Chavchavadzis gamziri 80, Vake; ☺10am-5.30pm Mon-Fri)

Israel (Map p30; ☑32-2556500; tbilisi.mfa.gov.il; Davit Aghmashenebeli 154; ☺10am-1pm Mon-Fri)

Kazakhstan (Map p30; ☑32-2997684; dmka-zaida@inbox.ru; Shatberashvili 23, Vake; ☺visa applications 11am-1pm Mon, Wed & Thu)

Netherlands (Map p36; ☑32-2276200; geor-gia.nlembassy.org; Sheraton Metechi Palace Hotel, Telavi 20; ☺consular section 9.30am-12.30pm & 2-6pm Mon-Thu)

Russia (Map p30; ☑32-2912782; www.georgia. mid.ru; Chavchavadzis gamziri 51 & 53, Vake; ☺9am-1pm Mon-Fri) Russian Interests Section of Swiss Embassy.

Turkey (Map p30; ☑32-2252078; tbilisi.emb. mfa.gov.tr; Chavchavadzis gamziri 35, Vake; ☺9.30am-1pm Mon-Fri)

UK (☑32-2274747; ukingeorgia.fco.gov.uk; Krtsanisi 5; ☺9am-1pm & 2-5pm Mon-Fri)

USA (☑32-2277000; georgia.usembassy.gov; George Balanchine 11, Didi Dighomi; ☺9am-6pm Mon-Fri)

Georgian embassies in other countries are listed on the website of the **Georgian Foreign Ministry** (mfa.gov.ge).

Maps

» By far the best maps of Georgia, including hiking maps and regional maps, are published and sold by **Geoland** (Map p36; www.geoland.ge; Telegrapis chikhi 3; ☺10am-2pm & 3-7pm Mon-Fri) in Tbilisi.

» The community mapping project **MapSpot** (www.mapspot.ge) has good online street maps of Georgian towns.

» Tourist Information Offices hand out useful regional and country maps.

Media

At least three weekly English-language newspapers, each with their own take on Georgian affairs and some events listings, circulate in Tbilisi. Brightest and breeziest is *Georgia Today* (www.georgia today.ge). Others are the *Georgian Times* (www.geotimes. ge) and *Financial* (finchannel.com).

Georgians get most of their news from TV. The government-funded **Georgian Public Broadcaster** (www.gpb.ge) operates two national channels, 1TV and 2TV, as well as **Kanal PIK** (pik.tv), a Russian-language satellite station designed to provide independent regional news to the Russian-speaking world. PIK's website has an English-language section including news clips with English subtitles.

Privately owned TV channels tend to get bigger audiences at home, especially **Rustavi 2** (www.rustavi2.com.ge) and **Imedi TV** (www.imedi.ge). Media freedom is protected by the constitution, but media critical of the government occasionally complain of harassment and inequities in licensing procedures.

International satellite channels are available on some hotel TVs.

Money

» Georgia's currency is the lari (GEL). It has been fairly stable since it was introduced in 1995. One lari is made up of 100 tetri.

» Banknotes come in denominations of one, two, five, 10, 20, 50, 100 and 200 lari; coins run from one tetri to two lari.

» ATMs, generally accepting MasterCard, Visa, Cirrus and Maestro cards, are plentiful in cities and most towns.

» There are also plenty of banks and small money-exchange offices in most towns and cities, where you can exchange US dollars, euros and sometimes sterling and the currencies of Turkey, Armenia, Azerbaijan and Russia.

» It's useful to have some cash US dollars or euros for times when there isn't a convenient ATM.

» You can make purchases with credit cards at the better hotels, restaurants and some shops in Tbilisi, but much less frequently outside the capital.

» Travellers cheques can be exchanged only in some banks.

» The common tipping practice in restaurants is just to round up the bill to the next round number.

» For information on costs and exchange rates, see p12 and p27.

Public Holidays

New Year's Day 1 January

Orthodox Christmas Day 7 January

Epiphany 19 January

Mother's Day 3 March

Women's Day 8 March

Orthodox Easter Sunday April or May (dates vary; see p296); Good Friday and/or Easter Monday may also be holidays

Independence Restoration Day 9 April

Victory Day 9 May

Independence Day 26 May

Mariamoba (Assumption) 28 August

Svetitskhovloba (Day of Svetitskhoveli Cathedral, Mtskheta) 14 October

Giorgoba (St George's Day) 23 November

Telephone

Area codes Given under city and town headings in this chapter.

Fixed cellular phone numbers (Networks such as Magtifix and Silknet) Nine digits, starting with 7.

Georgia country code ☏995

International access code (for calls from Georgia) ☏00

Landline numbers Seven digits in Tbilisi, six digits elsewhere; always starting with 2.

Mobile phone numbers Nine digits, starting with 5.

MOBILE PHONES

» Almost everyone in Georgia has a mobile phone and even some businesses no longer have landlines.

» The three main networks – **Magti** (www.magticom.ge), **Geocell** (www.geocell.ge) and **Beeline** (www.beeline.ge) – have shops in all sizeable towns (see p49 for their main downtown shops in Tbilisi).

» Magti is the overall best choice for coverage around the country, but only Geocell covers the Juta area outside Kazbegi.

» If you have a mobile phone that is unlocked for international use, you can easily buy a Georgian SIM card for 1 GEL

or 2 GEL from one of the three main networks. Take your passport when you go.

» If your mobile isn't unlocked for international use, you'll either have to pay roaming charges or buy a phone locally (new ones start around 35 GEL).

» Call rates from Georgian mobile networks are reasonable: for calls to other mobiles: Magti charges 0.24 GEL for the first minute, then 0.01 GEL per minute to other Magti mobiles and 0.10 GEL per minute to other mobiles. Magti texts to Western Europe cost 0.24 GEL.

» You can top up credit in shops and kiosks everywhere either with cash or by buying a top-up card, or by paying cash into grey iPAY machines (with on-screen instructions in English) in Tbilisi metro stations and some shops.

Tourist Information

» Georgia now has a good network of Tourism Information Centres in almost all main destinations. The country's official tourism website is www.georgia.travel.

Visas

» Citizens of EU countries, Australia, Canada, Israel, Japan, New Zealand, Norway, South Africa, Switzerland, Turkey and the USA are among those who need no visa to visit Georgia for up to 360 days.

» The full list of visa-free nationalities, and further information, is given on the websites of the **Georgian Foreign Ministry** (mfa.gov.ge) and **Georgian police** (www.police.ge).

» Those who do need visas can obtain one from a Georgian embassy or consulate (listed at mfa.gov.ge), or on arrival in Georgia by air or road. See p303 and p305 for lists of entry points.

HOW TO DIAL GEORGIAN NUMBERS

CALLING TO	FROM LANDLINE	FROM MOBILE	FROM FIXED CELLULAR PHONE	FROM OTHER COUNTRIES
landline	area code-number	area code-number	area code-number	IAC*-☏995-area code-number
mobile	☏05-number	number	☏5-number	IAC*-☏995-5-number
fixed cellular phone	☏5-number	☏5-number	number	IAC*-☏995-number

* IAC: International access code

» Single-entry 90-day visas on arrival cost 50 GEL; multiple-entry 360-day visas are 100 GEL.

» Visas are not available on arrival for travellers arriving in Georgia by train or sea, or for any travellers arriving from Abkhazia or South Ossetia.

» If you have entered Abkhazia or South Ossetia from Russia, Georgia considers this a crime subject to up to five years' imprisonment, so don't try to continue into undisputed Georgia from either of the breakaway enclaves.

» Visa-issuing procedures are pretty straightforward and are normally completed in minutes on arrival in Georgia. Consulates require a few days for processing.

VISAS FOR ONWARD TRAVEL

Armenia Tourist visas are issued in a few minutes at land entry points into Armenia. A 21-day visa costs AMD3000 (about US$8).

Azerbaijan Azerbaijan's visa regulations (p268) change frequently. At the time of writing, the embassy in Tbilisi required applicants to show a letter of invitation (LOI) individually validated by the Azerbaijan Foreign Ministry. It's easiest to use the services of **X-Tour** (Map p30; ☎32-2945579; www.xtour.ge; Chavchavadzis gamziri 68, Vake, Tbilisi), which can obtain a 30-day single-entry visa for US$200 in two or three working days. Even with a foreign-ministry-validated LOI, dealing with the embassy yourself takes at least three working days and involves three visits to the embassy and one to the **Transcaucasus Development Bank** (Map p30; Marjanishvili 4, Tbilisi; ⊙10am-5pm Mon-Fri), on the other side of the city, to pay the fee. Travellers have reported that the Azerbaijan consulate in Batumi was accepting travel-agency-issued LOIs without individual foreign ministry validation, but this could of course change.

Iran Tbilisi is convenient to collect an Iranian visa. The easiest method is to apply online several weeks ahead through an agency such as **Persian Voyages** (www.persianvoyages.com) or **IranianVisa**

(www.iranianvisa.com). The agency supplies an Iranian foreign ministry authorisation number to an Iranian embassy that you nominate. In Tbilisi, once the embassy has your number, you go there, fill in a form, provide two photos and your passport, and pay the fee at a nearby bank (€60 to €100 for a 30-day tourist visa for most Western nationalities). Your visa should be ready the following working day.

Kazakhstan The only Central Asian country with an embassy in Georgia. Citizens of 47 countries (including EU states, Australia, Canada, Israel, Japan, New Zealand, Norway, Switzerland and the USA) can obtain one-month single-entry visas without an LOI for US$30 to US$50, in about three working days. Unlike the Kazakh embassy in Baku, the Tbilisi embassy doesn't issue Kyrgyz visas.

Russia Some travellers have reported obtaining single-entry Russian visas at the Russian Interests Section of the Swiss Embassy in Tbilisi in four or five working days for US$60. You need an LOI.

Turkey Most Westerners either need no visa or can obtain it quickly at the border.

Work & Volunteering

» Fluency in English gives you a good chance of finding employment with NGOs, international organisations, some local companies or as a teacher in private schools. Ads for private language teachers appear in the paper *Sitqva da Sakme* (www.saqme.ge).

» The government's ambitious program **Teach and Learn with Georgia** (tlg.gov.ge, www.facebook.com/tlgeorgia) enlists hundreds of English-speakers as volunteers each year to teach English to Georgian schoolchildren. Volunteers live with host families and receive stipends of 500 GEL a month (more than their Georgian colleagues), plus flights to and from Georgia and one round-trip holiday flight per year. Minimum commitment is six months.

» **European Voluntary Service** (http://ec.europa.eu/youth) has a number of varied volunteer projects in Georgia.

Armenia

Includes »

Yerevan 124
Geghard Monastery.......145
Echmiadzin 148
Mt Aragats 151
Khor Virap Monastery ...151
Lake Sevan....................152
Dilijan 157
Vanadzor 163
Debed Canyon 167
Gyumri 169
Noravank........................174
Yeghegnadzor 174
Jermuk..........................178
Sisian 179
Goris.............................180
Tatev 184

Best Places to Stay

» Envoy Hostel (p135)

» Mirhav Hotel (p181)

» Gohar's Guest House (p176)

» Ananov Guesthouse (p157)

Best Places to Eat

» Maghay B&B (p163)

» Nina B&B (p158)

» Dolmama's (p138)

» Haykanoush (p158)

Why Go?

Although Armenians carry a lot of psychological baggage from a traumatic 20th century, you'd hardly notice it from a quick tour around the country. The rapidly modernising capital, the boutique tourism industry and the warm welcome you'll receive everywhere seem to belie the country's reputation for tragedy. Rather than letting past woes weigh it down, Armenia (ՀԱՅԱՍՏԱՆ) has built its memorials, dusted itself off and moved on. For travellers, easily visited highlights include ancient monasteries, candlelit churches and high-walled forts – but lasting impressions lie more with the Armenians themselves. You'll easily find friends among these gracious, humble and easy-going people, even without a common language. The travel experience is wide-ranging – you can have a four-star holiday in Yerevan and Sevan or a much simpler experience in rural towns like Dilijan and Goris. Many travellers only spend a week or less as they shuttle around the region but those with more time get to experience the best spots in crowd-free bliss.

When to Go

Most of Armenia has a dry, high-altitude climate except for verdant rainy pockets in Lori, Tavush and Syunik.

Spring (March to May) is a riot of flowers but does get a lot of rain.

Autumn (late September to early November) has long, warm days and more stable weather.

Summer (June to August) in Yerevan can be 40°C for days at a time, while conditions in the north are mild.

Winter weather lasts until late April through much of the country, with temperatures falling to -10°C in some areas. See p295 for details.

RESOURCES

Armenia Guide
(www.armeniaguide
.com)

Armenia Information
(www.armeniainfo.am)

Armenia Now (www.
armenianow.com)

**Discover Armenia
Tourist Magazine**
(www.touristmagazine
.am)

Tour Armenia
(www.tacentral.com)

Fast Facts

» **Country code** ☏374
» **Population** 3,262,200
» **Currency** Dram (AMD)
» **Languages** Armenian,
Russian
» **Emergency** ☏103

Exchange Rates

Australia	A$1	419.07 AMD
Canada	C$1	407.82 AMD
Euro zone	€1	548.93 AMD
Japan	¥100	433.83 AMD
NZ	NZ$1	340.61 AMD
UK	UK£1	635.77 AMD
USA	US$1	406.01 AMD

Set Your Budget

» **Guesthouse (per person)** AMD6000
» **Two-course evening meal** AMD3500
» **Museum entrance** AMD500–1000
» **Beer at a bar** AMD400
» **100km bus ride** AMD1200

Connections

The closed border with both Turkey to the west and Azerbaijan to the east means that connections to Armenia are somewhat limited. Land borders are open with both Georgia and Iran. As a result, many overlanders regard Armenia as something of a side trip from Georgia, heading south from Tbilisi for a week or two before returning to Georgia. *Marshrutka* (minibus) connections between Georgia and Armenia are fast and frequent, making it easy to pop between the two republics. Only a handful of travellers travel to/from Iran (given the visa restrictions of that country) but there are daily bus connections between Yerevan and Tehran. There are plenty of air connections between Yerevan and other regional cities, including Moscow, Dubai, Vienna, Prague, Paris, Rīga and London.

ITINERARIES

Three Days

There's lots to do and see around Yerevan: take in live music at a concert or restaurant, and shop for brandy, *oghee* (fruit vodka) and handicrafts. Take short day trips to Garni and Geghard, or Khor Virap, or a longer one to Lake Sevan and Dilijan.

One Week

Travel up to Lori to the awesome World Heritage–listed Haghpat and Sanahin churches, stay in Vanadzor or Dilijan, or concentrate on the best of the south – Tatev and Noravank in particular.

Two Weeks

Take some time around Yeghegnadzor and taste more of Yerevan's cosmopolitanism; organise a village or town homestay, explore more of Dilijan; visit Gyumri; or head for Sisian and Goris in the south. Take some time for day hikes, spelunking in Vayots Dzor or hiking on Mt Aragats.

Visas

Armenian visas are available at all entry points – 21-day tourist visas cost AMD3000 and a visa valid for 120 days costs AMD15,000. Most Western nationals require a visa to enter Armenia.

Armenia Highlights

1 Immerse yourself in the culture, cafes and museums of the capital **Yerevan** (p124)

2 Go exploring in the idyllic **Yeghegis Valley** (p177): old churches, quaint villages, a mysterious Jewish cemetery

3 Break in **Dilijan** (p157) for fine mountain scenery, hiking trails and its historic old town

4 Step back at **Echmiadzin** (p148), where St Gregory built Armenia's first church

5 Marvel the World Heritage–listed monasteries Haghpat and Sanahin in the steep-sided **Debed Canyon** (p167)

6 Get mystified at **Geghard Monastery** (p145), an ancient, historic cave church

7 Soar to the castlelike **Tatev Monastery** (p184) on the new cable car then hike down

8 Relax by the clear waters of **Lake Sevan** (p152) when temperatures soar in summer

9 Stretch your legs on **Mt Aragats** (p151), a 4000m snow-covered mountain with distant views of Mt Ararat

YEREVAN

📍10 / POP 1.1 MILLION

While it's the undeniable cultural, economic and political heart of the nation, Yerevan (ԵՐԵՎԱՆ) can at times feel like a city on permanent holiday. All summer long, Yerevanites saunter up and down the main boulevards, preening in high fashion and fast cars while occasionally popping into a parkside cafe to schmooze over a drink or two.

The city has some lovely 19th-century Russian edifices in its central core plus rings of parkland and handsome brick squares. Outer areas maintain an air of Soviet sprawl but these are limited by steep hills and gorges. Yerevan's museums and monuments could keep you busy for a few days but the best thing about the city is the people. Expressive black eyebrows, proud noses and classical Greek and Persian profiles appear everywhere, in a street culture somewhere between that of Marseilles, village Armenia and old Beirut. The cultural life is intense for a city of its size, including dozens of theatres, concert halls, galleries and live music clubs.

At the geographic heart of the country, the city also makes a perfect base to explore other areas. You could even make day trips as far afield as Lake Sevan, Mt Aragats and Vayots Dzor.

History

Yerevan's history dates back to 782 BC, when the Erebuni fortress was built by King Argishti I of Urartu at the place where the Hrazdan River widened onto the fertile Ararat Plains. It was a regional capital of Muslim khanates and Persian governors until the Russian annexation in 1828.

The Soviet rebuilding of the tsarist city removed most of its mosques and some of its churches, and hid others away in residential backwaters, but it kept some of the 19th-century buildings on Abovyan Poghots and left the old neighbourhood of Kond more or less alone.

Alexander Tamanyan developed the current grid plan in the 1920s with the idea that main avenues (Mashtots, Abovyan and Nalbandyan) should point in the direction of Mt Ararat.

◉ Sights

Yerevan has a dozen or so museums, plus several galleries and churches, all located in the city centre and easily reached on foot. We've broken down the sights into two main areas: the northern half of downtown, including Opera Sq (Operayi Hraparak) and the Cascade; and sights in the southern half of downtown, south of Republic Sq.

OPERA SQUARE, THE CASCADE & MOSCOVYAN POGHOTS

This leafy area of town is known for its fashion boutiques, upscale restaurants and outdoor cafes. It also has its share of small museums clustered between the Opera House and the Cascade.

Cascade   GALLERY

(Kaskad; Map p130) A vast flight of stone steps and flower beds, the Cascade leads up to a monument commemorating the 50th anniversary of Soviet Armenia. There are five recessed fountains along the Cascade, some with sculpted panels and postmodern *khatchkars* (carved stone crosses).

Construction of the Cascade came to a halt in 1991 when funds dried up. In 2001, diaspora philanthropist and art collector Gerald L Cafesjian took over the project, repaired the escalators, built galleries and planted flower beds. The top of the Cascade remains unfinished but you can skirt around the edge and walk up to a plaza holding the **50th Anniversary of Soviet Armenia Monument** (Map p126).

The new **Cafesjian Museum** (admission AMD1000; ⊙10am-5pm Tue-Thu, to 8pm Fri-Sun) inside the Cascade houses a vast collection of art and glassware. You can wander through most of the structure as you please but to get inside the galleries you need to buy a ticket. Concerts are held most nights in summer in the topmost gallery.

Fernando Botero's cheerfully fat sculpture *Cat* stands at the base of the Cascade, the first element of Cafesjian's collection put into place. Botero's naked *Roman Warrior* has a 'rigid' pose nearby.

Opera House   CULTURAL BUILDING

(Map p130; 📞52 79 92; 54 Tumanyan Poghots) The landmark of the northern part of the city, the Opera House is surrounded by parks, cafes, nightclubs and shops. The building has two main halls: the Aram Khachaturian Concert Hall and the National Academic Opera and Ballet Theatre.

Tastes have broadened a bit since Soviet Armenia, and the music scene here goes beyond opera and symphonies to Russian pop, MTV and a nightclub in the bowels of the Opera House itself. Tickets range in price from AMD2000 to AMD12,000 depending on the seat location and the performance itself.

Matenadaran
MUSEUM

(Map p130; www.matenadaran.am/en; 53 Mesrop Mashtots Poghota; admission AMD1000, guide AMD2500; ☺10am-4pm Tue-Sat) Armenia's ancient manuscripts library, the Matenadaran, stands like a cathedral at the top of Yerevan's grandest avenue. It preserves more than 17,000 Armenian manuscripts and 100,000 medieval and modern documents. The first Matenadaran for Armenian texts was built by St Mesrop Mashtots at Vagarshapat (Echmiadzin) in the 5th century.

By the early 19th century only 1800 manuscripts were kept at Echmiadzin, after centuries of invasion, looting and burning. The collection grew in importance after the Armenian genocide in WWI saw the destruction of countless tomes. The current Matenadaran was built in 1959, with a research institute dedicated to preserving and restoring manuscripts attached to it.

At the base of the building there is a statue of Mashtots teaching his alphabet to a disciple, while six other statues of great scholars and writers stand by the door. The outdoor gallery has carved rock tombs and *khatchkars* brought here from ancient sites around Armenia. Inside, the collection includes Greek and Roman scientific and philosophical works, Iranian and Arabic manuscripts, and the 15th-century Homilies of Mush, so heavy that it was ripped in half and carried away to safety by two women after the 1915 genocide. The book was not put back together until years later – one saviour had emigrated to America. The illuminated works on display show swirls of red and gold combining classical borders with luxuriant flowers and gardens.

Many of the rarer books in the collection are researched behind closed doors and are not on display. The ticket office has a gift shop with a nice collection of books and souvenirs.

Martiros Sarian Museum
MUSEUM

(Map p130; 3 Sarian Poghots; admission AMD600; ☺10am-5pm Fri-Tue, 10am-4pm Wed) This museum preserves the studio and some of the works of 20th-century painter Martiros Sarian. Some say the pick of his works adorns galleries in Moscow and Paris. Start your visit to the museum upstairs with his sombre early works, then watch the colours erupt as he falls in love with Persia and Egypt. His art seems to mature by fusing those colours into a vision of an Oriental Armenia, landscapes of stark mountains, green villages and plunging gorges. Sarian's large studio remains as it was when the artist died in the 1950s.

National Folk Art Museum of Armenia
MUSEUM

(Map p130; 64 Abovyan Poghots; admission AMD500; ☺11am-5pm Tue-Sun) Has a large display of Armenia's finest crafts, which reveal the exotic influence of the East in Armenian culture. There's also a nice lace exhibit and some interesting woodcarving.

Museum of Russian Art
MUSEUM

(Map p130; 38 Isahakyan Poghots; admission AMD500; ☺11am-4pm Tue-Sun) A collection of 200 works by 19th- and 20th-century Russian artists, donated by Professor Aram Abrahamian, who had a taste for cheerfully picturesque landscapes. Enter on Tamanyan Poghots.

Yervand Kochar Museum
MUSEUM

(Map p130; 39/12 Mesrop Mashtots Poghota; admission AMD600; ☺11am-5pm Tue-Sun) Features

ARMENIA YEREVAN

GETTING YOUR BEARINGS IN YEREVAN

Yerevan sits in a valley edged on three sides by hills, with the little Hrazdan River cutting a serpentine gorge west of the city centre. Downtown streets are laid out on a grid with several ring roads, intersected by the redeveloped Hyusisayin Poghota (Northern Ave). In the centre is Hanrapetutyan Hraparak (Republic Sq), while the Opera House, a few blocks north, is another focal point. Mesrop Mashtots Poghota (avenue) is one of the city's busiest thoroughfares.

The main bus station is the Kilikya Avtokayan west of town on the Echmiadzin highway, which also leads to Zvartnots Airport. *Marshrutky* (minibuses) to various parts of the country leave from all over the city centre, with a concentration around the Rossiya Mall on Tigran Mets Poghota.

The main train station is above Sasuntsi Davit metro station. Yerevan's metro has four stations in the city centre, with the last stop at Barekamutyun.

Yerevan

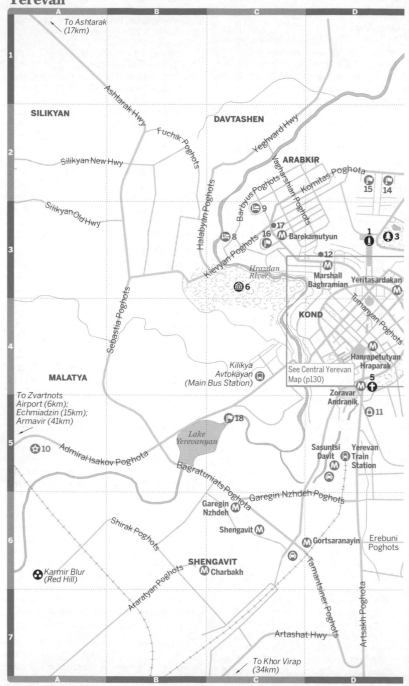

To Ashtarak
(17km)

SILIKYAN

DAVTASHEN

Ashtarak Hwy

Fuchik Poghots

Silikyan New Hwy

Yeghvard Hwy

ARABKIR

Vagharshyan Poghots

Komitas Poghota

Silikyan Old Hwy

Barbyus Poghots

Halabyan Poghots

15   14

9

Kievyan Poghots

8   16   17
Barekamutyun

1   3

12

Hrazdan
River

Marshall
Baghramian

Yeritasardakan

6

Sebastia Poghots

KOND

Tumanyan Poghots

Kilikya
Avtokayan
(Main Bus Station)

See Central Yerevan
Map (p130)

Hanrapetutyan
Hraparak

MALATYA

5

To Zvartnots
Airport (6km);
Echmiadzin (15km);
Armavir (41km)

Zoravar
Andranik

11

18

Lake
Yerevanyan

10

Admiral Isakov Poghota

Sasuntsi
Davit

Yerevan
Train
Station

Bagratuniats Poghota

Garegin Nzhdeh Poghots

Garegin
Nzhdeh

Shirak Poghots

Shengavit

Gortsaranayin

Erebuni
Poghots

Karmir Blur
(Red Hill)

SHENGAVIT
Charbakh

Araratyan Poghots

Tamantsiner Poghota

Artsakh Poghota

Artashat Hwy

To Khor Virap
(34km)

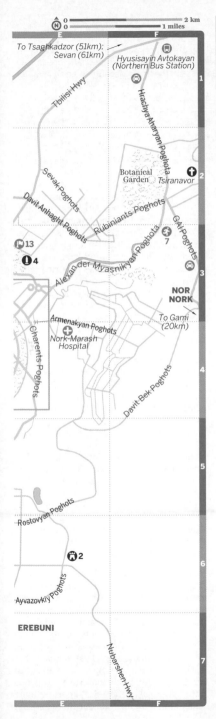

Yerevan

◎ Sights

1 50th Anniversary of Soviet
   Armenia Monument D3
2 Erebuni Fortress & Museum..............E6
3 Haghtanak Park..................................D3
   Military Museum........................ (see 4)
4 Mother Armenia (Mayr
   Hayastan)......................................E3
5 Surp Grigor Lusavorich
   Cathedral......................................D4
6 Tsitsernakaberd (Museum of
   the Armenian Genocide)................C3

◎ Activities, Courses & Tours

7 Water World..F3

◎ Sleeping

8 Boris Family B&B................................C3
9 Hostel Glide..C3

◎ Entertainment

10 Casino Strip A5

◎ Shopping

11 Shuka No 2..D5

◎ Information

12 American University of
   Armenia...D3
   Birds of Armenia Project............(see 12)
13 Georgian Embassy E3
14 Iranian Embassy D2
15 Permanent Representative of
   the Nagorno-Karabakh
   Republic..D2
16 Turkmenistan Embassy.....................C3
17 UPS Express-Hayk C3
18 USA Embassy C5

the sculpture and cubist-style 3-D paintings of the brilliant draughtsman and artist.

Hovhannes Tumanyan Museum MUSEUM
(Map p130; 40 Moscovyan Poghots; admission AMD500, guide AMD2500; ◎11am-4.30pm Tue-Sat, 11am-3pm Sun) Armenia's greatest poet, Hovhannes Tumanyan, is celebrated in this museum, with displays of his personal effects and journals. It's a must-visit if you have already been to (or planning a trip to) Tumanyan's home village of Dsegh (p167).

Churches
Churches in the area include the 1694 **Zoravar Church** (Map p130), one of the nicest little secrets in the city, tucked away

YEREVAN IN ONE DAY

Start off with breakfast at a cafe on Abovyan Poghots with some freshly ground *soorch* (coffee). Take a look around the grand buildings of Hanrapetutyan Hraparak (Republic Sq), and have a browse in the National Art Gallery and the State Museum of Armenian History. Walk up Hyusisayin Poghota to marvel at Yerevan's sparkling new pedestrian mall, then continue uphill to the Matenadaran, a fine building with a small but beautiful collection of manuscripts on display, or go up to the Cascade for a grand view over the city, surrounded by flower beds. If you have time (and energy) take a taxi to the genocide memorial. Then head out to a restaurant for a long dinner of Armenian *khoravats* (barbe-cued food) with salads, desserts and cognac. Check out a club or people-watch from any one of dozens of late-night cafes, around the Opera House or the Ring Park.

off Parpetsi Poghots. The tiny, 13th-century **Katoghike** (Map p130) is at the corner of Sayat-Nova Poghota and Abovyan Poghots. The Soviets were demolishing a later church here in 1936, which exposed the fine inscriptions on the chapel. Amazingly enough for that era, a public outcry let the chapel survive. Fragments from the dismantled church lie around it.

REPUBLIC SQUARE, SOUTHERN MASHTOTS & KHANDJIAN POGHOTS

Sights in this section are grouped in the southern part of downtown. The area around Republic Sq includes government ministries, as well as some of the better hotels and embassies.

Hanrapetutyan Hraparak
(Republic Square)   SQUARE

The former Lenin Sq is surrounded by the city's finest ensemble of buildings, particularly the Armenia Marriott Hotel, and the National Art Gallery and State Museum of Armenian History, where Stalinist scale meets Armenian architecture in a huge yellow-and-cream building facing some massive fountains. The centre of the square (more of an oval) is now a flat stretch of polished marble. New lights and repaired fountains make Hanrapetutyan Hraparak (Map p130) a focal point on warm afternoons and nights. In summer, the fountains dance to music and lights between 9.30pm and 11pm.

TOP CHOICE **State Museum of Armenian History**   MUSEUM

(National Museum; Map p130; Hanrapetutyan Hraparak; admission AMD1000, guide AMD5000; ☺11am-5pm Tue-Sun) This museum spans Stone Age cave dwellers in the Hrazdan Gorge to the astronomy and metallurgy of 3000 BC Metsamor, the Urartu Empire and

the gathering of the Hayk tribes into a nation in the 6th century BC. After that, centuries fly past through Hellenic Armenia, the arrival of Christianity and finally the long centuries under Muslim Turkish and Persian rule. There are medieval *khatchkars*, costumes, jewellery, coins, and models of buried settlements and lost churches. One of the most prized artefacts to join the collection is a 5500-year-old leather shoe discovered in a cave in Vayots Dzor region in 2008. Scientists have dubbed it the 'world's oldest shoe' (see the boxed text, p176).

National Art Gallery   GALLERY

(Map p130; Hanrapetutyan Hraparak; admission AMD800, guide AMD5000; ☺11am-5.30pm Tue-Sun) The National Art Gallery holds the third-biggest collection of European masters in the former USSR; many of the works here were appropriated in Europe during WWII. This national treasure includes works by Donatello, Tintoretto, Fragonard, Courbet, Theodore Rousseau, Rodin, Rubens and Jan Van Dyck. There are also many works by Russian painters, and Armenian painters, sculptors and graphic artists including Martiros Sarian, Yervand Kochar and Sedrak Arakelyan. If you can talk your way into visiting the roof there are opportunities here for sweeping city views.

Yerevan Brandy Company   BRANDY FACTORY

(Map p130; ☏54 00 00; www.ybc.am; Admiral Isakov Poghota; tour & tastings AMD3000; ☺10am-5pm Mon-Fri, tours by appointment) 'The fairyland of the world-famous Armenian brandy', Yerevan Brandy Company runs fun tours with generous tastings from its iconic premises by the Hrazdan River. The company has cellars of barrels dating back to the 19th century, including one that won't be opened until a Karabakh peace deal appears. Tours take 75 minutes, including tastings, and end at the souvenir shop. It's a pleasant walk across the Haghtanak Bridge or a short taxi ride (AMD600) from the city centre.

Blue Mosque
MOSQUE

(Map p130; 12 Mesrop Mashtots Poghota; ☉10am-6pm) Of the eight or so working mosques in Yerevan in 1900, the Blue Mosque is the only one remaining today. The **Iran Information & Communication Centre** next door has the key. It's appropriate to wear trousers and a long-sleeved shirt – no bare legs or shoulders.

The Soviets turned the mosque into the Yerevan City Museum until it was restored and somewhat 'modernised' by an Iranian religious-government foundation in the 1990s. It lives on as a sign of Armenia's necessarily good relations with Iran.

The mosque was built in 1765 by the Persian Governor Hussein Ali Khan as a place for Friday sermons and features a *medrese* (religious college) built around a garden courtyard, a 24m-high minaret and a brightly tiled turquoise dome.

Sergei Paradjanov Museum
MUSEUM

(Map p130; www.parajanov.com/museum.html; 15/16 Dzoragyugh Poghots; admission AMD700, guide in French AMD2500; ☉10.30am-5pm) This engaging, eccentric house-museum of an avant-garde film director and artist (see p190) stands by the Hrazdan Gorge near Surp Sargis. Paradjanov was born in 1924 in Tbilisi but retired to Yerevan after serving prison terms on charges of immorality in the 1970s and 1980s. This fine house showcases his colourful, amusing collages and framed found-object sculptures, as well as sketches and designs for his films. There's real wit and flair to his work, and the museum is well worth visiting even if avant-garde 20th-century film isn't normally your thing. There are postcards and videos of his major films for sale.

Yerevan Museum
MUSEUM

(Map p130; www.yerevanhistorymuseum.info.am; 1/1 Argishti Poghots; admission AMD500, guide AMD3000; ☉11am-5.30pm Mon-Sat) This new museum covers the foundation, expansion and development of Armenia's capital. The central display on the ground floor is an enormous scale model of 19th-century Yerevan (best seen from the balcony on the floors above). Other exhibits include knives, jewellery, pottery and other artefacts discovered during recent excavations.

FNPAK
GALLERY

(Map p130; www.accea.info; 1/3 Pavstos Byuzand Poghots; admission free; ☉10am-6pm Mon-Sat) The Norarar Pordzarakan Arvesti Kentovon (Armenian Centre for Contemporary Experimental Art) is a large, well-appointed gallery and art complex facing the big Vernissage market. Yervand Kochar's 1959 figure *Melancholy* pines at the entrance. Most of the artists in residence are in their 20s and 30s, and avant-garde concerts and performances are held in a huge auditorium. It's viewed with healthy suspicion by the more conservative arts audience – the next Armenian cultural revolution might start here.

Surp Grigor Lusavorich Cathedral
CATHEDRAL

Modern Yerevan's first real cathedral (Map p126) was built to celebrate 1700 years of Christianity in Armenia and was consecrated in 2001. This hulking building stands on a small hill where Khandjian Poghots meets Tigran Mets Poghota. It's a bit brutalist in execution, possibly because it hasn't been around for 1000 years and collected age, atmosphere and *khatchkars*. There's a statue of Zoravar (General) Andranik at the bottom of the stairs that lead to the church (Map p130). Zoravar Andranik led the army that defeated the Turks at Sardarapat in May 1918.

Museum of Modern Art
MUSEUM

(Map p130; 7 Mesrop Mashtots Poghota; admission AMD500; ☉10am-3pm Tue-Sun) Near the corner of Sarian Poghots is the main exhibition centre for contemporary Armenian artists, the Museum of Modern Art. It also has an impressive collection of works from the 1970s onwards. The museum is on a narrow lane just off Mashtots, hidden behind a row of shops.

State Museum of Wood-Carving
MUSEUM

(Map p130; 4-2 Paronyan Poghots; admission AMD400; ☉noon-6pm Tue-Sun) This is actually an interesting collection of some meticulous pieces, both modern and medieval. The entrance is slightly hidden, set back behind the food kiosk.

Surp Sargis Church
CHURCH

Near the Museum of Wood-Carving, look out for this 1853 church (Map p130; 1853), on Israeliyan Poghots off Mashtots, overlooking the Hrazdan River. The Sunday liturgy and choir are particularly good.

Central Yerevan

Presidential Palace

94

Marshall Baghramian Poghota

Aigedzor Poghots

33

Proshyan Poghots

Marshall Baghramian

Demirchyan Poghots

National Assembly (Azgayin Zogov)

Dzorap Poghots

84

3

69

Dzorap Poghots

5

21

49

Satian Poghots

70

87

53

39

Nairi Clinic

@

52

29

71

Mesrop Mashtots Poghota

67

81

Parpetsi Poghots

Tumanyan Poghots

Pushkin Poghots

47

90

Demirchyan Aram Poghots

P Byuzand Poghots

95

51

8

Paronyan Poghots

Amiryan Poghots

103

75

100

74

72

14

15

26

1

60

22

Hanrapetutyan Hraparak (Republic Square)

16

Momisea Khorenatsi Poghots

Grigor Lusavorich Poghota

Khorhrdaran Poghots

Hrazdan River

17

92

Haghtanak Bridge

Admiral Isakov Poghota

28

86

18

Yazgen Sargsyan Poghots

27

82

Italia Poghots

Zoravar Andranik

Rossiya Mall

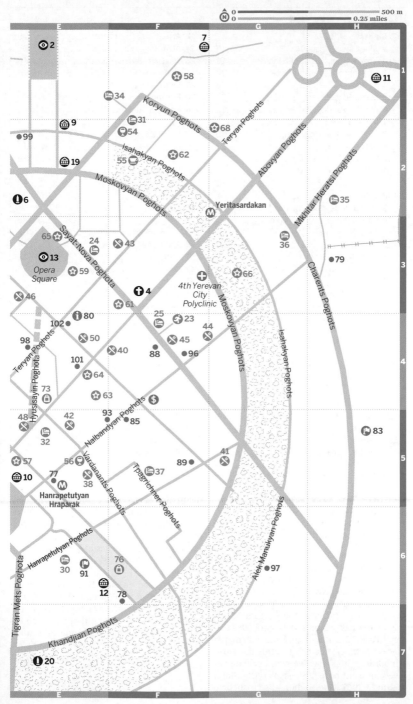

Central Yerevan

◉ Sights

1	Blue Mosque	C5
2	Cascade	E1
3	Hovannes Tumanyan Museum	D2
4	Katoghike	F3
5	Martiros Sarian Museum	C2
6	Martiros Sarian Statue	E2
7	Matenadaran	F1
8	Museum of Modern Art	C5
9	Museum of Russian Art	E2
10	National Art Gallery	E5
11	National Folk Art Museum of Armenia	H1
12	NPAK	E6
13	Opera House	E3
14	Sergei Paradjanov Museum	B5
	State Museum of Armenian History	(see 10)
15	State Museum of Wood-Carving	B5
16	Surp Sargis	B6
17	Yerevan Brandy Company	A6
18	Yerevan Museum	B7
19	Yervand Kochar Museum	E2
20	Zoravar Andranik Statue	E7
21	Zoravar Church	D3

◉ Activities, Courses & Tours

22	Arena Bowling Centre	B5
	Envoy Hostel	(see 29)
	Hyur Service	(see 85)
23	Lazaryn Dpratoon	F4

⬤ Sleeping

24	Anahit Stepanyan	E3
25	Ani Plaza Hotel	F4
26	Armenia Marriott Hotel	D5
27	AUA Suites	D7
28	Best Western Congress	C6
	Central Hostel	(see 38)
29	Envoy Hostel	D3
30	Europe Hotel	E6
31	Foreign Students Hostel	F2
32	Hotel Avia Trans	E5
33	Hotel Bass	B1
34	Meg Hotel	F1
35	Parev Inn	H2
36	Penthouse Hostel	G3
37	Yerevan Hostel	F5

⊗ Eating

38	Ankyun	E5
39	Artashi Mot	D3
40	Artbridge Bookstore Café	F4
41	Caucasus Tavern	G5
42	Dolmama's	E5
43	Karma	F3
44	Lagonid Bistro-Cafe	F4
45	Liban Restaurant	F4
46	Old Erivan	E3
47	Shah Pizza	D4
48	Square One	E5
49	The Club	D2
50	Tumanyan Shwarma	E4
51	Urartu	A5

◉ Drinking

52	26 Irish	D3
53	Calumet	C3
54	Ice Club	F2
55	Poplovok Jazz Café	F2
56	Stoyka	E5

OUTSIDE THE CENTRE

The following sights lie outside the central core and thus require a fair hike or a short cab or *marshrutka* ride.

Mother Armenia   MONUMENT
(Mayr Hayastan; Map p126) Symbolism abounds in the huge statue of Mother Armenia. She looms over the city in line with Mesrop Mashtots Poghota, on a classic Soviet plaza complete with tanks and jets set on pedestals at the eastern end of Haghtanak (Victory) Park. The 23m-high Mother Armenia glares out across the city towards the Turkish border with a massive sword held defensively in front of her. She replaced a Stalin statue in 1967. One soldier was crushed to death and several were injured when his statue was wrenched off unannounced one night, leading to grim muttering about Stalin still killing from beyond the grave.

Inside the 50m pedestal is a **Military Museum** (Map p126; admission free, photos AMD500; ☺10am-5pm Tue-Fri, to 3pm Sat & Sun). The interior is based on Surp Hripsime at Echmiadzin, a brave acknowledgment of religion by the architect during Stalin's lifetime. The space on the main floor is devoted to the Karabakh War. The basement houses a mothballed collection of WWII artefacts (300,000 Armenians died, half of those sent to fight). **Haghtanak Park** (Map p126), next to Mother Armenia, is a mostly overgrown patch of woods containing a small amusement park.

☺ Entertainment

Aram Khachaturian Concert
Hall .... (see 13)
57 Arno Babadjanian Concert
Hall E5
58 Chamber Theatre F1
59 Giza E3
60 Hakob Paronyan State
Musical Comedy Theatre D6
61 Hovhannes Tumanyan
Theatre of Marionettes F3
62 Hrachia Ghaplanyan Drama
Theatre F2
63 Kami E4
64 Kino Moskva E4
65 Kiosk for Opera Tickets E3
66 Komitas Chamber Music Hall G3
67 Malkhas Jazz Club D3
National Academic Opera &
Ballet Theatre .... (see 13)
68 One Club G2
69 Stop Club D2

☺ Shopping

Artbridge Bookstore .... (see 40)
70 Bureaucrat C3
71 Carpet Shop D3
72 Noyan Tapan D5
73 Salt Sack E4
74 Shuka No 1 .... B5
75 Treasures of Armenia D5
Vernissage Art Market .... (see 6)
76 Vernissage Market F6

ℹ Information

77 American Corner E5

78 Avarayr F6
79 Ayas Nautical Research Club H3
Canadian Embassy .... (see 26)
80 Caravan Tours E4
Envoy Tours .... (see 29)
81 FedEx/Transimpex D4
82 French Embassy C7
83 German Embassy H5
84 Greek Embassy C2
85 Hyur Service F5
Iran Aseman Airlines .... (see 93)
Iran Information &
Communication Centre .... (see 1)
86 Italian Embassy C7
87 Laundry Service C3
88 Levon Travel F4
Menua Tours .... (see 97)
89 Ministry of Culture F5
90 OVIR C4
91 Polish Embassy E6
92 Russian Embassy B6
93 Tatev Travel E5
94 UK Embassy C1

ℹ Transport

95 Aeroflot C5
Air France .... (see 97)
96 Armavia F4
97 Austrian Airlines G6
98 Baltic Air E4
BMI .... (see 97)
99 Czech Airlines E2
100 Fly Dubai C5
101 Hertz E4
102 S7 Airlines E4
103 Syrian Air C5

FREE **Tsitsernakaberd (Armenian Genocide Memorial & Museum)** MEMORIAL (Map p126; Tsitsernakaberd Hill; admission free; ☺11am-4pm Tue-Sun) Commemorating the agony of the 1915–22 genocide of Armenians during the death throes of the Ottoman Empire, the Museum of the Armenian Genocide and memorial create a moving experience. The museum lies underground in a grey stone bunker. Large photographs (many, but not all, with English explanations) tell the story of the genocide with stone-faced emotion. There's no effort to demonise the Ottoman authorities; the facts are allowed to speak for themselves. It starts with the massacres of 1896 and 1909 and the lack of an international response, and then moves on to the murder of Armenian labour conscripts in the Ottoman army in late 1914 and early 1915. The arrest and subsequent murder of community leaders and intellectuals on 24 April 1915 marks the beginning of that nightmare summer. All over Anatolia men were arrested, marched out of their towns and murdered in shallow graves.

A permanent exhibition of paintings of half-dead, naked survivors stands in the hall. The final image is an enlarged photograph of an orphanage in Syria after the genocide. Outside there's a magnificent view of Mt Ararat, the symbol of Armenia now 40km inside modern Turkish territory.

Nearby there is a *khatchkar* in remembrance of the 1988 Sumqayıt massacre in

Azerbaijan, and the graves of early victims of the Karabakh War (1989–94).

There is a row of trees planted by foreign leaders who recognise the genocide, despite the Turkish government's determination to punish any foreign power that does so.

A broad pathway flanked by a 100m-long wall engraved with the names of massacred communities leads to the **memorial**, consisting of a 40m-high spire next to a circle of 12 basalt slabs leaning over to guard an eternal flame. The 12 tilted slabs represent the lost provinces of western Armenia, land lost to Turkey in a post-WWI peace deal between Ataturk and Lenin, while the spire has a fine split dividing it into larger and smaller needles, the smaller one representing western Armenia. Set on Tsitsernakaberd Hill (Fortress of Swallows) across the Hrazdan Gorge from central Yerevan, the memorial was built in 1967 after unprecedented demonstrations on 24 April 1965, the 50th anniversary of the genocide. In a rare acknowledgement of public discontent, the Soviets deposed the local Communist Party boss in response and gave permission for the memorial to be built.

A taxi (AMD600 from the city centre) is the easiest way to reach Tsitsernakaberd. Or take *marshrutka* 70 or 87 from Mesrop Mashtots Poghota; these drop you by the road near the memorial, from where it's a 600m walk to the museum (after 200m take the road that forks left). From the memorial, continue walking down the steps, which leads back to the road where you can flag down a *marshrutka*.

Erebuni Fortress & Museum　　MUSEUM
Excavations began at the Erebuni Fortress (Map p126) site in 1959 after a farmer unearthed an inscribed stone tablet. Archaeologists swooped in and soon found a large cuneiform slab with the inscriptions of Argishti I, king of Urartu, setting the date the fortress was built at 782 BC. It reads, in part, 'Argishti, the son of Menua, has built this magnificent fortress as a house for Khaldi, the Lord, to the glory of the Biayni countries and to the horror of enemies', which says a bit about the nature of Armenian pride.

The view from the fortress takes in the city and Karmir Blur (Red Hill), where excavations have revealed similar ancient finds. Frescoes in the reconstructed palace wall are replicas. There are huge storerooms for wheat, along with gigantic pitchers

for wine and oil, and *tonir* (oven pits). There's also a place for animal sacrifices, and workshops (still buried) for making tools, including arrows for fighting and hunting. Sadly, ugly slabs of concrete now top most of the stone walls (preservation, Soviet-style).

The somewhat neglected **Erebuni Museum** (Map p126; 38 Erebuni Poghots; admission AMD1000, guide AMD3500; ☺10.30am-4.30pm Tue-Sun), at the bottom of the hill, has other cuneiform tablets and jewellery excavated from the site. It's housed in a striking 1960s Soviet building with huge apricot-coloured *tufa* (volcanic stone) friezes, with exhibits that probably haven't been updated since Brezhnev was in power.

To get here from outside the Armenia Marriott Hotel, take *marshrutka* 36, 86 or 76.

🏃 Activities

The local football league has a regular winter season. Basketball is popular among kids, while nardi (backgammon) is the elders' game of choice, along with chess.

Water World　　SWIMMING
(Map p126; ☎63 89 98; 40 Myasnikyan Poghota; admission AMD5000; ☺noon-8.30pm, nightclub until late Fri & Sat) The main sport and leisure facility in Yerevan is **Water World**, a large complex of pools and slides. Water World is open from June to September but next door is the **Aquatek** (☎58 88 88; www.aquatek.am; admission AMD5000), an indoor complex that stays open year-round. Women are required to wear a swimming cap. Both facilities are located on the outskirts of town on the road towards Sevan.

Arena Bowling Centre　　BOWLING
(Map p130; ☎53 61 01; www.bowling.am; 8 Mesrop Mashtots Poghota; ☺11am-4am) Yerevan's best bowling alley is modern and costs AMD6000 per lane per hour during the day, or AMD12,000 per hour after 6pm. On weekends it's AMD12,000 all day.

👉 Tours

The Envoy Hostel (p135) offers free walking tours several times a week (depending on demand). The tours last around 2½ hours and the guides do a great job of introducing Yerevan's unique history. They also do free night walking tours in summer. Three times a week the Envoy has a 'Communist History' tour for AMD8500, with visits to moribund factories, metro stations and other legacies of the USSR. Other recommended agencies for Yerevan tours include **Hyur Service** and Menua Tours (p142).

Courses

Lazaryn Dpratoon LANGUAGE
(☎52 37 78; www.ldt.am; 21a Sayat-Nova Poghota) An Armenian- and Russian-language school for all levels. It's in a building set back from Sayat-Nova Poghota. The door is on the southeast side of the building (but hard to find as there are many doors and no signs in English). It's best to call ahead before coming over here.

✿ Festivals & Events

Fireworks seem to celebrate a national holiday or commemorate some event or other every fortnight or so. The independence days sometimes see concerts on Republic Sq or in the parkland around the Opera House. The **Golden Apricot International Film Festival** (www.gaiff.am) is held in July. The **High Fest** (www.highfest.am), in early October, sees the arrival of international theatre groups for a variety of performances. For those willing to brave the cold, the **Armenia Winter Festival** takes place between December 25 and January 6 and features outdoor concerts in public parks.

🛏 Sleeping

Besides the following listings, travel agencies (p142) can organise a homestay for around AMD6000 per night or an apartment rental starting from around AMD15,000 per night. You can also check www.armeniainfo.am, which has listings for B&Bs. The hostel scene was developing rapidly at the time of research with new places popping up every month; expect changes in this category during the life of this book.

OPERA SQUARE, THE CASCADE & MOSCOVYAN POGHOTS

TOP CHOICE **Envoy Hostel** HOSTEL $
(Map p130; ☎53 03 69; www.envoyhostel.com; 54 Pushkin Poghots; dm AMD7000-8000, d AMD20,000-23,000, all prices incl breakfast; ☻✳@☎) This large, European-style hostel has eight dorm rooms spread over two floors. The beds are very comfortable and lockers in the rooms are available. The hot showers are legendary. Try to get a room on the main level as downstairs rooms are boxy, windowless cells. It has friendly English-speaking

staff and almost-daily tours to sites around the country (and free walking tours in the city). It even runs a weekly shuttle to Tbilisi (p142). It's a real hive of activity, as is the neighbourhood – there are loads of cafes and bars nearby. On the downside, it can get a bit noisy when big groups roll through. Kitchen facilities are available and the free breakfast includes bread, cheese and tea, and they sometimes add eggs or sausages. Despite the address, the door is actually on Parpetsi Poghots.

Meg Hotel HOTEL $$
(Map p130; ☎58 10 08; www.hotelmeg.com; 1 Jrashat Poghots; r from US$80; @☎) This smart little hotel has a business feel to it, with coffee-coloured furniture, polished fittings and all mod cons and services. Breakfast is served in your room. It's a roomy, comfortable place and a fine choice in this price range. It's a little hard to find: as you walk up Mashtots take a left just after the bookshop (into the small compound), and the hotel is up the little hill on the right.

Penthouse Hostel HOSTEL $
(Map p130; ☎094997794, 098894224; www.penthousehostel.org; 5 Koryun Poghots, apt 33; per person €11.30; @☎) This guesthouse, run by the friendly Yanaa and Artur Nazaryan, has modern double rooms and a three-bed dorm. The outgoing owners speak English and French and attempt to create a cosy, homelike atmosphere. The simple breakfast includes some Armenian dishes. You need

---

APARTMENT RENTALS

Renting an apartment is a common practice among visitors to Yerevan. Prices peak between June and October. At the time of writing, AMD15,000 a day got you a single-bedroom apartment with sporadic water supplies a *marshrutka* ride away from town. Upwards of AMD25,000 a day rented a two- or three-bedroom apartment in a more convenient location. Up to AMD40,000 a day earned a three- or four-bedroom renovated apartment or house. Besides the travel agencies (p142), which frequently arrange apartments, there are some specialists for standard and luxury apartments: www.hyurservice.com and www.visitarm.com.

to hike up five flights of stairs to reach the door but you will be rewarded with excellent views of Mt Ararat.

Parev Inn
GUESTHOUSE $$

(Map p130; ☑55 99 85; www.parev.am; 71 11th Aigestan Poghots; s/d incl breakfast AMD22,000/28,000;❋❂) A pleasant guesthouse just up from Mkhitar Heratsi Poghots (near the Nork cable car), run by a Canadian-Armenian couple. Generous discounts are available in the low season (from November to March). The rooms are large and comfortable, with splashes of colour, plus a kitchenette and modern bathrooms. The access road is a little hard to spot – take a sharp right before the CPS petrol station.

Anahit Stepanyan
HOMESTAY $

(Map p130; ☑52 75 89, 091502071; Apt 25, 5 Sayat-Nova Poghota; per person AMD6000) This popular homestay consists of two large dorm rooms, a private room and a loft. It has an authentic homestay feel – there is no front desk, just English-speaking Anahit greeting you at the door. It has a slightly dishevelled atmosphere but this somehow adds hominess – just don't come looking for a proper hotel. The entrance is on Sayat-Nova Poghota, between Our Village restaurant and a shoe shop called 'No One'. Press the button for apartment 25 and Anahit will buzz you inside. If it's full, you can try a more basic set-up at the home of Gayane Simonyan, in apartment 22 (just below Anahit).

Ani Plaza Hotel
HOTEL $$$

(Map p130; ☑58 95 00; www.anihotel.com; 19 Sayat-Nova Poghota; s/d AMD41,000/51,000, ste from AMD70,000, all incl breakfast;❋❂) This landmark in the heart of town has been updated to an upper-midrange hotel. Cheaper rooms have not seen renovation on the same scale as the deluxe rooms, but all are modern and comfortable. Rates include use of the indoor swimming pool.

Foreign Students Hostel
HOSTEL $$

(Map p130; ☑56 00 03; ysugh@xter.net; 52 Mesrop Mashtots Poghota; s/d AMD16,000/25,500) Simple and small rooms are on offer at this university hostel, usually occupied by exchange students. It's a handy option for budget travellers looking for more privacy than the hostels can offer. There is no reception desk, just go and talk to the administrator in room 106.

REPUBLIC SQUARE, SOUTHERN MASHTOTS & KHANDJIAN POGHOTS

⭐ Best Western Congress
HOTEL $$$

(Map p130; ☑58 00 95; www.congresshotelyerevan. com; 1 Italia Poghots; s/d AMD44,400/60,600; ❋@❂❂) Next to a pleasant park and overlooking leafy Italia Poghots, the Congress offers quiet serenity in the city centre. The 126 rooms are clean and modern, although the singles are a little poky. The hotel is best known for its big outdoor swimming pool; nonguests can swim for AMD7000 on weekdays and AMD9000 on weekends.

Europe Hotel
HOTEL $$

(Map p130; ☑54 60 60; www.europeho tel.am; 32-38 Hanrapetutyan Poghots; s/d AMD38,000/43,000, ste AMD61,000-71,000, all prices incl breakfast;❋❂) This quiet hotel in the centre of town has a flair for bright colours in its decor, and a groovy bar and cafe on the ground floor. The rooms are a little small but perfectly comfortable.

Armenia Marriott Hotel
HOTEL $$$

(Map p130; ☑59 90 00; www.marriott.com; Hanrapetutyan Hraparak; r from AMD75,000; ❋@❂) With its posh address on Republic Sq, the Marriott stands out as the place to be seen in Yerevan. The hotel includes a ritzy buffet breakfast (not included in room rates), a 24-hour gym (one of the best in town), an Italian restaurant and a popular streetside cafe. Wi-fi is free in the lobby but in the rooms you need to pay US$7 a day. Rooms in the back are quiet and have views of Mt Ararat.

Yerevan Hostel
HOSTEL $

(Map p130; ☑54 77 57; www.hostelinyerevan. com; 5 Tpagrichner Poghots; dm/d incl breakfast AMD6500/20,000; ❋@❂) This hostel is buried in the basement of a large apartment block, close to Republic Sq. It's a decent-sized place with bunk beds spread around two large dorm rooms plus a couple of private rooms. The set-up is a bit awkward, with the shared bathrooms and dorms at opposite ends of the hostel, so that you need to walk through the common areas to reach the showers. However, the atmosphere is clean and friendly and also quieter compared to some of its competitors. The English-speaking staff can help with logistics. The breakfast is a simple spread of bread, cheese and butter.

Central Hostel
GUESTHOUSE $

(Map p130; ☑52 86 39, 094484 673; Apt 31, 4 Vardanants Poghots; dm incl breakfast AMD6000; @) As the name indicates, this place has a good, central location near Republic Sq. However, despite the name, it resembles not so much a hostel but is more of a 'guesthouse' as it consists of just two rooms in a family apartment. Owner Susana Grigoryan prepares a basic breakfast and son Vahan speaks English. It is located above the Ankyun restaurant but the entrance is around the back of the building. Look for entrance III, apartment 31.

AUA Suites
HOTEL $$
(Map p130; ✐56 75 67; www.hybusiness.com; 8 Hanrapetutyan Poghots; s/d/ste AMD22,000/38,000/55,000; ✲@) Not a typical hotel, this place is designed for extended stays or families – rooms are large and come with kitchenettes. Internet is a pricey AMD2000 per day. It's associated with the American University in Armenia.

Hotel Avia Trans
HOTEL $$
(Map p130; ✐56 72 26; www.aviatrans.am; 4 Abovyan Poghots; s/d/tr incl breakfast AMD38,000/45,000/60,000; ✲@) An anonymous exterior belies an otherwise pleasant lobby and friendly reception in this central hotel. By comparison, the rooms are a bit bland and furnishings are dated but the bountiful breakfast buffet makes up for these shortcomings.

OUTSIDE THE CENTRE

Hotel Bass
HOTEL $$
(Map p130; ✐22 26 38; www.bass.am; 3/1 Aigedzor Poghots; s/d AMD32,000/36,000, ste AMD44,000; ✲@✆▨) A friendly boutique hotel in an interesting neighbourhood close to Marshall Baghramian metro station. Large and homey rooms are decked out with TVs and DVD players. Sauna and indoor pool are among the amenities. Ask for big discounts in the low season (November to March).

Hostel Glide
HOSTEL $
(Map p126; ✐27 40 27; www.hostelinyerevan.am; 16 Galents Poghots; dm/s/d AMD6000/12,000/18,000; @✆) This private home has several rooms, two common lounges and a big kitchen, all clean and well maintained. Paragliding, skiing, hiking and other adventurous activities can be organised. To get here, take the metro to Barekamutyun. In the underground mall, walk right to the third exit and take the right fork when going upstairs; this will lead you to Hakobyan Poghots. Walk up Hakobyan for 50m and turn left onto a little alley (Galents Poghots), and continue to number 16.

Boris Family B&B
GUESTHOUSE $
(Map p126; ✐27 37 27; sayvazyan@gmail.com; 42 Barbyus Poghots; r AMD6000; @✆) This huge private house has three guestrooms that share a clean bathroom. It's a little out of the centre but Boris and his family get high marks for hospitality. The excellent views of the Hrazdan River are a bonus. From Barekamutyun metro walk 600m along Kievyan Poghots, take the first right on Orbeli Poghots (also called Blur) and then a left on Barbyus Poghots.

🍴 Eating

Yerevan's dining scene continues to improve, with dozens of international offerings. Traditional fare is also thriving; there are plenty of places for carnivores to taste the best lamb, pork and beef *khoravats* (barbecued food) Armenia can offer. Street snacks like kebabs wrapped in lavash (thin flat bread) and pastries are sold from stalls and bakeries in every neighbourhood.

OPERA SQUARE, THE CASCADE & MOSCOVYAN POGHOTS

Lagonid Bistro-Cafe
MIDDLE EASTERN $
(Map p130; 37 Nalbandyan Poghots; meals AMD2000; ▥) A good-value restaurant serving terrific Syrian-Armenian cuisine, including tabouleh (AMD600), hummus (AMD600), and grills and kebabs for around AMD1300. The decor is fairly simple but the food is fresh and tasty.

The Club
FUSION $$
(Map p130; 40 Tumanyan Poghots; meals AMD3000-5000; ☉noon-1am; ✆▥) One of the classiest places in Yerevan, the Club fuses western Armenian and French cuisine into a fresh and tasty dining experience. It includes a main dining hall, a drinks-only room with cushions on the floor, and a hidden cafe in the back. Live music is occasionally on offer and there is a separate section selling books and handicrafts.

Old Erivan
ARMENIAN $$
(Map p130; 2 Tumanyan Poghots; meals AMD2500; ☉noon-midnight; ▥) Part spectacle, part restaurant, this place serves Armenian cuisine amid boisterous minstrels belting out folk music. The atmosphere is cavelike, with lots of antiques and crafts, although the winged centurions are a little over the top.

Liban Restaurant
LEBANESE $$
(Map p130; 23 Sayat-Nova Poghota; meals AMD2000-5000; ☉noon-1am; ▥) This casual

place is a great option for tasty, filling and delicious Lebanese food, with a huge array of grilled meats and tasty sides dishes. It makes a nice hummus and the speciality is *samke harra* (baked fish with nuts and garlic).

Karma
INDIAN $$
(Map p130; 65 Teryan Poghots; meals AMD2200-3500; 📖) North Indian restaurant offering excellent tandoori chicken and vegetarian dishes in beautifully decorated surrounds.

Artbridge Bookstore Café
CAFE $$
(Map p130; 20 Abovyan Poghots; sandwiches AMD1500-2500, coffee AMD600-1100; 📖) This is a comfy, arty cafe behind a bookshop that sells concert and drama tickets. The food is reasonably priced, the decor is very European and there are even nonsmoking tables. Foodwise, you can't go wrong with the excellent French toast, but the sandwiches and pastas we tried were mediocre for the price.

Artashi Mot
ARMENIAN $
(Map p130; Spendarian Poghots; shwarma AMD650) This midrange Armenian restaurant is divided into two parts: a takeaway shwarma joint on the main floor, and a sit-down restaurant in the basement. Try either for an excellent mushroom *khoravats*, or *putuk,* a mutton-and-veggie soup cooked in an individual glazed crock.

Tumanyan Shwarma
ARMENIAN $
(Map p130; 19 Tumanyan Poghots; shwarma AMD650; ⊙11am-2am) Popular Armenian fastfood place offering shwarma (AMD650) and *khoravats* (AMD2500), plus ice cream and smoothies.

REPUBLIC SQUARE, SOUTHERN MASHTOTS & KHANDJIAN POGHOTS

TOP CHOICE **Dolmama's**
ARMENIAN, EUROPEAN $$$
(Map p130; 10 Pushkin Poghots; meals AMD7000-10,000; 📖) This small, upmarket restaurant has a homey atmosphere and a kitchen that creates unique variations on local cuisine. Try the mountain lamb stew or chicken in wine and walnut sauce, made with the freshest produce available. Dolmama's is highly regarded among Yerevan's elite – the president dines here regularly and foreign dignitaries are often brought here. Smart casual dress is recommended.

Caucasus Tavern
GEORGIAN $
(Map p130; 82 Hanrapetutyan Poghots; meals AMD1500-3000; ⊙24hr; 📖) This is one of the more successful 'tourist' restaurants in town. Waiters in Georgian garb dish up cheap drinks such as mulberry *oghee* shots for AMD400, feasts of *khachapuri* (cheese pies) and main barbecue platters to the sound of live folk music. It claims to be open all night but may close in the wee hours.

Ankyun
ITALIAN $$
(Map p130; 4 Vardanants Poghots; meals AMD3500-6000; ⊙noon-11pm; 📖) Ask Yerevan foodies where to get the best Italian food in town and they will probably recommend this place. Excellent appetisers, steaks and pastas are available in a quiet, candlelit atmosphere.

Shah Pizza
MIDDLE EASTERN $
(Map p130; 34 Mesrop Mashtots Poghots; meals AMD1500-3000) This Middle Eastern hookah joint feels more like Damascus than Armenia. Most of the clientele are Arab businessmen, travellers and expats. It serves, salads, kebabs and of course pizza, as well as flavoured *nargile* (hookah).

Square One
AMERICAN $$
(Map p130; 1/3 Abovyan Poghots; meals AMD2500-3500; 📶📖) A handy, American-style place with sandwiches, pizzas, pastas, salads, burgers and tasty breakfasts (served all day). One section is blissfully nonsmoking.

Urartu
ARMENIAN $$
(Map p130; 17 Dzorap Poghots; meals AMD3000-5000; ⊙11.30am-midnight; 📖) The combination of atmosphere, views and traditional cuisine has made Urartu a popular place for a night on the town. It's perfectly set on the edge of Hrazdan Gorge and serves some delectable platters of *khoravats*. Service can be slow.

🍷 Drinking

Practically all restaurants and cafes serve drinks and are open late, so this is just a selection of specialist drinking spots.

OPERA SQUARE, THE CASCADE & MOSCOVYAN POGHOTS

Poplovok Jazz Café
OUTDOOR CAFE
(Map p130; Isahakyan Poghots) A cafe complex centred on a large pond. Poplovok is the one by the side of the pond, with live jazz most nights. Former president Kocharian is a jazz fan and sometimes drops by.

Ice Club
THEME BAR
(Map p130; 50 Mesrop Mashtots Poghota; admission AMD3000) This bar may give you the chills. It's entirely made of ice, right down to

OUTDOOR CAFES: LIVIN' THE GOOD LIFE

Cafe-hopping has become something of a freestyle sport in Yerevan. Before, after and sometimes during work locals crowd into the city's outdoor cafes, and there is no shortage. Take your pick from shady spots with umbrellas and cafe lattes to dimly lit mafia dens serving cakes and cognac. You hardly need this guide to tell you where to go; you'll spot them as you tour the city – just pick one that suits your style. Good places to look include the Cascade area and anywhere around the Opera House. Students tend to gather around the Ring Park near Surp Grigor Lusavorich Cathedral.

the bar, tables, chairs and walls. So that you don't freeze your bum off, the bouncer will give you a thick jacket to wear inside. Sure, it's a novelty but if you visit in August when temperatures are soaring this is one of the city's main attractions.

26 Irish PUB
(Map p130; 26 Parpetsi Poghots) About as Irish as you can get in Armenia, this wee pub has a smoky atmosphere, foosball, a dartboard and frothy glasses of beer.

Calumet BAR
(Map p130; Pushkin Poghots; ☺5pm-2am) Very casual bar owned by Hrach, a diaspora Armenian from Lebanon. The name is French for 'peace pipe', which is somewhat symbolic of this all-inclusive club. It's popular with locals, Peace Corps volunteers and travellers.

REPUBLIC SQUARE, SOUTHERN MASHTOTS & KHANDJIAN POGHOTS

Stoyka BAR
(Map p130; 46 Nalbandyan Poghots; ☺7pm-late) A cheerful, youthful pub popular with tourists, diaspora Armenians and locals. It's known for late-night hedonism and a lethal array of drinks.

☆ Entertainment

Theatre, Ballet & Classical Music

Billboards by the Opera House and on Abovyan Poghots advertise upcoming events; the Armenia Information office (p141) and the Artbridge Bookstore Café (p138) can help with tickets and information. Tickets are a steal at just AMD1000 to AMD2000 for most events. The Opera House (p124) has a concert hall and a theatre for opera and ballet. Most theatres close during July and August.

Theatres in Yerevan:

Aram Khachaturian
Concert Hall CLASSICAL MUSIC
(Map p130; ☎56 06 45; Opera House, 46 Mesrop Mashtots Poghota)

Arno Babadjanian
Concert Hall TRADITIONAL THEATRE
(Map p130; ☎58 27 73; 2 Abovyan Poghots)

Chamber Theatre COMEDY, DRAMA
(Map p130; ☎56 63 78; 58 Mesrop Mashtots Poghota)

Hakob Paronyan State
Musical Comedy Theatre COMEDY
(Map p130; ☎58 01 01; 7 Vazgen Sargsyan Poghots)

Hovhannes Tumanyan
Theatre of Marionettes PUPPET THEATRE
(Map p130; ☎56 32 44; 4 Sayat-Nova Poghota)

Hrachia Ghaplanyan
Drama Theatre DRAMA
(Map p130; ☎52 47 23; 28 Isahakyan Poghots)

Komitas Chamber
Music Hall CLASSICAL MUSIC
(Map p130; ☎52 67 18; www.ncoa.am; Isahakyan Poghots)

National Academic Opera
and Ballet Theatre OPERA
(Map p130; ☎52 79 92; www.opera.am; Opera House, 54 Tumanyan Poghots)

Nightclubs

The local club scene is well developed, with everything from Manhattan miniclubs to European-style techno caverns.

Giza CLUB
(Map p130; admission AMD3000; ☺until late Wed-Sun) This club is located in a huge underground space next to the Opera House. Anything goes here, from flying popcorn parties and lip-sync competitions to breakdancers and everything in between.

One Club CLUB
(Map p130; 1 Teryan Poghots, Citadel Business Centre; admission AMD3000; ☺until late Wed-Sun) Mixed music sets are pumped out of the sound system at this club for the 20-something crowd. Well-known DJs from Europe often spin here.

Kami

CLUB

(Map p130; 18 Abovyan Poghots; ☺until late) Small lounge and part-time disco with Mondrian art theme and dancing on Friday and Saturday. The rest of the week it hosts live music acts. It's back behind the Syrian sweet shop.

Live Music

Malkhas Jazz Club

JAZZ

(Map p130; 52 Pushkin Poghots; admission AMD2000; ☺11am-3am) Laid-back club with two levels: a bar upstairs, and a lounge in the basement where the bands perform. It also serves excellent food, including steaks, pork chops and pasta, plus a full range of drinks. Owner Levon Malkhasian is considered the father of Armenian jazz – he has a huge library of jazz books and CDs and often closes the club in the daytime so young musicians can rehearse.

Stop Club

JAZZ, ROCK

(Map p130; www.stopclub.am; 37 Moscovyan Poghots; admission AMD1000-4000; ☺noon-midnight) This place is a popular live-music venue for a variety of genres. The musical spectrum ranges from jazz to reggae and rock. Check the website for upcoming events.

Gay & Lesbian Venues

Gay life is fairly low-key in Yerevan and places are not well advertised – check www.gayarmenia.blogspot.com. The park in front of the Best Western Congress hotel is a popular cruising spot.

Cinemas

Kino Moskva

CINEMA

(Map p130; ✆52 12 10; 18 Abovyan Poghots; admission AMD1500) Tickets are cheap and there is a bar, an internet club and a nightclub. Nice Soviet-classical balcony. Documentaries are sometimes screened here.

Casinos

Looking like a Lego version of the Las Vegas Strip, Yerevan's low-rise casino strip (Map p126) stretches from the city limits out towards the airport along Admiral Isakov Poghota. For new arrivals, it makes for a somewhat surreal entry into Armenia as the neon signs flash past. Despite the novelty of it all, these places rank fairly low on the local entertainment scene and the empty sidewalks are testament to this. It's hardly worth the cab fare to get out here.

 Shopping

Cognac is a popular item to bring home (but you'll need to put it in your check-in baggage because of restrictions on taking liquid on aeroplanes). There are lots of cognac stores on the main streets (Mesrop Mashtots Poghota, Sayat-Nova Poghota and Abovyan Poghots).

There are two big *shukas* (food markets): **Shuka No 1** (Map p130; 3 Mesrop Mashtots Poghota) and **Shuka No 2** (Map p126; 35 Movses Khorenatsi Poghots), just off Tigran Mets Poghota.

Vernissage Market

MARKET

(Map p130; Pavstos Byuzand Poghots) The main weekend flea market is a popular place for antiques, old communist medals, chess sets, carved jewellery boxes and locally produced handicrafts.

Vernissage Art Market

MARKET

(Map p130; Mesrop Mashtots Poghota & Sayat-Nova Poghota) Around the Martiros Sarian statue across from Opera Sq, this market deals primarily with paintings; you can turn up some real gems here at negotiable prices. Purchases are made both from dealers and the artists themselves.

Salt Sack

HANDICRAFTS

(Map p130; 3/1 Abovyan Poghots) Better-than-average souvenir and handicrafts shop with some maps and books for sale, and a range of jewellery, pottery, items like woven salt sacks, carpets, dolls and T-shirts.

Treasures of Armenia

CRAFT

(Map p130; 1/1 Abovyan Poghots) Craft gallery run by local designer Nina Hovnanian, showcasing unique jewellery, crafts, cushions and clothing. Everything is handmade and of high quality, with high prices to match.

Carpet Shop

CARPETS

(Map p130; 27 Tumanyan Poghots) One of several carpet shops around town. Costs are inflated so you'll need to bargain like mad for a reasonable price.

Artbridge Bookstore

BOOKS

(Map p130; 20 Abovyan Poghots; ☺8.30am-midnight) Has a small but well-chosen range of titles and a book exchange.

Noyan Tapan

BOOKS

(Map p130; Hanrapetutyan Hraparak) Has a few English novels plus maps and books on Armenia.

Bureaucrat BOOKS
(Map p130; 19 Sarian Poghots) This chic little bookshop specialises in art books but also has a cafe serving snacks and drinks.

❶ Information

Cultural Centres

American Corner (Map p130; ☑56 13 83; yerevan@americancorners.am; 4 Nalbandyan Poghots; ⊗9am-5pm Mon-Fri, 10am-4pm Sat) Has a library, internet access and a series of films and lectures.

Emergency

Emergency services ☑103
European Medical Centre ambulance ☑54 00 03
Fire ☑101
Police ☑102

Internet Access

There are internet clubs scattered across the city; most stay open late into the night and charge around AMD400 per hour. You may also have to pay for the megabytes used, so costs rack up every time you click a new page or up-load/download something. **Nexus** (Map p130; 49 Pushkin Poghots; ⊗24hr) near the Envoy Hostel and the **Internet Club** (Map p130; 18 Abovyan Poghots; ⊗9am-10pm) at Kino Moskva are both decent options.

Fortunately, free internet and wi-fi come standard in many of Yerevan's hotels and cafes. Hotspots are indicated with a ⊚ icon.

Laundry

Most hotels, B&Bs and hostels can arrange clean laundry. If yours does not, try the following.
Laundry Service (Map p130; 56 Pushkin Poghots) Convenient if you are staying at the Envoy Hostel.

Media

The English-language weekly newspaper *Noyan Tapan* can be found at Artbridge Bookstore. There are a handful of tourist publications such as *Yerevan Scope*, which have short articles and local listings. These are available in hotels and some cafes. International magazines and newspapers are available at Artbridge and some upscale hotels.

Medical Services

Pharmacies, marked by the Russian word *apteka*, are common and there's one open late in every neighbourhood. For things like dental emergencies, embassies usually have a list of recommended specialists.

Yerevan has the best medical facilities in the country. Among the following, Nairi has the best reputation.

---

❶ **YEREVAN'S TEMPTING FOUNTAINS**

Drinking fountains are located all over Yerevan and across the country. While these may look tempting, especially on a hot summer day, we suggest avoiding them as the water is not filtered and may contain bacteria such as Giardia. If you are the unfortunate recipient of a Giardia bug go to the nearest chemist for a box of tinidazole (aka Tindamax).

4th Yerevan City Polyclinic (Map p130; ☑58 03 95; 13 Moskovyan Poghots)
Nairi Clinic (Map p130; ☑53 75 00; www. nairimed.mn; 21 Paronyan Poghots)

Money

There are moneychangers everywhere in Yerevan and ATMs dispensing drams are becoming quite common. Euros, US dollars and roubles can be changed nearly everywhere; the British pound and Georgian lari are less commonly traded. **HSBC** (9 Vazgen Sargsyan Poghots) is the leading international bank and has several branches with ATMs around the city. Handy ATMs that accept Visa and MasterCard include **Anelik Bank** (Map p130; 41 Pushkin Poghots) and **Arexim Bank** (Map p130; 20 Tumanyan Poghots). The airport arrivals hall has a moneychanger and an Armbusinessbank (ABB) machine that changes cash currency.

Post

The public mail service in Yerevan is slow but fairly reliable. The **Haypost Main Office** (Map p130; Hanrapetutyan Hraparak; ⊗9am-7pm Mon-Sat) is centrally located. Several local and international companies compete for the parcel business:
FedEx/Transimpex (Map p130; ☑53 00 29; tripex@arminco.com; 40 Mesrop Mashtots Poghota)
UPS Express-Hayk (Map p126; ☑27 30 90; omae@arminco.com; 1 Kievyan Poghots)

Telephone

Telephone services in Yerevan are reasonable, and your hotel will most likely allow local calls for free. Internet cafes offer cheap VoIP international calls. Many internet cafes also have **Skype** (www.skype.com).

Tourist Information

Armenia Information (www.armeniainfo.am), the local tourist office, was closed at the time of research. If and when a new office opens, the contact details should appear on its website.

INTERNATIONAL BUS & MARSHRUTKA SERVICES

The following services all originate and terminate at the Kilikya Avtokayan in Yerevan.

Batumi (Georgia) One weekly *marshrutka* (AMD12,500, 10 to 15 hours), departing Thursday at 6am.

Istanbul (Turkey) One weekly bus (US$60, 32 hours), departing Saturday.

Stepanakert (Nagorno-Karabakh) Four daily *marshrutky* (AMD5000, seven to eight hours), departing when full between 7.30am and 10.30am.

Tbilisi (Georgia) Seven daily *marshrutky* (AMD6500, six hours) departing when full between 7am and 2.30pm. In addition, Envoy Hostel (p135) offers a once-weekly shuttle-tour to Tbilisi departing on Friday (reservations are essential) for AMD23,500, stopping off at places of interest on the way.

Tehran (via Tabriz) (Iran) Daily bus (AMD22,000, 24 hours), departing at 10am; book in advance through Tatev Travel, p142.

Travel Agencies

There are lots of useful travel agencies offering everything from one-day minivan tours to private car tours, from a day to a week anywhere in the country. A selection of recommended agencies:

AdvenTour (☑48 22 71; www.armeniaexplorer. com) Specialises in adventure trips – hiking and mountain biking – plus speciality interests such as photography, bird-watching and archaeology. Call first as the location is hidden outside the centre but staff will meet you in town.

Ajdahag Mountain Hiking Club (www.ajdahag. narod.ru) Arranges one-day hikes up the southern peak of Mt Aragats and Mt Ara, a two-day climb up to Aragats' highest peak, plus hikes in the Geghama mountains to the petroglyphs on Mt Azhdahak and other peaks.

Avarayr (Map p130; ☑52 40 42; www.avarayr. am; 1 Pavstos Byuzand Poghots) Avarayr is an adventure-tour company offering hikes from three to 12 days (the latter covering much of the country), camping trips for groups, and some unusual cultural and archaeological tours.

Caravan Tours (Map p130; ☑56 52 39; www. caravanarmenia.com; 42/1 Teryan Poghots) Arranges apartments, homestays and tours; garners good reports for prompt individual service.

Envoy Tours (Map p130; ☑53 03 69; www. envoytours.am; 54 Pushkin Poghots) Runs day trips near Yerevan and into northern Armenia to popular places like Garni, Geghard, Echmiadzin and Mt Aragats. Operates out of the Envoy Hostel.

Hyur Service (Map p130; ☑56 04 95; www.hy urservice.com; 96 Nalbandyan Poghots) Rents apartments and does trips around the country including many day tours from Yerevan.

Levon Travel (Map p130; ☑52 52 10; www. levontravel.com; 10 Sayat-Nova Poghota) Good for outbound travel and booking airline tickets.

Menua Tours (Map p130; ☑51 20 51; www. menuatours.com; 9 Alek Manukyan Poghots) Does daily tours to sites around the country and is a reliable organiser of apartments, car rental, mobile-phone rental and other services.

Tatev Travel (Map p130; ☑52 44 01; www. tatev.com; 19 Nalbandyan Poghots) Specialises in travel to Iran, including arranging visas. It can also arrange bus and air tickets to Tehran.

❶ Getting There & Away

Yerevan can be reached by air from many countries, by road from Georgia and Iran, and by rail from Georgia. While there are a couple of arduous bus services to Turkey via Georgia, and flights to Istanbul, the land border is closed. There are no direct routes to Azerbaijan; it's most easily reached via Georgia.

Air

Zvartnots Airport (☑flight information 187), 11km from Yerevan, is Armenia's major airport. A multimillion-dollar overhaul of the airport was completed in 2011.

The arrivals hall has a money exchange and booths for mobile-phone companies if you want to buy a SIM card for your phone. See p302 for information on flights that serve Zvartnots.

AIRLINE OFFICES

Aeroflot (Map p130; ☑53 21 31; www.aeroflot. ru; 12 Amiryan Poghots)

Air France (Map p130; ☑51 22 77; www. airfrance.am; 9 Alek Manukyan Poghots)

Armavia (Map p130; ☑56 48 17; www.u8.am; 25 Sayat-Nova Poghota)

Austrian Airlines (Map p130; ☑51 22 01; www. aua.com; 9 Alek Manukyan Poghots)

Baltic Air (Map p130; ☑52 82 20; www.baltic air.com; 25 Teryan Poghots)

BMI (Map p130; ☑51 22 03; www.flybmi.com; 9 Alek Manukyan Poghots)

Czech Airlines (Map p130; ☑52 21 62; www. csa.cz; c/o Visa Concord Travel, 2 Marshall Baghramyan Poghota)

Fly Dubai (Map p130; ☑51 88 56; www.flydu bai.com; 7 Movses Khorenatsi Poghots)

Iran Aseman Airlines (Map p130; ☑52 44 01; info@tatev.com; c/o Tatev Travel, 19 Nalban-dyan Poghots)

S7 Airlines (Map p130; ☑54 41 10; www.S7.ru; 34 Tumanyan Poghots)

Syrian Air (Map p130; ☑53 85 89; c/o Astron Travel, 3 Movses Khorenatsi Poghots)

Bus

Buses are generally late Soviet models, and while they may be half the price of a *marshrutka* they're often twice as slow as well. Buses mostly serve on village and suburban routes. The main bus station is the **Kilikya Avtokayan** (Map p126; ☑56 53 70; 6 Admiral Isakov Poghota), past the Yerevan Brandy Company on the Echmiadzin road, which has international bus services and *marshrutky* to Sisian, Stepanakert, Jermuk and Stepanavan. The **Hyussisayin Av-tokayan** (Northern bus station; Map p126; ☑62 16 70; Tbilisian Mayrughi) is on the Tbilisi high-way, 4km from the centre, and serves Sevan and Dilijan.

Car & Motorcycle

Several agencies rent out cars in Yerevan, including big names like Sixt and Hertz. A three-day rental ranges between AMD56,000 and AMD176,000 depending on the make and model of the car. It's also possible to hire a driver with the car. Policies on taking the car out of Armenia (eg over the border to Georgia) vary between companies so be sure to clarify what is allowed.

Hertz (Map p130; ☑58 48 18; 7 Abovyan Poghots)

Sixt (☑59 31 53; Zvartnots Airport) The office is outside the centre but if you book a car it can be delivered to your hotel or you can pick it up at the airport. Sixt has a desk in the arrivals hall of the airport.

Marshrutka

Yerevan is the hub of the national network, and *marshrutky* (minibuses) leave from spots around the city. Try to arrive about 30 minutes before departure to make sure you get a seat. *Marshrutky* almost always leave on time and may even depart a few minutes early.

The following list outlines the destination, de-parture point in Yerevan, price, journey duration and departure times. Note that Araji Mas can be reached on bus 33 from Republic Sq.

Agarak (near Ashtarak) Kilikya Avtokayan, AMD300, 40 minutes, 9.55am, 11.55am, 1.55pm, 4pm and 5.55pm

Alaverdi Kilikya Avtokayan, AMD1500, three hours, hourly between 7am and 7pm

Armavir (Hoktemberyan) Kilikya Avtokayan, AMD400, 50 minutes, every 15 minutes from 7.30am to 8pm

Ashtarak Kilikya Avtokayan, AMD250, 40 minutes, one or two per hour between 8.40am and 6.40pm

Dilijan Hyusisayin Avtokayan, AMD1200, two hours, hourly between 10am and 6pm, plus Ijevan services

Echmiadzin Kilikya Avtokayan, AMD250, 20 to 30 minutes, every 10 minutes between 8am and 10pm

Goght (for Garni) GAI Poghots near Mercedes Benz showroom, AMD250, 25 minutes, every 50 minutes between 10am and 9.30pm

Goris Sasuntsi Davit metro, AMD2500, six hours, 8am. Most transport to Goris is by shared taxi.

Gyumri Kilikya Avtokayan, AMD1500, two hours, every 20 minutes between 7.30am and 7pm

Hrazdan (for Tsaghkadzor) Raykom Sta-tion, AMD400, 45 minutes, every 30 minutes between 9am and 6pm

Ijevan Hyusisayin Avtokayan, AMD1700, 2½ hours, hourly between 10am and 6pm

Jermuk Kilikya Avtokayan, AMD2000, two hours, 3pm

Kapan Sasuntsi Davit metro, AMD5000, eight hours, hourly between 7am and noon

Khor Virap Sasuntsi Davit metro, AMD400, 40 minutes, 11am and 3.30pm

Meghri Sasuntsi Davit metro, AMD7000, 10 hours, 7am

Sevan Raykom station, AMD600, one hour, hourly between 9.30am and 6.30pm

Sisian Kilikya Avtokayan, AMD2000, four hours, 10.30am, noon, 2.30pm

ⓘ YEREVAN MARSHRUTKA SHUFFLE

Every so often the authorities in Yerevan decide to shuffle around the departure points for *marshrutky* (mini-buses) leaving the city. Departure times are also subject to change. The list on this page was updated at the time of research but it's a good idea to consult with your hotel or guesthouse regard-ing possible changes to departure points and times.

ARMENIA YEREVAN

YEREVAN MARSHRUTKY

Handy in-town routes:

11 Erebuni Museum, Tigran Mets Poghota, Hanrapetutyan Hraparak, Haghtanak Bridge

13 Kilikya Avtokayan, Haghtanak Bridge, Mesrop Mashtots Poghota, Marshall Baghramian Poghota, Barekamutyun metro

18 Yerevan train station, Hanrapetutyan Hraparak, Nalbandyan Poghots, Marshall Baghramian Poghota, Ajapniak

43 Nor Zeytun, Azatutyan Poghots, Haghtanak Park, Yeritasardakan metro, Surp Grigor Lusavorich Cathedral, Gortsaranayin metro

51 Mesrop Mashtots Poghata, Abovyan Poghots, GAI Poghots (behind the Mercedes showroom)

75 Mesrop Mashtots Poghata, Kilikya Avtokayan

81 Avan, Nalbandyan Poghots, Tigran Mets Poghota, Erebuni

101 Hyusisayin Avtokayan (Northern bus station), Tbilisi Hwy, Komitas Poghota

108 Zvartnots Airport, Echmiadzin–Yerevan Hwy, Tigran Mets Poghota, Zoravar Andranik metro

Stepanavan Kilikya Avtokayan, AMD1500, three hours, 9am, 11am, 1.30pm, 2.30pm, 3.30pm

Vanadzor Kilikya Avtokayan, AMD1200, two hours, every 30 minutes between 7.30am and 7pm

Vayk Araji Mas, AMD1200, two hours, hourly between 8am and 7pm

Yeghegnadzor Araji Mas, AMD1200, two hours, hourly between 8am and 7pm

Train

The **Yerevan train station** (Map p126; ✆information 184; Sasuntsi Davit Hraparak) is off Tigran Mets Poghota south of the city centre, with the Sasuntsi Davit metro station underneath. The booking office is on the ground floor to the right as you enter the station. Information boards are in Armenian and Russian, but some of the staff speak English. The main rail route loops west and north through Gyumri (3½ hours), on through Vanadzor (8½ hours) and Ayrum near the border (11 hours), and on to Tbilisi (16 hours). There are a couple of local trains south to Yeraskh (near the Naxçivan border), and northeast to Hrazdan (continuing in summer to Sevan).

There are also daily *elektrichka* trains to Gyumri at 8am and 5.50pm; an open-seating (bench) ticket costs AMD950.

Train 372 departs for Tbilisi on even days at 10.35pm, arriving theoretically at 9am, though a couple of hours late is normal. In summer its run on a daily schedule and the train continues past Tbilisi to Batumi. Schedules and times are subject to periodic change so its best to get the latest departure times from the train station

(or ask your hotel or guesthouse for updates). There are separate classes for the train to Tbilisi: open seating costs AMD5000, *kupe* (standard) compartments cost AMD12,160, while SV (deluxe) compartments cost AMD16,800. There is an AMD500 booking fee when you buy the ticket.

The toilets aren't great and the carriages aren't new, but it's a very pretty ride. Book compartments a day ahead, and take food and drinks with you.

❶ Getting Around

To/From Zvartnots Airport

Minibuses from Zvartnots Airport leave from the car park 300m from the main terminal. Yerevan minibus 108 (AMD200, every 20 minutes, 7.30am to 10.30pm) runs between the airport and Barekamutyun Hraparak (which has the Barekamutyun metro station). The driver may charge you an additional AMD100 for your luggage. On the way the *marshrutka* makes a stop at Rossiya Mall, where you can hop on a *marshrutka* to other parts of the city, or get on the metro (Zoravar Andranik station)

The price of a taxi to and from the airport depends on whether you arrange it in advance or chance it with the cowboys outside arrivals. If you book the taxi inside the airport terminal it will cost around AMD6000, but if you walk outside to the parking lot the price drops to around AMD2000 (depending on your bargaining skills). Going to the airport from town you'll just pay around AMD2000. The trip takes about 15 to 20 minutes to/from central Yerevan.

Public Transport

The main way around Yerevan is by *marshrutka*. There are hundreds of routes, shown by a number in the van's front window. They stop at bus stops but you can flag one down anywhere on the street. You pay AMD100 when you leave. Ask to stop by saying '*kangnek*'. Women travellers should try to sit near the front and next to a female passenger if possible (or risk probing hands).

There are also buses and electric trolleybuses following numbered routes. Tickets cost AMD100.

Bus 259 is useful. It goes from Kilikya Avtokayan (the main bus station) up Mesrop Mashtots Poghota, past the Opera House, to Hyusisayin Avtokayan (Northern bus station) every 20 minutes or so.

Best of all there's the clean, safe and efficient **Yerevan metro** (AMD100; ☻6.30am-11pm), which runs roughly north–south through these underground stations: Barekamutyun, Marshall Baghramian, Yeritasardakan, Hanrapetutyan Hraparak, Zoravar Andranik near Surp Grigor Lusavorich Cathedral (and Rossiya Mall) and Sasuntsi Davit at the Yerevan train station. The line continues west and south on ground level to stations in the industrial suburbs. Trains run every five to 10 minutes.

Taxi

Taxis are cheap and plentiful, from well-loved Ladas to late-model Benzes. There are two types: street taxis and telephone or call taxis. Prices are AMD600 for the first 5km and then AMD100 per kilometre. Make sure the driver switches the meter on or you will be overcharged. You'll see numbers for call taxis stencilled on buildings everywhere. Tourist publications such as *Yerevan Guide* carry listings for many companies.

AROUND YEREVAN

Because Armenia has so much history centred on its capital, it's easy to see many sites on half-day excursions from Yerevan. You can easily hire a taxi to see many of these places, but it often works out to be cheaper and less hassle to take a day tour with a company like Hyur Service or Envoy Tours (p142).

Garni Temple ԳԱՌՆԻ

This comprehensively rebuilt **Hellenic temple** (adult/student AMD1000/250, guide AMD2500; ☻10am-8pm) was dedicated to the heathen sun god, Mitra. Armenia's King Trdat I built it in the 1st century. It became a summer house for Armenian royalty after the Christian conversion.

The area around Garni has been inhabited since Neolithic times, with archaeologists finding Urartian cuneiform inscriptions dating back to the 8th century BC. The high promontory site is protected on three of four sides by a deep valley with rock cliffs, with a wall of massive blocks on the fourth side.

The wall featured 14 towers and an entrance graced by an arch. Ruins of the fortress are on the left and right sides as you walk towards the temple from the parking area. The Avan Gorge, carved by the Azat River, lies below.

A **Roman bathhouse**, now partly covered by a modern structure, was built for the royal residence. In the 7th century a **church** was built nearby. The bathhouse features an intricate **mosaic**, made with 15 colours of natural stones, depicting the goddess of the ocean.

In the ruins of the church next to the temple is a **vishap** (carved dragon stone). This is a marker to show the location of water. Some marks on the middle of the stone are in fact writing from King Argishti from the 8th century BC, which reads: 'Argishti, son of Menua, took people and cattle from Garni to Erebuni [the original site of Yerevan] to create a new community.'

In summer, Garni stays open until 10pm, but you'll have to pay an additional AMD200 to see it illuminated by floodlights.

If you want to stay overnight, try **Chez Yvette B&B** (☏091357966, 093755811; www.armenie-voyages-garni.com; per person incl breakfast AMD7000), run by a French-Armenian family, located 1km up the road towards Geghard. This is a clean, comfortable house with shared bathroom. Meals are available on request.

In the village of Garni, **Tavern Restaurant** (☻11am-10pm) serves fish and meat *khoravats*. At the entrance to the temple is a horde of locals selling delicious dried fruit and locally produced honey.

See p147 for information on getting to and from Garni.

Geghard Monastery ԳԵՂԱՐԴ

Named after the holy lance that pierced Christ's side at the crucifixion, Geghard Monastery stands in a steep scenic canyon 9km beyond Garni. The spear itself was

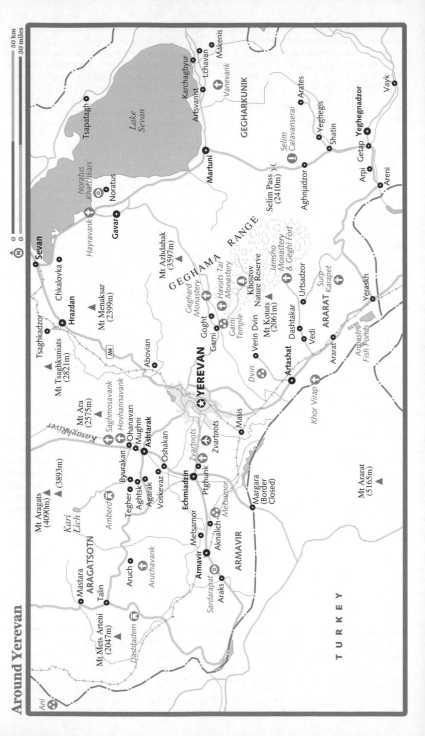

Around Yerevan

50 km
30 miles

TURKEY

ARAGATSOTN

Mt Aragats (4090m) ▲
▲ (3893m)

Mastara
Talin
Aruch
Aruchavank

Mt Mets Arteni (2047m) ▲

Dashtadem

Ani

Kari Lich

Amberd

Byurakan
Tegher
Aghtsk
Agarak
Voskevaz
Oshakan

Kasagh River

Mt Ara (2575m) ▲
Saghmosavank
Hovhannavank
Ohanavan
Mughni
Ashtarak

Tsaghkuniats (2821m) ▲

Mt Tsaghkadzor
M4
Abovian

Hrazdan
Mt Menaksar (2399m) ▲

Chkalovka
Sevan

Hayravank

Gavar
Noratus
Noratus Khatchkars

Lake Sevan

Tsapatagh

Karchaghbyur
Lchavan
Makenis
Artsvanist
Vanevank

GEGHARKUNIK

Arates
Yeghegis
Shatin

Yeghegnadzor
Arpi
Getap
Areni
Vayk

Martuni

Selim Caravanserai

Selim Pass (2410m)

Aghnjadzor

ARARAT

Yeraskh

Surp Karapet
Urtsadzor
Dashtakar
Vedi
Ararat

Artashni Fish Ponds

Mt Ararat (5165m) ▲

Khor Virap

Artashat

Verin Dvin
Mt Koruts (2061m) ▲

Dvin

Masis

YEREVAN

Zvartnots
Ptghunk
Ptghunk

Echmiadzin

Metsamor
Aknalich
Metsamor

Armavir
Araks
Sardarapat

Araks

ARMAVIR

Margara (Border Closed)

Metsamor

Goght
Garni
Garni Temple
Geghard Monastery
Havuts Tar Monastery
Khosrov Nature Reserve
Jamsho Monastery & Geghi Fort

GEGHAMA RANGE

Mt Azhdahak (3597m) ▲

once kept here but is now housed in the holy treasury at Echmiadzin.

Legend has it that Geghard Monastery was founded in the 4th century. The most ancient of the **cave churches**, St Gregory's, dates back to the 7th century. Once called Ayrivank (Cave Monastery), Geghard was burned by invading Arabs in 923.

As you approach the monastery, look to the left up the hill for caves that house monastic cells built by monks. Trees here are often dotted with strips of cloth, as are trees on the other side of the monastery near the river. It is said a person can say a prayer or make a wish and tie a strip of cloth to a tree near the monastery to make it come true.

Inside the monastery walls, Geghard's two main churches date from the 13th century. The principal structure, **Surp Astvatsatsin Church** (Holy Mother of God Church), was built in 1215. The adjoining vestibule, larger than the church itself, with an intricate carved ceiling and nine arches, dates from 1215 to 1225. Outside, above the south door, is a **coat of arms** of the family of the Zakarian prince who built it. The theme is a common Near Eastern one, with the lion symbolising royal might.

On the right-hand side of the vestibule are two entrances to **chapels** hewn from the rock. The left-hand one dates from the 1240s. It contains a basin with spring water believed to be lucky or holy. Splashing some of this water on your body is said to keep your skin youthful.

The right-hand chapel, constructed in 1263, includes the four-column **burial chamber** of Prince Papaq Proshian and his wife, Hruzakan. The family's **coat of arms**, carved in the rock above, features two lions chained together and an eagle.

Outside, steps on the left lead up the hill to a 10m passage into another **church** that has been carved out of the raw rock. The proportions in this room are nothing short of extraordinary, considering it was carved from the rock around it. The acoustics of the chamber are also quite amazing (on weekends, choir groups sometimes perform here). In the far corner is an opening looking down on the church below.

On the right-hand side of the church are steps that lead to some interesting **monastic cells** and **khatchkars**. Outside the monastery, next to the stream, is an active *matagh* (sacrifice) site.

ⓘ Getting There & Away

Marshrutky to Garni (AMD250, 25 minutes, every 50 minutes from 10am to 9.30pm) depart from GAI Poghots (behind the Mercedes Benz showroom) in Yerevan. You can get to the showroom by taking *marshrutka* 51 from Mesrop Mashtots Poghota.

In Garni the bus leaves you on the main road, a short walk to Garni Temple. The main road continues for 10km to Geghard, but public buses don't go that far. Bus 284 continues to Goght but then it's another 4.5km to Geghard (from where you could walk or hitch a ride the rest of the way). Alternatively, a taxi from Garni to Geghard and back with a one-hour wait is AMD3000 (drivers hang around Garni and will find you).

Zvartnots Cathedral
ԶՎԱՐԹՆՈՑ

Built from 641 to 661, the ruins of the **church** (admission AMD700; ◷10am-5pm) of Surp Grigor Lusavorich (St Gregory the Illuminator) at Zvartnots are different to every other set of ruins in Armenia. Catholicos Nerses II the Builder (building might have been his profession before joining the clergy) sponsored construction of the cathedral. Reputedly one of the most beautiful churches in the world, it housed relics of St Gregory, the first Catholicos (patriarch of all Armenians) of the Armenian Church.

A model of the partially reconstructed church in the State Museum of Armenian History in Yerevan shows it to have been a round creation with a hood-shaped dome 45m high. An earthquake in 930 caused the building to collapse. An arc of finely carved pillars and a massive stone floor are what remains, along with a profusion of decorated stone fragments. Architecture historians argue over whether the reconstruction in the museum is really true to the church's original design. Either way, the pillars evoke a feeling for a Greek- and Roman-influenced Levantine Christianity similar to many early-Syrian church ruins.

A pool in the centre of the building was used to baptise adults. Around the cathedral are the ruins of the palace of the Catholicos and the wine press and stone tanks of a massive medieval winery. Zvartnots lies in rich farmlands and orchard just south of the Echmiadzin–Yerevan highway, next to the delightfully named village of Ptghunk, 17km from Yerevan and 4km from the centre of Echmiadzin. It's easy to catch public transport either way along the highway.

Echmiadzin ԷՋՄԻԱԾԻՆ

☑231 / POP 52,000

Holy Echmiadzin is the Vatican of the Armenian Apostolic Church, the place where Surp Grigor Lusavorich saw a beam of light fall to the earth in a divine vision, and where he built the first Mayr Tachar (Mother Church of Armenia). For Armenian Christians, Echmiadzin (Descent of the Only Begotten Son of God) has unparalleled importance. Echmiadzin (sometimes spelt Ejmiatsin or Etchmiadzin) was the capital of Armenia from 180 to 340, when Christianity was first adopted by the Armenian nation. The seat of the Catholicos wandered across western Armenia for centuries before returning to the Mayr Tachar in 1441, with substantial rebuilding in the 15th century. The cathedral has sprouted more bell towers over the last 400 years, but the core is much as St Gregory's vision guided him. The Palace of the Catholicos in front of the Mayr Tachar is the home of the present Catholicos, Garegin II, enthroned in November 1999. He is the supreme prelate of the 1700-year-old Armenian Apostolic faith.

◉ Sights

Holy See of Echmiadzin MONASTERY
The main cathedral, **Mayr Tachar**, stands in a quadrangle of hedges and lawn surrounded by 19th-century buildings. The original church was built in 301–303. The building later fell in ruin and was rebuilt in 480–483. More work and expansion occurred in the 600s, 1600s and 1700s. By the main entrance at the southern end the large grey **2001 Papal Visit Monument**, built for Pope John Paul II's visit and Mass in 2001, stands next to the **Gevorgian Seminary**. The 19th-century **seminary** was closed in 1921 when Echmiadzin was swamped by refugees from the genocide, and it was forbidden to reopen under Soviet rule. The main gate leads past the **bookshop**, between buildings holding monastic cells, to the central compound. Bearded clergymen in hooded black robes glide along the garden paths around the Mayr Tachar.

The three-tiered bell tower at the entrance of the church is richly carved and dates from 1648. Inside, the church is modest in scale, about 20m by 20m, but the roof gleams with frescoes. At the centre is an altar at the place where St Gregory saw the divine light strike the ground.

At the rear of the church, through a door on the right of the altar, is the **treasury** (admission AMD1500; ⊙10am-5pm Tue-Sat, 1.30-5pm Sun); buy your ticket from the unsigned souvenir shop outside the church. It houses 1700 years of treasure collected by the church, including the Holy Lance (Surp Geghard), the weapon used by a Roman soldier to pierce the side of Christ while he was still nailed to the cross (to see if he was dead). It's a suitably brutish spearhead set into an ornate gold-and-silver casing. It was brought to Echmiadzin from Geghard Monastery. There is also an image of the Crucifixion, which, according to tradition, was carved by St John. The treasury has relics of the apostles Thaddeus, Peter and Andrew, some in hand or arm-shaped reliquaries, and fragments of the Holy Cross and Noah's Ark.

A door from the treasury leads under the main body of the church to a pagan shrine with a fire altar, seemingly left in situ in case this whole Christianity thing turned out to be a fad and the old faiths reasserted themselves. The shrine can be visited with a prior appointment through a travel agency, or with a bit of luck by asking one of the clerics in the treasury.

The gardens of Mayr Tachar have a **1915–23 Genocide Monument** and many fine *khatchkars* assembled from around the country. The **archway** leading to the Palace of the Catholicos was built by King Trdat III in the 4th century. The **Manougian Museum (Museum of the Old Residence)** stands next to the palace. It's off limits to casual visitors but if you have some clout with the Armenian Church it can be visited. Travel agencies in Yerevan can arrange visits to the church's private museum. There are some particularly fine *khatchkars* across the garden from the museum's entrance (some are also near the Papal Visit Monument), including examples from the recently destroyed cemetery in Culfa's old town in Naxçivan.

Other Churches
The **Surp Gayane Church** is a short walk past the main gate of the Holy See from the town's main square. St Gayane was the prioress of the 32 virtuous maidens who accompanied St Hripsime to Armenia. The original 6th-century chapel over her grave was rebuilt into a church in 1630. It's a fine

orange-toned building with a plain interior and some fine *khatchkars* scattered about.

The 17th-century **Surp Shogahat Church** rather pales beside the splendour of its neighbours in Echmiadzin, but it's a sturdy stone structure with simple, elegant lines. It was rebuilt on the foundations of a chapel to one of the companions of Hripsime and Gayane.

Surp Hripsime was originally built in 618, replacing an earlier chapel on the site where Hripsime was slain after she refused to marry King Trdat III, choosing instead to remain true to her faith – she was a pagan who had earlier fled marriage from the Roman emperor Diocletian. In the small chamber in the back of the church, look out for the niche that contains a few of the rocks purportedly used to stone Hripsime to death.

❶ Getting There & Away

Marshrutky for Yerevan (AMD250, 20 to 30 minutes, every 10 minutes), 21km east, leave from Atarbekyan Poghots, two blocks up from the main traffic circle. Transport further west towards Armavir (AMD250, hourly between 11am and 4pm) leaves from Tumanyan Poghots. The minivans to Echmiadzin leave from Sarian Poghots in Yerevan near the corner with Mesrop Mashtots Poghota.

Sardarapat ՍԱՐԴԱՐԱՊԱՏ

About 10km past the small city of Armavir (Hoktemberyan), in the orchards and farms of the Ararat Plain, stands the venerated war memorial site of **Sardarapat**. It was here in May 1918 that the forces of the first Armenian republic under Zoravar (General) Andranik turned back the Turkish invaders and saved the country from a likely annihilation. Built in 1968 with statues of giant bulls, a 35m stone bell-tower shrine to the fallen, five eagle statues built of tuff and a memorial wall, the site puts an Armenian twist on Soviet war memorials. Nationalist Armenians treat a visit here as a kind of pilgrimage. The nearby **museum** (admission AMD700, guide AMD1000; ⊗11am-5pm Tue-Sun) has relics from the battle itself in the first hall, as well as exhibits of items from the Neolithic Age up to the Middle Ages. Upstairs there is a treasure trove of carpets, jewellery, ceramics and handicrafts, the sum of which represents the country's best ethnography collection – a celebration of Armenian culture, survival and life.

❶ Getting There & Away

Sardarapat is about 10km southwest of Armavir, signposted near the village of Araks. Consider combing a visit with Echmiadzin. *Marshrutky* leave from Yerevan's Kilikya Avtokayan for Armavir (AMD400, 45 minutes to an hour, every 15 minutes, 7.30am to 8pm). A taxi from Armavir with two hours at Sardarapat should cost about AMD2000 with bargaining.

Ashtarak ԱՇՏԱՐԱԿ

🗐232 / POP 27,000

Ashtarak is a midsized regional town on the Kasagh Gorge, 22km northwest of Yerevan and somewhat higher at 1100m. Ashtarak is an interesting old town with lots of 19th-century buildings. There's a 16th-century stone bridge below the new bridge, and four churches around town. These include the little 7th-century Karmravor Church with intricate carvings and a cemetery with *khatchkars* a short way north, and the 6th-century Tsiranavor Church on the edge of the gorge. Ashtarak has some very rural neighbourhoods as well, full of fruit trees and haystacks in late summer. While there is no great need to come to the town itself, it does make a decent transit point for the Kasagh Gorge churches if you are travelling by local transport.

⊙ Sights

Kasagh Gorge Churches   CHURCHES

Churches from the 6th to the 16th century dot the landscape north and south of Ashtarak along the gorge of the little Kasagh River. Across the gorge from Yerevan on the northern outskirts of Ashtarak is the village of **Mughni**, with the splendid **Surp Gevorg Church**, finished in 1669, featuring striped bands of stone around its central drum and a classic half-folded umbrella cone on top. The village is an easy turn-off from the main highway that runs north to Spitak.

About 4km north of Mughi, along the same highway, is the village of **Ohanavan**. Perched on the edge of the village, overlooking the gorge, is the 7th-century monastery of **Hovhannavank**, famous for producing manuscripts and for its wealth of inscriptions and decorative carvings. It's right on the lip of the gorge, looking as though it pins down the flat volcanic grazing land, preventing it from tumbling into the chasm.

Getting back on the main road, another 5km north leads to perhaps the prettiest monastery of all, **Saghmosavank**, a cluster of drums and conical domes from the 13th century.

A trail at the bottom of the gorge links Hovhannavank and Saghmosavank – you can cover the distance on foot in less than 90 minutes. The trail begins at the new cemetery on the northern part of Ohanavan village. It's unlikely you'll find a taxi at Saghmosavank once you reach the end of the trail. You could arrange to have one from Ashtarak meet you at an appointed time, or just hitch back from the main highway, another 20-minute walk from Saghmosavank. Another option is to take a cab to Saghmosavank, do the walk in reverse and arrange transport back from Hovhannavank (which is close to Ashtarak).

About 8km southwest of Ashtarak in Oshakan is a 19th-century church built over the tomb of St Mesrop Mashtots, the genius who created the Armenian alphabet.

🛏 Sleeping & Eating

Ashtaraki Dzor HOTEL $$
(☑3 67 78; Kasagh Gorge, Ashtarak; per person incl breakfast AMD10,000; ❄) This midrange hotel, built on terraces down the walls of Kasagh Gorge, is best known for its dining and entertainment. *Khoravats* dinners cost AMD3000, and there's live music. The hotel rooms are modern with satellite TV, though the service is a bit rusty. It's about 4km north of the town centre.

❶ Getting There & Away

Ashtarak is on a major road, so public transport is easy. In Yerevan, Ashtarak *marshrutky* leave from Kilikya Avtokayan, (AMD250, 40 minutes, one or two per hour from 8.40am to 6.40pm). There are also *marshrutky* from here to villages such as Voskevaz and Agarak that go via Ashtarak. A bus travels to Ohanavan from Ashtarak around 3pm or whenever it's full. *Marshrutky* return to Yerevan from Ashtarak's main *shuka*.

To visit the local sites (eg Hovhannavank and Saghmosavank) by taxi you can save a little money by taking the bus from Yerevan to Ashtarak and then hiring a local taxi at a rate of AMD100 per kilometre.

Byurakan & Around
ԲՅՈՒՐԱԿԱՆ

The landscape around the village of Byurakan, about 14km northwest of Ashtarak on the southern slopes of Mt Aragats, includes a couple of astronomical observatories and the impressive remains of the fortress of Amberd, 15km up the mountain. The Surp Hovhannes Church in Byurakan is an interesting early basilica model. Other churches and villages in the vicinity have *khatchkars* and *vishap* scattered about.

The fortress of **Amberd** was constructed on a ridge above the confluence of the little gorges of the Amberd and Arkashen streams. The high stone walls and rounded towers are a rough but effective defence, rebuilt many times but mostly dating from the 11th century. It's easy to see why the site was chosen – at 2300m above sea level it commands a position above the farms and trade routes of the Ararat Plain. According to local lore no army ever breached the thick walls of the fortress. A church stands downhill from the fortress with the ruins of fortified houses and a substantial public bathhouse. A small kiosk here sells drinks and snacks.

The fortress is about a two-hour hike from the scout camp near the very end of Byurakan village. The scenery and the footpath is rewarding. Walk along the Mt Aragats road until you reach the ski house. A sign in Cyrillic and Latin script points ahead – take the left-hand fork anyway. The fortress can be seen from a distance, but you have to walk around a steep valley before reaching it. Although the fortress is geographically close to Byurakan, the paved road makes a 15km long circuitous route.

The first part of the road heads uphill towards Kari Lich (lake) and then branches off to the left 5km before the fortress. As you walk or drive through this landscape look for the large green or white tents owned by Armenian shepherds who graze their flocks here in summer.

The **Tegher Monastery** is about 5km uphill from the village of Aghtsk in the old village of the same name, on the far side of the Amberd Gorge from Byurakan. Mamakhatun, the wife of Prince Vache Vahutyan, built the church in 1232.

🛏 Sleeping

Byurakan Observatory Hotel HOTEL $
(☑094910986; per person AMD5000) This is an old Soviet establishment on the grounds of the observatory. The hotel itself is a lovely pink tuff building with basic but satisfactory rooms. For an extra AMD1000 you'll get a tour of the observatory at night.

ℹ Getting There & Away

There are four buses per day from Yerevan to Byurakan, departing at 10.30am, 12.45pm, 3.45pm and 5.30pm from the bus stand on Grigor Lusavorich Poghota in Yerevan (AMD350). If you don't catch one of these there are also a few buses to Agarak, 6km south of Byurakan on the Ashtarak–Gyumri highway. From Agarak you could walk, hitch or hire a taxi. There are very few, if any, taxis in Byurakan itself so if you need a cab to go to Aragats or Amberd its better to take one from Ashtarak or Yerevan. The four buses return to Yerevan at 7.30am, 9am, noon and 4pm.

Mt Aragats ԱՐԱԳԱԾ ԼԵՌ

Snow covers the top of the highest mountain in modern Armenia almost year-round, so climbing is best in July, August or September. Beware – even in August, clouds can gather in the crater by about 10am, so it's good to start walking as early as possible. It's not unusual for hikers to start on mountain ascents at 5am. The southernmost of its four peaks (3893m) is easy enough for inexperienced climbers, but the northern peak (4090m) is more challenging and requires crossing a snowfield (experienced hikers only). Check the Mt Aragats page on www.armeniapedia.org for details.

The road from Byurakan winds 27km up to the Cosmic Ray Institute observatory and the waters of Kari Lich. The scientists run an informal **B&B** (per person AMD8000) at the institute. Hot water and clean bathrooms are available. Alternatively, there are camping places for those suitably equipped with a tent.

The road ends at the lake, and uphill the route is rocky and strewn with debris. There's no path, but the peaks are visible so you basically slog it uphill. The northern summit can be reached in four to six hours. To get there, walk over the steep pass between the southern and western summits. From the southwest pass, the route descends into the crater where you navigate fields of volcanic stones, then up again to the ridge and northern summit. Alternatively, hike up to the southern summit in just two hours.

Several tour companies can arrange walks up Mt Aragats, including the Ajdahag Mountain Hiking Club and Avarayr (p142). A two-day trip including guide, transport and camping equipment costs around AMD45,000 per person. **Serzh Hovsepyan** (☎35 00 46; serzh_hovsepyan@yahoo.com) is also a recommended guide for climbing the mountain's peaks. Serzh is a member of the Spitak mountain-rescue team.

ℹ Getting There & Away

There is no public transport to Kari Lich. Hitchhikers usually take a bus to Byurakan and then try to thumb a lift, which is more likely on weekends. A better idea is to get a group together to climb the mountain and share the cost of a cab from Yerevan or Ashtarak.

Khor Virap Monastery ԽՈՐ ՎԻՐԱՊ

Khor Virap Monastery, 30km south of Yerevan, is a famous pilgrimage site with an iconic location at the foot of Mt Ararat. You'll see plenty of tempting pictures of the place on postcards and souvenir books long before you get there.

The monastery is on a hillock close to the Araks River, overlooking river pastures, stork nests and vineyards, 4km off the main highway through the village of Pokr Vedi (sometimes also called Khor Virap).

The pagan King Trdat III imprisoned St Gregory the Illuminator (Surp Grigor Lusavorich) in a well (*khor virap* means 'deep well') here for 12 years, where Christian women secretly fed him. The king was later cursed by madness (or, in a more colourful version of the tale, cursed by sprouting the head of a boar) and miraculously cured by St Gregory. Historians contend that Trdat may have switched allegiances to tap into the strength of Armenia's growing Christian community in the face of Roman aggression. In any case the king converted to Christianity and St Gregory became the first Catholicos of the Armenian Apostolic Church, and set about building churches on top of pagan temples and teaching the faith.

The ground-level buildings at Khor Virap have been repeatedly rebuilt since at least the 6th century, and the main Surp Astvatsatsin Church dates from the 17th century. Khor Virap is an important pilgrimage site and people often visit for a baptism or after a wedding to perform a *matagh* (sacrifice, often of sheep or chicken), which keeps the priests busy on weekends. It's a shivery experience to climb down the 7m-deep well. The well is lit, but you need to wear sturdy shoes to scale the metal ladder. Just outside the monastery walls are some excavations on the site of Artashat, Trdat's capital, founded in the 2nd century BC.

The **Armash Fish Ponds**, 25km downstream from Khor Virap near the border town of Yeraskh, are home to a great variety of migrating birds in spring and autumn as well as local species.

ℹ Getting There & Away

There are two *marshrutky* a day to Khor Virap from Yerevan (AMD400, 40 minutes, 11am and 3.30pm), and two buses per day (9am and 2pm), all from the Sasuntsi Davit metro station. Going the other way, the *marshrutky* leave at 1.20pm and 5.20pm while the buses leave at 10.20am and 3.20pm.

The main highway is 4km away, with lots of public transport to and from Ararat and towns further south. A return trip by car from Yerevan costs about AMD10,000 through a taxi service.

NORTHERN ARMENIA

Northern Armenia comprises the *marz* (provinces) of Shirak, Lori and Tavush, and also includes the rugged bare highlands of Gegharkunik around gorgeous Lake Sevan. We have listed the sights in the order they are most commonly visited from Yerevan – most travellers head up to Lake Sevan and then on to Dilijan with a side trip to Ijevan. Travellers usually overnight in Vanadzor

before going to Georgia via the Debed Canyon. Stepanavan and Gyumri are also worthy side trips.

Lake Sevan   ՍԵՎԱՆԱ ԼԻՃ

Perched at 1900m above sea level, the great blue eye of Sevana Lich (Lake Sevan) covers 940 sq km, and is 80km long by 30km at its widest. The lake is perfect for escaping Yerevan's summer heat. Its colours and shades change with the weather and by its own mysterious processes, from a dazzling azure to dark blue and a thousand shades in between. The freshwater lake supports a healthy fish population, including the *ishkhan* (prince trout), named for a row of spots like a crown on its head.

When Sevan's outlet, the Hrazdan River, was tapped for hydroelectric plants and irrigation in the 1950s, the lake fell and is now about 20m lower. Other Soviet plans to drain the lake down to one-sixth its size thankfully went nowhere. The retreating waters uncovered forts, houses and artefacts dating back some 2000 years, and made Sevan Island a peninsula.

The exposed land has been designated the Sevan National Park, although some of it is disappearing again as conservationists have convinced the government of the need

Northern Armenia

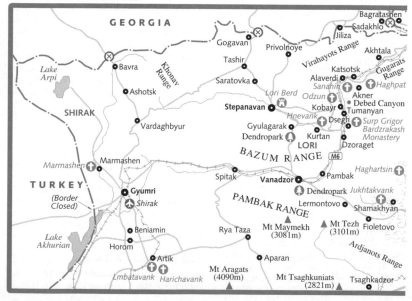

to raise the level of the lake. Since 2002 it has risen more than 2m, an environmental achievement that has meant cleaner water and more fish. Much to the consternation of local investors, the rising tide is also starting to flood into some of the beachside resorts.

Tourism is picking up around the lake, but except for a hectic 10 weeks in summer it's usually quiet. The stark volcanic highlands and plains around the lake endure a long winter, and except for a string of achievements in medieval church-building around the lake's edge, the hinterlands of Gegharkunik *marz* are not often visited.

Sevan ՍԵՎԱՆ

📞 261 / POP 16,000

The bustling little town of Sevan is 6km from Sevan Monastery, a short way inland from the lake's western shores. It was founded in 1842 as the Russian village of Elenovka; there are few signs of the past besides some Russian provincial houses at the western end of town. Sevan's main street, Nairyan Poghots, has a Haypost office, cafes, a *shuka,* moneychangers, and taxis to Sevan Monastery and lakeshore hotels.

The main beach strip is along the sandy south side of the Sevanavank peninsula, crowned by the much-photographed

churches on the hill at the end. This beach is suddenly transformed into the Armenian Riviera in the brief hot summers, with bars, beach volleyball, waterskiing and paddleboats. There are other, quieter beaches closer to Sevan town. There are fees in summer to use the beaches near Sevan, from AMD2000 to AMD3000 per person depending on the beach.

◉ Sights

Sevanavank   MONASTERY
Sevan Monastery is up a long flight of steps on the peninsula's turtle-backed hill and has commanding views of the lake. In summer and autumn a thick carpet of cloud pushes over the Areguniats mountains to the north and evaporates at the lake's edge.

The first monument on the steps leading up to the monastery is dedicated to a 20th-century navy captain, commander of the Russian fleet on Lake Sevan. The first church is **Arakelots** (Apostles), followed by **Surp Astvatsatsin** (Holy Mother of God) with a courtyard filled with *khatchkars.* St Mesrop Mashtots had a vision of 12 figures walking across the lake, who showed him the place to found a church. Queen Mariam, wife of Vasak of Syunik, built the churches in 874, and they have recently been restored. In the 19th century the monastery was a place to reform errant monks – there was a strict regime and no women were allowed.

Continue up the hill past the foundations of the **Surp Harutyun Church** to the highest point of the peninsula, with panoramic views. On the far side of the hill are two buildings: one belongs to the **National Writers' Union** (closed to the public), the other is the **president's vacation home**, protected by a high fence. The building on the north side of the peninsula is a new **seminary** for the Armenian Apostolic Church. The students sometimes play football in the car park near the stairs. There are a couple of souvenir stalls and the Ashot Yerkat Restaurant too.

Marshrutky (AMD100) to Sevanavank leave hourly between 9am and 5pm from the taxi stand 500m east of the *avtokayan* (bus station) in Sevan. Otherwise, taxis are plentiful in Sevan; a taxi to and from the monastery with 30 minutes' waiting time is AMD2000.

🛏 Sleeping & Eating

Sevan's beach resorts start to fill up – and raise their prices – around late May. Prices

ARMENIA SEVAN

may jump by 40% in the high season. The season slows down again in early September. In spring and autumn resorts remain open with reduced rates and in winter most are shut entirely. A unique form of shelter here are *domiki* (converted metal cargo containers), which gives you some insight into Armenian resourcefulness.

Local restaurants crank up the volume of their stereos extra loud when tourists arrive, so you may have a hard time finding a quiet place to enjoy the birdsong and lapping waters of Lake Sevan.

Kambuz   HOTEL $$
(☎2 00 76; Sevan peninsula; r AMD20,000-30,000) Located on the beach near Sevanavank, this is one of the few places to include a permanent structure, rather than *domiki*. Rooms are relatively modern and include either one or two bedrooms.

Ishkan   DOMIKI $
(Sevan peninsula; r AMD10,000) Very basic place next to Kambuz featuring colourful *domiki*. The buildings are flimsy and beds hard as a rock but it's the cheapest around. Food is available, including kebabs, salads, bread and beer (everything on the menu seems to cost AMD500).

Nirvana   COTTAGES $$$
(☎2 21 21; Yerevan Hwy; cottages AMD35,000) Between the Harsnaqar complex and the peninsula, Nirvana has five-person cottages with hot and cold water and a refrigerator. There's a cafe-bar here open late and a wide stretch of beach at the front.

Albatross   COTTAGES $$
(☎091485245; Yerevan Hwy; cottages AMD15,000) About 2.5km southeast of Sevan town, Albatross occupies a quiet stretch of beach with a few colourful *domiky*. Paddleboats and jet skis are available.

Harsnaqar Hotel Complex   HOTEL $$$
(☎2 00 92; www.harsnaqarhotel.am; Yerevan Hwy; s/d AMD30,000/40,000;✳) This is the large Holiday Inn–style hotel where the highway meets the lake. It has a water park, tennis courts, lawns and a private stretch of beach. It also has an excellent restaurant, with a terrace overlooking the lake.

Ashot Yerkat Restaurant   ARMENIAN $$
(meals AMD2000-3500; ⊘10am-9pm) You can feast on kebabs, grilled *ishkhan* trout, salads and lavash on the terrace of this restaurant out on the Sevan peninsula. Try the house speciality, 'eat and shut up' – a concoction of sautéed meat and potatoes.

Art Café   CAFE $
(Demirjan Poghots; snacks AMD1000-2500; ⊘11am-10pm; 🍴) Adding a splash of flair to Sevan, this place has loud music videos, big comfortable seating arrangements and a billiards room. The mostly Western menu includes pizzas, salads and sandwiches.

❶ Information

The **Tourist Information Centre** (☎2 02 20; 164 Nairyan Poghots; ⊘9am-noon & 2-5pm Mon-Sat), located in the Qaghaqapetaran (city municipality building), can supply you with a

---

THE AYAS NAUTICAL RESEARCH CLUB

One of the best stories about post-independence Armenia concerns a medieval sailing ship in a landlocked country. The Ayas project began back in 1985 when the club's founders became interested in the times of the Cilician Kings, from the 10th to 14th centuries, when Armenian naval vessels and traders plied the eastern Mediterranean from the ports of Ayas and Korykos. Club members discovered old plans of Armenian ships in the British Library. Armenia hasn't had a sea coast since 1375, but they set out to build a sailing ship the old way.

After independence, the fuel shortages made the timbers of the Ayas a target for people on the verge of freezing. Club members lived and slept in the boat for several years to protect it. The vessel survived to sail on Lake Sevan in 2002 and in 2004 sailed on the Black Sea then all the way to Portsmouth, England. In 2006 the ship continued its journey from Portsmouth to St Petersburg, Russia, and along a series of rivers all the way back to the Black Sea where the trip began. The **Ayas Nautical Research Club** (Map p130; ☎1-57 85 10; 1 Charents Poghots, Yerevan) has a substantial library of books on maritime Armenia and its fleets. The club's latest project is to build 10 small sailing vessels for use on Lake Sevan. When complete, an annual regatta is planned on the lake. More information is available at www.ayas.am.

Sevan

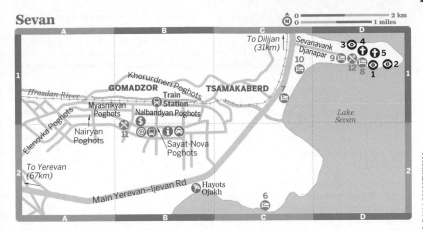

map of the area and ideas on activities or accommodation (note that the hours are pretty ad hoc so someone may or may not be there when you arrive). **Internet Club** (Nairyan Poghots; ⏱9am-1.30am) is on the corner opposite the *avtokayan*. **Converse Bank** (Nairyan Poghots) is one of many banks to offer an ATM service on the main street.

❶ Getting There & Away

By car Yerevan is only 60 minutes away by freeway. Transport to Yerevan (AMD600, one hour, every hour 8am to 5pm) leaves from the corner of Nairyan Poghots and Sayat-Nova Poghota in the centre of Sevan town.

There's a *marshrutka* to Vanadzor from the corner of Nairyan Poghots and Shinararneri Poghots at 10am (AMD1000) that can drop you in Dilijan. This corner is also a taxi stand. A taxi to Yerevan (67km) costs about AMD7000, to Dilijan AMD4000 and to Tsaghkadzor AMD3000. A taxi to one of the hotels around the peninsula costs AMD1000. A four- or five-hour tour of Sevanavank, Hayravank and the *khatchkars* of Noratus should cost around AMD7000.

In summer a train runs from Yerevan to Sevan (AMD200, four hours, 8am), though it's so slow that it could only be considered for the experience.

Around Lake Sevan

About 30km south of Sevan is the charmingly typical *tufa* monastery, **Hayravank** – 1100 years old, sturdy as the day it was built, and with *khatchkars* in the cemetery attesting to centuries of Armenian life. The promontory it stands on has a fine view of Lake Sevan. Further south is **Noratus**

Sevan

⊙ Sights

1	National Writer's Union	D1
2	President's Vacation Home	D1
3	Seminary	D1
4	Sevanavank	D1
5	Surp Harutyun Church	D1

⊟ Sleeping

6	Albatross	C2
7	Harsnaqar Hotel Complex	C1
8	Ishkhan	D1
9	Kambuz	D1
10	Nirvana	C1

⊗ Eating

11	Art Café	B2
12	Ashot Yerkat Restaurant	D1

(sometimes spelt Noraduz), an old village and a fine place to wander around. There's a tall chapel of **Surp Grigor Lusavorich** at one end of town and an ancient *khatchkar*-studded cemetery on the eastern side of the village. According to one legend, an Arab army was once forced to take cover nearby as the commander mistook the field of *khatchkars* for a battalion of enemy soldiers. They only moved on after a scout discovered the 'soldiers' were nothing more than harmless stone tablets. Noratus is a good area to find a **beach** away from the bustle of Sevan.

The provincial capital of Gegharkunik *marz* is **Gavar** (Kamo), population 30,000, on the cold slopes of the Geghama mountains west of Lake Sevan. It's a quietly poor town, similar to **Martuni** at the lake's southern end, with a few cafes, a Soviet-era hotel and a feeling that it is just struggling to survive. Hourly *marshrutky* travel between Yerevan and Martuni and between Yerevan and Gavar.

A paved road from Martuni heads south over the **Selim Pass** (2410m) to Yeghegnadzor in Vayots Dzor but it's impassable in winter (November to April). No public transport goes over the pass so you'll need your own vehicle to make the trip; a taxi will cost around AMD10,000.

About 20km east of Martuni is the handsome little **Vanevank** church (903), in a gorge south of the town of Artsvanist. Turn off at Karchagbyur and head up the valley through Lchavan to the centre of Makenis village to find the 10th- to 13th-century churches of **Makenyats Vank**, close to a gorge.

Further on, the road cuts inland to **Vardenis**. One road continues around the eastern side of the lake and another heads towards the mountains and the valuable **Zod gold mines**. A famously rough road used only by fearless truckers heads on from the mines over the Sodk Pass (2400m) into the wilds of Kelbajar and northern Karabakh.

Public transport around the lake is sporadic. For information on *marshrutky* from Yerevan to Gavar, Martuni and Vardenis see p143. The departure point in Yerevan is the Northern bus station. Vehicles depart hourly. To Gavar the cost is AMD1000, to Martuni AMD1200 and to Vardenis AMD1500. The best way to discover the lakeshore kilometres of quiet, clean beaches is with your own transport and perhaps camping gear.

Tsaghkadzor ԾԱՂԿԱՁՈՐ

☑223 / POP 1800

Back when Armenia was part of the USSR, Soviet athletes used to come to this tiny village to train for the Winter Olympics and other sport competitions. The ski centre is still here and, if you happen to be in Armenia in winter, Tsaghkadzor (Gorge of Flowers) makes an excellent weekend getaway. The little resort, 57km north of Yerevan, is a virtual ghost town in summer, which is great if you are looking for discount rates on hotels or some crowd-free nature spots.

The main road reaches a central square and veers left up to the House of Writers, or right and around to the active Kecharis Monastery. The road straight on from the monastery leads to the ski base where you can take a chairlift ride up the mountain, even in summer (per person AMD1500). It's a far cry from the Alps but good fun for a day on the slopes. You can hire ski equipment at the ski base or from the Kecharis Hotel.

The forests around the base of the mountain provide some nice walks. Horse riding can be organised directly through **Seran Mirzoya** (☑093340058), reached through the Kecharis Hotel.

The **Kecharis Monastery** is a finely carved 11th- to 13th-century complex with *khatchkars*, a *katoghike* (cathedral), a Surp Grigor church and a smaller Surp Nishan chapel. It's now the seat of the bishop of Kotayk *marz*.

🛏 Sleeping

Kecharis Hotel HOTEL $$
(☑6 04 09; www.kecharishotel.am; Orbeli Poghots; r incl breakfast AMD20,000-30,000;@🛜) A slick operation in the centre of town with topnotch facilities, modern rooms and lots of colourful art adorning the walls. Facilities include a business centre, a sauna and a branch of the popular Jazzve cafe chain. The English-speaking staff can also give tips on local activities or set up horse-riding trips. Prices increase by 30% during the ski season (November to March).

Jupiter Hotel HOTEL $$
(☑091407394; www.jupiter-hotel.info; Grigor Magistros; r incl breakfast from AMD15,000) The Jupiter is perhaps the best of several hotels on Tsaghkadzor's main square. It's a clean and quiet place with colourful rooms.

House of Writers HOTEL $
(☑1-28 10 81; www.writershotel.am; s/d AMD12,000/13,000, apt AMD40,000-50,000;🚗) This one-time Soviet-ministry hotel has seen significant renovations. Some rooms have been renovated to a respectable standard and even the unrenovated rooms are at least well maintained. Follow the main road into town and look for the sign on the left.

Arminay Akopyan B&B B&B $
(☑6 04 25, 093252 642; 35 Kecharetsu Poghots; r AMD10,000) Clean and friendly guesthouse with hot showers, located 200m downhill from the Kecharis Hotel. No English spoken.

ℹ️ Getting There & Away

Tsaghkadzor is only about 40 minutes' drive northeast of Yerevan. There are no direct buses or *marshrutky*, but a taxi to Yerevan costs about AMD5500.

There are frequent buses and *marshrutky* between Yerevan and Hrazdan (AMD400), 6km down the valley – a taxi up to Tsaghkadzor from here will cost AMD800. There are only a few taxis in Tsaghkadzor.

Dilijan ԴԻԼԻՋԱՆ

📋 268 / POP 17,000

It's billed as the 'Switzerland of Armenia', and although that may be a bit of a stretch, alpine Dilijan is still one of the most pleasant regions in the country.

During Soviet times this was the peaceful retreat for cinematographers, composers, artists and writers to come and be creative; today it's a centre for tourism with a number of fine B&Bs and a revitalised historic district.

There is certainly enough natural beauty to inspire creative thought: the lush oak and hornbeam forests surround the town with snowcapped peaks in the distance. In summer the villagers herd cattle down from the mountain pastures through the town, and people gather mushrooms and mountain herbs from the rich deciduous forests. Local architecture uses a lot of steep tiled roofs and wooden beams, along with some cute gingerbread-style structures. Even the local Soviet monuments have a touch of flair.

The gorgeous churches of Haghartsin and Goshavank are an easy day trip from Dilijan.

◉ Sights & Activities

Dilijan Historic Centre   AREA
(Sharambeyan Poghots) The Dilijan Historic Centre is a little cobbled street next to Myasnikyan Poghots. This collection of stone and wooden traditional buildings includes shops, a hotel, eateries, souvenir stalls and workshops for local craftspeople. As you walk along the main road into town you only see one part of it on the left; you need to turn down the stone steps to reach Sharambeyan Poghots, where most of the shops are located. The complex includes the modest **Dilijan Historic Museum** (Sharambeyan Poghots; admission AMD1000; ⊙10am-7pm), a mock 19th-century Dilijan

home with period furniture, photographs and crockery.

Dilijan Museum of Local History   MUSEUM
(Myasnikyan Poghots; admission AMD500, tour in English AMD2000; ⊙10am-5.40pm Tue-Sat, 10am-4.40pm Sun) This newly renovated museum houses a surprisingly varied collection of European and Armenian art from the 16th to 20th centuries. Some of the older works from Italian and French artists had been housed in museums in Moscow and St Petersburg but were moved to Dilijan during WWII for safekeeping.

Monuments

A crownlike monument to the **50th Anniversary of Soviet Armenia** stands near the main roundabout. The **WWII Memorial**, with the huge silver figures of a soldier holding a dying comrade, is on a hillock south of the river.

Walks

There are pleasant walks to the 11th-century **Surp Grigor Church** and **Jukhtakvank** monastery, both located near the Dilijan mineral-water plant, 3.2km east along the Vanadzor road and about 3.5km up to the right. They are well signposted and a trail continues past Jukhtakvank, through pastures and woods, and back to Dilijan (a three-hour hike).

Further on towards Vanadzor the scenery is gorgeous, passing the Russian **Molokan villages** of Fioletovo and Lermontovo. Molokans ('milk drinkers') are a Russian fundamentalist Christian sect that broke with the Russian Orthodox Church in the 17th century; they earned their moniker by not fasting on official holidays.

🛏️ Sleeping

There are lots of hotels and sanatoriums in and around town. Some beautifully located resorts, such as the House of Composers (where Khachaturian, Shostakovich and Prokofiev stayed), are still run by government ministries and often occupied by soldiers. There are a fair few B&Bs around town.

Ananov Guesthouse   BOUTIQUE HOTEL $$$
(📞70 59; www.tufenkianheritage.com; Sharambeyan Poghots; r AMD43,000-48,000; 🛜) This attractive heritage hotel features antique furnishings, high ceilings and a large wooden deck affording great views of Dilijan valley. It's a quiet, intimate place that sweeps you

back to an earlier age but does not give up conveniences like wi-fi and an updated bathroom. It's located in the Dilijan Historic Centre, a renovated confection of touristy shops and cafes.

Daravand Guesthouse   B&B $$

(☎78 57, 094420 965; www.daravand.com; 46 Abovyan Poghots; s/d without bathroom AMD10,000/16,000, with bathroom AMD16,000/22,000, all prices incl breakfast; @) This character-filled place has well-appointed rooms, a cosy common room and an outdoor deck with gorgeous views. The food is excellent. Owner Razmik is a diaspora Armenian with an Iranian upbringing and a German education. He can organise day trips to places of interest. The guesthouse is on the road toward Jukhtakvank, 360m off the main Dilijan–Vanadzor road. Look for the red garage and the stairs leading up to the house.

Nina B&B   B&B $

(☎23 30, 091767734; 18 Myasnikyan Poghots; per person AMD7000; @) Most backpackers end up at this friendly B&B consisting of seven guestrooms of varying size and quality. There's also a bright lounge were guests warm themselves with endless pots of tea. On the downside, the furnishings are a bit dated and the plumbing in the bathrooms isn't great, but overall it's a comfortable and homey experience. The best part of the place is mealtime; Nina spends half the day preparing a delicious dinner of soup, salads and either dolma (vine leaves with a rice filling) or *khoravats* (the main course switches each day). Dinner is an extra AMD3000. Meals for nonguests can be made with prior arrangement. At the *shuka* turn right and up the short hill (it's well signposted).

Magnit B&B   B&B $

(☎26 80, 093224725; bb_rima@mail.ru; 86 Kalinin Poghots; per person AMD7000; @) This huge villa has 10 clean guestrooms, all modern and carefully decorated. There is a large dining room and a backyard where *khoravats* meals are sometimes prepared by the staff. It's about 1km from the roundabout on the road to Vanadzor. Breakfast is overpriced at AMD3000.

Tateh Guesthouse   GUESTHOUSE $

(☎25 33, 093256430; 41 Komisarneri Poghots; r per person AMD5000) This family-run guesthouse is a no-frills operation (no breakfast, no internet, no English speakers). But rooms

are spacious, clean and comfortable and the place is rarely full. From the main road (just past the internet cafe), walk down the steps and look for the metal fence with the green trim.

 Eating

There are a couple of fast-food shwarma places at the bottom of the hill near the roundabout.

Artbridge   CAFE $

(Sharambeyan Poghots; meals AMD1500-3000; ⏱8.30am-10pm; 🛜📱) This branch of the Artbridge in Yerevan offers a short but sweet menu of soups, salads, pastas and sandwiches. It's a pleasant place to while away an afternoon with a book and a cup of tea or coffee.

Haykanoush   ARMENIAN $$

(Sharambeyan Poghots; meals AMD3000-5500; ⏱10am-10pm; 📱) This classy restaurant run by the Tufenkian Group has hardwood floors, cream-coloured walls and a muted traditional ambience meant to replicate 19th-century Dilijan. Speciality dishes include lamb and apricot stew, dolma rolled in raspberry leaves and warm *souboereg* (baked pasta and cheese). It's a great chance to sample some delicious Armenian authentic cuisine.

Getap Restaurant   ARMENIAN $$

(meals AMD2500-4000; ⏱9am-9pm) Located on the highway to Ijevan, this place consists of several wooden cabins overlooking the river. Food is typically *khoravats,* soups and fresh veggies.

Bistro Lchap   ARMENIAN $

(shwarma AMD800; ⏱9am-9pm) Located near the main roundabout, this is fine for a quick shwarma or kebab.

❶ **Information**

The **Dilijan Tourist Office** (Sharambeyan Poghots; ⏱10am-7pm Tue-Sun May-Oct; 🛜) is open for business in the Dilijan Historic Centre, a short walk uphill from the bus turnaround. It can provide lists of local homestays, B&Bs, craftspeople and artists.

Continue past the tourist enclave to reach the modern town centre. There's a **Haypost-Armentel** (58 Myasnikyan Poghots) in the town centre next to the plaza. The five-storey building behind the plaza contains an **internet cafe** (per hr AMD400). There are moneychangers on Myasnikyan Poghots as well as the **Ardshininvest**

ARMENIA DILIJAN

Bank (60 Myasnikyan Poghots), next to the Haypost office.

❶ Getting There & Around

Buses and *marshrutky* to Yerevan leave from the main roundabout by the river. Buses (AMD1000, three hours) leave hourly between 9am and 3pm – some of these are services starting further north from Ijevan or Noyemberyan. Services to Ijevan (AMD500, 45 minutes) run hourly between 9am and 6pm. Services to Vanadzor (AMD500, 40 minutes) run at 9am, 10.20am, 3.20pm and 4pm. One daily bus goes to the Georgian border at 10.30am.

There are taxis at the main roundabout (the fare is AMD400 around town). During the day a local bus trundles between the western side of town around Kalinin Poghots up to Shahumian Poghots (AMD100). A taxi to Haghartsin or Goshavank and back costs around AMD5000, or AMD7000 for both destinations combined.

Haghartsin ՀԱՂԱՐԾԻՆ

The handsome **Haghartsin Monastery** (Haghartsin means 'Dance of the Eagles') was built in the 12th century by two brothers, princes of the Bagratuni kingdom. It's hidden away in a lovely forest valley by some massive nut trees.

The monastery has three churches: the first for Gregory the Illuminator; the second for the Virgin Mary, named Surp Astvatsatsin (Holy Mother of God); and the last, a chapel to St Stepanos. The church is also famed for housing an image of the Virgin and Child, which has distinct Mongolian features –

ARMENIA HAGHARTSIN

HIKING FROM HAGHARTSIN TO SHAMAKHYAN

From Haghartsin, it's possible to walk on trails over the mountain to Shamakhyan, a village 3km northwest of Dilijan. Bring water, a hat and sunscreen, and be prepared for sudden bursts of rain.

Walk past the monastery to find the trailhead, which is marked with a sign that reads: 'Dilijan NP Eco-Tourist Route'. After five minutes the jeep trail reaches a creek and continues up the opposite bank. From here it's a one-hour uphill hike to the ridge. The path is a bit overgrown in places but the route is fairly obvious.

At the ridge you'll find another set of jeep tracks and you should follow these to the right. After a short distance, Dilijan will appear in the distance to your left. After about 30 minutes of level walking the jeep tracks start to head downhill below the treeline. After about 15 minutes of downhill walking (still on the jeep tracks) you'll see a fence made from branches. Stay on the road as it hooks left and continues downhill. Five minutes after seeing the fence an open meadow appears on the right. Just downhill from here is an artillery range used by the army.

At this point you should walk right, off the main jeep track, and down towards the meadow. Cross the gully and walk along the hillside in a southwesterly direction (veering away from the artillery range). The trail disappears for a while but after 10 minutes you hit an obvious jeep trail heading downhill (now the artillery range is more or less behind you). Continue downhill to a creek and a farmhouse on the opposite bank. There is a wood footbridge a little bit left of the jeep track.

On the other side of the creek is a little picnic area. Continue along the jeep trail for another 20 minutes and at the next clearing veer to the right. Shamakhyan village soon comes into view. The road leading to the village can be very muddy so look for the small break which leads down to the creek and up the other bank to the village. The walk takes less than four hours. From the village you can walk down to the highway and catch a lift back to Dilijan.

Alternatively, you can extend the hike by walking from Shamakhyan to Jukhtakvank (p157). Start by walking uphill from the taxi stand and follow this road as it wraps above the town to the cow farm *(kirova ferma)*. Just past the barns and sheds is a sign that says 'Nature Trail Jukhtak Vank – Shamakhyan'. Continue along this obvious jeep trail for about 50 minutes and you'll eventually reach Jukhtakvank. Note that few locals know this trail, so if you ask for directions most people will tell you to walk down to the highway and turn right up the next valley for Jukhtakvank. However, the shortest route is definitely along the 'Nature Trail'. Along the trail are some information panels that describe the flora and fauna of the area.

From Jukhtakvank you can walk 3km downhill to the main highway.

added to convince the next wave of Mongol invaders not to destroy the church (at the time of writing this carving was on display in an overseas museum and it is unknown when it will return to Haghartsin). The brothers' family seal can be seen on the back of St Stepanos chapel.

There are some stunning *khatchkars,* a sundial on the wall of the St Gregory Church, and a refectory (1248) with amazing arching interlocked stone beams. Mass is held in the Surp Astvatsatsin at 11am on Sunday. At the time of research the monastery was undergoing a massive renovation project funded by the Sheikh of Sharjah. In a somewhat controversial move, a hotel and cafe are also part of the building project. The project is to be complete by the time you read this.

The monastery is 4km off the main Dilijan–Ijevan road. You can get a lift to the turn-off and easily walk there the rest of the way (or possibly hitch there, especially on a weekend when there is more traffic).

Goshavank ԳՈՇԱՎԱՆՔ

Goshavank monastery stands in the mountain village of Gosh, founded in 1188 by the saintly Armenian cleric Mkhitar Gosh, who was buried in a little chapel overlooking the main complex. Goshavank features a main church (Surp Astvatsatsin) and smaller churches to St Gregory of Narek and St Gregory the Illuminator. The tower on the *matenadaran* (library) was once taller than the main church. With a school attached, the library is said to have held 15,000 books before it was burned by Timur's army in the 13th century.

Goshavank is considered one of the principal cultural centres of Armenia in its time; historians believe it was abandoned at the end of the 14th century. Goshavank then appears to have been reoccupied in the 17th to 19th centuries and restored from 1957 to 1963. The museum director Artur Osepian is usually available to answer questions and may show you a small **museum** (admission AMD250) behind the monastery.

🛏 Sleeping

Artur Osepian B&B B&B $
(☎093942491; per person AMD5000) This friendly B&B with three rooms is run by Artur Osepian, the director of the monastery complex. Artur can spin some yarns about the history of the area and give good advice on short hikes.

Makhital Gosh HOTEL $$
(093172777, 093758595; r AMD15,000-25,000) This 16-room hotel is next to the parking lot of Goshavank. The staff are quite helpful and will show you a variety of rooms; the best ones have excellent views of the monastery.

🛈 Getting There & Away

Goshavank is 6.5km off the main Dilijan–Ijevan highway. You can ride on a local bus or *marshrutka* to the turn-off and walk or hitch the rest of the way. One bus (AMD250) serves the monastery; on Tuesday and Friday it goes to Dilijan at 9am and returns at 1pm. On Monday and Wednesday it goes to Ijevan at 9am and returns at noon. A taxi from Dilijan or Ijevan (both 23km away) is the easiest option (about AMD4500 one way).

Ijevan ԻՋԵՎԱՆ

☎263 / POP 21,000

Surrounded by forested mountains and with the Aghstev River running through its centre, Ijevan is the attractive capital of Tavush *marz.* Ijevan means 'caravanserai' or 'inn' and the town has been on a major east–west route for millennia. The local climate is warmer than in Dilijan, and the town is the centre of a wine-growing district with some very acceptable white table wines. The town has some handsome early-20th-century buildings, a big *shuka,* a winery and a little museum. Outside the town there are opportunities for horse riding and hiking.

The local authorities are trying to encourage tourism, though the process has been slow: no one in the tourist office speaks English and most of the dozen or so listed B&Bs seem to only exist on paper. Still, there are some decent cafes in town and a friendly local populace.

Buses stop on the main highway close to the fountain; about 100m further is the police station, the Haypost office and the busy *shuka,* with plenty of moneychanging shops and stalls.

⊙ Sights

Locals enjoy whiling away the afternoon in the **Sculpture Park**, in the centre of town.

Ijevan Winery WINERY
(3 64 57; 9 Yerevanyan Poghots; ⊘by appointment) The Ijevan Winery presses much of the local harvest into dry white and sparkling wines under the Haghartsin, Gayane

and Makaravank labels. It offers free tours and tastings with advance notice, and has cellar-door sales. The winery also puts on lunches overlooking the river. It's about 1.5km from the town centre towards Dilijan.

Ijevan Local Lore Museum · · · MUSEUM
(5 Yerevanyan Poghots; admission free, donations appreciated; ☺10am-5pm Tue-Sun) On the road to the winery you'll pass this little museum, with a couple of rooms of ethnographical displays. The enthusiastic museum curator, Nariman Tananyan, enjoys showing off the ancient battle gear on display. Don't be surprised if he yanks a thousand-year-old sabre out of the display case and waves it around as if under attack!

🛌 Sleeping

The B&B scene is more than a little dysfunctional. About 10 properties are listed in a brochure at the tourist office but in reality only two or three operate (and even these are not well signed and are difficult to locate).

[TOP CHOICE] Gyulnara Meliksetyan · · · B&B $
(☑3 15 54, 093191211; 2 Nalbandyan Poghots; per person AMD7000) This B&B is in a big house about 1km north of the centre, with six bedrooms, satellite TV and modern plumbing. Home-cooked dinners cost about AMD1500. To get there, travel north along the main highway from the *shuka* for around 800m, turn left uphill and then take the first right on a dirt track. There are no signs at all, so it's best to take a taxi the first time or call first.

Vardan Vardanyan B&B · · · B&B $
(☑3 36 95, 093003695; 25 Proschyan Poghots; r per person incl breakfast AMD5000) This spacious home is run by the same man who owns the Vardanak Café near the bus stand; he'll probably approach you about accommodation if you eat there. A filling breakfast

with eggs and cheese is included. The B&B is on the hill behind the cafe.

Hotel Dok · · · HOTEL $
(☑4 01 71, 094515154; 40 Ankahutyan Poghots; r/deluxe AMD10,000/20,000; @) The Dok is the flashiest hotel Ijevan can offer. Rooms are spacious, fairly modern and cheap compared to others of this standard. There's an excellent restaurant downstairs that serves Armenian and international cuisine.

Hotel Mosh · · · HOTEL $
(☑3 56 11, 091452463; www.hotel-mosh.am; 3 Yerevan Poghots; r AMD7000, without bathroom AMD5000; 🖩) This eight-room hotel doesn't have much atmosphere, but it's conveniently located on the main road and prices are very reasonable. Hot showers, satellite TV and wi-fi are available. It's just past the large *shuka*.

🍴 Eating

Vardanak Café · · · CAFE $
(Yerevan Poghots; meals AMD600-1400; ☺11am-10pm; 🖩) Among the three cafes in the centre of town along the main highway, this one, next to the bus stand, is the only one that serves hot food. The owner Vardan also has a B&B nearby (see Sleeping) and is keen to assist travellers.

Yeritarsardakan Café · · · CAFE $
(3 Ankahutyan Poghots; meals AMD800-1600; ☺10am-10pm Tue-Sun; 🖩) Located opposite the Sculpture Park, this is the most popular spot in town for food and drinks. It serves decent *lahmajo* (minced-lamb minipizza), cutlets and soups, and claims to have wi-fi (though it never seems to work).

ℹ Information

The **Ijevan Tourist Information Centre** (☑3 32 58; 5a Melikbekyan Poghots; ☺10am-6pm Mon-Sat) gets our vote as the least-helpful tourist office in the country. No one speaks English and

---

PUNCH DRUNK

Oghee (pronounced something like 'orh-ee') are delicious fruit vodkas, sometimes called *vatsun* or *aragh*, made in village orchards everywhere. Around 60% alcohol, *oghee* is made from apples, pears, apricots, pomegranates, grapes, cherries, Cornelian cherries or cornels, mulberries and figs. The best mulberry (*t'te*) and Cornelian cherry (*hone*) *oghee* are intense, lingering liqueurs. Vedi Alco makes some *oghee* commercially, weaker than the village stuff. You won't need to go far to try some; it's a usual accompaniment to a *khoravats* dinner. The drink tastes best in autumn when homes turn into distilleries after the harvest.

WORTH A TRIP

SHAMSHADIN & AROUND

North of Ijevan, one road turns northwest at Azatamut through the captured Azeri enclaves of Upper and Lower Askipara (now Verin Voskepar and Nerkin Voskepar) to Noyemberyan and the Georgian border. Another road turns right just before the border to Berd in Shamshadin region. There are still landmines along this frontier; it's unwise to explore the shattered villages around here.

Just past the turn-off to Noyemberyan there's a road 4km to Achajur village and onwards another 6.5km to the 11th-century **Makaravank** monastery. The beautiful church is set deep in a forest, giving it a very peaceful atmosphere. There are some fine carvings on the exterior and interior of the structures, including ornate altar daises carved with eight-pointed stars, floral motifs, fish, birds and geometrical forms. There is no public transport here, but you may be able to get a lift with locals visiting the site.

The Shamshadin region east of Ijevan is a fertile stretch of woodlands, vineyards and farms carved by three valleys: the Khndzorut, Tavush and Hakhum. With Azerbaijan on two sides and rugged mountains dividing it from the rest of Armenia, it's also quite isolated.

As the crow flies it's just 21km from Ijevan to Berd; the mountains in between them, however, have forced the construction of a roundabout road that loops for 67km north and then south. About 44km into the trip you'll spot **Nor Varagavank** up the hillside – the 3km detour is worth the trip to see the ruined monastery. The oldest sections were started in 1198 by David Bagrtuni, son of King Vasak I; a Surp Astvatsatsin church was added in 1237. The monastery once contained a fragment of the True Cross until it was lost in fighting in 1915.

Berd (population 8000) itself is nothing special but does have a restaurant and a couple of hotels. The main reason to come to Berd is to hike here along the old road from Ijevan. The 35km road twists and winds through the mountains and past some attractive old villages. The hike takes about 12 hours in total, best spread over two or three days. There are no hotels, but you can ask in the villages for a homestay. It's best to have a taxi driver take you the first 5km or so out of Ijevan to get you on the right track. Just make sure they are taking you on the old road that heads east of town rather than the new road going north.

A daily *marshrutka* (AMD500) leaves from Ijevan to Berd (on the new road) at 9am. It returns from Berd at 2pm. A shared taxi between Berd and Ijevan is AMD1500 per person.

the most they might offer is a list of B&Bs, most of which no longer function. Banks are located on Melibekyan Poghots, which has a distinctive fountain and a couple of cafes. There is an **Internet Club** (per hr AMD300; ⏰8am-midnight) near the Sculpture Park. **Rouben Simonyan** (☎3 24 32) is a local historian who speaks Armenian and Russian and can arrange guides for road trips and hikes to unusual sites in the region.

ℹ️ Getting There & Away

The bus stand is in front of a decrepit hotel, just uphill from the Vardanak Café. There is a little ticket window displaying departure information.

There are *marshrutky* to Yerevan (AMD1700, 2.5 hours, every hour from 10am to 6pm) that stop in Dilijan 36km down the road. One bus (AMD1000) for Yerevan departs at 9.30am. The cost to be dropped in Dilijan is AMD400. There

are daily *marshrutky* to Vanadzor (AMD1000, 9.30am, 11am, 3pm and 5pm).

At the time of writing there was no public transport from Ijevan to Georgia, but you could get something to Noyemberyan and change there. If you are headed that way it's worth asking about a share taxi to the border or a resumption of bus services.

Yenokavan & Around
ԵՆՈՔԱՎԱՆ

The rugged mountains around Ijevan hide old roads, forts and churches in their many folds. The first part of the journey is a 9km road from Ijevan to the village of **Yenokavan**. On the southern edge of Yenokavan is a small church perched on a rock overlooking a gorge. Inside the nearby gorge is the 13th-century **Surp Astvatsatsin Church**.

A further 4km up the valley from Yenokavan is a unique tourist venture run by **Apaga Tour** (☎091290939, 091495834; www.apaga.info; s/d AMD42,000/66,000; ☎). There are horse stables here, and guided trail rides can be arranged for AMD3500 per hour or AMD25,000 per day (including meals). Guided hikes are also available if you prefer walking. Accommodation is available in newly built small cottages; the price includes three meals and horse riding. A taxi to Apaga from Ijevan costs around AMD2000 each way.

The drivable road ends at Apaga but if you are looking to get further off the beaten path, continue another 3km on foot from Apaga Tour down into the gorge to a separate tourist venture called **Anapat Tour** (☎094603010, 093365437; www.anapattur.nm.ru). This small operation, run by brothers Vahagn and Hovar Tananyan, is a simple bush camp near the Khachagbyur River in a beautiful spot they have dubbed 'Peace to the World'. Some locals also know it as 'Lastiver'. Bring a swimsuit as there are some wonderful bathing pools and cascades nearby. You can stay and eat at the camp for around AMD10,000 (less if you bring your own tent and food). Facilities consist of basic huts and even tree houses. If you arrive in the cooler months (October to April), accommodation is in caves. Activities include fishing, hiking and cave exploration. Some of the caves in the area contain unique pre-Christian carvings of faces and human forms.

The 3km hike from Apaga Tour to Anapat Tour takes about one hour and is mildly strenuous. It can be difficult to find the way so coming here on your own is not recommended; it's best to contact the brothers ahead of time so they can guide you to their camp.

Vanadzor ՎԱՆԱՁՈՐ

☎322 / POP 170,000

Lining the banks of the Pambak River, Vanadzor (formerly Kirovakan) is a post-industrial Soviet city and administrative centre for the Lori region. The main street, Tigran Mets Poghota, bustles with shops, cafes and the swishest clothes outside Yerevan. The young folk attending the teachers' college add a bit of nightlife to the city. The huge chemical works at the eastern end of town are mostly moribund, but some factories are reopening. The city is a useful base for visiting the classic churches of Debed Canyon, with good transport links to other cities.

⊙ Sights

There's not a whole lot to see, but there are parks and some interesting neighbourhoods to explore. A **regional museum** (admission AMD1000; ⊙11am-6pm Mon-Sat) at the western end of Tigran Mets Poghota is housed in an unattractive-looking building, just past the cinema (on the opposite side of the road). At the other end of town, the **Vanadzor Art Gallery** (Tumanyan Hraparak; admission AMD200; ⊙10am-5pm Tue-Sun) shows off local talent across widely divergent styles of painting and sculpture.

Vanadzor's **shuka** on Myasnikyan Poghots is one of Armenia's busiest regional markets. The old village neighbourhoods of **Dimats** and **Bazum** are east of the town centre, over the Tandzut River. The centre of town has the usual Soviet look, but south along Myasnikyan Poghots there are some elegant stone villas and country houses. There's a little **Russian Orthodox church** in the park by the train station, and the Armenian Apostolic church called the **Ghara Kilise** (Black Church), built from suitably black stone and surrounded by an elaborate cemetery. The Armenian church stands near the lower bridge on Tumanyan Poghots. There's an interesting walk up Abovyan Poghots along the little valley of the Vanadzor River, past boating ponds, tall trees and shuttered sanatoriums to an overgrown **Dendropark** (Forest Reserve).

🛏 Sleeping

TOP CHOICE **Maghay B&B**   B&B $

(☎4 52 59, 091380305; marined61@rambler.ru; 21 Azatamartikneri Poghots; per person AMD7000; @) This very welcoming B&B has two rooms and a communal bathroom, plus a second building that has rooms with bathroom. Dinners are available and the food is a delectable array of traditional Armenian salads and main courses. The family often eats with the guests, which creates a homey atmosphere. Meals for nonguests are available upon request. To find it, take the lane that goes left of the Nshkhark Hatsatun restaurant; it's at the end of the lane behind the big brown gate.

ARMENIA VANADZOR

Vanadzor

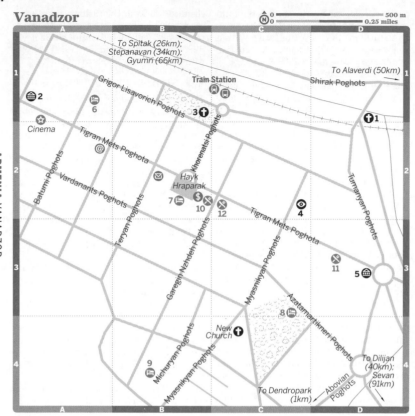

Hotel Argishti

HOTEL $$

(☎4 25 56; 1 Batumi Poghots; r incl breakfast AMD24,000; �wifi) Three blocks from Hayk Hraparak on a quiet street you'll find this reliable midrange hotel with high ceilings and a gated rose garden. The furnishings are new and comfortable, and there are some family rooms (for four people) for AMD35,000. It also has a restaurant, a bar and a billiards room.

Natasha & Lentrush's Guesthouse

GUESTHOUSE $

(☎4 63 43, 094914100; 24 Michuryan Poghots; per person AMD7000) A B&B with three rooms in an elegant two-storey villa with a garden. The couple's daughter, Kristine, speaks English. To get there, head up Garegin Nzhdeh Poghots, turn left at the army base and then take the first right after the Green House Hotel; number 24 is halfway up the street on the right, distinguished by a large grapevine and a little metal balcony.

Hotel Metropolina

HOTEL $$

(Gugark; ☎4 15 19; Hayk Hraparak; r per person AMD8000-15,000) This longtime Vanadzor hotel feels stuck in another age – USSR c 1978. A rickety elevator brings you up to the hotel and its scruffy rooms with temperamental plumbing. You may need to ask the 'administrator' to turn on the hot water before you hop in the shower. Some rooms have been renovated, which accounts for the cost difference between them. Note that the sign outside still displays the old name, the 'Hotel Gugark'. Despite its shortcomings, it's cheap, central and easy to find, and as a result sees a steady flow of budget travellers.

✕ Eating

Oasis

EUROPEAN, ARMENIAN $$

(48 Tigran Mets Poghota; meals AMD2500; �10.30am-11pm; �wifi) One of the most popular places in town, Oasis has an extensive

Vanadzor

◉ Sights
1 Ghara Kilise.................................... D1
2 Regional Museum.............................. A1
3 Russian Orthodox Church................. B1
4 Shuka... C2
5 Vanadzor Art Gallery........................ D3

⊜ Sleeping
6 Hotel Argishti.................................. A1
7 Hotel Metropolina (Gugark)............. B2
8 Maghay B&B..................................... C3
9 Natasha & Lentrush's
   Guesthouse B4

⊗ Eating
10 Jazzve.. B2
11 Oasis... D3
12 Shwarma... C2

menu with most items pictured so you know what you are in for. There are many European dishes and some Caucasian regional fare.

Jazzve   CAFE $
(22 Tigran Mets Poghota; meals AMD1800-2500; ⊙10.30am-11pm; 🛜🗐) This popular Armenian chain of coffee shops has made its way to Vanadzor. There's good coffee, desserts and light meals.

Shwarma   FAST FOOD $
(28 Tigran Mets Poghota; shwarma AMD400; ⊙10am-11pm) Handy fast-food place serving shwarma and cold drinks.

⊙ Information

Tigran Mets Poghota has lots of moneychangers' signs as well as an ATM at the **ACBA Bank** (22 Tigran Mets Poghota). There are also internet clubs and internet telephone offices along Tigran Mets Poghota, including the **Reborn Internet** (Tigran Mets Poghota; per hr AMD300; ⊙10am-10pm), near the corner with Batumi Poghots, and a post office. Wi-fi is available at Jazzve cafe and Oasis restaurant.

⊙ Getting There & Around

Vanadzor's *avtokayan* and train station (📞2 10 09) are at the bottom of Khorenatsi Poghots. *Marshrutky* to Yerevan (AMD1200, two hours, every 20 minutes from 7am to 7.30pm) take a 132km route via Spitak and Aparan to Yerevan. There's also transport to Dilijan (*marshrutka* or bus AMD500, up to one hour, hourly between 8am and 3.30pm), Stepanavan (AMD400, 45 minutes, 10am, 1pm, 2.30pm and 4.30pm),

Gyumri (AMD800, one hour, 9.30am, 11am, 1pm, 2pm, 3pm and 4.30pm) and Alaverdi (AMD500, up to one hour, 10am, 11am, noon, 1.30pm, 2.30pm, 3.30pm and 4.30pm). A *marshrutka* to Tbilisi (AMD3500) leaves at 8.30am.

The churches of the Debed Canyon can be visited on a day trip by taxi for around AMD6000 to AMD8000 for seven or eight hours, negotiate with drivers based at the *avtokayan*. Alternatively, head to Alaverdi and visit the sites on public transport.

Stepanavan & Around
ՍՏԵՓԱՆԱՎԱՆ

📞256 / POP 14,000

Stepanavan sits on a plateau above the steep-sided gorge of the Dzoragets River. It's fabled for its fine summer weather and, less proudly today, as one of the centres of Armenian communism. The area has been a site of settlement for millennia, on fertile fields above the river. The town is quiet, but it's a nice place for a wander (away from the usual monumental Soviet centre) and the locals are friendly.

An early cell of the Bolsheviks led by local lad Stepan Shahumian operated from hideouts and caves before the revolution. Shahumian died in a lonely corner of the Turkmenistan desert with the other 26 'Baku Commissars' in 1918, later sanctified in countless memorials across the region. (The Baku Commissars were Bolshevik leaders in the Caucasus in the early days of the revolution.) A rather dashing Shahumian poses on a pedestal in the main square, Stepan Shahumian Hraparak.

◉ Sights & Activities

The **Stepan Shahumian Museum** (Stepan Shahumian Hraparak; admission AMD100; ⊙11am-7pm) has an art gallery, plus displays on Stepanavan's history, and – excitement, comrades – the life story of the martyred commissar. It's completely built around the Shahumians' home, preserved like a doll's house in a giant box.

On the north bank of the Dzoragets River about 3km east of Stepanavan is the dramatically sited fortress **Lori Berd** (*berd* means fortress). The road from Stepanavan passes hillocks in the fields, which are actually **Bronze Age tumulus tombs**. The fort sits on a promontory between the gorges of the Dzoragets and Miskhana Rivers, with huge round towers and massive stone blocks along its exposed side. This was the capital of David Anhogin (949–1049) and later a local power base for the Orbelians and Zakarians, powerful families of Armenian nobles. There is a story that the Mongols captured the fortress after the defenders became distracted by alcohol. There is an ancient cemetery nearby and a 14th-century bridge in the gorge below. A taxi from Stepanavan takes about 15 minutes and costs AMD1000. From the fort it's a good idea to walk back to Stepanavan along a 4.5km trail in the steep-sided gorge. You can reach the trail from the north side of the fort.

The cool and tranquil 35-hectare **Dendropark** (admission free; ☉daily May-Oct, Mon-Fri Nov-Apr) is a botanical garden near Gyulagarak village, 11km south of Stepanavan. Established in the 1930s, it has a vast array of conifers and deciduous trees. It's especially popular in May when locals with respiratory problems come to inhale the pollen (not recommended for allergy sufferers!). A taxi should cost AMD2500 return. Cross the bridge in Gyulagarak and the park is about 2km away past the 6th-century Tormak Church.

You can make an interesting trip in this area by walking, hitching or bussing from Stepanavan to the village of Kurtan and staying overnight. The journey is 19km; to walk the whole route would take less than four hours. There are three or four basic B&Bs here; the most popular is run by **Anahit & Vanichka** (☎055454955), both of whom work at the local school. Activities include milking cows, making lavash and cheese, and if you are lucky, donkey rides.

If you are travelling from Stepanavan to Alaverdi, one sight worth visiting en route is the 7th-century monastery **Hnevank**, located 7km beyond Kurtan. The monastery has been ruined and rebuilt several times but most of what is visible today dates from the 12th century. It stands inside the gorge on the southern side of the canyon, near the confluence of the Gargar and Dzoragets Rivers.

Overnight camping trips in the mountains around Stepanavan were just getting underway at the time of research; inquire at the Stepanavan Information Centre.

🛏 Sleeping & Eating

There are three B&Bs on the north side of the river, costing around AMD7000 a night including meals. The hosts know the hospitality business but they may not speak English. Ask at the Information Centre for a recommendation.

Ruzanna Sargsyan B&B   B&B **$**
(☎093230320, 093226936; tag_sahakyan@yahoo.com; 9 Million Poghots; per person AMD7000) B&B offering a comfortable bedroom overlooking a garden. Ruzanna speaks Russian but her five daughters speak English and can provide information on the area (daughter Taguhi wrote a book about Stepanavan historical sites, and she can provide tours of the area with advance notice). Dinner is an additional AMD3000. It's the house behind the Information Centre.

Information Centre
Guesthouse   GUESTHOUSE **$**
(☎2 21 58, 093196096; stepanavaninfo@gmail.com; 11 Million Poghots; s/d incl breakfast AMD7000/10,000;@🖥) A convenient, low-priced option, the Information Centre has one room with bathroom, satellite TV and a laundry machine. The entrance is private so you don't need to go through the Information Centre each time you enter.

Lori Hotel   HOTEL **$**
(☎2 40 50; 9 Nzdheh Poghots; s/d incl breakfast AMD10,000/12,000) This hotel near the town square has clean, modern rooms. It's a little pricier than the B&Bs but you'll get a bit more privacy. There is a billiards room downstairs.

Anahit Pensionat   ARMENIAN **$$$**
(☎2 25 78; meals AMD4000-5000; 🍴) This Soviet sanatorium is in the forest on the ridge behind town. The restaurant here is probably the best in town, with unique Armenian cuisine including a tasty tandoori baked chicken. There is also a hotel on-site, and while the rooms are pretty neglected it does have a nice sauna.

ℹ Information

Several of the staff at the **Stepanavan Information Centre** (Language & Computer Centre; ☎2 21 58; www.stepanavaninfo.am; 11 Million Poghots) speak English and are happy to answer questions or perhaps arrange a tour for you. **Internet** (per hr AMD300) is available here as well as free wi-fi.

For more information see www.stepanvan.net or the blog www.sleeparoundstepanavan.blogspot.com.

There are banks and shops exchanging money around the main square and the *shuka*.

ℹ Getting There & Away

All transport departs from a parking lot near the main square. There are five *marshrutky* for Yerevan (AMD1500, three hours) between 7.30am and 3pm. For Vanadzor (AMD400, one hour) there are buses at 8.30am, 10.20am, noon and 4pm. Two daily buses go to Alaverdi (AMD700, 10.30am and 3pm). One daily bus goes to Gyumri (AMD1500, 1½ hours) at 2pm. Two *marshrutky* a day go to Tbilisi (AMD1500, 9am and 1pm). A taxi anywhere in town from the main square costs AMD400.

Debed Canyon
ԴԵԲԵԴԻ ՁՈՐ

This canyon manages to pack in more history and culture than just about anywhere else in the country. Nearly every village along the Debed River has a church, a chapel, an old fort and a sprinkling of *khatchkars* somewhere nearby. Two World Heritage–listed monasteries, Haghpat and Sanahin, justly draw most visitors, but there are plenty more to scramble around. Soviet-era infrastructure is noticeable, however, with electric cables and railway lines running through the canyon, plus an ugly copper mine at Alaverdi. The road through the canyon is also busy, as this is the main artery linking Armenia to Georgia. Tourist facilities include a highly rated Tufenkian hotel and a few B&Bs around Alaverdi and Sanahin.

🛏 Sleeping

Avan Dzoraget Hotel　　　　　HOTEL $$$
(☏10-54 31 22; www.tufenkianheritage.com; s/d AMD54,000/57,000; @🛜🏊) A 34-room luxury hotel run by the arty Tufenkian Group, near the confluence of the Debed and Dzoraget Rivers, midway between Vanadzor and Alaverdi. This is by far the best hotel in the region, with a spa, wi-fi, swimming pool and a restaurant, plus a bar in a Soviet bomb shelter.

ℹ Getting There & Away

Buses and *marshrutky* travel from Vanadzor to Alaverdi almost hourly between 10am and 4.30pm. But once you get to Alaverdi you'll still need transport to visit all the monasteries. Sanahin is easy to reach on your own (using the cable car) and there are regular *marshrutky* to Haghpat and Odzun. Akhtala is the only tricky one, with just one daily *marshrutka* at 1.30pm. To see the sights quickly it makes more sense to hire a taxi from Vanadzor or Alaverdi. Expect to pay around

AMD10,000 for the day. If your budget is tight or you prefer to explore the valley at a relaxed pace, hitching and bussing is still an option.

KOBAYR　ՔՈԲԱՅՐ
Don't blink or you might miss this charmingly ruined 13th-century convent, hidden just off the Vanadzor–Alaverdi highway. The convent lies above the hamlet of Kobayr (also spelt Khober or Kober) – hidden behind trees near the road. Most travellers pass right by having never seen it.

When you spot the signs for Kobayr keep an eye out for the access road that heads up the mountain. Another landmark is the tiny Kobayr train station, a white structure on concrete pillars. Walk over the railway line and find the stone steps that lead into the hamlet. The path continues uphill through the woods (follow the metal pipe); at the metal memorial spring go right and follow the path up the stone steps – in total the climb takes 10 to 15 minutes.

The main building has a bell tower and some elegant, partially restored frescoes. At the time of writing locals had begun the process of restoring the monastery – given their painstakingly slow work they are likely to still be there by the time you read this. The work has left a temporary metal roof over the building – quite the eyesore if you were hoping for a good photo.

Kobayr is about 18km from Alaverdi and 33km from Vanadzor. As it's on the main road you can hop on any passing bus or *marshrutka* between the two cities.

DSEGH　ԴՍԵՂ
In Dsegh, 9km from the main road, you can find the birthplace of writer Hovhannes Tumanyan (1869–1923). The home of his childhood has been converted to a **museum** (admission AMD200; ⊙10am-5pm), with period furniture and mementos. The stone memorial outside the museum contains the heart of Tumanyan (the rest of his body is buried in Tbilisi). From Dsegh it's 2km along a bumpy road to the edge of a steep canyon, and the footpath down to the ruins of the 8th-century **Surp Grigor Bardzrakash Monastery**. It's heavily overgrown but considered a masterpiece of Armenian architecture. The lost-temple feeling is very evident, as if you've made an extraordinary discovery. The walk down the path takes less than 15 minutes. The village of Dsegh is attractive and affords stunning views of the surrounding mountains.

You can stay the night at the simple **Mavneh B&B** (☏094318711; per person AMD3000) next to the museum.

Two *marshrutky* per day come here from Vanadzor (AMD400, 8.30am and 4pm).

ALAVERDI ԱԼԱՎԵՐԴԻ
☏253 / POP 10,000

The quiet, conservative mining town of Alaverdi is tucked into a bend in the canyon, with rows of apartment blocks and village houses cut into strata by the highway and the railway line. The town is rather poor with few jobs besides those at the half-open copper mine. A cable car (AMD50) climbs the lip of the inner canyon from the mine up to Sarahart and the nearby village of Sanahin. It runs according to work shifts at the mine – 7.45am to 9.45am, 11am to 2pm, 3pm to 7.30pm and 11.15pm to 11.45pm.

Tamara's bridge, about 1km down from the bus stand, was built by Queen Tamar of Georgia. This humpbacked stone bridge was used by road traffic until 30 years ago. There are four kitten-faced lions carved on the stone railing. Legend tells that when a 'real' man finally walks across, the lions will come to life.

🛏 Sleeping & Eating

Iris Guesthouse   GUESTHOUSE $
(☏2 38 39, 091088812; irinaisrayelian@gmail.com; per person AMD5000) Very popular among backpackers, this spacious house has several guestrooms and great views of the river. Owner Irina Israeliyan is an enthusiastic host and can prepare meals upon request: breakfast costs AMD2000 and dinner is AMD3000. The guesthouse is located right on the highway, about 2km south of Alaverdi (look for the small orange sign pointing to the left as you travel north).

Flora   ARMENIAN $$
(meals AMD2500; ◷10am-10pm; 🖻) Flora offers freshly prepared *khoravats,* kebabs, salads and sometimes dolma. To get here, cross Tamara's bridge, climb the stairs on the far side and turn right for a short walk along a road.

❶ Getting There & Away

The bus and *marshrutka* stand is a parking bay off the main road – taxis wait here and further up the hill. A bus ticket and information window is located in the back of the lot. *Marshrutky* and buses are available to Stepanavan (AMD700, two hours, 10am and 3.30pm), Vanadzor (AMD500, up to one hour, seven buses between 8am and 4.45pm) and Yerevan (AMD1700, three hours, 8am, 9am, 12.30pm and 2pm).

There's a bus to the Georgian border (AMD500) at 9am and 10am, or try to jump on a passing *marshrutka*. A taxi to Haghpat and Akhtala or to Odzun and Kobayr should cost between AMD4000 and AMD5000, or about AMD8000 to all of them.

ODZUN ՕՁՈՒՆ

Perched on a broad shelf that terminates at a sheer plunge down to the Debed River, Odzun is a substantial settlement of about 6000 with a magnificent 7th-century church in the centre of the village. The unusual monument next to it is a memorial but locals say it has the power to inspire fertility–approach with caution. The sturdy church features magnificent arches outside the main entrance. The custodian turns up sooner or later to unlock the church. There's another church on the edge of the cliff. One kilometre south of Odzun, at the edge of the canyon, is the three-chambered Horomayri Monastery, the well-camouflaged remnants of which are visible below the cliff on the right.

If you'd like to spend the night here, try **Alvard Nersisyan B&B** (☏0536-16 96, 091760858; r per person AMD5000) located near the upper school (where Alvard is a teacher). It's a large, comfortable house and breakfast is available for an additional AMD1000.

Buses come here from Alaverdi hourly between 10am and 5.30pm for AMD150. A taxi to and from Alaverdi should cost about AMD2000 return. Odzun is on the road to Stepanavan and a couple of times a day, around 10.30am and 3.30pm, an Alaverdi to Stepanavan bus passes through here.

SANAHIN MONASTERY ՍԱՆԱՀԻՆ

Moss-covered Sanahin is a fascinatingly detailed church and monastery complex, packed with ancient graves, darkened chapels and medieval gallery schools (study halls where pupils sat on benches on either side of a corridor). The inner sanctum of the Surp Astvatsatsin Church (Holy Mother of God Church), located in the middle of several buildings, is the oldest structure here, dating back to 928, while its adjoining *gavit* or entrance hall is one of the later buildings, built in 1211. A library was created at Sanahin in 1062, and a medical school flourished in the 12th century. Sanahin means 'older than that one', referring to its younger cousin at Haghpat.

From the cable-car station, walk up to the main square of Sarahart and take a left; after 900m you reach a T-junction in Sanahin village (separate from Sarahart). Sanahin Monastery is uphill, or follow the sign downhill to the **Mikoyan Museum** (admission AMD200; ◷10am-1pm & 2-6pm), a shrine to the Mikoyan brothers Anastas and Artyom. Anastas Mikoyan survived 60 years in the Politboro, outlasting even Stalin, and so deserves a museum. Artyom was the designer of the USSR's first jet fighter in WWII, the MiG. There's an early MiG jet outside the museum (no climbing allowed!). The charming administrator is unstoppable once she starts explaining every photo, medal and uniform on display – a tip is not required but would be a nice gesture after a tour.

🛏 Sleeping

In Sarahart, the best place to stay is **Lilit Guesthouse** (☏094671859; Apt 42, Bldg 2/30; per person AMD5000), located on the main square. Lilit speaks English, prepares a full breakfast and can arrange transport around the canyon.

❶ Getting There & Away

The cable car (AMD50) from Alaverdi is a fun way to reach Sarahart, which is a little more than 1km from Sanahin Monastery. There are also *marshrutka* and taxis from Alaverdi to Sarahart (AMD800, 5km). You can also inquire about an early-morning bus that travels from Sarahart straight to the Bagratashen–Sadakhlo border. If you are hitching, the turn-off from Alaverdi is 1km south of town at the bridge. Hikers may want to walk from Sanahin to Haghpat, via the village of Akner. The 7km walk takes less than three hours.

HAGHPAT MONASTERY ՀԱՂՊԱՏ

This pearl of a monastery, perched on the lip of the Debed Canyon, has Unesco World Heritage status, along with Sanahin. This place has atmosphere and architectural splendour in abundance and the views around the canyon alone are worth the trip. Founded around 976 by Queen Khosrvanuch, who built Surp Nishan at the centre of the walled complex, it really took off in the 12th century with a magnificent bell tower, library and refectory. An inscription on the *gavit* of Surp Nishan reads in part: 'You who enter through its door and prostrate yourself before the Cross, in your prayers remember us and our royal ancestors, who rest at the door of the holy cathedral, in Jesus Christ.' Further around past a cute Surp Astvatsatsin chapel is the freestanding *gavit* built by Abbot Hamazasp in 1257, which has glorious acoustics. Uphill is the bell tower, and off by the wall a stone refectory. *Khatchkars* and study halls surround the central church.

Gayane B&B (☏253-6 06 18; per person incl breakfast AMD8000) is a surprisingly pleasant hotel with several rooms, brand-new furnishings, hot showers and meals. It's a couple of kilometres back down the road from Haghpat Monastery (but before you reach the main road).

Marshrutky from Alaverdi run hourly between 10am and 5.30pm, costing AMD200. A taxi from Alaverdi to Haghpat and back, including wait time will cost AMD2000. Alternatively, walk to Sanahin Monastery if you are headed there anyway. It's 7km via Akner village.

AKHTALA MONASTERY ԱԽԹԱԼԱ

Situated at the edge of Akhtala village, this 13th-century complex is recommended for its fine decorative carvings and frescoes. A thick wall surrounds it. When you enter the wall, look left and you'll see two large caves that were used for smelting copper. Historians aren't sure if the church was dedicated to St Gregory (Surp Grigor) or the Apostles (Arakelots). Once inside, you can clearly see on the left side wall the image of bearded Persians, painted here so that invading armies would spare the church. Surrounding the church are a couple of well-preserved chapels and the ever-present graveyard with some new stones. Akhtala is about 18km northeast (downstream) of Alaverdi. A daily bus (AMD200) departs Alaverdi at 1.30pm. A taxi trip combined with a visit to Haghpat will cost about AMD4000. Alternatively, you can hitch to the signposted turn-off, then walk the final 3km up to the church (skirting around the edge of the copper-mine pond), which takes less than one hour.

Gyumri ԳՅՈՒՄՐԻ

☏312 / POP 120,000

A city of stately Russian architecture, cobbled streets and a bustling market, Gyumri is one of the most attractive towns in the country, and also one of the most tragic. The 1988 Spitak earthquake levelled large sections of the city and drove most of the survivors away. You can still see devastated buildings around town, as well as historic structures under careful reconstruction.

Twenty years after the quake, life is only beginning to normalise, although locals still seem to talk about it as though it occurred last week. Jobs have returned, permanent housing has replaced most of the cargo-container homes and the population has increased twofold.

The townsfolk of Gyumri have a distinctive accent with hints of western Armenian, and a famously ridiculous sense of humour in tandem with conservative social mores. Other Armenians like to tease Gyumritsis about local delicacies such as *kalla* (cow's head) and the particularly rich stew of *khash* made here in the cold seasons (made from animal parts). The winters last longer here than in Yerevan, until April or May.

History

Gyumri was first settled around 400 BC, possibly by Greek colonists. The town was inhabited periodically until the early 19th century, when the Russians moved in and built a large military garrison. It even received a visit from Tsar Nicolas I who, in 1837, renamed it Alexandropol after his wife. A steady influx of settlers arrived from Russia and the western Armenian cities of Kars and Erzurum (now within Turkey's borders). As the third-largest city in the South Caucasus, after Tbilisi and Baku, Gyumri was an important trading post between the Ottoman Empire and the rest of Asia and Russia. As a transport hub it was a stop on the rail journey from Tbilisi to Tabriz.

In 1920 the Turkish-Armenian war ended here with the signing of the Treaty of Alexandropol, an event that ceased the Turkish advance on Yerevan. In Soviet times the border was shut and Alexandropol became known as Leninakan.

The Spitak earthquake on 11 December 1988 put paid to much of Gyumri's historic splendour, as well as the myriad factories established here by the Soviets. Besides levelling large parts of the city and surrounding villages, it killed 50,000 people and made many more homeless. The botched recovery effort would haunt the city for years as successive winters passed without heating or electricity. Most of the city has been rebuilt, although a few patches remain under construction, most noticeably Amenaprkich Church in the city centre.

◉ Sights & Activities

The historic core of town, the **Kumayri** neighbourhood, is between Vardanants Hraparak and the City Park. While not as intact as those of Goris, the buildings of Kumayri are of a finer standard. Gyumri's atmospheric 19th-century Surp Astvatsatsin Church, locally called **Yot Verk** (Seven Wounds), stands on the northern side of the square. The battered and worn roof cones from an earlier incarnation of the church stand outside. On the south side of the square is the **Amenaprkich Church** (All Saviours Church), which is being ever-so-slowly restored to its pre-earthquake glory. Nearby, the *shuka* is something of an attraction with its endless piles of fruit, whirling coffee grinders and rows of cognac bottles.

A couple of blocks north of Yot Verk is the more modest **Surp Nishan Church**, built in 1870 and restored in 2003. The old buildings along Gorki Poghots and by the City Park are worth wandering around – some buildings are shells; others have been restored to their prime. On Teryan Poghots there is a 19th-century pyramid-shaped **Russian army chapel** with a peaked silver roof. The small park behind the chapel is actually a burial ground for 19th-century Russian soldiers who died fighting Ottoman Turkey.

Continuing over the hill for 500m or so brings you to the **Sev Ghul** or 'black sentry' fort. From here you can see the **Mother Armenia statue** on an adjacent hill, towards the Turkish border.

The **Museum of National Architecture and Urban Life of Gyumri** (47 Haghtanaki Poghots; admission AMD500; ☺10am-5pm Tue-Sun) is a substantial building set back from the corner with Teryan Poghots. The 1872 mansion of the Dzitoghtsyans includes fine furniture and authentic decor, plus an art gallery and displays on local history. An attached **gallery** (admission AMD500) of sculptures by Sergei Merkurov contains more Lenins and Stalins than you can shake a sickle at. The **Museum of the Aslamazyan Sisters** (232 Abovyan Poghots; donations accepted; ☺10am-5pm Tue-Sun), on what was once Kumayri's finest promenade, is another house-museum with a display of traditional furnishings and more contemporary artworks.

About 30km north of Gyumri, the village of **Ashotsk** offers a range of activities in both summer and winter, including kayaking, biking and cross-country skiing. **Artur Mikayelyan** (☎093352111; mika-ski@mail.ru) organises these activities and offers accommodation in his simple home. A weekend of food and lodging costs around AMD15,000.

Gyumri

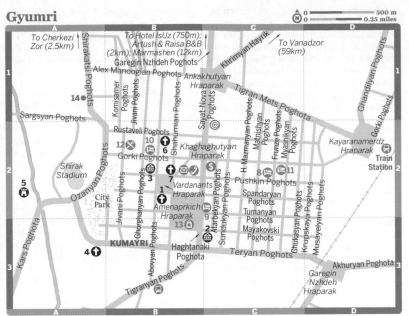

Gyumri

◉ Sights

1 Amenaprkich B2
2 Museum of National Architecture
   and Urban Life of Gyumri C3
3 Museum of the Aslamazyan
   Sisters B2
4 Russian Army Chapel A3
5 Sev Ghul A2
6 Surp Nishan B2
7 Yot Verk B2

⊜ Sleeping

8 Donara Kazaryan B&B C2
9 Gastehaus Berlin (Berlin Hotel) C2

10 Hotel Araks B2
11 Vanatur Hotel C2

⊗ Eating

Phaeton Alek .... (see 2)
12 Polos Mukuch B2

⊜ Shopping

13 Shuka B3

ⓘ Information

14 American Corner A1
Qaghaqapetaran (City Hall) .... (see 14)
Shirak Tours .... (see 9)

Marshrutky from Gyumri run to Ashotsk hourly during the day. It's a great way to experience rural Armenia and stay active too.

In the other direction, 40km south of Gyumri on the road to Yerevan, the region of **Talin** has scattered villages that are home to both western Armenians and Yezidi Kurds. The Yezidi practise their own unique religion (Yezidism), which combines traditional Kurdish beliefs and Islamic Sufi doctrine.

🛏 Sleeping

Gastehaus Berlin (Berlin Hotel)   HOTEL $$$
(☑ 2 31 48; www.berlinhotel-gyumri.am; 25 Haghtanaki Poghots; s/d incl breakfast AMD27,000/32,000; ✹ ☎) This hotel was built as an accommodation wing for a German hospital on the same premises. It seems odd to have doctors and patients outside, but the hotel is welcoming and colourfully decorated. The spacious rooms have comfy beds, satellite TV and minibar. The hotel is home to Shirak Tours, which can help with logistics in the area.

Hotel Araks
HOTEL $$$

(☏3 58 15; www.arakshotel.am; 25 Gorki Poghots; s/d AMD25,000/30,000; ❋@≋) High ceilings, frilly drapes and a huge staircase create an old-world feel at this hotel. Renovations have brought the rooms to a respectable standard. Amenities include a sauna and an indoor pool, rare sights anywhere in Armenia. The hotel also has an Italian restaurant and a disco.

Vanatur Hotel
HOTEL $$

(☏5 07 14; 70a Gorki Poghots; r AMD20,000, deluxe AMD30,000, prices incl breakfast) The centrally located Vanatur offers comfortable rooms with TV. Deluxe rooms have a Jacuzzi in the bathroom. The restaurant also serves lunch and dinner with a Georgian-inspired menu. Entrance to the hotel is on the side of the building.

Donara Kazaryan B&B
B&B $

(☏5 59 15, 093450557; rose-varduhi@yandex.ru; 142 Frunze Poghots; r per person AMD6000) Donara runs a homestay from her fine family house, with two chintzy bedrooms and a shared bathroom. Daughter Vartuhi speaks English and granddaughter Lily speaks German. It's about 100m south of the Vanatur Hotel.

Artush & Raisa B&B
B&B $$

(☏3 08 15, 093350314; artushdavtyan@yahoo.com 1-2 Ayvazovski Poghots; r per person incl breakfast AMD8000) Artush, an English-speaking local guide, runs this homestay with wife Raisa and son Martin. Three guestrooms are available, plus a piano room and garden. Breakfast includes bread, cheese, sausage, scrambled egg, jams and yoghurt. Artush, an accomplished musician, is very knowledgeable about the area and can provide good travel advice. Call ahead and the owners will meet you at Charles Aznavour Hraparak (from here it's a three-minute walk).

✖ Eating

There are cheap street snacks available from shops and stalls at the *shuka* and a wide range of new and historic restaurants around town. Besides the following, the Georgian restaurant in the Vanatur Hotel is recommended, as well as pizza joints at the Hotel IsUz and Hotel Araks.

Polos Mukuch
ARMENIAN $$

(75 Jivani Poghots; meals AMD2500; ☺9am-10pm) This establishment occupies a historic building and prepares a mix of Armenian and Georgian dishes – *khinkali* (spicy meat dumpling), dolma and kebabs are popular. Many locals prefer to sit around the bar swilling Gyumri beer and potent shots of *oghee*.

Phaeton Alek
ARMENIAN $$

(47 Haghtanaki Poghota; meals AMD2500-3500; ☺10am-7pm; 🍴) In the cellars of the Museum of National Architecture and Urban Life of Gyumri, this spot often hosts groups for an 'ethnic' experience, with old artefacts on the walls, and sometimes entertainment as well. Solo diners may not feel so welcome, but the food is hearty and good value.

Cherkezi Zor
ARMENIAN $$

(Fish Farm; meals AMD3000-5000; Bulvarayin Poghots; ☺10am-10pm) You'll be guaranteed fresh fish at the appropriately named Fish Farm. Pick what type of fish you want and the chef literally plucks your dinner out of the pool and sets it on the barbecue. It's on the western side of town and a little hard to find. From the stadium, cross the opposite bank and walk north up the canyon for 1.3km. Alternatively, go by taxi.

❶ Information

Shirak Tours (☏5 76 59; www.berlinhotel -gyumri.am; 25 Haghtanaki Poghota) is a useful local tour company run from the Gastehaus Berlin by Alex Ter-Minasyan. He arranges day trips by car to Marmashen for about AMD14,000 and to Harichavank for AMD21,000. It also does walking tours and can arrange visits to artist studios.

There are several internet cafes and banks along Sayat-Nova and Garegin Nzhdeh Poghots, including the **Ultra Net** (7 Sayat-Nova Poghots; ☺24hr). UniBank has an ATM at Khaghaghutyan Hraparak. You can also use the internet at **American Corner** (68 Shirakatsi Poghots; ☺9am-5pm Mon-Fri), located next to the City Hall.

❶ Getting There & Around

Buses and *marshrutky*, including those to Yerevan (AMD1500, two hours, every 20 minutes 7am to 7pm), leave from the *avtokayan* on Tigranyan Poghots. Transport to Vanadzor (AMD800, one hour) leaves almost hourly between 10am and 4.30pm. A *marshrutka* to Stepanavan (AMD1500, 1½ hours) leaves daily at 9am.

For Georgia, *marshrutky* travel daily to Tbilisi (AMD5200, 3½ hours, 10.30am) and to Akhaltsikhe (AMD3500, four hours, 10am). These will only set off if there is a minimum of five passengers.

Gyumri is on the train line between Yerevan and Tbilisi; there is a train every day in one direction (on odd days it goes to Tbilisi). A seat to Tbilisi is AMD5610 and a cabin berth costs AMD8810. The train departs at 12.30am and arrives in Tbilisi 10 to 12 hours later. The *elektrichka* train to Yerevan departs at 7.55am daily, takes 3½ hours and costs AMD950. Call the station (☎2 10 02) to confirm schedules.

Shirak Airport, which is 5km southeast of town, is served by Vim Airlines (Moscow three times weekly), Donavia (Sochi and Rostov-on-Don weekly, August to October) and RusLine (Krasnodar twice weekly). There are plenty of ticket agencies in town. A taxi to the airport is around AMD1500.

Marmashen ՄԱՐՄԱՇԵՆ

The monastery at Marmashen is about 10km northwest of Gyumri, just past the village of Varambert in the wide gorge of the Akhuryan River. There are three churches hewn from lovely apricot-coloured tuff clustered together next to an orchard, plus the ruins and foundations of other structures nearby. One of the ruins is of an unusual circular church.

The biggest church, Surp Stepanos, was built between 988 and 1029, with a 13th-century *gavit*. An Italian team led restoration work in the 1960s, so intricately carved old church stones have been incorporated into newer building blocks. Beautiful carved tombs and *khatchkars* dot the land around the churches, and it's a peaceful, rural environment typical of Shirak, with grassy horizons. The caretaker is here during daylight hours, and he can recite some of the inscriptions on the sides of the churches by heart.

A return taxi from Gyumri is about AMD3000. Make sure the driver understands that you want to see the monastery and not the nearby village of the same name. There are hourly buses from Gyumri's *avtokayan* to Varambert (AMD150) between 9am and 7pm (look for the bus to Kaps).

Harichavank ՀԱՌԻՃԱՎԱՆՔ

Harichavank monastery is in the sturdy old town of Harich, about 4km from the town of Artik. This complex was the summer residence of the Catholicos of Echmiadzin for a period after 1850 and is surrounded by 19th-century buildings. Harichavank is one of those monasteries where 13th-century *gavits* and domes have dramatically expanded a 7th- or 8th-century chapel. There is some beautiful geometric stonework over the main church door and around the dome of the *gavit*. It is still an active place; a new seminary was opened in 2011.

Inside, the church's caretaker can point out the anteroom/storeroom with a hole in the ceiling leading to a secret upstairs room. During times of invasion, the room was used to house women and children and sometimes even important local officials. A stone would be fitted exactly into the ceiling hole once everyone had climbed to safety.

Direct buses depart Gyumri's *avtokayan* for Harichavank (AMD350, 50 minutes) at 8.30am, 11.20am and 3pm. Alternatively, take a *marshrutka* or bus to Artik (AMD200, 30 minutes, hourly), from where you can wait around for another *marshrutka* to Harich, or take a taxi from Artik (AMD1800 return). If you have your own vehicle, the monastery is about 15km off the main Yerevan–Gyumri road.

If you are in the area, check out the well-preserved 7th-century **Lmbatavank** church southwest of Artik; it contains important early frescoes.

SOUTHERN ARMENIA

Armenia's remote southern regions, between Karabakh to the east and the Azeri enclave of Naxçivan to the west, are linked to Yerevan by a single, vital highway. Vayots Dzor (Gorge of Woes) centres on the headwaters of the wine-growing Arpa valley. The name comes from a history of ruinous earthquakes across these mountainous valleys and cliffs. It's a great area to explore off-the-beaten-track trails by foot, horse or 4WD jeep.

In the south, Syunik is full of ancient churches and monasteries, rustic villages making homemade fruit vodkas, forests and high pastures. The 19th-century town of Goris is a great base for visiting Tatev or Karabakh or as a break before the long haul to Iran.

Areni ԱՐԵՆԻ

Few grape varieties can thrive in Armenia's climatic extremes, but the Areni grape does. Most of the country's vineyards are on the Ararat Plain, but the valleys from the village of Areni up to Yeghegnadzor comprise a quality wine-growing region.

Wineries open for tastings (daily in summer, 10am to 6pm) include **Areni** in the town of Areni, **Ginetas** at Arpi and **Getnatep** on the main highway at Yeghegnadzor. The **Surp Astvatsatsin Church** across the river from Areni sits on a shelf below a cliff. **Getap**, just up the Yeghegis Valley before Yeghegnadzor, is also a local winemaking centre. **Hotel Noy** (☑0872-55 45; Arpi; r AMD7000-18,000;☒), on the main highway, is a motel-style complex with clean rooms, a bar, a buffet and a swimming pool. At the back of the hotel is a pleasant picnic spot by the river. There are frequent buses and *marshrutky* along the main highway.

Noravank ՆՈՐԱՎԱՆՔ

This church complex, by the 13th-century architect Momik, is a masterpiece both for its architecture and its dramatic setting. Noravank (New Monastery) was founded by Bishop Hovhannes in 1105, and was last restored in the 1990s. Climb the narrow stone stairs outside **Surp Astvatsatsin Church** (1339) to get a closer look at its dome. Astvatsatsin is also known as Burtelashen, after its patron, Burtel Orbelian, who is buried here with his family. Historians say the church is reminiscent of towerlike burial structures created in the early years of Christianity. There's a wonderful carving of Christ flanked by Peter and Paul above the door.

The smaller **Surp Karapet Church** (1227) next to Surp Astvatsatsin is the original shrine built by the miracle-working Bishop Hovhannes. Noravank once treasured a piece of the True Cross stained with the blood of Christ, acquired from a mysterious stranger. The side chapel of St Gregory includes a carved lion-human tombstone dated to 1300.

There are picnic spots and springs around Noravank, as well as an excellent restaurant by the car park. The valley really warms up in the middle of a summer's day, so come early, or late in the afternoon. During medieval summers the monks of Noravank retired to a mountain retreat. The site is at its most spectacular around sunset when the reddish hues of the cliffs are accentuated by the setting sun.

Noravank features on many travel-agency tours from Yerevan, about 90 minutes away by road – many combine a visit with a stop at Khor Virap and a winery. Public transport from Yerevan or Yeghegnadzor takes you as far as the turn-off on the highway, 6km from Noravank. Get out at the Edem restaurant and hitch the rest of the way, a fairly easy process on weekends.

About 4km from the turn-off to Noravank is an unusual cave-cafe dug out of the side of the cliff. There is no sign, but you'll see the metal grating between the boulders on the right side of the road.

Yeghegnadzor & Around ԵՂԵԳՆԱՁՈՐ

☑281 / POP 8200

An overgrown country town built on twisting lanes that wind into the hills, Yeghegnadzor (yeh-*heg*-nadzor) is the peaceful administrative centre of Vayots Dzor. The town is a mainly Soviet-era confection of wide civic spaces and *tufa* apartment blocks. A few small factories (eg a diamond-cutting plant) have opened, but remittances and agriculture provide the biggest incomes. There isn't much to see in the town itself, but it does make a good base from which to explore the region – you could easily spend two or three days here in between trips to Yeghegis village, Noravank and the wineries in Areni and Spitakavor.

The town has moneychangers, a UniBank with an ATM (accepting Visa cards) and the **Arpa Net Internet Café** (per hr AMD300; ☺9am-9pm) just downhill from the *avtokayan*.

◉ Sights

The **Vayots Dzor Regional Museum** (4 Shahumian Poghots; admission AMD200; ☺10am-5pm Tue-Sat) in the centre of town describes local history but was closed for renovation at the time of research.

There is a good walk from town down to the river and a 13th-century stone bridge, designed by the same architect who built Noravank. To get there, walk down the highway, turn right and walk for 400m, then turn left down a dirt track (just before the 256km post) and follow it for 1.3km to the bridge.

Another possible diversion is the **Museum of Gladzor University** (admission AMD500; ☺10am-5pm Tue-Sun) in the village of Vernashen, 5km uphill from the Yeghegnadzor *avtokayan*. The museum has displays on monasteries across the country, plus old

manuscripts and descriptions of Armenia's various schools and universities. The museum is housed inside a 17th-century church called Surp Hagop. If the museum is closed, get the key from the family in the house in front of the museum. There are buses to Vernashen at 10am, noon, 2.30pm, 3.30pm and 5.30pm from the *avtokayan*.

The Vernashen museum marks the end of the village and just past it is a T-junction. The road to the left leads to **Spitakavor Monastery**, about 9.5km along a winding dirt track for vehicles or 5km along a more direct walking path. To find the trail, walk through the village and carry on straight up the western bank of the gorge past a small dam on the river (ignore the vehicle road, which switches back). The 20th-century Armenian military commander Garegin Nzhdeh was buried at Spitakavor in 1987 (his remains were secretly taken to Armenia from his grave in Russia). Nzhdeh fought in the Balkan Wars against the Ottoman Empire and commanded a force of Armenian volunteer fighters in WWI. In 1921 he was prime minister of the short-lived Republic of Mountainous Armenia before it was swallowed up by the USSR.

The **Boloraberd** fortress crowns a rocky crest across from the monastery. Some hikers have tried to walk over the pass and down to Yeghegis but the other side of the mountain is a steep and dangerous hike.

Back at the T-junction, the road to the right winds for 6km to Tanahati Vank. The impressive main **Surp Stepanos Church** was built by the Orbelians. There are significant stone reliefs of animals on the exterior of the church, including the crest of the Orbelians (a bull and a lion) on the tambour. All around the church are ruins that once made up the actual site of Gladzor University.

Another 3.5km along the road leads to the **Monastery of Arkaz**. It is well known

IF THE SHOE FITS

In 2008 an archaeologist exploring a cave in Vayots Dzor found an ancient leather shoe buried under a pile of animal dung. She estimated that the shoe was around 700 years old and dated from the Mongol period. But once the shoe reached the laboratory a new story began to unfold. Testing dated the shoe to around 3500 BC, thus making it the world's oldest leather shoe (300 years older than a shoe found on a frozen mummy in the Alps in 1991).

The shoe is about a women's size 7 (US), designed for the right foot and is made from leather sewn together like a moccasin. It was found stuffed with grass as if its owner wanted to maintain the shape of the shoe. (The whereabouts of the left shoe are unknown.) The shoe is now on display at the State Museum of Armenian History in Yerevan.

The cave where the shoe was found is known as Areni-1 and is located not on some distant mountaintop, but rather just behind the Edem restaurant, where the main southern highway intersects with the road to Noravank. At the time of writing the cave was closed to casual tourists as researchers continue to excavate. However, it's possible that the cave will reopen for tourism during the lifetime of this book; inquire at the information centre in Vayk (p177).

Areni-1 is just one of thousands of caves around Areni and Arpi, some of which contain a kilometre or more of chambers. About 1km up the canyon from Areni-1 is Magili Karandzav, one of the deepest caves in the area and significant as the home of a large colony of fruit bats; Neolithic-era stone tools have also been found here.

Some caves are filled with a wonderful collection of stalactites and stalagmites, including the Arjeri, Mozrovi and Jerovank caverns. These caves are not for the inexperienced, so it's best to visit on a guided tour (the caves are also locked to casual visitors). Travel agencies in Yerevan (p142) can arrange cave exploration tours or contact **Gor Hovhannishyan** (☑093265576), a member of the Armenian Extreme Club.

for holding a piece of the True Cross under a stone marker in the back of the church. The church sees many visitors during the last two Sundays of October, when locals arrive in droves to sacrifice animals after the harvest.

🛌 Sleeping

Arpa HOTEL $$

(☑2 06 01; www.arpatour.com; 8/1 Narekatsky Poghots; s/d AMD10,500/16,500, deluxe AMD19,500, all incl breakfast; 🛜) This new hotel is the best in town. Rooms are small but modern, clean and well appointed with satellite TV and wi-fi. The friendly management speaks English and can provide travel assistance. A filling breakfast of potatoes, crepes and eggs is included. It's located next to the *avtokayan*.

Gohar's Guest House GUESTHOUSE $$

(☑2 33 24; 44 Spandaryan Poghots; s/d incl breakfast AMD8000/15,000; @🛜) Gohar Gevorgyan offers rooms in her large, comfortable home. It's set in a lovely spot in the upper part of town, with great views of the valley. Rooms are clean and modern and meals are available upon request. Gohar can arrange a 4WD

taxi if you want to head to some off-road destinations. To get there, walk up Spandaryan Poghots towards the football field. When you reach the T-junction, turn left and then a quick right (so that you are walking next to the field) and walk 200m to Gohar's house. Call ahead as the place fills up fast.

Artak & Ruzan Guest House GUESTHOUSE $$

(☑2 22 75, 094878990; 5 Spandaryan Narpansk; s/d incl breakfast AMD8000/15,000) Ruzan (a history teacher) and her husband run this quiet, comfortable guesthouse, surrounded by a garden. There are four rooms, hot water and excellent food. To find it, walk past Gohar's Guest House and after about 150m take the second left up a short hill to house number 5. Note that the house is on Spandaryan Narpansk, not Spandaryan Poghots.

🍴 Eating & Drinking

If you have your own transport, there are several riverside restaurants along the main highway that set a good Armenian table for around AMD2500 per person, including kebabs, *khoravats* (including venison and fish), salads and drinks. They are open

8am until late outside of winter. A popular place for vehicles to stop is **Karitak** (☉10am-8pm), about 5km west of town on the road to Yeghegnadzor. **Edem Café** (☉10am-midnight), on the road to Noravank, is another excellent choice; it has live music from 9pm on weekends.

In the various seasons there are roadside stalls selling watermelons, fruit, honey, nuts and homemade wines and conserves.

Aygi   CAFE-BAR **$**
(☉11am-midnight May-Oct) This popular outdoor cafe has simple dishes like pizza and *khachapuri*. It's a good spot for a cold beer or ice cream. It's located next to the Ferris wheel, about 150m past the Arpa Hotel.

❶ Getting There & Away

Marshrutky and buses to nearby villages leave from the *avtokayan* in the centre of town, next to Arpa hotel. A daily bus to Jermuk (AMD700, 40 minutes) leaves at 2pm. There are *marshrutky* to Vayk (AMD200, 20 minutes) twice hourly between 9am and 5pm. *Marshrutky* to Yerevan (AMD1200, 90 minutes to two hours, hourly 8am to 6pm) usually leave from the junction with the main highway. Space permitting, you can also flag one down here to go to Goris. As yet there is no public transport to Martuni on the shore of Lake Sevan, but hitching is not too much of a struggle. Taxis can be hired near the *avtokayan* for AMD100 per kilometre. Noravank is about 20km west, while Jermuk is 53km east.

Yeghegis & Around
ԵՂԵԳԻՍ

The beautiful **Yeghegis Valley** (yer-ghiz) is surrounded by towering peaks and contains a rare concentration of churches. This and the surrounding valleys are well worth exploring for a day or two.

To reach the area, turn north off the Yerevan–Goris highway at Getap and after 12km turn right (east) towards Shatin village. The sights are well signposted off the road.

About 2km up from Shatin village, a road branches up the valley to the west towards Artabuynk. About 1km past the village of Artabuynk a sign points to the right for the 10th-century **Tsakhatskar Monastery**, a crumbling agglomeration of churches and old *khatchkars*. From the stream, continue up the main track to the right (the side of the valley with the power poles); the monastery eventually comes into view on the left.

From the monastery, head back down the way you came and at the fork in the path head left up the slope to **Smbataberd** fortress. The stretch up to the fort takes about 30 minutes. On the other side of Smbataberd you can look down on the Yeghegis Valley.

Yeghegis village is reached by taking the right fork after Shatin (ie away from Artabuynk). The village looks as though it's been inhabited forever; it has a couple of churches, including the very unusual Surp Zorats, where worshippers gathered before an outdoor altar. It's believed this courtyard was created so that horses and soldiers could be blessed before going off to battle.

Across the river from the village, a metal footbridge leads to an 800-year-old **Jewish cemetery** – Hebrew inscriptions are clearly visible on some of the grave markers. The engravings are biblical verses and the names of the deceased. Prior to the discovery of the cemetery there had been no evidence of Jews inhabiting Armenia. The cemetery was in use for about 80 years – the oldest tombstone is dated 1266 and the newest is dated 1346. Researchers theorise that this community of Jews arrived from Persia, having travelled up the Silk Road. The reason for their disappearance remains a mystery.

The next village up the valley is **Hermon**, where a rough track north up the valley (on the left) leads to Arates and **Arates Vank**, a monastery with three churches (from the 7th to the 13th centuries). Arates is about 10km beyond Yeghegis.

Public transport to the area is limited. Each day a couple of buses go from Yeghegnadzor to Yeghegis, Hermon and Artabuynk. You could catch a bus one way and hitch or walk back. At the time of writing buses to Yeghegis departed at 7.30am from the bottom of the hill and 4.30pm from the *avtokayan*. Taxis from Yeghegnadzor cost the standard AMD100 per kilometres.

The only place to stay in the area is the simple **Lucy Guest Camp** at Hermon, which was under construction at the time of research. Managers at the camp were planning to offer activities such as hiking and horse riding.

Vayk & Around   ՎԱՅՔ
☏282 / POP 5400

The rugged hills and valleys around this overgrown village hide lots of artfully positioned churches, monasteries and chapels from the 8th to the 12th centuries. Heading 6km up the valley, the first turn-off left leads 10km north to Herher and a cluster of churches at the **Surp Sion Monastery** 1km beyond it. There are the ruins of **Kapuyt Berd** (Blue Fortress) and *khatchkars* around Herher as well.

The **Tourism Centre Hotel** (☑9 28 09; vayktour@info.am; r per person AMD5000-8000; @ 🛜) is conveniently located on the highway. It has 24 comfortable rooms, great rates, English-speaking staff and wi-fi. As indicated by the name, the hotel also has a regional information centre and can direct you to B&Bs in the region, including one in Herher.

You'll find *marshrutky* to Yerevan (AMD1400, less than two hours, every two hours 8am to 7pm) from the main road.

Jermuk ՋԵՐՄՈՒԿ

☑287 / POP 7000

This small resort town, 2080m above sea level on the upper Arpa River, was popular in the USSR as a vacation spot for mineral-water treatments and hot springs, some of them very hot. The landscape around Jermuk is very pretty, and excellent for walks and hikes.

The spa business gets most of its customers in the July and August holidays, and largely hibernates outside this season. Some of its sanatoriums have immersion pools and treatment areas. The spa attendants take their job seriously – in the old days people would sign up for 18-day courses with medically supervised immersions in Jermuk's waters.

Open to the public is the **Gallery of Waters**, with a facade of archways and a pleasant view. Water runs into stone urns from pipes set in the wall and the temperature of the water is printed next to its pipe. The various waters are said to have different properties, good for curing stomach and liver problems, heart disease and cancer.

The **Armenia Hotel and Health Spa** (⊙9am-5pm) has hot baths, mud treatments, sauna, hydrotherapy rooms and various other treatment rooms. Treatment costs range between AMD600 and AMD2500. Even better, try the Jacuzzi at the Olympia Health Spa across the road.

The **Jermuk Ski Resort** (⊙ Nov-Mar) next to the town is smaller than the one in Tsaghkadzor but the facilities are new and

the equipment in good condition. It makes for a fun day of swishing down the slopes if you happen to be here in season.

The town is entered via a bridge spanning a deep gorge high above the Arpa River; turn left at the end of the bridge, and a few hundred metres along is the taxi and bus stop that serves as a main square of sorts. The Haypost and Telecom offices are here. Just north of the taxi stand is the Armenia Hotel and Gallery of Waters. South of the taxi stand is the short main road with shops and an internet cafe.

🛏 Sleeping & Eating

There are lots of informal pensions and spas open in July and August, but options thin out in the winter. Prices following represent low season – in July and August prices can double based on demand.

Nairi Hotel   HOTEL $
(☑2 20 08; www.jermuknairi.am; 5 Myasnikyan Poghots; per person AMD6000-8000) Jermuk's newest hotel has functional rooms with modern furnishings and a big patio in the back that overlooks the canyon. If you don't mind somewhat gaudy colour schemes (rooms range from lime green to maroon), it's probably the best-value place in town. Breakfast is an additional AMD2000.

Armenia Hotel   HOTEL $$$
(☑2 12 90; 2 Myasnikyan Poghots; s/d incl 3 meals AMD20,000/40,000) Located next to a scenic park and the Gallery of Waters, the Armenia is the best hotel in town. However, it also doubles as sanatorium so it can be a little creepy to see doctors and patients shuffling about in smocks. The price includes a range of diagnostic treatments – just keep reminding yourself it's all part of the Armenia experience.

Gndevank Restaurant   ARMENIAN $$
(meals AMD2500; ⊙10am-midnight; 🅿) This *khoravats* place stands out for its succulent grilled meats. The fresh-fruit dessert also deserves a special mention. Coming across the main bridge, turn right (away from the centre); it's about 400m straight ahead in a wood-fronted building.

❶ Getting There & Away

Jermuk is 177km from Yerevan, about two hours by the main highway and then 26km off the main highway on a spur road. In the low season there is one *marshrutka* to Yerevan each day

(AMD2000, 2½ hours) at 7.30am. At 8am there is a bus to Yeghegnadzor (AMD700, one hour) and at 4pm a bus goes to Vayk (AMD500, 30 minutes). More buses and *marshrutky* operate in July and August.

Sisian ՍԻՍԻԱՆ

📞283 / POP 18,000

Sisian sits on a high plateau where it snows as late as March or April, and the autumn ends early here too. This quiet country town has a core of early-20th-century buildings and is divided into two districts by the wide Vorotan River.

The region was inhabited long before the town was built, evidenced by nearby Neolithic observatories and animal petroglyphs. Some examples have been gathered in the town's *karadaran* (stone museum) park.

Sisian is mostly laid out on a grid and is small enough for walking around. The centre of town is on the northern side of the Vorotan. *Marshrutky* leave from the junction on the northern end of the bridge. The main street, Sisakan Poghots, runs parallel to the river, one block inland.

One end of Sisakan has a Soviet memorial cheerfully celebrating the crushing of the Dashnaks in 1920; from here a road swings to the right and up to Sisavan Church.

◎ Sights

Originally built in the 6th century, **Sisavan Church** was restored as recently as the 20th century. It combines an elegant square-cross floor with some striking sculptures of royal and ecclesiastical patrons inside and out. Inside there's a display of microsculptures by local artist Eduard Ter-Ghazaryan. Seen through a microscope, one features 17 images of the cross on a human hair coated with metal.

The road up from town passes a Soviet war memorial with a Karabakh War monument – local men were some of the first to volunteer to join their kin over in the next mountain range when the war began, and paid a heavy price for it.

The **karadaran** park in town one block from Sisakan Poghots gathers together stone carvings from different millennia, with sarcophagi, phallus stones, ram stones and megaliths. You can spot the evolution of the pagan *khatchkars* to rough stone crosses and finally medieval Armenian *khatchkars*.

Facing the park is the **Museum of History** (admission AMD500; ◎10am-5pm Tue-Sat), with some carpets and ethnographical displays beside maps and historical information, mostly labelled in Armenian with some English. It also has some interesting photos taken after an earthquake levelled the town in 1931.

On the main road, a few doors west of Hotel Lalaner, is the **Sisian Art School** (📞091584 485; admission free), run by local artist Ashot Avagyan. Visitors are welcome to wander through the studios and Ashot is happy to show off his work. The school organises an annual local arts festival on 11 August that attracts artists and musicians from around the country.

🛏 Sleeping & Eating

Hotel Dina HOTEL $

(📞33 33, 093334392; www.dinahotel.am; 35 Sisakan Poghots; s/d AMD6000/9000, s/d without bathroom AMD3000/6000, deluxe AMD14,000) A handsome 1930s building with basic shared rooms and nicer double rooms with private bathrooms. The receptionist usually won't offer the cheaper rooms unless you ask. Given the low price, quality rooms and central location, this is easily the best deal in town. Breakfast costs AMD1500. The managers speak some English and can help with arranging tours and onwards transport.

Aminhanyan Shavash B&B GUESTHOUSE $$

(📞41 42, 077414277; 9 Tigran Mets Poghota; per person AMD8000) A large house on the outskirts of town managed by English-speaking Gayane. Laundry is available and breakfast is an extra AMD2000. It's 2km from the bus stop on the eastern side of town and difficult to find on your own. A taxi here will cost AMD400.

Hotel Lalaner HOTEL $$

(📞66 00; www.lalahotel.am; 29 Sisakan Poghots; s/d/deluxe AMD10,000/20,000/35,000; @) Overlooking the town square, this clean and comfortable hotel has 16 rooms and a restaurant. Deluxe rooms have a Jacuzzi in the bathroom. The hotel also organises trips to local sights.

Jira Hars ARMENIAN $

(Israeliyan Poghots; ◎10am-10pm) Nestled by the river just next to the bridge, this local *khoravats* joint serves up grilled meat, goulash, soups and salads. You can sit inside or in cabanas next to the river.

ARMENIA SISIAN

❶ Information

An internet club is opposite Hotel Dina and a better one is opposite Hotel Lalaner. You can change money at stores and kiosks near the main bridge.

Sasun Badasarian (☎093821 472) is a guide who arranges jeep trips up the mountains to Ughtasar.

❶ Getting There & Away

There are three *marshrutky* to Yerevan (AMD2000, four hours, 10am, 12.30pm and 2.30pm) and one to Goris (AMD800, 45 minutes, 9.30am) each day, where the bridge meets Israeliyan Poghots (along the north bank). Taxis wait at this junction too. There's also a bus stop at the turn-off from the Yerevan–Goris road into town, where people often wait for rides.

Local tours can be negotiated directly with the taxi drivers or through one of the hotels. A trip to Shaki Waterfall or Zorats Karer costs about AMD700 to AMD1000, a ride to Goris AMD5000, and a longer tour to Tatev Monastery and back about AMD9000.

Around Sisian

Two hundred and twenty upright basalt stones up to 3m high set along sweeping lines and loops, some punctured with sight holes aligned with stars, make up the ancient site of **Zorats Karer** (also known as Karahundj or Carahunge, which means 'speaking stones'). The site, situated on a rise above the river plains ringed by mountains, is dotted with tombs dated to 3000 BC. The astronomical design of Zorats Karer is most evident at the solstices and equinoxes. Lines of stones define an egg-shaped area with a burial tumulus in the centre, with a north arm stretching 170m and a southern alley 160m long. About 70 stones are pierced with finger-sized holes. The builders had a deep knowledge of astronomy, including the zodiac and the lunar phases, combined perhaps with worship for stars such as Sirius. The site won't blow you away (there's no balancing stones like you'd see at Stonehenge) but the pleasant walk here from town and excellent panoramas make it a worthwhile trip. Zorats Karer is 6km north of Sisian, signposted on the left about 700m before the main highway. The stones are in the fields about 400m from the turn-off. It's a pleasant one-hour walk from Sisian or a short drive in a taxi (AMD1000 including waiting time).

The **Shaki Waterfall** lies about 4km from Sisian near the village of the same name. About 18m high, it sluices down a wide expanse of stones above the Shaki River. The water is used for Shaki's hydroelectric power station, so the waterfall isn't always 'on'.

About 6km down the Vorotan River from Sisian in **Aghitu** (Aghudi) village is a distinctive 7th-century **tower-tomb**. There are dragon stones nearby from the 2nd to 3rd century BC. The road continues as the canyon deepens past Vaghatin to **Vorotnavank**, 12km from Sisian on the south side of the Vorotan. Vorotnavank is a striking 9th- to 11th-century fortress and church complex built by Queen Shahandukht and her son Sevada.

The petroglyphs of **Ughtasar** (Pilgrimage Mountain) in the mountains north of Sisian are even older than Zorats Karer. They lie at an altitude of 3300m around a lake on Mt Tsghuk, accessible between June and September – and even then only if it's not a cold summer. Carvings of leaping, dancing animals and hunters adorn rocks and boulders everywhere around the small lake. It's a haunting place surrounded by isolated peaks, and you can only wonder why ancient people would hike to such an inhospitable place to leave their mark on stone. The tracks are steep, rocky and hopeless without a jeep (Villis) and a guide. Sasun Badasarian (see p180) can probably get you up here, with some advance notice. A round trip will cost around AMD20,000 to AMD25,000 per vehicle for a trip of eight to 10 hours – the ascent takes at least three hours.

The ruins of **Tanahati Vank** are 17km southwest of Sisian past the Tolors Reservoir. A university was established here in 1280. Called Karmir (Red) Vank by locals, Tanahat Monastery is on a high promontory by a gorge. The monks here were so pious and ascetic they refused soup, cheese and oil, eating only vegetables, hence the name Tanahat, meaning 'deprived of soup'.

Goris ԳՈՐԻՍ

☎284 / POP 25,000

The endlessly winding roads that leap through the gorges over the mountains of Syunik come to a major junction at Goris, making this an inevitable stop between Yerevan, Stepanakert and the Iranian border. But it's hardly a place to pass through – Goris is a destination in itself. Boasting fine stone houses with arched windows and balconies on tree-lined avenues, it's a great place for strolling and chatting with locals. Goris is known for its variety of homemade fruit *oghee* including the deliciously potent mulberry and Cornelian cherry *(hone) oghee* – explore the *shuka* on Syuniki Poghots or ask at a B&B to find some.

There is plenty to see around the town too, including a weird cave city on the other bank of the river and equally bizarre sets of volcanic pillars that spear through the steep grassy slopes above town. Longer day trips can be made to Tatev, the Vorotan Canyon and the caves at Khndzoresk.

There is a fine selection of hotels and B&Bs in town, plus a couple of museums and a busy little *shuka*. All this plus the scenic surrounds make Goris a fine place to unwind for a couple of days.

◉ Sights

Locals say the cave shelters and stables of **Old Goris** carved into the hillside on the east side of town were built and inhabited in the 5th century. Several trails lead up over a saddle where there are more volcanic pinnacle clusters to explore. Many of the rooms are linked together, and arched 'shelves' grace some walls. The caves are sometimes used to house cattle – watch your step.

The **Museum of Axel Bakounts** (41 Mesrop Mashtots Poghots; admission AMD200; ⊙10am-5pm Tue-Sun) is a typical Goris villa with stone walls and a veranda looking onto a courtyard. The museum was the home of writer Axel Bakounts (or Bakunts), who died in Stalin's 1937 purges. It features his personal effects and furnishings from the late 19th and early 20th centuries. The friendly director of the museum, Mikaelyan Kajik, may invite you into his office to sample some of the local mulberry vodka.

The **Museum of Ancient History** (Ankakhutyan Poghots; admission free; ⊙10am-5pm) displays Bronze Age knives, traditional costumes, carpets and other locally found artefacts. The most unique item is a five-sided stone with carved faces that represent the sun, moon, water, earth and sky, believed to date back 4000 years. The museum is dimly lit and everything is labelled in Armenian, but it's still worth a look.

About 2km northwest of the *avtokayan* is the village of **Verisheen**, which houses the ancient Surp Hripsime Church. The barrel-vaulted structure saw restoration in 2007 and is believed to have been built on top of an old pagan temple. Continuing on

the main road northwest you'll spot plenty of cave dwellings by the road.

🛏 Sleeping

Mirhav Hotel HOTEL $$
(☑2 46 12; 100 Mesrop Mashtots Poghots; s/d/tr incl breakfast AMD17,400/21,600/26,700; @�;⚡) This tastefully designed boutique hotel is probably the best place to stay in southern Armenia. The brick floors, antiques hanging from the walls, wood furnishings and stone facade all blend with Goris' historic character. While providing a rustic atmosphere it maintains modern bathrooms, cable TV and internet. It's run by an Iranian-Armenian named Shahen Zeytourtchian, a retired surgeon who speaks five languages including English.

Hostel Goris B&B $
(☑2 18 86, 093287902; jirmar28@freenet.am; 55 Khorenatsi Poghots; per person incl breakfast AMD7000; @⚡) This hostel is run by the affable Jirayr Martirosyan, an accomplished artist. There are two rooms, one with three beds and one with a double bed that is suitable for couples; the atmosphere is homey and old-fashioned but comfortable enough. There is a hot shower, freshly brewed coffee and a filling breakfast. The hostel is well signed and right next to the partially restored Hotel Olympia.

Khachik Mirakyan B&B B&B $$
(☑2 10 98, 091204012; www.khachikbb.com; 13 Davit Bek Poghots; s/d/tr incl breakfast AMD11,000/15,000/21,000;@⚡) Situated near the park where Davit Bek Poghots meets Syuniki Poghots, Khachik Mirakyan B&B is welcoming, comfortable and the owners speak English. There are seven bedrooms with private bathrooms (and excellent hot showers), and a great balcony for resting up. On the downside, a constant parade of vehicles along this stretch of road disturbs an otherwise peaceful location.

Hotel Gyorez HOTEL $
(☑3 00 12; Garegin Nzhdeh Poghots; s/d incl breakfast AMD7000/13,000; @⚡) Clean, functional and somewhat bland hotel with a decent location near the river. It's excellent value for solo travellers who want a private room. No English is spoken but the manager is friendly enough.

Lyova Mezhlumyan B&B B&B $
(☑2 16 00, 091753010; mlyova@rambler.ru; 7 Makichi Poghots; per person incl breakfast AMD7000;@⚡)

Goris

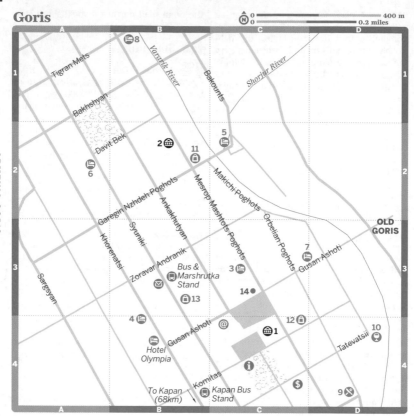

A fine stone house close to the Vararik River. It is 200m east of the main square and well signed. The large home includes six bedrooms, a spacious living room and nice bathrooms. However, it's not as well maintained as some other places in town. Mrs Mezhlumyan's daughter Nairi speaks English.

Andranik B&B   B&B $
(✆2 16 39; sevadamalincyan@mail.ru; Mesrop Mashtots Poghots; per person incl breakfast AMD7000) This centrally located guesthouse consists of three clean and quiet rooms. It's in a large stone house with a big garden out back. No English is spoken.

✗ Eating & Drinking

The best place to eat in Goris is the restaurant at the Mirhav Hotel, which serves a variety of items including rice pilaf and pork chops. However, the kitchen only does advance orders so it can take up to an hour to prepare

a meal. You can probably kill a little time while you wait by visiting the traditional lavash factory, right next to the hotel.

▨ KS restaurant   ARMENIAN $
(Narekatsi Poghots; meals AMD2000; ⊕10.30am-midnight) If you don't mind loud music, this place is fine for dinner, offering the usual array of *khoravats,* kebabs and salads. The clean bathroom is a bonus.

Turbaza Café   CAFE $
(Tatevatsii Poghots; meals AMD1500-3000; ⊕9am-1pm) This lush garden-cum-cafe overlooks Old Goris. It's a popular place for drinks but snacks are also served, including shwarma and boiled crayfish.

🔒 Shopping

Locally produced handicrafts are available at the **Goris Women's Centre** (grcentre@rambler.ru; 26a Komitas Poghot), which supports

Goris

⊙ **Sights**
1 Museum of Ancient History.............. C4
2 Museum of Axel Bakounts.................B2

⊞ **Sleeping**
3 Andranik B&B.......................................C3
4 Hostel Goris.......................................B4
5 Hotel Gyorez......................................C2
6 Khachik Mirakyan B&B A2
7 Lyova Mezhlumyan B&B....................C3
8 Mirhav Hotel B1

✖ **Eating**
Mirhav Hotel ....(see 8)
9 SKS Restaurant................................... D4

⊖ **Drinking**
10 Turbaza Café.................................... D4

⊚ **Shopping**
11 Armenian Souvenirs..........................B2
12 Goris Women's Centre......................C4
13 Shuka..B3

ℹ **Information**
14 Tatev Link C3

a cooperative of low-income handicraft makers. **Armenian Souvenirs** (cnr Mesrop Mashtots & Garegin Nzhdeh Poghots) is another good place to browse antiques and shop for local handicrafts.

ℹ Information

The **Tourist Office** (✆2 26 50; goristourism@gmail.com; 4 Ankakhutyan Poghots; ⊙10am-5pm Mon-Sat) can provide basic tips on things to do around Goris. The English-speaking manager Anush is helpful but sometimes out of the office. It is located just south of the park in the centre of town.

Tatev Link (✆2 22 23; tatevlink@gmail.com; Gusan Ashoti Poghots) organises a variety of trips around Goris and Tatev, including horse-riding, biking and hiking trips.

The banks, the **Haypost office** (19 Syuniki Poghots), restaurants and shops are within a few blocks of the main square. The **Armeconombank** (4 Mesrop Mashtots Poghots) has an ATM that accepts MasterCard.

The **Zakyus Internet cafe** (Gushan Ashoti Poghots; per hr AMD400; ⊙10am-midnight) just west of the taxi stand is clean and has a good connection. Wi-fi is available in almost every hotel and B&B and you can also get wi-fi at the Tourist Office.

ℹ Getting There & Away

There are three main stands for onward transport. The old *avtokayan* is on the highway into town (where the highway continues to Yerevan in one direction and Stepanakert in the other direction).

Most *marshrutky* and taxis gather on Syuniki Poghots, near the post office. The *marshrutka* to Kapan leaves from a corner near the Tourist Office.

At the time of writing the *marshrutka* service from Goris to Yerevan was indefinitely suspended. You'll most likely have to take a share taxi (per person AMD3500), which leave when full from the post office. Arrive as early as possible and if nothing is available, ask at the Tourist Office to help arrange a ride.

One daily *marshrutka* departs for Stepanakert (AMD1500) at 10.30am from the top of Mesrop Mashtots Poghots. If you miss this one, you can wait at the same spot for a *marshrutka* to pass through from Yerevan (four or five will pass per day in the afternoon). A taxi to Stepanakert, 104km away, will cost AMD10,000.

Marshrutky to Kapan (AMD1500, two hours, noon and 3pm) depart from the corner of Komitas and Syuniki Poghots.

The *marshrutka* to Sisian (AMD800) departs at 1.30pm from the town square.

Buses for nearby villages, including Tatev (AMD500, 3pm), leave from the *shuka* on Syuniki Poghots.

Around Goris

There are several historic villages around Goris, many with ancient artificial caves that are still used as stables.

Khndzoresk, 10km east of Goris, perches above the ruins of Old Khndzoresk, which was dug into a grassy gorge of soft volcanic sandstone. Whole walls of rock are dotted with caves; you could spend several hours exploring the area.

There are more caves around **Tegh** on the Stepanakert road, and around **Hartashen**, a tough but rewarding 3km on foot from Old Goris or about 8km by road. A smattering of **standing stones** similar to the ones at Zorats Karer is visible from the main road towards Sisian.

The **Sev Lich Nature Reserve**, 14km northeast of town on the shoulder of Mt Mets Ishkhanasar, protects a lake (Sev Lich means 'Black Lake') at 2666m. The track up requires a jeep and a guide. The reserve can also be reached from Sisian.

Tatev ՏԱԹԵՎ

📞284 / POP 600

Built on a fairy-tale natural fortress of rock on the edge of the Vorotan Canyon, Tatev is as jaw-dropping as any of the World Heritage–listed churches in Lori. The views down the gorge reach to the peaks of Karabakh.

The bishops of Syunik built the main church of **Surp Poghos-Petros** (St Paul and St Peter) in the 9th century to house important relics. There are faint signs of **frescoes**, intricate carvings and portraits of the main donors on the northern side. The 11th-century **Surp Grigor Church** nestles next to it, and there's a masterfully miniaturised chapel above the gatehouse. The fortifications, added in the 17th century, have been restored and are full of dining halls, towers and libraries. At the monastery's peak some 600 monks lived and worked at Tatev, and national icon Surp Grigor Tatevatsi (St Gregory of Tatev, 1346–1409) is buried here.

In the courtyard, look for the 8m octagonal pillar topped by a *khatchkar*. The 9th-century monument is said to have predicted seismic activity (or the roar of hooves by approaching armies) by shifting.

Outside the main gate, have a look at a newly constructed **oil press exhibit**, an excellent display of seeds, tools and ancient machinery used in the process of oil extraction.

Just uphill from the monastery is a cafe and an **Information Centre** (📞9 73 32,

093845632; annshik14@yahoo.com; ⊙9am-9pm), run by the English-speaking Anna Arshakyan. This is the place to ask about hikes in the area or B&Bs where you can spend the night. More information can be found at www.tatev.org.

See p185 for information on travelling the new cable car to the monastery.

The scenery around Tatev is gorgeous and there is plenty of scope for short hikes. One trail leads to **Svarants** (population 250), a hamlet 20 minutes' walk away on the other side of the valley. Another trail heads north to the top of **Petroskhatch mountain**, 4km from Tatev (the round-trip hike takes under three hours).

The most popular walk is downhill from Tatev to **Mets Anapad**, an overgrown 17th-century church. The cable car soars directly over Mets Anapad so you can get an idea of its location on the way up to Tatev.

The Information Centre has a copy of *Hiking in Armenia,* which describes this and other routes in the area. A knowledgeable hiking guide in Tatev is **Saro Martirosyan** (📞093575960).

Another attraction in the area is **Satan's Bridge**, located deep in the canyon below Tatev. Legend tells that centuries ago, villagers fleeing a rebel army were blocked by the raging river. Before the invaders attacked, a bridge was magically created by a huge falling rock and the people were saved. The site includes two natural spring pools, so bring a swimsuit. There are also beautiful natural pools and caves in the canyon below the bridge but at the time of research the canyon was off-limits. Local authorities plan to build a staircase down to the canyon.

Satan's Bridge is on the road, halfway between the cable car and Tatev village.

🛌 Sleeping

There are at least four B&Bs in tiny Tatev, each charging around AMD3500 to AMD6000 per person. They are not signed, but the hamlet is small so just ask around or contact the Information Centre. The main B&Bs include **Gago** (📞9 74 48), **Norik** (📞098104145), **Raffik** (📞093854632) and **John & Lena** (📞9 73 92). As it happens, Gago drives the bus from Goris so if you take the bus up to Tatev he'll probably deliver you straight to his doorstep.

FOLLOW THE ZANGEZUR TRAIL

A new tourist initiative in southern Armenia is the creation of a network of hiking trails between Noravank (near the village of Arpi) to Tatev. The ambitious project is still in its early stages but when complete it will be an epic 21-day journey on foot between the two legendary monasteries. The first section is to be established around Tatev Monastery. The route connects villages, so in theory you don't even need a tent or sleeping bag – it should be possible to stay at B&Bs during the entire journey. For details on the trail see www.zangezurtrail.am.

WORTH A TRIP

GORIS TO MEGHRI HIGHWAY

Travellers continuing from Goris to Meghri on the Iranian border will need to steel their stomach against approximately 160km of nonstop hairpin turns as the road climbs and dips through the mountains of southern Syunik. Most people coming this way are over-landers heading to Iran or curious road-trippers wanting to cover every inch of Armenian soil.

The first stretch is a 68km drive from Goris to Kapan. The most interesting sight along this route is the **Bgheno-Noravank** monastery, which was lost to the world until 1920 when writer Axel Bakounts happened upon it in the forest. The main church dates to 1062 and contains intricately carved biblical reliefs. It's a great camping spot or a logical break for cycle tourists. The turn-off from the highway has a sign directing you towards Bardzravan, a nearby village. After 3.1km, turn off the road to the right and the church is visible after 150m.

Further down the highway, there is a military base (Karmerkar) and a turn-off for the 3km access road to the village of **Davit Bek**. The village is another pleasant stopover and sports a couple of old churches and a pristine river with cascades and swimming holes. From the village there is a pleasant 40-minute walk to a pagan temple.

On the final plunge towards Kapan a bizarre turquoise lake comes into view. This is an artificial lake created by the tailings of a nearby copper mine so while it might look like the Caribbean Sea, swimming is not recommended.

Kapan marks the halfway point to Meghri and is thus a logical place to spend the night. From Kapan there are two roads to Meghri: a 75km road via Kajaran; and a newer, more scenic 94km route through the **Shikahogh Nature Reserve**. The most attractive part of the reserve is the valley of the Tsav River, where at the hamlet of Nerkin Hand there's an ancient grove of massive plane trees. The oak and hornbeam forests either side of the Tsav comprise the nature reserve, though you'll need a Niva or Villis jeep to explore the 100 sq km of gorges and forests.

① Getting There & Away

Each day a single bus leaves Goris for Tatev (AMD700, 3pm). The bus returns to Goris the next morning at 9am.

The most novel way to get to and from the monastery is to use the brand-new **cable car** (one way/return AMD2000/3000; ⊙10.30am-5.30pm), which travels 5.7km from Halidzor village to Tatev (purported to be the world's longest aerial tramway).

The cable car leaves once per hour (on the half-hour) but will also leave as soon as 15 passengers are assembled. A bus departs Goris for Halidzor (AMD350, 45 minutes) at 7.30am and 2.30pm (daily except Sunday). A taxi from Goris to the cable car costs AMD6000 return (plus AMD1000 per hour waiting time). A taxi from Goris to Tatev costs AMD6000/9000 one way/return.

It's a good idea to take the cable car one way and travel by road in the other direction, giving you both the aerial and ground views. Another option is to take the cable car up, then hike down to Mets Anapad church and hitch a ride from Devil's Bridge back to Goris (or arrange for your taxi driver to meet you at Devil's Bridge).

There is also a bus from Tatev to Kapan (AMD750) on Friday at 8am and Sunday at 3.30pm. The same bus leaves Kapan for Tatev on Friday at 4pm and Sunday at 8am from outside the Lernogratz Hotel.

Kapan ԿԱՊԱՆ

✏ 285 / POP 45,700

The largest city in Syunik, Kapan is wedged between high mountains and splintered by numerous valleys. The name itself is derived from the Armenian word *kapel* (to lock), in reference to the interlocking mountain chains that converge here.

During the 18th century Kapan was a base for Davit Bek, an Armenian freedom fighter who took on Muslim invaders encroaching Armenia's southern border. The village grew rapidly during the Soviet era when Russian geologists, seeing the potential for mineral extraction, arrived with blueprints for a massive mining complex. There is so much unrefined metal underground that compasses won't work in some parts of town.

Despite its industrial background, Kapan has a pleasant downtown with leafy parks, outdoor cafes and fast-flowing streams. There are banks and shops on Shahumian Poghots and an internet cafe in Hotel Lernagordz.

Mighty **Mt Khustup** (3210m) is visible high above the town. The approach to the peak is via the village of Verin Vachagan, about 3km southwest of Kapan. There are various routes up from here, so ask in the village. It's about 7km to the base of the peak, where a small church has been built. You can get fine views from here; another three hours of hiking is required to reach the peak.

The main site in the immediate area is the remains of 9th-century **Vahanavank**, about 7km from Kapan just off the Kajaran road. The monastery was once the religious centre for Syunik's kings. An attempt to restore the monastery in 1978 was later abandoned and what remains is a roofless structure of red limestone.

🛏 Sleeping & Eating

Hotel Mia & Max　　　　　　　HOTEL **$$**
(📞2 03 00; 9th fl, 2 Demirchyan Poghots; s/d incl breakfast AMD18,000/25,000; 📶) The nicest hotel in town is located on the 9th floor of Hotel Lernagordz, making this a hotel within a hotel. Rooms are completely remodelled with all new furnishings. The price includes wi-fi.

Hotel Lernagordz　　　　　　　HOTEL **$**
(📞6 20 86; 2 Demirchyan Poghots; dm AMD3000, s AMD5000-6500, d AMD8000-12,000; 🅿) This place has been around since Soviet times and not much has changed since then. Although dated, rooms are reasonably comfortable and come with TV and a nice balcony.

Khach Meruk Café　　　　　　　CAFE **$**
(🕓9am-midnight) For food, try Khach Meruk Café, in the little park near Hotel Lernagordz. It serves salads, sandwiches and pizzas.

❶ Getting There & Away

There is one daily *marshrutka* to Yerevan (AMD5000, six/eight hours in summer/winter, 7.30am) from in front of Hotel Lernagordz. Shared taxis depart when full from the same location for AMD6000. There are two *marshrutky* to Goris (AMD1500, 90 minutes to two hours, 9am and noon). For Meghri (AMD1500) there are *marshrutky* at 7.30am and 3pm departing from a stop at the Davit Bek statue.

Meghri ՄԵՂՐԻ
📍286 / POP 4500

Strategic Meghri, Armenia's toehold on Iran, is worth exploring for its fine stone houses and stark but beautiful scenery. The town sits deep in the rocky, lushly irrigated gorge of the Meghri River surrounded by sawtooth peaks. The border crossing (open all day) is at the Araks bridge near Agarak (population 3500), 8km from Meghri.

The brick domes of **Surp Hovannes** at the Meghri town monastery date from the 17th century. In the centre of the main part of town is the fine **Surp Astvatsatsin Church** with a distinctive octagonal dome, built in the 17th century with later frescoes. There's also the **Surp Sargis Church** across the river in Pokr Tagh, the smaller side of town, with two rows of columns and some delicately restored frescoes.

In Iran, just across the river from Agarak, is the ancient village of Noordoz (also spelt Noghdoz or Norduz) – the minarets of the local mosque are visible in the distance. This is a sensitive border area so be careful where you point your camera.

Haer B&B (📞4 30 54, 093545414; info@bedandbreakfast.am; 14 Karakert Poghots; r per person AMD5000) in Meghri is a cosy homestay run by Marieta Azatyan. The B&B is 900m from the town square. Walk past the Haypost and follow the road as it curves along the hillside; turn right just after the abandoned stone-and-brick army fort – it's 50m uphill on the right.

❶ Getting There & Away

A Yerevan-bound *marshrutka* (AMD7000, nine/11 hours in summer/winter) departs at 9am from Hotel Meghri, just off the central square, on Block 2. A bus to Kapan (AMD1000) departs at 7.30am. A taxi to Kapan should cost AMD8000 to AMD10,000 (90 minutes) from Agarak or Meghri. A taxi between Meghri and Agarak costs about AMD2000.

On the other side of the border, buses are rare or nonexistent, but a taxi to Jolfa (Julfa, Culfa) should cost US$5 to US$8 (40 minutes) with bargaining. A shop just outside Iranian immigration exchanges currencies. See p142 for information on buses to Iran, which leave from Yerevan.

UNDERSTAND ARMENIA

Armenia Today

Despite its limited resources, Armenia has become a master at geopolitics. What other country in the world can say it maintains good relations with the USA, Russia *and* Iran? Each international giant has made moves to forge ties. The US has built a huge new embassy in Yerevan (on 8.9 hectares of land). Iran continues to bolster trade ties with Armenia and has signed multimillion-dollar energy and transit deals, including a natural gas pipeline and oil refinery. Russia, the main energy supplier until now, has upped the ante with a deal to build a new nuclear reactor at Metsamor. Russia also maintains a military base near Gyumri and posts its soldiers along Armenia's borders with Turkey and Iran.

While Armenia shoulders up to the big boys of international trade and energy, it remains mired in old feuds with its neighbours that make the Montagues and the Capulets seem like bosom buddies.

On the one side stands Turkey and the long-simmering genocide argument. The issue flares up every so often; in 2006 the French Parliament voted to make it a crime to deny the genocide (the bill did not become law), and in 2010 a US congressional committee branded the killings a 'genocide' even though the US is not one of the 20 countries to officially recognise the genocide. More often than not it is the diaspora that pushes this agenda. As the actual events slide into history, modern Armenians still pay the price as diplomatic relations are frozen and the border closed. Still, free-marketeers have found ways around the blockade and manage to import Turkish goods via Georgia.

Recent political efforts between Turkey and Armenia hold promise of a thaw. In 2008 and 2009 the countries engaged in a round of 'football diplomacy' that involved national sides competing against each other in the World Cup qualifiers. There were two matches; Turkey came to Yerevan for one game, and Armenia travelled to Bursa for the second match. The presidents of each respective country accompanied their players and the matches included high-level talks between Turkish President Abdullah Gül and Armenian President Serzh Sargsyan. The sides discussed normalising relations, establishing embassies and opening the border. In the end, talks broke down over the

A SURNAME PRIMER

The vast majority of Armenian surnames end in '-ian' or '-yan'. The spelling depends on the whether the root ends in a vowel or consonant (Saro + yan = Saroyan or Gregor + ian = Gregorian). The suffix means 'from' or 'of', either from a town (Marashlian from Marash; Vanetsian from Van), from a parent (Davidian, son of David), from an occupation (Najarian, son of a carpenter; Boyajian, from the Turkish word 'boyaj' for someone who dyes fabrics), or from status or personal traits (Melikyan, son of a king; Sinanian, from a Turkish term for a well-endowed gent). Names with the prefix 'Ter' mean a married priest (Ter Hayr) was an ancestor, eg ex-president Levon Ter-Petrossian. Western Armenian names may spell it 'Der', as in Der-Bedrossian. There are also families with the suffix '-runi', such as Siruni and Artsruni. These families were once aristocrats.

Karabakh issue. Turkey said it would only normalise relations if the conflict was finally settled, and talks have been suspended.

Armenia was unable to move forward with Turkey because its relationship with Azerbaijan is in a shambles. Official fighting between the two countries ended in 1994, but the matter still feels closer to war than peace. A sniper war still brews along the border and brief skirmishes occurred in 2008 and 2010, with both sides suffering casualties. The status quo – with Armenia officially occupying 16% of Azerbaijan and negotiations at a standstill – is likely to last for some time.

Closer to home, domestic news is often centred on public dissent in the wake of the disputed 2008 presidential elections. The election pitted Sargsyan against Levon Ter-Petrossian, Armenia's first president (1991 to 1998). Sargsyan won 52% of the vote in an election largely condemned as fraudulent by international observers. There were allegations of vote buying, ballot rigging and media suppression. Protestors gathered on Freedom Sq (Opera Sq) near the Opera House but were violently dispersed. At least 10 people died and Sargsyan called for a 20-day state of emergency. In the years since, Yerevan has seen a large number of political protests aimed at increasing democratic reforms, press freedom and other civil liberties.

On the economic front, Armenia was posting 13% growth until economic recession in 2008–9. The figure has since shrunk to around 4%. Critics point to Armenia's over-dependence on resource exports and remittances as problematic for stable, long-term growth. But the streets of Yerevan and other cities display superficial improvements, with international brand-name stores and flashy SUVs at every turn.

With per capita income at around US$3090 and inflation at a crippling 9%, Armenia has a long way to go to catch up with Europe. The idea of joining the EU has been thrown around with much interest but, given the level of poverty that still exists (around 30%), the high levels of corruption and the shaky democracy, no one is holding their breath.

History

In the Beginning...

Like all countries ancient, Armenia has a murky origin. According to Bible lore Armenians are the descendants of Hayk, great-great-grandson of Noah, whose ark grounded on Mt Ararat after the flood. In recognition of their legendary ancestry, Armenians have since referred to their country as Hayastan, land of the Hayk tribe. Greek records first mention Armenians in the 6th century BC as a tribe living in the area of Lake Van.

The Armenian highlands north of the Fertile Crescent had long been inhabited, and historians believe that local advances in mining, chemical and metallurgical technologies were major contributions to civilisation. With invasion routes open in four directions, the early Armenian kings fought intermittent wars against Persia and the Mediterranean powers. Greek and Roman cultures mixed with Persian angel-worship and Zoroastrianism.

In the 1st century BC the borders of Armenia reached their greatest extent under Tigranes II, whose victories over the Persian Seleucids gave him land from modern Lebanon and Syria to Azerbaijan.

Christianity & the Written Word

The local religious scene in Armenian villages attracted Christian missionaries as early as AD 40, including the apostles Bartholomew and Thaddeus. According to lore, King Trdat III declared Christianity the state religion in AD 301. His moment of epiphany came after being cured of madness by St Gregory the Illuminator, who had spent 12 years imprisoned in a snake-infested pit, now located under Khor Virap Monastery. A version preferred by historians suggests that Trdat was striving to create national unity while fending off Zoroastrian Persia and pagan Rome. Whatever the cause, the church has been a pillar of Armenian identity ever since.

Another pillar of nationhood arrived in 405 with Mesrop Mashtots' revolutionary Armenian alphabet. His original 36 letters were also designed as a number system. Armenian traders found the script indispensable in business. Meanwhile, medieval scholars translated scientific and medical texts from Greek and Latin.

Kingdoms & Conquerors

Roman and Persian political influence gave way to new authority when western Armenia fell to Constantinople in 387 and eastern Armenia to the Sassanids in 428. The Arabs arrived around 645 and pressure slowly mounted from Baghdad to convert to Islam. When the Armenians resisted they were taxed to the point where many left for Roman-ruled territories, joining Armenian communities in a growing diaspora.

Better conditions emerged in the 9th century when the caliph (Muslim ruler) approved the resurrection of an Armenian monarch in King Ashot I, the first head of the Bagratuni dynasty. Ani (now in Turkey) served as capital for a stint. Various invaders including the Seljuk Turks and Mongols took turns plundering and at times ruling and splitting Armenia.

By the 17th century Armenians were scattered across the empires of Ottoman Turkey and Persia, with diaspora colonies from India to Poland. The Armenians rarely lived in a unified empire, but stayed in distant mountain provinces where some would thrive while others were depopulated. The seat of the Armenian Church wandered from Echmiadzin to Lake Van and further west for centuries.

The Armenian Question

The Russian victory over the Persian Empire, around 1828, brought the territory of the modern-day Armenian republic under Christian rule, and Armenians began returning to the region. The tsarist authorities tried to break the Armenian Church's independence, but conditions were still preferable to those in Ottoman Turkey, where many Armenians still lived. When these Ottoman Armenians pushed for more rights, Sultan Abdulhamid II responded in 1896 by massacring between 80,000 and 300,000 of them.

The European powers had talked often about the 'Armenian Question', considering the Armenians a fellow Christian people living within the Ottoman Empire. During WWI some Ottoman Armenians sided with Russia in the hope of establishing their own nation state. A triumvirate of *pashas* (Ottoman governors) who had wrested control of the empire viewed these actions as disloyal, and ordered forced marches of all Armenian subjects into the Syrian deserts. What is less certain – and remains contentious to this day – is whether they also ordered pogroms and issued a decree for Armenians to be exterminated. Armenians today claim that there was a specific order to commit genocide; Turks strenuously deny this. What is inescapable is the fact that between 1915 and 1922 around 1.5 million Ottoman Armenians died.

The first independent Armenian republic emerged in 1918, after the November 1917 Russian Revolution saw the departure of Russian troops from the battlefront with Ottoman Turkey. The republic immediately faced a wave of starving refugees, the 1918 influenza epidemic, and wars with surrounding Turkish, Azeri and Georgian forces. It fought off the invading Turks in 1918, and left the final demarcation of the frontier to Woodrow Wilson, the US president. Meanwhile, the Turks regrouped under Mustafa Kemal (later Kemal Ataturk) and overran parts of the South Caucasus. Wilson's map eventually arrived without troops or any international support, while Ataturk offered Lenin peace in exchange for half of the new Armenian republic. Beset by many other enemies, Lenin agreed.

The Armenian government, led by the Dashnaks, a party of Armenian independence fighters, capitulated to the Bolsheviks in 1921. They surrendered in order to preserve the last provinces of ancient Armenia. The Soviet regime hived off Karabakh and Naxçivan (Nakhchivan) for Azerbaijan. Forced from their homes, hundreds of thousands of survivors of the genocide regrouped in the French-held regions of Syria and Lebanon, emigrating en masse to North America and France. Remarkably, the Armenians who stayed began to rebuild with what was left, laying out Yerevan in the 1920s. Armenia did

ARMENIA HISTORY

KOMITAS & SOGHOMIAN TEHLIRIAN

Two figures from the genocide are particularly well remembered by Armenians. Komitas represents the losses. A *vardapet* (monk) of the Armenian Church, Komitas travelled through Armenian villages collecting folk songs; he was the first great ethnomusicologist. He also worked on deciphering the mysteries of medieval Armenian liturgical music. His concerts in Europe in the early 1910s were hailed as the arrival of a distinct national musical tradition. His Liturgy remains unfinished. On 24 April 1915 Komitas was in Istanbul when he was rounded up with 250 other Armenian community leaders and intellectuals. He was one of possibly two to survive – his life was literally bought from the Young Turks by a benefactor and he was smuggled to France. But the atrocities he witnessed broke his mind, and he died in an asylum in Paris in 1937 having never again spoken. His ideas for breathing life into the ancient harmonies and chorales were lost with him.

Soghomian Tehlirian represents a different face of the genocide. After losing his family to the killings, he ended up in Berlin in the early 1920s, where, on 15 March 1921, he assassinated the man most responsible for the genocide, Mehmet Talaat Pasha. Talaat Pasha was Minister of War in 1915, and founder of the covert Teshkilati Mahsusa (Special Organisation), which among other things recruited psychotic killers from prisons to serve on the deportations. Tehlirian's trial was one of the few public vindications of the genocide. Survivors and witnesses gave testimony on the marches, massacres, tortures and rapes, and Talaat Pasha's prime role. After two days the German jury found Tehlirian not guilty and released him. Other senior Turkish officials were killed in the early 1920s in Operation Nemesis, a secret Dashnak (Armenian Revolutionary Federation) plan to execute their own justice. Tehlirian later settled in the US and remains a kind of Armenian icon of revenge.

well in the late Soviet era, with lots of technological industries and research institutes.

Independence

The debate over the Armenian-majority region of Nagorno-Karabakh inside Azerbaijan brought a new wave of leaders to the fore under Gorbachev's *glasnost* (openness) reforms. Armenians voted for independence on 21 September 1991, and Levon Ter-Petrossian, a 40-year-old scholar and leader of the Karabakh Committee, became president. The war with Azerbaijan over Karabakh exploded just as the economy went into free-fall. See the Nagorno-Karabakh chapter (p277) for more information on the conflict.

After the war, rumours of coups and assassination attempts prompted Ter-Petrossian to reverse civil rights and throw Dashnak leaders and fighters from the Karabakh War into jail, where some spent three years as political prisoners. Ter-Petrossian was re-elected for another five-year term in 1996 but resigned in 1998, isolated and unpopular.

He was replaced by Robert Kocharian in March 1998, a war hero from southern Karabakh. Kocharian entered the war with one tank and amassed 13 more by the time of the ceasefire. Kocharian quickly moved to woo back the diaspora, especially the influential Dashnak faction.

By the end of the 1990s the new class of wealthy import barons stood out in shocking contrast to the country's poverty. Anger over this disparity was at least partly responsible for the terrible 1999 massacre in the national assembly, when gunmen, screaming that the barons were drinking the blood of the nation, murdered eight members of parliament and wounded six others. The event sparked a wave of emigration and endless recriminations, but the 1700th anniversary of the founding of the Armenian Church in 2001 marked something of a turning point in the country's fortunes. Memories of the suffering and upheaval since independence linger on, but the rapid economic revival through the first decade of the 21st century has raised spirits.

Arts

Cinema

The ArmenFilm studios on the Ashtarak road out of Yerevan once thrived with productions but are now mostly moribund. Sergei Paradjanov (Parajanian) was born in Tbilisi and was 'encouraged' by Soviet authorities to adopt the Russian -ov suffix to his name. Frequently out of favour with the culture moguls, he still managed to unleash camp-visionary theatrical films including *Colour of Pomegranates.* The reward for his genius was four years' hard labour in a Soviet prison camp. After his release in 1977 he went on to produce *Ashough Gharib* and *The Legend of Souram Fortress,* but his final masterpiece, *The Confession,* was left unfinished with his own death. While the films may not have seen success in the USSR, he won fans internationally including Fellini and Bertolucci.

Canadian-Armenian director Atom Egoyan has made several films on Armenian themes, including 1993's *Calendar* and 2002's *Ararat,* a film within a film on the genocide. *Ararat* is typical of Egoyan's art-house leanings, leaving you wondering about how it all fits together more than the subject matter. You could say the interweaving plot structure is intrinsically very Armenian. *Calendar,* another Egoyan arthouse classic, describes the story of a photographer sent to Armenia to shoot Armenian churches for a calendar. The plot, one of lost love, is filled with twists. Much of the dialogue between the characters was improvised.

Here (2010), directed by Braden King, is an American arthouse film set in Armenia that focuses on the romantic interlude between an American mapping engineer and a diaspora Armenian returning to her homeland.

Music

Armenian religious music's mythically complex harmonies are partly lost, though there are many fine, melancholy choirs of the Armenian liturgy. The great composers of the 19th and 20th centuries include Komitas, whose works for choir and orchestra put Armenian music on an international stage, and Armen Tigranyan for his opera *Anush.* Aram Khachaturian is best known for his *Sabre Dance* and the ballet *Spartacus.* Sayat Nova, often considered the greatest singer-songwriter in the South Caucasus, began his career in the court of Erekle II of Georgia but was exiled for his forbidden love of the king's daughter (see p284). The country is still a centre for classical music, with a ballet theatre, an opera company, orchestras for chamber music and symphonies, and an active world of composers and performers.

Folk music is alive and well in town troupes and late-night clubs and *khoravats* palaces. Spend a night at a popular venue like Ashtarak's Ashtaraki Dzor complex (p150) and marvel at the range of talent. The *duduk*, a double-reed instrument made from apricot wood, will become the soundtrack to your journey in Armenia. Its inescapable trill features in traditional music and many modern pop tunes blaring from the speakers of taxi cabs.

For good traditional music try the Real-World label, which has albums by *duduk* master Djivan Gasparian. Also try Parik Nazarian, Gevorg Dabagian and the album *Minstrels and Folk Songs of Armenia* by Parseghian Records.

Current artists of note include Lilit Pipoyan, a Joni Mitchell–esque singer and songwriter, and Vahan Artsruni, a composer with folk-guitar pickings who also rocks out in Yerevan's small live music scene.

There are plenty of emerging young singers, including Hasmik Karapetyan, Armenia's version of Celine Dion, and at the opposite end of the sound spectrum, the speed metal band Vordan Karmir.

Visual Arts

There are enough art galleries, artists' studios and house-museums to fill several weeks in Yerevan. Miniaturisation and microsculpture are peculiarly Armenian pursuits, with a number of impressive artists, including Eduard Ter-Ghazaryan of Sisian, whose pieces require a microscope to be appreciated. You can see examples of his work at Sisavan Church (p179).

Martiros Sarian is one of Armenia's most famous painters, and a museum in Yerevan preserves his studio (p125). Suitably enough, a Sarian sculpture in a Yerevan park is the focus of Yerevan's art market, where painters gather to offer a critique of each other's work and sell their paintings (p140). Most of the paintings have religious iconography or capture familiar Armenian landscapes. Yervand Kochar has his own gallery filled with portraits nearby on Moscovyan Poghots (p125).

Yousef Karsh was one of the great portrait photographers, and once achieved a famously defiant photo of Winston Churchill after snatching away his cigar.

The illustrated manuscripts preserved in Yerevan's Matenadaran (p125) and the libraries of Echmiadzin are testament to centuries of monastic endeavour.

Theatre & Dance

Theatre runs deep in Armenian culture – a 10th-century fortress at Saimbeyli in Cilicia had three storeys of theatres and two storeys of libraries.

The Hellenic kings of Armenia patronised theatre in the 3rd century BC, and Greek dramas played to King Tigran the Great. There are about a dozen active theatre houses in Yerevan specialising in musical comedy, contemporary plays and drama revivals. The musical comedies and shows for kids are easy to follow and very professionally done (for booking details, see p139).

Armenia has a rich tradition of folk dancing, and chances are you'll stumble across a performance in a public square. Revellers at country weddings might not be so professional, but then it is the real thing. Armenia has a rich diversity of dances and costumes, straight out of a medieval spring festival. There are also dance and ballet companies in Yerevan.

RABIZ MUSIC

Rabiz is a contraction of the Russian words 'rabochee iskusstvo' (workers' art). It's entertainment and it's also a lifestyle – the guys in the silk shirts and gold chains driving too fast while smoking and talking on their mobile phones. If you ask a hip student, they'll say that Armenian popular culture is divided between loud, showy, raucous *rabiz* culture on one hand, and everything of good taste on the other. *Rabiz* also covers a lot of highly inventive slang. *Rabiz* music is *marshrutka*-driver music, a mix of brainless pop and over-the-top tragic ballads (girl has cancer, boy says he'll kill himself before she dies) that strike a sentimental Middle Eastern chord in Armenian hearts. Fans want music that will make them cry, as well as impassioned love songs and arms-aloft dancing music. This kind of music booms from taxis in Greek, Russian, Turkish and Arabic. The Armenian variety comes from Los Angeles, Beirut and Moscow as well as Yerevan, where it plays in neighbourhood bars, clubs and *khoravats* (barbecued food) joints late into the night.

Food & Drink

Staples & Specialities

Armenian cuisine is a national treasure, a delicate mix of lightly spiced meats, fresh salads, lots of chewy light lavash and homemade specialities dating back centuries. It combines elements of the cuisines of all its historic neighbours – Arabic, Russian, Greek and Persian – but remains distinctive. Scientists believe the first wheat was grown on the southern flanks of historic Armenia, south of Lake Van, while the Romans dubbed the apricot *prunus armeniaca* (Armenian prune). The freshness of Armenian produce is another trait – crops are often grown on a small scale in villages and backyards across the country.

If there's one word for dining, it's *khoravats* (barbecued food). Pork is the favourite, though lamb, beef and sometimes chicken are usually available too. *Ishkhan khoravats* is grilled trout from Lake Sevan. *Siga* is another good grilled-fish dish. Kebabs are also very common.

Broadly speaking, western Armenian cuisine is more similar to Lebanese and Turkish cooking, while eastern Armenian has more Russian and Georgian influences. Besides *khoravats,* staples include dolma (rice wrapped in vine leaves), soups, vegetable stews and lavash fresh from the oven. *Khash* is a thick winter stew made from animal parts. Hors d'oeuvres include cold salads, salty cheeses and dips such as *jajik* (yoghurt with cucumbers and fennel). Cured meats include *sujukh* or *yeghchik* (dark, cured spicy sausage) and *basturma* (finely cured ham).

There are few strictly vegetarian restaurants in Armenia but any restaurant will offer numerous veggie dishes, made from tomatoes, rice, eggplants (aubergines), zucchinis (courgettes) and a profusion of herbs and spices. Western Armenian cuisine has hummus, tabouleh and other dishes associated with Lebanese cuisine, and lots of homemade ratatouilles are made from beans, carrots and onions with olive oil. Adventurous eaters might want to consider *kartofel atari graki mej* – baked potatoes cooked in cow dung (which is said to boost flavour).

Drinks

The most popular drink is *soorch* (Armenian coffee), also claimed by Georgians, Greeks and Arabs. It's a potent, finely ground cup of lusciously rich coffee, with thick sediment at the bottom. It goes well with honeyed pastries such as baklava. Tea is also popular. There is an interesting array of mineral and table waters, ranging from salty, volcanic Jermuk to lighter Noy and Dilijan waters. Fruit juices are cheap and delicious.

The two main lagers are Kilikia and Kotayk, widely available and quite refreshing on a hot summer afternoon. Kilikia is a typical middle-European lager, very good when fresh. Its main rival, Kotayk, is sold everywhere and is a little more reliable, if bland, while Erebuni has more flavour and is made by the same company.

The country's national liquor is cognac (around 40% alcohol). There are several other producers, such as Great Valley, but the Yerevan Brandy Company's Ararat label is the real thing, a smooth, intense liquor with a smoky aroma similar to whisky. Armenian *konyak* (cognac) has a huge following in Russia and Ukraine. Even Winston Churchill favoured it over the French stuff, and Stalin used to send him cases of Ararat cognac.

Most red wines are made from the Areni grape, well suited to the hot summers and harsh winters. Some reputable Areni makers are Vayots Dzor, Vedi Alco, Getap and Noravank, and new wineries are springing up. White wines are produced from vineyards in Tavush, Lori and Karabakh, and are generally sweet or with extra tannins from the skins.

If you want to propose a toast it's polite to ask the permission of the *tamada* (main toastmaker). There's a custom in clinking glasses of holding your glass lower than the next person's, as a sign of deference. This can develop into a game until the glasses are at table level. If you empty a bottle into someone's glass, it obliges them to buy the next bottle – it's polite to put the last drops into your own glass.

EATING PRICE RANGES

The following price ranges have been used in our reviews of restaurants and cafes in Armenia. Prices are based on one main dish and a drink.

Budget ($)   <AMD2000

Midrange ($$)   AMD2000–4000

Top End ($$$)   >AMD4000

ACCOMMODATION PRICE RANGES

The following price ranges have been used in our reviews of places to stay in Armenia. Prices are based on accommodation for two people without meals, in high season.

PRICE RANGE	YEREVAN	ELSEWHERE
Budget ($)	<AMD21,000	<AMD15,000
Midrange ($$)	AMD21,000–45,000	AMD15,000–28,000
Top End ($$$)	>AMD45,000	>AMD28,000

SURVIVAL GUIDE

Directory A–Z

Accommodation

Peak season runs from June through July. Even outside these months it's a good idea to book your room ahead of time. This is especially true for B&Bs so that the hosts can organise food and be available at the time of your arrival. Discounts are usually available in the low season (November to March).

Some definitions of terms used in this chapter:

B&Bs Private apartment or home occupied by a local family with rooms available for guests. Breakfast is sometimes just bread, jam and tea, although some places offer full meals. Some B&Bs offer dinner for an additional cost. Local tourist offices usually keep an updated list of B&Bs. Prices range around AMD5000 to AMD7000 per person.

Cottages & Domiky These are typically located around Sevan for summer holidaymakers. Construction quality is often poor but lakeside location is generally good. Expect to pay AMD10,000 to AMD35,000.

Homestays These are similar to B&Bs but do not offer breakfast or other meals. Prices are similar to B&Bs.

Hostels At the time of writing there were four or five hostels in Yerevan, with more on the horizon. They are locally run but somewhat more institutional compared to the B&Bs, with a reception desk that opens during the day and some travel services. Dorms and private rooms are available but bathrooms are usually shared. Breakfast is usually included in the price, with costs often AMD6000 to AMD7500 per person.

Hotels There is a wide variety of hotels across the country, from old Soviet dinosaurs in rural areas to five-star international chains in Yerevan. Prices are considerably higher in the capital, with a midrange double in Yerevan costing around AMD30,000, while a similar room in the other areas might cost AMD15,000 or AMD20,000. Top-rated hotels cost up to AMD60,000 per room. There are a few excellent boutique hotels in Yerevan, Dilijan and Goris. For upmarket hotels we've included government taxes in the prices.

Resorts Resort areas such as Dilijan, Tsaghkadzor, Jermuk and Lake Sevan have a range of Soviet-era hotels and sanatoriums either recently privatised or owned by government ministries.

Activities

Armenia is quickly building a reputation among bird-watchers – 346 species have been recorded here, including one-third of Europe's threatened species, and 240 species breed here. The Birds of Armenia Project at the **American University of Armenia** (Map p126; ✆1-27 45 32; 40 Marshall Baghramian Poghota, Yerevan) has maps and books on the country's profusion of avian plumage. *A Field Guide to Birds of Armenia* and *Handbook of the Birds of Armenia* are both by Martin S Adamian and D Klem. For further information, see the informative website www.armeniabirding.info.

Hiking to the top of Mt Aragats is possible in summer, and there are great walking trails in the forests and mountains around Dilijan. Country hikes are made easier by the profusion of piped springs. *Adventure Armenia: Hiking and Rock Climbing* by Carine Bachmann and Jeffrey Tufenkian will serve you well. It details 22 hiking routes and several rock-climbing spots. The book is produced by the **Kanach Foundation** (www.kanach.org), which supports environmental protection programs in Armenia. A new initiative called Zangezur Trails aims to connect villages between Tatev and Noravank monasteries (see the boxed text, p184).

Horse riding is becoming more popular and is a great way to explore out-of-the-way places; a good place to start is Yenokavan Canyon near Ijevan (p162). Sailing and fishing on Lake Sevan on a mild summer's day is idyllic – inquire at the Harsnaqar hotel (p153). Underground there are karst (limestone) caves in Vayots Dzor, largely unexplored and for experienced spelunkers only. The cave villages around Goris are an easier challenge.

Business Hours

Most churches are open 9am to 6pm daily, though in winter you might have to wait a while for the key to appear. Fairs and markets open daily. Museums and galleries often close Monday.

Reviews in this chapter only list opening hours where they differ significantly from the following typical hours:

» Banks 9.30am-5.30pm Mon-Fri, 10.30am-1.30pm Sat
» Bars 7pm until last customer (times can vary)
» Cafes 10am-midnight (times can vary)
» Churches 9am-6pm
» Government offices and international organisations 9am-5pm Mon-Fri
» Restaurants 11am-midnight (times can vary)
» Shops 9am or 10am, closing between 7pm and 10pm

Customs Regulations

The usual restrictions apply (one carton of cigs, 2L of booze, no guns) and there's no currency declaration to keep. If you plan to take something out of the country considered to be of cultural, historical or national value (eg a rug, a samovar or similar), a certificate is required from the Ministry of Culture (Map p130; ☑1-52 93 49; 5 Tumanyan Poghots, Yerevan). You'll find it's much easier if the shop you bought the item from arranges the permit for you, or if you can speak Armenian. Otherwise the bureaucracy can be quite baffling.

Dangers & Annoyances

Armenia is one of the safest countries in the region. Health and safety precautions are minimal, just exercise the same type of caution you would if travelling in Europe. One common problem, however, is stomach bugs that come from drinking untreated water. Avoid the water fountains found in most cities. Be aware that the transport system in Armenia tends to run early in the day so don't plan on making any long-distance journeys in the late afternoon. When dealing with taxi drivers use a meter or set an agreed price prior to departure or risk being overcharged.

Embassies & Consulates

A full list of Armenian embassies and consulates can be found at www.mfa.am.

The following are all in Yerevan (phone code 1):

Canada (Map p130; ☑56 79 03; aemin@freenet. am; Armenia Marriott Hotel, 1 Amiryan Poghots)

France (Map p130; ☑59 19 50; www.ambafrance -am.org; 8 Grigor Lusavorich Poghots)

Georgia (Map p126; ☑20 07 42; geoemb@netsys. am; 2/10 Babayan Poghots)

Germany (Map p130; ☑52 32 79; germemb@ arminco.com; 29 Charents Poghots)

Greece (Map p130; ☑53 00 51; grembarm@ arminco.com; 6 Demirchyan Poghots)

Iran (Map p126; ☑28 04 57; www.iranembassy.am; 1 Budaghyan Poghots, Arabkir Park)

Italy (Map p130; ☑54 23 35; www.ambjevervan. esteri.it; 5 Italia Poghots)

Nagorno-Karabakh (Map p126; ☑24 99 28, 52 64 28; www.nkr.am; 17a Zaryan Poghots)

Poland (Map p130; ☑54 24 93; polemb@arminco. com; 44/1 Hanrapetutyan Poghots)

Russia (Map p130; ☑56 74 27; 13a Grigor Lusavorich Poghots)

Turkmenistan (Map p126; ☑22 10 29; serdar@ arminco.com; 52 Erznkian Poghots)

UK (Map p130; ☑26 43 01; www.britishembassy. gov.uk; 34 Marshall Baghramian Poghota)

USA (Map p126; ☑46 47 00; http://yerevan.usem bassy.gov; 1 American Poghota)

Food

For coverage of Armenian food and drink, see p192.

Maps

The maps made by Yerevan-based company Collage are the best available, with a full-colour foldout map *Armenia & Mountainous Karabakh*; the nifty, brochure-sized, 26-page *Roads of Armenia*; and the brilliant *Yerevan Atlas,* with new and old street names, street numbers and lots besides. They cost AMD3000 to AMD6000 from souvenir shops and bookstores in Yerevan.

MENU DECODER

abour	soup
ankius	pilaf made with rice, walnuts, apricot and lavash
basturma	cured beef or ham
biber	capsicum, pepper
bourek	flaky stuffed pastry
dolma	rice and meat parcels in vine leaves
hats	bread
hav	chicken
hummus	ground chickpea paste with oil
gata	breakfast croissant
gov	beef
ishkhan	Sevan trout
kebab	ground meat cooked on a skewer
kedayif	crunchy dessert pastry
khaghogh	grapes
khamaju	a meat pie similar to *khachapuri* (Georgian cheese pie)
khash	winter stew of animal parts
khashlama	lamb stew cooked in beer or wine
khoravats	barbecue, usually pork, lamb or beef, also vegetables and fish, does not include kebab
khoz	pork
kyufta	meatballs mixed with onion and egg
lahmajo (lahmajoon)	minced-lamb minipizza
lavash	thin flat bread
matsoon	yoghurt
oghee	fruit vodkas
paneer	cheese
patlijan	eggplant (aubergine)
pomidor	tomato (also *loleek*)
shaker	sugar
siga	river trout
suchush	plum-and-walnut sweet
sujukh	cured sausage
tabouleh	diced green salad with semolina
tan	yoghurt
tsiran	apricot
vochkhar	lamb
zarazogon	mushrooms stir-fried with egg and butter

Media

The main English-language weekly newspaper is *Noyan Tapan*. *Armenia Now* (www.armenianow.com) is an online newspaper.

Armenian-language dailies include *Aravot, Azg* and *Yerkir*.

Hye-FM (91.1 FM) plays a good mix of popular music on international playlists and some local music as well.

INTERNET RESOURCES

See also the Need to Know section (p13) for additional travel resources.

Armenia Diaspora (www.armeniadiaspora.com) An excellent portal for news, travel, business and listings.

Armenia Guide (www.armeniaguide.com) A strong links website, with connections to the sites listed here and many more.

Armeniapedia (www.armeniapedia.org) The best resource on everything you ever wanted to know about Armenia.

Blogrel (www.blogrel.com) Ongoing blog that keeps a finger on the pulse of modern Armenia.

News.am (www.news.am) Good source of daily news.

PanArmenian.net (www.panarmenian.net) Online community site carrying comprehensive news bulletins on Armenia, Karabakh and regional issues.

The only TV channel with an independent editorial policy, A1 is constantly at odds with government and often dragged through the courts. CNN is broadcast over public TV in Yerevan. Big hotels carry satellite TV.

Money

Armenia's currency is the dram (AMD). Coins are available in denominations of 10, 20, 50, 100, 200 and 500 dram. Paper currency is available in notes of 1000, 5000, 10,000, 20,000 and 50,000 dram.

A strong dram means that Armenia is no longer the bargain it once was, but prices are still moderate by European standards. For a list of exchange rates, see p122; for an idea of costs, see p12 and p122.

EXCHANGING MONEY

The best cash currencies are US dollars, euros and Russian roubles, roughly in that order. Georgian lari can also be changed in Yerevan and border towns. Other currencies are hard to change except at a handful of major banks in Yerevan. There are money-changing signs waving flags and rates at customers everywhere in Yerevan and around *shukas* (markets) in all major towns. Virtually any shop can change money legally, and many food stores and smallgoods vendors do. Scams seem to be rare, and transactions straightforward.

Travellers cheques are rare in Armenia and not recommended. Bring cash or an ATM or Visa card. Some local ATMs are linked to the Plus system and others to the Maestro system. ATMs are in prominent locations around Yerevan, including half a dozen HSBC branches. You can withdraw money in US dollars from HSBC machines and sometimes from local bank ATMs as well. All other main cities and even some small towns have ATMs, though you may have to poke around to find one that matches your card. Western Union money transfer is not available in Armenia.

TIPPING & BARGAINING

The usual tipping rule at cafes and restaurants is 10%. Taxi drivers won't complain if you set the price when getting in and stick to it when getting out. Shops have set prices, but *shukas* (markets) and outdoor fruit and vegetable stands are more negotiable.

Post

National postal service Haypost has offices in every major town. A letter might take anything from two weeks to six weeks to reach North America or Australia, but the service is fairly reliable. If you're sending out something of value you might feel safer with UPS, FedEx or a local courier company in Yerevan (p141).

Public Holidays

Annual public holidays in Armenia:

New Year's Day 1 January

Christmas Day 6 January

International Women's Day 8 March

Good Friday varies, from mid-March to late April

Motherhood and Beauty Day 7 April

Genocide Memorial Day 24 April

Victory Day 9 May

Republic Day 28 May

Constitution Day 5 July

Independence Day 21 September

Earthquake Memorial Day 7 December

Telephone

The country code is ☎374, while Yerevan's area code is ☎10. It's possible to make calls from central call centres.

International calls using either landlines or mobile phones can be expensive. Internet clubs in Yerevan often have VoIP calls at much lower rates (about AMD100 per minute anywhere).

For calls within Armenia, dial ☎0 + city code + local number; for mobile numbers dial the ☎09 prefix first (most people will give you this along with their mobile number), then the number. Note that the 0 is not dialled when calling from overseas. For international calls, dial ☎00 first.

MOBILE PHONES

Mobile-phone services, operated by Viva-Cell, Orange and Beeline, are fairly priced and wide-ranging. You can get mobile-phone service just about anywhere in the country these days, unless you are hiking in the backcountry. There is little difference between the providers, although there seem to be more subscribers to VivaCell (and calling other VivaCell phones is a little cheaper).

Tourist Information

The main tourist office is the Armenia Information centre (p141), which was closed at the time of research and there is no indication if or when it will reopen. Tourist information offices are also located in Dilijan, Goris, Ijevan, Sevan and Stepanavan.

Visas

Armenian visas are available at all entry points – 21-day tourist visas cost AMD3000 and a visa valid for 120 days costs AMD15,000. The officials might not speak much English, but it's just a matter of filling out a form and paying. You'll need one empty page in your passport for the visa and you must also pay in dram (moneychangers are available at border points and the airport).

It's also possible to get an e-visa by applying through the website www.mfa.am. However, since it's easier to just pick up a visa upon arrival, few travellers bother with the e-visa. If you do buy an e-visa, it's a good idea to print out a copy of your receipt just in case the border officials can't locate your records on their computer.

See p303 and p305 for lists of entry points into Armenia.

VISA EXTENSIONS

You can get a visa extension at the Passport and Visa Department of **OVIR** (Map p130; ☎1-53 07 22; 090007 007; 13a Mesrop Mashtots Poghota, Yerevan; ⌚2-6pm Mon-Fri). At room 211 you fill in a form and provide a photocopy of the picture page in your passport and return the next day to confirm authorisation of the extension. Once you have confirmation you pay AMD500 for every day you want to extend (maximum 60 days).

You will be given an account number for you to make the deposit, which can be done at any bank (the ABB across the street will do this for an AMD100 fee). You then go back to room 211 and leave your receipt and passport. You can pick up the extension the following day.

For people of Armenian descent and their partners, OVIR issues 10-year residency permits. The process takes about three months and costs around US$300.

VISAS FOR ONWARD TRAVEL
Georgia

The **Georgian Embassy** (Map p126; ☎1-58 55 11; geoemb@netsys.am; 2/10 Babayan Poghots, Yerevan) provides visas for 100 GEL (US$60). However, many Western nationals can enter Georgia visa-free (see p119). Those who need a visa can get one at road borders, but not at railway borders, so train travellers needing visas must get one in advance.

Iran

The **Iranian Embassy** (Map p126; ☎1-28 04 57; www.iranembassy.am; 1 Budaghyan Poghots, Arabkir Park, Yerevan) provides visas only after you have received approval from the Iranian Ministry of Foreign Affairs, and for this you'll need to go through a travel agent. The whole process can last two weeks or more. Contact Tatev Travel (p142).

Work & Volunteering

Wages are very low in most sectors, but there is a ton of NGO and volunteer work going on. NGOs have bloomed everywhere – international relief agencies are well represented, and there are many local and diaspora bodies as well, covering everything from health to the environment to teaching. The website www.armeniadiaspora.com is a good place to start investigating.

Azerbaijan

Includes »

Baku..............................202
Abşeron Peninsula........224
Qobustan.....................227
Quba............................230
Lahıc............................234
Mt Babadağ..................235
Qəbələ.........................236
Şəki..............................238
Qax..............................244
Zaqatala.......................245
Balakən........................247
Masallı & Around..........250
Lənkəran......................251
Lerik............................253
Astara..........................254
Naxçivan......................255

Best Places to Stay

» Karavansaray Hotel (p239)

» Rustam Rustamov (p234)

» Şəki Saray Hotel (p239)

» John & Tanya Howard's Guesthouse (p236)

» Afra Hotel (p238)

Best Rural Getaways

» İlisu (p244)

» Xınalıq (p231)

» Lahıc (p234)

Why Go?

Neither Europe nor Asia, Azerbaijan (Azərbaycan) is a tangle of contradictions and contrasts. A nexus of ancient historical empires, it's also a 'new' nation rapidly emerging on a petroleum-funded gust of optimism.

Surrounded by semidesert on the oil-rich Caspian Sea, the cosmopolitan capital, Baku, rings its Unesco-listed ancient core with mushrooming new skyscrapers.

Yet barely three hours' drive away are timeless rural villages, clad in lush orchards and backed by the soaring Great Caucasus mountains. Here, aimlessly wandering cattle trump Baku's flashy limousines while potbellied bureaucrats scratch their heads in confusion on finding that an outsider has wandered into their territory.

When to Go

Lowland Azerbaijan is especially lovely from April to June as showers interspersed by clear skies enliven bright-green, flower-dappled fields. In October, Baku is particularly pleasant though much of the rural countryside is parched brown.

Summer gets oppressively hot and humid in low-lying areas but late July is by far the best trekking season in the higher mountains.

Winters are relatively mild around the Caspian shores, but do bring heavy sweaters for Şəki.

In January, brass monkeys may panic in Xınalıq or Lahıc while remote Caucasian villages like Qrız can be cut off for months by snow.

Connections

By air, Baku has numerous connections to Europe and Central Asia, plus to China and Dubai. There are additional air links to Moscow from Lənkəran, Naxçivan and Gəncə.

Direct international buses from Istanbul run three days a week to Baku (via Georgia and Gəncə) and six times daily to Naxçivan. Between Naxçivan and the rest of Azerbaijan you'll need to fly, or transit Iran.

All borders between Azerbaijan and Armenia are closed and seriously militarised. Similarly, Nagorno-Karabakh and the occupied areas are entirely inaccessible from the rest of Azerbaijan.

Borders with Russia are closed to foreigners but locals can cross by road/rail at Samur/Yalama.

Between Baku and Tbilisi there are direct buses and overnight trains but it's far more satisfying (and scenic) to travel in bus hops via İsmayıllı, Oğuz, Şəki and Zaqatala.

To reach remote mountain villages you may need to rent a 4WD.

ITINERARIES

Three Days

Soak up the atmosphere of bustling Baku and make trips to Qobustan and the Abşeron Peninsula.

One Week

Work your way between Tbilisi (Georgia) and Baku via Zaqatala, Şəki and Lahıc or head up from Baku to Quba and explore its mountain hinterland.

Two Weeks

Combine the suggestions above and consider adding a trip to Lənkəran and Lerik, perhaps en route to Iran.

Visas

Most nationalities require a visa, and getting one requires an awkward-to-procure letter of invitation (see p268). Applying in Georgia is generally the easiest option.

Visas on arrival are not available.

RESOURCES

Azerbaijan International (www.azer.cm)

TEAS (www.visions.az, www.teas.eu)

Window to Baku (www .window2Baku.com)

News (www.news.az, www.today.az, www.apa.az)

Az.az (www.azerbaijan.az)

BTIC (www.bakutourism.az)

MCTAR (http://azer baijan.tourism.az)

Navigator (www.navigator.az)

Fast Facts

» **Country code** ☑994
» **Population** 9 million
» **Currency** Manat (AZN)
» **Language** Azerbaijani (Azeri)
» **Emergency** Police ☑102, Ambulance ☑103, Baku 012-4970911

Exchange Rates

Australia	A$1	0.81 AZN
Canada	C$1	0.79 AZN
Euro Zone	€1	1.06 AZN
Japan	¥100	0.84 AZN
NZ	NZ$1	0.66 AZN
UK	UK£1	1.23 AZN
USA	US$1	0.78 AZN

Set Your Budget

» Budget accommodation AZN40 double
» Two-course meal AZN15
» Museum free–AZN10
» Beer 70q–AZN5
» Baku bus ride 20q

Azerbaijan Highlights

1 Discover the grand stone architecture, medieval walled city centre and modernist tower skyline of Azerbaijan's capital **Baku** (p231), a dynamic boom town.

2 Seek out an 18th-century palace, unforgettable caravanserai-hotel and picturesque old town in **Şəki** (p238), cupped in beautiful wooded mountains.

3 Take in Stone and Bronze Age petroglyphs then a nearby 'family' of wonderfully weird mud volcanoes at **Qobustan** (p227).

CASPIAN SEA

Border open to CIS citizens only

Yalama
Nabran
Samur
Xudat
Qusar
Xaçmaz
ahdağ (4243m)
Quba
Laza
Şabran (Deveçi)
Mountain Villages
Siyəzən
Xınalıq
Babadağ (3629m)
Çırax Qala
Lahıc
Xızı
Besbarmaq Dağ (520m)
İsmayıllı
Pirqulu
Alti Ağaç National Park
Şamaxı
The Abşeron Peninsula
Ağsu
Mərdəkan
Artyom Island
Abşeron National Park
Kürdəmir
Suraxanı
SUMQAYIT
BAKU (BAKI)
Şah Dili
To Aktau (Kazakhstan)
Şixov Beach
Qobustan
To Turkmenbashi (Turkmenistan)
Qazıməmməd
Mud Volcanoes
Sabirabad
Ələt
Şirvan (Əli Bayramlı)
Şirvan National Park
Salyan
Biləsuvar
M3
Neftçala
Cəlilabad
Masallı
Kür Dili
M3
Yardımlı
Lerik
Lənkəran
MOUNTAIN
Hırkan National Park
Astara
To Tehran (Iran)
Astara

1994 Ceasefire Line

0   60 km
0   40 miles

4 Venture into high-altitude shepherd **villages in the Quba hinterlands** (p231) – with unique languages and dramatic canyonland scenery.

5 Explore **Lahıc** (p234), where copper beaters' and carpet weavers' workshops line the cobbled main street of this mountain hideaway.

BAKU (BAKI)

📑 012 / POP 2.1 MILLION

Azerbaijan's capital is the South Caucasus' largest and most cosmopolitan metropolis. Few cities in the world are changing as quickly and nowhere else in Eurasia do East and West blend as seamlessly or as chaotically. Battered Ladas race SUVs and shiny Mercedes past illuminated stone mansions, shiny glass towers and tatty old Soviet apartment blocks. In Baku's elegant centre, pedestrianised tree-lined streets are increasingly filled with exclusive boutiques. Unesco World Heritage status has helped kerb the corporate gentrification of the fascinating Old City (İçəri Şəhər), hemmed in by an exotically crenellated arc of fortress wall. And romantic couples defy Islamic stereotypes by canoodling their way around wooded parks and handholding on the Caspian-front bulvar (promenade), whose greens and opal blues make a mockery of Baku's desert-ringed location.

History

Though it was already ancient, Baku first came to prominence after an 1191 earthquake destroyed the region's previous capital, Şamaxı (p233). Wrecked by Mongol attacks, then a vassal to the Timurids, Baku returned to brilliance under Shirvanshah Khalilullah I (1417–65), who completed his father's construction of a major palace complex. However, the Şirvan dynasty was ousted in 1501 when Shah Ismail I (remembered as poet 'Xatai' in Azerbaijan) sacked Baku and then forcibly converted the previously Sunni city to Shia Islam. When Peter the Great captured the place in 1723, its population was less than 10,000, its growth hamstrung by a lack of trade and drinking water. For the next century Baku changed hands several times between Persia and Russia, before being definitively ceded to the Russians with agreements in 1806, 1813 and 1828.

Oil had been scooped from surface diggings around Baku since at least the 10th century. However, when commercial extraction was deregulated in 1872 the city rapidly became a boom town. Workers and entrepreneurs arrived from all over the Russian Empire, swelling the population by 1200% in under 30 years.

Baku's thirst was slaked by an ambitious new water canal bringing potable mountain water all the way from the Russian border, and the city's desert image was softened by parks nurtured using specially imported soil. By 1905 Baku was producing around 50% of the world's petroleum and immensely rich 'oil barons' built luxurious mansions outside the walls of the increasingly irrelevant Old City. Meanwhile, most oil workers lived in appalling conditions, making Baku a hotbed of labour unrest and revolutionary talk. Following a general strike in 1904, the Baku oil workers negotiated Russia's first-ever worker-management contract. But tensions continued to grow.

In the wake of the two Russian revolutions Baku's history became complex and very bloody with a series of brutal massacres between formerly neighbourly Armenian and Azeri communities. When the three South Caucasus nations declared their independence in 1918, Baku initially refused to join Azerbaijan's Democratic Republic, a position bolstered by a small British force that secretly sailed in from Iran hoping to defend the oilfields against the Turks (Britain's WWI enemies). Turkish and Azeri troops eventually stormed the city as the British ignominiously withdrew by sea under cover of darkness. In the end game of WWI, the Turks were forced to evacuate too and Baku became capital of independent Azerbaijan for almost two years until, on 28 April 1920, the Red Army marched into Baku.

In 1935 the search for oil moved into the shallow coastal waters of the Caspian. A forest of offshore platforms and derricks joined the tangle of wells and pipelines on land. Investment dwindled after WWII and only really resumed in earnest after independence in 1991.

Since 1994, however, foreign oil consortia have spent billions exploring these resources and for reasons as much political as economic, the world's second-longest oil pipeline, BTC, was built to Ceyhan in Turkey, ensuring that Azeri oil could be exported safely and quickly to the West without transiting Russia or Iran. Since BTC went online in 2005, Baku has boomed once more. Fountains, flagpoles and countless new multistorey towers (some of questionable earthquake resilience), have been mushrooming while those grand older buildings that avoided demolition have been cleaned and up-lit. Ambitious future plans include a proposed causeway to encircle Baku Bay, several futuristic skyscrapers, plus a giant ecological theme park for Nargiz Island.

Greater Baku

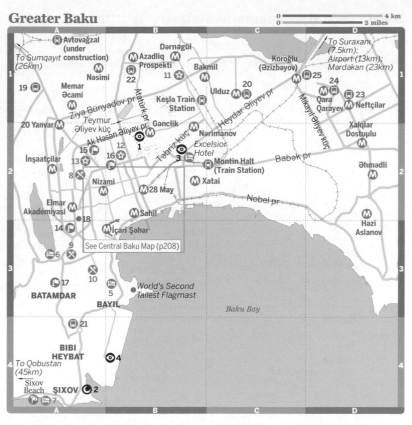

Greater Baku

◉ Sights
1 Azər-İlmə	B2
2 Bibi Heybat Mosque	A4
3 Heydər Əliyev Cultural Centre (under construction)	B2
4 James Bond Oil Field	B4

🛏 Sleeping
5 East Legend Hotel	B3
6 Kempinski Hotel Batamdar	A3
7 Ramada Şixov Beach	A4

🍴 Eating
8 Qorodok	A2
9 Şəki	A3
10 Tele-Qüllə (TV Tower)	A3

🎭 Entertainment
11 Baku Karting	B1
12 Megapolis	B2
13 Opera Lounge	A2

ℹ Information
14 Georgian Embassy	A3
15 Kazakhstan Embassy	A2
16 Russian Embassy	B2
17 Uzbekistan Embassy	A3

ℹ Transport
18 Avis	A2
19 Avtovağuzal (Main Bus Station)	A1
20 Bus 101 to Türkan	C1
21 Bus 105 for Qobustan	A4
22 Bus 98 to Novxani	B1
23 Marshrutka 141 to Mərdəkan Beach	D1
24 Marshrutka 231 to Suraxanı via Əmircan	D1
25 Pick-up point for most Abşeron-bound buses	D1

Baku – Old City & Fountains Square

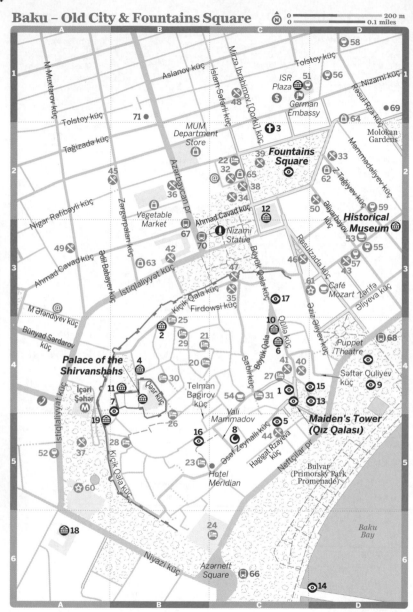

◉ Sights

OLD CITY

Baku's historic heart is İçəri Şəhər, the Unesco-listed, walled Old City. It contains the city's most accessible sights and its quieter back alleys are minor attractions in their own right, as are the tree-lined streets of 'oil-boom' mansions just beyond.

Several modest mosques and blunt stone **minarets** date back centuries. Best known is the recently restored AD 1079 **Sınıq Qala** (broken tower), whose nickname

Baku – Old City & Fountains Square

◉ **Top Sights**
Fountains Square C2
Historical Museum D3
Maiden's Tower (Qız Qalası)............... C4
Palace of the Shirvanshahs B4

◉ **Sights**
1 17th Century Market Square C4
2 Ali Shamsir's Gallery B4
3 Armenian Church C2
4 Bakı Gallery B4
5 Carpet Sellers C5
6 Centre of Contemporary Art C4
7 Coin Museum.. B4
8 Cuma Mosque... C5
9 Giant Screen D4
10 İçeri Şəhər Archaeological
    Museum.. C4
11 Museum of Miniature Books................. B4
12 Nizami Literature Museum................... C2
13 Old City Audio Guide Booth................. D4
14 Pleasure-Boat Cruises D6
15 Qız Qalası Gallery................................. D4
16 Siniq Qala Mosque................................ B5
17 Site of former Khan's Palace C3
18 State Art Museum A6
19 Vahid Garden & Bust............................. A5

⌕ **Sleeping**
20 Altstadt Hotel... B4
21 Atropat Hotel B4
22 Azcot Hotel C2
23 Caspian Hostel....................................... B5
24 Four Seasons Hotel............................... C6
25 Hotel Kichik Gala B4
26 King Palace Hotel B5
27 Museum Inn C4
28 Noah's Ark Hotel.................................... B5
29 Old City Inn B4
30 Qonaq Evi Buta B4
31 Sultan Inn C4

✕ **Eating**
32 Adams Curries.. C2
33 Ali & Nino Cafe D2
34 Cafe City (Fəvvarə) C2
35 Chocolate 2.. C3
36 Çudo Peçka 1.. B2

37 Filarmoniya Cafe A5
38 Kafe Araz C2
39 Kafe Fəvvarə... C2
40 Karvansara Restaurant.......................... C4
41 Karvansara Restaurant (Cellar
    Section).. C4
42 L'Aparté B3
43 Maharaja D3
44 Muğam Club C5
45 Paul's.. B2
46 Sunset Café C3
47 Tandir.. C3
48 U Dali C1
49 Xutor A3
50 Yeni Bəh Bəh Club................................. D2

◯ **Drinking**
51 Azza Bar C1
52 Brewery... A5
53 Café Caramel.. D3
54 Café Caramel (Old City) C4
55 Finnegans D3
56 Garaj... D1
57 Otto D3
58 Pivnushka Beer House........................... D1
59 Soviet Union D2

✪ **Entertainment**
60 Filarmoniya.. A5
61 Theatre Ticket Booth D3

🛍 **Shopping**
62 Ali & Nino Bookhouse D2
63 Chiraq Books B3
64 Subterranean Souvenir Stalls.............. D1
65 Suvenir Noffel.. C2

🛈 **Transport**
66 Azneft Bus Stop C6
    Bus 14 to Azneft & Araz Hotel..... (see 70)
67 Bus 162 to Şahidlər Xiyabani................ B3
    Bus 3 to Batamdar .... (see 67)
    Bus 65 North .... (see 70)
68 Bus 88... D4
69 Iran Air... D1
70 MUM Bus Stop B3
    Northbound Bus 88 .... (see 66)
71 Turkish Airlines...................................... B1

dates from damage inflicted during a 1723 Russian naval bombardment (since repaired). Several stone **caravanserais** have been converted into atmospheric restaurants and the many **carpet-souvenir** **shops** are attractions in their own right. A small, semi-hidden **booth** (⊘9am-6pm) rents rewarding audio-tour headsets (AZN5 plus deposit) that present the old city's highlights in a self-guided walk taking around 90 minutes.

TOP CHOICE **Maiden's Tower** HISTORIC BUILDING
(Map p204; adult/student/child AZN2/60q/20q; ⊙10am-7pm) This tapering 29m stone tower is Baku's foremost architectural icon. Possibly millennia old, its original date of construction is the subject of much debate, though much of the present structure appears to be 12th century. The Azeri name, Qız Qalası, is usually rendered 'maiden's tower' in English, leading to plenty of patently fictitious fairy tales. A popular version has a wealthy ruler falling in love with his own daughter. He asks the girl to marry him. Revolted by the thought of incest but unable to disobey her father she stalls, commanding that he build her a tower high enough to survey the full extent of his domain before she decides. When it's finally complete she climbs to the roof and throws herself off.

A better translation of Qız Qalası would be 'virgin tower', alluding to military impenetrability rather than any association with tragic females. It was certainly an incredibly massive structure for its era, with walls 5m thick at the base and an unusual projecting buttress. Today, the eight-storey interior contains some old photographs, a souvenir shop and a costume photography opportunity (AZN10 extra), but the highlight is the rooftop viewpoint surveying Baku Bay and the Old City.

Palace of the Shirvanshahs PALACE
(Map p204; admission/guided tour AZN2/6; ⊙10am-6pm) This sandstone palace complex was the seat of northeastern Azerbaijan's ruling dynasty during the Middle Ages. Mostly 15th century in essence, it was painstakingly (over)restored in 2003.

Enter via the main ceremonial courtyard. A small gateway on the left leads into the courtyard of the 1428 **Divan Xanə**, an open-sided, octagonal rotunda where Shirvanshah Khalilullah I once assembled his court: a decidedly small court it would seem, judging from the structure's diminutive size.

Entered through a towering if plain portal are the main **palace apartments** (Saray binası) whose renovation has almost amounted to full-scale rebuilding. Inside is a collection of old coins, pots,

sepia photos, paintings and crafts, mostly unlabelled.

Down one level, around the so-called **Dervish's Mausoleum**, are many carved stone blocks inscribed with Arabic calligraphy, animal figures and human faces. These **Bayıl Stones** were recovered in the 1950s from the 13th-century ruins of Sabayil Qala, a castle that once stood on an island that's now submerged near Baku's southern Bayıl Peninsula.

The next level down includes the small cubic **Shah Mosque**, a stone minaret, and the **Mausoleum of the Shirvanshahs**, where calligraphic carvings grace the portal gateway.

Vahid Garden SQUARE
(Map p204) Behind İçeri Şəhər metro, an arched gateway through the Old City wall leads into a handkerchief of garden dominated by one of Baku's most imaginative busts, that of poet Vahid incorporating characters from his work into the lines of his hair. The simple stone cube behind him is the 1378 Chin Mosque, now used as a tiny **coin museum** (admission AZN2; ⊙9am-6pm). A lane leading up from here towards the Palace of the Shirvanshahs passes a **Museum of Miniature Books** (admission free; ⊙11am-5pm, closed Mon & Thu).

CENTRAL BAKU

TOP CHOICE **Fountains Square** PIAZZA
(Map p204) Endlessly popular with strollers, this leafy boutique-ringed piazza forms Central Baku's natural focus. The fountains for which it is named include one topped by shiny silvered spheres giving fish-eye reflections of the trees and stone facades. Outside the large McDonald's (whose faithfully transliterated menu includes *dabl çizburqers*), notice the bronze statue of a young lady with umbrella, bare midriff and mobile phone. Very Baku. Approached down a wide tree-shaded stairway from the other (southwestern) side, the square is given an artistic aspect by the **Nizami Literature Museum** (İstiqlaliyyət küç 53; admission AZN10; ⊙11am-4pm Mon-Sat), whose exterior facade is a series of ogive arched niches set with statues of the nation's literary greats. The museum's entry fee includes an hour-long guided tour (English available) introducing the history of Azerbaijan through the prism of its poets.

Bulvar
WATERFRONT

Full of cafes, fountains and fairground rides, this central sweep of seafront park is eternally popular with families, amateur musicians and courting couples. Striking modernist buildings here include the **International Muğam Centre**, the **Baku Business Centre** and the four-storey **Park Bulvar Mall**. Behind the photogenic old **Puppet Theatre** (Map p204), a giant screen often projects fun time-lapse footage of Baku at night. Looking out across the oil-filmed waters, you'll see the **World's Second Tallest Flagmast** (Map p203). To get closer, you could join a noisy 30-minute **pleasure-boat cruise** (adult/child AZN2/1; ⊙from 11am during fine weather May-Oct). Amid a variety of funfair rides, contrast the ponderously slow-moving old **big wheel** (per rotation AZN2) with the high-tech **5-D Cinema** (10min AZN5), a miniature don-the-specs simulator experience.

Carpet Museum
MUSEUM

(Map p208; Xalça Muzey; Neftçilər pr 123; admission AZN5; ⊙9.30am-5.30pm) This column-fronted neoclassical building once honoured Lenin. Now it's a multimuseum centre whose most interesting section charts the history of Azeri carpet making. The collection includes over 1000 rare and beautiful rugs from Azerbaijan, as well as Iran and Dagestan. A guided tour (AZN5 extra) helps to put the designs in context and to explain the significance of their symbols. In the same building are the far less compelling **Theatre Museum** (admission AZN2) and **Museum of Independence** (admission AZN2). Note that by 2013 the carpet section is due to move to a new home on the bulvar where it will occupy a building shaped like a partly unfurled roll of cloth.

Historical Museum
MUSEUM

(Map p204; Z Tağiyev küç 4; adult/student AZN5/2, audio/human guide AZN3/10; ⊙11am-6pm Mon-Sat, last entry 4.30pm) Well-presented exhibits on Azerbaijan's history and culture might miss the odd century here and there, but there's more than enough to fill several hours if you're really interested. If not, it's still worth a brief trot through to admire the building – an opulent 1896 mansion. Its dazzling neo-Moorish 'Oriental Hall', along with some attached apartments, form a submuseum (no extra charge) honouring HZ Tağiyev, one of Baku's greatest late-19th-century oil barons for whom the house was built.

Şahidlər Xiyabani (Martyr's Lane)
CEMETERY, VIEWPOINT

(Map p203) High above the city centre's southwest corner lies a sombre row of **grave-memorials** – Bakuvian victims of the Red Army's 1990 attack and early martyrs of the Karabakh conflict. There's also a memorial to Turkish WWI soldiers, and (more controversially) to the British and Commonwealth troops killed fighting them. The viewpoint beside the **eternal flame** offers splendid panoramas across the bay and city; the site is newly overshadowed by a vast trio of sinuous blue-glass skyscrapers known as the **Flame Towers**. Access is easiest using the aging funicular (20q, every 15 minutes 10am to 9pm) starting from opposite the Muğam Centre on the Bulvar. For pedestrians a parallel stairway leads up beside, but don't take photos while walking up the first section. Bus 162 drives up from near Fountains Sq.

State Art Museum
GALLERY

(Map p204; Niyazi küç 11; adult/youth/student AZN10/5/2; ⊙10am-5pm Tue-Sun) Baku's foremost art collection counterpoints staid 19th-century Russian and European works with a much more interesting overview of Azeri modern art. The gallery is housed in two impressive oil-boom mansions but one is currently closed for long term renovation.

Art Galleries
GALLERIES

(Map p204) There are several commercial mini-galleries in the old city (all with free admission). The most imaginative include **Qız Qalası** (www.qgallery.net; Qüllə küç 6; ⊙10.30am-7pm), **Center of Contemporary Art** (Qüllə küç 15; ⊙11am-8pm Tue-Sun) and **Ali Shamsir's Gallery** (Kiçik Qala küç 84).

Taza Bəy Hamami
BATHHOUSE

(Map p208; ☑4373444; Şeyk Şamil küç 94; bathing AZN17; ⊙10am-11pm) This 1886 stone-vaulted bathhouse (men only) is merrily overloaded with knick-knacks and kitschy statuettes. The bathing fee includes towel-gown and disposable shorts, but as the bar areas are actually more evocative than the sauna and small modern pool, you might prefer to simply come for an AZN2 beer.

BEYOND THE CENTRE

MIM
GALLERY

(Modern Art Museum; Map p208; www.mim.az; Yusuf Səfirov 5; adult/student AZN5/2; ⊙11am-9pm, last entry 8pm) Brilliantly designed

Central Baku

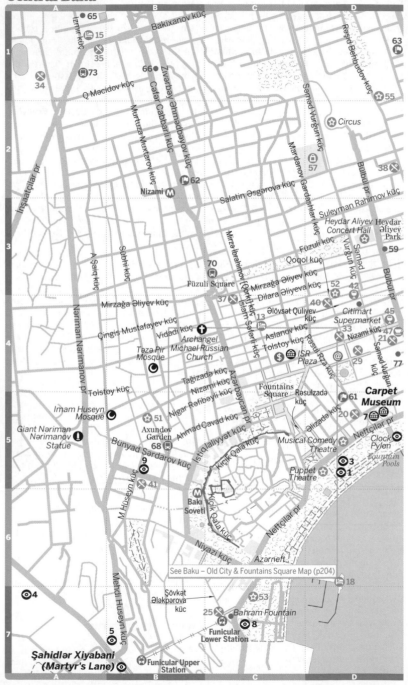

65

İzmir küç

15

35

73

34

Q Məcidov küç

66

Bakıxanov küç

Zivarbəy Əhmədbəyov küç

Cəfar Cabbarlı küç

Murtuza Muxtarov küç

Rəşid Behbudov küç

63

55

Circus

Səməd Vurğun küç

62

Nizami

Mardanov Qardashlari küç

57

Salatin Əsgərova küç

38

Bülbül pr

Suleyman Rahimov küç

Heydar Aliyev Concert Hall

Heydar Əliyev Park

59

A Saiq küç

Subhi küç

Mirzağa Əliyev küç

Çingis Mustafayev küç

70

Füzuli Square

37

Fuzuli küç

Qoqol küç

Mirzağa Əliyev küç

Dilara Əliyeva küç

52

42

13

Ələvsat Quliyev küç

40

Citimart Supermarket

45

Aslanov küç

Tolstoy küç

33

Nizami küç

Rasul Rza küç

21

47

Mirza İbrahimov [Qorki] küç

İslam Səfərli küç

Azərbaycan pr

Səməd Vurğun küç

Səməd Vurğun küç

Vidadi küç

Archangel Michael Russian Church

Tağizadə küç

Nizami küç

Nigar Rəfibəyli küç

Ahmad Cavad küç

Təzə Pir Mosque

İSR Plaza

29

77

Narıman Nərimanov pr

Tolstoy küç

Imam Huseyn Mosque

51

Axundov Garden

68

Istiqlaliyyat küç

Fountains Square

Rəsulzadə küç

61

20

Əlizadə küç

Carpet Museum

7

Giant Nəriman Nərimanov Statue

Bünyad Sardarov küç

9

41

Baki Soveti

Kiçik Qala küç

Musical Comedy Theatre

Puppet Theatre

3

1

Clock Pylen

Fountain Pools

M Hüseyn küç

Niyazi küç

Neftçilar pr

Azərneft

See Baku – Old City & Fountains Square Map (p204)

18

4

Mehdi Huseyn küç

Şövkat Ələkpərova küç

25

Bahram Fountain

8

53

Funicular Lower Station

5

Şahidlər Xiyabani (Martyr's Lane)

Funicular Upper Station

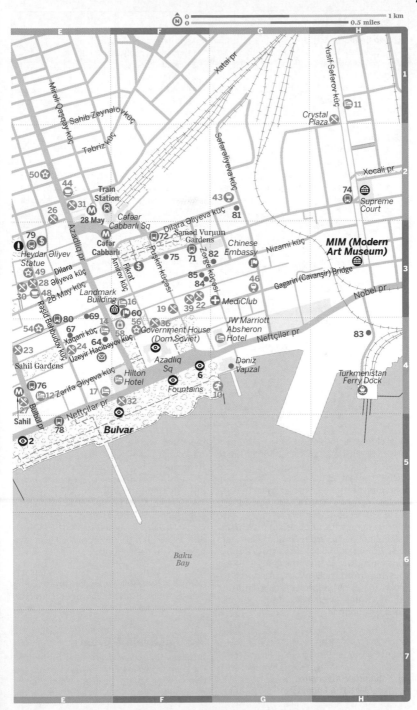

Central Baku

◉ **Top Sights**

Bulvar F4
Carpet Museum................................. D5
MIM (Modern Art
  Museum)... H3
Şahidlər Xiyabani
  (Martyr's Lane)................................. B7

◉ **Sights**

1 5-D Cinema D5
2 Baku Business Center...........................E5
3 Big Wheel D5
4 Faxri Xiyəbani Cemetery...................... A7
5 Flame Towers B7
6 Funfair F4
  International Muğam
  Centre....................................(see 53)
7 Museum of
  Independence D5
  Park Bulvar Mall...........................(see 32)
8 Site for New Carpet
  Museum... C7
9 Taza Bəy Hamami B5
  Theatre Museum ....(see 7)

◉ **Activities, Courses & Tours**

10 Pleasure Boat Cruises...........................G4

◉ **Sleeping**

11 Araz Otel..H1
12 Cənub Hotel E4
13 Hotel Hale Kai......................................C4
14 Hotel Respublika Lyuks E4
15 Hyatt Hotels... A1
16 Landmark Hotel...................................... F3
17 Park Inn.. E4
18 Yacht Club D6

◉ **Eating**

19 Anadolu 1 .... F3
20 Anadolu 2..D5
21 Art Restoran D4
22 Blinnaya Bistro F3
23 Brot Haus... E4
24 Cafe City (Sahil) E4
25 Çinar...C7
26 Çudo Peçka (Station) E2
27 Cudo Peçka 3.. E4
28 Fayton Club E3
29 Imereti..D4
30 La Strada Trattoria................................ E3
31 Nənəmin... E2
32 Park Bulvar Mall F4
33 Pizza Gusto...D4
34 Qoradoq A1
35 Scalini.. A1
36 Taboo F4
37 Tbilisi..C4
38 Tiflis Taverna...D2
39 Trin Trava.. F3
40 Yolki Palki (Central) D4
41 Yolki Palki (Yasamal) B5

by architect Jean Nouvel, this brand-new gallery creates a wide variety of intimate viewing spaces, in many of which you can recline on leather bean-bag sofas as you contemplate the extensive collection of predominantly post-1980 Azerbaijani art. Some earlier 20th-century canvases also appear, along with three original Picassos. Eastbound bus 1 (from Vurğun Gardens) or 14 (from the Bulvar) stop across a thundering major road from the gallery. To get back into town, walk two blocks north towards the grand Supreme Court building (Ali Məhkəmə) then take buses 1 or 232 buses westbound.

Azər-İlmə   CARPET FACTORY
(Map p203; ☑4659036; www.azerilme.az; Şəmsi Rəhimov küç 2; ☺9am-1pm & 2-6pm) Hand-woven carpets using wool coloured with vegetable dyes are created before your eyes in this characterful suburban factory that's decorated with a museumlike selection of traditional handicrafts. Tours are free even if you don't buy anything. It's around 20 minutes' drive northeast of the centre. Using bus 288, alight where it turns left in front of Kontinental Supermarket, walk two blocks right along Ak Həsən Əliyev küç, and the factory-gallery is tucked behind Kral Wedding Palace. Bus 6 (106) from the Hyatt area passes right beside Kral.

Faxri Xiyəbani   CEMETERY
(Map p208; Parlament pr) Heydar Əliyev's tomb here is the first place that any dignitary is likely to be taken to on an official visit to Baku.

✦ Festivals & Events

Business hotels are overloaded during the **Caspian Oil & Gas Show** (www.caspianoil-gas. com, www.cog.az), the biggest of many international trade fairs held in early June at the

⊜ **Drinking**
42 2/5 Mərtəbə.............................D3
43 3 Boçki...................................G2
   Caspian Terrace ....(see 16)
44 cheap çayxana......................E2
45 Dafne....................................D4
46 Mamounia Lounge................G3
47 Travellers Coffee..................D4
48 Xəlifə....................................E3

⊜ **Entertainment**
49 Baku Jazz Center..................E3
   Bowling................................(see 32)
50 Dövlət Pantomima Teatrı.......E2
   e11even...............................(see 17)
51 Face Club..............................B5
52 Gold/Infiniti Club..................D3
53 International Muğam Centre....C7
54 Opera & Ballet Theatre..........E4
   Park Cinema........................(see 32)
55 Rock Club..............................D1
56 Theatre Ticket Booth.............F4

⊜ **Shopping**
57 Təzə Bazar............................D2
58 Xəzər Balıqı...........................F4

ⓘ **Information**
59 Aptek Həyat...........................D3
60 British Embassy......................F3

61 French Embassy.....................D5
62 Iran Consulate.......................B2
63 US Embassy...........................D1

ⓘ **Transport**
64 Aeroflot.................................E4
65 AeroSvit.................................A1
66 Air Astana..............................B1
67 AST Turizm (Istanbul bus)......E4
   Austrian Airlines...................(see 65)
68 Axundov Bağ bus stop............B5
69 AZAL (Azerbaijan Airlines)......E3
70 Beş Mərtəbə Bus Stop............C3
71 Bus 116 to Airport.................F3
72 Bus 136 to Mərdəkən.............F3
73 Bus 6 (106) towards Kral.........A1
74 Buses 1 and 14 to Centre.......H2
75 China Southern......................F3
76 Kavaşoğlu (Istanbul Bus).......E4
   Lufthansa.............................(see 65)
77 Mahmut Turizm.....................D4
78 Northbound Bus 288..............E5
79 Northbound Buses.................E3
80 Northbound Buses.................E4
81 S7 Airlines............................G2
82 SCAT Kazakhstan Airlines......G3
83 Turkmenistan Ferry
   Ticket-Window.......................H4
84 Ural Airlines..........................F3
85 Uzbekistan Airlines................F3

AZERBAIJAN BAKU (BAKI)

new **Baku Expo Centre** (Binə Hwy), beyond the Buta Palace near Suraxanı. The world-class **Baku Jazz Festival** is usually held in October.

🛏 Sleeping

Many Baku hotels are shockingly overpriced at walk-in rates but online brokers and travel agencies often offer discounts. Even in pricier places service is often overfamiliar and sometimes incompetent, if friendly and willing. Much is likely to change in the top-end price range with six major hotel openings slated by 2013.

OLD CITY

Sultan Inn   BOUTIQUE HOTEL $$$
(Map p204; ☎4372305; www.sultaninn.com; Böyük Qala küç 20; s/d AZN271/295; ❄🛜) This luxurious 11-room boutique hotel hits a fine balance between opulent elegance, cosy comfort and trendy modernism. The perfectly central Old City location is a great plus, but prices

are steep – AZN10 for a coffee in its rooftop restaurant, though that does get you unparalleled views of the Maiden's Tower.

Qonaq Evi Buta   GUESTHOUSE $$
(Map p204; ☎4923475; www.butahotel.com; Qasr küç 16; s/d incl breakfast AZN70/80; ❄🛜) Enter this well-kept little gem via a lounge decked with cushions and traditional copperwork. Climb the stairs past etchings and a few antiques to well-presented modern rooms with silk paintings on the walls and rugs on the wood-effect floors. Breakfast is in the 4th-floor rooftop view-room, but there's no lift.

Hotel Kichik Gala   HOTEL $$
(Map p204; ☎4371950; www.hotelkichik gala.com; Kiçik Qala 98; s/d/tw incl breakfast AZN120/130/140; ❄🛜) While room sizes vary, most are unusually large for the Old City, the linens are high quality and autumnal decor was refreshed during 2011. Advance bookings can score major discounts (around AZN90).

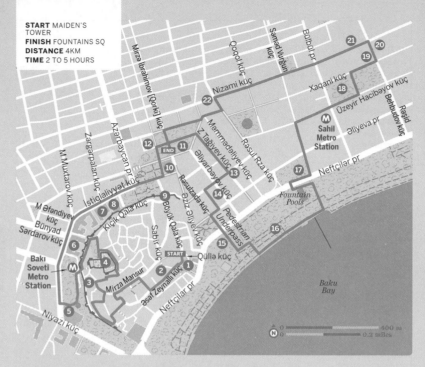

START MAIDEN'S TOWER
FINISH FOUNTAINS SQ
DISTANCE 4KM
TIME 2 TO 5 HOURS

Walking Tour
Exploring Baku

Start by wandering the alleyways of **İçəri Şəhər**, Baku's Unesco-protected Old City, possibly using the info booth's interesting audio guide if you have a couple of hours to spare. In any case, be sure to climb the ① **Maiden's Tower**, compare colourfully touristy ② **Zeynallı küç** with still-lived-in ③ **backstreet areas** and ④ **Palace of the Shirvanshahs**.

Exit into grand İstiqlaliyyət küç, near the handsomely renovated ⑤ **Filarmoniya** concert hall. Curving northeast you'll pass the noble, late-19th-century ⑥ **Baku City Hall**, the equally grand ⑦ **Institute of Manuscripts** and ⑧ **Ismailiya Palace**. Beyond lies the Old City's sturdy, castle-style ⑨ **Double Gateway**, while on your left is the statue-inlayed facade of the ⑩ **Nizami Literature Museum**.

Behind that, ⑪ **Fountains Square** is a great place for people-watching where you can find inexpensive refreshment at male-dominated ⑫ **Kafe Araz** or more indulgently (yet still reasonably) at the nearby

⑫ **Cafe City**. The surrounding tree-lined streets are full of pubs, restaurants and century-old 'oil-boom' mansions, including one that houses the ⑬ **Historical Museum**.

Backtrack via the historic, if over-renovated, ⑭ **Jewellery Arcade** to an underpass beneath thundering Neftçilər pr and emerge beside the dinky old ⑮ **Puppet Theatre**.

Stroll along the ⑯ **bulvar**, gazing across the Caspian's oil-rainbowed waters towards the world's tallest flagmast.

When traffic allows, cross back across Neftçilər pr to the colonnaded ⑰ **Carpet Museum**. Continue through Baku's commercial centre to ⑱ **Sahil Garden** ringed by several fine buildings including the statue-encrusted ⑲ **Axundov Kitabxana** (national library) and the classically styled ⑳ **Rəşid Behbudov Song Theatre**, once Baku's main synagogue.

From the city's twin-spired 1911 ㉑ **Opera House**, Baku's most cosmopolitan pedestrianised shopping street, ㉒ **Nizami küç**, leads you back to Fountains Sq.

Old City Inn

HOTEL **$$**

(Map p204; 4974369; www.oldcityinn.com; 10-ci Kiçik Qala alley, 16; s/d/king AZN70/80/90; ✳@🖑) Friendly and well run by students of the Western University's tourism course, the 15 rooms are assorted shapes and sizes – biggest but still not enormous are the 'king' options. Those residents who can manage five flights of stairs enjoy breakfast with 360-degree city views,

Museum Inn

BOUTIQUE HOTEL **$$**

(Map p204; 4971522; www.museuminn.az; Q Mahammad küç 3; r AZN160-200; ✳🖑) Selling points of this eight-room hideaway are the Maiden Tower views, the vine-draped rooftop and the playful Disney-Tuscan interior with lashings of ironwork and stone cladding. Rooms come with stripy wallpaper and rugs on cork floors, but two of them are windowless and there's no lift.

Noah's Ark Hotel

HOTEL **$**

(4373996; www.noahsark-hotel.com; İlyas Əfəndiyev küç\ç; s/d from AZN50/70; ✳@🖑) Worth considering in preference to a hostel, this friendly nine-room place goes out of its way to be helpful, provides free bicycle rental (only one) and has brilliant city views from its basic rooftop cafe. No lift, breakfast costs extra, mind your head on the stairway.

Atropat Hotel

HOTEL **$$**

(Map p204; 4978950; www.atropathotel.com; Magomayev küç; s/d/tr/ste AZN150/170/200/250; ✳🖑) Pleasant, calm, upper-market option with golden bedspreads and curtains, a small fitness and subterranean fitness room. It's a step up from many Old City hotels but overpriced at rack rates given the skeleton staff, malfunctioning lamps and less-than-fluffy towels.

King Palace Hotel

HOTEL **$$**

(Map p204; 4980000; www.kingpalace.az; İlyas Əfəndiyev küç; s/d AZN60/80; ✳🖑) Good-sized rooms at very fair prices. A few lamps need fixing and corridor walls are far from stylish but staff are enthusiastic – one a Sherlock Holmes fan, another a regular Babadağ climber. Breakfast comes with decent real coffee in the sizeable, well-appointed restaurant.

Altstadt Hotel

GUESTHOUSE **$**

(Map p204; 4933492; aae@box.az; Mammadyasov küç 3/2A; s/d/tr incl breakfast AZN40/50/60; ✳🖑) Simple eight-room homestay-style guesthouse. Rough edges include hidden mini-steps, collapsing shower curtains and some carpet scuffing, but it's peaceful and has the cheapest private rooms you'll find in the Old City.

Caspian Hostel

HOMESTAY HOSTEL **$**

(Map p204; 4921995; seyf@box.az; Əsəf Zeynallı küç 29; dm AZN16; ✳🖑) Although bookable on international hostelling sites, Baku's minuscule backpacker bastion is certainly not a youth hostel – just a communal room in a friendly family's low-rise old-town apartment. Six thin, hard, dorm bunks plus one double bed share a kitchenette and a shower-toilet. Washing-machine usage costs AZN3.

CITY CENTRE

Hotel Hale Kai

HOTEL **$$**

(Map p208; 5965056; hotelhalekai.com; Mirza Ibrahimov küç 18; r incl breakfast €120; ✳🖑) Smart, central, American-owned 25-room hotel with decor inspired by Frank Lloyd Wright and featuring Modigliani-style paintings by a Georgian artist. Rooms are big and even the smallest comes with kitchenette. The small lobby bar has an art deco vibe.

Azcot Hotel

GUESTHOUSE **$$**

(Map p204; 4972507; www.azcothotel.com; N Rəfibəyli 20; r from AZN100; ✳🖑) In a fabulously central 1885 mansion, period settees, large Chinese vases and tasteful landscape paintings make the bright new corridors feel homely. The comfortable rooms have kettles and minibars. But don't expect a big business hotel; the experience is more like having a room in a large private house.

Yacht Club

HOTEL **$$**

(Map p208; Yaxt Klub; 5981895; yclub@caspar.az; s/d/ste AZN120/140/210; ✳🖑) Colours don't always match and the 26 rooms are functional rather than stylish but the selling point of this blue-glass arc is that it's perched on stilts above the Caspian waters. Receptionists dress in naval uniform to emphasise the nautical theme.

Cənub Hotel

CRASH PAD **$**

(Map p208; 5981152; Zərifə Əliyeva küç 31; r AZN30-40; 🖑) If you're on a serious budget, the Cənub's low prices and central location might just about make up for the rotting walls, inconsistent hot-water supply and broken air-con. Some corridors and landings retain a distant memory of Soviet-era grandeur but the whole place is desperately in need of renovation and might even be demolished before you read this.

TRAIN STATION AREA

The gleaming new Hilton and JW Marriott Absheron tower hotels, facing off across Azadlıq Sq, are due to open shortly.

TOP CHOICE Landmark Hotel BUSINESS HOTEL $$$
(Map p208; ☑4652000; www.thelandmarkhotel.az; Nizami küç 90A; s/d AZN230/295 ste AZN259-324; ✱@◌⟐) Stunning views complement suave minimalist decor in huge rooms making this discreet hotel one of Baku's most sought-after business lodgings. Impressive bathrooms come with giant rainforest shower and rather silly electronic self-flushing toilets. The whole 10th floor of the tower is given over to a gym and infinity pool with more great views.

Hotel Respublika Lyuks HOTEL $$$
(Map p208; ☑5981056; www.hotelrespublika.com; Xaqani küç 24; ste AZN180-450; ✱◌) This impressive latter-day stone mansion makes no attempt to advertise that it's a hotel, but standards are high and prices fair by Baku standards. Large, plush rooms have deep-brown bedclothes, parquet floors and small chandeliers. Bathrooms include a bidet. Each pair of standard suites shares a large lounge (with desk and big, flat-screen TV) and smaller kitchen. Wi-fi costs a cheeky AZN4 per hour.

OUTER SUBURBS

Kempinski Hotel Batamdar BUSINESS HOTEL $$$
(Map p203; ☑5389090; www.kempinski.com/en/baku Muşfiq küç 1c; r internet/rack rates from AZN149/220; ✱◌⟐) Just beyond the Botanical Gardens, this brand-new five-star hotel complex comes with seasonal Aqua Park, spa and entertainment centre.

Hyatt Hotels BUSINESS HOTELS $$$
(Map p208; ☑4961234; www.baku.hyatt.com; 1033 İzmir küç; from s/d Park AZN295/319, Regency AZN224/248; ◌⟐) Baku's longest-standing business stalwarts. Prices may fall during 2012 as several big new competitors open.

Araz Otel HOTEL $
(Map p208; ☑4905063; www.arazhotel.az; Yusif Səfərov küç 30; r AZN40-80; ✱◌) Popular with Turkish traders and a trickle of travellers, the Araz was refitted in 2009 and offers about the best-value budget accommodation in Baku. Even the smallest rooms have high ceilings and full bathroom facilities but

be warned that the cheapest versions face a thunderingly busy road. Getting here takes around 15 minutes on bus 1 (from outside the train station) or bus 14 (from the bulvar). Receptionists speak English. Wi-fi costs AZN1 per day.

East Legend Hotel HOTEL $$
(Map p203; ☑4916717; www.eastlegent.az; Xanlar küç 38; s/d AZN100/120; ✱◌⟐) This professionally managed midrange hotel has comfy rooms, pseudo-antique elements and a tiny swimming pool in the central quadrangle. Baku Bay views are memorable from the rooftop **restaurant** (mains AZN6-12, cocktails AZN5.50-7). The downside is the hotel's Bayıl location: it's just off the bus 20 route, one block east of the visible Crown Hotel, but getting back into town can be annoying due to heavy traffic and the one-way system. Internet rates start around AZN60.

Ramada Şixov Beach RESORT $$$
(Map p203; ☑4917303; www.ramadabaku.com; Salyan Highway, Km 8; s/d/ste AZN180/220/310; ✱◌⟐) The closest beach hotel to central Baku is an arc of stepped modern glass where sea-view rooms all have a decent balcony. An excellent pool has connecting indoor-outdoor sections and jet-skis can be rented in season. Room decor is typical international style with full-sized king beds and ample space. Music can prove noisy during parties. Bus 124 passes outside. Four free guest-shuttles run to Azneft Sq (last return 11.45pm).

Apartment Rental

Numerous rental agents focus on the expat market but can offer daily rates for short stays. Quality varies but many properties are central and all are likely to have hot water and a kitchenette. English-speaking agents include the following:

Rena Salmanova APARTMENT SERVICE $
(☑050 3142439; http://travelazerbaijan.land.ru; 1-/2-room apt from US$30/45) Five-night minimum.

Baku Services APARTMENT SERVICE $$
(☑4189661; www.bakuservices.com; from US$90)

Marina Mednikova APARTMENT SERVICE $
(☑050 4507740; www.bakurealestate.net; from US$40) Three-night minimum.

 Eating

Baku is a culinary treat, but prices in top restaurants are equal to any in Western

Europe, and you'd be wise to always check before ordering a cup of tea or coffee which, in the most extreme cases, might add AZN30 to the bill! Fortunately there are plenty of bargains to seek out, and if you want to save money many very good midrange restaurants offer bargain lunch menus from Monday to Friday.

OLD CITY & FOUNTAINS SQUARE

Muğam Club   AZERBAIJANI $$$

(Map p204; ✑4924085; Rzayeva küç 9; meals/beers from AZN20/5, kebabs AZN15-20; ☺11am-11pm; ◙) Historic two-storey caravanserai with stone alcoves and a colourful coverable courtyard complete with two dwarf fig trees. Except on Sundays, dinners are accompanied by an impressive cabaret showcasing various Caucasian musical and dance styles. The Azeri food is excellent but prices can be exorbitant; there's a 15% service charge too. Often closed for private functions.

Cafe City   INTERNATIONAL $$

(www.cafecity.az; mains AZN5-15, coffees/beers from AZN2.90/2.80; ☺11am-midnight, to 2am Fri & Sat; ✳◙) Fəvvarə (Map p204; İslam Səfərli küç 1A); Sahil (Map p208; Rəşid Behbudov küç 8) Fashion-conscious without pretentions, Cafe City adds tasteful carved screenwork to two elegant Baku buildings. The picture menu offers a mouthwatering array of international cuisine; there's an AZN8 weekday lunch deal and a regional 'cuisine of the month'. Its Fountains Sq (Fəvvarə) branch has an in-demand outdoor terrace.

Yeni Bəh Bəh Club   AZERBAIJANI $$

(Map p204; ✑4988734; www.bah-bahclub.com; Əliyarbəyov küç 9; mains AZN6.50-14; ☺1.30-11.30pm; ✳◙) Kilims on walls, heavy wooden tables and costumed waiters serving up an excellent selection of regional food including *sac* (sizzler roast) dishes, Şəki dolma (miniature dolma served in a clay pot) and *ləvəngi* (Talysh stuffed chicken). The live music is low key.

Chocolate 2   INTERNATIONAL $$

(Map p204; Kiçik Qala 124; mains AZN10-17, coffee/cocktails from AZN3/6; ☺noon-11.30pm, kitchen to 10.30pm; ✳◙) With unusually high vaulting, Chocolate 2 hits the right balance between suave casual calm and a certain refined elegance. Meal options cover a gamut of styles, but this is also a fine spot if you just want a relaxed drink.

Paul's   GERMAN $$

(Map p204; ✑055 5200092; www.pauls-baku.com; Zərgəpalan küç; mains AZN12.50-30, beers AZN4-7; ☺6pm-late Mon-Sat; ◙) Hidden away in an ivy-draped, tree-shaded yard this genuinely German beer garden has a short menu of what expats swear to be the best sausages, pork and steaks (the T-bone is AZN29) in town washed down with real Weissbier. For winter there's a wooden cottage area inside.

Karvansara Restaurant   AZERBAIJANI $$

(Map p204; Böyük Qala küç 11; mains AZN6-10; ☺10am-9.30pm; ◙) Choose from two 14th-century caravanserais, one offering atmospheric stone cell-rooms around an open courtyard, the other an intriguing dungeon-like cellar.

L'Aparté   INTERNATIONAL, AZERBAIJANI $

(Map p204; İstiqlaliyyət küç 51; mains AZN2.50-6, beers from AZN1.60; ☺24hr; ✳◙) Descending into this colourfully panelled three-room basement feels like entering an upmarket club, yet the prices are ultrabudget and the food is perfectly acceptable, albeit without much flair.

Ali & Nino Cafe   INTERNATIONAL, CAFE $$

(Map p204; www.alinino.az; Z Tağiyev 16; meals from AZN5; ☺9am-11pm; ✳🛜◙) Just off Fountains Square, this small, attractive cafe is painted to evoke Baku of the WWI era and decorated with Molla Nasreddin cartoons. Food ranges from English breakfasts to grilled trout via burgers, sandwiches and many coffee-cake possibilities. The AZN5 weekday lunch mini-buffet is a great deal. In the block south of here you'll find a steakhouse, Mexican restaurant, a decent Italian eatery and several pubs.

Adams Curries   INDIAN $$

(Map p204; Fountains Sq; mains AZN8-15, rice AZN3-8, beers AZN2-4; ☺11am-1am; ✳◙) Arguably Baku's best curries served at a new location on the edge of Fountains Sq. The outdoor seating makes it popular as an expat drinking spot.

Kafe Araz   AZERBAIJANI, TEAHOUSE $

(Map p204; İslam Səfərli küç 3; beers/teas from AZN1.20/2, snacks 60q-AZN4; ☺24hr) For little more than the price of a takeaway, the Araz offers decent doner kebabs that you can eat on a shaded, open-air terrace on the edge of Fountains Sq. Though clientele is predominantly male, women aren't unknown here.

Sunset Café
AMERICAN $$

(Map p204; Əziz Əliyev küç 9; sandwiches AZN8.80-11.50; ⊗noon-11pm Mon-Sat, noon-10.30pm Sun; ✳️💵) The ugly glass-fronted building is an eyesore, but the cinema-themed interior is perfectly pitched, while generous salads, giant burgers and excellent sandwiches keep a faithful clientele happy.

Kafe Fəvvarə
SANDWICHES, CAFE $$

(Map p204; Fountains Sq; snacks AZN4.50-7, pizza AZN5.40-8, mains AZN9-14; ⊗noon-11pm; ✳️🛜💵) Modern minimalist cafe with sturdy air-conditioning, ample outdoor seating and great views over Fountains Sq. There's a great-value AZN6 weekday lunch deal (soup, pasta/pizza and drink).

Xutor
UKRAINIAN $$

(Map p204; M Muxtarov küç 9/3; mains AZN5-10; ⊗11am-11pm; ✳️) Cottage atmosphere with costumed waitresses and great value AZN6 lunch. Menus in Cyrillic.

Maharaja
INDIAN $$

(Map p204; Əlizadə küç; veg/meat mains AZN8/15; ⊗11am-11pm; ✳️💵) Curry prices include rice in this gently upmarket Indian restaurant decorated with giant metal-filigree *aftafas* (water jugs), upstairs in the Shakespeare Pub.

Tandir
AZERBAIJANI TAKEAWAY $

(Map p204; Kiçik Qala; qutab 70-90q, mains AZN4-6; ⊗8am-8pm) Aproned grannies serve up fresh *qutab* (Azeri stuffed pancakes), *düşbərə* (mini-ravioli) and *çığırtma* (glorified chicken omelette) at this pleasant but simple open-sided chalet-stall with just four bench seats.

CENTRAL BAKU

TOP CHOICE Çinar
ASIAN FUSION $$

(Map p208; www.chinar-dining.com; Şövkət Ələkpərova küc 1; snacks AZN6.50-12.50, mains AZN7.50-21, beers/cocktails from AZN3/8; ⊗noon-2am, kitchen noon-3pm & 6-11pm; ✳️💵) At the foot of the funicular, this fashion-conscious lounge-restaurant sports a 'theatre kitchen' producing imaginative Asian-fusion food, including designer sushi (try the mackerel with olive and pine nuts). There's a hip cocktail bar and a plush garden area with lime-green sofa seats shaded with white drapes. An extraordinary range of exotic teas (AZN5) is served in artistically sculpted pots.

Trin Trava
RUSSIAN $$

(Map p208; ☎4379857; Xaqani küç 42; mains AZN5-9.50, fish dishes AZN8-16; ⊗12.30-11pm; ✳️💵) Decked out in *izba* (Siberian cottage) style, Trin Trava creates a merrily festive mood with log-panelled walls, tavern lanterns and plenty of Russian village atmosphere. The food is excellent and sensibly priced. Bookings are advised for dinner. Music from 7pm. Next door, the co-owned **Blinnaya Bistro** serves Baku's best pancakes (from 40q) until 10.30pm.

Park Bulvar
FOOD COURT $$

(Map p208; www.parkbulvar.az; Bulvar; ⊗10am-midnight; ✳️💵) This ultramodern shopping mall seems an odd addition to a nationally 'protected' park but its 3rd-floor food court offers a vast selection of cuisines that you can take out to eat on the open balcony (beside KFC) for super Baku Bay views. One storey above, bustling brasserie-winebar **Kitchenette** has similar views albeit at far higher prices (coffee AZN4, Chassagne-Montrachet AZN195 a bottle) while **Zeytun** serves refined Azeri favourites.

Fayton Club
AZERBAIJANI $$

(Map p208; ☎4988101; www.fayton.az; Rəşid Behbudov küç 17; meals AZN6-18, beers from AZN2; ✳️🛜💵) Handicrafts, a pair of pony-carts and a fake well make an almost-successful attempt to create a feel of 18th-century Azerbaijan, though this jars with the plush velveteen chairs and ironed tablecloths. The menu is classic Azeri and there's a varying program of local music from 7.30pm (AZN5 admission). Can get loud.

U Dali
GEORGIAN $$

(Map p204; ☎4949356; Mirzə İbrahimov küç 7; mains AZN6-8; ⊗10am-11pm; ✳️) Tasty Georgian home-cooking served at sweetly unsophisticated wooden booths in a basement full of drinking horns, shepherd costumes and a few budgies. The house wine (AZN12 per litre) is a dry red Saperavi, and *khachapuris* (cheese pies) come in large multiperson size (AZN10). Other good choices for Georgian cuisine include stylistically challenged **Imereti** (Xaqani küç 13; ✳️💵) and cosy little **Tiflis Taverna** (mains AZN4-6; Rəşid Behbudov küç 33; ⊗noon-midnight; ✳️) where menus are only in Russian.

Art Restoran
INTERNATIONAL, AZERBAIJANI $

(Map p208; Xaqani küç 19; mains AZN2.40-6, kebabs AZN3-4, beers AZN1.80; ⊗24hr; ✳️💵) Open all hours with a wide-ranging menu and surprisingly plush decor given the bargain price range. Add AZN1.20 or so for the garnish with most main courses. Local Azerbaijani wine from AZN4.80 a bottle.

La Strada Trattoria
ITALIAN $$
(Map p208; www.lastrada.az; D Əliyeva küç; pastas AZN12-14, pizza AZN7-14, mains AZN15-26; ☺noon-11.30pm; ✹🌐) Wine boxes, herb jars and checkerboard floors bring life to the high, whitewashed vaults of this relaxed Italian restaurant. There's a good-value AZN8 weekday lunch menu.

Çudo Peçka
BAKERY $
(snacks 20q-AZN1.60; ☺8am-11pm) Çudo Peçka Station (Map p208; Füzüli küç 79); Çudo Peçka 1 (Map p204; Azərbaycan pr 5); Çudo Peçka 3 (Bülbül küç 5) Twelve branches of this citywide bakery chain offer seating and/or stand-to-eat ledges for nibbling a wide range of pastries and snacks. Prepay your order before collection. The station branch has old photos and an amusingly satirical painted frieze of Baku circa 2004.

Taboo
MEDITERRANEAN $$$
(Map p208; ☎5981910; www.taboo-baku.com; F Əmirov, 1st fl; mains AZN16-35, pizza AZN10-14; ✹🌐) Mediterranean food with a Caspian twang served in a large, colourful Tim Burton-style fantasy dining room with surreal furniture set around a gilded zebra.

Anadolu
TURKISH $
(Map p208; www.anadolu.az; meals incl 1 side dish AZN6.30-8.50; ☺7am-11pm; ✹📶🌐) Anadolu 1 (Puşkin küç 5); Anadolu 2 (Rəsul Rza küç 3/5) Best known of numerous Turkish restaurants serving comparatively inexpensive precooked meals in pleasantly appointed premises.

Tbilisi
GEORGIAN $
(Map p208; Rezaoğlu küç 44; mains AZN3-7, bread AZN1, beers from 75q; ☺11am-10pm; ✹) Although one of the city's cheapest Georgian eateries, the food is reliable, there's a vague attempt at interior decor and a small yard offers outdoor seating.

Yolki Palki
RUSSIAN $$
(Map p208; Ëlki Palki; mains AZN5-10, beers AZN4; ☺noon-11pm; ✹🌐) Central (☎4942492; Qoqol küç 15); Yasamal (☎4926427; M Hüseyn küç 58) This jolly, if cramped, log-walled cellar restaurant fills with whooping live Romani music after 7pm.

Brot Haus
GERMAN BAKERY $
(Map p208; www.brothaus.az; Nizami küç 78; bread AZN0.60-4.50; ☺8am-10pm) Baguettes, seeded rolls, German wholegrain bread and the most unctuous blueberry muffins (AZN1.10) in town. Takeaway only.

Pizza Gusto
PIZZERIA $
(Map p208; ☎050 3165489; www.pizzagusto.az; Qoqol (Mardanov Kardəşləri) küç 7; pizza AZN5-10; ☺11.30am-11pm; ✹🌐) Inexpensive thin-crust pizza, eat in or delivered to your door. Lunch bargains available.

Nənəmin
AZERBAIJAN TAKEAWAY $
(Map p208; Süleyman Rəhimov küç; pirojki/qutab from 20/30q; ☺8am-8pm) Queue at this takeaway window for excellent fresh-cooked *qutabs*.

OUTER SUBURBS
Hyatt Area
Scalini
ITALIAN $$$
(Map p208; ☎5982850; Bakixanov küç 2; pizzas AZN9.50-18, mains AZN21-30; ☺noon-2.30pm & 7-11pm; ✹🌐) Baku's longest-lasting and most convincing Italian restaurant, Scalini remains congenial if pricey with soaring high ceilings and a decor of classic Martini and film posters.

Qorodok
AZERBAIJANI $$
(off Map p203; www.qorodok.az; A Şaiq küç 245A; mains from AZN5, small/large beers AZN1.50/2.50; ☺noon-2am; ✹) If you're staying at the Hyatt but want something a little more local in atmosphere, walk a block southwest (past Japanese and Chinese restaurants) then uphill to the right to find a trio of possibilities. Qorodok is the most interesting of the three with pirate-ship interior and a range of Azeri and Russian meals. Before 4pm there's a range of precooked 'bistro' dishes (AZN3 to AZN8) but the leatherbound menus are only in Russian.

Batamdar
Şəki
AZERBAIJANI $$
(Map p203; ☎5024481; kebabs AZN5-9; ☺11am-11pm) This small row of garden dining-booths is a bit of a trek from the centre and the decor is nothing fancy. However, the quality of kebabs is unbeatable, the salad selection includes a spicy aubergine paste and the *dovğa* (yoghurt soup) is the best we tasted anywhere. Note that there's no written menu and pricing, while fair, is opaque. It's beside the Botanical Gardens, relatively handy for the new Kempinski. Bus 3 from Monolit/Fountains Sq passes outside.

Tele-Qüllə
INTERNATIONAL $$$

(☎5370808; Ak Abbaszadə küç 2; mains AZN25-50, kebabs AZN10-25, beers AZN8; ☺noon-midnight; ✽🍽) Dining at this revolving restaurant is the only way to gain access to Baku's iconic Soviet-era TV Tower. Views are sensational and the upscale menu includes beef in cognac, pepper-and-lemon tiger prawns and various lobster dishes. Reservations are essential. Note: if you don't eat a meal there'll be an AZN30 minimum fee for your drinks. Bus 6 (106) from Şahidlər Xiyabani stops within seven minutes' walk of the entrance.

Drinking

Stroll along the bulvar on a warm evening and you'll find countless cafes. The cheapest serve tea/beer from AZN2/1 but always double-check prices as variation can be enormous. Central Baku's suave coffee houses rarely charge less than AZN3/4 for an espresso/cappuccino or AZN5 for one of those scrumptious cake slices to accompany it. There are many expat bars in the centre, especially west of Fountains Sq between Tolstoy and Əlizadə streets. Plush new lounge bars and superexpensive tea parlours are scattered far more widely out into the suburbs.

OLD CITY & FOUNTAINS SQUARE

Otto
PUB

(Map p204; Facebook ottoefesbeercafe; Məmmədaliyev küç; small/large Efes beers AZN3/4; ☺noon-3am) The beer tap is a saxophone, the walls are bare stone vaults and the big windows slide open to allow a cooling through draught. Live rock music from 10.30pm nightly.

Garaj
PUB

(Map p204; Məmmədaliyev küç; beers from AZN2.20, Boddingtons AZN4; ☺11am-4am) Expat pub decorated with tool kits, graffiti wallscapes and a car chassis flying through the ceiling. The stand-and-drink tables outside catch evening sunshine.

Brewery
MICROBREWERY

(Map p204; İstiqlaliyyət küç 27; small/large beers AZN2/3, meals AZN12-18; ☺10am-midnight) Baku's brew-pub creates three varieties of very acceptable ale, served in a stone-vaulted basement with heavy wooden furniture. Germanic meals and pricey beer snacks are available.

Finnegans
PUB

(Map p204; Əlizadə küç; beers from AZN2.50; ☺11am-1am) Old faithful Anglo-Irish pub decorated with diving helmets and big wrought-iron lamps in high vaults. Draught Guinness is AZN6 a pint.

Café Caramel
CAFE

(Map p204; coffee AZN3-5; ☺11am-11pm) Old City (Böyük Qala 21); Centre (Əlizadə küç 7) Great coffee and fresh cakes in two contrasting locations – the city centre branch is small and modern with a bridgelike upper level, albeit beneath century-old vaulting. The Old City branch is more indulgent with a vaguely 1930s feel and window seating that allows for some interesting people-watching.

Soviet Union
BAR

(Map p204; Z Tağiyev küç; beers from AZN3; ☺5pm-2am) Smoky basement nostalgia bar with a downmarket youthful vibe, sparsely decorated with a few Red Army garments and some fun photos of USSR's politburo stars.

Pivnushka Beer House
PUB

(Map p204; Rəsul Rza küç; beers from 50q, snacks 50q-AZN4; ☺11am-4am) Baku's cheapest beer attracts a boisterous mix of locals and foreigners. There are several other popular pubs around the same corner, which was nicknamed 'the Darkside' in early 2011 after a few expats suffered late-night, postpub muggings nearby.

Azza Bar
LOUNGE

(Map p204; ISR Plaza, 17th fl, Nizami küç 340; ☺6pm-1am) It's past its best, but the city views are hard to beat. Live soft jazz at 10.30pm on Fridays.

CENTRAL BAKU

Dafne
CAFE, RESTAURANT

(Map p208; Nizami küç; cocktails/coffee from AZN7/4.50; ☺11am-1am) Expertly mixed cocktails and luscious künəfə (a heated Turkish cake made of sweetened wheat strands, filled with melted cheese and topped with ice cream) are drawcards at this luxuriously relaxed lounge-cafe. It's mostly spread across a large open-air rooftop with dreamy night-time views of up-lit classic buildings.

2/5 Mərtəbə
AZERBAIJANI PUB

(Map p208; B Səfiroğlu küç; beers AZN2-4, mains AZN5-14, sausages AZN3-6; ☺9am-2am; ✽) Ropes, terracotta pots, strings of dried fish and cowhide seats make a lively decor at this congenial pub-restaurant. No English menu.

Xəlifə
TEAHOUSE

(Map p208; Rəşid Behbudov küç 17; tea set AZN30, beers AZN4-5, qalyan AZN15; ⊙7pm-2am) Lushly exotic Moroccan-themed tea lounge with belly dancers at 9pm and midnight.

Caspian Terrace
COCKTAIL BAR

(Map p208; Landmark Hotel, 20th fl, Nizami küç 90A; beers/wines/cocktails/coffees from AZN4/7/9/4; ⊙7am-midnight) This little-advertised open-air balcony offers jaw-dropping views across the Escheresque Dom Soviet (Government House) building and Baku waterfront. It's accessed through Shin-Shin Chinese restaurant at the Landmark.

Mamounia Lounge
LOUNGE

(Map p208; Hacibəyov küç 51; mains AZN9-21, beers/cocktails from AZN4/9; ⊙noon-midnight) Suave, upmarket lounge with lush gilded sofa seating, sushi snacks and DJs spinning beats after 7pm (cover charges possible on big nights).

3 Boçki
PUB

(Map p208; D Əliyeva küç 251; snacks AZN2.20-7, mains AZN5-20, beers AZN3-5; ⊙24hr) All-night Germanic beer and cocktail pub with seating inside giant barrels.

Travellers Coffee
CAFE

(Map p208; Nizami küç; coffees AZN4-7, mains AZN3.50-9, steaks AZN11-15; ⊙8am-10pm) Split-level Starbucks-style coffee house with some of Baku's best (if pricey) coffee and contrastingly inexpensive snack meals (quesadillas, sandwiches, pastas). AZN7 weekday lunch.

☆ Entertainment

For extensive what's on listings see www.bakucitylife.com.

Live Music

The Muğam Club (see p215) includes a cabaret of traditional music and dancing to accompany your meal. Other up-market restaurants, typically those in large suburban gardens, offer top Azeri pop stars singing at full blast. Many Westerners consider this more like punishment than entertainment.

International Muğam Centre
CONCERTS

(Map p208; www.mugam.az; Neftçilər pr 9) Although built with *muğam* in mind, this stylish new concert hall hosts a sparse schedule of concerts in an eclectic variety of styles.

Rock Club
ROCK, THRASH

(Map p208; www.facebook.com/therockclubbakili; Behbudov küç 66-68) Alternative music scene. Check the website for schedules.

Baku Jazz Center
JAZZ

(Map p208; ☏4936196; http://jazzcenter.jazz.az; Rəşid Behbudov küç 19; cover AZN7, mains/beers/cocktails from AZN7/3/6; ⊙7pm-midnight daily, live music from 9pm Tue-Sun) High-quality jazz performances feature almost every night (unless booked for private parties) in this large, if staid, venue with table seating. Meals available but not recommended.

Buta Palace
CONCERT VENUE

(Map p226; www.butapalace.az; Binə hwy, Suraxanı) When 50-Cent hits Baku it's to play the Buta Palace, way out towards the airport. Major DJ parties and similar events are often held here too.

Theatre & Classical Music

Baku has a vibrant arts scene. The theatre season runs from mid-September to late May, with the month's listings for 10 major venues on www.ryl.az/teatr.html.

Tickets for several venues are sold at the **theatre ticket booths** (Teatri və Konsert Biletləri; ⊙10am-2pm & 3-6pm) opposite Dom Soviet and beside Cafe Mozart.

Opera & Ballet Theatre
OPERA, BALLET

(Azərbaycan Dövlət Akademik Opera və Balet Teatrı; Map p208; ☏4931651; www.tob.az; Nizami küç 95) Most productions are lavish at this recently refurbished 1910 theatre and even the less exciting repertory performances are worth seeing, if only to admire the classically grand interior.

Dövlət Pantomima Teatrı
MIME

(Map p208; ☏4414756; Azadlıq pr 49; tickets AZN5) Superbly creative mime performances in a tiny theatre fashioned from a former chapel. Generally weekends only.

Filarmoniya
CONCERT VENUE

(Map p204; ☏4972901; www.filarmoniya.az; İstiqlaliyyət küç 2) With its twin Mediterranean-style towers, this Baku landmark was originally built as an oil-boom-era casino. The interior is as impressive as its architecture and there's an eclectic, if unpredictable, concert program.

Nightclubs

Face Club
CLUB

(Map p208; www.face.az; Nizami küç 10; cover varies; ⊙10pm-6am) Under renovation at the time

FREE NEWS

Several free English-language newspapers are available through restaurants and hotels. Their 'news' content is sometimes written in an impenetrable, propagandist English which is almost comical to decipher. They are more helpful if you want advertisements for apartment rentals, expat services, lunch deals and the latest new restaurants. Titles come and go but currently **Baku Weekly** seems the most commonly available.

of research, Face Club has been the most popular central club in recent years. Expect a stringent dress-code policy, hefty cover charge and significant minimum per-table spend.

Baku Karting   CLUB, KARTING
(Map p203; www.baku-karting.az; Dərnəgül) Party nights as well as go-karting sessions.

Up-market lounge bars like **Mamounia** (p219), **Megopolis** (Map p203), **Opera Lounge** (Map p203; www.facebook.com/Opera Lounge) and **e11even** (Map p208; Park Inn, 11th fl) sometimes have guest DJs. The **Buta Palace** has big 'Freedom Music' parties (AZN20) a few times a year.

Many other city-centre 'Disko Klubs' are contrastingly down-market basement dives, predominantly seen as prostitute pick-up spots. However, there are some (partial) exceptions, where groups of revellers will feel comparatively comfortable. **Gold/Infiniti** (Map p208; Qoqol (Mardanov Kardəsləri) küç; cover AZN5; ⊙7.30pm-6am) is less sleazy than most.

When not in Lahıc, youthful English-speaking guide **Ruslan Haciyev** (⊅050 6120553; rusik071@hotmail.com) offers visitors accompanied nocturnal rambles around a selection of Baku clubs.

Website www.hg2.com/cities/azerbaijan/baku/clubs has several club reviews.

Other

Park Bulvar Mall   ENTERTAINMENT CENTRE
(Map p208) On the 4th floor there's a **bowling alley** (AZN10 per person per game; ⊙10am-2am) and brand-new multiplex **cinema** (www. parkcinema.az; AZN3-8; ⊙10am-11pm) showing some films in 3-D.

Shopping

The main shopping street is pedestrianised Nizami küç, commonly still known by its Soviet-era moniker of Torgovaya (Trade St). There's an alluring array of upmarket boutiques along southern Rəsul Rza küç, western 28th May küç and on Ə Əliyev küç where the once great Karvan Jazz Club has become a D&G Store.

Carpets & Souvenirs

Carpets, along with Azeri hats and traditional copperware, might prove cheaper purchased in the provinces but they are conveniently sold though Ali Baba-esque shops around Baku's İçəri Şəhər. These are great places to browse with very little sales pressure. Dealers here will be familiar with the annoying carpet-export procedures – don't buy anything 'antique' and beware that any carpet bigger than 2 sq m will need an export permit.

Several stands in the old city sell a selection of (often tacky) souvenirs, along with old Soviet-era badges, medals and buttons. More of the same are available in subterranean shops beneath the passage leading east from Fountains Sq and at **Suvenir Noffel** (İslam Səfərli 3; ⊙11am-8pm), the well-stocked souvenir-section of a general book-and-clothes shop.

Caviar

During WWI, British soldiers found caviar to be 'cheaper than jam'. These days it's seriously pricey but still barely a third of the price you'd pay in western Europe. Officially packed 113g pots of 'legal' caviar sold at **Xəzər Balıqı** (Xaqani pr) cost AZN90/130 for sevruga/beluga.

At Baku's central market, **Təzə Bazar** (Map p208; Səməd Vurğun küç), you might find cheaper 'illicit' caviar in the fish section, hidden away behind the area of photogenically piled fruit. However, prices aren't necessarily much better and quality can be dodgy. Expats suggest buying reliable caviar through Paul's (see p215).

Bookshops

Ali & Nino Bookhouse   BOOKS
(Map p204; www.alinino.az; Z Tağiyev 19; ⊙11am-9pm) Stocks maps, postcards and a selection of books in English.

Chiraq Books   BOOKS
(Map p204; Zərgərpalan küç 4) English-language bookshop with decent range of classics,

bestsellers, travel guides and locally relevant titles.

Information

Dangers & Annoyances

The crime rate is very low. Overinquisitive police are more likely to bother you than criminals, though in 2011 there were a few late-night cases of single foreigners being robbed while exiting 'Darkside' pubs. Baku has a **Police Office of Crimes By & Against Foreigners** (☎4909532). Avoid photography on the metro, near the Presidential Administration Tower and halfway up the steps beside the funicular.

Internet Access

Internet cafes are very common, though often hidden away in basements.

Castle VIP (Map p208; Xaqani küç, per hr AZN1; ☺24hr; ▣) The fastest (if priciest) of three options on the north side of Molokan Gardens. Price drops to 20q per hour after midnight.

C@Z (Map p204; M Əfəndiyev küç; per hr 60q; ☺10am-2am; ▣) Vast subterranean internet club with Skype-phone options.

VIP Internet Klub (Map p204; Ü Bünyadzadə küç 3; per hr 80q-AZN1; ☺24hr) Very central and costs only AZN2 for an eight-hour session starting at midnight.

Left Luggage

At the train station are two **baggage rooms** (Saxlama Kameralari; small/large bag per day AZN1.10/2; ☺24hr). The bigger one is in the tunnel corridor accessed behind the main ticket-selling concourse.

Maps

Bookshops stock several city maps. Heron's (typically AZN8) is the most detailed but the 1:24,000 Turist Sxemi (AZN3.50) is cheaper and covers more of the suburbs.

Medical Services

A regularly updated list of emergency medical services appears on the US Embassy's website at http://azerbaijan.usembassy.gov/medical _services.html.

Aptek Həyat (Map p208; Bülbül pr 30; ☺24hr) All-night pharmacy.

MediClub (Map p208; ☎4970911; www.medi club.az; Üzeyir Hacıbəyov küç 45) Attractively appointed English-speaking clinic. Doctors' consultations from AZN29.50 by appointment 8am to 6pm, without appointment 6pm to 8am.

Money

ATMs are common throughout Baku. Exchange facilities are nearly as ubiquitous and don't charge commission. Rate-splits are excellent for US dollars (under 1%), good for euros, poorer but still competitive for Russian roubles and pounds sterling (around 4%). Various other currencies (including Georgian lari) can be changed in some change booths but on far less favourable terms. Some exchanges open late into the evening but most banks shut by 4pm. The best rates are usually available on 28 May küç at Vurğun Gardens (Map p208).

Post

Main post office (Map p208; Üzeyir Hacıbəyov küç 36; ☺stamp sales 9am-7pm)

Telephone

The few long-distance pay phones charge double what you'd pay in the central **Call Centre** (Beynəlxalq Telefon Danışıa Mərtəqəsi; Map p208; Şeyx Şamil küç 1; ☺9am-9pm), where calls cost 9q per minute to provincial Azeri towns and 27q to most international numbers.

Tourist Information

Tourist Information Office (Map p208; ☎4981244; www.tourism.az, www.bakutou rism.az; ☺9am-1pm & 2-6pm Mon-Fri) Gives away a range of glossy pamphlets but some information is (perhaps predictably) out of date.

Getting There & Away

Air

Baku's Heydar Əliyev International Airport (Map p226) is the busiest in the South Caucasus, with flights to/from plenty of European, Russian and Central Asian cities, plus Dubai, Tehran, Trabzon and Tbilisi. For many more Asian destinations, connect via Tashkent (Daşkənd) or Ürümqi using **Uzbekistan Airlines** (Map p208; ☎5983120; www.uzairways.com; Nizami küç 98) or **China Southern** (Map p208; ☎5981166; www.csair. com, www.flychinasouthern.com; 28 May küç 54; ☺9.30am-5pm Mon-Fri, 11am-4pm Sat) respectively.

Only **AZAL** (Azerbaijan Airlines, SW Travel; Map p208; ☎5988880; www.azal.az, www. swtravel.az; Nizami küç 66-68; ☺8am-8pm) offers domestic flights: at least four times daily to Naxçivan (AZN70/140 one-way/return for non-Azeris) and thrice weekly to Gəncə, Lənkəran and Zaqatala.

Boat

In principle, ferries run to Turkmenbashi, Turkmenistan (per metre-length passenger/motorbike/vehicle AZN72/90/70) several nights a week and to Aktau Kazakhstan (AZN80/100/75) every week or so. Berths are available for a token extra fee but these are primarily cargo ships so strict timetables don't exist – ferries leave as soon as sufficient cargo is loaded.

TURKMENISTAN Bus 1 stops within five minutes' walk of the port. If you have a vehicle, buy tickets at the first white door on the right after passing the Həyat Restaurant. The passenger ticket office is a minuscule window marked KASSA just beyond. Even though it looks permanently closed, it is usually manned from 9am till noon and for much of the afternoon – bang on the door or shutter! You'd be advised to visit a day before your planned departure to gauge the frequency of sailings and to return at 9am the day you want to leave, by which point, if a boat is slated to run that evening, it should be possible to buy the ticket. Even then the departure time will be only very approximate – be prepared for interminable delays both leaving Baku and arriving in Turkmenbashi. In past years passengers have waited as long as five days offshore. Fortunately, growing trade with Central Asia has improved ferry frequency of late and delays are rarely so hideous. In 2011 average waits were under 12 hours, but it's still wise to take ample supplies of food and water.

KAZAKHSTAN The Aktau ferry now leaves from a different port several kilometres further east. Ask a taxi for 57 Prichal (Göyərtə Eli Yeddi) in Əhmədli. However, given the long potential wait, it is often cheaper to fly (both AZAL and SCAT fly across the Caspian to Aktau).

Bus & Marshrutka

AVTOVAĞZAL (MAIN BUS STATION)

The big **main bus station**, nearly 10km north of central Baku, handles almost all intercity destinations except for Salyan, Qobustan and towns on the Abşeron Peninsula. Timetables are approximate, especially for the smaller Hyundai buses which tend to leave when almost full, whatever the electronic departure board might claim. If no bus is due to leave you might still find a nontimetabled *marshrutka* (minibus) gathering passengers in one of the numbered bays directly across from the bus stands.

Reaching the departure gates (floor 3) from entry-level (floor 2) requires transiting a labyrinthine shopping mall. Oddly, the tickets sold by the ticket desks (hidden on floor 1) are sometimes underpriced such that drivers demand a supplement: despite appearances this is not a scam!

There's usually no reason to book ahead except for overnight and international services, or on peak holiday weekends.

IRAN

Iranian bus companies offering daily services to Tabriz and Tehran include the following:

Seiro Safar Baku (☏055 4053883); Tabriz (☏0411 5552531)

DSG (Baku (☏4080929); Tehran (☏021 44693051)

Aram Safar (Baku ☏055 6022030); Tabriz ☏0411 5560597)

ISTANBUL

Several Turkish bus companies have services to Istanbul (AZN80) via Trabzon (AZN50), all departing at around 3pm on Tuesday, Thursday and Saturday from the main bus station. Most have conveniently central ticket offices around Sahil Gardens. Examples:

AST Turizm Central Baku (☏4931033; ast_baku@ hotmail.com; Xaqani küç 35); Bus station (☏4997168); Istanbul (☏0212-5886423)

Kavaşoğlu (Map p208; ☏4932280; Bülbül küç 10)

Mahmut Turizm (Map p208; ☏050 6886008, Istanbul ☏0212-6329979)

TRAINS DEPARTING BAKU

DESTINATION	VIA	DEPARTS	ARRIVES	FARE
Ağstafa	Gəncə	10.05pm	9.30am	AZN14 *kupe**
Astara	Lənkəran	7.40am	3pm	AZN5 seat**
Astara	Lənkəran	11pm	8.55am	AZN8 *kupe*
Balakən	Şəki	9.15pm	10.15am	AZN10 kupe
Gəncə	'express'	7.20am (not Thu)	3pm	AZN6 seat**
Qazax	Gəncə	10.20pm	11.50am	AZN10 *kupe*
Tbilisi	Gəncə	9pm	12.15pm	AZN36 *kupe*

*2nd-class train, no *platskart* (3rd class) available **day trains, no sleeper berths

BUSES DEPARTING BAKU BUS STATION

DESTINATION	DURATION (HR)	COST	NOTES
Gəncə	6½	AZN5.70	hourly
İsmayıllı	4	AZN4.20	hourly
Istanbul	36	AZN80	Tue, Thu, Sat
Lənkəran	5	AZN5	hourly
Qala Altı (for Çirax Qala)	3½	AZN5	10am; returns 6.45am next morning
Quba	2½	AZN4	hourly
Qusar	3	AZN4	hourly
Qırmızı Körpü (Georgian border)	10	AZN9.60	nine daily
Şamaxı	2	AZN3	8 daily
Şəki	6½	AZN6	hourly, mostly via Ağdaş
Sumqayıt direct	1	50q	every few minutes
Tbilisi (Georgia)	12	AZN12	seven daily, *kassa* 26
Tehran (via Tabriz)	19 (12)	AZN32 (AZN23)	9am, *kassa* 15 to 18

Train

All overnight trains give you a sleeping berth, so you can cross the country and wake up next morning in (or near) your destination for a price that's less than a hostel dorm. Fares include sheets that are handed out once the train is underway.

You'll need your passport both to buy a ticket and to board the train.

Trains also run regularly to many Russian and Ukrainian cities, but at the time of writing the Azerbaijan–Russia border remained closed to foreigners, limiting such routes to local travellers.

According to press reports the main train station might eventually move way out of town to Biləcəri.

ⓘ Getting Around

To/From Heydar Əliyev International Airport

Midsized bus 16 runs to the airport from the southeast corner of Vurğun Gardens (30q), every half hour between 7am and 8pm. From the airport it operates 6.30am to 7.30pm starting from a far-from-obvious spot at the far side of the car park from the terminal.

Taxis to the city centre cost around AZN25. Between 7.30pm and 11.30pm you could save money by paying a taxi around AZN10 to get you to Əzizbəyov metro station then continue by public transport.

Public Transport

BUS

As we go to press, Baku is starting to totally renumber the city bus routes. The full list is not yet clear but 288 becomes 88, 253 goes to 33, 106 is now 6 and 207 will become 17. There are likely to be many more changes by the time you read this so double-check carefully. A dauntingly vast network of buses runs from virtually anywhere to anywhere else within Baku for just 20q, though the complex one-way system makes for certain gaps and surprises. In some central areas and on major highway sections there are fixed *astanovki* (stopping points). Elsewhere the driver can usually squeal to a halt when someone shouts '*sakhla*' (stop) or, more subtly, taps a coin on the bodywork. Pay as you get off. A deeply ingrained code of bus chivalry often demands giving up one's seat to older or less able passengers. On packed-full buses don't be surprised if a seated stranger grabs your bag – they're not stealing it, just helpfully holding it to help you cope with the crush.

METRO

The metro's main line forms a vast rotated S from Dərnəgül to Həzi Aslanov with a couple of small spur lines. One such spur links the train station (metro 28 May) to the Old Town (metro İçəri Şəhər) via metro Sahil (for the Cənub Hotel). From İçəri Şəhər, direct trains run to Həzi Aslanov via Ulduz, Əzizbəyov, Qara Qarayev and Neftçilər metros (each with bus connections to certain Abşeron towns) but you'll need to change at 28 May for

BAKU BUS STOPS

Some key stops as they appear on bus sign boards:

» **28 May** Loosely interpreted to mean anywhere near the train station (Map p208).

» **Axundov Bağ** (Map p208) A triangular garden just north of İçeri Şəhər.

» **Azneft** (Map p204) The big traffic circle directly southwest of the Old City.

» **Beş Mərtəbə** (Map p208) Füzuli Sq.

» **Çimərlik** 'Beach', usually implying Şixov.

» **M xxxx** Suggests a stop near xxxx metro station .

» **MUM** (Map p208) Handy for western side of Fountains Sq.

» **Təzə Avtovağzal** (Map p203) Main Bus Station.

» **Vurğun Bağ** Anywhere around Vurğun Gardens (Map p208), just south of the train station.

20 Yanvar. That's currently the nearest metro to the bus station though a new spur line is under construction. Metro Azadlıq Prospekti (buses for Novxanı) is the stop before Dərnəgül.

Fares (AZN1 for six rides) must be credited to a smart card. These cost AZN2 which you can eventually recoup.

TAXI

The majority of taxis that wait street corners are not metered, many demanding around AZN5 minimum fare. However, the metered London-style cabs, introduced in 2011, are an exception with a flag fall of only AZN1 and very sensible kilometre rates. For longer rides call **Taxi189** (☑189; www.taxibaku.az; ☺24hr) which charges AZN3 minimum for up to 3km, or AZN3.80 for 4km plus 50q per km. Pay 20% more for a plusher 'bizniz' vehicle. You'll need to preorder by phone and they'll quote the total fare in advance.

AROUND BAKU

Abşeron Peninsula

☑012

The Abşeron confounds easy definition. Agricultural land is blanched by salt lakes, sodden with oil runoff and poisoned by pesticide abuse. Platoons of rusty oil derricks fill horizons with abstract metallic 'sculptures'. And where ever you look, new boxy houses are filling up the remaining areas of former sheep pasture. Yet despite mesmerising ugliness and a traditionally conservative population, the Abşeron still manages to be Baku's seaside playground. Meanwhile several historic castle towers peep between the *dachas,* fires that inspired Zoroastrian and Hindu pilgrims still burn, and beneath the cultural surface lie some of Azerbaijan's oddest folk beliefs. It's a perversely fascinating place.

SURAXANI

Hidden away in otherwise dismal Suraxanı is the unique **Ateşgah Məbədi** (☑4524407; admission/camera/guided tour AZN2/2/6; ☺9am-6pm). Part caravanserai, part fire temple, it stands on the site of a natural-gas vent that was sacred to Zoroastrians for centuries, though the temple's current incarnation was built by 18th-century Indian Shiva devotees. They lived in the surrounding pentagonal courtyard and reputedly performed extreme ascetic practices such as lying on hot coals or carrying unbearably heavy chains. Such eccentric behaviour is depicted by a number of mannequins in the museum section. But the temple's centrepiece is the flaming stone hearth with four stone side flues that also spit dragon breath...at least when the caretaker bothers to turn up the gas pressure. The original natural vent has long been exhausted, so today the flame comes courtesy of Baku's main gas supply.

There are areas of photogenically ugly oil derricks in fields nearby but several travellers report being hassled by security staff for taking pictures. Tourists aren't supposed to be interested in ugly things!

Access is by bus 84 that picks up from the south exit of Baku's metro station Əzizbəyov. From where it terminates, cross the railway through the almost abandoned commuter train station, turn left and walk three minutes along Atamoğlan Rzayev küç which turns right into the temple square.

Alternative access suggestions include bus 77 from Mərdəkən, *marshrutka* 231 from Qara Qarayev metro (via the historic town of Əmircan) or the extremely slow, convoluted bus route 33 starting behind Baku train station (70 minutes). The latter drops you at a junction that's five minutes' walk west of Suraxanı station.

QALA

Since 2008 the centre of historic little Qala village has been dominated by an impressive **Ethnographic Museum Complex** (☑4593714; admission/tour AZN2/8; ⊙10am-7pm), an open-air park featuring several furnished traditional buildings (house, smithy, potters workshop) set amid a wide range of archaeological finds and petroglyphs (many are reconstructions). Call to check which days it has craft demonstrations.

A shiny new metalcraft museum plus a convincing medieval-style stone **fortress** are nearing completion opposite.

Türkan-bound bus 101 from Baku's Ulduz metro passes within 200m of the museum complex.

Mərdəkən–Zirə bus 252 stops 400m further away at the main Qala crossroads.

MƏRDƏKƏN & ŞÜVƏLAN

Sprawling twin towns **Mərdəkən** and **Şüvəlan** together form a popular weekend *dacha* getaway for wealthy Bakuvians. The townscape is largely forgettable but hides a handful of interesting discoveries. At the east end of Şüvəlan, around 4km east of central Mərdəkən, **Mir Mövsöm Ziyarətgah** is one of Azerbaijan's most impressive new Muslim shrines replete with beautifully patterned Central Asian–style domes and an interior spangled with polished mirror mosaic facets. Most Azeris firmly believe that a wish made will come true. And when it does they return in droves, offering suitable donations to show their gratitude.

Take a bus back to central Mərdəkən to find the pleasant but overpriced **Arboretum** (Mərdəkən Dendrarisi; http://dendrary.in-baku.com; Yesenin küç 89; foreigners/locals AZN5/AZN2; ⊙9am-6pm), which has a cactus garden, boating pool, mini-zoo and fine century-old **oil-boom villa** in which sex-obsessed Russian poet Sergei Yesenin once wrote odes to the local womenfolk. Entry to the park is from the west gate down a side alley.

At the traffic light directly west of the arboretum, turn north, swing west again on Ramin Qazimov küç and next turn north once more to find **Pir Həsən**, a shrine area where superstitious locals queue up to have

AZERBAIJAN ABŞERON PENINSULA

Baku Metro

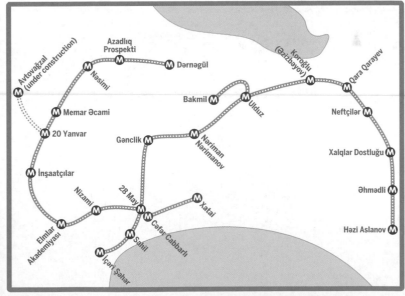

bottles smashed over their heads. Honestly. It's considered a cure for nervousness of spirit. The smashing occurs at the back of a little view-garden whose focus is the grave of oil baron Zeynalabdin Tağiyev beneath an egg-shaped stone pavilion, surrounded by archaeological fragments.

Hidden away in some vaguely interesting backstreets, Mərdəkən has two crenellated **castle towers** (admission free; ☉sporadic). The more interesting is the large square tower, set within a walled park along with a historic little mosque. The tower itself is rarely open but you can get close enough to take some good photos. It is accessed off Kolxoz küç, about 15 minutes' walk from Pir Həsən following Ramin Qazimov küç west. For buses back to Baku, continue 50m west on Kolxoz küç then walk south to re-find Yesenin küç, the main Baku road.

ℹ️ Getting There & Away

Little bus 36 from Baku's Vurğun Gardens runs to the Ziyarətgah via Mərdəkən, passing within walking distance of all of the sites. Bus 77 connects the Ziyarətgah, Mərdəkən and Suraxanı. For Nardaran change in Maştağa. Bus 144 runs directly between Mərdəkən and Maştağa. Alternatively, *marshrutka* 21 bumps through Şagan (passing a very ruined shard of 14th-century castle) to Buzovna's revered if unpretentious

Əliayağı Shrine where you could switch to (painfully slow) bus 7 for Maştağa.

NARDARAN

Nardaran is the closest that Azerbaijan comes to having a centre of conservative Islam, with women scarf-clad (if visible at all). The town's spiritual heart is the huge 1990s **Rehime Khanım Mosque**, built above the grave of the 7th Shiite Imam's sister. A two-minute walk beyond is a genuineif relatively plain **castle tower**. Bus 89 via western Maştağa picks up from the south exit of Baku's Əzizbəyov metro station and terminates right at the mosque's gates. To reach Yanar Dağ, change from the 89 to the 227 at the Zabrat roundabout.

YANAR DAĞ

In the 13th century Marco Polo mentioned numerous natural-gas flames spurting spontaneously from the Abşeron Peninsula. Most, as at Suraxanı, petered out when the drilling of oil wells reduced underground pressure. However, **Yanar Dağ** (Fire Mountain; admission AZN2) lives on, a 10m-long wall of fire that's been blazing away on this inconspicuous hillock since it was accidentally ignited by a shepherd's cigarette back in the 1950s. The site is not pristine: a broken-down old teahouse overlooks the scene and a new rubbish disposal plant looms nearby, but this

Abşeron Peninsula

remains one of the Abşeron's stranger sights. By public transport use clunky little bus 227 (30q, 30 minutes) departing from the northern exit of Əzizbəyov metro.

ABŞERON BEACHES

In summer, fearless local swimmers crowd the grey-brown beaches of the northern Abşeron coast. Though infamously polluted, the Caspian waters do often look temptingly turquoise and there are well-manicured sections of sand near **Mərdəkən** (bus 341 from metro Neftçilər) and on the pay beaches of **Amburan** (bus 72 from metro Əzizbəyov). Good alternatives lie north of **Novxanı** (bus 98 from metro Azadlıq Prospekti, 50q, 40 minutes) where you'll find the resort-style **AF Hotel** (✐4483030; www.afhotel.az; s/d AZN90/120; ✸🛜✚). It's built around an **Aquapark** (day use for nonresidents AZN15; ◷8am-8pm, summer only) where a busy trio of swimming pools and several tall waterslides are supplemented by various table and video games. The nearby beaches are packed in summer with snack stalls renting shade, 40q box toilets and AZN1 showers (*duş*) while close-packed locals bury each other in sand, splash in the waves, trot along on horseback or just picnic with the family.

Baku to Qobustan

The most popular day trip from Baku takes visitors to the mud volcanoes and petroglyphs around Qobustan, 60km south of the capital. En route is a fascinating collage of beaches, oil workings, shimmering seascapes, spirit-crushing Soviet townships and desolate semideserts. At Baku's southern limits, the **James Bond Oil Field** was so nicknamed after featuring in the opening scenes of the movie *The World Is Not Enough*. The area has been considerably tidied up since then but there are still plenty of nodding-donkey oil pumps at work. The scene is best surveyed from near **Bibi Heybət Mosque**, which was for centuries the region's holiest shrine. The original 13th-century mosque was demolished by the Soviets in 1934 and today's neo-Ottoman style structure dates from 1998. Bus 20 gets you here.

Just beyond is **Şixov Beach**, fascinating for photographing bathers gambolling on the 'sand' with a romantic backdrop of giant offshore oil rigs. There are hotels, restaurants and disco-beaches here should you

BUS NUMBERS

Bus numbers within Baku and to the Abşeron towns were correct at the time of research. However, a wholesale renumbering process is planned so while departure points are likely to stay the same don't be surprised the bus you need has a new number.

wish to stay awhile. In summer, most beach areas charge an access fee of around AZN3.

QOBUSTAN

PETROGLYPHS

Around 12,000 years ago, when the Caspian coast was lusher and sea levels far higher, Stone Age hunter-gatherers settled in a series of caves that they etched with around 6000 simple stone engravings. Now high above the shore, the cave sites have crumbled into a craggy chaos of boulders but the ancient etchings remain, protected in the Unesco-listed **Qobustan Petroglyph Reserve** (✐5444208; admission/tour AZN2/5; ◷10.30am-4.30pm). There's a brand-new museum and English-speaking staff offer guided tours to assist you spotting and deciphering the petroglyphs whose themes include livestock, wild animals and human figures, notably shamans. Don't miss the spindly **reed boat** sailing towards the sunset. Comparing this with similar ancient designs in Norway led controversial ethnologist Thor Heyerdahl to suggest that Scandinavians might have originated in what is now Azerbaijan.

Even if you have no particular interest in ancient doodles, Qobustan's eerie landscape and the hilltop views toward distant oil-workings in the turquoise-blue Caspian are still fascinating.

ROMAN GRAFFITI

Around 2km from the petroglyphs at the bottom of Böyük Dash Mountain, a fenced-in rock sports the easternmost Roman inscription ever discovered. It was chipped out by Julius Maximus, a centurion of the 12th Legion, probably on a reconnaissance mission from Roman Syria during the reign of Emperor Domitian (AD 51–96).

MUD VOLCANOES

Some 10km south of Qobustan is a weird collection of baby **mud volcanoes** (*palcik vulkanlar*), a whole family of 'geologically

AZERBAIJAN BAKU TO QOBUSTAN

flatulent' little conical mounds that gurgle, ooze, spit and sometimes erupt with thick, cold, grey mud. It's more entertaining than it sounds – even when activity is at a low ebb, you get the eerie feeling that the volcanoes are alive. And normally the peaceful site is completely deserted.

The site is on top of utterly unpromising Daşgil Hill. If driving, the easiest access is from the old Ələt junction, 15km south of Qobustan.

Follow 'Şpal Zavodu' signs, but keep straight ahead after crossing the railway. Keep to this unpaved track for 3km then climb the hill to your right. Note that these directions will change once the new M3 highway interchange is completed, and the old Ələt junction is bypassed.

❶ Getting There & Away

Take city bus 20 to the Yiriminçi Sahə (20-ci Sahə) roundabout, then swap to the Ələt-bound bus 195 (80q, one hour). Get off at the south end of depressing Qobustan town, just before the overpass bridge. From here the petroglyphs site is 5km inland: by taxi it's AZN10 return via the Roman graffiti site, or AZN20 if also including the mud volcanoes. Taxis direct from Baku want at least AZN40 return to see all of the above, but be aware that many Baku drivers won't know how to find the mud-volcano site.

Şirvan National Park

Around 100km south of Baku, this **park** (Ələt-Salyan hwy Km 33; admission foreigners/locals AZN4/2; ◷9am-6pm) is outwardly just a featureless flat plain but it provides Europe's last remaining natural habitat for wild Caucasian antelopes *(ceyran)*. The area is very large and to stand any chance of seeing these lovable creatures you'll need your own vehicle, preferably a 4WD.

NORTHERN AZERBAIJAN

Most of Azerbaijan's scenic highlights lie in the spectacular, snowcapped Great Caucasus or its luxuriantly forested foothills. Some of these zones are accessible from the Baku–Balakən road, others from the Quba–Qusar area, but unless you're prepared to hike via 3000m passes (see p235) there's no direct way to cross between these two regions.

Baku to Quba

Northern Azerbaijan's real highlights start behind Quba. Nonetheless there are some mildly interesting diversions en route, best suited to those with a vehicle. From the main Quba road, around 50km out of Baku, you'll glimpse hauntingly awful acres of rusty pipe-workings and factory chimneys. This is **Sumqayıt**, Azerbaijan's third-largest city, a dystopian nightmare created after WWII when much of the Soviet chemical industry was plonked in what might otherwise have become Azerbaijan's foremost beach resort. At **Giləzi**, a side lane runs west towards the gently attractive woodland of the **Altı Agaç National Park** (foreigners/locals AZN4/2). It passes an eye-catching area nicknamed the **Candycane Mountains**, where vivid pink-and-white striped hills are full of little conical fossils.

North of Giləzi the dull main-road scenery gets an emphatic boost from the looming silhouette of 520m **Beşbarmaq Dağ** (Five Finger Mountain). High on a super-steep grassy ridge top, this mystical fistful of phallic crags attracts local (mostly female) pilgrims dressed in their Sunday best. They climb rickety metal ladders, kiss rocks and speak in tongues hoping to score spiritual merit, good fortune and/or divine assistance in getting pregnant. Holy men lurk in rocky nooks ready to help out – but only with prayers.

Another possible excursion swings past **Çirax Qala**, one of rural Azerbaijan's best-preserved castle ruins. Its spindly, three-storey keep rises on a forested bluff, high above **Qala Altı**, a decrepit sulphur-water sanatorium that is slated for major renovation during 2012.

❶ Getting There & Away

Baku–Xızı buses pass the Candycane Mountains. For Beşbarmaq, take Baku–SDK, Baku–Xaçmaz or Baku–Quba buses and get off at a roadside rest area near Km 90. From there, taxis charge AZN15 to AZN20 to a car park at the base of the holy crag. Climbing to the summit takes a further 20 minutes on foot.

To reach Qala Altı, start from either Siyəzən or Şabran (formerly Dəvəçi), both towns newly bypassed by the busy Baku-Quba highway. Taxis from either cost around AZN20 return using horribly potholed roads. In dry conditions vehicles can continue another 3km from Qala Altı leaving you just 15 minutes' hike away from the Çirax Castle ruins.

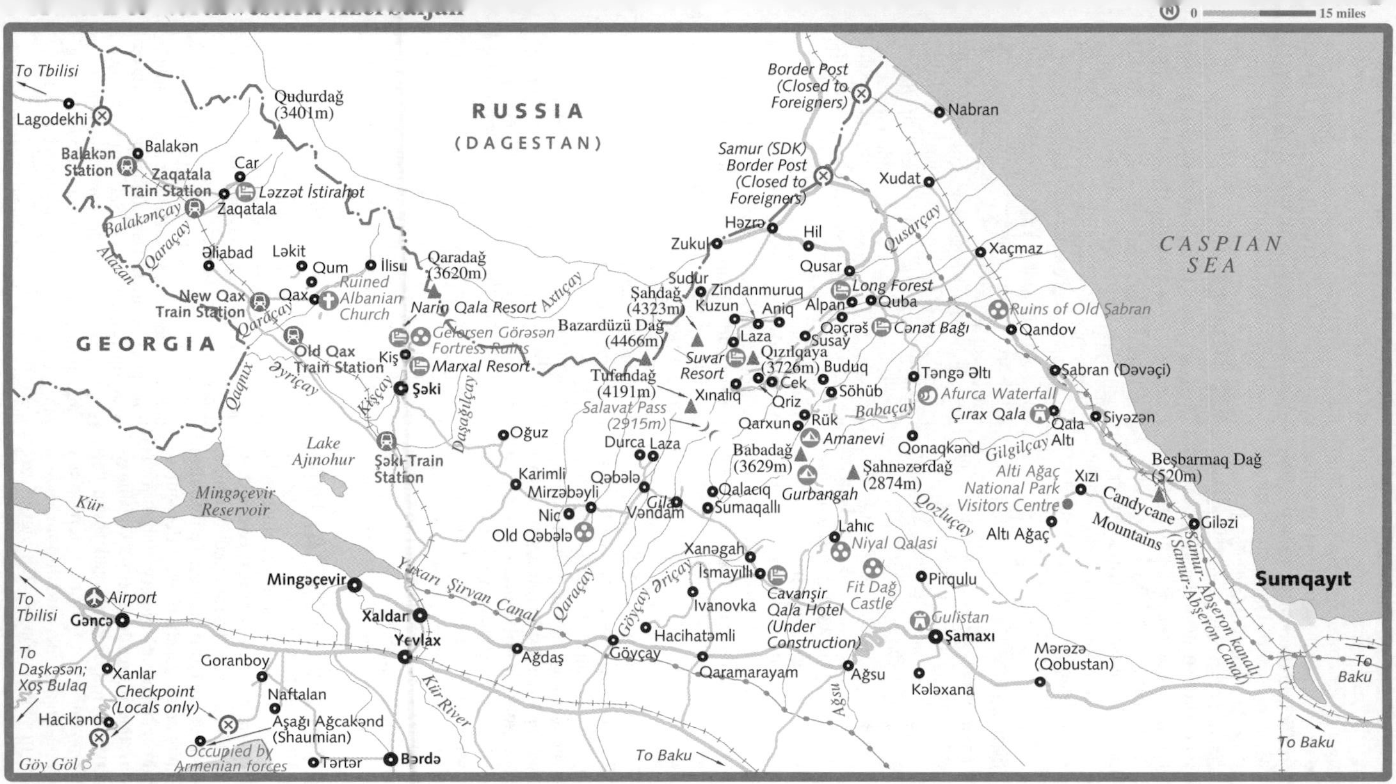
0
15 miles
RUSSIA
(DAGESTAN)
GEORGIA
CASPIAN SEA
To Tbilisi
Lagodekhi
Qudurdağ (3401m)
Balakən Station
Balakən
Car
Zaqatala Train Station
Ləzzət İstirahət
Zaqatala
Balakənçay
Alazan
Qaraçay
Əliabad
Ləkit
Qum
İlisu
Qaradağ (3620m)
Ruined Albanian Church
Qax
New Qax Train Station
Old Qax Train Station
Nariŋ Qala Resort
Axtıçay
Gələrsən Görəsən Fortress Ruins
Marxal Resort
Kiş
Şəki
Qaqnıx
Əyriçay
Kişçay
Daşağılçay
Lake Ajınohur
Şəki Train Station
Oğuz
Mingəçevir Reservoir
Kür
Border Post (Closed to Foreigners)
Nabran
Samur (SDK) Border Post (Closed to Foreigners)
Xudat
Həzrə
Hil
Zukul
Qusarçay
Xaçmaz
Qusar
Sudur
Şahdağ (4323m)
Zindanmuruq
Kuzun
Long Forest
Quba
Alpan
Aniq
Bazardüzü Dağ (4466m)
Laza
Qəçrəş
Cənət Bağı
Susay
Ruins of Old Sabran
Qandov
Suvar Resort
Qızılqaya (3726m)
Buduq
Şabran (Dəvəçi)
Tufandağ (4191m)
Xınalıq
Cek
Söhüb
Təngə Əltı
Salavat Pass (2915m)
Qriz
Afurca Waterfall
Qarxun
Rük
Babaçay
Çırax Qala
Qala Altı
Siyəzən
Amanevi
Qonaqkənd
Gilgilçay
Durca Laza
Babadağ (3629m)
Şahnəzərdağ (2874m)
Beşbarmaq Dağ (520m)
Alti Ağaç National Park Visitors Centre
Xızı
Karimli
Qəbələ
Mirzəbəyli
Qalacıq
Gurbangah
Candycane Mountains
Gilə
Vəndam
Sumaqallı
Qozluçay
Altı Ağaç
Giləzi
Nic
Old Qəbələ
Lahıc
Niyal Qalasi
Samur-Abşeron kanalı (Samur-Abşeron Canal)
Sumqayıt
Xanəgah
İsmayıllı
Pirqulu
Fit Dağ Castle
Cavanşir Qala Hotel (Under Construction)
Göyçay Əriçay
Ivanovka
Gulistan
Qaraçay
Yuxarı Şirvan Canal
Mingəçevir
Airport
To Tbilisi
Gəncə
Xaldar
Hacihatəmli
Şamaxı
Yevlax
Ağdaş
Göyçay
Qaramarayam
Ağsu
Mərəzə (Qobustan)
To Baku
Kələxana
To Daşkəsən; Xoş Bulaq
Xanlar
Goranboy
Checkpoint (Locals only)
Naftalan
Kür River
Ağşu
Hacikənd
Ağaşı Ağcakənd (Shaumian)
Occupied by Armenian forces
Göy Göl
Tərtər
Bərdə
To Baku
To Baku

Quba

🔌 0169 / POP 55.000

Famous for apples and carpetmaking, Quba is a flat grid of low-rise streets raised above the deep-cut Qudiyalçay River. Founded as the 18th-century capital of local potentate Fatali Khan, Quba became a provincial backwater once the khanate had been absorbed into the Russian Empire (1806). A fair scattering of Tsarist-era buildings remain and across the river is a unique Jewish settlement. But Quba's main attraction is as a gateway to Azerbaijan's most interesting and remote mountain villages.

◎ Sights

Quba's main attraction is just wandering the quiet leafy streets. From the bus station take any 'Şəhər' *marshrutka* along the main street to the grassy central square (Meydan). On the square's south side, a drab lump of Soviet concrete hides the obliging **tourist office** (📞 53618, 070 2383038; www.guba-tim.com; ⊙9am-1pm & 2-6pm Mon-Fri).

Across the road, through the Meydan's decorative archway, you'll spy Quba's most distinctive mosque – the octagonal **Cümə Məscid** with its metallic dome shaped like a lemon squeezer. A block behind, Ardəbil küç couldn't be called beautiful but if you follow it west you'll discover a representative selection of Quba's older architecture including 19th-century homes with rounded door shields, the colourful **Hacı Cəfər Mosque** (Ardəbil küç 60), a working **bathhouse** (Ardəbil küç 43) and the decrepit, century-old **Günbəzli hammam** (Ardəbil küç 33) with its big, grass-sprouting beehive dome. Two blocks further west, turn right to find **Nizami Park**, dotted with statues. Many are literary based and recently repainted to look like bronze. Others of Greco-Soviet Adonis youths lead down a long stairway to the river bridge, across which **Qırmızı Qəsəbə** (Krasnaya Sloboda) is a wealthy and much celebrated Jewish village with two active **synagogues**. From Nizami Park, if you instead continue walking west past the Şahdağ Hotel, after 15 minutes you'll reach a steep descent to the right labelled 'Cemetery'. This leads down to the excavation site of a heavily politicised **mass grave** (admission free; ⊙9am-7pm Mon-Fri). Beneath temporary plastic sheeting, skulls and human bones protrude in awful profusion. The victims are

thought to have died in one of numerous 1918 massacres perpetrated by Azerbaijan's first, short-lived communist regime. According to the brochure, these saw a total of 16,782 civilian deaths and the destruction of 122 villages in the Quba region alone.

🛌 Sleeping

There are many bungalow resorts along the road to Qəçrəş and others around a little canyon at Təngə Əltı.

Cənət Bağı　　　　　　　　RESORT $$
(📞 51415; contact@cannatbagi.com; d/mini-ste/ste AZN50/80/160; ☒) In a woodland clearing 7km south of Quba, this popular complex is the area's nearest approximation to a real hotel – at least until the luxurious 'seven-star' Rixos Hotel is completed nearby. The eye-catching entrance boasts parquet floors, wrought ironwork and a candlelit piano, but rooms are more generic. Odd-numbered rooms overlook streamside picnic tables. The outdoor swimming pool only opens in midsummer. Vahid speaks English.

Oskar Hotel　　　　　　　GUESTHOUSE $
(📞 51516; Baku Hwy; r AZN30) Between the bus station and bazaar, this is not so much a hotel as a set of modern motel-style rooms above a pleasant kebab restaurant. They're reasonably new, with private hot showers, frilly curtains and partly tiled floors, though the whole place feels slightly jerry-built.

Xınalıq Hotel　　　　　　GUESTHOUSE $
(📞 54445; xinaliqotel@mail.ru; s & tw/tr AZN15/30) This trader's guesthouse is basic and male-orientated but the 19 rooms cover a variety of qualities and styles – a few even have private toilet and shower. Look at several before deciding. It's perched above the chaotic market area: a five-minute walk back down the main road towards Baku from the bus station, then right through a brick archway.

Şadağ Hotel　　　　　　　CRASH PAD $
(📞 52927; Yusif Qazimov küç; s/d AZN5/10) This two-storey Soviet-era establishment, right beside Nizami Park, is Quba's only genuinely central option. In serious need of renovation, it's currently a sad old crash pad with shared 'toilets' and dribbling taps, though not quite as awful as you might surmise from the price.

🍴 Eating

Several cheap beer-and-tea places lie around the bazaar area, the Meydan and Nizami

Park. Oscar Hotel has a little open-air garden serving fair-priced kebabs and beer from 75q. Should you have a vehicle, consider the many forest kebab places that stretch for several miles along the Qəçrəş road.

Çinar Kafé　　　　　AZERBAIJANI $
(Heydar Əliyev pr 168; mains & kebabs AZN3-4, beers AZN1.50; ◎9am-11pm) Despite its dogged lack of decor, this long-lasting eatery is probably the most reliable place for food quality in central Quba. It's two blocks east of the Meydan.

🛍 Shopping

Qadim Quba　　　　CARPET WORKSHOP
(✐53270; Heydar Əliyev pr 132; ◎8am-6pm Mon-Fri) Watch carpets being woven in the workshop or just peruse the boutique, which also sells handicrafts and local pastries.

ℹ Getting There & Away

Quba's bus station is 2km east of the town centre.

BAKU Buses (AZN4, 2½ hours) depart at least hourly till 5.30pm. Other Baku-bound services from Qusar pick up passengers outside the bus station when not full.

QUSAR (FOR LAZA) Marshrutky/shared taxis (30q/AZN1) take around 25/20 minutes.

XINALIQ A marshrutka (AZN5, 1¾ hours) departs around 2pm from opposite Xınalıq Hotel when customer numbers and road conditions allow. Shared jeeps (AZN7 to AZN10) leave from the same point as full, usually around 8am.

ℹ Getting Around

By day, marshrutky (20q) run from the bus station roundabout, up Heydar Əliyev pr, finally turning left to the hospital around 100m before reaching the turning for the mass grave site. They return through town along Əliqulu Nərimanov küç.

Around Quba

Amid sheepy Caucasian foothills and dramatic canyons lie Azerbaijan's grandest mountain panoramas and its most fascinating villages. Perhaps the most memorable hamlets are mysterious, whitewashed **Buduq** and cragtop **Qriz**, whose name means 'dagger' (from an 8th-century massacre) and whose melodramatic central feature is an ancient graveyard. However, neither Buduq nor Qriz have formal accommodation or public transport and even

4WDs struggle to cope with their muddy access tracks. Far easier to reach are the fabled ancient village of **Xınalıq** and the architecturally neutral village of **Laza**, whose jaw-dropping setting counterpoints emerald meadows, high green crags and long mountain waterfalls. The Quba–Xınalıq road is narrow and precarious in places but it's asphalted and remains what's arguably Azerbaijan's most scenically glorious route.

XINALIQ
POP 800 (1700 IN SUMMER) / ELEV 2335M
By some definitions Xınalıq is Europe's highest village. Remote in its mountain fastness, for years just getting here was the holy grail of Azerbaijan tourism. Since 2006, however, a new asphalt road has removed that sense of adventure. The road has also allowed local families the luxury of bringing in new metal roofing, which has diminished the architectural integrity of Xınalıq's ancient stone houses. But they still form distinctively austere stepped terraces up a steep highland ridge. And the whole scene often remains magically wrapped in spooky clouds that part sporadically to reveal 360-degree views of the surrounding Caucasus. Apart from examining the one-room **museum** (admission AZN1; ◎on request) and gazing at the hypnotic views, the main attraction is meeting Xınalıq's hardy shepherd folk who have their own language (Ketsh) and still live much of their lives on horseback. Bring warm clothes – nights can be icy cold.

In future, foreign visitors to Xınalıq might be charged AZN4 'entry charge' to the controversial Şahdağ National Park.

Hiking to Laza (full day) or to **ateşgah**, a small ever-burning natural fire-vent (two hours), is currently forbidden. For a short, legal hike try following the village water pipe part-way up the northern slopes of Qizilqaya. For a multiday walk head east to Alpan (two or three days) via Qalay Xudat, Qriz, Susay and Long Forest (http://longforest.az/eng). Four daily buses link Alpan to Quba.

Charming **Xeyraddin Gabbarov** (✐050 2259250; www.xinaliq.com) usually works in Quba but comes from Xınalıq, speaks fluent English and for a relatively modest profit can organise tailor-made visits.

🛏 Sleeping
There's no hotel, but several families can offer informal homestays for around AZN15 including breakfast and plenty of tea. The

HIKING HURDLES

Ludicrous new regulations, introduced by both national park authorities and the border defence force, have essentially shut down Azerbaijan's three most popular longer-distance hikes – the scenically spectacular Laza–Xınalıq and Laza-Sudur trails and the two-day Xınalıq–Vandəm cross-Caucasus trek. Even the shorter stroll to Xınalıq's Ateşgah (fire pit) is currently out of bounds. Soldiers keep watch and don't accept 'innocent foreigner' excuses. It is still possible, however, to climb Babadağ (p235) as part of a cross-Caucasus walk between Lahıc and Qarxun (the latter reached by a lurching half-day 4WD drive from Quba). And rough tracks between the villages east of Xınalıq make for hikes that are interesting and relatively trouble-free (apart from sheepdogs). Qrız Dahmə–Qrız–Cek makes a lovely full-day loop starting and ending on the Quba–Xınalıq road. CBT Azerbaijan (www.cbtazerbaijan.com) is developing village homestays and hikes in the region while quad-bike tours through the same trails are planned by the folks at Baku's Hotel Hale Kai (p213).

best homestays are likely to be highlights of any Xınalıq visit, their ultrathick walls decorated with richly coloured carpets.

Vugar Həzərov's Homestay
HOMESTAY $
(070 9121124) Directly behind the main water-collection point at the top of the village, this is much more traditional inside than you'd guess from the new facade.

Qonaq Evi
HOMESTAY $
(050 3722986; r per person incl breakfast AZN20) At the far end of town in the valley is this clean, if sparse and unsophisticated, house where you pay per bed, hostel-style, to stay in one of the four large guestrooms. So far it's the only Xınalıq option with a hot shower but the toilet's at the end of the garden. Breakfast is cursory. Lacklustre dinners cost AZN5. Call ahead.

❶ Getting There & Away
Assuming it runs, Rajab's *marshrutka* (050 6152740) to Quba (AZN5, two hours) leaves at around 7am from near the upper water-collection point. Otherwise ask around to find a paid hitchhike into Quba.

LAZA (QUSARÇAY LAZA)
0138 / POP 150
The soaring mountain valley surrounding Laza is one of the most stunning sights anywhere.

Grass-clad slopes drop precipitously from noble Şahdağ (4243m) and craggy Qızılqaya (3726m). A series of ribbon waterfalls cascades over perilous cliff edges, and carpets of wildflowers add to the vivid greens throughout late spring and summer.

Tiny Laza village is diffuse and its houses somewhat banal, but a rocky pinnacle beside the rusty-roofed little mosque adds foreground for photos of the mind-blowing panorama.

Nonsensical new regulations have recently snuffed out Laza's former role as Azerbaijan's hiking and climbing base, but hopefully these problems will be resolved in coming years. Just 3km east, but invisible from Laza, the vast new Şahdağ Ski Resort is under construction. Although one short piste has been officially opened, works aren't due to be complete until 2019.

🛏 Sleeping & Eating

Suvar
RESORT $$
(53671, 57033; www.suvar.az; s/d/ste AZN60/100/150) Suvar's well-appointed mountainside bungalows incorporate rustic design features and survey one of the finest panoramas in Azerbaijan. The restaurant has stone fireplaces, wood mosaics and big view-windows. Prices increase during peak weekends and holidays.

Azizov family
HOMESTAY, BUNGALOWS $
(57035, 57406; per person AZN12-18) As you enter Laza, the first homestead you'll find is Zahir Azizov's great-value homestay with an indoor shared bathroom and sitting area. Across the road, teacher Khaled Azizov also runs the village shop and has his own homestay beds plus a couple of smarter, newly built cottages with bathroom (one/two-bedroom bungalow AZN40/50) close to the waterfalls, part-way towards Suvar. A third brother, Mevlud (57421, 050 6844374) speaks English and sometimes acts as a hiking guide.

❶ Getting There & Away

Start by heading from Baku or Quba to the Lezgin town of Qusar. From there driving to Laza currently takes 1½ bumpy hours but times will reduce once the road is asphalted for the ski-resort project. The route is far less scenic than the Quba–Xınalıq road until shortly before your arrival in Laza. Share taxis cost around AZN3/5 per person in a Zhiguli/Niva. Chartering costs at least AZN20. You might have to walk the last 500m down into the village, as the steep last descent is troublesome for smaller cars. Hitching with construction traffic to the ski resort site, 3km short of Laza, is relatively easy from the far western end of *marshrutka* route 1 in Qusar.

There's no bus to Laza but services leaving Qusar at 11.20am and 3.40pm do run to Əniq (80q, 1¼ hours) where CBT Azerbaijan (www.cbtazerbaijan.com) has a homestay. Walking Əniq to Laza takes around four hours. The 3.30pm Qusar–Kuzun bus gets you to within two hours' walk of Laza but the hiking route is less obvious. Beware of sheepdogs.

NABRAN

Azeris often recall summers of love in Nabran with a fondness that may lead you to expect a Soviet Ibiza. Don't get carried away. In July and August it certainly has the party vibe with a tidal wave of Azeri holidaymakers at play. But with sand like topsoil, the beach is far from idyllic. And with over 30 resorts spread out along 20km of coastal woodlands, you'll really need a vehicle.

NORTHWESTERN AZERBAIJAN

The road between Baku and Balakən traverses a whole spectrum of scenic and climatic zones and offers by far the most interesting way to transit between Georgia and Azerbaijan. The landscape reaches several climaxes between İsmayıllı and Şəki where, in spring, wildflowers and fields full of poppies add impressionistic splashes of colour to the woodland foregrounds.

Baku to İsmayıllı

This remarkable three-hour drive starts off across parched badlands and a rolling semidesert that sprouts a first dusting of greenery around Mərəzə. In 2008, Mərəzə was bizarrely renamed 'Qobustan', a move seemingly designed to confuse tourists heading for the 'real' Qobustan south of Baku. If you're driving by, it's vaguely worth a quick detour to see the Diri Baba Mausoleum, a 15th-century stone tomb clinging to a little canyon 1km north of the Heydar Məscidi (a roadside mosque in Mərəzə's northeast corner). At the opposite end of town, a discordant glass pyramid suggests Louvre ambitions for the Heydar Əliyev Irsini Arasdirma Mərkəzi.

ŞAMAXI

☏ 0176 / POP 30,100

For centuries, Şamaxı (Shemakha) was the royal seat of the Shirvanshahs and thus one of northern Azerbaijan's most prominent cultural and trading cities. However, fire, earthquakes and invasions have left virtually no visible historical signs. One minor exception is Yeddi Gümbaz, a handful of domed tomb towers (mostly 19th century) set on a small rise across the main Baku–Şəki road from town. The surrounding graveyard is older.

Above Xinişli village, 2km west of Şamaxı's busy bazaar (Rəsulzadə küç), is the site of Gulistan Castle on the further crest of an abrupt cleft hilltop. This was the 12th-century residence of the Shirvanshahs but only a few utterly unrecognisable stones remain.

Şamaxı's sturdy Cümə Mosque (Şirvani küç) is dubbed the 'second-oldest mosque in the trans-Caucasus' (after Derbent in Dagestan). However, the 8th-century structure disappeared centuries ago, and during 2011 even the grand 1902 rebuild was largely demolished as part of a massive reconstruction project that should eventually create a 21st-century masterpiece.

Minor attractions around Şamaxı include a group of ancient *turbe* (tomb towers) at Kələxana and the popular weekenders' getaway of Pirqulu whose high, windswept hills are reminiscent of Yorkshire's 'Brontë Country'. Note that Pirqulu's extensive Soviet-era Astronomical Observatory (Rasiatxana) is closed for major reconstruction until at least 2013.

West of Şamaxı, most traffic descends the looping Ağsu Pass to the dusty lowland plain. But continuing westward towards İsmayıllı is quieter and far more scenic, crossing the deep, wide Ağsu River valley then following a long, bucolic ridgetop.

İsmayıllı

☏ 0178 / POP 13,800

If you're visiting Lahıc on public transport, diffuse İsmayıllı makes a useful transit point. The town's landmark is a 1km-long

fortress-style wall complete with round turret effects and proud battlements. Looking towards the northern mountain ridges, the wall adds indisputable extra interest to photos. But it's a very obvious sham, built in 2010 with absolutely no historical pedigree. The wall parallels Heydar Əliyev pr north from the leafy town centre to the point on the main Baku–Qəbələ road where through transport to Qəbələ and Oğuz picks up passengers should there be any space. At a roundabout 100m east of that point is the run-down **Motel Talistan** (☑070 3695604; s/d AZN20/28, without bathroom per person AZN9) with squat toilets and a shared shower. Or you can sleep in Ivanovka or Lahıc, at least until the smart new **Cavanşir Qala Hotel** (Baku Hwy) opens.

The **bus station**, 1km south of Niyal Hotel, has an 11.30am bus to Qəbələ and hourly departures for Baku (AZN5, three hours) via Şamaxı (AZN3, one hour). Last at 5pm. If not already full, these also pick up passengers opposite **Çaldas Petrol** (Baku hwy) at the eastern edge of town, 500m east of Motel Talistan. Use the same point for shared taxis to Baku (AZN7) and for crushed-full *marshrutky* to Lahıc (AZN1.40, 1½ hours) departing at 7am, 11am and 2pm.

For Şəki change in Qəbələ or Oğuz.

Around İsmayıllı

LAHIC
☑0178 / POP 905

Azerbaijan has many delightful mountain villages, but tourist-savvy Lahıc is quainter and more accessible than most. It is locally famous for its Persian-based dialect and its traditional coppersmiths. Hiking and regional scenery is inspiring and, at least in summer, there's an unusually good smattering of English speakers to help you get a feel for rural life.

◉ Sights

Hüseynov küç　　　COPPERSMITH STREET

Lahıc's main street is unevenly paved with smooth pale river-stones. Houses, many with wooden box-balconies, are built traditionally with interleaving stone and timber layers to improve earthquake resilience. Lahıc's famous **workshops** have mostly been superseded by little boutiques but the smithy at Hüseynov küç 47 is almost a museum, Hüseynov 83 remains relatively active, and at Hüseynov 50 blind Mr Azada mans an antiquated little harnessmaker's

shop. During summer the **village school** welcomes visitors to look around and has a tiny little 'museum room'.

Lahıc History Museum　　MUSEUM, MOSQUE
(Nizami küç; donation expected; ☺9am-2pm & 3-6pm Tue-Sat) This quaint little one-room collection of cultural artefacts is housed in a former mosque next door to the tourist office. Posted opening times are far from fixed.

⚡ Activities

Hiking up the steep wooded hillsides you emerge on bare mountaintop sheep meadows *(qaylağ)* with views towards snow-topped Caucasus peaks that are simply majestic on clear days. Of the region's (very) ruined fortresses, the most accessible is **Niyal Qalasi**, a barely recognisable heap of stones about 1½ hours' sweaty climb up the Kişcay valley. The relatively easy-to-follow walk starts up the stream beside Cənnət Bağı guesthouse. With a horse and guide you could make a full-day excursion to more impressive **Fit Dağ castle ruins**. The tourist office offers many more suggestions.

🛏 Sleeping & Eating

Numerous families offer homestay rooms from AZN10 per bed, many in archetypal village homes, though be aware that most will have only outdoor toilets. Camping is possible for a fee in many village gardens.

TOP CHOICE **Rustam Rustamov**　LUXURY HOMESTAY **$$**
(☑050 3658049; rustam-48@mail.ru; Aracit; d AZN60-70) Affable Rustam speaks good English and offers by far the most comfortable homestay in Lahıc. Nine European standard rooms have central heating, (slow) internet and excellent private bathrooms with underfloor heating. The verandah seating overlooks an orchard, and a great private bar-lounge is tastefully decorated with local handicrafts.

Cənnət Bağı Guest House　HOMESTAY, CAMPING **$**
(Garden of Paradise; ☑77200, 050 5870140, 070 2870140; mr.casarat@mail.ru; per person homestay/camping AZN15/7.50, half board AZN25-30) This large, simple homestay is set in lovely landscaped orchards right at the entrance to the village. The attractive house has shared outdoor toilets but its private 320-year-old *hammam* is a popular bonus. English-speaking Cəsarət İsmailov is almost always in residence and can rustle up guides and horses at relatively short notice. Meals (extra cost) are available in the garden cafe.

Haciyev Family HOMESTAY $
(☑77357, 050 6320732 Hidayat; per person AZN10) This traditional old house has superfriendly hosts and very simple rooms including one that's a verandah box with views across a small garden towards the river. The shared outdoor toilet should soon be joined by a *banya* (sauna). To find the house, enter the second garden to the left as you walk towards İsmayıllı from the main square along the clifftop road.

Evim Otel HOTEL $$
(☑77111; www.evimotel.net; r AZN90, without bathroom AZN60) Well-signed mini-hotel with fancy furniture and style-conscious bathroom fittings near the central bridge.

Haji Mohammad's HOTEL $
(☑77494, 050 5283227; Aracit Sq; d/q/ste AZN30/50/60) Facing Aracit Mosque, this unmarked house-'hotel' is being steadily upgraded with bathrooms added to most of

CLIMBING MT BABADAĞ

Babadağ is Azerbaijan's 'holy mountain', a 3629m bald peak with 360-degree views and a reputation for making climbers' wishes miraculously come true. While steep and tiring, the walk to the summit is entirely nontechnical and in **season** (☉mid-Jul–mid-Aug) there's the added fascination of meeting an assortment of pilgrims as you hike.

Of several routes up, the three commonest all start from **Gurbangah**, a seasonal camp where a concrete-floored shed doubles as a basic cafe. From Lahıc, reaching Gurbangah takes two hours by 4WD (one-way/return AZN80/100 per vehicle), much longer by pilgrim truck-bus (hitchhiked ride around AZN5). Most walkers camp at Gurbangah then start the climb before dawn. In clear weather the well-trodden main trail takes around six hours up, four hours back and is easy to follow without a guide. Around halfway, a scenic highlight is the awesome **Şeitan Daşatan** (Devil Gets Stoned) viewpoint, appearing quite unexpectedly after a long climb. It's a breathtaking overlook made all the more intriguing when pious climbers send forth a volley of stones into the void. Their action symbolically apes Həzərət Baba, Babadağ's legendary 12th-century saint who supposedly used a similar technique to ward off the Devil. The Baba eventually 'disappeared' from the mountaintop, a tale taken literally by some pilgrims though it's probably metaphorical for his reaching a kind of Sufi nirvana. Reaching the physical mountaintop is far less ambitious – simply follow a clear knife-edge ridge. At the summit there's no monument, just a pair of shepherd-style shelters to protect some gruff policemen and a mullah who daubs a 'lucky spot' on pilgrims' foreheads (free) or says requisite prayers to unlock your good fortune (donation expected).

Around an hour before reaching the summit, a less-frequented alternative path signposted Губа (Quba) leads north towards Rük, allowing summer hikers a legal route to traverse the Caucasus. This descends in around seven hours to a much more basic camp called **Amanevi**, 11km from the nearest village, **Qarxun**, via a very rough riverbed where any semblance of road has been washed away. Locals generally walk or ride horses, though 6WD trucks do arrive occasionally in Amanevi carrying local student/pilgrim groups. From Qarxun there's a 6am shared 4WD service to Quba via Rük, Söhüub and the Tangi Altı Canyon.

Babadağ Miscellaneous Tips

» In peak season there are a few tea tents along the Gurbangah and Amanevi routes (tea 50q per cup) but no food or water is available.

» Bring sunscreen, a hat, and warm waterproof clothes. The climb can be very sweaty in sunshine but you'll rapidly feel the cold when it's cloudy or wet. Outside pilgrimage season, unexpected blizzards can be a danger.

» Locals often climb at night to watch the sunrise from the top but unless you have a good moon, guide or both, it's a little risky.

» As the day breaks, pilgrims get hot and temporarily discard sweaters along the path. They'll collect them when coming down again so don't pick them up!

» The easiest time to find a shared ride to the trailheads is on Saturday afternoons, best of all during the week after the midsummer full moon.

WORTH A TRIP

WINE-TASTING EXCURSION

At Hacıhatəmli, some 15km west of Ivanovka, **Şato Monolit** (☑050 3064252, www.ismailliwine.com) is the first Azerbaijani winery to offer tours (AZN10 including tasting) and to offer a comfortable on-site hotel (per person AZN50). Don't miss the extensive cellars, which look ancient though dating from just 2009.

---

the sizeable rooms. One downstairs triple is retained as a 'budget' option (AZN20).

Mikail Humbatov's Restaurant RESTAURANT, ROOMS $
(☑050 3119475, 055 5322233; mikail_humbatov@ mail.ru; per person AZN20, kebabs AZN4) The greatest glory of Lahıc's biggest (yet unsigned) restaurant is its tree-shaded garden seating with mountain views high across the river. Above the main dining hall are four colourful new guestrooms, two spacious and comfy, two contrastingly small and basic yet oddly the same price. The four rooms share two bathrooms so tiny that the shower inevitably sprays straight onto the toilet.

❶ Information

The **tourist office** (☑77571; Nizami küç; ⊙10am-2pm & 3-7pm mid-May–mid-Sep) organises homestays, guides and horses (AZN10 short ride, AZN25-35 per day) and sells basic village maps (AZN2), T-shirts, postcards and photo DVDs (AZN4) to fund its existence. Out of season, the keen English-speaking director **Dadaş Əliyev** (☑050 6777517) reverts to his role as school -teacher, but can still offer assistance. To find the tourist office, take the narrow alley-stairway beside the tiny **Internet Klub** (40 Hüseynov küç; per hr AZN1; ⊙10am-midnight) and turn right on Nizami küç.

❶ Getting There & Away

İSMAYILLI Buses depart at 8.30am, 12.30pm and 4pm (AZN1.50, 1½ hours). Consider paying a taxi at least one-way, to allow photo stops (around AZN15 to or from İsmayıllı) en route: the drive has some spectacular sections passing perilous drops, geological wizardry and the wobbly, vertigo-nightmare that is the suspension footbridge to Zərnava. Sometimes the road is rendered impassable by landslides.

BAKU There's one bus at 8am from the central square (AZN7, four hours). Ask the driver to save you a seat the night before. Or change in İsmayıllı.

ŞƏKİ Taking the 8.30am bus to İsmayıllı should allow time to cross that town for the 11.30am Qəbələ bus and then the 3pm to Şəki or Oğuz. A direct taxi to Şəki/Oğuz costs from AZN40/35. Ask at your homestay.

IVANOVKA
☑0178 / POP 3500

Although lacking specific 'sights', Ivanovka has a time-warp fascination: it's one of the last remaining *kolxoz* (collective farms) to have survived from the Soviet era and even retains the CCCP rosette on its welcome sign. The population has a high percentage of blond-haired, blue-eyed Russians – mostly descendants of various puritanical protestant sects who had been effectively banished from Russia proper in the mid-19th century. Many houses also have a Russian look with red-tiled roofs and wooden uppers. Locals produce some of the country's best cheeses, robust homemade wines (AZN5 per litre) and excellent honey. But come quickly: dissatisfaction with profit sharing and regional management has led to a steady economic migration to Russia. Much of Ivanovka's attraction is staying at **John & Tanya Howard's Guesthouse** (☑050 3771273; Sadovaya ul 86; r per person with/without breakfast AZN25/15), a wonderful homestay where five purpose-built rooms have bathroom, supercomfy beds, framed-lace decor and a shared kitchen room in the garden behind the traditional main house.

A taxi from İsmayıllı costs AZN5. Or take İsmayıllı–Mingəçevir buses for 5km and then a shared taxi (AZN1) for the last 6km, climbing through vast fields of sunflowers. If the haze clears, the horizon presents a wonderful mountain panorama en route.

Qəbələ
☑0160 / POP 12,100

Nowhere better expresses Azerbaijan's 21st-century economic transformations than Qəbələ. Five years ago it was a dowdy market town whose main attractions were the quaint but unsophisticated cottage getaways in a wooded valley around 5km north. Today the city is a vast construction site. Soviet-era structures have been demolished or refurbished, grand new public buildings are rising and that once-quiet wooded valley has been largely overwhelmed by tourism complexes: the pharaonic **Qafqaz Riverside** (☑54330;

www.qafqazriversidehotel.com; d/ste AZN160/180) and its sister property, **Qafqaz Resort** (☑54200; www.qafqazresorthotel.com; s/d from AZN119/149) along with the sprawling **Qabaland Amusement Park** (www.qabaland.com; admission from AZN2; ⊙10am-10pm). Reportedly further developments are planned towards **Durca** but for now that remains an unspoilt seasonal village (and quad-biking destination for resort guests) where shepherd families' old stone houses are only occupied during the midsummer grazing season.

In the Qəbələ town centre, the only really historical building is the colonnaded 19th-century **mosque** (Heydar Əliyev küç). Around 500m south is the new **Historical Museum** (Tarix Muzeyi; Qutqaşınlı pr; admission AZN1; ⊙10am-6pm). It displays finds from Old Qəbələ but its most unusual feature is the fake Stone Age–style swing gate through which one enters. Next door is a typically grand, wordless **Heydar Əliyev Museum** (Qutqaşınlı pr; admission free; ⊙10am-6pm Tue-Sat, to 4pm Sun-Mon).

Qəbələ has launched an **international music festival** (www.gabalainternational musicfestival.com, http://gilanpianos.com/4.html) in July and the town's soccer team, **Gabala FC** (www.gabalafc.az) is rapidly gaining stature, managed during 2010 and 2011 by ex-Arsenal defender Tony Adams.

If you don't have the budget for Qəbələ's megaresorts, try **Qəbələ Xanlar** (☑050 6207341; d/cottage AZN50/90). Its family size cottages are set in one remnant area of beautiful mossy woodland directly before the Qafqaz Resort. Cheaper 'cabin' rooms with bathroom are big, if slightly worn.

In the town centre there are two hotels within two minutes' walk of the mosque.

Hotel Qəbələ (☑52408; http://qebelewelcome syou.wordpress.com; 28 May küç 31; s/d AZN30/50; ☒☏) has a few flaws (damp sheets, smelly drains) but is more spacious than the oddly conceived **Karvan Otel** (☑50673; Heydar Əliyev küç; d AZN40-50; ☒), which stands beside the telecom building.

❶ Getting There & Away

The shiny new **bus station** (avtovağzal; Qutqaşınlı pr) is 2km south of the centre, 20q/AZN1 by shared/flag-down taxi. Despite all the ticket windows you simply pay onboard.

BAKU Buses (AZN6, five hours) around twice hourly from 7.20am to 6pm, fewer in afternoons. You may have to pay the full Baku fare even if you get off at İsmayıllı or Şamaxı. At busy times (eg Sunday evenings) locals book ahead by phoning the driver, so all services may prove full. A list of relevant drivers' numbers is displayed in the redundant ticket hall.

İSMAYILLI One bus (AZN2, 40 minutes) at 9.50am.

GƏNCƏ Buses (AZN5) at 8.15am, 8.40am, 9.30am and 3pm.

ŞƏKİ Buses (AZN2, two hours) via Oğuz at 9am, 11.10am, 3pm.

Oğuz

☑0111 / POP 6700

Using public transport between İsmayıllı and Şəki, it often makes sense to change buses in Oğuz. Known until the 1990s as Vartashen, Oğuz has a backdrop of mighty mountain ridges both forested and rocky that beckon with satisfying hikes and climbs. The town's population still includes small minorities of Jewish and Udi people and its most important historic building is a

---

WORTH A TRIP

OLD GABALA

Formerly known as Kutkashen, the town we now call Qəbələ was renamed as such in the early 1990s to honour an ancient city of Caucasian Albania. But the original Qəbələ (Gabala) was in fact some 20km further southwest. Mentioned in Pliny the Elder's *Natural History* (AD 77), Old Gabala was so comprehensively trashed by the 18th-century invader Nader Shah that even its location was entirely forgotten. Rediscovered in 1959, the almost featureless **site** (admission AZN2; ⊙9am-1pm & 2-6pm) is a raised grassy field with a few archaeological diggings and the brick-and-stone stumps of two massive brick gate-towers at the southern end. These are a 10-minute walk from the site's ticket wagon, itself tucked around the corner from a big new hotel construction site (4km off the Qəbələ–Şəki road, turn at Mirzəbəyli). There's no public transport. Consider chartering a taxi (around AZN15) between Qəbələ and Oğuz with added side trips to Old Gabala and to the three Albanian churches in the ethnically Udi village of **Nic**.

beautifully preserved ancient Udi-Albanian Church, now housing a quaint little everything **museum** (S Qaziyev küç; admission 40q; ⊘9am-1pm & 2-6pm Mon-Sat). If you're just in transit, consider dumping your gear at the bus-station baggage room (Saxlama Kamerası, 20q) and jumping on *marshrutka* 1 to the church-museum (near the top end Heydar Əliyev küç). After visiting, walk two minutes around the top of Heydar Parkı and grab *marshrutka* 2 back downhill again via the small but effusively friendly **bazaar** (M Əzizbəyov küç). From the bazaar, walk one block south then west to find the **synagogue** (A Əliyev 25), easily missed as it's architecturally little different from other Oğuz houses.

🛏 Sleeping

Afra Hotel   HOTEL $$
(⊉52673; http://afra-hotel.com; 20 Yanvar küç 6; s/tw AZN50/70; ✳🛜✸) Around 600m north then 400m east from the bus station, this smart resort hotel is one of provincial Azerbaijan's best accommodation deals. Rooms are large and new without undue glitz and most have mountain-facing balconies. Rates include use of a large indoor swimming pool, fitness centre and a range of indoor games (foosball, billiards, Playstations etc) should the weather turn sour.

LT Hotel   MOTEL $
(⊉53773; Heydar Əliyev pr; tw/tr/ste AZN30/40/50; ✳) This very neat, family motel has five brand-new rooms and makes a handy budget choice if you've simply missed the day's bus connection. It's 200m south of the bus station, facing Oğuz's fanciful new park.

❶ Getting There & Away

BAKU Buses via Qəbələ and İsmayıllı (AZN5, six hours) 8am, 9am, 10am, noon, 3pm, 4pm, 5pm.

QƏBƏLƏ (AZN1, one hour) 8am, 12.40pm, 2.30pm.

ŞƏKI (80q, 40 minutes) hourly 8am-3pm plus 5pm.

Şəki

☏0177 / POP 62,800

Snoozing amid green pillows of beautifully forested mountains, Şəki (Sheki) is Azerbaijan's loveliest town, dappled with tiled-roof old houses and topped off with a glittering little khan's palace.

History

Historic Şəki was originally higher up the valley around the site now occupied by Kiş (see p244). That town was ruined by floods in 1716 but rebuilt by rebellious Khan Haci Çələbi, who set up a defiantly independent khanate there in the 1740s. He built a second fortress at Nukha (today's Şəki). When the original Şəki was obliterated by a second, even more catastrophic flood in 1772, Nukha became the new royal capital.

After 1805, when the khanate was ceded to Russia, Nukha continued to flourish as a silk-weaving town and was a trading junction between caravan routes to Baku, Tbilisi and Derbent (Dagestan), with five working caravanserais at its peak. Nukha was renamed Şəki in the 1960s.

◎ Sights

WITHIN THE FORTRESS WALLS

The sturdy stone perimeter wall of Haci Çələbi's Nukha Fortress today encloses an 18th-century palace, tourist office, craft workshops, several museums and a decent cafe-restaurant, all set in patches of sheep-mown grass.

Xan Sarayı   PALACE
(admission AZN2; ⊘9am-7pm) This small but vividly colourful palace is Şəki's foremost 'sight' and one of the South Caucasus' most iconic buildings. When completed in 1762 it was used as the khan's administrative building, just one of around 40 royal structures within the fortress compound, though none now of the others survive. It's set in a walled rose garden behind two huge plane trees supposedly planted in 1530. The fa ade combines silvered stalactite vaulting with strong geometric patterns in dark-blue, turquoise and ochre. The only light filters in through intricate wood-framed, stained-glass windows known as *şəbəkə*. Only one room deep, the palace's petite interior is lavished with intricate, colourful murals. Most designs are floral but in the central upper chamber you'll find heroic scenes of Haci Çələbi's 1743 battle with Persian emperor Nader Shah complete with requisite swords, guns and severed heads. No photos are allowed inside: postcards of the murals cost AZN5 for 10.

FREE **Şəbəkə Workshop**   WORKSHOP
(⊘9am-1pm & 2-7pm) Those *şəbəkə* stained-glass windows you'll have seen at the palace are laboriously made by slotting together hundreds of hand-carved wooden pieces to

create intricate wooden frames without metal fastenings. See them being made at this no-nonsense family workshop (no English). Small examples are sold as souvenirs.

Historical-Regional Ethnography Museum named after Raşidbey Əfəndiyev
MUSEUM
(admission AZN2; ⊙10am-7pm) Tour groups are marched dutifully around this dowdy museum whose name is its most impressive feature. Exhibits include archaeological oddments, ethnographical artefacts and the usual emotive panels on WWII, Karabakh and Xocalı.

Museum of National Applied Art
MUSEUM
(admission AZN2; ⊙10am-7pm) Across the road is a late-19th-century Russian church in unusual cylindrical form, built on the site of a 6th-century Caucasian Albanian original. It now hosts this very limited museum displaying haphazard collections of Şəki crafts. It's hardly worth the money.

BEYOND THE WALLS
A canalised stream parallels Axundov küç from the fortress area and the new town's main square, passing two **19th-century mosques** and numerous *halva* shops en route. Away from this road, it's fun to delve into the maze of residential old town alleys full of typical tiled-roof homes.

Karavansaray
CARAVANSERAI
(MF Axundov pr 185) Even if you don't stay here, do peep inside this historic caravanserai whose twin-level arcade of sturdy arches encloses a sizeable central courtyard. Stride through the imposing wooden gateway door and if questioned say you're heading for the restaurant in the garden behind, a relaxing place for a 20q cup of tea, perhaps accompanied by a slice of signature Şəki *halvasi* (local *paxlava*).

Çingis Klubu
CULTURAL BUILDING
(☑47700; MF Axundov pr 91; admission 40q; ⊙10am-7pm) This polished new centre remembers TV journalist and national hero Çingis Mustafayev who died in 1992 filming the Karabakh War. Photos of his life are complemented by a small but well-chosen gallery of modern Azerbaijani paintings. A basement ethnographic room illustrates typical crafts.

Yuxari Baş
AREA
A pleasant stroll into this villagelike area takes you past a small 1880 octagonal minaret in around 10 minutes' walk heading east from the fortress walls.

Activities

Azeri Mountain Adventures
ROCK CLIMBING
(www.azerventures.com; Aydin Məmmədov küç; climbing wall 1hr/day AZN1/2; ⊙1pm-10pm) This American-run outfit organises a selection of four-hour rock-climbing trips into some beautiful local valleys (AZN60 for six people). In a Şəki warehouse, one block south then east of the bus station, its 7m-high climbing wall has six runs, a bouldering section and rents full professional safety gear.

Xan Yaylağı
WALKING
A 12km switchback track zigzags up from Marxal Resort to a spectacular viewpoint on a mountain plateau whose summer pastures are known as Xan Yaylağı. Ideal for a day's walk (some short cuts possible) or horse ride. Marxal is around 1km off the Kiş road; turn beside the Soyuq Bulaq cafe-complex.

Sleeping
A big new Ramada Hotel is nearing completion, opposite the Karavansaray. Work on the fanciful castle-style Nagorny Resort appears to have stalled. There are several rural alternatives around Kiş.

TOP CHOICE Karavansaray Hotel
INN $
(☑44814; reseil_karavan@mail.ru; MF Axundov pr 185; s/d/tr/q/ste AZN20/30/38/48/80) Staying in this converted caravanserai is justification enough to visit Şəki. Rooms have wonderful arched brickwork ceilings and while they're certainly not luxurious, all have sitting areas and Western loos in the humorously dated little bathrooms. Booking ahead can be wise, especially for single rooms, of which there are only two. Just down the road is the larger Aşağı Karavansaray: it had lain in ruins for decades but is now under renovation as a second, more luxurious caravanserai hotel.

TOP CHOICE Şəki Saray Hotel
BOUTIQUE HOTEL $$
(☑48181; www.shekisaray.az; ME Rəsulzadə küç; s/d/tw/ste AZN80/90/100/250; ❇☎) Oriental touches counterpointed with smart Western facilities make this 21st-century hotel the most stylish anywhere in provincial Azerbaijan. Staff speak English, standards are tip-top and the inviting bar brews Şəki's best coffee.

AZERBAIJAN ŞƏKİ

Şəki

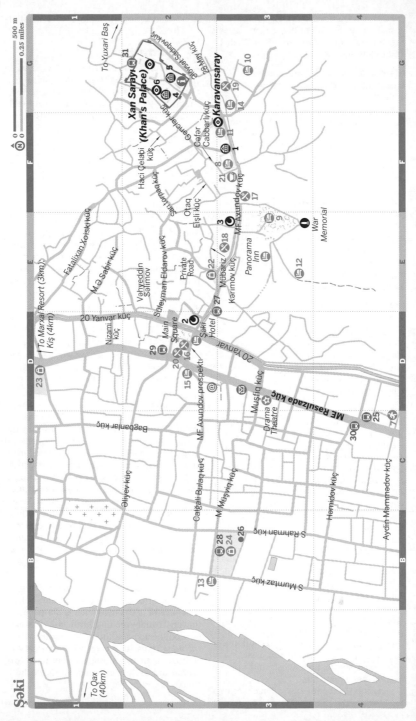

0 0
500 m
0.25 miles

Xan Sarayı (Khan's Palace)

Karavansaray

To Yuxarı Baş

To Qax (40km)

To Marxal Resort (3km);
Kiş (4km)

War Memorial

Panorama Inn

Şəki Hotel

Main Square

Drama Theatre

MƏ Rəsulzadə küç

20 Yanvar

MF Axundov prospekti

Bağbanlar küç

Əliyev küç

S Rəhman küç

S Mumtaz küç

Çalgali Bulaq küç

M Muşviq küç

Müşfiq küç

Həmidov küç

Aydın Məmmədov küç

Nizami küç

Vəhyeddin Sälimov

Süleyman Eldarov küç

Private Road

Fatalixan Xoyski küç

MƏ Sabirli küç

Otaq Eşli küç

Şah Tepedi küç

Həcı Çələbi küç

Cəngər küç

Dibəsər Sağlidinov küç

28 Mefi küç

Cəfər Cabbarli küç

MF Axundov küç

Mübariz Karimov küç

20 Yanvar küç

Şəki

◉ Top Sights

Karavansaray F3
Xan Sarayı (Khan's Palace).................G2

◎ Sights

1 Çingis Klubu......................................F3
2 Cümə Mosque D2
3 Omar Əfəndiyev Mosque.....................E3
4 Raşidbey Əfəndiyev
  Historical-Regional
  Ethnography Museum......................G2
5 Russian Church/Musuem of National
  Applied Art....................................G2
6 Şəbəkə Workshop................................G2

◔ Activities, Courses & Tours

7 Azeri Mountain Adventures.................C4

⊜ Sleeping

8 Aşağı Caravanserai...............................F3
9 Greenhill Inn E3
10 İlqar Ağayev's Homestay G3
11 Kəravansaray Hotel..............................F3
12 Nagorny Resort (Under
   Construction)................................E3
13 Pensionat Sahil B2
14 Ramada Hotel (under construction)....G3
15 Şəki Saray Hotel.................................. D2

⊗ Eating

16 Çələbi Xan Restoran D2
17 Marry Brown F3
18 Ovuçlar Məkanı...................................E3
19 Qaqarin Restoran................................G3
20 Sehirli Təndir.....................................D2
   Şəbəkə Restaurant.......................(see 15)

⊖ Drinking

21 Babamin Çayxanasi F3

⊛ Entertainment

Cinema...(see 1)

⊜ Shopping

22 Halva Shops E2
23 Şəki İpek (Silk Factory) D1
24 Təzə Bazaar B3

❶ Transport

25 Bus Station..C4
26 Cahid (Train Tickets)............................B3
27 Marshrutka 11 to Karavansaray............E2
28 Marshrutka 15 to Kiş B3
29 Marshrutka 8 to Dodu............................D2
30 Marshrutkas to Town Centre................C4
31 Terminus of #11 Marshrutka.................G2

İlqar Ağayev HOMESTAY $
(☏055 6238295; ilqaragayev77@hotmail.com; www.cbtazerbaijan.com/sheik; M Magomayev 20; beds AZN12-16) Kindly, pious and proficient in English, İlqar can arrange beds in a selection of Şəki homes including his own family's place, a quintessential Şəki traditional house with garden and a great old-town location. There's a hot shower but the squat toilet is across the garden, squeezed improbably into a superthick wall. Ask about local hikes and horse riding.

Greenhill Inn HOTEL $$
(☏050 4224619 Taleh; www.greenhillinn.az; d/ste AZN60/120; ☷) Doubtless things will improve but for now, staying in this unfinished five-storey tower is a distinctly odd experience. The brand-new, oversized rooms come with a neo-retro feel and most have sweeping city views. But as yet there's no reception, nor any apparent staff apart from a local caretaker who speaks no English and only appears if you phone him.

Pensionat Sahil MOTEL $
(☏45491; S Mumtaz küç; d/ste AZN20/35) The Sahil has simple but perfectly survivable older rooms with garish wallpaper and private if sometimes musty bathrooms. Suites are better renovated and some have balconies with views of snow-topped peaks, albeit seen through electricity cables. There's air-con in corridors but not rooms. Access is through tall iron gates directly west of the bazaar. Enter from the back of the building through the good-value restaurant-garden where draught Napoleon beer costs just 80q.

✗ Eating

There are numerous very cheap, if forgettable, eateries around Təzə Bazaar. Şəki is famous for its confectionery. Shops along lower Axundov pr flog lurid *nöğul* (sugar-coated beans) and much more palatable *mindal* (nuts in a crisp caramel coating). But by far their best-known offering is *Şəki halvasi,* a misnomer for a kind of *paxlava* (baklava). *Piti* (two-part stew) is a popular

---

EATING PITI

So you've taken our suggestion and ordered *piti*. But all you can see in the conical earthenware *dobu* (pot) is a lump of lamb fat floating lugubriously in broth. Don't panic! Before eating anything, start by tearing up pieces of bread into a separate bowl. Sprinkle with sumac (the purple condiment you'll see on the table) and then pour the *piti* broth over the top. Eat the resultant soup as a first course. Then transfer the remaining *piti* solids to the dish and mush together using spoon and fork. Yes. Including that lump of fat. Without it the dish just won't taste right. Another sprinkling of sumac and your 'second course' is ready to eat. Delicious.

---

main course here but before digging in, read the boxed text.

Çələbi Xan Restoran AZERBAIJANI $$
(main square; mains AZN3-8; ❄) The restaurant's striking exterior combines classic *şəbəkə* with modern smoked glass. The pine interior is as eccentric as a cuckoo clock with dining spaces in huge barrel-booths. In summer there's lots of tree-shaded outdoor seating too and for just AZN1.60 you could fill up on bread and borscht. The *piti* (AZN3) is excellent but if you fancy the *aş* (a multiperson platter of fruity *plov*, AZN30) you'll need to preorder. There's a 15% service charge.

Şəbəkə Restaurant INTERNATIONAL $$
(Şəki Saray Hotel; meals AZN4.50-8; ❄🍴) Despite the ironed, snow-white tablecloths, suede chairs and chandelier, this suave restaurant is nowhere near as expensive as it looks. The short but varied menu includes pastas, pizza, *ləvəngi*, kebab sets and veal in mushroom sauce. Meal prices include garnish.

Xan Bağı AZERBAIJANI $
(Fortress Grounds; mains AZN3-5; ☺9am-11pm; 🍴) This cafe has outside dining booths draped in living ivy and the menu includes AZN3 pots of mini vine-leaf dolma, tasty *piti* (AZN3) and good chicken soup (AZN1.40) but before ordering double-check prices with the English-speaking manager and watch for salads arriving unannounced (extra cost).

Ovuçlar Məkanı AZERBAIJANI $
(Axundov pr; beers 80q, snacks/mains from AZN0.50/3; ☺9am-10pm; ❄) If you're not put off by the sorry trophies and the ultratacky tiger portraits, this new 'hunters restaurant' makes a relatively comfortable place to sink beers. It also does kebabs (AZN2.40), *qutab* (50q) and Georgian-style *khinkali* (40q).

Qaqarin Restoran AZERBAIJANI $$
(mains AZN3-8; ☺9am-10pm) The outdoor garden seating surveys Old Şəki but service seems to strongly favour local clientele and menus are unpriced. No sign.

Marrybrown FAST FOOD $
(Axundov pr; burger/meal from AZN2.50/3.50; ❄📶) Chicken fast food enlivened by starburst ball lamps and bare stone-and-brick walls. Wi-fi is free if staff can remember the access code.

Sehirli Təndir BAKERY $
(Rəsulzadə küç; piraşqi/qutab 20/30q) Bright patisserie for pastries, cakes and a small selection of takeaway snacks.

🍷 Drinking

Babamın Çayxanası BOUTIQUE TEAHOUSE
(Axundov pr 20; tea sets AZN1-10; ☺variable) Sepia photos, stone walls and a decorative old brass samovar make this a tasteful little designer teahouse. If it's closed try calling 'uncle' Seyran on 📞050 5834986.

Babayaga BREWERY
(beers from 50q) Oddly hidden away behind the military compound 4km south of the centre, Şəki's first microbrewery already brews two excellent ales but has yet to finish its planned beer garden. *Marshrutka* 1A gets you near.

🛍 Shopping

Təzə Bazaar MARKET
Everything from pottery, metalwork and carpets to masses of fresh food – saffron comes in a wide variety of qualities, the cheapest just AZN1 a cupful. Get there by southbound *marshrutka* 11, 8 or 5.

Axundov pr STREET
Axundov pr is peppered with halva shops. Up by the caravanserais are a wildly contrasting range of stores: crusty old hat

sellers, tourist-trinket merchants and greengrocers purveying giant jars of pickled cucumbers, but also Tissot and Longines boutiques selling designer watches and AZN700 pens.

Şəki İpek
SILK

(Rəsulzadə küç; ☺9am-6pm) Şəki's silk factory (*kombinat*) still doesn't offer tours but its plush new showroom stocks a range of products including some attractively simple silk scarves from AZN10.

☆ Entertainment

The Çingis Klubu has an air-conditioned **cinema room** (40q; hshows 3pm & 5pm). Some screenings have English subtitles.

❶ Information

The **tourist office** (☎46095; tic_sheki@box. az; Sənətkarlar Evi; ☺10am-5pm daily Apr-Oct, Mon-Fri only Nov-Mar) gives away a good free city map. Staff can organise homestays, help you book rail tickets and arrange horse riding. The office is in a renovated historic building, upstairs above an interesting collection of craft workshops – woodwork, carving, *şəbəkə* (intricately carved, wood-framed stained-glass windows) and sculpture.

MONEY Several banks directly south of Şəki Saray Hotel have ATMs and currency exchange. There are exchange booths around the bazaar. In the old city there's an ATM on Axundov pr near Çingis Klubu.

INTERNET There are several internet cafes around the main square. **@vusal** (Budokan Lane; per hr 60q; ☺9am-10.30pm) has fast connections, new computers and ample space.

❶ Getting There & Away

Bus & Taxi

From the **bus station** (☎44617; Rəsulzadə küç) Baku *marshrutky* (AZN6, seven hours) depart at least hourly between 6.30am and 7pm, most travelling via Qaramarayam, Ağdaş, Göyçay, Ağsu and Şamaxı. Big buses run five times daily via Kürdamir, last 6.15pm. A shared taxi costs AZN12 per person.

For İsmayıllı change at Oğuz and/or Qəbələ.

Train

Şəki train station is a whopping 17km south of town (AZN6 by taxi). A nightly train to Baku departs at 8.30pm. To buy tickets without going all the way there, call Cahid (☎055 2085828) or find his tiny window-room, one door back from the Aviakassa at the southeast corner of Təzə Bazaar. You'll need a photocopy of your passport and should apply by lunchtime one day ahead. Alternatively, the tourist office can try to make a phone reservation in your name that you pick up and pay for at the station directly before departure.

Arriving by train at Şəki station, if you don't manage to find a shared taxi into town, you could walk 700m east to the AzPetrol roundabout then flag down any northbound bus (40q).

❶ Getting Around

Marshrutky (20q) run till around 8pm, or 9pm in summer. *Marshrutky* 8 and 11 both connect Təzə Bazaar to the centre, picking up at the Hämidov küç/Rəsulzadə küç junction a half block north of the bus station. The 11 continues to the Karavansaray and passes near the Xan Sarayı. The 8 goes on past the Silk Factory and terminates at the Makan Motel in Dodu. Rarer route 3 cuts

ŞƏKI BUSES

DESTINATION	DURATION (HR)	COST	DEPARTURES
Balakən	3	AZN2.15	10.10am, 2pm
Qəbələ	2½	AZN2	6.50am, noon, 2pm
Gəncə	3	AZN2.60	8am, 8.30am, 1.30pm
Oğuz	1¼	80q	7.20am, 10.30am, 11.40am, 1.20pm, 3pm, 4pm, 5.30pm
Qax via Şəki station	1½	AZN1.60	7.40am, 10.30am, 1.40pm, 4.10pm
Qax direct* (köhnə yöl)	1	AZN1	8.30am, 2.30pm
Zaqatala	2½	AZN2	7am, 9am, 11am, 11.40am, 3pm, 4.30pm, 5pm

* departs from the east side of Təzə Bazaar; call to book a seat on ☎055 5861799

across town from the Karavansaray to the Silk Factory via Fatalixan Xoiski küç.

Taxis charge AZN1 for a short hop, AZN2 for rides over 2km or if you cross an invisible line drawn east–west around the Drama Theatre. That means from bus station to centre costs AZN2, centre to Karavansaray costs AZN1. Taxis to the train station cost between AZN4 and AZN6.

Around Şəki

KIŞ
📞 0177 / POP 1300

Kiş village has plenty of tile-roofed homes, cobbled streets and views up the valley towards snowcapped peaks. But it is best known for its round-towered **Albanian church** (adult/student AZN2/1; ⊙9am-8pm). Lovingly converted into a very well-presented trilingual museum, it's the best place anywhere to learn about mysterious Caucasian Albania, the Christian nation that once covered most of northern Azerbaijan. In fact, the church site goes back well beyond the Christian era and glass-covered grave excavations allow visitors to peer down on the excavated bones of Bronze Age skeletons.

Outside is a bust of Thor Heyerdahl, the Norwegian explorer and ethnographer who postulated cultural links between the peoples of ancient Azerbaijan/Caucasian Albania and those of Scandinavia, based mainly upon their rock art (see p227).

In the northern part of Kiş you might still observe women fetching water in traditional *guyum* containers. And from there, a pleasant afternoon's walk leads up the river valley towards the minimal ruins of **Gelersen Görəsən Fortress**.

Back near the church, English-speaking **Ilhamə Hüseynova** (📞98833; ilhame633@ mail.ru) can readily organise a **homestay** (AZN10, or AZN25 to AZN30 with three meals) and is building a simple mini-hotel in her own attractive orchard-garden. She's usually to be found working at the church or in the seasonal cafe opposite.

Several more sophisticated bungalow resorts, aimed at vacationing Bakuvians, form an arc around Kiş.

Overcrowded daytime *marshrutky* 15 and 23 run about three times hourly from Şəki's Təzə Bazaar (20q, 20 minutes) until around 5pm. To find the church get off where Kiş's main street becomes cobbled, take the first right and walk 800m, a doubleback loop following the signs to Kiş Alban Məbadi.

Qax
📞 0144 / POP 12,200

Famed for its bottled **mineral water**, three historic **churches** and its partly Georgian-speaking population, Qax is most useful as the gateway to İlisu 15km beyond. But before you jump on a connecting bus, it's worth strolling up **İ Mustafaeyev küç** which starts directly beside the bus stand. Though the street's shops are banal, the road hugs a canalised stream and is overhung by trees and the wooden box-windows of traditional houses. After around 10 minutes' walk turn right one block on Azərbaycan pr to find **Içəri Bazaar**. Despite the name (meaning Old Bazaar), this is a 2011 for-tourists redevelopment where older houses have been refaced in stone along a cobbled street bracketed by big, new faux-castle style gateways guarded by slightly tacky warrior statues (as at Zaqatala fortress). An **open-air theatre** and series of boutiques selling traditional specialities should be operational by the time this book goes to press.

Three small blocks west on Azərbaycan pr, turn right just after the **Heydar Əliyev Museum** to find the simple little **Hotel Qax** (📞54865; Nərimanov küç; per person AZN5) with shared squat toilets.

Cranky *marshrutky* to Zaqatala (70q, 1¼ hours) depart roughly hourly. Most *marshrutky* to Şəki (AZN1.60, 1½ hours) loop circuitously past Qax's new train station. Those leave the bus station at 7.40am, 10.30am, 2pm and 4.10pm. However two direct Şəki services (AZN1, one hour, 9.45am and 3.45pm) start from the bazaar and use the recently patched-up A20 road: prebook these on 📞055 5861799.

Around Qax

Near Qax you'll find the remains of 6th-century Albanian churches in **Qum** village, in the hills above **Ləkit** and most accessibly perched above the A20, 3km southeast of Qax. But the most popular excursion is to İlisu, nicknamed Qax's 'mini-Switzerland'.

İLISU
📞 0144 / POP 1350

Set at the junction of two beautiful high-altitude valleys, diminutive İlisu was once the capital of a short-lived 18th-century sultanate. It's a narrow ribbon of photogenic old houses with box windows, arched doorways and red-tiled roofs with only a few Soviet and 21st-century blemishes. Towards the southwestern end of town the square-plan, five-storey **Summaqala Tower** commands a picture-perfect valley view towards distant snow-topped peaks. Opposite the unusual triple-arched **Ulu Mosque**, the lane towards Saribaş leads past the drum-shaped stone **Qala**, a remnant bastion of İlisu's historic fortress. At the northernmost end of the village, the main road dead-ends at the good-value **Uludağ Resort** (Uludağ İstirahət Mərkəzi; [✎]93425; per person AZN25; [✕]), with pine-fresh, apartment-sized rooms; some (like 35 and 36) have mountain panoramas from their balconies. A jeep track from here leads steeply up the mountainside to **Şəlalə**, a much-photographed ribbon of **waterfall** cascading over upturned strata. Allow around 40 minutes' steadily uphill walking or pay a whopping AZN20 to hop in a Niva jeep (horribly bumpy). Hikes deeper into the mountainous **İlisu Nature Reserve** aren't permitted as the reserve is a closed zone and the peaks behind form the sensitive Russian border.

Several summer-only restaurants and bungalow resorts lie on riverside meadows 3km south of İlisu village, close to a 17th-century bridge. Best value is **Ulu** ([✎]54140; per person from AZN10) whose bungalows were refitted in 2011. Around 1km further north, **Sangar Qala Restaurant** ([✎]050 3502131 Magomed) is an unmissable new fantasy castle built within crenellated dark stone walls.

Marshrutky leave from Qax (40q, 20 minutes) at 7.30am, 10.30am, noon, 2pm and 5pm, returning almost immediately on arrival in İlisu.

Zaqatala

[✎]0174 / POP 18,400

Azerbaijan's hazelnut capital sits at the confluence of two wide mountain rivers descending steeply from the Great Caucasus. The lower town (bazaar, bus station) is unremarkable but 2km uphill, beyond the small **Historical Museum** (30 Heydar Əliyev pr; [◷]9am-1pm & 2-6pm Wed-Sun) and tourist office, is a pretty little **old town square** featuring some noble **ancient çinar trees**. Hidden close by is the maudlin shell of a drum-towered **church**. Directly above, Zaqatala's 1830 **Russian fortress** originally guarded against attacks from the Dagestan-based guerrilla army of Shamil and later

imprisoned sailors from the battleship *Potёmkin,* whose famous 1905 mutiny at Odessa foreshadowed the Russian revolution. The large but sparse fortress site has recently been vacated by the Azerbaijani military and is partly open to visitors.

🛏 Sleeping

Hotel Qafqaz HOTEL $$
([✎]53353; qafqaz-hotel@mail.ru; Heydar Əliyev Pr 100; s/d/tr/ste AZN50/60/75/140; [✱][✿]) The best choice in town, this European-standard hotel has polished marble floors and large, high-ceilinged rooms whose bathrooms have good closable shower booths. Töhfə speaks English.

Hotel Zaqatala HOTEL $
([✎]55709; www.hotelzaqatala.com; Heydar Əliyev Pr 92; dm/tw/tr/ste AZN8/25/35/40; [✱][✿]) Despite rucked corridor carpets, standards are pretty good for the price in this well-renovated old Soviet hotel. Even the six-bed dorm (men only) has a private bathroom. Choose even-numbered rooms to reduce road noise. Only the suites have air-conditioning. Kamran speaks good English.

Turqut Motel INN $
([✎]56229; Imam Şamil küç; r AZN30-50) Recently redecorated rooms come with functioning bathrooms and toiletries provided but reception is dormant: for keys seek out a waiter in the fountain tea-garden behind. No English.

Motel Görüş CRASH PAD $
([✎]050 3225289; r AZN10-12) Three super-cheap, slightly dysfunctional rooms have off-line floors and are perfumed with eau-de-drain. One has a private bathroom but not necessarily any water. 'Check in' with the waiters at the very simple Görüs Restaurant directly across the tarmac behind the bus station.

🍴 Eating & Drinking

There are several shady tea-places in the Old Town Square and Heydar Parki.

Qala Düzü TEAHOUSE, AZERBAIJANI $
(Heydar Əliyev Park; mains AZN2-7, tea AZN1; [◷]summer) The big main building is a wedding palace, not a regular restaurant, but food and tea are served at clifftop pavilion seats in the park outside. Some tables have views across the river valley and of the forested mountains beyond.

Zaqatala

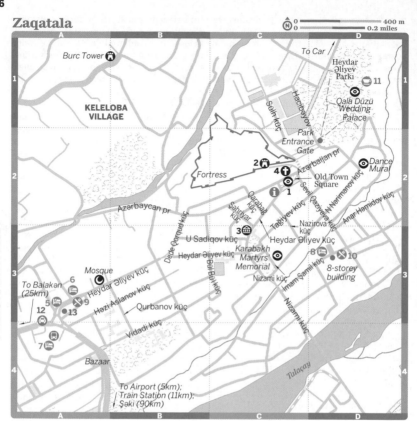

Qaqaş Restoran　　　　　AZERBAIJANI $

(Imam Şamil küç; kebabs AZN3; ⊙10am-11pm) Zaqatala's most original restaurant has a façade of bottle-ends, an interior of timber rooms and a series of wooden perches out the back as dining platforms. Cheap NZS beer on draught. No menu.

Bərəkət　　　　　　　　TURKISH $

(Heydar Əliyev küç 161; meals AZN3-5; ⊙10am-11pm) Neat yet inexpensive eatery for doner (AZN1.50), *lahmajun,* fresh-baked *pide* etc.

ℹ Information

The **tourist office** (Heydar Əliyev pr 2; ⊙9am-1pm & 2-4pm Mon-Fri) is friendly and English-speaking but poorly informed.

Several banks around the bus-station roundabout have **ATMs** and change euros, US$ and Russian roubles.

Internet cafes are sprinkled along Heydar Əliyev pr.

ℹ Getting There & Away

Air

The airport is beside the main Yevlax road, about 5km east. Flights go to Baku (AZN52) on Monday and Wednesday at 11.30am, and Friday at 9.30pm.

Bus & Shared Taxi

Marshrutky to local villages start from the bazaar. Other road transport starts from the bus station or various points around the roundabout outside it. Town- and Car-bound *marshrutky* link both points then shuttle into the town centre.

BAKU VIA AĞDAŞ (6.80AZN) 9.40am, 10am, 11am, noon, 3pm, 3.30pm, 4pm

BAKU VIA ŞAMAXI 9am, 1pm

BAKU VIA İSMAYILLI Shared taxi per seat/car AZN15/60

BALAKƏN *Marshrutky* (60q, 35 minutes) leave when fairly full. Shared taxis (per seat/car AZN1/4) sometimes continue to the Georgian border (AZN2/8).

Zaqatala

⊙ **Sights**
1 Ancient Çinar (plane) trees C2
2 Fortress Entrance C2
3 Historical Museum C3
4 Ruined Church C2

⊜ **Sleeping**
5 Hotel Qafqaz...............................A3
6 Hotel Zaqatala............................A3
7 Motel Görüş A4
8 Turqut Motel..............................D3

⊗ **Eating**
9 Bərəkət A3
10 Qaqaş Restoran D3

⊝ **Drinking**
11 Qala Düzü Summer Cafe D1

ⓘ **Transport**
12 Shared Taxis to Balakən.................A3
13 Transport to town centre and
Car A3

GƏNCƏ (AZN3.60) 8.15am, 8.45am, 11am, 3pm, 4.30pm

QAX (80q, 1¼ hours) 7.50am, 8.30am, 9.30am, 10.15am, 12.20pm, 2pm, 3.30pm, 5.05pm. Pay aboard.

ŞƏKI (AZN1.70, 2½ hours) 8am, 8.30am, 9.15am, 10.30am, noon, 1.15pm, 3pm, 5pm. Bypasses Qax.

Train

BAKU (*platskart/kupe* AZN7/10, 11 hours) Departs at 7pm. The station is 8km southeast of town.

Around Zaqatala

CAR

Half hidden in blossoms and greenery, Car (pronounced *jar*) is a chocolate-box village of picturesque houses tucked behind mossy dry-stone walls in abundant orchards of chestnut and walnut. But hurry to enjoy it before corrugated roofs and new buildings spoil the effect. Surrounding woodland foothills lead up eventually to bald ridges high above, but the trails can be hard to find and the 3000m-plus peaks of the remote **Zaqatala Nature Reserve** are out of bounds.

Ləzzət İstirahət Zonası (📞050 3133199; per person AZN20; ⊙May-Sep; 🅿) has a series of rustic dining pavilions including one

in a tree house. It also offers good value accommodation in stone-and-wattle cottages with old-tiled roofs, polished wooden floors and functional bathrooms. These form a circle around a gaudy goat statue in a grassy woodland clearing. Find it by following the signs to better-marked Daşliq teahouse.

Marshrutky (30q, 15 minutes) shuttle up from Zaqatala bazaar three or four times an hour from 7am to 6.30pm.

Balakən

📞0119 / POP 9100

The first town you'll reach on arrival from Georgia (via Lagodekhi), Balakən is essentially a 3km-long ribbon following Heydar Əliyev pr east–west. Two blocks south of the western end, Balakən's 19th-century **mosque** has a unique brick **minaret** that's free to climb if you can track down the mullah for the key. Around 1km east along Heydar Əliyev pr, the central roundabout is marked by a huge flagpole. The bazaar is just to the south, while a large manicured park leads north past the snazzy new **Hotel Qubek** (📞51599; www.qubekhotel.az; Səttar Gözəlov küç; s/d from AZN50/60; 🕸🛜🏊) to a merrily waving **statue of Heydar Əliyev** on a hillock. You could save the 15-minute walk by using the **cable car** (AZN1; ⊙7pm-9.30pm), assuming somebody fixes it.

The bus station is around 1.5km further east, 500m before the clean little **AzPetrol Motel** (📞52401; Zaqatala Rd; dm/tw/d AZN15/24/30; 🕸) at the far end of the city *marshrutka* route.

⊕ Getting There & Away

Bus

FROM THE BUS STATION

ŞƏKI (AZN1.95, three hours, 8.20am)

GƏNCƏ (AZN4.10, 9.30am)

BAKU (AZN8, 8½ hours, 9.20am)

OTHER SERVICES

ZAQATALA *Marshrutky* (60q, 40 minutes) leave when nearly full from a point two blocks west of the main (flagpole) roundabout, usually once or twice an hour.

GEORGIA Transport from MMOil Petrol station at the flagpole roundabout includes shared/private taxis to the border (AZN1/4), a 2pm bus to Telavi (AZN3 or 7GEL, two to three hours) and Qax–Tbilisi *marshrutky* (usually already full).

AZERBAIJAN AROUND ZAQATALA

Train

The train station is 2.5km south of AzPetrol Motel, AZN2 by taxi. The overnight Baku train (*platskart/kupe* AZN7/10) departs at 6.30pm.

CENTRAL AZERBAIJAN

Central Azerbaijan is mostly monotonous flat steppe, semidesert and salt marsh. The scenery gets much more interesting in the beautiful Lesser Caucasus Mountains, southwest of the nation's second city, Gәncә. However, the areas with most tourism potential are in (or sensitively close to) Armenian-occupied Karabakhand, thus inaccessible. If you're heading to Georgia it is far more pleasant to transit via Şәki and Balakәn, but the shorter route between Gәncә and Tbilisi via Krasny Most (Qırmızı Körpü; Red Bridge) is perfectly feasible.

Gәncә

☑022 / POP 309,000

Despite a certain Soviet grandeur, Azerbaijan's second city has relatively little to show for 25 centuries of history. Most proudly it was home to Azerbaijan's national bard Nizami Gәncәvi (1141–1209), but was razed by the Mongols in 1231 and levelled by earthquakes. It rebounded as capital of an 18th-century khanate before falling into the Russian orbit from 1804. From a building that is now the city's agricultural institute, the Azerbaijan Democratic Republic first declared the nation's independence in 1918. Gәncә served for a few months as the capital of that short-lived republic until Baku was recaptured from the socialist revolutionaries.

◉ Sights

The vast, central Heydar Әliyev (former Lenin) Sq is lined by powerful Stalinist architecture including the arcade-fronted **City Hall**,

---

WHERE'S THE STATION GONE?

Several popular train stations, including Şәki, Qax, Zaqatala and Astara, are many kilometres from the towns they purport to serve. Sometimes a single *marshrutka* awaits disembarking passengers, but hurry off the train as even taxis don't wait around long.

---

the **Academy of Sciences** building and the grand **Hotel Gәncә**. The twin-minareted 1620 **Cümә Mosque** is credited to Persian Shah Abbas. From here you could stroll **Cavadxan küç**, the city centre's almost-quaint pedestrian lane, or explore some patches of wooded parkland. On a quiet residential street, the quirky **Bottle House** (Qәmbәr Hüseynli küç) is a building-cum-artwork created as a memorial using beer, champagne and water bottles.

The **Imamzade**, around 11km north of central Gәncә, is the mausoleum of an 8th-century Muslim 'saint' (*seyid*). Until 2011, all you could see here was a graveyard and a relatively humble blue-domed shrine dating from the 1870s. However, major funding is transforming it into an impressive new multi-domed pilgrimage complex. For now, access is by rickety, twice-hourly bus 18 from opposite the train station, but connections will probably improve as pilgrim numbers increase.

East of town, the **Nizami Mausoleum** (Baku Hwy; admission free) is a 1991 tomb tower shaped like a space shuttle and flanked by a series of bold **sculptures** depicting scenes from Nizami's works. A vast aluminium smelter forms an incongruous backdrop.

🛏 Sleeping

My Way Hotel   HOTEL $$

(☑671019; www.myway-hotel.com; Adil İskәndәrov küç 59; s/tw/ste AZN60/90/170; ❉🛜) Down a quiet but relatively central lane, this family hotel has comfy, colourful rooms with some stylish elements to the bathrooms and original, local-themed watercolours on corridor walls.

Ramada Plaza Hotel   BUSINESS HOTEL $$$

(☑670005; www.ramadaplazagence.com; Nizami 237; s/d AZN140/160, large s/d AZN170/190; ❉🛜🏊) Pinging glass elevators whisk you to business-standard rooms that feature Nizami miniatures, imaginative swing-out desks and supercomfy beds. Large indoor and outdoor swimming pools are a soothing bonus. Prebooking online can slash rates to below AZN100.

Hotel Gәncә   HISTORIC HOTEL $$

(☑565106; Xatai küç; d/ste AZN60/200; ❉🛜) This grand stone-fronted Stalinist edifice has a Brezhnevian tendency to underilluminate the grand lobby and corridors, but rooms have been upgraded to roughly Western standards. It's wonderfully central and the restaurant is decent value, even if meal

Gəncə

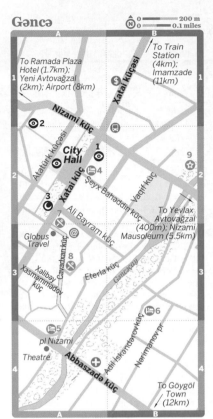

Gəncə

◉ Top Sights
City Hall A2

◉ Sights
1 Academy of Sciences A2
2 Bottle House A1
3 Cümə Mosque A2

▭ Sleeping
4 Hotel Gəncə A2
5 Kəpəz Hotel A4
6 My Way Hotel B3

✕ Eating
7 Elegance A2
8 Kafe Magara A3

◉ Entertainment
9 Şah Sarayı B2

prices are approximately double what the menu claims.

Kəpəz Hotel HISTORIC HOTEL **$**
(✆566013; Abbaszadə küç; r AZN15-30) Within this monstrous Soviet-era hulk of decomposing concrete, only the 6th to 8th floors function, and even then only a few rooms have running water. It might prove foolhardy to test the stability of one's balcony. The lifts work but their call mechanism doesn't! Price negotiable.

✕ Eating

In summer, anyone with a vehicle should consider driving up towards Hacikənd to dine at one of the woodland eateries along the way.

Kafe Maraga AZERBAIJANI **$$**
(Cavadxan küç; mains AZN3-10; ☉10am-11pm; ❄️📶) A handicraft cart and heavy wrought-iron lantern lamps add to the vaguely cave-

like effect in this subterranean cellar cafe. Good food but double-check prices.

Elegance TURKISH, PIZZA **$**
(Cavadxan küç; mains AZN1.80-5, drinks 30q; ☉noon-11pm; ❄️) Arched windows, autumnal colours and photos commemorating the restaurant's record-breaking giant pastries. No alcohol.

🍷 Drinking & Entertainment

The relaxed bar of the My Way hotel offers sensibly priced drinks including wine from AZN6 a bottle. The VIP basement beneath **Şah Sarayı** wedding hall is Gəncə's nearest approximation to a nightclub. There are popular tea spots in the manicured main park and a few tea-tables overlooking the river beside the main theatre.

❶ Information

Several moneychangers north of the Univermaq department store open late.
Internet Klub 65-65 (Cavadxan küç 26; per hr 40q; ☉24hr)

❶ Getting There & Away

Air

Globus Travel (✆521121; Cavadxan küç 41; ☉10am-11pm) sells all air tickets and organises a 10pm shuttle-bus to Tbilisi airport connecting with Pegasus (www.flypgs.com) budget flights to Istanbul and beyond.

Gəncə's airport is 8km northwest of centre, AZN6 by taxi plus 40q gate fee. Save half the taxi

BUSES FROM GƏNCƏ'S 'YEVLAX AVTOVAĞZAL'

DESTINATION	DURATION	COST	DEPARTURES (HR)
Baku	6½	AZN6	every half hour 7.30am-4.30pm plus overnight
İsmayıllı	4	AZN3	8am, 3pm
Lənkəran	8	AZN7 AZN10	9.30am 6pm
Qəbələ	3½	AZN2.60	1.30pm, 2.15pm
Şəki	3	AZN2.50	8.20am, 1.45pm, 4.30pm
Zaqatala	4¼	AZN3.50	8am, 11am, 4pm, 5pm

fare by starting from the Yeni Gəncə junction opposite Ramada Plaza hotel. Flights from Gəncə:

BAKU (AZN44, thrice weekly) AZAL

KYIV (AZN227, Tuesdays) AeroSvit

MOSCOW (AZN130, daily) Moskovia (www. ak3r.ru)

NAXÇIVAN (AZN41, thrice weekly) AZAL

ST PETERSBURG (AZN258, Mondays) Ural Airlines

Bus

All three main bus stands are linked by city bus route 20.

Yevlax Avtovağuzal (Nizami küç) handles most major destinations including Baku. Turkish bus companies have their office across the road while *marshrutky* to Göygöl Town (Xanlar, 50q, 25 minutes) leave when full from a block further west, 200m south down Nərimanov küç.

Yeni Gəncə junction opposite Ramada Plaza hotel is the pick-up point for through buses to Krasny Most (Qırmızı Körpü, the Georgian border, three hours).

Yeni Avtovağzal, 300m southwest of the Ramada, handles *marshrutky* to Daşkəsən (80q, last 6.30pm) and Qazax (AZN2, last 7.30pm).

Train

The train station is 4km north of the centre by *marshrutka* 1. Sleepers run overnight to Baku (nine hours) at 10.30pm (*kupe* AZN11), 11.30pm (*platskart/kupe* AZN6/9) and around 2am (*kupe* AZN9). The daytime 'express' departs 3.35pm (AZN5, not on Thursdays) arriving in Baku antisocially at 11.40pm.

Around Gəncə

GÖY GÖL TOWN (XANLAR)

📞 0230 / POP 17,800

For a surreal slice of transplanted Teutonic history, visit this agreeable small town founded as Helenendorf by German winemakers in the 1830s. Stalin bundled the Germans' descendants off to permanent exile in Kazakhstan during WWII. However, several photogenic old homes on the tree-lined central streets have Germanic keystone inscriptions and the old **church** now houses a small museum. The town, known till recently as Xanlar, was re-renamed Göygöl in 2010. This causes pointless confusion as the region's most celebrated beauty spot is a mountain lake also called **Göy Göl**. The lake is currently out of bounds to foreigners for security reasons (too near the ceasefire line) but driving around 45 minutes towards it is allowed. You'll wind through woodland picnic spots near **Hacikənd** then emerge onto a ridge with magnificent views of the Lesser Caucasus range, crowned by the beaklike peak of **Mt Kəpəz**.

SOUTHERN AZERBAIJAN

Southern Azerbaijan's coastal strip is the lush breadbasket of the country, where tea plantations line the roadsides and trees are heavy with citrus fruit. Inland, bucolic forested mountains offer tempting streamside getaways and plenty of hiking potential. The area is home to the hospitable Talysh people, famed for living to great ages. Using the overnight train to Lənkəran avoids the long bus ride through dreary plains south of Salyan, making an easy escape from Baku or a pleasant stop en route to Iran.

Masallı & Around

📞 0151 / POP 9800

Although less appealing than the Lənkəran–Lerik route (p251), the **Masallı–Yardımlı road** offers an alternative gateway to the Talysh Mountains. Local weekenders head for the popular picnic site overlooking **Vilaş Lake** (Masallı–Yardımlı road, Km 10), whose woodlands are now increasingly crammed with cafes and mini-resorts. Further towards Yardımlı, **Yanardağ** (☏050 2089895, 5385228; Km 15; cottages from AZN30) is a more isolated rest zone with a wooden dining platform that bridges the river. On the far side the river water 'catches fire' due to all the dissolved methane, though disappointingly the most flammable waters have recently been diverted into a decorative pool and a series of medicinal bathing booths. If you climb five minutes up the steep stairway to the right, you'll reach a small bald area of hillside where local tourists scrabble to reignite three minuscule gas vent-holes.

Further towards Yardımlı you'll pass a seasonal, two-level **waterfall** (şəlalə; Km 27) that's one of Azerbaijan's more impressive. And there are several rough tracks leading into forgotten highland villages. With a guide it is possible to hike across eventually to Lerik, but driving this without a 6WD you'll probably get stuck in the mud. Little **Yardımlı** (Km 50) has a carpet factory and mini-hotel and the pleasant backdrop of grassy hills is split by a picturesque chasm.

Southern Azerbaijan

ⓘ Getting There & Away

Baku–Lənkəran buses are generally easy to flag down at the eastern end of Masallı's Heydar Əliyev pr, 2km east (AZN1 by taxi) of the main bazaar. A return taxi direct from the main road junction to the waterfall/Yanardağ costs around AZN15/10.

Lənkəran

☏0171 / POP 48,500

Although it's the region's biggest town, likeable Lənkəran (Lenkoran) exudes a laid-back, docile charm. Famous for flowers and tea, its social hub is **Dosa Park**, full of fountains and minutely clipped shrubberies, and sporting the refreshingly air-conditioned **Heydar Əliyev Museum** (admission free; ⏰10am-1pm & 2-6pm Mon-Sat). The two-room **History Museum** (S Axundov küç; admission free; ⏰10am-1pm & 2-6pm Tue-Sun) is housed in a century-old brick mansion built in 'Scooby-Doo Gothic' style, and formerly home to a Talysh playboy prince. Lənkəran's **Dairəvi Qala** is a sturdy brick-barrel tower that once imprisoned Joseph Stalin during his early revolutionary days. Though recently renovated, it has yet to open to general visitors.

There's a somewhat similar **lighthouse tower** near the train station along with a statue of local WWII hero **Həzi Aslanov**, shown atop a stylised concrete tank.

Lənkəran's **bazaar** is an architecturally drab concrete hangar but it's loaded with big jars of pickled fruit and veg sold by a welcoming cast of comical characters.

Before the Caspian water levels started rising in the later Soviet era, Lənkəran had a beachfront promenade. Now the centre's beaches can't be recommended for swimming due to chunks of concrete and submerged ruins. Marginally better beaches lie around 4km north in front of the new **Qafqaz Sahil Hotel** (www.qafqazsahilhotel. com; Tofiq İsmailov küç 11) but they're still narrow strips of green-black sand and hardly worth the trip.

The town's new **Xazar Stadium** plays host to major league soccer and even occasional international matches.

🛏 Sleeping & Eating

A southern speciality is *ləvəngi*, chicken or fish stuffed with nut paste, sold relatively cheaply from little stalls and house windows around the region. *Ləvəngi* makes a great picnic best savoured with hot bread (*isti*

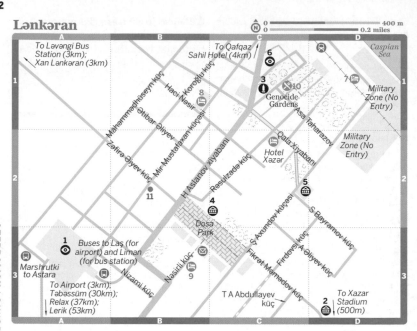

Lənkəran

◉ Sights
1 Bazaar A3
2 Dairəvi Qala (Stalin's Prison)...........D3
3 Hazi Aslanov Statue C1
4 Heydar Əliyev Museum.......................C2
5 History Museum C2
6 Lighthouse Tower...............................C1

⊟ Sleeping
7 Dalğa Restaurant & Hotel D1
8 Otel Qala..B1
9 Otel Yeni Tac B3

⊗ Eating
10 Uzbek Kafesi C1

ⓘ Transport
11 Air Tickets B2

çörək) fresh-baked in the same *tandir* (hive-shaped clay stove).

Xan Lənkəran   HOTEL **$$**
(✆42580; xanlankaran@gmail.com; Ləvəngi Bus Station; s/d from AZN40/48; ❄) If you don't mind staying out by the bus station, this fairytale complex combines a village-style dining room, a Tolkienesque garden restaurant

and a hidden hotel section whose reception desk is fashioned from two vast tree trunks. The whole place is dotted with handicrafts. Some walls are made of traditional mud-wattle and in sitting areas you can lounge like a khan on piles of carpets and *mutəkə* (elbow cushions). Despite the air of well-contrived antiquity, rooms have all modern conveniences including flat-screen satellite TV and underfloor heating.

Otel Yeni Tac   GUESTHOUSE **$$**
(✆41664; Nəsirli küç 2; s/d/tr AZN30/50/60; ❄) There's neither reception nor sign for this collection of brand-new rooms, attached to Zamin Bank. Nonetheless standards are as high as the ceilings except in one simpler single (AZN15) that has a separate toilet and lacks air-con. It's noticeably better value than Otel Qızıl Tac next door.

Otel Qala   HOTEL **$$**
(✆50284; www.abqala.az; Mir Mustafaxan küç; s/d/tw/ste AZN51/72/92/123; ❄) Qala has a certain restrained elegance, monogrammed towels and rugs spread over attractive terracotta-tiled floors. English is spoken but the place is often eerily empty, the lift doesn't work, some lights now dangle off-line and the stylish bar-restaurant only seems to operate

when groups are booked (usually during football matches).

Dalğa Restaurant & Hotel   INN $
(☑51769, 050 3409203; s/tw/tr/q AZN25/30/40/50; ❇) Five rooms with bathroom and scuffed carpets are set above the courtyard dining chambers of this sprawling low-key restaurant (kebabs/beers from AZN3/1), whose nicest dining area is a tree-shaded rose garden. Bring mosquito repellent.

Uzbek Kafesi   LUNCH RESTAURANT $
(mains AZN2.50; ⊘11am-3.30pm) Entirely unmarked but widely known for its inexpensive, hearty lunches (perhaps *plov* with *ləvəngi* or vegetable dolma – known here as *giymə*) served at outside tables in parkland near the train station.

❶ Getting There & Away

AIR Lənkəran International Airport is just off the bypass on the Lerik road. Flights to Moscow Domodedovo (AZN125, Friday) and Moscow Vnukovo (AZN130, Wednesday) are operated by UT Air. **AZAL** (☑3121593) flights to Baku (AZN40) are timetabled for Tuesday, Friday and Sunday but don't necessarily operate.

BUS Ləvəngi bus station (Lənkəran bypass), 3km northwest of the centre, handles long-distance bus services. Baku-bound services (AZN5) leave at least hourly until 6pm, with *marshrutky* adding capacity. There's a Gəncə-bound *marshrutka* at 8am (AZN6).

LOCAL BUSES Most depart from around the bazaar. Take Laş buses for the airport, Liman buses for Ləvəngi bus station (20q, last around 4pm). *Marshrutky* to Astara (AZN1) leave from Sabir küç, one block further north.

For Lerik, shared taxis (per person/car AZN3/10) start from Dört Yol Lerik, the bypass junction near the airport.

TRAIN The sleeper train to Baku (AZN5.50 *platskart*, AZN7 *kupe*, 10 hours) departs daily at 8.30pm arriving 6.25am next morning. The seat-only 'express' to Baku (AZN5, seven hours) leaves at 4.30pm but not on Monday.

Lerik & Around

The Talysh Mountains are not as high nor as spectacular as the Caucasus but their attractive mix of forest, canyon and sheep-mown uplands makes the area a delightful place to hike, as long as you don't stray too close to the sensitive Iranian border. The hub of this upland region is the overgrown village of Lerik. In summer Lerik is refreshingly cool but spring can be foggy and in winter it can get seriously cold, so remember to bring appropriate clothing.

LƏNKƏRAN TO LERIK

The Lənkəran–Lerik road leads up through extensive forests then continues into the bare, rolling Talysh Mountains. Several rest areas offer accommodation and/or refreshments and can be used as the starting point for random strolls or longer hikes.

In the lower woodland areas, **Təbəssüm** (☑91302, 050 3000313; Lerik–Lənkəran Rd Km 27; d AZN40-80) is a particularly appealing small-scale rural restaurant-resort that prides itself on not cutting any trees. Indeed fine foliage grows right 'through' the kitchen buildings. Wooden footbridges link tea pavilions nestled into the mossy rocks, some overlooking a minor waterfall. Its series of pine-fragrant huts come with dining platforms and neat little shower-toilets set into an attractive stream gully.

In glaring contrast to Təbəssüm's natural approach, the plush but gruesomely over-sized resort **Relax** (☑050 2508464; www.relax.com.az; Km 34; ❇❇) is now disfiguring its once pristine area of valley with a discordant water park. Less intrusive than Relax, but more manicured and upmarket than Təbəssüm, is the new **Cənub Resort** (☑050 4333636; www.cenub.com; Km 36; d/q AZN80/120; ❇) with its pirate-ship bar and various childrens attractions.

LERIK
☑0157 / POP 6900

Often lost in the clouds, Lerik climbs a steep Talysh mountainside and makes a great starting point for regional hikes. Behind the central Heydar Əliyev statue, a long stairway leads up the main suburban ridge affording wide panoramas over highland fields and serrated crags. Otherwise the town's most interesting sight is the new two-room museum, **Uzunömürlülər Muzeyi** (local/foreigner 40q/AZN1; ⊘9am-1pm & 2-5pm Tue-Sun), celebrating the region's famously long-lived residents (see the boxed text, p254). While not in English, most exhibits are self-explanatory. The simplest way to find the museum is using the steps that start around halfway between the shared-taxi stand and the main square. Follow signs for the culture house (Mədəniyyet Evi), then walk around that grey-clad building to the left.

Several bracing walks are possible by simply striding out of town in any direction. Simple maps of some well-tested options

LIVING LONGER IN LERIK

When he died in 1973, Şirəli Müslümov (aka Shirali Muslimov) was hailed as the world's oldest man. According to his Soviet passport he had chalked up an astounding 168 years. The *Guinness Book of Records* later dropped Müslümov due to uncertainties over that passport's accuracy, but his fame led National Geographic to visit his home region around Lerik. Here they reported what the Soviets had long since known – that this part of Azerbaijan had a statistically high proportion of centenarians. An international yoghurt company even based an advertisement on the place, hinting, without any real proof, that their products could make you live longer. In fact, researchers credit regular exercise coupled with sturdy genetics as the main factors of local longevity. These days you can still meet centenarians in the Talysh region, but their numbers are dwindling, as you'll see in Lerik's Uzunömürlülər Muzeyi.

are available to guests at the **Heydarov Homestay** (B&B/full-board per person AZN18/26), which can be booked through **CBT Lənkəran** (☎051 5293537; www.cbtazerbaijan.com/lerik). This relatively comfortable house is tucked behind a memorial garden, accessed by the first alley on the right as you walk into town from the shared taxi stand. Father and son are *meyxana* performers and might show you DVDs of the art, but no English is spoken.

There's no hotel per se in Lerik. However, **Gussein Baba's Cafe** (☎44276; Heydar Əliyev meydanı 4; mains AZN2.50, dm AZN3-6, tw/q AZN15/20) has acceptable if basic rooms. The best two share an indoor squat toilet and shower but the small dorm's facilities require a short walk across the garden. The place has been run since 1974 by ebullient, Russian-speaking Gussein who's now nearly 70 and doesn't see why it would need a sign. Opposite the central hospital take the short road that leads past the Royal Bank (ATM) and Gussein's place is behind a wall where the road dead-ends at a car repair workshop.

Getting There & Away

Shared taxis to Lənkəran (per person/car AZN3/10) start from a stone-columned bus shelter at the eastern edge of town, five minutes' walk from the main square. A few direct buses to Binə bazaar (AZN7 to AZN10, six to eight hours) near Baku airport leave around dawn from the *avtovağzal* (bus station), an area of teahouses around 1km steeply downhill at the bottom of a valley south of town.

Astara

☎0195 / POP 15,400

Its beaches are relatively decent by Caspian standards but Astara is a slightly sensitive border town so unless you're transiting to or from Iran, it's probably be best not to linger too long here. The pedestrian **border crossing** (⏲9am-1pm & 2.30-6pm) is an intimidating, unmarked series of grey metal gratings from which Astara's central square is five minutes' walk away, straight ahead up Azərbaycan küç. On the square, Royal Bank has an international ATM and the **Hotel Şindan** (☎54177; Azərbaycan küç 11; d/ste AZN50/70; ❄) is Astara's smartest, with a pleasant beer garden. Budget travellers may prefer **Hotel Xəzər** (☎53530; H Əliyev pr 69; dm/tw AZN10/20) whose eight clean, bright no-nonsense rooms share a well-maintained squat toilet and shower. It faces Kapital Bank, one block west of the Şindan, though walking between them requires doing three sides of a square.

Marshrutky to Lənkəran (AZN1, 50 minutes) depart regularly till 3pm from beside Azərbaycan küç 36, just two minutes' walk north of Hotel Şindan. A taxi to Lənkəran shouldn't cost more than AZN10, including a brief roadside stop to watch water burn at **Yanar Bulağ** (Arçivan village). This is a standpipe beneath a concrete pergola, bubbling forth water made 'flammable' by bubbles of partly dissolved methane.

Buses to Baku (AZN6) start from a bus stand 2km north of the centre, accessed by Dairəvi *marshrutka* (20q). The inconveniently located train station is an AZN3 taxi ride up the coast. The sleeper train to Baku departs at 7.30pm (AZN8 *kupe*) arriving at 6.25am.

NAXÇIVAN

This cradle of Azeri culture and history is now a disconnected lozenge of Azerbaijan wedged uncomfortably between hostile

Armenia and ambivalent Iran. Historical monuments and oasis villages are dotted about a fascinating landscape of deserts and melon fields rimmed by craggy barren mountains.

It's a memorable place but visiting requires resourcefulness and imagination. Westerners are an extreme novelty and even Russian speakers are comparatively rare. While much of the population is extravagantly hospitable, officials beyond Naxçivan City tend to regard lone travellers with a deep suspicion that borders on aggression.

Transiting Naxçivan would make an interesting alternative route when travelling between Iran and Turkey (with which the territory has a short but crucial border) but without an Iranian visa, the only way to get here from the rest of Azerbaijan is to fly.

History

Extravagant local legends claim that Noah founded Naxçivan after his biblical ark had crash-landed on Mt Ararat (Ağrıdağ, Turkey), whose twin cones loom powerfully above the western tip of the enclave. Or even, according to some Azeri sources, on Naxçivan's own Mt Gəmiqaya. In the 12th century Naxçivan was one of three capitals of the Atabey dynasty, which controlled much of western Persia. Throughout medieval times it flourished as an important centre of trade, emerging as an independent khanate in the 18th century. Like many Azeri khanates, Naxçivan was sucked into the Russian Empire following a series of Russo-Persian wars, sealed by the 1828 treaty of Turkmenchay.

When Azerbaijan was briefly independent from 1918 to 1920, it stretched uninterrupted from Baku to Naxçivan. However, in the early Soviet era that followed, Lenin's divide-and-rule policies gave Armenia the province of Zangezour, thus isolating Naxçivan from the rest of Azerbaijan. In 1924 Naxçivan was declared an Autonomous Soviet Socialist Republic.

In January 1990, as the Soviet Union began to crack, Naxçivan became the first part of the Soviet Union to formally declare independence, beating Lithuania by a matter of weeks. It didn't last. Naxçivan soon rejoined the rest of Azerbaijan and remains an integral (if dislocated) part of the nation.

Naxçivan City

036 / POP 68,700

Ordered and compulsively neat, Naxçivan City's streets are lined with shiny new facades, yet a strange torpor reigns. That's especially true in blisteringly hot summers, which render most activity impossible beyond the playing of nard and drinking of tea in soothingly shady parks. There's a plethora of free museums and a scattering of historic buildings, but many of those have been so heavily renovated with brassy metallic roofs that they appear to be reconstructions.

◉ Sights

Mömina Xatun TOMB TOWER
(admission free; ⊙9am-1pm & 2-6pm Tue-Sun) Perfectly proportioned, if gently leaning, Naxçivan's architectural icon is a 26m brick tower dating from 1186. It's decorated with geometric patterns and Kufic script (a stylised, angular form of Arabic) picked out in turquoise glaze. The mausoleum originally entombed Shemseddin Eldeniz, the founder of the Atabey dynasty, along with his beloved wife, for whom the monument is named. Today the tower's hollow interior features a small exhibition of relevant photos and drawings. Outside, a paved open-air 'museum' displays historic **stone rams** and grave markers. From the nearby **promenade**, Ağrıdağ (Mt Ararat) is distantly visible on exceptionally clear days.

FREE **Xan Sarayi** PALACE
(Mömina Xatun Park; ⊙9am-1pm & 2-6pm Tue-Sun) The promenade culminates in a formal garden containing the heavily rebuilt palace of Ehsan Khan, one of Naxçivan's 18th-century monarchs. It features şəbəkə windows and attractive exterior porches but feels virtually new and lacks the atmosphere of the Şəki's equivalent (p238).

Citadel ARCHAEOLOGICAL SITE
The Naxçivan khans were buried in a squat, brick tomb complex with a simple blue-glaze dome, now over-restored and known simply as the İmamzadə. Directly above is a large graveyard and the mudbrick walls of what was once the city's **citadel**. Until recently these walls were barely visible undulations. However, a major reconstruction effort is reviving them. There's also a brassy-spired tomb tower that was revealed by '2006 research' to be the **tomb of Noah**. Amusingly

the structure is even dated 'VI-millennium BC' even though it's essentially brand new. History and myth are rarely more incongruously muddled than they are in Naxçivan.

FREE **Hüseyn Cavidin Ev Muzeyi** MUSEUM
(www.huseyncavid.com; Istyqlalyyət küç 8; ◎9am-1pm & 2-6pm) This little house-museum commemorates Hüseyn Cavid (1882–1941), a progressive Azeri playwright who died in Stalin-era Siberian exile. The museum's collection is of limited appeal to foreigners but the wooden homestead makes an appealingly calm oasis. The writer's remains were very symbolically brought back to Naxçivan in 1982 and are now entombed in a conspicuous white marble **mausoleum** outside.

FREE **Heydar Əliyev Muzeyi** MUSEUM
(◎9am-1pm & 2-5pm) This modern palace of shiny marble is more interesting than other such hagiographic shrines elsewhere in Azerbaijan, if only because Naxçivan was Heydar's home region.

FREE **Xalça Muzeyi** CARPET MUSEUM
(Heydar Əliyev pr; ◎9am-1pm & 2-6pm Tue-Sun) Recognise the four main styles of Azeri carpetmaking or seek out the apparently non-ironic silk-wool carpet portrait of a young Heydar Əliyev, replete with Soviet medals.

FREE **Dövlət Tarix Muzeyi** MUSEUM
(İstiqlal küç; ◎9am-1pm & 2-6pm) If you have time to kill, this is an attractively presented, if fairly standard, historical museum showing off the usual Azeri artefacts.

🛏 Sleeping

If you're travelling as a couple, the Hotel Grand is far better value than any of the city's budget dives, which are mostly aimed at Iranian traders and charge per person.

Hotel Grand HOTEL $$
(☏5445930; N Əliyev küç 5; d with/without breakfast AZN60/50; ❄) Large, stylishly sparse modern rooms come in coffee-and-cream colours, enhanced by oversized mirrors and giant flat-screen satellite TV. Expansive bathrooms feature stone basins and great showers. Some 5th-floor rooms survey the mountain-spiked southeastern horizon.

Otel Avtovağzal GUESTHOUSE $$
(☏5456290; bus station; s/d AZN30/50; ❄🛜) If you're travelling alone this new guesthouse

Naxçivan City Centre

attached to the bus station is the best deal in town. Rooms have the same walk-in showers as the Grand and there's free wi-fi in the lobby. The incidental tea-and-cake art is a little odd.

Duzdag Hotel RESORT $$$
(☏5444901; www.duzdag.com; d AZN130, ste AZN250-350; ❄🛜🏊) Some 10km north of town on an arid hillside, Duzdag sees itself as Naxçivan's top hotel, with indoor and outdoor swimming pools, sauna (included), games room and English-speaking staff. The suites are expansive and come with a basket of Bvlgari toiletries, but standard rooms are smaller and less stylish than those at the Grand, despite costing more than double. A major part of Duzdag's clientele are asthma sufferers spending much of their cure package (s/d AZN195/260 full board) sleeping in a disused salt mine 1.3km beyond. Non-residents can usually visit the mine on

Naxçivan City Centre

◉ Top Sights
Mömi̇nə Xatun		A3
Tomb of Noah		B4
Xan Sarayi		A3

◎ Sights
1	Citadel	B4
2	Dövlət Tarix Muzeyi	B2
3	Heydər Əliyev Muzeyi	A2
4	Huseyn Cavid Ev Muzeyi	B2
5	Huseyn Cavid Mausoleum	B2
6	Mausoleum of Yusif Hüseynoğlu	B4
7	Stone Rams	B3
8	Xalça Muzeyi (Carpet Museum)	B2

🛏 Sleeping
9	Hotel Gartal	B2
	Otel Avtovağzal	(see 19)

✖ Eating
10	Cağ Kebab	A3
11	Gənclik Kafesi	B2
12	Restaurant Təbriz	B3

⊘ Drinking
13	Çay Evi	A2
14	Kafe Göl	A3
	Marakesh Club	(see 11)
15	Şarq Hamam	B3

⊕ Entertainment
	Əyləncə Mərkəzi	(see 13)

ℹ Information
16	Iranian Consulate	B2
17	Turkish Consulate	B2

ℹ Transport
18	Aviakassa	B4
19	Avtovağzal (Bus station)	A1
20	Shared taxis to Culfa	B4

AZERBAIJAN NAXÇIVAN CITY

request – a fascinating experience. You can even take tea in an illuminated midtunnel buffet (AZN1).

Hotel Gartal HOTEL $
(☏5452124; per person AZN20; ✻) Cheap, central bed-in-a-box rooms that share hot showers and two communal squat toilets. Not recommended for women.

✖ Eating

Restaurant Təbriz AZERBAIJANI, IRANIAN $$
(13th fl, Hotel Təbriz; mains AZN2-8, beers/wines from AZN2.50/5; ☺8am-midnight; ✻📶) Dine at the top of the otherwise overpriced Hotel Təbriz for spectacular views towards İlan Dağ and a capable selection of Azeri and Iranian favourites, cryptically described in amusingly impenetrable English. Alcoholic drinks are served and it's female-friendly.

Gənclik Kafesi TURKISH $
(Heydar Əliyev pr; mains AZN2.50; ☺10am-9pm; ✻) Point-and-pick precooked Turkish dishes plus a salad bar, of sorts. Staff are friendly and women do venture in (usually chaperoned) but there's little atmosphere and no alcohol.

Cağ Kebab TURKISH $
(Nizami küç; mains AZN3-6; ☺8.30am-midnight; ✻) Semismart Turkish diner.

🍷 Drinking

Marakesh Club BAR, TEAHOUSE
(Atatürk küç; beers AZN1; ☺10am-midnight) Spacious cellar bar that's comparatively bohemian by Naxçivan standards. Beneath Gənclik Kafesi, but entered from the opposite side.

Şarq Hamam TEAHOUSE
(Cəlilov küç; tea AZN2; ☺9am-midnight) From the outside this 18th-century bathhouse looks like a modern fake. But inside there's oodles of atmosphere and such a museumlike collection of old handicrafts that it can take some effort to track down one of the napping waiters.

Kafe Göl CAFE
(tea/coffee/snacks from 60q/AZN1.20/2.50; ☺10am-9pm) New park cafe overlooks a pond.

☆ Entertainment

Əyləncə Mərkəzi RECREATION CENTRE
(bowling AZN5; ☺10am-midnight) Tenpin bowling alley with attached games room.

ℹ Information

There are currency exchanges and ATMs throughout the town. Naxçivan City has both Iranian and Turkish consulates.
Aliheydar Paşayev (☏050 5672506; www.natigtravel.com, www.natigllc.co.cc) This

well-connected translator, guide and travel fixer speaks decent English and is passionate about Naxçivan.

Internet Klub (Heydar Əliyev pr; per hr 60q; ☺8am-1am) Decent internet connection.

🛈 Getting There & Away

Air

AZAL (www.azal.az) flies several times daily to Baku (local/foreigner AZN50/70, 55 minutes) and thrice weekly to Gəncə (AZN41, 40 minutes). Return tickets cost double. Purchase from the **Aviakassa** (N Əliyeb küç; ☺8am-8pm) where you can also get tickets for UTAir's Sunday flight to Moscow (AZN240).

Anadolu Jet (☑4442538; www.anadolujet. com; Naxçivan Airport) flies to Istanbul (from €95, 2½ hours) at 5.30am on Sunday and Tuesday. Tickets sold online or, before 6pm, at the airport.

Bus & Marshrutka

Almost all services start from the renovated *avtovağzal* (bus station).

ISTANBUL İğdırlı Turizm (☑050 5890977; www.igdirliturizm.com.tr) operates six daily buses to Istanbul (AZN41, around 26 hours) via İğdır (AZN5, five hours) departing 6am, 8am, 9am, 10am, 3pm and 11pm even if almost empty.

BAKU Five morning buses (AZN14, 12 hours) drive via Iran but for foreigners who need visas to transit Iran and re-enter Azerbaijan it's usually far cheaper to fly.

ORDUBAD *Marshrutky* (AZN2, 80 minutes) leave Naxçivan roughly hourly until 5pm.

CULFA (AZN1, 40 minutes) Hourly *marshrutky* from 9am to 1pm. Thereafter use a shared taxi from the roadside lay-by just beyond the Aviakassa.

Train

No international service. Domestic trains leave both Şəhrur and Ordubad at around 7am to Naxçivan City (3½ hours) returning at 3pm. The Ordubad line traverses some superb canyon scenery directly northwest of Culfa as both routes skirt right alongside the sensitive Iranian border, tourists taking any train can expect to be bombarded with questions and might endure a full-scale interrogation.

🛈 Getting Around

Taxis charge AZN1 per hop in town, AZN2 at night. For the airport (4km) some drivers ask AZN3 plus the *kapı* gate fee that you can avoid by walking the last 350m. A relatively comprehensive bus/*marshrutka* network operates till around 8.30pm but don't expect any service to return the way it came. All cost 20q per trip.

Useful route 6 links the bus station to the airport via the Turkish consulate, returning via the bazaar. More frequent route 3 circles the city anticlockwise passing the Grand Hotel, Aviakassa, Hotel Təbriz, Iranian consulate and Hüsein Cavid memorial northbound then heading east and returning south past the bazaar. Route 2 circles clockwise, going south down Nizami küç past Möminə Xatun then doing an out-and-back side trip to the train station before continuing past the Grand Hotel and returning eventually past the bazaar.

Naxçivan City to Ordubad

The drive to Ordubad takes you past some of Naxçivan's finest scenery. Arid crags rise powerfully in the middle distance and once you're past Culfa, sections of painted desert sprout lion-paw ridges. In between lie just a handful of surreally green oasis villages.

AŞƏBI KEYF

Contrasting with the thrusting masculinity of Beşbarmaq Dağ (p228), the womblike rocky folds of Aşəbi Keyf are decidedly feminine. But both reveal an interestingly animist side to Azeri Islam. A series of restaurant terraces leads up to a cleft cliff that gives something of the feeling of entering Petra (Jordan), albeit on a much smaller scale and without the carvings. Steps lead past a tiny blackened cave that was once the improbable abode of seven legendary holy men. Quite how they all managed to fit in it is as miraculous as their mythical 309-year sleep. More stairs lead up to somewhat bigger caves, passing a prayer area and two miniature shrines, one of which displays a tooth-shaped holy rock on a wooden stand. Some devotees puff their way to the top of a metal-ladder stairway to make miniature prayer cairns at the top.

Allow at least half an hour up and back from the car park, which is 14km north of the Ordubad road from a turning 8km southeast of Naxçivan City. Taxis want AZN10 return.

İLANDAĞ

Dramatic İlandağ (Snake Mountain) is a 2415m rocky peak that juts abruptly out of the central Naxçivan plains like a gigantic eroded tombstone. It's clearly visible from Naxçivan City almost 30km away. Legend has it that the cleft in the summit was created by the keel of Noah's Ark crashing through as the biblical floodwaters were abating.

DON'T MENTION ARMENIA

Given the unconcluded war, it's perfectly understandable that Azeri officials are a little edgy about visitors nosing about in border areas. However, in parts of Naxçivan, many officials treat visitors with quite unguarded suspicion. Expressing the merest interest in church sites or any other historical monuments built by the now-vanished Armenian community is likely to land you in hot water. It appears that most such sites have themselves 'disappeared' (see http://forum.openarmenia.com/index.php?showtopic=8751) and some straight-faced officials farcically claim that there 'never were any Armenians here'. Plainclothes police watch travellers closely, will probably interview your taxi driver and might check your bags for 'pro-Armenian' material. Comically enough, during questioning, a popular technique is to bark at you in Armenian to see if you understand it, as though speaking Armenian were a crime.

On a separate rocky outcrop above the village of Xanəgah are the minimal, widely scattered remains of the 7th-century **Alinca Fortress**, where the main attraction is a series of stupendous views towards İlandağ.

CULFA
📞0136 / POP 11,100

Unless you're crossing the Iranian border, it's unwise to stop in lacklustre Culfa. Eversuspicious bureaucrats are liable to get apoplectic if you attempt to visit the windswept site of Ancient Jolfa (Cuğa), 3km northwest. Ancient Jolfa was sacked in 1604 by Persian Shah Abbas who ruthlessly exported its talented Armenian craftsmen to build his glorious new capital at Esfahan. The Armenian quarter of Esfahan is still known as 'New Jolfa'.

ORDUBAD
📞0136 / POP 9800

An improbable oasis set amid rugged mountainous deserts, Ordubad is brought to life by *qanats* – ancient underground canals known locally as *kahriz* and accessed by *ovdan* stairways (see www.viewchange. org/videos/the-last-kankan-of-nakhchivan). These provide water for homes and lush orchard gardens, many of which lie inscrutably hidden behind crumbling mud walls. The village centres on the **Cümə Mosque**, which started life as the office of a 17th-century vizier. It still looks more palace than mosque. Outside, a *çayxana* (teahouse) sits beautifully shaded by ancient plane trees (*çinar*) while across the road Ordubad's interesting **history museum** (Heydar Əliyev pr 18; admission free; ⊙9am-1pm & 2-5pm Mon-Fri) is housed in a domed 18th-century building. From the museum's northwest corner, cross the stream and follow a stone-flagged footpath for two minutes to find the **house museum** (admission free; ⊙9am-1pm & 2-6pm) of scientist and photographer Yussuf Mammedaliyev. Heavy-handed reconstruction renders the building almost contemporary but budding artists might be tempted to linger on the two-storey wooden balcony and paint the view.

Ordubad has several old, if heavily overrenovated, **mosques** and attractive alleys to explore but be careful where you point your camera, as virtually any landscape will include a bit of sensitive border and police are quick to smell 'spies'. Within the remote Ordubad National Park, **Mt Gəmiqaya** (http://gemiqaya.nakhchivan.az/gemienglish) is famed for its ancient petroglyphs but getting to see them is effectively impossible for casual visitors.

Most *marshrutky* for Naxçivan City leave Ordubad before 9.30am but there are also three afternoon services (1pm, 3pm, 5pm). The bus station is around halfway down the main street from the museum towards the small **bazaar** where Ordubad's famously fragrant and flagrantly pricey lemons can easily cost AZN4 a piece.

Naxçivan City to Turkey

A recently upgraded 86km highway links Naxçivan City to the **Sədərək border post**, Azerbaijan's only border crossing to Turkey. The route is less picturesque than that to Ordubad, but the looming approach of **Ağrı Dağ** (Mt Ararat) gives a constantly mesmerising focus when visibility allows. Around 35km from Naxçivan City, a 5km spur road leads to **Qarabağlar**, where a famous 14th-century tower, crusted with blue glazework, entombs a wife of the great Mongol-Persian ruler Hulugu Khan.

UNDERSTAND AZERBAIJAN

Azerbaijan Today

In the last decade Azerbaijan has witnessed an astonishing economic recovery. Helpfully, the US$4 billion Baku–Tbilisi–Ceyhan (BTC) pipeline began pumping Caspian oil to Turkey just as petroleum prices peaked. And while Azerbaijan's oilfields have not proved as abundant as originally hoped for, there have been some important finds of natural gas. As money floods into state coffers there has been a building boom, especially in Baku and Qəbələ. All across the country, roads are being upgraded, buildings renovated and parks studded with new Heydar Əliyev statues.

Development optimism has been tinged by widespread reports of nepotism, corruption and press-gagging, though Transparency International reports an improvement since 1999. Political freedoms remain restricted and elections aren't necessarily fully fair, but few doubt that president Əliyev is genuinely admired by a wide proportion of the population. Nonetheless, many older folk look back fondly to the 'fairer days' of the USSR when everyone had work and there was not today's gulf between poor farmers and Pajero-driving ultrarich biznizmen. Apart from economics, the overwhelming political issue is still Nagorno-Karabakh. Few Azeris understand why the world isn't rallying to help restore Azerbaijan's territories occupied by Armenians since the early 1990s. The continued dispossession of hundreds of thousands of refugees and IDPs (internally displaced persons) remains an issue that is felt very personally by all Azeris. Armenians are frequently made a scapegoat for any national ill, and the idea of a war to regain the lost territories is not entirely inconceivable in coming years.

History

Early History

From the 6th century BC (and indeed for much of its later history) proto-Azerbaijan was part of the Persian Empire, with Zoroastrianism developing as the predominant religion. Around the 4th century BC the ill-defined state of Arran emerged also known as 'Caucasian Albania' (no link to the present-day Balkan republic). From about AD 325 these Albanians adopted Christianity, building many churches, the ruins of some of which still remain today. The history of the Caucasian Albanians is of great political importance to modern-day Azeris, largely for the disputed 'fact' that they weren't Armenian.

The Muslim Era

Islam became the major religion, starting with the Arabs' 7th-century advance into Albania. For later waves of Turkic herder-horsemen, proto-Azerbaijan's grassland plains presented ideal grazing lands. So it was here that the Caucasus' Turkic ethnicity became concentrated while original Caucasian Christians tended to retreat into the mountain foothills.

A classic cultural era bloomed in the 12th-century cities of (old) Qəbələ, Bərdə and Naxçivan. Şamaxı emerged as the capital of Şirvan and Gəncə's regional pre-eminence was symbolised by the classical 'national' poet Nizami Gəncəvi. However, from the 13th century these cities were pummelled into dust by the Mongols, Timur (Tamerlane) and assorted earthquakes.

After two centuries and an improving caravan trade, Şirvan had revived. Its rulers, the Shirvanshahs, scored an important home victory in a 1462 battle against Arbadil (southern Azerbaijan, now in Iran) only to lose in the 1501 rematch. Converted to Shia Islam as a result of that defeat, Şirvan bonded with (south) Azerbaijan under the Azeri Safavid shahs who came to rule the whole Persian Empire.

In the early 18th century, a collection of autonomous Muslim khanates emerged across Azerbaijan. However, to preserve their independence against a rebounding Persia, several khanates united and asked Russia for assistance. They got more than they bargained for. The Russian Empire swiftly annexed many northerly khanates. Persia's bungled attempts to grab them back ended with the further Russian annexation of the Şirvan, Karabakh, Naxçivan, Talysh and Yerevan khanates, recognised under the humiliating treaties of Gulistan (1813) and Turkmenchay (1828).

The Russian Era

To consolidate their rule over their new conquests the Russians encouraged the immigration of Christians, particularly non-Orthodox religious sects from Russia, Germans from Würtemburg and Armenians from the Ottoman-Turkish Empire. This indirectly sowed the seeds of ethnic conflicts that broke out in 1905, 1918 and 1989.

In the 1870s, new uses for petroleum suddenly turned little Baku into a boom town. By 1905 it was supplying half the world's oil, creating immense wealth, a cultural renaissance but also an underclass of workers suffering appalling conditions. Exploited by a young Stalin, their grievances ballooned into a decade of revolutionary chaos that resulted in several horrific interethnic clashes.

Independence & Soviet Conquest

The Russian revolution of 1917 saw the end of the Tsarist empire. With WWI still undecided, Azerbaijan collapsed into internal conflict. In Gəncə, 1918, Azerbaijan was declared the Muslim world's first 'democracy'. Baku only joined this formulation once its socialist revolutionary leaders were driven out, helped by an invading Turkish army. The Turks rapidly withdrew, leaving the Azerbaijan Democratic Republic (ADR, Azərbaycan Xaiq Cümhuriyyəti) independent. This forward-thinking secular entity, of which Azeris remain intensely proud, lasted barely two years.

The Bolshevik Red Army invaded in 1920, creating the short-lived Transcaucasian Soviet Socialist Republic in 1922 (along with Georgia and Armenia) as a prelude to the USSR. A series of border changes during this era progressively diminished Azerbaijan's borders in favour of Armenia, and eventually left Naxçivan entirely cut off from the rest of Azerbaijan SSR. The passionate insistence of Azerbaijan's 'father of communism', Nəriman Nərimanov, kept Nagorno-Karabakh within the nation, but for his pains Nərimanov was poisoned in 1925. His replacement, Mir Jafar Bağirov, unquestioningly oversaw Stalin's brutal purges, in which over 100,000 Azeris were shot or sent to concentration camps, never to return. Following the Khrushchev 'thaw' Bağirov was himself arrested and shot.

During WWII, Hitler made no bones about his priority of grabbing Baku's oil wealth for energy-poor Germany. Luckily for Baku, the German army became divided and bogged down trying to take Stalingrad on the way. Nonetheless, realisation of Baku's potential vulnerability encouraged Soviet engineers to develop new oil fields in distant Siberia after the war.

Perestroika (Soviet restructuring) in the late 1980s was also a time of increasing tension with Armenia. Tit-for-tat ethnic squabbles between Armenians and Azeris over the status of Nagorno-Karabakh bubbled over into virtual ethnic cleansing, as minorities in both republics fled escalating violence. On 20 January 1990, the Red Army made a crassly heavy-handed intervention in Baku, killing dozens of civilians and turning public opinion squarely against Russia. Azerbaijan declared its independence from the Soviet Union in 1991.

Independent Again

The massacre of over 600 Azeri civilians by Armenian forces at Xocalı (26 February 1992) turned public opinion against dithering postindependence president Ayaz Mütəllibov, who was ousted and replaced in June 1992 by Əbülfəz Elçibəy. Elçibey himself fled a year later in the face of an internal military rebellion. This was comeback time for Parliamentary Chairman Heydar Əliyev, who had been Azerbaijan's communist party chairman in the 1970s and a USSR Politburo member in the 1980s. Əliyev stabilised the fractious country, kickstarted international investment in the oil industry and signed a ceasefire agreement with Armenia and Nagorno-Karabakh in May 1994. However, around 16% of Azerbaijan's territory remained (and remains) under Armenian occupation. For two decades the 'frozen conflict' has left around 800,000 Azeris homeless or displaced and, although Azerbaijan's 21st-century oil boom has seen a vast economic transformation since 2005, these folks still remain in limbo… permanently rehousing them could be seen as an admission of defeat. And, judging from the constant media drumbeat coupled with a vast spurt of military spending, Azerbaijan appears to be intent on one day getting back at least part of the Karabakh 'lost territories'.

Heydar Əliyev (www.Heydar-Aliyev.org) is still unblinkingly referred to as Azerbaijan's 'National Leader' even though he died in 2003, aged 80. His photos appear everywhere and each town has a new museum and park in his honour. Meanwhile the dynasty continues under his son İlham.

AZERBAIJAN HISTORY

Arts

Azerbaijan's cultural greats are revered across the country. Their busts adorn Baku's finest buildings, their names are commemorated as streets and their homes are often maintained as shrinelike 'house-museums' (*ev-muzeyi*), where fans can pay homage.

Cinema

Film-making in Azerbaijan dates back to footage of the Abşeron oil wells dated 1898. Baku has offered a tailor-made set for many directors. In *The World Is Not Enough*, Pierce Brosnan as James Bond drove a BMW Z8 through the oil fields at Bayıl. In the 1968 Soviet cult classic *Brilliantovaya Ruka* (Diamond Arm, www.youtube.com/ watch?v=cibzTYr-PSs), Baku's Old City formed the exotic backdrop to a De Funes–style comedy farce about an accidental gem smuggler. Baku also features heavily in Ayaz Salayev's *Yarasa* (The Bat, www.youtube. com/watch?NR=1&v=qozngjNA-dE), a contrastingly slow-moving art-house film which won the Grand Prix at the 1996 Angers Film Festival (France).

Kinozal (www.kinozal.az) is an online resource for Azerbaijani cinema-lovers while the Azerbaijan Film Commission (http:// afc.az/eng) has an English-language history of the local movie industry (http://afc.az/ eng/az_films/tarix.shtml). The only venue that regularly shows movies with English subtitles is the Çingis Klubu in Şəki.

Literature

Azerbaijan has a long and distinguished literary tradition. Best known is the Azeri 'Shakespeare', Nizami Gəncəvi (1141–1209), whose ubiquitous statues almost outnumber those of Heydar Əliyev. Nizami wrote in Persian rhyming couplets, but Mehmed bin Suleyman Füzuli (1495–1556) was the first to write extensively in Azeri-Turkish. His sensitive rendition of Nizami's classic 'Leyli and Majnun' (a Sufi parable wrapped up as a tale of mad, all-engrossing love) influenced many later writers, including poet Khurshudbanu Natavan (1830–97), playwright Mirza Fatali Axundov (1812–78) and satirist Mirza Sabir (1862–1911), as well as inspiring Eric Clapton's 'Layla'. Azerbaijan's 20th-century star writer was Səmət Vurğun, who remains especially popular in his native Qazax district. One of the current deputy

prime ministers, Elçin Əfəndiyev, is himself a celebrated playwright.

Music

MUĞAM

Azerbaijan's *muğam* music is recognised by Unesco as being one of the world's great forms of intangible cultural heritage. To some Western ears it sounds more like pained wailing than singing, but at its best it's intensely emotional, an almost primal release of the spirit. This generation's greatest *muğam* superstar is Alim Qazimov. Listen online to a range of performers of various eras and styles on Mugam Radio (www.mu gamradio.az). Traditionally *aşıgs* (wandering *muğam* singers) would compete with each other in contests similar to the bardic competitions of the Celtic world. Such competitions continue today in a more upbeat and light-hearted form known as *meyxana*, with bantering lyrics and cantering synthesiser accompaniment.

JAZZ

In Baku, jazz grew popular in the 1950s and '60s and took an original local flavour under Vaqif Mustafazadeh (1940–79), who fused American jazz with traditional Azeri *muğam* improvisation. His multitalented daughter Aziza Mustafazadeh (www.azi zamustafazadeh.de; b 1969) has further blended *muğam* jazz with classical music. Other contemporary jazz-*muğam* pianist sensations include Shahin Novrasli and Isfar Sarabski, who triumphed respectively in the 2007 and 2009 Montreux Jazz Festivals.

ROCK & POP

Much of Azerbaijani pop is based firmly on the Turkish mould. There is also a minor rap, R&B and rock scene. Musically skilful rockers New Skin have the feel of an Azerbaijani Muse and are often featured on the website www.rockzone.az.

Painting & Sculpture

Azerbaijani art blossomed in the later Soviet era and today the works of neo-impressionist superstar Səttar Bəhlulzadə cost hundreds of thousands of dollars. Tahir Salaxov's work ranges from thoughtful Soviet realism to densely coloured portraiture and semicubist landscapes. Much of the expressive pre-Independence public statuary has been removed of late in favour of fountains or replaced by images of Heydar Əliyev, but great works do remain, notably by Omar

Eldarov, whose swirlingly creative statue of Hüseyn Cavid dominates Baku's Landau Sq.

Food & Drink

Azeri cuisine lacks the garlic-walnut fascination of Georgian cookery but has great strengths in fruity sauces, wonderful fresh vegetables and mutton-based soups. Outside Baku, the main problem can be getting beyond restaurants' obsession with barbecued meat.

Price ranges used in our reviews are for a typical main course with garnish. Budget ($) <AZN6, midrange ($$) AZN6-15, top end ($$$) >AZN15.

Staples & Specialities

The cornerstone of Azeri restaurant cuisine is the flame-grilled kebab. Standard *tikə* kebabs consist of meaty chunks, often including a cube of tail-fat that locals consider a special delicacy. *Lülə* kebab is minced lamb with herbs and spices. Both will almost automatically be served with a series of fresh vegetables, fruits, salads, cheese and bread (all costing extra) unless you specify otherwise. Pricier kebab types include *antreqot* (ribs) and *dana bastirma* (marinated beef strips), which are generally leaner. Barbecued vegetables are often available too, though vegetarians might be alarmed to find lurking morsels of lamb fat inserted into barbecued aubergines to make them more succulent.

The classic nonkebab dish is dolma, where various vegetables, *kələm* (cabbage leaves) or *yarpaq* (vine leaves) are stuffed with a mixture of rice and minced lamb, ideally infused with fresh mint, fennel and cinnamon.

Various stews incorporating potato and soft-boiled mutton include *buğlama* (sometimes with cherries), *bozbaş* (with *köfte* meatballs) and *piti* with chickpeas (see p242).

Typical of southern Azerbaijan, deliciously fruity Talysh cuisine is best known for *ləvəngi* (chicken or fish stuffed with walnuts and herbs).

Azerbaijani breakfast foods (*səhər yeməkləri*) are bread (*çörek*), butter (*yağ*) and cheese (*pendir*), maybe with some honey (*bal*) or sour cream (*xama*), all washed down with plentiful sweet tea (*çay*). Scrambled egg (*qayğana*) or fried eggs (*qlazok*) might be available on request.

Quick Eats

Azerbaijan's foremost fast food is the doner kebab. Much as in Europe, a large cone of compounded meat (*ət*, essentially mutton), or perhaps chicken (*tovuq*), is flamed on a rotating grill then sliced into small morsels that are served with mixed salad in *lavaş* (thin flour tortilla) or *çörək* (bread). Judge the quality by the queue. The *qutab* is a very thin semicircular folded bready-pancake lightly stuffed with either ground meat or sorrel-greens. *Peraşki* are greasy, Russian-style savoury doughnuts.

 Drinks

The national drink is *çay* (tea), usually served in pear-shaped *armudi* glasses and sucked through a sugar lump for sweetness, or accompanied by jams and candies. Coffee is a pricey fad in Baku but little seen in the provinces. Azerbaijan makes decent *konjak* (brandy) and its wines (*şərab*) are steadily improving. Xırdalan lager is the best known of several unsophisticated beers (*piva*), though Naxçıvan Beer and a couple of microbrewed ales are arguably much better. Toasting with vodka (*arak*) remains an important social ritual between older men with significant social standing (and bellies) to maintain. However, it is less formalised than in Georgia and less compulsive than in Russia.

Drinking water (*su*) from the tap is fine in mountain villages, but not recommended in

---

BLESSED BREAD

If you look carefully behind any apartment block you're likely to see bags of discarded stale bread hanging on trees or hooks, separate from the domestic trash. That's because bread is considered holy and can't simply be binned or even placed on the ground, leaving superstitious Azeris with a disposal problem.

Eating bread with someone is considered to seal a bond of friendship, while it's necessary to share sweets or pastries with strangers (or give it to a mosque) when a wish-prayer has been granted.

lowland towns. Bottled water is widely available: choose from sparkling (*qazli*) or still (*qazsiz*).

Where to Eat & Drink

Baku restaurants offers a wide, ever-changing range of cuisines from Mexican to mushy peas via Georgian, European and oriental alternatives. Prices can approach European levels but 'bizniz lunches' (from noon to 3pm Monday to Friday) are often a good deal. Beyond the capital, Azerbaijani and Turkish food is almost all you'll find. Eateries divide into four main types:

İstrahət Guşasi (rest corner) or **İstrahət Zonası** ('rest zone' with attached accommodation) Rustic eateries along country lanes, generally tucked into woodland clearings or beside streams. Usually kebabs will be the only choice (AZN3 to AZN5 per kebab plus around AZN1 to AZN2 per basic garnish).

Restoran (restaurant) Generally more refined than a *yeməkxana* but outside Baku meal choices are often limited to kebabs and accompanying salads, perhaps with additional choices of fish or *tabaka* (flattened whole chicken). To check if there are other non-kebab options, ask what *qazan-yeməkləri* (plate foods) are served.

Şadlıq saray Ostentatious 'palace' banqueting halls used almost exclusively for weddings or large, prebooked groups. Getting invited to a wedding offers a brilliant insight into Azeri culture, but bring earplugs to combat superloud music and be aware that guests are expected to give a financial gift on arrival: from around AZN25 in country weddings, but often AZN100 in Baku.

Yemekxana Simple eating house, typically providing basic cheap meals like *piti, buğlama, çığırtma, borş, kotlet* and *sosiska*. You'll usually pay a little extra for bread and the garnish of *qreçka* or *püre*.

Vegetarian & Vegan

Whether Göychay pomegranates, Balakən persimmons, Ordubad lemons or Gədəbəy potatoes, Azerbaijan's seasonal fresh fruit is utterly packed with flavour. Perfect-looking but tasteless Western equivalents can't compare to the condensed sunshine of an Azeri tomato. *Çoban,* a green 'shepherd' salad of chopped tomato, cucumber, raw onion, dill and coriander leaves, is served

as a preamble to most meals. If you eat fish, try *sudak* (pike-perch) or *balıq* (sturgeon), best smeared with tangy sauces made from sour-plum or pomegranate juice (*narşərab*). *Doğrama* and *dovğa,* both dairy-based soups, are possibilities for nonvegans though hardly a meal in themselves. *Göyərti qutab* are spinach-filled pancake-snacks. Baku's Western, oriental and Georgian restaurants serve meat-free options.

SURVIVAL GUIDE

Directory A–Z

Accommodation

Azerbaijan's accommodation scene is being transformed at a mind-boggling speed. In Baku alone, six new five-star properties are slated to open in time for the 2012 Eurovision Song Contest, with several more under construction in the provinces. Glitzy new resorts have already started transforming Qəbələ into a regional tourist centre.

Camping The nearest thing to an organised campground are the private orchard gardens at Lahıc. In the mountains one can generally pitch a tent almost anywhere but do be sensitive about damaging meadows (that flower-filled grass is a crop) and beware of fierce sheepdogs.

Guesthouse (*qonaq evi*) This is a term rarely used in Azerbaijan and generally falls somewhere between a homestay and a small family hotel.

Homestay A well established idea in Lahıc, Laza and Xınalıq but a new concept elsewhere in Azerbaijan. Rural homestays (typically AZN10 to AZN20) are now gaining an important impetus thanks to CBT Azerbaijan (www.cbtazerbaijan.com) but outside Şəki, city homestay options are so far limited to couch surfers (www.couch surfing.com)

Hostel There are only two places in Azerbaijan that call themselves hostels. These are essentially homestays with less space.

Hotel (*mehmanxana* or *otel*) Can mean anything from the (now rare) unreconstructed Soviet era dives (usually under AZN20) to one of Baku's rapidly expanding fleet of stylish five-star palaces (usually over AZN200). A new breed of

MENU DECODER

antreqot	lamb ribs
aş	fruity rice-pilaf meal generally served on huge multi-person platters
badımcan	aubergine
balıq	fish, usually sturgeon
borş	borscht, hearty cabbage-based soup
bozbaş	stew-soup usually featuring a meatball formed around a central plum
buğlama	mutton-and-potato stew slow-cooked to condense the flavour
çığırtma	soft omelette incorporating chicken, tomato and garlic (not a soup as in Georgia)
cız-bız	fried tripe and potato
çörek	bread
doğrama	a cold soup made with sour milk, potato, onion and cucumber
dolma	various mince-stuffed vegetables
dovğa	a hot, thick yoghurt-based soup
düşbərə	lightly minted broth containing tiny bean-sized ravioli and typically served with sour cream and garlic
düyü	rice
gurcu xinqal	Georgian spiced dumplings
kabablar	kebabs
kotlet	meat patties
kuftə	köfte
kuku	thick omelette cut into chunks
lahmacun	wafer-thin version of *pide* that you should fill with salad then squeeze on lemon juice
lavaş	very thin bread-sheets
ləvəngi	Talysh-style *toyuq* (chicken) or *balıq* (fish) stuffed with a paste of herbs and crushed walnuts
qızıl balıq	salmon
qovurma	mutton fried in butter with various fruits
qreçka	boiled buckwheat
qutab	limp pancake turnover half-heartedly filled with spinach (*göyərti*) or meat (*ətlə*)
pide	Turkish 'pizza' but without the cheese
piti	two-part soupy stew
püre	mashed potato
sac	sizzler hot-plate meal, usually served for multiple diners
sosiska	frankfurter-style sausage
tabaka	pricey, flattened whole chicken
xama	sour cream
xaş	heavily garlic-charged soup made from bits of sheep that Westerners prefer to avoid; wash down with a hair-of-the-dog vodka
xinqal	meaty chunks served with lasagnelike leaves of pasta
yağ	butter

ACCOMMODATION PRICE RANGES

The following price ranges are used in reviews. Ranges are based on the cost of typical accommodation for two people, including taxes but without meals.

PRICE RANGE	BAKU	ELSEWHERE IN AZERBAIJAN
budget ($)	<AZN70	<AZN40
midrange ($$)	AZN70-180	AZN40-100
top end ($$$)	>AZN180	>AZN100

neat mini-hotels has begun appearing across the country offering generic but clean rooms that rarely cost much over AZN60. Many are to be found in market areas or near bus stations. Relatively few have much personality.

Resort Gleaming new resort hotels are sprouting along the Abşeron coast and in Qəbələ, while the Caspian's summer playground at Nabran has a range of widely spread holiday complexes for locals on summer holidays. In woodland areas popular with weekending Bakuvians you'll also find a range of more modest rural resorts known as *istrahət zonası* (rest zones) offering wooden cottages with bathroom – many are big enough to sleep a family. Costs typically range between AZN60 and AZN200, though price isn't always a fair guide to quality. These rest zones often cite their idyllic, natural settings as an attraction while paradoxically having a penchant for blaring music.

🏃 Activities

As disposable income grows, activity tourism is likely to develop apace. Possibilities include the following:

Climbing Indoor wall- and cliff-climbing excursions start from Şəki. The mountaineering options formerly available around Laza are temporarily inaccessible (see the boxed text, p232).

Quad biking Short rides possible from Qəbələ's big resorts. Multiday explorations of Azerbaijan's untouched mountain villages should soon be possible through Baku's Hotel Hale Kai.

Skiing A vast ski-mountain resort is under construction between Quba and Laza, but low precipitation means that pistes will probably depend on artificial snowmaking when it is finally completed (estimated for 2019).

Spa cures Oil bathing in Naftalan, sulphur-water springs at Altı Ağaç (p228) and salt-mine accommodation at Duzdag near Naxçıvan (p256) are seen as valuable potential niche markets by Azerbaijan's tourism authorities.

Swimming & watersports Pollution means that the Caspian isn't the most pristine sea for swimming but in summer, locals flock to the make-do beaches at Nabran and on the Abşeron Peninsula. Jet-skis are also available. The beach at Şixov (p227) is curious for its offshore backdrop of oil rigs.

Wine tourism Şato Monolit near Ivanovka.

Business Hours

Reviews in this chapter list opening hours where they differ significantly from the following typical hours.

Office hours 9am to 5pm Monday to Friday, but late starts, early closing and long lunch breaks are common.

Shops 10am to 7pm or later, seven days a week.

Bazaars 8am to 2pm.

Restaurants 11am to 11pm in Baku, variable elsewhere

Customs regulations

Export restrictions include these:

Artworks & artefacts Export can prove awkward, as you'll often need written permission from the Ministry of Culture.

Carpets Exporting new carpets bigger than 2 sq metres requires a certificate from the Baku Carpet Museum (AZN46/26 issued in one day/week). Baku carpet shops can usually organise this for you. Antique carpets may not be taken out of Azerbaijan at all.

Caviar Limit of 250g per person.

Embassies & Consulates

Addresses of Azeri embassies abroad are listed in the 'useful information' section of www.tourism.az.

Embassies and consulates (in Baku unless stated), include the following:

France (Map p208; ☑012-4931286; www.ambafrance-az.org; Rəsul Rza küç 7)

Georgia (Map p203; ☑012-4974558; Suleyman Dadaşev küç 29, Baku) Bus 177.

Germany (Map p208; ☑012-4654100; www.baku.diplo.de; 10th fl, ISR Plaza)

Iran Baku (Map p203;☑012-4980766; www.iranembassy.az; Cəfər Cabbarli küç 44); Naxçivan (Atatürk küç 13, Naxçıvan; ◷10.30am-noon Mon-Thu)

Kazakhstan (Map p203; ☑012-4656247; Ak Həsən Əliyev [İnqilab] küç 15-ci kecid 8-10; ◷9.30-11.30am Tue-Fri)

Russia (Map p208; ☑012-4986016; Bakixanov küç 17)

Tajikistan (☑012-5021432; www.tajembaz.tj; Baglar küç 2-pr 20; ◷9am-noon Tue, Thu, Fri)

Turkey Baku (Map p208; Azadlıq pr 3/28); Naxçivan (Map p257; ☑012-444 7320; Heydar Əliyev pr 17, Naxçıvan City)

Turkmenistan (☑012-4654876; Şamsi Rahimov küç 14; ◷9am-noon & 3-5pm Mon-Fri) Just north of Həsən Əliyev küç a block west of Atatürk pr. Eastbound bus 6 (106) from the Hyatt area passes very near.

UK (Map p208; ☑012-4377878; http://ukinaz erbaijan.fco.gov.uk; Xaqani küç 45) Represents Commonwealth citizens.

USA (Map p203; ☑012-4980335; http://azerbai jan.usembassy.gov; Azadlıq pr 83)

Uzbekistan (Map p203; ☑012-4972549; Badamdar Şosesi, 9th Lane, 437) Access by bus 3 from Ahmad Cavad küç.

Money

Azerbaijan's new manat (AZN1) is divided into 100 *qəpiq* (100q). Very occasionally locals still quote prices in *shirvan* (AZN2) and *məmməd* (20q), nicknames for the pre-2006 'old manat' banknotes.

For information on costs and exchange rates, see p12.

Public Holidays

New Year's Day 1 January

Noruz Bayramı 20–24 March

Genocide Day 31 March (mourning day for those killed in Baku, 1918)

Victory Day May 9th

Republic Day 28 May (founding of first Azerbaijan Democratic Republic in 1918)

National Salvation Day 15 June (parliament asked Heydar Əliyev to lead the country in 1993)

Armed Forces Day 26 June (founding of Azerbaijan's army in 1918)

Ramazan Bayram The day after Ramazan (p296)

National Independence Day 18 October (date of Azerbaijan's breakaway from the USSR)

Flag Day 9 November (celebrates the 2010 unfurling on what was then the world's tallest flagmast)

Constitution Day 12 November (framing of constitution in 1995)

National Revival Day 17 November (first anti-Soviet uprising in 1988)

Gurban Bayramı (p296)

Solidarity Day 31 December (breaking down of border fences between Azerbaijan and Iran in 1989)

Telephone

Azerbaijan's country code is ☑994.

Landline numbers Five, six or seven digits. Area codes are given under city and town headings in this chapter.

Mobile phone numbers Seven digits plus a three-digit code denoting the provider, 050 or 051 for Azercell, 055 for Bakcell, and 070 for Nar Mobile. SIM cards cost from AZN5 for the least popular numbers. To buy one you'll need your passport and possibly proof of residency.

Payphones Rare outside Baku. Usually only call local numbers. Use 10q and 20q coins.

Call Centres For calling international, regional or mobile numbers. Standard price calls to most of the world cost 54q per minute, though there's a cheaper option in Baku.

3G Nar Mobile is so far the only 3G network.

Tourist Information

Dedicated tourist information offices are a relative novelty in Azerbaijan, and as yet many are still finding their feet. Most are friendly and generous with glossy pamphlets but few really understand the concept of individual travel and virtually none offer decent city maps. The best offices are in Lahič and Şəki.

Visas

Visas are required for most visitors and obtaining one can be an expensive headache (US$58 to US$131 depending on nationality). Since October 2010, visas are no longer available on arrival at Baku airport. Almost all applications now require a **letter of invitation** (LOI) from an agency like Baku Travel Services (www.azerbaijan24.com) or from a contact or business in Baku. But even this might not be enough: an increasing percentage of consulates now demand that the LOI be approved by the Azerbaijani foreign ministry, adding considerably to the cost and annoyance of procuring one. In most embassies allow at least two weeks to apply and be aware that you might need to prove residency in the country where you apply. At present this is not the case in Georgia, where visas are comparatively quick and easy to procure even if you don't have well-placed connections, see p120. Elsewhere, express processing is rarely possible for tourist visas but can be organised for some business visas. Tourist visas are all single entry but for business visas a double entry costs exactly the same price so is well worth requesting. Generally you'll need to pay the visa fee into a local bank then return with the pay-in slip, so don't apply late in the day.

Note that the Azerbaijan embassy in London has outsourced its visa issuing to www. visaforazerbaijan.org.uk.

In the USA, some travellers have been able to get tourist visas with only a hotel booking and no LOI, but don't believe outdated website information that claims you can apply online. At least one report suggests that getting a visa in Tehran (Iran) is possible in a single day and without any kind of invitation or letter whatever. All in all the situation remains highly unpredictable and your best bet for up to date information will be through lonelyplanet.com/thorntree.

Registration

If you plan to stay more than 30 days, police registration (*müveqqəti qeydiyat*) is a legal requirement at the local police station.

Visas for Onward Travel

Turkmenistan In Baku it is now possible to get a Turkmen transit visa or e-visa/ permission code – the latter authorises the issuance of a five-day transit visa on arrival in Turkmenbashi, very useful for those crossing the Caspian by notoriously unpredictable ferry. Before applying make sure you have an onward visas (eg for Uzbekistan) and be prepared to wait around two weeks. Beware that no visas are issued when the consul is away. That can be over a month in summer.

Kazakhstan & **Kyrgyzstan** Visas available without invitation letter in three working days. For both, use the Kazakh embassy in Baku which can process both visas simultaneously. Visa fees must be paid into an IBA bank (nearest is at the Hyatt complex).

Uzbekistan Friendly and helpful if hard to find. LOI requirement depends on nationality.

Tajikistan Single entry visa usually takes only two days with three passport photos and no LOI.

Iran Always hit and miss; Westerners are often refused visas. Note that the Baku consulate is separate from the embassy. You'll usually do much better applying in your country of residence with an invitation organised through a reputable agency such as www.persianvoyages.com.

Nagorno-Karabakh

POPULATION: 150,000 | ☑0479 | AREA 10,700 SQ KM

Includes »

Stepanakert.................270
Shushi..........................273
Azok Cave.....................275
Tigranakert...................275
Agdam..........................275
Gandzasar Monastery..276
Kelbajar........................276
Understand Nagorno-
Karabakh.....................277
Directory A–Z..............278

Best Historic Sites

» Tigranakert (p275)

» Dadivank (p276)

» Shushi (p273)

» Gandzasar (p276)

Best Places to Stay

» Saro B&B (p274)

» Park Hotel (p271)

» Hotel Armenia (p271)

» Eclectic Hotel (p276)

Why Go?

Nagorno-Karabakh is an enigma wrapped up inside the South Caucasus. It is a self-declared republic recognised by no one. It is Armenian culture on land claimed by Azerbaijan. Even the name is something of a mystery, being made up from words of three different languages: *nagorno* means mountainous in Russian, *kara* means black in Turkish and *bakh* means garden in Persian. To confuse things further, the locals refer to their region as Artsakh.

While there exist many questions about Nagorno-Karabakh and its political status, the beauty and cultural richness of this remote mountain landscape are undeniable. The Karabakh War left deep psychological and physical scars on the people and their landscape but the Karabakhtis are moving on, rebuilding their land stone by stone. Travel here is still an adventure, involving special permits and military-occupied no-go zones, but rapidly improving infrastructure means better hotels, restaurants and facilities in the main tourist areas. Karabakhti hospitality makes wading through the challenges a joy, even in difficult times.

When to Go

Nagorno-Karabakh is just one mountain range over from Syunik province in Armenia, so you can expect similar weather to what you'll experience in Goris. An excellent time to visit is the 9 May Victory Day, which also marks the Day of Liberation in Shushi. You'll see lots of military hardware paraded on the streets and an evening concert. Book accommodation ahead of time as rooms are in short supply. Summer and early autumn (June to September) are the best times for hiking. Spring (March to mid-May) is often wet and foggy.

Nagorno-Karabakh Highlights

1 Visit the **Gandzasar Monastery** (p276): excellent Armenian architecture with rich friezes and magnificent detail.

2 Wander around the lovely hilltop town of **Shushi** (p273), Karabakh's cultural capital with revitalised museums, churches and historic sites.

3 Explore the ancient remains of **Tigranakert** (p275) one of the four cities built by Tigran the Great, now home to an excellent new museum.

4 Eat, drink and be merry in **Stepanakert** (p270), home to a surprisingly good choice of hotels, restaurants and bars.

5 Wind your way through Karabakh's rugged landscape to reach little-visited **Dadivank Monastery** (p276), an overgrown masterpiece on the edge of Kelbajar.

6 Travel south of Stepanakert to explore the remarkable **Azokh Cave** (p275), with tunnels and six chambers.

7 Contemplate the tragedy of **Agdam** (p275), a city ravaged by the Karabakh War, located on the still sensitive frontline.

Stepanakert

📞 0479 / POP 55,000

Stepanakert, Karabakh's capital, stands above the Karkar River, surrounded by a typical landscape of forest, pasture and fields backed by craggy mountains. The city is not much different from a typical Armenian town, though it does have a bit more vibrancy. There are lively local arts and music scenes, modern shopping malls are popping up and cafés and restaurants, some surprisingly sleek, are often busy. A lot of reconstruction has occurred since the end of the war and it's hard to believe that it was under siege not long ago. A military presence is still evident but this doesn't impede your movements around the city.

☉ Sights

FREE Artsakh State Museum MUSEUM
(4 David Sasuntsi Poghots; ☉9am-5pm Tue-Sun) Rich in local artefacts, this contains particularly interesting displays on the Karabakh War, including homemade weapons used in the crushing early days of the fighting.

FREE Museum of Fallen Soldiers MUSEUM
(btwn N Stepanyan & Vazgen Sarksyan Poghots; ☉9am-6pm Mon-Sat) This stunning museum honours those men who died in battle during the 1990–94 war with Azerbaijan. The walls are lined with photographs of soldiers killed in action and there are displays of weaponry and other memorabilia. The entrance to the museum is in the back of a white building that stands on Vazgen Sarksyan Poghots. The door is slightly hidden by trees but the cannons and other military hardware outside act as a landmark. On the north side of the same courtyard (behind a pink building) is the **Museum of Missing Soldiers** (admission free; ☉9am-6pm Mon-Sat), which is similar to the Fallen Soldiers museum, but just one room instead of three.

Amusement Park AMUSEMENT PARK
(☉May-Sep) For something a little more lighthearted, this has rides and live music on warm summer nights.

Papik Tatik MONUMENT
On the outskirts of the town towards Mayraberd (Askeran) is the tuff statue of a bearded elder and a woman with a veil. It is named 'We are our mountains', their stony gaze embodying the indomitable local spirit.

✨ Festivals

National holidays are celebrated on 9 May. The day commemorates the liberation of Shushi and the foundation of Karabakh's army. Concerts, military parades, fireworks and related ceremonies are held in Stepanakert and Shushi. Accommodation can be tight at this time.

🛏 Sleeping

The homestay business is not well developed in Stepanakert; try contacting the English-speaking guide **Susanna Petrossian** (☏097246673; susanna_petrossian@yahoo.com), who has contacts in the city and can help find a host family for around AMD5000 per person.

🔝TOP Park Hotel   HOTEL $$$
CHOICE
(☏7 19 71; www.parkhotelartsakh.com; 10 Vazgen Sargsyan Poghots; s/d incl breakfast AMD20,000 /30,000; @🛜) Opened in 2011, this boutique hotel has been tastefully built in the classic Karabakhti style. The distinctive stone and wood facade lends a traditional atmosphere but facilities inside are thoroughly modern.

Hotel Yerevan   HOTEL $$
(☏7 15 03; www.yerevanhotel.travel; 62 Tumanyan Poghots; s/d AMD15,000/21,000; ✳@🛜) This new hotel has a quiet location, reasonable rates and modern rooms with flat panel TVs and wi-fi. There is a decent restaurant on the ground floor.

Raffo & Karine Guesthouse   GUESTHOUSE $
(☏097335288, 097261616; 27 Nalbandian Poghots; r per person AMD4000) This unsigned guesthouse has two basic guestrooms in a family house. The rooms are clean and comfortable, just a little old. Breakfast is an extra AMD1000. The house has two parts; the front side that overlooks the street is for guests. You need to walk around the back of the building to find the separate entrance where the host family lives.

Ella & Hamlet Guesthouse   GUESTHOUSE $
(☏4 77 38, 5 21 55; 10 Kamo Narpansk; r per person AMD5000) Budget travellers will find a safe haven in this spotless guesthouse. It has five spacious rooms with new furnishings, TV and shared bathroom in a huge villa. It gets busy with groups so book ahead if possible. To find it from the Ministry of Foreign Affairs, take the steps down to Kamo Poghots and walk northwest for 300m. After crossing the bridge take the first right onto a narrow road marked Kamo Narpansk (Kamo Lane). Near the end of the alley, look for the grey concrete building on the right with the high chain-link fence.

Armenia Hotel   HOTEL $$$
(☏5 09 10; Hraparak Veratsnound; s/d/ste AMD29,000/35,000/60,000; ✳@🛜) The plushest hotel in town is right on the main square, near the Presidential Palace and Parliament. Amenities include fitness centre, sauna and cable TV (with BBC news).

Sofia Hotel   HOTEL $$
(☏7 70 37; 15 David Sasuntsi Poghots; s/d AMD15,000/21,000) This reliable hotel is on the 3rd floor of the Sofia Shopping Mall. Rooms are clean and nicely furnished, just a little bland.

Hotel Heghnar   HOTEL $$
(☏4 86 77, 097266666; www.heghnarhotel.com; 39-41 Kh Abovyan Poghots; s/d/deluxe AMD18,000/ 24,000/45,000) Has 12 rooms in two buildings, which can be combined into apartments. It's quite cosy and comfortable with decent beds and big couches, and all the rooms have a balcony. The caretakers speak only Armenian and Russian.

YMCA   HOTEL $
(Kars Hotel; ☏4 71 67; 22 Nalbandian Poghots; s/d AMD6500/10,000, s/d deluxe AMD10,000/20,000) This is certainly not an official YMCA but that is what the sign reads outside the building. To confuse things further the management says the place is actually called Kars Hotel. Rooms are small, the carpets are filthy and the walls are starting to crumble. But budget travellers often end up here when the B&Bs are full.

✗ Eating

In addition to the following, you can get fresh fruits, bread and *khorovats* (barbecue) at the *shuka* (market).

Viaggio   ITALIAN $$
(10 Lusavorich Poghots; meals AMD2000-4500; ⏱11am-midnight; 🛜) Stepanakert's first and only Italian restaurant features an array of pastas, plus grilled chicken, steaks and fish fillets. The pizzas are big enough for two.

Petachok   CAFE $
(1 Azatamartikneri Poghota; snacks AMD400-1000; ⏱11am-midnight) This small cafe on Shahumian Hraparak has sandwiches, cold drinks and *ponchik* (powdered doughnuts).

NAGORNO-KARABAKH STEPANAKERT

Stepanakert

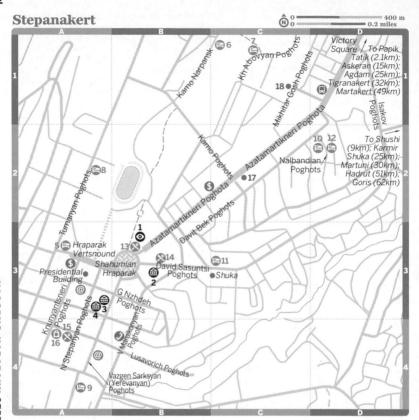

Russia RUSSIAN $$$
(1 David Sasuntsi Poghots; meals AMD3000-5000; ⊘noon-1am) One of the more popular places in town, this upscale restaurant serves excellent Russian and Armenian dishes. It has indoor seating but most people dine on the gorgeous, shady patio.

 Shopping

Nereni Arts & Crafts CRAFTS
(www.nereni.nk.am; 10 Lusavorich Poghots; ⊘10am-7pm) Run by a diaspora Iranian and his Australian wife, this shop carries a range of unique handicrafts created by local jewellers and artisans.

ⓘ Information

There's no official tourist office, but the **Ministry of Foreign Affairs** (☑4 14 18; info@mfa.nkr. am; 28 Azatamartikneri Poghota; ⊘9am-1pm & 2-6pm Mon-Fri, noon-4pm Sat) can suggest

routes and places to visit – you have to register there on arrival anyway (see p278).

A good contact is **Susanna Petrossian** (☑097246673; susanna_petrossian@yahoo. com), a local teacher who speaks excellent English and French. She can help organise homestays, tours (including hiking and camping trips) and a visit to a local school. Another good place for information is Shushi (p273), where you can link up with the helpful Armen de Shushi.

Moneychangers everywhere have rates posted outside shops – rates are much the same as in Armenia. An ABB cash exchange machine is located at the Armenia Hotel.

Stepanakert has at least a dozen Internet Clubs, all charging around AMD300 per hour. Try no-name places at 68 G Nzhdeh Poghots or 16 Vazgen Sarksyan Poghots.

There are several open wi-fi hotspots around Stepanakert, including the Armenia Hotel, Viaggio Restaurant and even in the outdoor park at Shahumian Hraparak.

Stepanakert

Sights
1 Amusement Park.................................B3
2 Artsakh State Museum.......................B3
3 Museum of Fallen Soldiers................A3
4 Museum of Missing Soldiers.............A3

Sleeping
5 Armenia Hotel....................................A3
6 Ella & Hamlet Guesthouse................C1
7 Hotel Heghnar...................................C1
8 Hotel Yerevan...................................A2
9 Park Hotel...A4
10 Raffo & Karine Guesthouse..............D2
11 Sofia Hotel..C3
12 YMCA..D2

Eating
13 Petachok...B3
14 Russia...B3
15 Viaggio..A4

Shopping
16 Nereni Arts & Crafts.........................A4

Information
17 Ministry of Foreign Affairs................C2
18 University of Karabakh......................C1

Karabakh Telecom has several phone offices around town (with attached internet cafes). You can also make calls from the main **Telecom Office** (30 V Mamikonyan Poghots; ⊙9am-6pm). Note that if you bought a SIM card in Armenia it will not work in Karabakh. Local mobile phones work on the Karabakh Telecom network but SIM cards are cheap; a card costs AMD1200 and includes AMD600 units.

If you are interested in hiking in Karabakh and need a guide, try contacting **Dima Ekorov** (☎097306833; mazzoniguide@gmail.com). Dima is actually based in Kelbajar but can meet you in Stepanakert; email is best to contact him.

🛈 Getting There & Away

Buses and *marshrutky* (minivans) depart from the **station** (☎4 06 61) near Victory Sq on Azatamartikneri Poghota. There are at least three *marshrutky* per day to Yerevan (AMD4500, seven to eight hours) leaving when full between 8am and 11am. These all pass through Goris (AMD1500, two hours). Daily *marshrutky* also travel to Sisian at 10am and to Goris at 2.30pm. Chartering a taxi to Goris/Yerevan costs AMD15,000/43,000.

Marshrutky to Shushi depart once or twice per hour between 7am and 7pm (AMD200, 30 minutes). Two buses a day run to Gandzasar

(AMD500, one hour) at 9am and 4pm. Nine buses a day go to Martakert between 8.30am and 4pm (AMD600, 1½ hours). Buses to Martuni (AMD600, one hour) leave at 9.30am, 12.30pm, 1.30pm and 3.30pm. Buses to Karmir Shuka (AMD500, 50 minutes) depart at 9am, 9.30am, 2pm and 3pm. Buses to Hadrut (AMD1200, two hours) leave at 9am and 3.30pm.

The airport in Stepanakert, closed during the war, was reopened in 2011. Flights are expected to run between Stepanakert and Yerevan and possibly even Russia.

🛈 Getting Around

There are plenty of *marshrutky* (per ride AMD50) that ply the main boulevards of Stepanakert. Nos 10, 13, 14 and 17 shuttle up and down Azatamartikneri Poghota.

Shushi

☎0477 / POP 3500

Shushi (Şuşa) stands on a plateau 9km south from Stepanakert, with high walls and views over a wide swath of central Karabakh. The city was once a centre of Armenian and Azeri art and culture, and during the 19th century it was one of the largest towns in the South Caucasus. The city suffered badly during the war and most people left, but recovery is under way. There are some excellent B&Bs in town so if you want to experience village life in Karabakh consider spending a couple of nights up here. For further info: www.shoushi.nk.am.

⊙ Sights

A fine **medieval wall** protects the eastern ramparts of the town – you'll see it on the left as you approach the town from the highway. The fortress was built in 1750 by Panah Khan. During the Karabakh War the Azeri army used the town heights to fire barrages of Grad missiles down onto Stepanakert and surrounding villages. It was conquered by a stunning night assault up the cliffs on 8–9 May 1992, a crucial turning point in the conflict.

The scarred centre of town has the restored **Ghazanchetsots Cathedral**, the obvious white church near the Hotel Shoushi. Another church, the 1818 **Kanach Zham** (Green Church) stands up the hill.

Down the hill, in the older part of town, is a damaged **mosque** that is slowly being restored. Close by is a recently restored **Iranian Bathhouse** (admission AMD5000; ⊙10am-5pm Mon-Sat), and an outdoor vegetable market.

KARABAKH STATUS QUO

According to nearly all international protocols, the territory of Nagorno-Karabakh is still legally part of Azerbaijan. It is not officially recognised as a sovereign state and we do not regard it as such. It is an independent state only according to the Nagorno-Karabakh Declaration of Independence and can only be visited from Armenia, which controls the territory. To visit you must buy a Nagorno-Karabakh Republic visa. Note that in addition to Nagorno-Karabakh, this chapter includes other areas controlled by Armenia but claimed by Azerbaijan, including Kelbajar and Agdam. Travellers should be aware that visiting Nagorno-Karabakh is illegal under Azerbaijan law and evidence of a visit could bar entry into Azerbaijan.

As for the terminology, the term 'Karabakh' was amended during the Soviet-era to 'Nagorno-Karabakh Autonomous Oblast', with nagorno meaning upper or mountainous in Russian. Nagorno-Karabakh had defined borders that did not match historic Karabakh, ergo, the term 'Karabakh' can refer to upper Karabakh plus surrounding areas such as Kelbajar and Shahumian. In practice, few people today say 'Nagorno-Karabakh', shortening it to just 'Karabakh'.

The **museum** (admission free; ⊙10am-5pm Mon-Sat), about 350m south of the mosque, is also newly renovated and holds a wonderful collection of local artefacts. English-language descriptions of the exhibits help to make sense of it all but to get a better understanding of Shushi history have a chat with curator Ashot Harutunyan, a historian and war veteran. Ashot was even born in the building that now houses the museum (it used to be a hospital).

Near the Shushi Municipality building are several old buildings, including the **residence of the Panah Khan**.

Jerderduz, grazing land for horses, is 1km south of the mosque on the edge of a beautiful gorge. Take a walk out here for some stunning views.

🛏 Sleeping & Eating

Hotel Shoushi HOTEL $
(☑3 13 57; 3 Amiryan Poghots; s/d incl breakfast AMD14,000/18,000; ❄@) You wouldn't guess there would be a boutique hotel here, but the extremely comfortable Hotel Shoushi stands across from the Ghazanchetsots Cathedral. It has 12 very tasteful, spacious rooms, lots of interesting artwork and a good restaurant. Dinners cost around AMD3500.

Armen & Christina B&B GUESTHOUSE $
(☑097240 712; shoushi.nk.am@gmail.com; Apt 36, 9 Aram Manoukyan Poghots; r per person incl breakfast AMD6000;@) Armen Rakedjian (French) and wife Christina (Romanian) run this B&B out of their apartment in upper Shushi. Armen speaks French, English and Armenian and is a mine of information on the area. His apartment is right next to the corner where the bus terminates. Send an email or call ahead and he will arrange to meet you.

Saro's B&B GUESTHOUSE $
(☑097231 764; saro.saryan@gmail.ru; r per person incl breakfast AMD6000) English-speaking owner Sarasar (Saro) Saryan is an enthusiastic host and knows much about Shushi's history. He is also the president of the Union for Armenian Refugees. His tranquil home has large rooms and a garden out back. It's in the lower part of Shushi near the hospital but Saro can usually be found at his office in the Municipality. Staying here is a great opportunity to experience traditional village life in Karabakh.

Hovik Gasparyan B&B GUESTHOUSE $
(☑097261 736; r per person incl breakfast AMD6000) Located near Saro's B&B, this large house has four guestrooms. Russian and Armenian languages spoken.

Ludwig Restaurant ARMENIAN $
(⊙10am-midnight) Traditional Armenian cuisine featuring salads, cutlets and *khoravats* (barbecued food). It is located in upper Shushi opposite the church.

ⓘ Information

The **Tourism Office** (☑3 32 96; ⊙10am-2pm & 3-7pm Mon-Fri) has some brochures and books on Karabakh but can't offer much practical travel info. It's located in lower Shushi near the old bus station. You can get better travel advice from Armen Rakedjian at the Armen & Christina B&B.

ⓘ Getting There & Away

Buses between Shushi's main square and the *avtokayan* (bus station) in Stepanakert, 9km downhill, leave every 30 minutes or so during the day (AMD200). By taxi the trip costs about AMD2000.

Southern Karabakh

There are two main routes into southern Karabakh, one towards Martuni and the road to Hadrut.

The first point of interest on the Hadrut road is the village of **Sarushen**, 26km from Stepanakert, which contains the ruins of Pirumashen Church. The 12th-century relic is near the road but hidden by trees. Next is **Skhtorashen**, about 2km north of Karmir Shuka (Krasni Bazar) and home to a 2000-year-old platan (plane) tree so large you could hold a party inside its core.

From the small town of Karmir Shuka you can turn off the main road and visit **Amaras Monastery**, founded by St Gregory the Illuminator and completed by his grandson, Bishop Grigoris. Mesrop Mashtots also founded a school here to educate people in the new alphabet in the 5th century. The current structure is a modest church surrounded by monastic cells. Amaras is 15km from Karmir Shuka.

Back on the main road, head 14km south of Karmir Shuka to reach the extraordinary **Azokh cave**, not far from the village of Azokh. About 200m before the village look for the trail to the right that leads uphill to the cave. The cave has six bat-filled chambers connected by tunnels. Remains of ancient humans have been found here, as well as tools and pottery shards. The cave entry is large and stunning, but you'll need a strong torch (flashlight) to view the inner chambers.

The route continues south to Hadrut, which has a **museum** portraying local history and ethnography. The road loops north through to **Fizuli (Varanda)**, a war-ravaged town on the front line that is off-limits to foreign travellers.

Southeast of Stepanakert is **Martuni** (population 4000), a market town with a few palm trees and a statue of Monte Melkonian, a native of Fresno, California, who became a hero in the Karabakh War. Markar Melkonian chronicled his brother's fascinating life story in the book *My Brother's Road: An American's Fateful Journey to Armenia*. Note that if you take public transport to Martuni some vehicles take a roundabout way via Agdam.

Northeast Karabakh

The road heading northeast of Stepanakert goes 14km to the town and fortress of **Mayraberd (Askeran)**, which has huge medieval walls and towers. Built by Panah Khan in the 18th century, it once stretched 1.5km across the valley. Further north you'll spot abandoned buildings and a tank monument as you approach Agdam. The road branches before Agdam, one road going north to Martakert.

The restored 18th-century fortress of **Shah Bulart** appears on the left side of the road, 32km out of Stepanakert. Nearby, archaeologists uncovered the remains of **Tigranakert**, one of the four cities founded by Tigran the Great but the only one known to historians today. A new **Archaeological Museum** (☑097208678; admission free; ☉10am-6pm Tue-Sun) inside the fort details

AGDAM

Karabakh and the occupied land around it has many deserted villages and towns, but no others are quite like this former city of 150,000 people. The city was captured in 1994, sacked and looted. Tall, shattered tower blocks stand in the distance, past a sprawling city centre of one- and two-storey buildings. Shredded playgrounds sprout with shrubs, the streets are cracking open with trees, and ponds fill in bomb craters. The city was picked clean by people from Stepanakert looking for building materials, and by professionals who took out everything from copper wires to bathroom fittings.

Despite its unofficial town nickname, 'the Hiroshima of the Caucasus', Agdam is not completely dead. Soldiers, scrap-metal hunters and a handful of permanent residents can be seen here. Conditions are primitive – no electricity, running water or public services. The main point of interest is the mosque (defaced, sadly) in the town centre. You can climb one of the rickety minarets for a 360-degree view of the overgrown city.

The travel permit from the Ministry of Foreign Affairs does not include a visit to Agdam, though some travellers do visit without incident – you just need to keep a low profile. A taxi from Stepanakert will cost around AMD5000. Bear in mind that cameras are not welcome so you'll need to use a fair amount of discretion when taking photos.

the existence of Tigran's great kingdom. A 15-minute film covers the history of the city and the recent excavations. Pottery shards, carved stones and bronze tools are a few of the items on display. The museum curator, Vahram Loretsyan, will most likely guide you to the two main archaeological sites, an excavated church and a fortress wall.

There is a good one-hour (each way) hike to **Vankasar Church**, on the hilltop above Vankasar.

To visit these sites, take a bus to Martakert and ask the driver to let you off at Tigranakert. If you want to combine a trip to Tigranakert and Agdam, organise a taxi.

Northwest Karabakh

The road northwest of Stepanakert winds 40km through low hills to reach the 13th-century **Gandzasar monastery**, probably the most important structure in Karabakh. The church of **Surp Hovhannes Mkrtich** (St John the Baptist) is the largest in the grouping, with beautiful friezes around the central drum. There are well-preserved inscriptions and *khatchkars* (stone crosses) in the church's *gavit* (antechamber), which is filled with the floor-slab tombs of former bishops and nobles of the region.

Vank, the village below Gandzasar, is unlike any other village in Karabakh, thanks to the patronage of native son Levon Hairapetian. The Moscow-based lumber baron has funded large-scale redevelopment of the town, including a new road from Stepanakert, a school, hospital and an enormous hotel that resembles the *Titanic*. The **Eclectic Hotel** (☑097330099; per person AMD8000) is great value and has loads of surreal atmosphere, including a totally out-of-place Chinese restaurant run by three chefs from Guangxi province. For more information about Vank and the hotels here see www.gandzasarecotour.com.

There are two buses a day from Stepanakert to Vank (AMD300, one hour), departing at 9am and 3pm. From the village you need to walk the last 2.5km uphill to Gandzasar, or hire a taxi. When the bus arrives in Vank it stays for about 10 minutes and heads back to Stepanakert. If you are stuck you can hitch back or hire a taxi (AMD5000).

On the way back to Stepanakert you can stop by the village of Ghshlagh to visit the unique **Nikol Duman Memorial Museum** (☑0479-4 47 58; ☉10am-6pm), which honours the life of the renowned Dashnak leader. The home, once occupied by Duman himself, is fully restored to its 19th-century condition. Drinks are available and meals are often prepared for groups.

A more remote destination is **Dadivank monastery**, 30km further northwest of Gandzasar (some backtracking on the Gandzasar road is required to get there). This overgrown masterpiece has a bell tower, fine *khatchkars* and monastic cells around the main 13th-century Surp Dadi church. Watch out for holes into underground cisterns and chambers as you walk around. The princes of Upper Khachen are buried under the floor of the main church's *gavit*. The road continues up the Tartar River into the Kelbajar region.

A taxi to/from Gandzasar is AMD10,000 and a taxi to/from Stepanakert (with a side trip to Gandzasar) is AMD20,000.

Kelbajar

This wild, mountainous region between Armenia and northern Karabakh is ringed by 3000m peaks, with rivers cutting through high gorges and a scattering of villages being resettled by Armenians. Most of the population before the war were Muslim Kurdish farmers and herders – the Bolsheviks toyed with the idea of creating a Red Kurdistan here in the 1920s.

The main artery through here is a rough road (jeep only) that leads across the Sodk Pass to the Zod gold mines and Vardenis near Lake Sevan. Because this is occupied Azerbaijan (not Nagorno-Karabakh) the region falls under a restricted military zone and getting a permit to travel here can be difficult. However, some hardy travellers have made it through the area without a permit. Some Armenian or Russian will be handy if the police stop you, as there won't be anyone to act as a translator.

The largest town in the region is **Karvachar** (population 600). It's populated with people from the Shahumian district north of Karabakh proper, driven out of Azerbaijan in the early 1990s. Around 8km past the town are a hot spring and geyser.

The southern part of Kelbajar is technically the region of Berdzor (Lachin), which contains the strategic Goris–Stepanakert highway. Entering the region is possible as long as you have listed it on your travel permit. Close to the checkpoint a sign points to the north up to the **Tsitsernavank Monastery** (Monastery of Swallows), a modest but ancient church dating back to the 5th century. A one-way journey from the checkpoint takes about one hour.

UNDERSTAND NAGORNO-KARABAKH

History

In this region, names and history are as contested as the land itself. Azeris claim 'Qarabaq' as their cultural heartland, and point to the role of Şuşa (Shushi) in the growth of their literature and language. In Azeri accounts, the Christian inhabitants of Karabakh are descendants of the Christian nation of Albania (unrelated to the present-day state of Albania). Caucasian Albania lost independence after the Arab invasion in the 7th century, and most Albanians converted to Islam, while the remnants of the Albanian Church were usurped by the Armenian Church. Certainly the locals say they're culturally as Armenian as anyone, with 4000 churches, monasteries and forts on their hills to attest to this.

During the Middle Ages the region was under the control of Persia, with local rule in the hands of five Armenian princes known as Meliks. The Karabakh Khanate, with Panahabad (Shushi) as its capital, passed into Russian hands in 1805. During the 19th century many native Muslims left for Iran while Armenians from Iran emigrated to Karabakh.

Stalin separated Karabakh from Armenia in the 1920s and made it an autonomous region within Azerbaijan. The natural growth of the Azeri population outpaced growth of the Armenian one and Azeri settlers were moved to Armenian villages. By the 1980s the territory's population was down to about 75% Armenian.

Demands to join Armenia SSR grew in 1987–88, until the local assembly voted for independence from Azerbaijan SSR in December 1989, and hostilities commenced. From 1989 to 1994 the area was racked by war, which, in its first stage, pitted the Karabakhtis against overwhelming Azeri and Soviet forces. Grad antitank missiles fell on Stepanakert from Shushi until 1993, while bands of local men, organised into *fedayeen* (irregular soldier) units, scavenged for weapons and ranged them against the Soviet army. After the fall of the USSR, the war escalated into a heavily armed clash between Armenian troops and *fedayeen* commandos on one side and the Azeri army assisted by Turkish officers on the other. A ceasefire was declared in May 1994 and the territorial lines have remained constant since then. The war cost around 30,000 lives. It also resulted in a mass emigration of Azeris: figures for those who fled Nagorno-Karabakh and surrounding war-affected areas of Azerbaijan range between 500,000 and 750,000, in addition to 150,000 other Azeri refugees from Armenia.

International negotiations have repeatedly failed but there are plenty of options on the table. The hope is that at some point an internationally recognised referendum can be held, but this would only be considered legitimate after the return of Azeri refugees who fled the region during the war. Armenia wants the referendum to be held as soon as possible, while Azerbaijan prefers a timetable of 15 to 20 years. Clearly there are issues to be sorted out.

Bako Sahakyan, Nagorno-Karabakh's president, won his job with a more than 85% mandate in July 2007 elections. Running on a pro-independence platform, the win was also seen as a referendum for his cause. Despite Sahakyan's lofty title, all political decisions and economic reforms are essentially handed down from Yerevan. New elections are scheduled for 2012.

Nagorno-Karabakh Today

Stepanakert, the self-proclaimed capital, is a town of about 55,000, with a parliament, presidential palace, ministries and a national museum. The local economy includes subsistence farmers and diaspora-funded projects such as the highway to Goris in

ACCOMMODATION PRICE RANGES

The following price ranges are used in our reviews of places to stay in this chapter. Prices are based on double rooms with private bathroom, in high season.

Budget ($)	<AMD21,000
Midrange ($$)	AMD21,000–25,000
Top End ($$$)	>AMD25,000

southern Armenia. The spike in investment has brought new life to Karabakh but the region still faces high levels of unemployment and poverty. The government believes increasing the population will stimulate development and pays large cash handouts to newlyweds and newborns.

Visitors should be aware that because of the region's disputed status, foreign embassy staff can't visit Nagorno-Karabakh. That said, if you stay away from the frontline areas and any military exercises it's no less safe than Armenia. The front line traces along the edge of the hills of Karabakh, where they spread into the plains. The northern frontier is along the Mrav range, with 3724m Mt Gyamish. Around 25,000 Armenians are slowly settling the occupied territories between Armenia, Karabakh and Iran. These areas are virtually off-limits to tourists.

SURVIVAL GUIDE

Directory A–Z

Dangers

Unexploded ordnance (UXO) continues to injure people and livestock and it is unwise to venture into open pastureland anywhere near the front line. Warning signs are prominently displayed in areas close to the main roads. Regarding personal safety, crimes against visitors are almost unheard of – Stepanakert is as safe as Yerevan or any part of Armenia.

Internet Resources

www.shoushi.nk.am Presents the culture and history of Shushi.

www.nkr.am The website of the Nagorno-Karabakh Republic (NKR) Ministry of Foreign Affairs.

EATING PRICE RANGES

The following price ranges have been used in our reviews of restaurants and cafes. Prices are based on one main dish and a drink.

Budget ($)   <AMD2000

Midrange ($$)   AMD2000–4000

Top End ($$$)   >AMD4000

---

www.nkrusa.org Website of the NKR office in Washington, with a list of NKR representatives in 10 or so countries.

Visas

Most people get their visas at the Ministry of Foreign Affairs (p272) in Stepanakert. You need to fill out a single-page form including every destination you're heading to in Karabakh. You don't need passport photos but perhaps bring one just in case. A 21-day visa is issued on the spot for AMD3000. Multiple-entry visas valid for up to 90 days are available. Consul staff will ask how you're travelling in Karabakh and where you intend to stay.

If you are in a group the Consul might prepare one group visa, which involves less paperwork. However, this pretty much requires your group to stick together for the duration of your stay and requires you to leave in the same vehicle; so don't do this if there is a chance your group will split up.

Note that you will not be permitted to enter Azerbaijan if you have a Karabakh visa on your passport, so if you plan to visit Azerbaijan, request that the visa be left outside the passport.

Visas are also available in Yerevan at the **Permanent Representative of the Nagorno-Karabakh Republic** (☏24 97 05; nkr@arminco.com; www.nkr.am; 17a Zaryan Poghots; ◷10am-1pm & 2-5pm Mon-Fri).

VISA REGISTRATION

In Stepanakert you must register on arrival (or the next day if it's after hours) at the Ministry of Foreign Affairs (p272). This will happen automatically if you are getting your visa in Stepanakert. But if you already received your visa in Yerevan you will need to come here for registration anyway. Your registration paper states the areas you intend to visit.

While no checks on your papers are likely to be made while travelling in Nagorno-Karabakh, the permit will be checked (and taken) on departure at the checkpoint on the Aghavno River between Berdzor and Goris. There are also checks if you are going into Kelbajar.

This bureaucracy is unnecessary if you happen to have a 10-year Armenian residency pass.

Understand Georgia, Armenia & Azerbaijan

GEORGIA, ARMENIA & AZERBAIJAN TODAY....280
The fallout of regional conflicts still looms large; economic and democratic progress is patchy.

HISTORY 282
South Caucasus history is ultracomplex and endlessly fascinating. We sort the Seljuks from the Soviets, and Saakashvili from Shevardnadze.

PEOPLE OF GEORGIA, ARMENIA & AZERBAIJAN 287
The South Caucasus region is one of the world's most difficult ethnic jigsaws, but its people have a surprising amount in common.

LANDSCAPE 289
A spectacularly varied canvas for hikers, horse riders, skiers, rafters and everyone else.

ARCHITECTURE 291
From quaint, ancient churches and towers to bold statements of the 21st century.

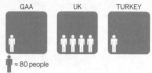

population per sq km

GAA   UK   TURKEY

≈ 80 people

Georgia, Armenia & Azerbaijan Today

Unneighbourly Conduct

The consequences of post-Soviet conflicts still loom large. Armenia and Azerbaijan are as far as ever from agreement over Nagorno-Karabakh, the Armenian-majority region within Azerbaijan that has been de facto independent since the Karabakh War of 1989 to 1994. Occasional skirmishes still break out along the Armenia–Azerbaijan border and the ceasefire line, and Azerbaijan's recent hike in military spending may suggest that it intends one day to regain at least part of its lost territory.

Karabakh also bedevils any efforts at rapprochement between Armenia and its western neighbour Turkey, who have long been divided over the early-20th-century genocide issue. Turkey is Azerbaijan's firmest ally and refuses to normalise relations with Armenia before the issue is settled.

Any prospect of Georgia coming to terms with its breakaway regions, Abkhazia and South Ossetia, all but vanished with the 2008 South Ossetia War, when Russia briefly invaded Georgia then recognised the independence of these two territories, stationing thousands of troops in them. Many Georgians fear that Russia is waiting for an opportunity to impose its will yet more strongly. Meanwhile most of the hundreds of thousands of refugees from these conflicts within Azerbaijan and Georgia remain in temporary accommodation of varying degrees of squalor.

Income per head 2010

» **Georgia**
US$2700 (year 2000: US$673)

» **Armenia**
US$3090 (year 2000: US$613)

» **Azerbaijan**
US$5180 (year 2000: US$636)

The Rich and the Poor

All three countries have made big economic strides since the desperate 1990s, especially Azerbaijan which is riding a boom based on exporting its Caspian Sea oil to the West. Economic progress in Georgia and Armenia was knocked by the world recession of 2008–09 (and in Georgia's case the 2008 war), but has made a comeback of sorts – although Armenia was still judged the world's second-worst economy by *Forbes* magazine in 2011.

Dos & Don'ts

» In religious buildings, covered shoulders are obligatory; long skirts for women, long trousers for men. Headscarves for women demonstrate respect.

» Public kissing and physical affection are frowned on and will offend near religious buildings.

» Shorts are widely considered very odd: in Azerbaijan shorts on men can actually cause offence anywhere except central Baku.

» Short skirts are rare, especially in rural areas.

» Women don't have to cover their hair in Muslim Azerbaijan.

Films

The Loneliest Planet (2011) Backpacking duo go awry in the Caucasus (dir: Julia Loktev)

Here (2011) Couple discovers Armenia (dir: Braden King)

The Legacy (2006) French travellers entangled in a Georgian blood feud (dir: Gela Babluani)

belief systems
(% of population)

52 — Muslim

46 — Christian

2 — Other

if Georgia, Armenia & Azerbaijan were 100 people

48 would be Azeri
25 would be Georgian
21 would be Armenian
1 would be Russian
1 would be Dagestani
4 would be Other

Throughout the region there is a gulf between those who gain from the new economies (typically well-educated, well-connected urbanites working in the private sector, along with powerful bureaucrats and politicians) and those who have been left behind (the older, the unqualified, government employees and those in the countryside). Impressive new buildings, glitzy shops and flashy cars in the cities do nothing to help farmers subsisting on the produce of their own fields. Many older folk look back nostalgically to the late Soviet era when there was a job and security for everyone.

Free and Fair?

Georgia has the strongest democratic credentials, although Mikheil Saakashvili, who led the Rose Revolution of 2003, is often criticised by opponents for too much top-down decision-making, and Georgia has been criticised by international bodies for using excessive force against political demonstrators. Georgia has certainly attacked corruption and crime head-on: almost its entire police force was replaced soon after the Rose Revolution.

Armenia still suffers the fallout of its 2008 presidential election, won by Serzh Sargsyan but largely condemned as fraudulent by international observers. Yerevan sees plenty of protests in favour of democratic reforms and greater press freedom.

Political freedoms remain restricted in Azerbaijan, where ex-Communist boss Heydar Əliyev died in 2003 but is still revered as the 'National Leader' and was seamlessly succeeded by his son İlham. But Azerbaijan's economy is booming and democratic dissent is thin on the ground.

While Georgia was ranked 64th best of 182 countries in Transparency International's 2011 corruption league table, Armenia stood 129th and Azerbaijan 143rd. In the 2011 press freedom rankings of Freedom House, the three countries stood respectively 118th, 146th and 171st.

LOCAL SENSITIVITIES

It's not a good idea to come out with strong opinions on political issues unless you know someone pretty well. Locals can, unsurprisingly, be very sensitive about these matters.

Greetings

» A handshake is the normal greeting between men.

» Women generally don't shake hands, though if foreigners don't follow this it won't be an insult.

» Friends (of whatever sex) normally give each other a peck on the cheek.

Books

Bread and Ashes Tony Anderson walking the Caucasus
Georgia: In the Mountains of Poetry Peter Nasmyth roaming
Azerbaijan with Excursions to Georgia Mark Elliott
Rediscovering Armenia Brady Kiesling and Raffi Kojian

Etiquette

» When visiting someone's home, take a gift, and offer to remove your shoes.

» Don't be ashamed to say you can't eat or drink any more.

» If invited to a dinner or overnight stay, tactfully offer some money, but don't insist.

History

This mountainous isthmus between the Black and Caspian Seas stands at the frontiers of Europe and Asia and of Islam and Christendom. Innumerable waves of conquerors and colonists washing into the region from all directions make its story one of the most complicated, and most fascinating, in the world – and have left one of the world's trickiest ethnic jigsaws. The three South Caucasus nations today are just the latest of scores of republics, kingdoms, principalities, emirates, khanates and satrapies that have blossomed and died here down the centuries. Recognisably Georgian, Armenian and Azerbaijani states have only existed at certain times, as the numerically small local peoples have played pawns in the grand games of Macedonian, Roman, Persian, Byzantine, Arab, Mongol, Ottoman, Russian and other empires.

Georgia did not come together with approximately its current extents until several small principalities were united in the 11th century. It disintegrated by the 15th century, and was not reunified until the 19th.

What's now Azerbaijan was for centuries part of a jigsaw of small khanates on the northern fringe of the Persian empire. The first unified, independent Azerbaijan, or indeed any sense of an Azerbaijani nationality, did not emerge until the 20th century.

Modern Armenia is just a small eastern part of historic Armenia, much of which lay in what are now eastern Turkey and northwest Iran. Ancient Armenia once held sway from the shores of the Caspian Sea to those of the Mediterranean, but for many later centuries there was no Armenian state at all.

Early Empires

Some aver that South Caucasus history began at the unspecified time when Noah's Ark grounded on Mt Ararat (in modern-day Turkey, just west of the Armenian border). What is known is that the 1.8-million-year-old early human remains found a few years ago at Dmanisi, 80km

Top History Sites

» Tsitsernakaberd, Yerevan

» Stalin Museum, Gori

» Mtskheta

» Shirvanshahs' Palace, Baku

» Vardzia

» Armenian History Museum, Yerevan

» Shushi

» Echmiadzin

» Historical Museum, Baku

» Gelati

TIMELINE

1st Century BC

Tigranes the Great builds an Armenian empire stretching from the southwest corner of the Caspian Sea to the eastern shores of the Mediterranean, with its capital at Tigranakert.

» *Vankasar Church (p276), Nagorno-Karabakh*

southwest of Tbilisi, are the oldest discovered outside Africa. It may also be that the world's first wine was made in the region: archaeologists have found evidence of wine-making in eastern Georgia about 7000 years ago.

Greeks, Persians and Romans brought the classical pagan faiths and philosophies to the South Caucasus in the 1000 years before Christianity took hold, helping to create rich local cultures. The Greeks established colonies in Colchis (western Georgia) perhaps as early as the 8th century BC. The Armenians trace their origins back to the Urartu kingdom of about 1000 to 600 BC centred on Lake Van in eastern Turkey. They were incorporated successively into the Persian Achaemenian Empire, the Macedonian Empire and the Seleucid Empire. After the Romans defeated the Seleucids, Tigranes the Great (r 95–55 BC) built an Armenian empire stretching from the Caspian Sea to the Mediterranean. But Rome moved into Armenia and Georgia after Tigranes ill-advisedly allied against it with Mithradates of Pontus (in northern Turkey). Armenia ended up as a buffer between the Romans and the Persians, who fought long wars for control of the region.

First Christian Kingdoms

Christian apostles were already visiting the South Caucasus in the decades after the death of Jesus. In 301 Armenia's King Trdat III was converted to Christianity and Armenia became the first nation officially to embrace the religion. The eastern Georgian kingdom of Kartli (or Iveria), and the state of Albania in what's now Azerbaijan (no relation to Balkan Albania), followed suit within the next 30 years or so.

As the Christian Byzantine Empire expanded eastward from Constantinople, western Armenia and western Georgia fell under its sway, while their eastern areas came under Persian control.

Islam & Asian Conquerors

Arabs, carrying Islam beyond the Arabian Peninsula after the death of the Prophet Mohammed in 632, took over the South Caucasus by 661. In the 9th century the Arabs recognised a local prince of the Bagratid family, Ashot I, as king of Armenia. By the 11th century another Bagratid branch controlled most of Georgia.

Nomadic Turkic herders arriving from Central Asia around the 9th century were probably the ancestors of modern Azerbaijanis. Another group of Turks from Central Asia, the Seljuks, brought death, plunder and destruction to the Caucasus region in the 11th and 12th centuries, but Georgian king Davit Aghmashenebeli (David the Builder, 1089–1125) managed to drive the Seljuks out of Georgia, initiating its medieval golden age. David's great-granddaughter Queen Tamar (1184–1213) controlled

Top History Reads

» **The Caucasus** Thomas de Waal

» **The Ghost of Freedom** Charles King

» **The Crossing Place** Philip Marsden

» **Black Dog of Fate** Peter Balakian

HISTORY FIRST CHRISTIAN KINGDOMS

AD 301	642–661	11th to 13th centuries	16th century
Armenia becomes the first state officially to embrace Christianity, after King Trdat III's conversion. The eastern Georgian kingdom of Kartli (Iveria) follows suit in 327.	Muslim Arabs take over the South Caucasus, reaching Azerbaijan in 642, setting up an emirate in Tbilisi in 654 and gaining control of Armenia in 661.	Georgia enjoys a golden age under rulers like Davit Aghmashenebeli (David the Builder, 1089–1125) and Tamar (1184–1213). The South Caucasus is then devastated by the Mongol invasion and Black Death.	The Constantinople-based Ottoman Turks take over nearly all of Armenia; the Azeri/Persian Safavids take control of Azerbaijan and the khanate of Yerevan; Georgia is divided between the Ottomans and Safavids.

A TANGLED WEB

Just how interwoven are the stories of the South Caucasus' different peoples is well illustrated by the life of the famed 18th-century poet and Armenian cultural hero Sayat Nova. Though Armenian, Sayat Nova was part of the court of the Georgian king Erekle II in Tbilisi. Exiled for his forbidden love of the king's daughter, Sayat Nova lived as a wandering troubadour and as a monk in Armenian monasteries. He wrote over 200 songs, some of them still sung today, in Armenian, Georgian, Persian and, most of all, in Azeri, which was spoken by Armenia's large Muslim population of the day and was also a *lingua franca* for much of the South Caucasus. Sayat Nova died helping defend Tbilisi from the Persians in 1795 and his tomb stands outside the city's Armenian Cathedral of St George. His life is the subject of one of the great Soviet-era films, *The Colour of Pomegranates,* directed by another Tbilisi-born Armenian, Sergei Paradjanov.

A Hero of Our Time (1840), Mikhail Lermontov's masterpiece about a bored, cynical Russian officer in the Caucasus, was the first – and shortest – Great Russian Novel. An entirely different fictional experience, *The Girl King* (2011) is Meg Clothier's hard-to-put-down imagining of the great medieval Georgian Queen Tamar's life.

territory from western Azerbaijan to eastern Turkey, including many Armenian-populated regions.

The whole region was floored by the next great wave from the east, the Mongols, who invaded in the 1230s. They were followed in the late 14th century by another ruthless Asian conqueror, Timur (Tamerlane). Şirvan, a Muslim khanate in modern Azerbaijan, managed to retain some autonomy and by the 15th century Baku was a prospering trade-route centre. In 1501 Şirvan was conquered by fellow Azeris from what's now northern Iran, who converted it from Sunni to Shia Islam.

The next pair to compete for the South Caucasus were the Azeri Safavid dynasty from Persia and the Ottoman Turks, who had taken Constantinople and swept away the Byzantine Empire in 1453. In 1514–16 the Ottomans took over nearly all of Armenia, and kept most of it for nearly 400 years. After the Safavid collapse in 1722, a new Persian conqueror, Nader Shah, installed Bagratid princes in eastern Georgia, while autonomous Muslim khanates emerged in Azerbaijan.

Russia Arrives...& Stays

Peter the Great began the great Russian push into the Caucasus region in the 1720s. Russia took over the whole of South Caucasus in the 19th century, wresting the Yerevan khanate and those comprising modern Azerbaijan (including Karabakh and Naxçivan) from Persian claims, annexing the Georgian princedoms one by one, and taking the Batumi area (southwest Georgia) as well as Kars and Ardahan (northeast Turkey) from the Turks in the 1870s.

A good half of historic Armenia and perhaps 2.5 million Armenians remained in the Ottoman Empire after the Russo-Turkish War in the

1783	1915	1918–21	1930s
Treaty of Georgievsk: east Georgian King Erekle II accepts Russian control in exchange for protection from Muslim foes. Russia goes on to take over the whole South Caucasus in the 19th century.	The Young Turk government in Istanbul orders the killing or deportation of virtually all the Armenian population in the Ottoman Empire. Well over a million people are thought to have died.	Following the Russian Revolution, Georgia, Armenia and Azerbaijan exist briefly as independent nations, before being taken by the Red Army and incorporated into the new USSR in 1922.	Antinationalist repression, led by Georgian Bolsheviks Stalin, Beria and Ordzhonikidze, and the Great Terror see hundreds of thousands of people from the region executed or imprisoned.

1870s. Unrest among them led to massacres of Armenians in the 1890s, and in 1915 the Young Turk government in Istanbul ordered the killing or deportation of virtually all Armenians within the Ottoman Empire. Deportation meant walking into the Syrian deserts. In all, well over a million are thought to have died.

Following the Russian Revolution, the South Caucasus declared itself an independent federation in 1918, but national and religious differences saw it split quickly into three separate nations: Georgia, Armenia and Azerbaijan. The Turkish army pushed into the region before the Red Army came south to claim it 1920–21. Georgia, Armenia and Azerbaijan were thrown together in the Transcaucasian Soviet Federated Socialist Republic, one of the founding republics of the Soviet Union in 1922. This in turn was split into separate Georgian, Armenian and Azerbaijani Soviet Republics in 1936.

The later Soviet period, after Stalin's death in 1953, was relatively calm, despite worsening corruption. But the wider Soviet economy stagnated, and Mikhail Gorbachev's efforts to deal with this through *glasnost* (openness) and *perestroika* (restructuring) unlocked nationalist tensions that would tear both the Caucasus region and the whole Soviet Union apart.

> **Post-Soviet Wars & Politics**
>
> » **Black Garden: Armenia and Azerbaijan through Peace and War** Thomas de Waal
>
> » **Azerbaijan Diary** Thomas Goltz
>
> » **Georgia Diary** Thomas Goltz

HISTORY INDEPENDENCE

Independence

In 1988, Azerbaijan's Armenian-majority region of Nagorno-Karabakh declared its wish for unification with Armenia. Armenians were massacred in the Azerbaijan town of Sumqayıt, violence spiralled in both republics, and Azeris in Armenia and Armenians in Azerbaijan started to flee. By 1990 Armenian and Azerbaijani militias were battling each other in and around Nagorno-Karabakh.

In Georgia, the national independence movement became an unstoppable force after 19 hunger strikers died as Soviet troops broke up a protest in Tbilisi in 1989. Georgia, Armenia and Azerbaijan all declared independence in 1991, and the Soviet Union formally split into 15 different nations in December that year.

Strife in the South Caucasus only got worse. Independent Georgia's first president, Zviad Gamsakhurdia, was driven out in a civil war in 1991–92, and bloody interethnic fighting left the Georgian regions of South Ossetia and Abkhazia effectively independent by 1993. In Karabakh, several years of vicious fighting ended with a 1994 ceasefire and a victory for the Armenian and Karabakhtsi forces over the Azeri army. Nagorno-Karabakh has been de facto independent ever since. These wars cost around 40,000 lives and displaced hundreds of thousands of people.

All the region's economies nosedived in the 1990s, but took an upturn in the 2000s. In Georgia, President Eduard Shevardnadze, formerly Gorbachev's Soviet foreign minister, managed to stabilise the political

> The 2011 film *5 Days of War*, directed by Renny Harlin, tells a story of Western journalists covering the 2008 South Ossetia War. Despite glaring factual inaccuracies, it has an exciting plot and paints a chilling picture of ethnic warfare. Andy Garcia plays Georgia's President Saakashvili.

1989–94	1991	1991–93	1990s
Nagorno-Karabakh War: Fighting over Azerbaijan's Armenian-majority region kills 30,000, displaces hundreds of thousands. Nagorno-Karabakh becomes independent; Armenia occupies areas of Azerbaijan.	Georgia, Armenia and Azerbaijan all declare independence from the USSR, which formally dissolves itself in December. The region is already wracked by interethnic unrest.	Interethnic conflict in Georgian regions South Ossetia (1991–92) and Abkhazia (1992–93) leaves both regions independent. Abkhazia ethnically cleanses its ethnic-Georgian population (about 230,000 people).	Economic collapse throughout the region due to internal wars, refugee problems, corruption, infrastructure collapse and the end of Soviet state support for industry and agriculture.

situation but lost popular support as Georgians grew sick of crime and corruption. He was booted out in the peaceful Rose Revolution of 2003 led by the modernising, pro-Western Mikheil Saakashvili. In 2008 Saakashvili's attempt to regain control of South Ossetia by military force ended disastrously in a brief, humiliating Russian invasion of Georgia.

In Azerbaijan, another ex-Communist boss, Heydar Əliyev, who had returned to power in 1993, negotiated a lucrative deal with Western oil companies over Azerbaijan's Caspian Sea oil reserves. The oil deal was the seed of the economic boom which his son İlham has presided over, after a seamless transition of power on his father's death in 2003.

<table>
<tr><td>

2003

İlham Əliyev succeeds his father Heydar Əliyev as Azerbaijan's president, inheriting an economic boom based on the country's large reserves of oil and natural gas.

</td><td>

2003

Georgia's peaceful Rose Revolution brings in a pro-Western, anti-Russian, modernising government led by Mikheil Saakashvili to replace the regime of former Soviet boss Eduard Shevardnadze.

</td><td>

</td><td>

2008

Russia inflicts a humiliating defeat on Georgia in a brief war over South Ossetia, then recognises South Ossetian and Abkhazian independence and starts military buildups in both territories.

</td></tr>
</table>

» *Mikheil Saakashvili*

People of Georgia, Armenia & Azerbaijan

The Caucasus region is home to so many peoples and languages that the Arabs called it the 'Mountain of Languages'. Kept alive by rugged terrain that divides every valley from its neighbours, over 40 mutually incomprehensible tongues are spoken between the Black and Caspian Seas. Each defines a people. The southern side of the Caucasus, subject of this book, is home to at least 16. Some number only a few thousand, isolated in remote mountain valleys.

Strained Relations

The region's major peoples give their names to the region's three countries: the Georgians, Armenians and Azeris, who form more than 90% of the region's nearly 17 million people. Differentiated by religion, language, alphabets, geography and more, these three peoples have nevertheless lived interwoven existences for centuries, which makes it all the sadder that the region today is riven by intractable ethnic and territorial quarrels.

Until the 1990s, communities of (Muslim) Azeris and (Christian) Armenians had coexisted for centuries across much of what are now Armenia and Azerbaijan, under Persian, Turkish or Russian rulers. Before WWI Muslims outnumbered Armenians in what is now Armenia's capital, Yerevan – and Armenians outnumbered Georgians in the Georgian capital, Tbilisi.

Today, Armenians and Azerbaijanis are deeply divided over the Karabakh issue; Armenians and Georgians harbour a strange mutual distrust, while Georgians and Azerbaijanis rub along OK, without having too much to do with each other. Only Georgia has sizeable communities of the other two main nationalities – 250,000 to 300,000 each of Azeris and Armenians, chiefly close to their respective borders.

Origins

The Armenians are an ancient people who trace their origins back to the Urartu kingdom of about 1000 to 600 BC, centred on Lake Van in eastern Turkey. Historic Armenia was a much larger area than today's Armenia, encompassing large areas of what are now eastern Turkey and northwest Iran.

Georgians' origins are shrouded in the mists of distant antiquity, and they still identify strongly with their local regions (Samegrelo, Adjara, Svaneti, Kakheti and so on), but they are united by shared, or similar, languages, and a shared culture and history going back at least 1500 years.

Azeris are a Turkic people, whose animal-herding ancestors probably arrived on the southwestern shores of the Caspian Sea from Central Asia around the 9th century AD.

Kurban Said's *Ali and Nino* is not only a wonderful story of a love affair between an Azeri Muslim and a Georgian Christian a century ago, but also a fascinating observation of life on the frontier between Europe and Asia, and of South Caucasus peoples' perceptions of each other.

After centuries of emigration, more Armenians (about eight million) live outside Armenia than in it. Diaspora Armenians include Cher, Andre Agassi, the members of System of a Down, Charles Aznavour, Gary Kasparov, William Saroyan, Herbert von Karajan and US billionaire Kirk Kerkorian (a big benefactor of Armenia).

RELIGIOUS REVIVAL

For seven decades until 1991, the South Caucasus was part of an officially atheist state, the USSR. Its churches, monasteries and mosques were used as museums, schools, hospitals and much else. But underlying religious sentiments never died and were a major part of the national independence movements in the late Soviet years. Today Christianity in Georgia and Armenia, and Islam in Azerbaijan, are ubiquitous; very few people call themselves atheists, and religious authorities are now strong, socially conservative forces. Churches and mosques, many of them newly built or recently renovated, are busy with worshippers; monasteries and convents have been repopulated by monks and nuns. Old traditions of tying bits of cloth to wishing trees, visiting shrines and graves, and spending lavishly on funerals, remain common everywhere.

The Armenian Apostolic church was the first legal Christian church in the world, dating back to AD 301. The Georgian Orthodox church was the second, dating from the 320s. While the Georgian church is part of the Eastern Orthodox tradition, like the Greek and Russian Orthodox churches, the Armenian church belongs to the separate Oriental Orthodox branch of Christianity, along with the Coptic Egyptian and Ethiopian churches.

The Armenians diverged from Eastern Orthodoxy back in AD 451, when they disagreed with the authorities in Constantinople over the nature of Jesus Christ: the Armenian church sees Christ's divine and human natures combined in one body (monophysite), while the Eastern Orthodox churches see each nature as separate.

Azerbaijan is the only Turkic country to follow Shia Islam, established there in the 16th century by the Safavid dynasty. Unlike the Sunni Muslims of Turkey or south Asia, Shia Muslims consider the descendants of the Prophet Mohammed's son-in-law Ali to be the true bearers of Mohammed's message. In contrast to its Shia neighbour Iran, Azerbaijan is religiously very tolerant, with little fundamentalism. Women are not obliged to cover their hair and few do. Restaurants stay open during the fasting month of Ramazan.

Common Traditions

Despite ethnic differences, the way of life around the region has much in common. The three large capital cities, home to a quarter of the total population, are large, cosmopolitan places (above all, oil-boom Baku) with layers of 21st-century Western lifestyle over seven decades' worth of attempted Soviet regimentation, and much older traditional ways at their foundation.

With their pubs, clubs and contemporary fashions, city dwellers might appear to live like Londoners or Parisians, but deeply ingrained social traditions keep the paternalistic family, and extended-family loyalties, supreme. Even in Georgia, the most socially liberal of the three countries, women are generally considered to be failures, or weird, if they are not married by 26, and the concept of unmarried couples living together is unheard of.

Most city dwellers still have roots in the countryside, where life remains slow paced and very conservative. Family homesteads often house three or more generations. Wives are expected to have food ready whenever their husband appears, and in Azerbaijan women never even set foot in the teahouses that are the hub of male social life. Wedding and funeral customs, and rituals held 40 days after death, are similar throughout the region.

Equally strong are traditions of hospitality and toasting (wine and brandy are produced in all three countries). Throughout the region it is both a custom and a pleasure to welcome guests with food and drink. People everywhere enjoy meeting, helping and hosting foreigners: as a visitor you will see the locals' warmest side, which will undoubtedly provide some of the best memories of your trip.

Main Minorities

» Abkhaz (Abkhazia) 70,000–90,000

» Avars (northern Azerbaijan) 50,000

» Lezgins (north, northwest Azerbaijan) 200,000

» Ossetians (South Ossetia) 30,000

» Talysh (south Azerbaijan) 80,000

» Yezidi Kurds (Armenia,Georgia) 50,000–60,000

Landscape

Longer and higher than the Alps, the main Caucasus range strides from the Black Sea to the Caspian in an endless sequence of snowcapped, rocky peaks, high passes, mountain pastures, deep, green valleys with rushing rivers and a scattering of remote villages. Its beauty is perhaps the greatest of all the region's attractions – but the varied landscape to the south has plenty to offer too.

Though scarred and scratched by the environmental insouciance of the Soviet past, the South Caucasus countries are lightly populated and mostly fertile and verdant. About a quarter of the land is still classed as natural habitat. With a few exceptions, such as large hotels on Georgia's coast and resorts in Azerbaijan, tourism development is mostly small scale and low impact.

The Lie of the Land

The Great Caucasus separates Russia from Georgia and Azerbaijan. Some contend that it also separates Europe from Asia, although the nations that are the subject of this book would dispute that. Several of its peaks reach above 5000m, and in all its 700km length, the Caucasus is crossed by only three motorable roads. Its rugged topography, with valleys connected only by high, often snowbound passes, has yielded fascinating ethnic diversity. Yet feet and hooves can travel where tyres cannot: mountain peoples on both flanks of the Caucasus share cultural traits, and historically have always had contact with each other. That contact has not always been amicable, as is testified by the hundreds of ancient defensive towers standing in villages along the south side of the range.

The Caucasus' fertile lower slopes give way to broad plains running west–east along central Georgia and Azerbaijan, and it's these lower areas (along with Armenia's valleys) that are home to the region's all-important agriculture. Most of central Azerbaijan is monotonous steppe, semidesert and salt marsh, though it's intensively irrigated for cultivating cotton and grain.

The Rioni River drains the western Georgian plains into the Black Sea. The Mtkvari flows eastward through Tbilisi and on into Azerbaijan where it becomes the Kür (Kura) and enters the Caspian Sea. The Araz (Araks, Araxes) River forms the western and southern borders of Armenia and Azerbaijan along much of its course from eastern Turkey, before joining the Kür in Azerbaijan.

South of the plains rises the Lesser Caucasus, stretching from southwest Georgia across Armenia to Nagorno-Karabakh. Less lofty than the main Caucasus range, the Lesser Caucasus still packs in some spectacular mountain, gorge and forest scenery and has plenty of peaks above 3000m. Western Armenia and the Azerbaijani enclave of Naxçivan sit on the edge of the Anatolian Plateau, with historic Armenia's highest peak, Mt Ararat (5165m), sometimes in view across the border in Turkey.

Animal herders still move their flocks up and down between the lowlands and mountains seasonally, but Azeri herders can no longer take their livestock up to Nagorno-Karabakh in summer as a result of the Karabakh conflict.

To learn more about the Caucasus region's special ecological value, check www.biodiversityhotspots.org.

HOTSPOT

GETTING OUT INTO NATURE

For the most scenic hiking in the Great Caucasus, home in on Georgia's Svaneti, Tusheti, Khevsureti and Kazbegi areas, and the Quba hinterland and Mt Babadağ in Azerbaijan. Georgia's Borjomi-Kharagauli National Park and Armenia's Mt Aragats and Dilijan, Ijevan and Tatev areas offer further excellent walking. Trail marking is most advanced in Borjomi-Kharagauli, Svaneti and Tusheti. If you like to enjoy scenery from a saddle, horses are available in most of the same Georgian areas, and at places such as Lahıc and Şəki (Azerbaijan), and Tsaghkadzor and Yenokavan Canyon (Armenia).

Mt Kazbek (5047m) on the Georgia–Russia border is the most popular high summit for mountaineers – a serious challenge but technically uncomplicated, and easy enough to organise locally, or from Tbilisi. Mt Chaukhi, east of Kazbegi, presents good technical challenges. Twin-peaked Ushba in Svaneti is the greatest and most perilous challenge of all.

Skiers can pick from three quite up-to-date resorts in Georgia (Gudauri, Bakuriani and Mestia), while Armenia has new facilities at Jermuk and older ones at Tsaghkadzor.

Rafting on Georgia's upper Mtkvari and the branches of the Aragvi River north of Tbilisi (see p41) is rapidly growing in popularity.

With 380 known bird species, the region has a reputation among birdwatchers too. Raptors including the majestic lammergeier (bearded vulture), with its 2.5m wingspan, love the craggy, mountainous zones, while the Black Sea and Caspian coastlines are key summer and autumn migration corridors. There are well-developed visitor facilities at the wetlands of Kolkheti National Park on Georgia's coast.

Beasts of the Hills & Forests

With habitats embracing deserts and glaciers, alpine and semitropical forests, steppe and wetlands, the South Caucasus is a biodiversity hotspot. Mountain areas are home to brown bears (2000 to 2500 in the region), wolves, lynx, deer, chamois and more.

Many of the most exciting species are, sadly, endangered. Perhaps 20 to 25 Persian leopards survive in places like Azerbaijan's Hirkan National Park and Armenia's Khosrov Nature Reserve (the leopard's stronghold is Iran, where 600 to 800 remain). The two species of Caucasian *tur* (large mountain goats found in the Great Caucasus) are down to about 4000 for the eastern species and 6000 to 10,000 for the western one.

Until recently Azerbaijan's Şirvan National Park was the last South Caucasus habitat for the elegant little goitred gazelle (also called the Persian gazelle or ceyran); further gazelles have been reintroduced from Turkey into the Georgia–Azerbaijan border area.

Deforestation had been going on for millennia – the stark plains around Georgia's Davit Gareja monastic complex were once covered in woodlands – but increased with the energy shortages of the 1990s. Fuelwood collection, illegal logging and poaching are among the biggest threats to wildlife here.

Parks & Reserves

National parks, nature reserves and other protected areas cover about 8% of the total land area. The degree of genuine protection these areas receive ranges from skeletal upwards. Georgia has the most visitor-friendly network, with good or improving infrastructure in places like Borjomi-Kharagauli, Mtirala and Kolkheti National Parks and the Tusheti, Lagodekhi and Vashlovani Protected Areas. Azerbaijan's much-expanded parks network is unfortunately proving more of a hindrance than a help to visitors in the Caucasus: park and border regulations have, at the time of writing, effectively shut down Azerbaijan's three most popular longer-distance hikes, in the Laza–Xınalıq–Vandəm area.

Architecture

Quaint, conical-towered churches perched on hilltops, tall cathedrals visible from afar across flat plains, high tomb towers rising above the roofs of Azerbaijani towns...builders in the South Caucasus have always (except during the aesthetically brutal Soviet era) had a talent for creating structures that are not just beautiful in themselves but also enhance the landscapes they are part of.

Georgia & Armenia

Armenia and Georgia, the world's first two Christian kingdoms, have been building churches since the 4th century. Historically, most other buildings were constructed in perishable materials and have not survived, the chief exceptions being defensive constructions such as the impressive forts at Amberd, Armenia (11th century) and Nariqala, Georgia (founded in the 4th century) and the picturesque towers that dot high Caucasus valleys in Georgia.

Early Christian Architecture

Georgian and Armenian church architecture developed out of common roots. The earliest churches were basilicas, rectangular edifices (often divided into three parallel naves) that were originally devised by the Romans as meeting or reception halls. In Armenia and Georgia they usually had vaulted stone roofs in contrast to the wooden roofs usual elsewhere, and the domes typical of Armenia and Georgia began to appear above these roofs as early as the 6th century.

Church designs soon began to transmute from the rectangular basilican shape to symmetrical constructions with a dome above the centre. Such churches could be square, or take the form of an equal-armed cross, or of a four-leafed clover (known as a quatrefoil or tetraconch). Tall, windowed drums supporting the domes let light into the church.

In some churches a quatrefoil inner space is enclosed within a rectangular or square exterior by the addition of chambers in the corners. Such are the very typical and architecturally influential Surp Hripsime Church at Echmiadzin, Armenia, and Jvari Church at Mtskheta, Georgia, both completed in the early 7th century. Symmetrical design reached its ultimate form with Armenia's circular Zvartnots Cathedral (641–661), which was as high as it was wide (about 45m).

Almost all the key features of Armenian and Georgian church design were established before the Arab invasion of the 7th century and new churches even today still imitate these original forms.

Later Christian Architecture

Church building revived under the Bagratid dynasties of both Armenia and Georgia from the 9th century onwards. Quite a lot of this new work, especially the Armenian, took place in areas that are now in Turkey – buildings like the 10th-century Holy Cross Cathedral on Akhtamar

World Heritage Sites in Georgia & Armenia

» Mtskheta (Georgia)

» Bagrati Cathedral & Gelati Monastery (Georgia)

» Ushguli (Georgia)

» Geghard Monastery (Armenia)

» Zvartnots Cathedral (Armenia)

» Echmiadzin (Armenia)

» Haghpat & Sanahin Monasteries (Armenia)

World Heritage Sites in Azerbaijan

» Baku's Walled City

» Qobustan Petroglyph Reserve

CONTEMPORARY TENDENCIES

Much of the architectural energy of post-Soviet Georgia and Armenia has gone into building new churches and restoring old ones. Tbilisi's Tsminda Sameba (2004) and Yerevan's Surp Grigor Lusavorich (2001) are, respectively, the biggest Georgian and Armenian cathedrals. Georgia has a few other eye-catching contemporary edifices such as Tbilisi's Presidential Palace and Peace Bridge, and the zigzag glass tower that is Batumi's Radisson Hotel (all designed by Italian Michele De Lucchi), but it is oil-rich Baku where the most impressive contemporary building is being done.

The Baku skyline has sprouted dozens of concrete, steel and glass towers, and some of them are genuinely stunning to the eye. The three blue-glass Flame Towers (a hotel, offices and apartments) twist their way up to pointed tips 28 or more storeys high, while the Korean-designed Hotel Full Moon and Hotel Crescent are projected to adorn the bayside with, respectively, a giant glass disc and a crescent moon resting on its two tips – both 30-plus storeys high. More down to earth, in a sense, is the Zaha Hadid– designed Heydar Əliyev Cultural Centre that ripples sinuously over the contours of its site in a form vaguely reminiscent of a large conch shell.

Island in Lake Van (on the Hripsime model), and the 11th-century cathedral of the ruined Armenian capital Ani.

In Georgia the old basilican form was further developed into the elongated-cross church, with a drum and pointed dome rising above the crossing. Such are the beautiful tall Alaverdi, Svetitskhoveli (Mtskheta) and Bagrati (Kutaisi) cathedrals. This was also the major era of monastery construction in Georgia and Armenia, and the time when the ubiquitous Armenian tradition of carving *khatchkars* (elaborately engraved headstones) took off.

The Mongol and Timurid invasions brought another hiatus in Christian construction, but it revived again under Persian Safavid rule from the 16th century.

Cave Cities & Monasteries

» Uplistsikhe (Georgia)

» Davit Gareja (Georgia)

» Vanis Qvabebi (Georgia)

» Vardzia (Georgia)

» Geghard Monastery (Armenia)

» Goris (Armenia)

» Khndzoresk (Armenia)

19th- & 20th-Century Architecture

The 19th and early 20th centuries brought international influences via Russia, with Georgia putting a quirky twist on styles like neoclassicism and art nouveau. Yerevan was almost totally rebuilt in heavy Soviet style in the 20th century. Gyumri's old quarter, Kumayri, is the most complete 19th-century urban area in Armenia. Tbilisi's Open-Air Museum of Ethnography is the best place to get a feel for some of the region's traditional wooden domestic architecture.

Azerbaijan

Sadly, little early architecture survives in Azerbaijan thanks to earthquakes and invaders like the Mongols and Timur. The few churches remaining from the early Christian Albanian culture, in places like Nic, Oğuz and Kiş, bear a notable resemblance to Georgian and Armenian churches. Outstanding among Azerbaijan's medieval Islamic buildings are some tomb towers, notably the 26m-high, 12th-century Mömina Xatun in Naxçivan, with its turquoise glazing, and some of old Baku's stone buildings, notably the 12th-century Maiden's Tower and the 15th-century Palace of the Shirvanshahs.

The country's most aesthetically interesting mosques, such as Quba's Hacı Cəfər, and the colonnaded mosque at Qəbələ, are mostly 19th century, an exception being Gəncə's twin-minareted, 17th-century Cümə Mosque, credited to Persian Shah Abbas.

The finest 18th-century buildings are secular affairs such as the beautiful Xan Sarayı (Khan's Palace) and Karavansaray in Şəki. Baku's first oil boom a century ago saw the construction of numerous fine mansions in eclectic European styles, some of which are now open as museums.

Survival Guide

DIRECTORY A–Z... 294

Accommodation.........294
Children................295
Climate.................295
Electricity 295
Embassies & Consulates ..295
Gay & Lesbian Travellers..296
Insurance...............296
Internet Access.........296
Legal Matters 297
Maps...................297
Money..................297
Photography 297
Safe Travel.............298
Telephone 298
Time...................298
Toilets.................298
Travellers
with Disabilities 298
Visas...................299
Women Travellers........299

TRANSPORT 300

GETTING THERE & AWAY..300
Entering the Region......300
Air.....................300
Land...................301
Sea 303
GETTING AROUND 305
Air.....................305
Bicycle 305
Bus & Minibus 305
Car & Taxi 306
Hitching................306
Local Transport.........306
Train 306

HEALTH.......... 308

LANGUAGE 310

Directory A–Z

Accommodation

The price indicators **$** (budget), **$$** (midrange) and **$$$** (top end) are used in sleeping listings throughout this book. See under Accommodation in Directory A–Z in each country chapter for the price ranges that each indicator refers to, and for a rundown of the types of accommodation available in each country.

Lodgings in the capital cities tend to be considerably more expensive than elsewhere. Outside the capitals, the range of accommodation is smaller, but value for money is generally much better.

Budget

Plenty of inexpensive hostels, homestays, guesthouses and B&Bs (generally with shared bathrooms boasting hot showers), welcome budget travellers, especially in Georgia and Armenia – in Azerbaijan budget travellers sometimes have to resort to cheap hotels. These places are often happy to dispense local information, help you find transport and generally make your stay enjoyable. The more popular of them are also very good places to meet other travellers.

Camping There are very few commercial campsites and most of those have pretty basic facilities. There are few restrictions on wild camping, but be sensible and sensitive about where you camp – it's not always safe to camp just anywhere, so get good information on local conditions, and if you're near a village, ask if it's OK to camp there.

Camping gas is available in Tbilisi but hard to find elsewhere.

Couch surfing A budget option with great scope for getting an inside angle on local life.

Homestays, Guesthouses and B&Bs Home-cooked meals often available and the opportunity to get a feel for local life.

Hostels Generally provide dormitory beds or bunks, and guest kitchens and hang-out areas.

Midrange

There's a good selection of comfortable midrange hotels around all three countries, many of them on a refreshingly small scale, with professional, amiable staff. They range from Finnish-style wooden cottages in the woodlands of Azerbaijan to modern art nouveau mansions in Batumi, Georgia. They'll offer comfortable rooms (air-conditioned where necessary) and usually a decent restaurant, and often a bar and a couple of leisure facilities. Most of the dreary old Soviet hotels have closed down or have been totally rebuilt.

PRACTICALITIES

» All three countries fall into DVD Region 5 and the predominant video format is SECAM.

» Electric power is 220 volts AC, 50Hz. Sockets are designed for European-style plugs with two round pins. Power cuts still happen sometimes, but with nothing like the frequency of the 1990s.

» All three countries use the metric system of measurements.

» ISIC cards bring a surprising number of discounts on entertainment, museums, shops, restaurants, medical services and even some places to stay in Tbilisi and Baku – see www.isic.org.

» Smoking is near universal among local men, less common among women; only Georgia has a significant number of lodgings with nonsmoking rooms or eateries with nonsmoking areas.

Climate

Baku

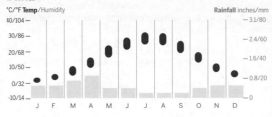

Tbilisi

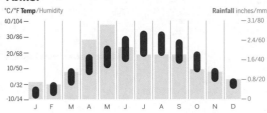

Yerevan

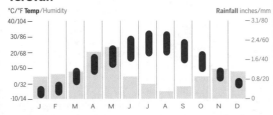

Top End

International top-end chains such as Hyatt, Radisson and Marriott have set up shop in the three capitals and Batumi.

Children

Family is important in the Caucasus, and children are considered treasured gifts from God. Local people love meeting children and are very relaxed with them – it's perfectly normal for strangers to strike up a conversation over kids, and for the most part people will be extremely considerate towards travellers with children.

» Children are only likely to enjoy travel in the region if they enjoy the things most travellers do here, such as

hiking, horse riding and visiting monuments.

» Journeys in sweltering, crowded minivans and buses can be trying, and delays and minor inconveniences can make life difficult travelling on a budget.

» Capital cities and the Georgian coastal resort of Batumi have a few child-friendly attractions.

» Disposable nappies are sold in the larger towns, but

may be hard to come by elsewhere.

» Extra beds for children sharing a parents' room are often available at no, or low cost.

Lonely Planet's *Travel with Children* is full of practical tips on both planning and travelling with kids.

Electricity

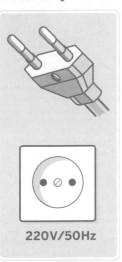

220V/50Hz

Embassies & Consulates

» Embassies in the three countries encourage visitors to register with them and this is a particularly good idea if you are going to isolated or sensitive areas.

» In Nagorno-Karabakh, Abkhazia and South Ossetia, you're on your own: assistance

BOOK YOUR STAY ONLINE

For more accommodation reviews by Lonely Planet authors, check out hotels.lonelyplanet.com. You'll find independent reviews, as well as recommendations on the best places to stay. Best of all, you can book online.

RELIGIOUS FESTIVAL DATES

Some Christian and Muslim festivals have movable dates. The exact dates of Muslim festivals that are calculated by the Islamic lunar calendar must be pronounced locally by clerics, based on moon sightings. Dates given below are for the predicted dates. See Month by Month (p16) for more information on these festivals and other events in Georgia, Armenia and Azerbaijan.

YEAR	ARMENIAN EASTER	GEORGIAN EASTER	RAMAZAN	GURBAN BAYRAMI	AŞURA
2012	8 Apr	15 Apr	20 Jul-18 Aug	26 Oct	24 Nov
2013	31 Mar	5 May	9 Jul-7 Aug	15 Oct	14 Nov
2014	20 Apr	20 Apr	28 Jun-27 Jul	4 Oct	3 Nov
2015	5 Apr	12 Apr	18 Jun-16 Jul	23 Sep	23 Oct

from your embassy is not possible as these de facto independent territories are outside the control of their nominal national governments and are not recognised internationally.

» Foreign embassies in Tbilisi, Yerevan and Baku are listed in the Directory A–Z sections of this book's country chapters.

» Some countries may only have one embassy in the region, or none at all. For Australia, Canada and Ireland, responsibility for the South Caucasus countries is taken by their embassies in Moscow, Ankara or Sofia (Bulgaria).

Gay & Lesbian Travellers

Homosexual acts are legal in all three countries, but social acceptance or understanding is minimal and extremely few gays or lesbians openly display their orientation. Traditional and religious values and a patriarchal society make homosexuality pretty much taboo. There are small gay-rights movements in Georgia and Armenia, but no public gay scenes, and homophobia is still quite widespread, even in Georgia which is generally the most open-minded of the three

societies. In one bizarre incident reported by news media in 2011, three gay German tourists were tied up and thrown into a river near Omalo, Tusheti, after kissing each other on the lips during a dinner with Georgian tourists.

In general gay travellers should encounter no problems if they are discreet – and two men or women sharing a bed will often be considered far less scandalous than an unmarried straight couple doing the same.

Websites

Gay Batumi (http://gaybatumi.com) Practical information for Georgia, with an active message board.

Unzipped: Gay Armenia (www.gayarmenia.blogspot.com) Wide-ranging blog.

ADVOCACY & SUPPORT GROUPS

Inclusive Foundation (www.inclusive-foundation.org) Georgia.

Lesbi.org.ge (www.lesbi.org.ge) Georgia.

We for Civil Equality (www.wfce.am) Armenia.

Pink Armenia (www.pinkarmenia.org) Armenia.

International Lesbian and Gay Association (www.ilga-europe.org) Useful information on all three countries.

Insurance

It is important to be properly insured against theft, loss and medical problems. Health insurance should cover you for visits to private clinics in the capitals, which generally provide the best medical care, but can be expensive, and emergency air evacuations. Check that your policy covers any activities you plan, such as horse riding, climbing, skiing and even hiking. Worldwide travel insurance is available at lonelyplanet.com/travel_services. You can buy, extend and claim online anytime – even if you're already on the road. See also p308.

Internet Access

Many places to stay, at all price levels, have wi-fi and/or internet-connected computers for guests to use. These services are usually, though not always, free. Some cafes, restaurants and bars also offer wi-fi. Almost all towns have internet cafes, typically charging around the equivalent of US$1 per hour. In this book the 🛜 icon indicates wi-fi availability; @ means internet-connected computers for guests.

Legal Matters

Police harassment of foreigners is a thing of the past, but you might be questioned by police or soldiers if you visit sensitive areas, such as near the Azerbaijan–Armenia border, the Nagorno-Karabakh ceasefire line (including Agdam), the Kelbajar region in Armenian-occupied Azerbaijan, Naxçıvan, or the borders of Russia, Abkhazia or South Ossetia. The same goes for military installations anywhere, and in Azerbaijan even for some government buildings and economically strategic installations such as oilfields. Outsiders can be viewed with some suspicion in less-visited areas of Azerbaijan.

» Visiting Nagorno-Karabakh is illegal under Azerbaijan law. Evidence that you have done so, such as a Nagorno-Karabakh visa in your passport, could prevent you from entering Azerbaijan.

» Entering Abkhazia or South Ossetia from Russia is illegal under Georgian law, with a maximum penalty of five years' imprisonment. If you have entered Abkhazia from Russia, don't attempt to continue across Abkhazia's southern border into undisputed Georgia.

» It's sensible always to carry at least a photocopy of your passport and visa, and the real thing if you are going anywhere where you might be questioned. In Azerbaijan it's a good idea always to carry the passport itself and preferably a copy too.

» There is a zero limit on blood alcohol for drivers in all three countries. Traffic police are unlikely to try to extract bribes from foreigners for fabricated or marginal driving offences.

» Cannabis grows in the region and the seeds are sometimes used as a cooking ingredient, but consuming drugs in any other way carries the risk of long prison sentences.

Maps

A good regional map such as ITMB's *Caucasus Region* (1:650,000 scale) or Freytag & Berndt's *Caucasus* (1:1 million) is invaluable for planning. See the Directory A–Z in the Georgia and Armenia chapters for information on country-specific maps.

Money

The easiest way to carry money is with an ATM card, with US dollars or euros in cash as a backup. The greenback is still the most popular foreign currency in the region, now closely followed by the euro. ATMs are plentiful in the cities and can be found in almost every town. They normally accept MasterCard, Visa, Cirrus and Maestro cards. Visa and MasterCard cash advances are also possible at major banks. Most towns have almost as many money-changing offices as ATMs. There are Western Union offices in many places in case you need to arrange a money transfer.

You can't change Azeri manat in Armenia or Armenian dram in Azerbaijan, but both can be exchanged in Georgia. Georgian lari are exchangeable in both countries. Capital cities and border areas are generally the easiest places to make these intra-Caucasian transactions, although it can be difficult to change Armenian dram into lari on the Georgian side of Armenia/Georgia borders.

Travellers cheques are often a real pain to change except at some banks in the three capitals. You can make purchases with credit cards at the better hotels, restaurants and some shops in the capitals, but less frequently elsewhere.

In this book prices are given in whatever currency they are normally quoted in – usually the local currency but sometimes (chiefly at the more expensive hotels and travel agencies) US dollars or euros.

For further information on money, see under Money in Directory A–Z in each country chapter.

Photography

It's unwise to start pointing your camera anywhere near border areas that might be considered sensitive. This includes pretty much anywhere near the Azerbaijan–Armenia border, the Armenia–Iran border, the Nagorno-Karabakh ceasefire line (including Agdam), Naxçıvan, or the borders of Russia, Abkhazia or South

GOVERNMENT TRAVEL ADVICE

These government websites have information on potential danger areas and general safety tips.

» **Australia** www.smartraveller.gov.au
» **Canada** www.voyage.gc.ca
» **Germany** www.auswaertiges-amt.de
» **Japan** www.mofa.go.jp
» **Netherlands** www.minbuza.nl
» **New Zealand** www.safetravel.govt.nz
» **UK** www.fco.gov.uk
» **USA** travel.state.gov

Ossetia. Nor is it a good idea to point a camera at military vehicles or army bases. Be sensitive if photographing at religious sites.

There are some spots in Baku, including the metro system, where police might bother you if you start waving a camera about; also see p259. Azerbaijani police and security guards can get suspicious at anyone photographing what they consider 'unflattering' or 'inappropriate' scenes (ugly buildings, factories, transport infrastructure, etc). Naçxivan seems especially sensitive.

When photographing people, extend the usual courtesies – people will often happily pose if you ask their permission to snap them, and it's a good way to break the ice.

Lonely Planet's *Travel Photography* is a comprehensive, jargon-free guide to getting the best shots from your travels.

Safe Travel

» These are now generally safe and low-crime-rate countries. Police corruption is much less of a problem than in the past, and virtually nonexistent in Georgia.

» Take normal precautions for travelling anywhere – don't flash large amounts of cash, keep a close eye on your belongings in crowded places and transport, don't walk alone along dark, empty streets.

» You do need to be careful near volatile border areas such as the Nagorno-Karabakh ceasefire line, the borders of Abkhazia and South Ossetia, and the Armenia–Azerbaijan border. Tensions and conflicts may flare up at any time in or around these areas. Keep an ear to the ground.

» Landmines or unexploded ordnance (UXO) still lie near sections of the Armenia–Azerbaijan border and the Nagorno-Karabakh ceasefire line. Away from the ceasefire line and any military exercises, Nagorno-Karabakh is as safe as Armenia.

» Clearing of Abkhazia's last minefields, mostly in the upper Kodori Gorge, was due to be completed in 2011.

» The area between South Ossetia and the Georgian town of Gori has been cleared of UXO, but there is still danger from mines and UXO in some parts of South Ossetia itself.

» Climbing and hiking in the mountains have their potential risks. Seek local advice and go with company or take a guide, especially if you're heading into isolated areas. Give dogs a wide berth: mountain dogs are bred for fending off wolves!

Telephone

» Many local people and businesses now mainly use mobile phones, which are inexpensive and provide virtually country-wide coverage.

» All three countries use the GSM standard, and if your mobile is unlocked for international use you can buy local SIM cards for very little – well worth doing if you are spending more than a few days in any country.

» Landline telephone systems in all three countries have been updated and now generally provide efficient service.

» See the Telephone sections in Directory A–Z in each country chapter for information on dialling codes, costs and further useful tips.

Time

All three countries are four hours ahead of Greenwich Mean Time (GMT+4), making them three hours ahead of most of Western Europe, four hours ahead of the UK and nine hours ahead of New York. Like most of Europe and North America, Armenia and Azerbaijan – but not Georgia – switch to Daylight Saving Time from the last Sunday in March to the last Sunday in October. This puts Armenia and Azerbaijan five hours ahead of GMT, and one hour ahead of Georgia, for that period (which includes the main tourist season).

Toilets

Public toilets are rare across the region, and where they exist they may not have paper, so it's a good idea to carry some. Larger bus and train stations usually have toilets – often the squat variety – where you may have to pay a nominal fee to the attendant.

The best places for clean, seat toilets when you are out and about are modern restaurants, cafes and bars in the cities. Some of the more basic homestays and guesthouses have squat toilets, which may be in an outhouse.

Travellers with Disabilities

There are few facilities to make life easier for travellers with disabilities. Even in the main cities, cracked and potholed pavements make wheelchair use problematic, although the growing number of modern hotels is a positive factor. Public transport generally has no wheelchair access. The cost of a car and driver-helper, however, isn't extortionate. Some of the best local travel agencies will be able to discuss specific needs.

These organisations can provide general info for travellers with disabilities:

Access-able Travel Source (www.access-able.com)

Mobility International USA (www.miusa.org)

Visas

Georgia Many nationalities need no visa for visits of up to 360 days. Those who need visas can get them at road and air entry points into the country (50 GEL for 90 days), or from Georgian embassies or consulates. See p119.

Armenia Almost all visitors need visas: 21-day (AMD3000) and 120-day (AMD15,000) visas are issued at all entry points. See p197.

Azerbaijan Visas (US$58 to US$131 according to nationality) must be obtained in advance from an Azerbaijan embassy or consulate. A letter of invitation from an agency, contact or business in Azerbaijan is usually required, adding to the cost. See p268.

Nagorno-Karabakh You need a visa from Ministry of Foreign Affairs in Stepanakert (obtainable on arrival there) or the Nagorno-Karabakh representative in Yerevan. See p274 . Important: you will not be permitted to enter Azerbaijan if you have a Karabakh visa in your passport, so if you plan to visit Azerbaijan after Nagorno-Karabakh request that the visa be left outside the passport.

Abkhazia You must get a visa from one of Abkhazia's representatives in other countries, or, more complicated, from the Abkhazia Foreign Ministry in Sukhumi. See p69.

Visas for Onward Travel

Central Asia Kazakhstan visas are available for many nationalities without a Letter of Invitation (LOI) in three to five working days at the Kazakhstan embassies in Tbilisi, Yerevan and Baku. The Baku embassy will also issue Kyrgyz visas simultaneously with a Kazakh visa. Baku also has Turkmenistan, Uzbekistan and Tajikistan embassies: obtaining a Turkmen 'permission code', which authorises issuance of a five-day transit visa on arrival, can take two weeks or more; Tajik visas are straightforward; Uzbekistan requires an LOI from some nationalities.

Iran To obtain a visa you need a foreign ministry authorisation number obtainable through agencies such as **Persian Voyages** (www.persianvoyages.com) or **Iranian Visa** (www.iranian visa.com). Start the process a few weeks in advance. You can nominate the embassy at which you will collect your visa: Tbilisi is a convenient collection point, Baku can be difficult.

China & Pakistan Visas are awkward to procure in South Caucasus countries.

Turkey Most Westerners either need no visa or can obtain it quickly at the border.

See Visas sections in each country's A–Z directory in this book for further information on onward voyages.

Women Travellers

While women are least restricted in Georgia and more so in Azerbaijan, attitudes throughout the region are conservative. The big cities might appear to be open and liberated places, but this is something of a veneer. Even in Tbilisi it is rare for unmarried couples to go out together unaccompanied, and almost unheard of for them to live together. So female travellers, especially if travelling alone, may find they have to ward off some unwanted male attention.

» It's a good idea to sit near the front in *marshrutky* (minivans), and not next to a strange man.

» If you're alone it's unwise to accept an invitation to a man's house or office unless he's with a female relative; it could be misinterpreted as strong interest on your part.

» It's a good idea to keep your legs and shoulders covered in all public places. This is obligatory in mosques and churches, where also wearing a headscarf demonstrates respect for local culture.

» Drunkenness is very bad form generally, but for women even being tipsy is frowned upon. Women aren't expected to drink heavily during toasts – a sip will suffice.

» Sitting alone at male-dominated restaurants can be uncomfortable, especially Azerbaijan's *çayxanəs* (teahouses) and *yeməkxanas* (cheap local restaurants). Local women do not go into *çayxanəs*. Some restaurants and cafes offer private booths or rooms or discreet vine-covered pavilions or tables.

» Some cheaper lodgings in Azerbaijan are also uncomfortably male-dominated.

» Islam in Azerbaijan is not generally fundamentalist and in most areas women do not cover their hair.

» In the Georgian mountain region of Tusheti, women are not permitted to approach the traditional animist shrines known as *khatebi*.

» In off-the-beaten-track places, women travellers may get some strange looks if they smoke. Local women smoking in public are often considered to have loose morals.

Transport

The South Caucasus countries are accessible by air, sea and land. All three national capitals have busy international airports.

Politics complicate matters a little on the ground. Armenia's borders with Turkey and Azerbaijan are sealed, and Georgia's and Azerbaijan's borders with Russia are closed to most foreigners. This means the only routes right through the region are from Turkey into Georgia, then either south through Armenia to Iran, or east into Azerbaijan and then south to Iran or across the Caspian Sea to Kazakhstan or Turkmenistan – or vice versa.

GETTING THERE & AWAY

Most visitors fly into the region, but it's also possible to enter by road from Turkey or Iran and by sea from Ukraine, Bulgaria, Turkmenistan or Kazakhstan. Flights, tours and rail tickets can be booked online at lonely planet.com/bookings.

Entering the Region

Procedures at arrival points are generally straightforward and quick. It might take a couple of hours to get through the Turkish–Georgian road border at Sarpi on a busy weekend.

The Turkey–Armenia border is closed, and the Russia–Georgia and Russia–Azerbaijan borders are open only to local or CIS citizens. With the requisite visas it is possible to enter the breakaway Georgian region of Abkhazia from Russia, but this is illegal under Georgian law, with a maximum penalty of five years' jail, so don't attempt to continue into undisputed Georgia from Abkhazia if you have come this way.

See the Directory A-Z in each country chapter for detail on visa requirements.

Air

There are direct flights to Tbilisi, Yerevan and Baku from many cities in Europe, the Middle East and Russia, and from a few Central Asian cities. A few international flights also go to Batumi and Kutaisi in Georgia, Gəncə, Lənkəran and Naxçivan in Azerbaijan, and Gyumri in Armenia.

Routes from Europe involving a transfer in Riga (with Air Baltic), Istanbul (with Pegasus Airlines) or Kiev (with Aerosvit or Ukraine International Airlines), are often good value. Turkish Airlines has worldwide connections through Istanbul and can be competitive. Fly Dubai, China Southern Airlines and Uzbekistan Airlines have widespread Asian connections via Dubai, Ürümqi and Tashkent respectively.

CLIMATE CHANGE & TRAVEL

Every form of transport that relies on carbon-based fuel generates CO_2, the main cause of human-induced climate change. Modern travel is dependent on aeroplanes, which might use less fuel per kilometre per person than most cars but travel much greater distances. The altitude at which aircraft emit gases (including CO_2) and particles also contributes to their climate change impact. Many websites offer 'carbon calculators' that allow people to estimate the carbon emissions generated by their journey and, for those who wish to do so, to offset the impact of the greenhouse gases emitted with contributions to portfolios of climate-friendly initiatives throughout the world. Lonely Planet offsets the carbon footprint of all staff and author travel.

FLYING TO GEORGIA

AIRLINE	WEBSITE	FROM	TO
AeroSvit	www.aerosvit.com	Dnepropetrovsk, Donetsk, Kiev, Odessa	Tbilisi
		Kiev	Batumi
Air Astana	www.airastana.com	Almaty	Tbilisi
Air Baltic	www.airbaltic.com	Riga	Tbilisi
Airzena Georgian Airways	www.georgian-airways.com	Amsterdam, Athens, Dubai, Frankfurt, Kharkov, Kiev, Minsk, Moscow, Paris, Tehran, Tel Aviv, Vienna	Tbilisi
		Donetsk, Kharkov, Kiev, Odessa, Moscow, Tel Aviv	Batumi
Arkia Israel Airlines	www.arkia.com	Tel Aviv	Tbilisi
BelAvia	http://belavia.by	Minsk	Batumi, Tbilisi
BMI	www.flybmi.com	London	Tbilisi
China Southern Airlines	www.flychinasouthern.com	Ürümqi	Tbilisi
Czech Airlines	www.csa.cz	Prague	Tbilisi
Fly Dubai	www.flydubai.com	Dubai	Tbilisi
Lot	www.lot.com	Warsaw	Tbilisi
Lufthansa	www.lufthansa.com	Frankfurt, Munich	Tbilisi
Pegasus Airlines	www.flypgs.com	Antalya, Istanbul	Tbilisi
Qatar Airways	www.qatarairways.com	Doha	Tbilisi (planned)
SCAT	www.scat.kz	Aktau, Astana	Tbilisi
S7 Airlines	www.s7.ru	Moscow	Kutaisi, Tbilisi
Turkish Airlines	www.turkishairlines.com	Istanbul	Batumi, Tbilisi
Ukraine International Airlines	www.flyuia.com	Kiev	Tbilisi
Ural Airlines	www.uralairlines.ru	Moscow	Kutaisi

None of the South Caucasus countries' main airlines – state-owned Azerbaijan Airlines (AZAL) and privately owned Airzena Georgian Airways and Armavia – are world class, though they can offer good fares.

To fly to Ashgabat (Turkmenistan), it's normally much cheaper to go via Dubai with Fly Dubai than take the direct Lufthansa flight from Baku (though a potential new direct service by Turkmenistan Airlines will be worth investigating). For fares from North America check Georgia and Armenia specialist **Levon Travel** (www.levontravel.com).

Since 2000 there have been three fatal crashes of scheduled passenger flights flying to/from the region's airports: in 2005 an AZAL Antonov 140-100 flying from Baku to Aktau (Kazakhstan) crashed near Nardaran; in 2006 an Armavia Airbus A-320 from Yerevan to Sochi (Russia) crashed into the Black Sea; and in 2009 a Caspian Airlines Tupolev 154M from Tehran to Yerevan crashed in Iran. All passengers and crew died in each case.

Land

Bus & Minibus

Buses from various cities in Turkey and Iran cross the Sarpi, Posof/Vale, Agarak, Sədərək and Astara border points. You can just as easily cross all land borders by a sequence of hops by local bus, minibus, taxi or train – which is sometimes preferable given the long journeys involved on intercity buses.

FLYING TO ARMENIA

AIRLINE	WEBSITE	FROM	TO
Aeroflot	www.aeroflot.ru	Moscow	Yerevan
AeroSvit	www.aerosvit.com	Kiev	Yerevan
Air Baltic	www.airbaltic.com	Riga	Yerevan
Air France	www.airfrance.com	Paris	Yerevan
Air Italy	www.airitaly.it	Rome	Yerevan
Armavia	www.u8.am	Aleppo, Amsterdam, Athens, Beirut, Berlin, Donetsk, Dubai, Istanbul, Kharkov, Kiev, Krasnodar, Larnaca, Lyon, Marseille, Minvody, Moscow, Nizhny Novgorod, Novosibirsk, Odessa, Paris, Rome, Rostov-on-Don, St Petersburg, Samara, Simferopol, Sochi, Stavropol, Tehran, Tel Aviv, Venice, Volgograd, Voronezh, Warsaw, Yekaterinburg	Yerevan
Austrian Airlines	www.austrian.com	Vienna	Yerevan
BMI	www.flybmi.com	London	Yerevan
Czech Airlines	www.csa.cz	Prague	Yerevan
Donavia	www.aeroflot-don.ru	Minvody, Rostov-on-Don, Sochi	Yerevan
		Rostov-on-Don, Sochi	Gyumri
Fly Dubai	www.flydubai.com	Dubai	Yerevan
Iran Aseman Airlines	www.iaa.ir	Tehran	Yerevan
Kuban Airlines	www.kuban.aero	Krasnodar	Yerevan
Lot	www.lot.com	Warsaw	Yerevan
RusLine	www.rusline.aero	Krasnodar	Gyumri
S7 Airlines	www.s7.ru	Chelyabinsk, Moscow, Novosibirsk	Yerevan
SCAT	www.scat.kz	Aktau	Yerevan
Syrian Air	www.syriaair.com	Aleppo	Yerevan
Ural Airlines	www.uralairlines.ru	Yekaterinburg	Yerevan
Vim Airlines	www.vim-avia.com	Moscow	Gyumri

See the relevant city transport sections in this book for further details on these services.

IRAN
Daily buses run between Tehran and Yerevan (US$60, 24 hours) via Tabriz and the easy-to-cross Agarak border point near Meghri. Tatev Travel (p142) is the Yerevan agent for this bus. There is also a bus service between Tehran and Baku (about US$40, 19 hours) via Tabriz.

TURKEY
Georgia Several Turkish bus companies run from Istanbul, Ankara, Trabzon and other Turkish cities to Batumi, Kutaisi and Tbilisi via the Sarpi border crossing. There are normally at least two daily buses from Istanbul to Tbilisi (typically US$40, 26 hours), and more in summer. Buses or minibuses run almost round the clock between Trabzon and Batumi (US$12, about 3½ hours).

Özlem Ardahan (http://ozlemardahan.com.tr) runs buses from Istanbul to Tbilisi via Ankara, Erzurum, Ardahan and the Posof/Vale border crossing near Akhaltsikhe, Georgia. They are scheduled daily from mid-June to mid-September, and at least once weekly at other times. The Ardahan to Tbilisi stretch (US$35) takes seven hours. Koch Ardahan company also travels between Ardahan and Akhaltsikhe. Some Tbilisi-bound buses have been known to terminate across this border in Vale or Akhaltsikhe, leaving travellers to continue by minibus or taxi.

Azerbaijan Companies including **Öz Nuhoğlu** (www.oznuhogluseyahat.com) and Öz Gülhan run buses between Istanbul and Baku (around US$60, 40 hours), via Trabzon and Georgia, three days a week. **Iğdırlı Turizm** (www.igdirliturizm.com.tr) has six buses a day from Istanbul to Naxçivan (about US$32, 26 hours) via Iğdır.

Armenia Buses from Istanbul to Yerevan (US$60, 32 hours), via Georgia, run once a week.

Car & Motorcycle

Drivers bringing vehicles into the region will need the vehicle's registration papers and liability insurance. If your motor insurance policy from home is not extendable to cover the South Caucasus countries, try to organise some insurance in advance. **Ingosur** (www.ingosur.nl) is one insurance company providing motoring coverage for former Soviet states. Failing that, you'll have to buy insurance as soon as possible after you cross the border. You may have to pay a small amount for obligatory minimum third-party insurance when entering some countries.

You should contact automobile associations in your home country, and embassies of the countries you plan to visit, well in advance for information on vehicle documentation and regulations. South Caucasus countries do not require the *carnet de passages en douane* (a document that some countries require for duty-free temporary vehicle importations). But Azerbaijan for example normally only allows visitors to bring in foreign-registered vehicles for a maximum 30 days (sometimes less) without leaving a hefty deposit on entry. There is also a road tax of US$15 payable on entry to Azerbaijan.

Some drivers have been refused entry into Azerbaijan in right-hand-drive vehicles (from Britain and other countries where driving is on the left-hand side of the road); others have got through customs with right-hand-drive vehicles after paying special 'fees' (US$30 in one reported case).

For information on driving inside the region, see p306.

Train

The only trains running beyond the three South Caucasus countries are between Baku and Russia and Ukraine, and are open to citizens of CIS countries only. But a new 98km line is being built between Kars, Turkey, and Akhalkalaki in Georgia (which has a line to Tbilisi), creating a potential rail link between Turkey and all three South Caucasus countries. It may open in 2013.

Sea
Georgia

The Ukrainian company **UkrFerry** (www.ukrferry.com) operates approximately weekly passenger ferries between Ilyichevsk, near Odessa, and Batumi (p78), and between Kerch, on the Crimean Peninsula, and Poti (p66). Most sailings between Ilyichevsk and Batumi also carry vehicles. UkrFerry also has a passenger ferry from Varna, Bulgaria, to Batumi (but not vice versa at the

---

ENTRY POINTS

Official entry points into Georgia, Armenia and Azerbaijan from other countries are as follows:

Georgia
Batumi International airport and seaport.
Kutaisi Airport. Flights from Russia.
Larsi (Verkhny Lars) Road border with Russia, open to CIS and Georgian citizens only.
Poti Seaport.
Sarpi/Sarp Road border with Turkey.
Tbilisi International airport.
Vale/Posof Road border with Turkey.

Armenia
Agarak Road border with Iran.
Gyumri Shirak Airport. Flights from Russia.
Yerevan Zvartnots Airport. International airport.

Azerbaijan
Astara Road border with Iran.
Baku Heydar Əliyev International Airport. Seaport with ferries from Turkmenbashi, Turkmenistan and Aktau, Kazakhstan.
Culfa (Naxçivan)/Jolfa Road border with Iran.
Gəncə International airport.
Lənkəran Airport. Flights from Moscow, Russia.
Naxçivan City Airport. Flights from Istanbul, Turkey and Moscow, Russia.
Samur Road border with Russia, open to CIS citizens only.
Sədərək (Naxçivan) Road border with Turkey.
Yalama Railway border with Russia, open to CIS citizens only.

FLYING TO AZERBAIJAN

AIRLINE	WEBSITE	FROM	TO
Aeroflot	www.aeroflot.ru	Moscow	Baku
AeroSvit	www.aerosvit.com	Kiev	Baku, Gəncə
Air Astana	www.airastana.com	Astana, Almaty	Baku
Air Baltic	www.airbaltic.com	Riga	Baku
Anadolu Jet	www.anadolujet.com	Istanbul	Naxçivan
Austrian Airlines	www.austrian.com	Vienna	Baku
Azerbaijan Airlines (AZAL)	www.azal.az	Aberdeen, Aktau, Ankara, Dubai, Istanbul, Kabul, Kiev, London, Milan, Moscow, Paris, Prague, Tel Aviv, Trabzon, Ürümqi, Vienna	Baku
BelAvia	http://belavia.by	Minsk	Baku
BMI	www.flybmi.com	London	Baku
China Southern Airlines	www.flychinasouthern.com	Ürümqi	Baku
Fly Dubai	www.flydubai.com	Dubai	Baku
Iran Air	www.iranair.com	Tehran	Baku
Lufthansa	www.lufthansa.com	Ashgabat, Frankfurt	Baku
Moskovia	www.ak3r.ru	Moscow	Gəncə
Qatar Airways	www.qatarairways.com	Doha	Baku (planned)
Rossiya	www.rossiya-airlines.ru	St Petersburg	Baku
S7 Airlines	www.s7.ru	Moscow, Novosibirsk	Baku
SCAT	www.scat.kz	Aktau, Atyrau	Baku
Turkish Airlines	www.turkishairlines.com	Istanbul	Baku
Ural Airlines	www.uralairlines.com	Moscow	Baku
		St Petersburg	Gəncə
Utair	www.utair.ru	Khanty-Mansiysk	Baku
		Moscow	Lənkəran, Naxçivan
Uzbekistan Airlines	www.uzairways.com	Tashkent	Baku

time of writing). Schedules and routes fluctuate and information on the website can be inaccurate: email Ukr-Ferry for current schedules and reservations.

Bulgaria's **Intership-ping** (www.intershipping.net) runs a passenger-carrying vehicle ferry from Burgas to Poti (three days), but at the time of writing this was suspended pending acquisition of a new ship.

Ferries between Sochi (Russia) and Batumi were open only to CIS and Georgian citizens at the time of writing: check www.seaport-sochi.ru for latest information. **Olympia-line** (www.olympia-line.ru) operates two or three weekly hydrofoils from Sochi to Trabzon (US$130, 4½ hours) in Turkey, about 180km from the Georgian border.

Azerbaijan

In principle, ferries sail from Baku to Turkmenbashi, Turkmenistan, several nights a week, and to Aktau, Kazakhstan, every week or so. They carry passengers and vehicles, but are primarily cargo ships, so strict timetables don't exist: they leave when they have enough cargo. You could wait as long as two weeks for the Aktau ferry to depart (save time by flying instead). The crossing takes about 12 hours to Turkmenbashi, and 18 hours to Aktau, though the Turkmenbashi ferries often wait many hours offshore before finally docking there. See p221 for more on these services.

GETTING AROUND

Air

INTRA-REGIONAL FLIGHTS
Tbilisi has daily connections with Baku by AZAL (Azerbaijan Airlines), and with Yerevan by Armavia. Airzena Georgian Airways operates summer flights between Baku and Batumi.

DOMESTIC FLIGHTS
Georgia Airzena Georgian Airways has several flights a week between Tbilisi and Batumi. One-way fares bought in advance start at 50 GEL (US$30). There are also Tbilisi–Mestia flights almost daily (see p82).
Azerbaijan AZAL flies from Baku to Naxçivan several times daily (AZN70–US$90; one-way for non-Azeris), and to Gəncə, Lənkəran and Zaqatala three or four times weekly. It also operates three Gəncə–Naxçivan flights per week.

Bicycle

Cycling is growing in popularity as a way to travel in the South Caucasus. For some, this is one leg of a cross-Asia trip. Obviously take plenty of care on the roads – local driving styles are somewhat less predictable than in Western countries, and some road surfaces are awful (though there is a gradual overall improvement). On the plus side, traffic is light away from the few busy highways, the scenery is mostly gorgeous and wild camping is practicable in much of the region.

There's a lot of hilly terrain, but you can store your bike at a guesthouse or hostel if you want to resort to motorised transport for a bit. The weather is pretty hot in July and August. Bring all your spare parts – and beware of the dogs!

You can enjoy some local riding on rented bikes or bike excursions in several places in Georgia and a few in Armenia.

Bus & Minibus

The minibus (*marshrutka*; short for the Russian *marshrutnoe taxi*) is king of public transport in Armenia and Georgia, while buses are a bit more common in Azerbaijan. One or other of these forms of transport reaches almost every village in the region, and there are frequent services between larger towns and cities. Cross-border routes include Tbilisi–Vanadzor–Yerevan, Tbilisi–Gəncə–Baku and Akhaltsikhe–Gyumri–Yerevan.

Marshrutky are 10- to 20-seat minibuses that can pick up and drop off passengers anywhere along their route. They typically charge around US$1.50 per hour of travel. There are some reasonably comfortable and modern buses on intercity routes, but most buses are ageing Soviet workhorses or recycled Western European buses. Buses are usually cheaper than *marshrutky* and have more baggage space, but also slower. Both *marshrutky* and buses can get loaded up with freight (sacks of potatoes, crates of drinks) as well as people.

It's not necessary (and often not possible) to book ahead for buses or *marshrutky*, except for a few international services. *Marshrutky* usually have a sign in the windscreen with

---

BORDER CROSSINGS

Border crossing points within the region are as follows.

Georgia/Azerbaijan
Böyük Kəsik Railway-only border, southeast of Tbilisi.
Matsimi–Postbina Road border between Lagodekhi and Balakən.
Krasny Most (Tsiteli Khidi, Qırmızı Körpü, Red Bridge) Road border southeast of Tbilisi.

Georgia/Armenia
Guguti–Tashir Road border southwest of Marneuli.
Sadakhlo–Bagratashen Road and rail border south of Tbilisi.
Zhdanovi–Bavra Road border between Ninotsminda and Gyumri.

All Armenia–Azerbaijan borders are closed. Nagorno-Karabakh can only be accessed from Armenia, and this is illegal under Azerbaijani law. You will not be permitted to enter Azerbaijan with a Nagorno-Karabakh visa in your passport, so if you plan to visit both places, go to Nagorno-Karabakh second, or request that the Nagorno-Karabakh visa be put on a separate piece of paper.

Abkhazia can be entered at the Enguri River checkpoint northwest of Zugdidi; South Ossetia's border with undisputed Georgia is closed to foreigners.

the destination in the local alphabet. To hail one out on the road, stick out your arm and wave.

If you want to get off, say *gaacheret* (stop) in Georgia, *kangnek* in Armenia and *sakhla burada* in Azerbaijan.

Car & Taxi

Driving styles in the South Caucasus are less regimented than in Western countries, or more anarchic if you see it that way. But if you can get used to the way locals overtake, weave around potholes and like to go fast – and keep a permanent eye on every vehicle that's anywhere near you – driving here is quite possible. Off the main highways and outside the cities, traffic is generally light, although road surfaces are worse, and other road users often include animals. It's now far less common, and unheard of in Georgia, for traffic police to try to extract bribes or 'fines' for spurious driving infringements. If you are fined for a genuine infringement, you should be given a receipt.

The capital cities have branches of major international car-rental companies as well as local outfits, and self-drive rental is becoming more popular in Georgia, though less so in Azerbaijan and Armenia.

It is, however, often no more expensive, and quite common practice, to hire a local driver for intercity trips or excursions. You can find drivers around bus and train stations, but most accommodation places can also find you one, often at a better price. A typical rate for long-distance taxis in Georgia and Armenia is around US$0.30 per kilometre, which is quite economical, especially if shared between three or four people.

Exploring unsurfaced tracks often calls for a 4WD, which can be hired, if you're game, from rental agencies in the capitals. It's often easy enough to find a local driver with their own 4WD who will drive you at reasonable cost. If you plan to drive yourself in mountain areas, it's safest to travel in a convoy of at least two vehicles. Mountain roads are often very poorly surfaced and sometimes blocked or washed away by landslides or flash floods.

» Driving is on the right-hand side of the road.

» The legal maximum blood-alcohol level for driving in all three countries is zero.

» It is acceptable to drive on a licence from an EU country in Georgia and Azerbaijan, but otherwise it's a good idea to carry an International Driving Permit as well as your home-country driving licence.

» Many road signs in Georgia now have Latin script alongside the Georgian; Azerbaijan's are now all in Latin; in Armenia signs might be in Russian, Latin or Armenian script.

» Fuel is generally plentiful along main roads, but if you are going into remote areas ask about availability first and fill up beforehand.

Hitching

In rural areas with poor public transport, local people sometimes flag down passing vehicles and it's quite acceptable for travellers to do the same. It's good to offer a little money (the equivalent of the bus or *marshrutka* fare), as local people often do. Hitching along main roads between cities is less common, although some local students and a few international budget travellers do it in Georgia and Armenia. If you look like a foreign backpacker, locals may pick you up because they're interested to talk with you.

Hitching is never perfectly safe anywhere. Refusing rides from drunk drivers is crucial, and in general you can never be too careful.

Local Transport

All three capitals have cheap, easy-to-use metro systems. Other urban transport comprises a mixture of *marshrutky* and buses. *Marshrutky* will stop to pick up or drop off passengers anywhere along their routes, but they can get very crowded.

In Georgia and Armenia route boards are in the local alphabets. Try to ascertain in advance what route number you need. Otherwise, passers-by and drivers are usually pretty helpful: just say where you want to go, and a nod or shake of the head will give you your answer.

Taxis are plentiful. Most Yerevan taxis, and some in some other cities, have meters, though you may need to remind the driver to turn them on. For other taxis, you need to agree on the fare before you get in. A ride of 3km or so normally costs around US$2 in Tbilisi or Yerevan, but about US$4 (metered) or US$9 (unmetered) in Baku.

Train

Trains in the South Caucasus are slower and much less frequent than road transport. But they're also cheap, and many intercity trains run overnight so you can save money on accommodation. The main railway line in the region runs from Batumi in the west, through Kutaisi and Gori to Tbilisi, and on to Gəncə and Baku in Azerbaijan. A branch south from Tbilisi heads to Yerevan via Vanadzor and Gyumri. Other lines reach towns such as Poti, Zugdidi and Borjomi in Georgia, Yeraskh and Hrazdan in Armenia, and Şəki, Balakən, Gəncə, Qazax, Lənkəran and Astara in Azerbaijan.

International sleeper trains run every night from Tbilisi to Baku and vice versa (2nd class around US$40, about 16 hours), on odd dates from Tbilisi to Yerevan (2nd class about US$30, 13 hours), and on even dates from Yerevan to Tbilisi. From mid-June to mid-September the normal Tbilisi–Yerevan and Yerevan–Tbilisi services are usually replaced by faster, daily Batumi–Tbilisi–Yerevan and Yerevan–Tbilisi–Batumi trains. All international trains may be held up for two or three hours at the borders due to customs searches.

Georgia has some modern rolling stock but most trains in the region are traditional Soviet-style affairs, refurbished in some cases. On most trains some or all of the following ticket classes are available:

1st class or *luks* (in Russian *spalny vagon*; SV) – has upholstered berths and only two people to a compartment; only available on a few trains.

2nd class or *kupe* (short for Russian *kupeyny*, compartment) – four to a compartment, harder berths and fold-down upper bunks; the best compromise between cost and comfort for overnight journeys.

3rd class or *platskart* (reserved) – open bunk accommodation, more crowded and less comfortable.

4th class or *obshchy* (general) – unreserved bench seating.

Take your passport when you go buy tickets, and have it handy when you board trains.

Some day trains have more comfortable seating-only accommodation. An *elektrichka* is a local service with single-class seating, linking a city and its suburbs or groups of nearby towns.

Once a night train is under way and bedtime approaches, an attendant will dole out sheets for you to make up your own bed. The attendant will also wake you up before arrival and collect the used bed linen. Bring any food and drink, though you may be able to buy overpriced snacks on the platform at stops.

Health

Websites

There is a wealth of travel-health advice on the internet. The following include country-specific information:

www.mdtravelhealth.com Full travel-health recommendations for every country, updated daily.

wwwnc.cdc.gov/travel The US Centers for Disease Control and Prevention.

www.nathnac.org The UK's National Travel Health Network and Centre.

Prevention is the key to staying healthy while travelling. A little planning before departure will save trouble later: visit a doctor in good time to discuss vaccinations and prepare any medications that you need to take with you; carry spare contact lenses or glasses.

While you're on the road, take care to avoid dodgy food and water, as well as insect and animal bites, to minimise the risk of problems.

BEFORE YOU GO

Insurance

It's a very good idea to have comprehensive travel insurance with medical evacuation cover. A policy that will make payments directly to providers, rather than reimburse you later, is usually preferable.

Standards of public health care in the region are very patchy. If you need medical attention you may well want to go to one of the expensive Western-standard clinics in the major cities, in which case good insurance coverage is essential.

EU citizens are entitled to free public medical and some dental care in Georgia, Armenia and Azerbaijan under reciprocal arrangements, though they still have to buy prescribed medicines.

IN GEORGIA, ARMENIA & AZERBAIJAN

Availability of Health Care

The capital cities have some expensive, Western-standard clinics. Public medical care is available in all towns, though clinics and hospitals may be ill supplied, and nursing care limited (families and friends

RECOMMENDED VACCINATIONS

You should be up-to-date with the vaccinations that you would normally have back home, such as diphtheria, tetanus, measles, mumps, rubella, polio and typhoid. Further vaccines may be advisable for children or the elderly.

» **Hepatitis A** Classed as an intermediate risk in the region: vaccination may be recommended for those who are staying for long periods, or with family or friends, or in areas with poor sanitation.

» **Hepatitis B** Has high endemicity: vaccination may be recommended for some groups, including people who are likely to have unprotected sex.

» **Tuberculosis (TB)** Vaccination is a good idea for those likely to be mixing closely with the local population or planning a long stay.

» **Rabies** Exists in all three countries. Consider vaccination if you plan a lot of activities that might bring you into contact with domestic or wild animals, such as cycling, hiking or camping, especially in remote areas where postbite vaccine may not be available within 24 hours.

are often expected to provide this). In Georgia some formerly public hospitals have been privatized and will charge fully for treatment, although the cost is still modest by Western standards.

The old custom of giving a tip in cash to nurses or doctors for hospital treatment is no longer common. In places where it does still happen, foreigners would usually be forgiven for not knowing about it. If you want to give a cash tip for special attention, do it discreetly by putting money in an envelope, with a card saying something like 'for coffee and cakes in the office'.

Traveller's Diarrhoea

If you develop diarrhoea, be sure to drink plenty of fluids, preferably in the form of an oral rehydration solution such as Gastrolyte. If diarrhoea is bloody, persists for more than 72 hours or is accompanied by fever, shaking, chills or severe abdominal pain, seek medical attention.

Environmental Hazards

Altitude Sickness

Altitude sickness may develop in anyone who ascends quickly to altitudes above 2500m. It is common at 3500m and likely with rapid ascent to 5000m. The risk increases with faster ascents, higher altitudes and greater exertion. Symptoms may include headaches, nausea, vomiting, dizziness, fatigue,

insomnia, undue breathlessness or loss of appetite.

Severe cases may involve fluid in the lungs (the most common cause of death from altitude sickness), or swelling of the brain. Anyone showing signs of altitude sickness should not ascend any higher until symptoms have cleared. If symptoms get worse, descend immediately.

Acclimatisation and slow ascent are essential to reduce the risk of altitude sickness. Drink at least 4L of water a day to avoid dehydration: a practical way to monitor hydration is to check that urine is clear and plentiful. Avoid tobacco and alcohol. Diamox (acetazolamide) reduces the headache pain caused by altitude sickness and helps the body acclimatise to the lack of oxygen. It is normally only available on prescription.

Hypothermia

Hypothermia occurs when the body loses heat faster than it can produce it. Even on a hot day in the mountains, the weather can change rapidly so carry waterproof garments, warm layers and a hat, and inform others of your route. Hypothermia starts with shivering, loss of judgement and clumsiness. Unless rewarming occurs, the sufferer deteriorates into apathy, confusion and coma. Prevent further heat loss by seeking shelter, warm dry clothing, hot sweet drinks and shared bodily warmth.

Insect Bites & Stings

Mosquitoes are found in most parts of the Caucasus. Malaria is present, though uncommon, from May or

TAP WATER

Tap water is generally safe to drink in Georgia but not in Armenia. It's also OK in Azerbaijan's mountain areas, but not Baku or lowland Azerbaijan. Bottled water is plentiful. Alternatively, boil tap water for 10 minutes, use water purification tablets, or use a filter.

There are many piped springs in rural areas. Many are safe (ask locals), but there can always be a slight risk of contamination.

June to October in southeast Georgia, the rural lowlands of southern Azerbaijan and some parts of Armenia. Bring a good insect repellent, preferably one containing DEET, which can be applied to exposed skin and clothing.

Travelling with Children

Make sure children are up to date with routine vaccinations, and discuss possible travel vaccines well before departure as some are not suitable for children.

Be extra wary of contaminated food and water. If your child has vomiting or diarrhoea, lost fluid and salts must be replaced.

Children should be encouraged to avoid and mistrust dogs or other mammals because of the risk of rabies and other diseases.

Language

WANT MORE?

For in-depth language information and handy phrases, check out Lonely Planet's *Russian Phrasebook*. You'll find it at **shop .lonelyplanet.com**, or you can buy Lonely Planet's iPhone phrasebooks at the Apple App Store.

This chapter offers basic vocabulary to help you get around the south Caucasus. If you read our coloured pronunciation guides as if they were English, you'll be understood.

RUSSIAN

Russian is widely spoken in all three countries, and few people will ever object to being spoken to in it. If you speak passable Russian, you'll be able to get by. Note that kh is pronounced as in the Scottish *loch,* zh as the 's' in 'pleasure', r is rolled in Russian and the apostrophe (') indicates a slight y sound. The stressed syllables are shown in italics.

Basics

Hello.	Здравствуйте.	*zdrast*·vuyt·ye
Goodbye.	До свидания.	da svee·*dan*·ya
Excuse me./ Sorry.	Извините, пожалуйста.	eez·vee·*neet*·ye pa·*zhal*·sta
Please.	Пожалуйста.	pa·*zhal*·sta
Thank you.	Спасибо	spa·*see*·ba
Yes./No.	Да./Нет.	da/nyet

What's your name?
Как вас зовут? kak vaz za·*vut*

My name is ...
Меня зовут ... meen·*ya* za·*vut* ...

Do you speak English?
Вы говорите
по-английски? vi ga·va·*reet*·ye pa·an·*glee*·skee

I don't understand.
Я не понимаю. ya nye pa·nee·*ma*·yu

Accommodation

campsite	кемпинг	*kyem*·peeng
guesthouse	пансионат	pan·see·a·*nat*
hotel	гостиница	ga·*stee*·neet·sa
youth hostel	общежитие	ap·shee·*zhi*·tee·ye

Do you have a ... room?	У вас есть ...?	u vas yest' ...
single	одноместный номер	ad·nam·*yes*·ni *no*·meer
double	номер с двуспальней кроватью	*no*·meer z dvu·*spaln*·yey kra·*vat*·yu

How much is it ...?	Сколько стоит за ...?	*skol'*·ka *sto*·eet za ...
for two people	двоих	dva·*eekh*
per night	ночь	noch'

Eating & Drinking

What would you recommend?
Что вы
рекомендуете? shto vi ree·ka·meen·*du*·eet·ye

Do you have vegetarian food?
У вас есть овощные
блюда? u vas yest' a·vashch·*ni*·ye *blyu*·da

I'll have ...
..., пожалуйста. ... pa·*zhal*·sta

Cheers!
Пей до дна! pyey da dna

I'd like the ..., please.	Я бы хотел/ хотела ... (m/f)	ya bi khat·yel/ khat·ye·la ...
bill	счёт	shot
menu	меню	meen·yu

(bottle of) beer	(бутылка) пива	(bu·til·ka) pee·va
(cup of) coffee/tea	(чашка) кофе/чаю	(chash·ka) kof·ye/cha·yu
water	вода	va·da
(glass of) wine	(рюмка) вина	(ryum·ka) vee·na

Emergencies

Help!	Помогите!	pa·ma·gee·tye
Go away!	Идите отсюда!	ee·deet·ye at·syu·da

Call ...!	Вызовите ...!	vi·za·veet·ye ...
a doctor	врача	vra·cha
the police	милицию	mee·leet·si·yu

I'm lost.
Я потерялся/ ya pa·teer·yal·sa/
потерялась. (m/f) pa·teer·ya·las'

I'm ill.
Я болею. ya bal·ye·yu

Where are the toilets?
Где здесь туалет? gdye zdyes' tu·a·lyet

Shopping & Services

I'd like ...
Я бы хотел/ ya bi khat·yel/
хотела ... (m/f) khat·ye·la ...

How much is it?
Сколько стоит? skol'·ka sto·eet

That's too expensive.
Это очень дорого. e·ta o·cheen' do·ra·ga

Numbers – Russian		
1	один	a·deen
2	два	dva
3	три	tree
4	четыре	chee·ti·ree
5	пять	pyat'
6	шесть	shest'
7	семь	syem'
8	восемь	vo·seem'
9	девять	dye·veet'
10	десять	dye·seet'

bank	банк	bank
market	рынок	ri·nak
post office	почта	poch·ta
tourist office	туристическое бюро	tu·rees·tee· chee·ska·ye byu·ro

Transport & Directions

Where's the ...?
Где (здесь) ...? gdye (zdyes') ...

What's the address?
Какой адрес? ka·koy a·drees

Can you show me (on the map)?
Покажите мне, pa·ka·zhi·tye mnye
пожалуйста (на карте). pa·zhal·sta (na kart·ye)

One ... ticket, please.	Билет ...	beel·yet ...
one-way	в один конец	v a·deen kan·yets
return	в оба конца	v o·ba kant·sa

boat	параход	pa·ra·khot
bus	автобус	af·to·bus
plane	самолёт	sa·mal·yot
train	поезд	po·yeest

ARMENIAN

Armenian is an Indo-European language, with its own script and heavy influences from Persian evident in its vocabulary. It has also borrowed many words and phrases from Russian, Turkish, French and Hindi. The standard eastern Armenian is based on the variety spoken in Ashtarak, close to Yerevan. People from Lori *marz* have a slower, more musical accent, while speakers from Gegharkunik and Karabakh have a strong accent that can be difficult for outsiders to understand, and vocabulary that is sometimes unique to one valley.

Below we've provided pronunciation guides (in blue) rather than the Armenian script. Note that zh is pronounced as the 's' in 'measure', kh as the 'ch' in the Scottish *loch*, dz as the 'ds' in 'adds', gh is a throaty sound and r is rolled.

Basics

Hello.	barev dzez (pol) barev (inf)
Goodbye.	tsetesutyun (pol) hajogh (inf)
Yes.	ayo/ha (pol/inf)
No.	voch/che (po/inf)

Numbers – Armenian	
1	mek
2	yerku
3	yerek
4	chors
5	heeng
6	vets
7	yot
8	ut
9	eenuh
10	tas

Please.	khuntrem
Thank you.	shnorhakalutyun
No problem.	problem cheeka
How are you?	vonts ek/es? (pol/inf)
I'm fine, thank you.	lav em shnorhakalutyun
And you?	eesk' duk?
What's your name?	anunut eench eh?
My name is ...	anuns ... e
Do you speak English?	khosum es angleren?
I don't understand.	chem haskanum

Accommodation

Do you have a room?	unek senyak?
guesthouse	panseeonat
hotel	hyuranots

Emergencies

Where is the toilet?	vortegh e zugarane?
I'm sick.	heevand em
doctor	bjheeshk
hospital	heevandanots
police	vosteegan

Shopping & Services

How much?	eench arjhey?
bank	bank
chemist/pharmacy	deghatun/apteka
currency exchange	dramee bokhanagum
expensive	tang
market	shuka
open	bats
post office	post
shop	khanut
telephone	herakhos

Time & Dates

When?	yerp?
yesterday	yerek
today	aysor
tomorrow	vaghe
Monday	yerkushaptee
Tuesday	yerekshaptee
Wednesday	chorekshaptee
Thursday	heengshaptee
Friday	urpat
Saturday	shapat
Sunday	keerakee

Transport & Directions

When does ... leave?	yerp jampa gelle ...?
When does ... arrive?	yerp gee hasne ...?
Stop!	kangnek!
airport	otanavakayan
bus	avtobus
bus station/stop	avtokayan/gankar
car	mekena
minibus	marshrutny/marshrutka
petrol	petrol/benzeen
plane	eenknateer/otanov
taxi	taksee
ticket	doms
Where?	ur/vortegh?
here	aystaeegh
left	dzakh
right	ach

AZERI

Azeri is a member of the Turkic language family, and shares its grammar and much of its vocabulary with Turkish. Originally written in a modified Arabic script, and during the Soviet rule in Russian Cyrillic script, it's now written in a modern Azeri Latin alphabet (used below).

Note that r is rolled, ğ is pronounced at the back of the throat, g as the 'gy' in 'Magyar', ç as the 'ch' in 'chase', c as the 'j' in 'jazz', x as the 'ch' in the Scottish loch, j as the 's' in 'pleasure', q as the 'g' in 'get', ş as the 'sh' in 'shore', ı as the 'a' in 'ago', ə as in 'apple' (short), ö as the 'e' in 'her', and ü as the 'ew' in 'pew'. In many parts of the country, the hard 'k' is pronounced more like a 'ch'. Words are lightly stressed on the last syllable.

Basics

Hello.	Salam.
Goodbye.	Sağ olun/ol. (pol/inf)
How are you?	Necəsiniz? (pol)
	Necəsən? (inf)
Yes.	Bəli./Hə. (pol/inf)
No.	Xeyr./Yox.
Please.	Lutfən.
Thank you.	Təşəkkür edirəm.
You're welcome.	Buyurun.
Excuse me./Sorry.	Bağışlayın.
Do you speak English?	Siz ingiliscə danışırsınız?
I don't understand.	Mən anlamıram.
Cheers!	Deyilən sağlığa!

Accommodation

hotel	mehmanxana
room	otaq
toilet	tualet

Emergencies

ambulance	tacili yardım maşını
doctor	hakim
hospital	xastaxana

Shopping & Services

How much?	Nə qədər?
bank	bank
chemist/pharmacy	aptek
currency exchange	valyuta dayışma
expensive	baha
market	bazar
open	açıq

Numbers – Azeri

1	bir
2	iki
3	üç
4	dörd
5	beş
6	altı
7	yeddi
8	səkkiz
9	doqquz
10	on

post office	poçt
shop	dukan/mağaza
telephone	telefon

Time & Dates

When?	Nə vaxt?
yesterday	dünən
today	bu gün
tomorrow	sabah
Monday	Bazar ertəsi
Tuesday	Çərşənbə axşamı
Wednesday	Çərşənbə
Thursday	Cümə axşamı
Friday	Cümə
Saturday	Şənbə
Sunday	Bazar

Transport & Directions

When does ... leave?	... nə zaman gedir?
When does ... arrive?	... nə zaman gəlir?
Stop!	Saxla!
airport	hava limanı
bus	avtobus
bus station	avtovağzal
bus stop	avtobus dayanacağı
car	maşın
ferry	bərə
minibus	mikroavtobus
petrol	benzin
plane	təyyarə
port	liman
taxi	taksi
ticket	bilet
train	qatar
train station	damir yolu stansiyası
Where?	Hara?/Harada?
	(for verbs/nouns)
avenue	prospekt
lane/alley	xiyaban
square	meydan
street	küçə

GEORGIAN

Georgian belongs to the Kartvelian language family, which is related to the Caucasian languages. It is an ancient language with its own cursive script.

Below we've provided pronunciation guides (in blue) rather than the Georgian script. Note that q is pronounced as the 'k' in 'king' but far back in the throat, kh as the 'ch' in the Scottish *loch*, zh as the 's' in 'pleasure', dz as the 'ds' in 'beds', gh is a throaty sound (like an incipient gargle) and r is rolled. Light word stress usually falls on the first syllable.

Basics

Hello.	gamarjobat
Goodbye.	nakhvamdis
Yes.	diakh/ho (pol/inf)
No.	ara
Please.	tu sheidzleba
Thank you.	madlobt
How are you?	rogora khart?
Excuse me.	ukatsrovad
Sorry.	bodishi
It doesn't matter.	ara ushavs
Do you speak English?	inglisuri itsit?
I don't understand.	ar mesmis
Cheers!	gaumarjos!

Accommodation

hotel	sastumro
room	otakhi
toilet	tualeti

Emergencies

doctor	ekimi
hospital	saavadmqopo
police	politsia/militsia

Shopping & Services

How much?	ramdeni?
bank	banki
chemist/pharmacy	aptiaqi
expensive	dzviri
market	bazari/bazroba
open	ghiaa
post office	posta
shop	maghazia
telephone	teleponi

Time & Dates

When?	rodis?
yesterday	gushin

Numbers – Georgian

1	erti
2	ori
3	sami
4	otkhi
5	khuti
6	ekvsi
7	shvidi
8	rva
9	tskhra
10	ati

today	dghes
tomorrow	khval

Sunday	kvira
Monday	orshabati
Tuesday	samshabati
Wednesday	otkhshabati
Thursday	khutshabati
Friday	paraskevi
Saturday	shabati

Transport & Directions

When does it leave?	rodis midis/gadis?
When does it arrive?	rodis modis/chamodis?
Stop here!	gaacheret!
airport	aeroporti
boat	gemi
bus	avtobusi/troleibusi
bus station	avtosadguri
bus stop	gachereba
car	mankana
minibus	marshrutka
petrol	benzini
plane	tvitmprinavi
port	porti
taxi	taksi
ticket	bileti
train	matarebeli
train station	(rkinigzis) sadguri

Where?	sad?
avenue	gamziri
road/way	gza
square	moedani

GLOSSARY

You may encounter some of the following words during your time in Georgia (Geo), Armenia (Arm) and Azerbaijan (Az). Some Russian (Rus) and Turkish (Tur) words, including the ones below, have been widely adopted in the Caucasus.

abour (Arm) – soup
ajika (Geo) – chilli paste
alaverdi (Geo) – person appointed by the toastmaster at a *supra* to elaborate on the toast
Amenaprkich (Arm) – All Saviours
aptek/apteka/aptiaqi (Az/Rus & Arm/Geo) – pharmacy
Arakelots (Arm) – the Apostles
ARF (Arm) – Armenian Revolutionary Federation; the Dashnaks
aşig (ashug) (Az) – itinerant musician
astodan (Az) – ossuary
Astvatsatsin (Arm) – Holy Mother of God
avtosadguri (Geo) – bus station
aviakassa (Rus) – shop or window selling air tickets
avtokayan (Arm) – bus station
avtovağzal (Az) – bus station

baklava – honeyed nut pastry
baliq (Az) – fish, usually sturgeon, often grilled
basturma (Arm) – cured beef in ground red pepper
berd (Arm) – fortress
bulvar (Az) – boulevard

caravanserai – historic travellers inn, usually based around a courtyard
Catholicos – patriarch of the Armenian or Georgian churches
çay (Az) – tea
çayxana (Az) – teahouse
chacha (Geo) – powerful grappalike liquor

chakapuli (Geo) – lamb and plums in herb sauce
churchkhela (Geo) – string of nuts coated in a sort of caramel made from grape juice and flour
chvishdari (Geo) – Svanetian dish of cheese cooked inside maize bread
CIS – Commonwealth of Independent States; the loose political and economic alliance of the former republics of the USSR (except Georgia and the Baltic states)
çörək (Az) – bread

dacha (Rus) – country holiday cottage or bungalow
darbazi (Geo) – traditional home design with the roof tapering up to a central hole
doğrama (Az) – cold soup made with sour milk, potato, onion and cucumber
dolma (Arm, Az) – vine leaves with a rice filling
domik (Rus) – hut or modest bungalow accommodation
dram – Armenian unit of currency
duduk (Arm) – traditional reed instrument; also *tutak* (Az)
dzor (Arm) – gorge

elektrichka (Rus) – local train service linking a city and its suburbs or nearby towns, or groups of adjacent towns
eristavi (Geo) – duke

gavit (Arm) – entrance hall of a church
ghomi (Geo) – maize porridge
glasnost (Rus) – openness

halva (Az) – various sweet pastries, often containing nuts
hraparak (Arm) – square

IDP – internally displaced person
Intourist (Rus) – Soviet-era government tourist organisation

ishkhan (Arm) – trout from Lake Sevan
istirahət zonası (Az) – rural bungalow resort

jvari (Geo) – religious cross; spiritual site in mountain regions

kamança (Az) – stringed musical instrument
kartuli – Georgian language
Kartvelebi – Georgian people
kassa (Rus) – cash desk or ticket booth
katoghike (Arm) – cathedral
khachapuri (Geo) – savoury bread or pastry, usually with a cheese filling
khamaju (Arm) – meat pie
khash/khashi (Arm/Geo) – garlic and tripe soup; also *xaş* (Az)
khashlama (Arm) – lamb or beef stew with potato
khatchkar (Arm) – medieval carved headstone
khati/khatebi (Geo) – animist shrine in Tusheti, Georgia
khevi (Geo) – gorge
khidi (Geo) – bridge
khinkali (Geo) – spicy meat, potato or mushroom dumpling
khoravats (Arm) – barbecued food
kişi (Az) – men (hence 'K' marks men's toilets)
köfte/kyufta/küftə (Tur/Arm/Az) – minced beef meatballs with onion and spices
körpü (Az) – bridge
koshki/koshkebi (Geo) – defensive tower in Georgian mountain regions
kubdari (Geo) – spicy Svanetian meat pie
küçəsi (Az) – street
kupe/kupeyny (Rus) – 2nd-class compartment accommodation on trains
kvas (Rus) – beverage made from fermented rye bread

LANGUAGE GLOSSARY

lahmacun/lahmajoon (Tur/Arm) – small lamb and herb pizzas

lari – Georgian unit of currency

lavash/lavaş (Arm/Az) – thin bread

ləvəngi (Az) – casserole of chicken stuffed with walnuts and herbs

lich (Arm) – (lake)

lobio/lobiya/lobya (Geo/Rus/Az) – beans, often with herbs and spices

luks (Rus) – deluxe; used to refer to hotel suites and 1st-class accommodation on trains

manat – Azerbaijani unit of currency

marani (Geo) – wine cellar

marshrutka/marshrutky (Rus) – public minivan transport

marz (Arm) – province, region

matagh (Arm) – animal sacrifice

matenadaran (Arm) – library

matsoni (Geo) – yoghurt drink

mayrughi (Arm) – highway

mehmanxana (Az) – hotel

merikipe (Geo) – man who pours wine at a *supra*

meydan (Az) – square

mədrəsə (Az)- Islamic school

moedani (Geo) – square

most (Rus) – bridge

mtsvadi (Geo) – shish kebab, shashlyk

muğam (Az) – traditional musical style

mushuri (Geo) – working songs

muzhskoy (Rus) – men's toilet

nagorny (Rus) – mountainous

nard, nardi (Az/Arm) – backgammonlike board game

obshchy (Rus) – general-seating class (unreserved) on trains

oghee (Arm) – delicious fruit vodkas; sometimes called *vatsun or aragh*

OSCE – Organisation for Security and Co-operation in Europe

OVIR (Rus) – Visa and Registration Department

paneer (Arm) – cheese

paxlava (Az) – honeyed nut pastry

pendir (Az) – cheese

perestroika (Rus) – restructuring

pir (Az) – shrine or holy place

piti (Az) – soupy meat stew with chickpeas and saffron

pivo (Rus) – beer

pkhali/mkhali (Geo) – beetroot, spinach or aubergine paste with crushed walnuts, garlic and herbs

platskart/platskartny (Rus) – open-bunk accommodation on trains

plov – rice dish

poghota (Arm) – avenue

poghots (Arm) – street

prospekti (Az) – avenue

qadım (Az) – woman (hence 'Q' marks womens toilets)

qala, qalasi (Az) – castle or fortress

qəpiq – Azerbaijani unit of currency (100 qəpiq equals one manat)

qucha (Geo) – street

qutab (Az) – stuffed pancake

rabiz (Rus) – Armenian workers' culture, party music

rtveli (Geo) – grape harvest

sagalobeli (Geo) – church songs

sagmiro (Geo) – epic songs

sakhachapure (Geo) – café serving *khachapuri*

sakhinkle (Geo) – café serving *khinkali*

saxlama kamera (Az) – left-luggage room(s)

satrap – Persian provincial governor

satrpialo (Geo) – love songs

satsivi (Geo) – cold turkey or chicken in walnut sauce

şəbəkə (Az) – intricately carved, wood-framed, stained-glass windows

shashlyk – shish kebab

Shirvan – old Azerbaijani unit of currency, equal to two manat

shkmeruli (Geo) – chicken in garlic sauce

shuka (Arm) – market

soorch (Arm) – coffee

spalny vagon/SV (Rus) – two-berth sleeping compartment in train

suchush (Arm) – plum and walnut sweet

sulguni (Geo) – smoked cheese from Samegrelo

supra (Geo) – dinner party; literally means 'tablecloth'

supruli (Geo) – songs for the table

surp (Arm) – holy, saint

tabouleh (Arm) – diced green salad with semolina

tamada (Geo) – toastmaster at a *supra*

tan (Arm) – yoghurt

tetri – Georgian unit of currency (100 tetri equals one lari)

tikə kəbab (Az) – shish kebab; commonly called *shashlyk*

tqemali (Geo) – wild plum, wild plum sauce

tonir (Arm) – traditional bread oven

tsikhe (Geo) – fortified place

tufa – volcanic stone famous to Armenia

tur – large, endangered Caucasian ibex

tutak (Az) – traditional reed instrument; also *duduk* (Arm)

vank (Arm) – monastery

virap (Arm) – well

vishap (Arm) – carved dragon stone

xaş (Az) – garlic and tripe soup; also *khash/khashi* (Arm/Geo)

xəzri (Az) – gale-force wind in Baku

yeməkxana (Az) – food house, cheap eatery

zhensky (Rus) – womens toilets

behind the scenes

SEND US YOUR FEEDBACK

We love to hear from travellers – your comments keep us on our toes and help make our books better. Our well-travelled team reads every word on what you loved or loathed about this book. Although we cannot reply individually to postal submissions, we always guarantee that your feedback goes straight to the appropriate authors, in time for the next edition. Each person who sends us information is thanked in the next edition – the most useful submissions are rewarded with a selection of digital PDF chapters.

Visit **lonelyplanet.com/contact** to submit your updates and suggestions or to ask for help. Our award-winning website also features inspirational travel stories, news and discussions.

Note: We may edit, reproduce and incorporate your comments in Lonely Planet products such as guidebooks, websites and digital products, so let us know if you don't want your comments reproduced or your name acknowledged. For a copy of our privacy policy visit lonelyplanet.com/privacy.

OUR READERS

Many thanks to the travellers who used the last edition and wrote to us with helpful hints, useful advice and interesting anecdotes:

Grzegorz, Julian, Wojciech, Ashley Adrian, Asli Akarsakarya, Simone Appert, Alik Arzoumanian, Marc Bokma, Ido Brickner, Yuliono Budianto, Silvio Calvi, Linda Campbell, Erik Carapetian, Francisco Chong Luna, Sonny Colin, Roslyn Coltheart, Greg Cornwell, Marco Crisafulli, Andrew Cullen, Paddy Davison, Michiel De Graaff, Evan Decorte, C Denton Brown, Janine Downes, Randell Drum, Michael Falvella, Andreas Fertin, Richard Frank, Damien Galanaud, Kees Geselschap, John Gilchrist, Steve Goldberg, Irena Grzegorczyk, Xavier Guezou, Rainer Hamet, Graham Hamilton, Judith Harrison, Jim Holroyd, Henry Howard, Mabon John, Benzi Kahana, Patricia Knox, Dvir Koenigstein, Jorg Lauberbach, Maxime Leloup, Ed Lunken, Petter Magnusson, Marcel Medek, Alex Miller, Andy Mitchell, Giorgio Mori, Ilka Morse, Alejandra Navarro Rueda, Emily Nelson, Greg O'Hern, Kimberly Palmer, Esther Parigger, Mario Pavesi, Wladimiro Perez Ortigosa, Niklas Petersen, Vieri Riccardo Salvadori, Steve Rigden, Taguhi Sahakyan, Tony Schneider, Ben Schottland, Barbara Schumacher, Christopher Sexton, Betty Smallwood, Silvia Spies, Lene Steen, Victoria Stefaniuk, Farid Subhanverdiyev, Valeria Superno Falco, Laurel Sutherland, Andreas Sveen Bjørnstad, Trevor Sze, Ann Tulloh, Gerbert Van Loenen, Martin Van Der Brugge, Robert Van Voorden, Wouter Van Vliet, Michael Weilguni, Arlo Werkhoven, Barbara Yoshida, Ian Young, Anne Zouridakis.

AUTHOR THANKS

John Noble

Special thanks to Sofo Ghoghoberidze, everybody at Dodo's, William Dunbar, Tuta Balavadze, Hans Gutbrod, Tim Blauvelt, Roza Shukvani and family, Regina Jegorova, Giorgi Gardava, Roma Tordia, Besik Basaria, David Luashvili, Jason Thake, Felix Tomlinson, Miri and Itamar Shinin, Svea and Joerk, Funky Henning, Christian Portelatine, Anthony Schierman, Eka Chvritidze, Dan Bingham-Pankratz, Kate Ortenzi; Natalia Bakhtadze, Tamuna Giorgadze, Nutsa Totadze (GNTA); Information Centres all around Georgia; Alan Saffery, Nutsa Abramishvili (EPI); and, above all, supercolleagues Danielle Systermans and Michael Kohn.

Michael Kohn

In Armenia, thanks to Gevorg Babayan, Gohar Mirzoyan, Nick Wagner, Taguhi Sahakyan, Gor Aleksanyan, Lennart Lehmann, Nyree Abrahamian, Syuzanna Azoyan and the staff at *Armenia Now*. Cheers to fellow travellers Franziska Laue, Edward Cheng, Steve Gibbs and Chris Khachatourian. Armenia's gang of Peace Corps volunteers deserves special recognition for guiding me in their respective cities, in particular: Beckey (Yeghegnadzor), Greg (Stepanavan), Hayley (Sevan), Mary (Dsegh), Lizzie (Kapan), Patrick (Goris) and Zoe (Goris). My love as always to Baigal and Molly.

Danielle Systermans

Many, many, many thanks to Ian, Saadat, Narmin, Vasif, Micah and Mason, Jeffrey, Taleh, Zaur, Fiona, Tanya in Ivanovka, Mark, Rebecca, Dustin and Kelly in Ganja, Humbat and his $100,000 BMW, Aliheydar, Rustam, Askar and friends in Amanevi, Larissa and

Sandy, Ilqar, Martin, Andrei and friends, Sander, John, Zahid, Samid, Mevlud and Khaled in Laza, the Haciyev and Ismailov families, and to Mark Elliott for 15 memorable years.

ACKNOWLEDGMENTS

Climate map data adapted from Peel MC, Finlayson BL & McMahon TA (2007), 'Updated World Map of the Köppen-Geiger Climate Classification', *Hydrology and Earth System Sciences*, 11, 1633–44.

Cover photograph: Ananuri fortress, Georgia (p84), W Korall, Imagebroker.

Many of the images in this guide are available for licensing from Lonely Planet Images: www.lonelyplanetimages.com.

THIS BOOK

This 4th edition of Lonely Planet's *Georgia, Armenia & Azerbaijan* guidebook was researched and written by John Noble, Michael Kohn and Danielle Systermans. The previous edition was also written by John, Michael and Danielle. This guidebook was commissioned in Lonely Planet's London office, and produced by the following:

Commissioning Editors Katie O'Connell, Glenn van der Knijff

Coordinating Editors Jackey Coyle, Tasmin Waby

Coordinating Cartographer Alex Leung

Coordinating Layout Designer Kerrianne Southway

Managing Editors Imogen Bannister, Angela Tinson

Senior Editor Susan Paterson

Managing Cartographers Adrian Persoglia, Amanda Sierp

Managing Layout Designer Chris Girdler

Assisting Editors Janet Austin, Carolyn Bain, Kate Evans, Paul Harding, Andi Jones, Kristin

Odijk, Alison Ridgway, Sophie Splatt

Assisting Cartographers Julie Dodkins, Xavier di Toro, James Leversha, Jacquie Nguyen

Cover Research Naomi Parker

Internal Image Research Aude Vauconsant

Language Content Branislava Vladisavljevic

Thanks to Helen Christinis, Ryan Evans, William Gourlay, Imogen Hall, Kate James, Yvonne Kirk, Trent Paton, Kirsten Rawlings, Nelly Rukhadze, Gerard Walker

index

A

Abanotubani 33, 41
Abashidze, Aslan 72
Abkhazia 68-74, 109, 111, 280, 285
Abşeron Peninsula 224-7, **226**
accommodation 294-5, see also
    individual locations
    apartment rentals 135
    online bookings 295
Achara, see Adjara
activities 14, 16-19, see also individual
    activities
    Armenia 193-4
    Azerbaijan 266
    Georgia 116
Adishi 81
Adjara 72-9
Agarak 186
Agdam 275
Aghitu 180
Aghmashenebeli, Davit, see David
    the Builder
Ağrı Dağ, see Mt Ararat
agriculture 289
air travel
    to/from the region 300-1, 302,
        304
    within the region 305
Ajara, see Adjara
Ajaria, see Adjara
Akhali Shuamta 97
Akhaltsikhe 106-7
Akhtala 169
Alaverdi 168
Alexandropol 170
altitude sickness 309
Amberd 150
amusement parks
    Batumi Ferris wheel 72
    Borjomi Mineral Water Park 102
    Haghtanak Park 132
    Qabaland 237

000 Map pages
000 Photo pages

Stepanakert 270
Tbilisi Ferris wheel 38
Ananuri 84
Anhogin, David 165-6
animals 290
archaeological sites
    Armaztsikhe-Bagineti 56
    Erebuni Fortress 134
    İmamzadə 255-6
    Naxçıvan City 255
    Nokalakevi 67
    Old Gabala 237
    Tigranakert 275-6
    Uplistsikhe 59
    Vani 64-5
architecture 14, 291-2
Areni 173-4
Argishti I 124, 134, 145
Arkhoti 88
Armash Fish Ponds 152
Armenia 23, 121-97, **123**
    accommodation 121, 193
    activities 193-4
    airlines 302
    architecture 291-2
    arts 190-1
    business hours 194
    cinema 190, 280
    climate 121, 295
    costs 122
    culture 187-8, 280-1, 287-8
    customs regulations 194
    dangers 194
    drinks 192
    economy 280-1
    environment 289-90
    exchange rates 122
    food 121, 192
    highlights 123
    history 188-90, 282-6
    internet resources 122
    language 311-12
    menu decoder 195
    money 122, 196
    names 187
    northern Armenia 152-73, **152-3**
    planning information 121-2
    politics 187-8, 280-1
    population 280
    postal services 196
    religion 281
    southern Armenia 173-86
    telephone services 197
    travel seasons 121
    travel to/from 122
    travel within 305-7
    visas 122
    Yerevan 9, 124-45, **126-7**, **130-1**, 9

art galleries, see museums
Art-Gene Festival 17, 41
arts
    Armenia 190-1
    Azerbaijan 262-3
    Georgia 112-14
Artsruni, Vahan 191
Aşəbi Keyf 258
Ashot I 188
Ashotsk 170-1
Ashtarak 149-50
Astara 254
Ateşgah Məbədi 224-5
atheism 288
ATMs 12
Atsunta Pass 90
Avlabari 34-5
Ayas Nautical Research Club 154
Azerbaijan 23, 198-268, **200-1**
    accommodation 198, 264, 266
    activities 266
    airlines 304-5
    architecture 292
    arts 262-3
    Baku (Bakı) 202-24, **203**, **204**,
        208-9, 10
    border areas 259
    business hours 266
    central Azerbaijan 248-50
    cinema 280
    climate 198, 295
    costs 199
    culture 280-1, 287-8
    drinks 263-4
    economy 260, 280-1
    environment 289-90
    exchange rates 199
    food 242, 263, 264
    highlights 200-1
    history 260-1, 282-6
    language 312-13
    menu decoder 265
    money 267
    Naxçivan 254-9
    northern Azerbaijan 228-33, **229**
    northwestern Azerbaijan 233-48,
        229
    planning information 198-9
    politics 260, 280-1
    population 280
    public holidays 267
    religion 281
    southern Azerbaijan 250-4, **251**
    telephone services 267
    travel seasons 198
    travel to/from 199
    travel within 305-7
    visas 199, 268

Azerbaijan Democratic Republic 261
Azokh cave 275

B
Babluani, Gela 114
Bagrat III 109
Bakounts, Axel 185
Baku (Bakı) 202-24, **203**, **204**, **208-9**, **10**
  accommodation 211, 213-14
  climate 295
  dangers 221
  drinking 218-19
  entertainment 219-20
  festivals & events 210-11
  food 214-18
  history 202
  internet access 221
  medical services 221
  metro **225**
  Old City 10, 204-6, 211, 213, 215-16, 218, **204**, **10**
  shopping 220-1
  sights 204-10
  travel to/from 221-3
  travel within 223-4
  walking tours 212, **212**
Baku Commissars 165
Bakuriani 105-6
Balakən 247-8
ballooning 41
Baratashvili, Nikoloz 113
bargaining 196
Barisakho 89
bathhouses
  Abanotubani 33, 41
  Amberd 150
  Iranian 273
  Quba 230
  Taza Bay Hamami 207
  Roman 145
bathrooms 13, 298
Batumi 72-8, **74**
beaches 78
  Abşeron 227, **226**
  Adjara 72-3
  Astara 254
  Gagra 71
  Gonio 78
  Lənkəran 251
  Nabran 233
  Noratus 155
  Sevan 153
  Şixov 227
Becho 83-4
beer 115, 263
Bəhlulzadə, Səttar 262
Berd 162
Beşbarmaq Dağ 228

bicycle travel, see cycling
birds 290
bird-watching 116, 290
Blue Horn poets 113
books 281, 283, 284, 285, see also literature
border areas 259
border crossings 303, 305
Borjomi 102-4
Borjomi-Kharagauli National Park 104-5
brandy 15, 192, 263, 288
  Yerevan Brandy Company 128-9
BTC pipeline 260
budget 12, 27, 122, 199
Buduq 231
bungee jumping 41, 44
bus & minibus travel 301-3, 305-6
business hours, see individual locations
Byurakan 150-1

C
Car 247
car travel 13, 303, 306
cathedrals, see churches & cathedrals
cave cities 292, see also monasteries & convents
  Uplistsikhe 59-60
  Vanis Qvabebi 107
  Vardzia 107-8
Cavid, Hüseyn 256
caving 176
cell phones 13, 298
  Armenia 197
  Azerbaijan 267
  Georgia 49, 119
  Nagorno-Karabakh 273
Charkviani, Irakli 112
Chavchavadze, Ilia 113
Chavchavadze, Prince Alexander 96-7
Chesho 92
children, travel with 295
  health 309
Christianity 188-9, 260-1, 277, 283, 288
  holy dates 296
churches & cathedrals
  Akhali Shuamta & Dzveli Shuamta 97
  Alaverdi Cathedral 95
  Albanian 244
  Anchiskhati Basilica 33
  Ateni Sioni 60
  Bagrati Cathedral 60
  Church of Simon the Zealot 71
  Echmiadzin 148

Jvari Church 55-6
Kasagh Gorge churches 149-50
Noravank 174
Samtavro Church 56
Surp Gayane Church 148-9
Surp Grigor Lusavorich Cathedral 129, 155
Surp Hripsime 149, 291
Surp Sargis Church 129
Surp Shogahat Church 149
Svetitskhoveli Cathedral 54-5
Tsminda Sameba Cathedral 34
Tsminda Sameba Church 88, **2-3**, **9**
Vankasar Church 276, **282**
Zoravar Church 127
Zvartnots Cathedral 147, 291
cinema 280
  Armenia 190
  Azerbaijan 262
  Georgia 113-14
Çırax Qala 228
climate 12, 16-19, 295, see also individual regions
  charts 295
climbing, see mountaineering
cognac, see brandy
conservation 152-3
consulates, see embassies
convents, see monasteries & convents
coppersmithing 234
corruption 109, 111, 188, 281, 285-6
country codes 13
Culfa 259
culture 280-1, 287-8
customs regulations 266
cycling 305

D
dance 3
  Armenia 191
  Georgia 112
dangers, see safety
Dartlo 92
Dashnaks 189
dates, religious 296
Datvisjvari Pass 89
David the Builder 64, 95, 283
Davit Bek 185
Davit Gareja 10, 100-1, **11**
daylight saving 12
De Lucchi, Michele 33, 35, 292
Debed Canyon 167-9
Dilijan 157-8
disabilities, travellers with 298
discounts 294
drama 191
  High Fest 18-19
  Rustaveli Theatre 48

drinks 15, *see also* brandy, wine
  Armenia 192
  Azerbaijan 263-4
  chacha 99
  beer 115, 263
  Georgia 115
  oghee 161
Dsegh 167-8
Duman, Nikol 276
Dumbadze, Nodar 113
DVDs 294
Dzveli Shuamta 97

E
Echmiadzin 148
ecology 289-90
economy 280-1
Əfəndiyev, Elçin 262
Egoyan, Atom 190
Eldarov, Omar 262-3
Əliyev, Heydar 260, 261, 281, 286
Əliyev, İlham 281, 286
electricity 294, 295
embassies 295-6
  Armenia 194
  Azerbaijan 267
  Georgia 116-18
emergencies 13, 113, 141, 199
  in Armenian 312
  in Azeri 313
  in Georgian 314
  in Russian 311
entry points 303
environmental issues 289-90, 300
Erekle II 284
ethnographic museums
  Ethnographic Museum Complex
    225
  Ijevan Local Lore Museum 161-2
  Museum of History &
    Ethnography 80
  Open-Air Museum of
    Ethnography 39
  Ushguli 83
etiquette 280-1
events, *see* festivals & events
export permits 220

F
Fellini, Federico 113
festivals & events 16-19, 296, *see also*
  individual locations
  Gabala International Music
    Festival 18
  Kakheti Grape Harvest 18

000 Map pages
000 Photo pages

film, *see* cinema
Fizuli (Varanda) 275
food 15, *see also individual locations*
  Armenia 121, 192, **15**
  Azerbaijan 242, 263, 264
  Georgia 114-15
  khachapuri 45
  menu decoders 117, 195, 265
  piti 242
fortresses
  Amberd 150
  Ananuri 84
  Boloraberd 175
  Erebuni Fortress & Museum 134
  Gonio-Apsarus Fortress 78
  Gori Fortress 58
  Gremi 96
  Lori Berd 165-6
  Nariqala Fortress 34
  Nukha Fortress 238
  Shah Bulart 275-6
  Tmogvi Castle 107
Fountains Sq 206
Füzuli, Mehmed bin Suleyman 262

G
Gabala International Music Festival 18
Gagra 71-2
Gamsakhurdia, Konstantin 113
Gamsakhurdia, Zviad 32, 111, 285
Garni Temple 145
Gavar 155-6
gay travellers 296
Geghard Monastery 8, 145-6, **8**
Gəncə 248-50, **249**
Gəncəvi, Nizami 248, 262
geography 289
geology 289
Georgia 22, 26-120, **28-9**
  Abkhazia 68-74, 109, 111, 280, 285
  accommodation 26, 115-16
  Adjara 72-9
  airlines 301
  architecture 291-2
  arts 112-14
  cinema 280
  climate 26, 295
  costs 27
  culture 280-1, 287-8
  dialling codes 119
  drinks 114-15
  economy 280-1
  environment 289-90
  exchange rates 27
  food 26, 114-15
  Great Caucasus 79-92
  highlights 28-9

history 109-12, 282-6
  Kakheti 92-100
  language 313-14
  media 118
  menu decoder 117
  money 118
  planning information 26-7
  politics 108-9, 280-1
  population 280
  religion 281
  Samtskhe-Javakheti 101-9,
    103
  street names 34
  Tbilisi 30-54, **30-1**, **36-7**, **6-7**
  travel seasons 26
  travel to/from 27
  travel within 305-7
  visas 27, 119-20
  western Georgia 60-8, **61**
Georgian Military Hwy 84-9
Ghshlagh 276
Giorgi III 107, 108
Giorgi the Brilliant 110
glaciers
  Chalaadi 81
  Gergeti 87
  Svaneti 83
glasnost 190, 285
Golden Fleece 65
Gonio 78
Gorbachev, Mikhail 285
Gori 57-9
Goris 180-3, **182**
Goshavank 160
Göy Göl Town 250
grape harvest 96
Great Caucasus 79-92
Gudauri 84
Gül, Abdullah 187
Gyumri 169-73, **171**

H
Hacı Cəfər 292
Hadid, Zaha 292
Hadrut 275
Haghartsin 159-60
Harichavank 173
health 308-9
Heydar Əliyev Cultural Centre 292
Heyerdahl, Thor 244
High Fest 18-19
hiking 290, *see also* walking
  Azerbaijan 231, 232, 239
  Borjomi-Kharagauli National Park
    104-5
  Juta 87-8
  Nagorno-Karabakh 273
  northern Armenia 157, 159, 162

Oreti Lake 91
southern Armenia 184
history 282-6, *see also individual locations*
hitching 306
Hitler, Adolf 261
holidays
Armenia 196
Azerbaijan 267
Georgia 118-19
holy days 296
horse riding 14
hypothermia 309

I

Ijevan 160-1
Ikaltoeli, Arsen 95
İlandağ 258, 258-9
İlisu 244-5
insect bites & stings 309
insurance 296
car 303
health 308
internet access 296
internet resources 13, 122
government travel advice 297
health 308
Iprari 81
Islam 260, 277, 283-4, 288
holy dates 296
İsmayıllı 233-4
itineraries 20-1, 27, 122, 199
Ivanovka 236

J

James Bond Oil Field 227
Jason, Prince of Thessaly 65
Javakhishvili, Mikheil 113
Jermuk 178-9
Juta 87-8
Jvari Church 55, 291
Jvari Pass 84

K

Kakheti 92-100
Kakheti Grape Harvest 18
Kancheli, Gia 112
Kapan 185-6
Karabakh War 17, 132, 134, 179, 280, 285
Karavansaray (Şəki) 239, 292
Karvachar 276
Kazbegi 8, 84-6, **9**
Kazbegi, Alexander 85, 113
Kelbajar 276
Kələxana 233
Ketevan, Queen 96

Khachaturian, Aram 190
Khalilullah I, Shirvanshah 202
Khan Haci Çələbi 238
Khevsureti 89-90, **90**
Khndzoresk 183
Khor Virap Monastery 151
King Giorgi III 107
Kiş 244
Kochar, Yervand 125-7, 129
Kocharian, Robert 190
Kolkheti National Park 66
Komitas 189, 190
Korsha 89
Koruldi Lakes 81
Kumayri 292
Kutaisi 60-3, **62**
Kvariati 78

L

Lagodekhi Protected Areas 101
Lahıc 234-6
Lake Ritsa 71
Lake Sevan 152-3
landscape 15
languages 310-16
Armenian 195, 311-12
Azeri 265, 312-13
Georgian 117, 313-14
Russian 310-11
Laza 231, 232-3
legal matters 297
Ləkit 244
Lenin, Vladimir 35, 57, 134, 189, 255
Lənkəran 251-3, **252**
Lerik 253-4
lesbian travellers 296
literature
Armenian 125
Azeri 262
Georgian 113
Matenadaran 125
Nizami Literature Museum 206
local transport 306
longevity 254
Lori Berd 165

M

Maiden's Tower 206
maps 297
Armenia 194
Georgia 118
Marmashen 173
marshrutka travel, *see* bus & minibus travel
Martuni 156, 275
Masallı 250-1
Matenadaran 125
Mayraberd (Askeran) 275

measurements 294
medical services 308-9
Meghri 186
Melkonian, Monte 275
menu decoders
Armenia 195
Azerbaijan 265
Georgia 117
Mərdəkən 225-6, 227
Mərəzə 233
Mestia 79-81
Mikoyan, Anastas & Artyom 169
mineral springs
Borjomi 102
Samegrelo 67
minibus travel, *see* bus & minibus travel
Mirzaani 100
mobile phones 13, 298
Armenia 197
Azerbaijan 267
Georgia 119
Nagorno-Karabakh 273
Molokan villages 157
Mömina Xatun 255, 292
monasteries & convents
Akhtala Monastery 169
Armenian 11
Bgheno-Noravank 185
Bodbe Convent 100
Dadivank 276
Davit Gareja, **11**
Gandzasar 276
Geghard Monastery 8, 145-6, **8**
Gelati 64-5
Goshavank 161
Haghartsin 159-60
Haghpat Monastery 169
Harichavank 173
Hayravank 155
Hnevank 166
Holy See of Echmiadzin 148
Hovhannavank 149
Ikalto Monastery 95
Kecharis Monastery 156
Khor Virap Monastery 151
Kobayr Convent 167
Lavra 100-1
Marmashen 173
Martvili Monastery 67
Motsameta 63-4
Nekresi Monastery 96
Noravank 174
Novy Afon Monastery 71
Saghmosavank 149-50
Sanahin Monastery 168-9
Sapara Monastery 108
Sevanavank 153
Shamshadin 162

monasteries & convents continued
Surp Grigor Bardzrakash
Monastery 167
Tatev Monastery 184, **11**
Tegher Monastery 150
Tsitsernavank Monastery 277
money 12, 297
Mongols 110
monkey colony 70
Morchiladze, Aka 113
mosques
Batumi 73
Bibi Heybət Mosque 227
Blue Mosque 129
Cümə Məscid 230
Cümə Mosque 292
Qəbələ 292
motorcycle travel 303
mountaineering 290
Azerbaijan 235
Mt Kazbek 89
Mt Aragats 151
Mt Ararat 259, 289
Mt Babadağ 235
Mt Chaukhi 87
Mt Kazbek 89
Mt Mtatsminda 38
Mt Ushba 81
Mtirala National Park 78-9
Mtskheta 54-7, **56**
muğam 262
Mughni 149
museums 35, see also ethnographic
museums
Artsakh State Museum 270
Cafesjian Museum 124
Carpet Museum 207
Erebuni Fortress & Museum 134
Historical Museum 207
Hovhannes Tumanyan Museum 127
Ivane Javakhishvili Samtskhe-
Javakheti History Museum 106-7
Kutaisi Historical Museum 61
Martiros Sarian Museum 125
Matenadaran 125
MIM 207-10
Museum of Fallen Soldiers 270
Museum of Georgia 35
Museum of History &
Ethnography 80
Museum of Modern Art 129
Museum of Russian Art 125
National Art Gallery 128
National Folk Art Museum of
Armenia 125
National Gallery 35

000 Map pages
000 Photo pages

Niko Pirosmanashvili State
Museum 100
Nikol Duman Memorial
Museum 276
Nizami Literature Museum 206
Nobel Technological Museum 73
NPAK 129
Sergei Paradjanov Museum 129
Sighnaghi Museum 97
Stalin Museum 57-8
State Art Museum 207
State Museum of Armenian
History 128
State Museum of Wood-Carving
129
Stepantsminda History Museum 85
Tsitsernakaberd (Armenian
Genocide Memorial &
Museum) 133-4
Uzunömürlülər Muzeyi 253
Yerevan Museum 129
Yervand Kochar Museum 125-7
music
Armenian 190-1
Azeri 262
Georgian 112
muğam 262
rabiz 191
Mustafazadeh, Aziza 262
Mustafazadeh, Vaqif 262
Mütəllibov, Ayaz 261
Mutso 90

N
Nabran 233
Nagorno-Karabakh 23, 269-78, **270**
conflict 260, 261, 274, 275, 277,
280, 285
Nardaran 226
Nariqala Fortress 34
national parks & reserves 64, 66,
104-5, 228, 290
Naxçivan 254-9
Naxçivan City 255-8, **256**
Nərimanov, Nəriman 261
Noah's Ark 258, 282
Noratus 155
Noravank 174
Nova, Sayat 190, 284
Novy Afon 71

O
Odzun 168
Oğuz 237-8
Ohanavan 149
Old Gabala 237
opening hours, see business hours
under individual locations
Ordubad 259

Oshakan 150
outdoor cafes 139

P
palaces
Palace of the Shirvanshahs 206
Xan Sarayi 238, 255
Paliashvili, Zakaria 112
Paradjanov, Sergei 113, 129, 190, 284
paragliding 41
perestroika 261, 285
Peter the Great 284
phone services, see telephone
services
photography 297-8
Pipoyan, Lilit 191
Pirosmani 97, 100
Pirosmani, Niko 113
Pirqulu 233
planning 12-13, see also individual
regions
calendar of events 16-19
Georgia, Armenia & Azerbaijan's
regions 22-3
itineraries 20-1, 27, 122, 199
travel seasons 12
politics 280-1
Armenia 187-8
Azerbaijan 260
Georgia 108-9
Poti 65-6
Prometheus cave 64
Pshavela, Vazha 113
public holidays, see holidays
puppet theatre 48, 207
Putin, Vladimir 112

Q
Qala 225
Qarabağlar 259
Qax 244
Qazimov, Alim 262
Qəbələ 236-7
Qızılqaya 232
Qobustan 227-8
Qriz 231
Quba 9, 230-1
Qum 244

R
rabiz 191
rafting 41, 290
religion 288, see also Christianity,
Islam
Romanov, Duke Mikhail 102
Rose Revolution 32, 111, 286
Roshka 89
Russo-Turkish War 284-5

Rustaveli 35-6, 42-3, 46
Rustaveli, Shota 95, 113

S
Saakashvili, Mikheil 111-12, 281, 286, **286**
safety 297, 298
Sahakyan, Bako 277
Şahdağ 232
Salaxov, Tahir 262
Şamaxı 233
Samegrelo 67
Samtskhe-Javakheti 101-9, **103**
Sardarapat 149
Sargsyan, Serzh 187, 281
Sarian, Martiros 125
Sarushen 275
Sataplia Nature Reserve 64
sea travel 303-5
Şəki 238-44, **240**
Seljuks 283
Sevan 153-5
Shahumian, Stepan 165
Shamshadin 162
Shatili 89
Shenaqo 92
Shevardnadze, Eduard 111, 285
Shia Islam 288
Shushi 273-4
Sighnaghi 97-100
Şirvan National Park 228
Sisian 179-80
Şixov Beach 227
Skhtorashen 275
skiing 170, 290
    Bakuriani 105
    Gudauri 84
    Hatsvali Ski Station 80
smoking 294
Sno Valley 87-8
South Ossetia 85, 112, 280, 285, 286
spa cures 178, 266
St George 110
St Gregory the Illuminator 151
St Mesrop Mashtots 150, 188
St Nino 54, 88, 100, 109
Stalin, Joseph 35, 57-8, 59, 110, 251, 261, 277
Stepanakert 270-3, **272**
Stepanavan 165-7
Stepantsminda, see Kazbegi
stone towers 79
    Maiden's Tower 206
    Zemo Omalo 91
Sturua, Robert 114
Sukhumi 69-70
Sumqayıt 228
supras 15, 112, 115

Suraxanı 224-5
Surp Hripsime Church 149, 291
Şüvəlan 225-6
Svaneti 6, 79-83, **80**, **7**
Svetitskhoveli Cathedral 54-5
swimming 41
synagogues
    Akhaltsikhe 106
    Quba 230
    Oğuz 238
    Tbilisi 33
Syunik 173-86, **175**

T
Tabidze, Galaktion 113
Talin 171
Tamar, Queen 35, 59, 64, 80, 107-8, 283-4
Tanahati Vank 180
Tatev 184-5
Tatev Monastery 184, **11**
taxi travel 306
Tbilisi 30-54, **30-1**, **36-7**, **6-7**
    accommodation 42-4
    activities 41
    climate 295
    drinking 47
    entertainment 47-8
    festivals & events 41-2
    food 44-6
    history 31-2
    internet access 49
    medical services 49
    shopping 48-9
    sights 32-9
    tourist offices 49-50
    travel agencies 50
    travel to/from 50-3
    travel within 53-4
    walking tours 40, **40**
Tbilisoba 19, 41
teahouses 15
Tehlirian, Soghomian 189
telephone services 298
    Armenia 197
    Azerbaijan 267-8
    Georgia 119
Tengiz Abuladze 114-15
Tergdaleulebi movement 113
Ter-Petrossian, Levon 190
theatre
    Armenia 139, 191
    Azerbaijan 219
    Georgia 48, 114
    High Fest 18-19
Tigranakert, 275-6
Tigranes 283
Tigranyan, Armen 190
time 12

Timur (Tamerlane) 110
Tinatin, Queen 97
toilets 13, 298
tourist information
    Armenia 197
    Azerbaijan 268
    Georgia 119
    Nagorno-Karabakh 272
tours, see also travel agencies
    archaeological 142, 150
    bird-watching 50, 142
    quad bike 232
    walking 40, 134-5, 172, 212, **40**, **212**
    wine 98, 99, 236
train travel 306-7
Transcaucasian Soviet Federated Socialist Republic 285
travel agencies
    Armenia 142, 172
    Georgia 50, 91, 100
travel to/from the region 13, 301-5
travel within the region 13, 305-7
traveller's diarrhoea 309
Trdat III 151, 188
trekking, see hiking, walking
Truso Valley 88-9
Tsaghkadzor 156-7
Tsereteli, Akaki 113
Tsinandali 96-7
Tsminda Sameba Church 88, 2-3, **9**
Tsunda 107
Tumanyan, Hovhannes 127, 167
Turashvili, Davit 113
Turkey 187, 280, 282
Tusheti 90-2, **90**
TV
    Armenia 196
    Georgia 118

U
Udabno 101
Ughtasar 180
unexploded ordnance 278, 298
Uplistsikhe 59-60
Urartu kingdom 287
urban centres 14
Ushguli 82-3

V
vaccinations 308
Vahid 206
Vake 38-9, 46
Vanadzor 163-5, **164**
Vani 64-5
Vank 276
Vankasar Church 276, **282**
Vardenis 156

Vardzia 107-8
Vayk 177-8
Vayots Dzor 173-7, **175**
Verisheen 181
video systems 294
visas 299
Armenia 197
Azerbaijan 268
Georgia 119-20
visual arts
Armenia 191
Azerbaijan 262-3
Georgia 113
Vorontsov, Count 102
Vurğun, Səmət 262

W
walking 14, 116, *see also* hiking
Baku 212, **212**
Becho 83
Dilijan 157
Gergeti 87
Lerik 254-5
Mestia 81
Tbilisi 40, **40**
Tusheti 91
Ushguli 83
Vardzia 107
war memorials
Şahidlər Xiyabani (Martyr's Lane) 207

Sardarapat 149
Sisian 179
water, drinking 13, 141, 309
weather 12, 16-19, 295, *see also individual regions*
websites *see* internet resources
wildlife, *see* animals, birds
wine 283
Armenia 160-1
Azerbaijan 236
Georgia 99
tours 98, 99, 236
women in the region 3, 91, 153, 173, 182-3, 224, 280, 281, 288
Women's Day 17
women travellers 299
work
Armenia 197
Georgia 120
World Heritage sites 291

X
Xan Sarayı 292
Xınalıq 9, 231-2, **9**

Y
Yanar Bulağ 254
Yanar Dağ 226-7
Yeghegis 177
Yeghegnadzor 174-6
Yenokavan 162-3

Yerevan 9, 124-45, **126-7**, **130-1**, **9**
accommodation 135-7
activities 134-5
climate 295
courses 135
cultural centres 141
drinking 138-9
emergencies 141
entertainment 139-40
festivals & events 135
food 137-8
history 124
internet access 141
itineraries 128
music 124-5
postal services 141
shopping 140-1
sights 124-34
tours 134-5
travel to/from 142-4
travel within 144-5
Yesenin, Sergei 225

Z
Zaqareishvili, Levan 114
Zaqatala 245-7, **246**
Zenon 95
Zorats Karer 180
Zoroastrians 224
Zugdidi 66-8
Zvartnots Cathedral 147, 291

how to use this book

These symbols will help you find the listings you want:

- ⊙ Sights
- 🏊 Beaches
- 🏃 Activities
- 🛶 Courses
- ☛ Tours
- 🎊 Festivals & Events
- 🛏 Sleeping
- 🍴 Eating
- 🍷 Drinking
- ☆ Entertainment
- 🛍 Shopping
- ℹ Information/Transport

These symbols give you the vital information for each listing:

- 📞 Telephone Numbers
- ⊙ Opening Hours
- P Parking
- ⊖ Nonsmoking
- ✴ Air-Conditioning
- @ Internet Access
- 📶 Wi-Fi Access
- 🏊 Swimming Pool
- 🌱 Vegetarian Selection
- 🗒 English-Language Menu
- 👪 Family-Friendly
- 🐾 Pet-Friendly
- 🚌 Bus
- ⛴ Ferry
- Ⓜ Metro
- Ⓢ Subway
- ⊖ London Tube
- 🚊 Tram
- 🚆 Train

Reviews are organised by author preference.

Look out for these icons:

- TOP CHOICE — Our author's recommendation
- FREE — No payment required
- 🍃 — A green or sustainable option

Our authors have nominated these places as demonstrating a strong commitment to sustainability – for example by supporting local communities and producers, operating in an environmentally friendly way, or supporting conservation projects.

Map Legend

Sights
- Beach
- Buddhist
- Castle
- Christian
- Hindu
- Islamic
- Jewish
- Monument
- Museum/Gallery
- Ruin
- Winery/Vineyard
- Zoo
- Other Sight

Activities, Courses & Tours
- Diving/Snorkelling
- Canoeing/Kayaking
- Skiing
- Surfing
- Swimming/Pool
- Walking
- Windsurfing
- Other Activity/Course/Tour

Sleeping
- Sleeping
- Camping

Eating
- Eating

Drinking
- Drinking
- Cafe

Entertainment
- Entertainment

Shopping
- Shopping

Information
- Post Office
- Tourist Information

Transport
- Airport
- Border Crossing
- Bus
- Cable Car/Funicular
- Cycling
- Ferry
- Metro
- Monorail
- Parking
- S-Bahn
- Taxi
- Train/Railway
- Tram
- Tube Station
- U-Bahn
- Other Transport

Routes
- Tollway
- Freeway
- Primary
- Secondary
- Tertiary
- Lane
- Unsealed Road
- Plaza/Mall
- Steps
- Tunnel
- Pedestrian Overpass
- Walking Tour
- Walking Tour Detour
- Path

Boundaries
- International
- State/Province
- Disputed
- Regional/Suburb
- Marine Park
- Cliff
- Wall

Population
- Capital (National)
- Capital (State/Province)
- City/Large Town
- Town/Village

Geographic
- Hut/Shelter
- Lighthouse
- Lookout
- Mountain/Volcano
- Oasis
- Park
- Pass
- Picnic Area
- Waterfall

Hydrography
- River/Creek
- Intermittent River
- Swamp/Mangrove
- Reef
- Canal
- Water
- Dry/Salt/Intermittent Lake
- Glacier

Areas
- Beach/Desert
- Cemetery (Christian)
- Cemetery (Other)
- Park/Forest
- Sportsground
- Sight (Building)
- Top Sight (Building)

OUR STORY

A beat-up old car, a few dollars in the pocket and a sense of adventure. In 1972 that's all Tony and Maureen Wheeler needed for the trip of a lifetime – across Europe and Asia overland to Australia. It took several months, and at the end – broke but inspired – they sat at their kitchen table writing and stapling together their first travel guide, *Across Asia on the Cheap*. Within a week they'd sold 1500 copies. Lonely Planet was born.

Today, Lonely Planet has offices in Melbourne, London and Oakland, with more than 600 staff and writers. We share Tony's belief that 'a great guidebook should do three things: inform, educate and amuse'.

OUR WRITERS

John Noble

Coordinating Author; Georgia John, from the UK, first arrived in Georgia in 1990 when it was still officially part of the Soviet Union and he was writing Lonely Planet's first (and last) guide to that now-defunct empire. Entering Georgia from Russia through the Dariali Gorge to Kazbegi was like taking a big breath of fresh air. John was thrilled by the Georgians' love of freedom and the outstanding warmth of their hospitality, and every visit since then has deepened his own love for this utterly unique and stunningly beautiful country, which is now finally gaining the place in travellers' consciousnesses that it deserves. John has written on many ex-Soviet states for Lonely Planet, but none quite like Georgia.

Michael Kohn

Armenia, Nagorno-Karabakh Michael first visited the Caucasus in 2006, having travelled there the hard way on a turbulent crossing of the Caspian Sea to Baku. After zigzagging through the region he returned a year later to cover Armenia and Nagorno-Karabakh for the 3rd edition of this guide. Struck by the kindness of the Armenian people on his previous visit, Michael was thrilled to take a second tour of duty of Armenia and NK in 2011. He specialises in writing Lonely Planet guides to Silk Road regions from China to the Levant.

Danielle Systermans

Azerbaijan Born in Belgium, Dani has spent the last 25 years travelling the globe, both modestly for pleasure and more luxuriously in the world of international finance. She first arrived in Baku back in 1995 with an improbable mission: to explain the 'new idea' of credit cards to an audience of sceptical ex-Soviets. Judging from all the ATMs in town these days she was quite successful. Friendships and an unquenchable traveller-curiousity keep bringing her back to the region in a series of visits that have been as stormy as any love-affair, and just as compulsive.

Contributing Author

William Dunbar: Tbilisi Drinking & Entertainment William is a freelance journalist who has worked in Georgia since 2006. When not travelling the country covering political unrest or obscure mountain tribes, he likes to unwind in the less salubrious Tbilisi nightspots and then complain about the service.

Published by Lonely Planet Publications Pty Ltd
ABN 36 005 607 983
4th edition – June 2012
ISBN 978 1 74179 403 8
© Lonely Planet 2012   Photographs © as indicated 2012
10 9 8 7 6 5 4 3 2
Printed in China

Although the authors and Lonely Planet have taken all reasonable care in preparing this book, we make no warranty about the accuracy or completeness of its content and, to the maximum extent permitted, disclaim all liability arising from its use.